# JAPAN AND AMERICA IN THE PRE-WAR ERA

## POLITICAL AND BUSINESS RELATIONS

TSUNAO NAKAMURA

JAPAN AND AMERICA IN THE PRE-WAR ERA
POLITICAL AND BUSINESS RELATIONS

2024年9月5日　初版発行

著　者：中村綱雄
発行者：伊藤秀樹
発行所：株式会社ジャパンタイムズ出版
　　　　〒102-0082 東京都千代田区一番町2-2 一番町第二TGビル 2F
ISBN978-4-7890-1862-3
本書の無断複製は著作権法上の例外を除き禁じられています。

Copyright©2024 by Tsunao Nakamura

All rights reserved. No part of this publication may be reproduced, stored in a retrieval
system, or transmitted in any form or by any means, electronic, mechanical, photocopying,
recording, or otherwise, without the prior written permission of the publisher.

First edition: August 2024

Editing services: Time & Space, Inc.
Editing and copyreading: Katherine Heins
Cover art: Hirohisa Shimizu (Pesco-Paint)
Editorial design and typesetting: Soju Ltd.
Printing: Nikkei Printing Inc.

Published by The Japan Times Publishing, Ltd.
2F Ichibancho Daini TG Bldg., 2-2 Ichibancho, Chiyoda-ku, Tokyo 102-0082, Japan

Website: https://jtpublishing.co.jp/

ISBN 978-4-7890-1862-3
Printed in Japan

# Table of Contents

Preface...................................................................................................... vii

*Chapter 1* Japan before Opening the Country, Hegemonic Britain, and
America from Colonial Time............................................... 1
1.1. Japan before Opening the Country...................................... 1
1.2. Hegemonic Britain ............................................................. 7
1.3. America from Colonial Times ........................................... 11
Notes........................................................................................ 19

*Chapter 2* Japan's Opening of the Country and the Fall of the *Bakufu* ..... 27
2.1. Japan's Opening of the Country ........................................ 27
2.2. The Aftermath of the Treaty of Amity and Commerce ....... 33
2.3. The Fall of the *Bakufu* ...................................................... 39
Notes........................................................................................ 44

*Chapter 3* Early Mutual Impressions ............................................... 51
3.1. Successful American Diplomacy ........................................ 51
3.2. Japan's Ratification Embassy of 1860................................. 54
3.3. The Iwakura Embassy of 1871........................................... 58
3.4. Americans in Japan .......................................................... 62
Notes........................................................................................ 67

*Chapter 4* Treaty Revision ............................................................. 73
4.1. Early Negotiations ........................................................... 73
4.2. Extraterritoriality............................................................. 77
4.3. Negotiations in the 1890s ................................................ 84
Notes........................................................................................ 87

*Chapter 5* The US and Japanese Economies, and Their Economic
Relations in the 19th Century ........................................... 93
5.1. The United States and Japan in the World Economy in the 19th
Century............................................................................ 93
5.2. Early Japanese Foreign Trade............................................ 99
5.3. The Tea, Raw-Silk, and Raw-Cotton Trade between the US and
Japan ...............................................................................103
Notes........................................................................................115

*iii*

**Chapter 6 Imperialism in East Asia and the Japanese and American Responses** ...................................................................................... 123

6.1. Imperialism in the Late 19th Century ........................................ 123

6.2. The Sino–Japanese War and Subsequent Developments ............ 125

6.3. The Anglo–Japanese Treaty and the Russo–Japanese War ......... 133

6.4. Developments after the Russo–Japanese War ............................. 136

6.5. US Foreign Policy; Expansionism and the Open Door .............. 142

Notes ................................................................................................ 147

**Chapter 7 Friction and Cooperation between Japan and the United States in the 1910s and Early 1920s** ..................................... 157

7.1. Dollar Diplomacy ...................................................................... 157

7.2. The Twenty-One Demands ........................................................ 161

7.3. Japan's Relations with the Powers during WWI and the Paris Peace Conference ................................................................................. 167

7.4. The Washington Conference ...................................................... 172

Notes ................................................................................................ 179

**Chapter 8 US–Japanese Immigration Disputes** ................................ 191

8.1. The Roots of Immigration Question in California ...................... 191

8.2. The San Francisco School Incident and the Gentlemen's Agreement ................................................................................... 195

8.3. The Alien Land Laws in California ............................................ 198

8.4. The Legislation of the Japanese Exclusion Law of 1924 ............ 203

8.5. The 1924 Law and US–Japanese Relations ................................ 210

Notes ................................................................................................ 215

**Chapter 9 The Economies of the US and Japan in the Early Decades of the 20th Century** ........................................................ 223

9.1. The Economic Growth and Industrial Development of the US and Japan ......................................................................................... 223

9.2. Foreign Trade in the US and Japan ........................................... 231

9.3. Japan's Return to the Gold Standard after WWI ....................... 242

9.4. The International Financial Positions of the United States and Japan ......................................................................................... 249

Notes ................................................................................................ 253

*iv*

*Chapter 10*  Foreign Investments in the US and Japan and by the US
   and Japan in the Pre-WWII Period ..............................265
10.1. Foreign Investments in the United States ...........................265
10.2. US Foreign Direct Investments ......................................268
10.3. Foreign Investments in Japan .......................................272
10.4. Japan's Foreign Direct Investments .................................283
Notes ......................................................................291

*Chapter 11*  The New China and the Powers ...............................305
11.1. China in the 1910s and 1920s ......................................305
11.2. US and British China Policy ........................................309
11.3. Japan's China Policy in the 1920s .................................315
11.4. The London Naval Conference and Its Unfortunate
   Consequences ..........................................................324
Notes ......................................................................327

*Chapter 12*  The Great Depression, the Impasse in China, and the
   Road to Mukden ......................................................337
12.1. The Great Depression ...............................................337
12.2. Japanese Economy and Society before the Manchurian Incident ....344
12.3. The Impasse in Japan's China Policy ...............................352
12.4. The Road to Mukden .................................................356
Notes ......................................................................360

*Chapter 13*  Developments after the Mukden Explosion ..................369
13.1. The Japanese Government, Army Leadership, and the Kwantung
   Army ..................................................................369
13.2. The Reactions of China .............................................375
13.3. The Shanghai Incident ..............................................379
13.4. Stimson's Challenge to Japan ......................................382
13.5. Japan's Withdrawal from the League of Nations ...................385
Notes ......................................................................390

*Chapter 14*  Japan's Militarism, War with China, and the US Position ....403
14.1. The Rise of the Army in Japanese Politics .........................403
14.2. Japan's China Policy in the Mid-1930s and the Xian Incident ........411

*v*

14.3. The Sino–Japanese War and US–Japanese Relations ........................415

Notes..........................................................................................................423

**Chapter 15  US and Japanese Economies, Their Economic Policies, and Their Trade Relations in the 1930s** ...........................................437

15.1. The US Economy in the 1930s................................................437

15.2. The New Deal...........................................................................443

15.3. The Japanese Economy and Economic/Industrial Policies in the 1930s.......................................................................................447

15.4. Trade Relations between the United States and Japan in the 1930s.......................................................................................456

Notes..........................................................................................................463

**Chapter 16  Japan, the United States, and China on the Eve of the Pacific War** ..........................................................................475

16.1. The War in Europe ..................................................................475

16.2. Japanese China Policies and the US Reactions in the Late 1930s....480

16.3. Japan's Southward Advance and the Tripartite Pact, and the US Reaction in 1940 ....................................................................489

16.4. US–Japanese Relations in 1941 ...............................................496

Notes..........................................................................................................515

Figures: Map of Manchuria in 1900 .................................................. 129

Map of China in 1920 ......................................................... 131

Chronology of Events ..............................................................................534

Index ..........................................................................................................540

*vi*

# Preface

This book discusses pre-war US–Japanese relations from Commodore Perry's visit to Japan in the mid-1850s until Japan's attack on Pearl Harbor in 1941. In that it ended with the disastrous war, the prewar bilateral relationship was nothing but a tragedy. What drove the two countries to war is, naturally, the main subject of this book. But I also write about various positive developments in their prewar bilateral relations.

The two countries made a good start in their relations after Japan's opening of the country in 1854. During the crucial early stages of the relationship, they established a very friendly relationship, which continued until the early 20th century. In terms of business relations, in both trades and investments, the two countries maintained close ties throughout almost the entire prewar period.

It was fortunate for Japan that the first foreign country it encountered was the United States. As observed in chapter 1, Americans viewed themselves as having a special mission to serve as an example in the world, whereas the European nations were pursuing selfish imperialistic policies. Americans believed that they were destined to build a "City upon a Hill" on which the world would shape itself.[1]

The Japanese found Americans sincere and friendly, while Americans

*vii*

found Japanese courteous and hardworking. Michio Morishima argues that the Confucianist education in the Tokugawa era was responsible for the diligence and discipline of Japanese in the Meiji era and after.[2] Americans were genuinely helpful to the Japanese, who were trying hard to build a modern nation out of the ruins of old feudal system. The Japanese eagerly learned from America. Their relationship was something like that of a benevolent teacher and an eager student (chapter 3).

In 1872, the Japanese government sent a large study mission, the Iwakura Mission, to the United States. Americans received the mission very warmly, and took the visitors to various facilities and institutions for inspections. In Philadelphia, a group of Japanese engineers visited forty-three factories in three weeks thanks to arrangements by the municipality. The mission stayed in the United States for seven months.

Fukuzawa Yukichi described America in 1866 as the foremost nation of "civilization and enlightenment."[3] Though he later revised his view of America, the earlier image of America as an admirable incarnation of liberty remained a deep undercurrent in the minds of many Japanese, and was handed down to their descendants.

In the treaty revision negotiations in the 1870s and 1880s, as well (chapter 4), while European powers refused to relinquish the rights that they had acquired through unequal treaties, only the United States was supportive to Japan.

The very friendly US–Japanese relationship lasted until about the time when President Theodore Roosevelt left office in 1909. The imperialism of the European powers, which expanded to East Asia in the late 19th century, had a serious effect on Japanese diplomacy (chapter 6). Unless Japan joined the group of the rulers, the alternative was to become the ruled. Japan joined the rulers' group by winning wars with China (1895) and Russia (1905). Roosevelt was supportive of such Japanese efforts, but his successors were not friendly to Japan. They asserted that the United States should weaken Japan's hold on China and tried to strengthen the political and economic position of the US in China (chapter 7).

The decades of the 1910s and the 1920s saw both friction and cooperation between the two countries. The United States supported the new Republican China (chapter 11) and criticized Japan's aggressive acts in China, but the two countries cooperated in other fields. For example, during WWI, both governments supported a deal between American steel makers and Japanese shipbuilders to exchange the former's steel for the latter's shipping (chapter 9). In the Washington Conference in 1921–1922, Japan showed its willingness to go along with the US new diplomacy (chapter 7). But the passage of the anti-Japanese immigration law in 1924 greatly disheartened the pro-American Japanese and strengthened the position of the proponents of anti-American policies in Japan (chapter 8).

The Manchurian Incident of 1931 ushered in the tense decade of the 1930s, as discussed in chapters 12 and 13. In 1933, Japan left the League of Nations, which refused to recognize Japanese control of Manchuria. In 1937 the Sino–Japanese War began (chapter 14). The United States started partial embargoes against Japan in July 1940, and a de facto oil embargo in August 1941 (chapter 16). Japan had its back to the wall.

Although US–Japanese relations culminated in an unfortunate war, I consider important the fact that the two countries had very close and friendly relations for more than half a century after the commencement of the relationship. Most Japanese people fought the war not out of hatred for Americans, but because they were trained to do so. It is my view that the memory of the good old days survived the difficult years and even the wartime, and helped the two countries to reconcile smoothly after the war.

\* \* \*

Although political relations worsened over the course of the 1910s, 1920s, and 1930s, the two countries continued actively conducting business transactions throughout this time. Considerable portions of this volume are devoted to analysis of both countries' economic and industrial situations and their trade and investment relations in the prewar period (chapters 5, 9, 10, 12, and 15). The United States remained the biggest buyer of Japanese exports from the mid-1870s until 1939. Exports of Japanese raw silk to the United States were particularly important to the Japanese economy. The United States was the biggest investor in Japan in both direct investments and portfolio investments in the prewar period.

When close business relations are maintained over a long time, they not only create mutual respect and confidence between those engaged in the business, but also help foster a positive image of the trade partner in the minds of

*ix*

the people at large. In this book, I write about various contacts between American and Japanese businessmen, including the case of a pioneering raw-silk exporter from Gunma Prefecture (chapter 5); Western Electric's NEC venture, the first foreign direct investment in Japan; and General Electric's ventures that led to the formation of Toshiba (chapter 10).

American and Japanese businessmen were intent on continuing their business dealings until the outbreak of the war, and were ready to resume their relationships as soon as hostilities ended. The president of Mitsubishi Goshi Kaisha, in a speech to all the managers of Mitsubishi companies two days after the Pearl Harbor attack, said, "We were opposed to the war . . . The war started, however . . . When peace is restored, we shall revive our old friendships and work together. . . ."[4] In another case, the Japanese executive of a US–Japan joint venture used to tell his assistants in the company during the war period that the war was a fight between governments, not between people, so they should keep their confidence in their American partner.[5] In the United States, in the September 1940 issue of *Fortune* magazine, a survey was published showing that about three-quarters of 15,000 American executives opposed measures that would antagonize Japan.[6] Business leaders on both sides were instrumental in the early resumption of good bilateral relations after the war.

\*　　\*　　\*

Regarding the question of what drove the two countries to war, I consider the following three factors to be crucial: American diplomacy based on moral globalism, the Japanese–German alliance of 1940, and the unique Japanese system of independence of the right of supreme command.

The United States persistently condemned Japanese military aggression in China. But it condemned Japan's actions not because they posed a threat to American security, but rather because it judged them immoral and unjust in light of America's moral globalism, or diplomacy based on principles. To allow the Japanese military occupation of China would mean a denial of America's principle-based diplomacy. The US administration knew, however, that liberating China from Japanese occupation was a goal that could not be achieved by peaceful means. With no threat to American security, the US Congress would not approve any action that would lead to war with Japan.

The Japanese–German military alliance concluded after the German spring offensive in 1940 changed the situation, however, as it made Japan a threat to US security. According to Akira Iriye, the security considerations gave moral globalism an official status.[7] American public opinion supporting stronger measures to block Japanese control of China increased drastically after the alliance. The Roosevelt administration was now in a position to take decisive measures against Japan. In November 1941, the United States presented the Hull Note to Japan, demanding that Japan move out of China.[8]

Japanese military leaders, as well as some civilian government officials, being students of the diplomacy of British-style imperialism, failed to correctly interpret American diplomacy based on moral globalism. They mistakenly believed that the alliance would warn the United States away.

Many Japanese government leaders opposed the alliance with Germany, but the army did not allow them to serve as important cabinet ministers, let alone in the role of prime minister. As chapter 14 discusses, the Japanese military had veto power against the cabinet, thanks to the rule that the army minister and the navy minister must be military men. This rule was derived from the cabinet ordinance that the ministers and chiefs of staff of the Japanese army and navy could report directly to the emperor regarding the supreme command without prior consultation with the prime minister. This system made the right of supreme command independent from the government, allowing the military to act without being restricted by the government. The right of supreme command was originally the right to move the armed forces during times of war, but the Japanese military interpreted it more broadly.

The Japanese army's time-honored practice of allowing field commanders to act flexibly was also derived from the concept of the independence of the right of supreme command. The Kwantung Army used this privilege effectively in the Manchurian Incident.

The political power balance in Japan between the government and the army, which shifted in favor of the latter in the 1930s as a result of the government's harsh economic policies (chapter 12) and the army's successful operations in Manchuria (chapter 13), helped allow this rather arbitrary use of the privilege by the army.

\*    \*    \*

I began writing this book while I was teaching at Takushoku University, which I had joined in 1997 at the age of sixty. Before that time, I worked at a Japanese trading company, the Sumitomo Corporation, which I had entered in 1959 after completing my undergraduate education in the law department of Kyoto University. I did not receive any scholarly training when I was young, but I consider the business experiences and personal acquaintances gained during my professional life to have been invaluable in writing this book. I wrote this book in English because I wanted it to be read not only by Japanese, but also by Americans and other English-language readers. References I consulted have been cited in the endnotes to each chapter so that readers can refer to them easily.

I would like to extend my sincere appreciation to Dr. Ellen Frost, without whose encouragement I would not have written this book. She kindly read my draft in the early stages and improved it. I am also very thankful to Professor Hugh Patrick, who kindly read part of my draft and gave me valuable suggestions. I met both individuals when I was with the Sumitomo Corporation. Mr. Katō Yasuya, a colleague at Sumitomo, kindly gave me various suggestions for publishing this book. Professor Kimura Hiroshi, having read part of my draft, encouraged me to write the book in English. I must also say thanks to Mr. Rodney Armstrong, who patiently assisted me to write this book from chapter 1 through 16. My thanks also go to Mr. Michimata Takatoshi of The Japan Times Publishing, Ltd. and Mr. Saito Junichi of Time & Space, Inc., who have been kind enough to offer to undertake publication of this book, as well as Ms. Katherine Heins, the copy editor. Lastly, I would express my gratitude to the International House of Japan, whose library and other facilities were helpful to me in writing this book.

Tsunao Nakamura

---

1    As discussed in sub-section 1.3.1 in chapter 1, "City upon a Hill" is a phrase John Winthrop, the first governor of Massachusetts Bay Colony, used in a speech he delivered to his group of settlers on a ship bound for Boston in March 1630. Winthrop quoted the phrase from the Gospel of Matthew (5:14), which goes, "You are the light of the world. A city upon a hill cannot be hidden." Harry Carman and Harold Syrett, *A History of the American People, vol. I, to 1865* (New York: Alfred A. Knopf, 1952), 530. Michael Corbett and Julia Corbett, *Politics and Religion in the United States* (New York: Garland Publishing,1999), 33. Sylvia Söderlind and James Carson, eds., *American Exceptionalisms: From Winthrop to Winfrey* (Albany, NY: State

Preface

University of New York Press, 2011), 53.

2    Michio Morishima, *Why Has Japan 'Succeeded'?* (Cambridge: Cambridge University Press, 1982), 60.

3    See sub-section 3.2.2 in chapter 3.

4    The president of Mitsubishi Shoji was Iwasaki Koyata (岩崎小弥太). Mitsubishi Shoji Kabushiki Kaisha, *Mitsubishi Shoji shashi* (Tokyo: Mitsubishi Shoji Kabushiki Kaisha, 1986), 547.

5    The Japanese executive was Nakagawa Suekichi (中川末吉). See chapter 10, note 87.

6    *Fortune* asked the panel, "In dealing with Japan, should we: Appease them? Let nature take its course? Attack them?" Reportedly, 40.1 percent chose "Appease them"; 35.0 percent answered, "Let nature take its course"; and 19.1 percent said, "Attack them." Mira Wilkins, "The Role of U.S. Business," in *Pearl Harbor as History*, eds. Dorothy Borg and Shumpei Okamoto (New York: Columbia University Press, 1973), 350–351. Wilkins speculates that the survey was conducted in early July 1940.

7    Akira Iriye, *Across the Pacific* (Chicago: Printing Publications, 1967), 203.

8    The United States had prepared a general agreement consisting of ten basic proposals including withdrawal of the Japanese forces from China, and a short-term temporary agreement (a *modus vivendi*) to avoid war for the time being. The *modus vivendi*, which proposed settlement of some issues but left the China issue unsettled, was to last for three months, during which period conversations were to continue on the general agreement. The original plan had been to present the *modus vivendi* to Japan together with the ten-point proposals. It was dropped at the last moment, however, and only the ten-point proposals were presented. See sub-section 16.4.6 in chapter 16.

*xiii*

# Chapter 1
# Japan before Opening the Country, Hegemonic Britain, and America from Colonial Times

## 1.1. Japan before Opening the Country

### 1.1.1. Japan under *Sakoku*

Japan had been under the policy of *sakoku* (鎖国 national isolation) for over two hundred years, when it decided to open the country in the middle of the 1850s. The Tokugawa (徳川) government—henceforth the *bakufu* (幕府) — through a series of edicts in the 1630s gradually closed Japan to the world. The goal of *sakoku* was mainly to keep out Christianity. The Christianity the *bakufu* knew was the Catholicism introduced by Jesuit missionaries from Spain and Portugal in the mid-16th century. The *bakufu* regarded it as a belief system that threatened the feudal social structure of Japan. They suspected that missionaries' activities might be intended to rule the Japanese spiritually for the benefit of their home countries' imperialistic purposes.[1]

The first shogun, Tokugawa Ieyasu (徳川家康), had imposed the military authority of his family upon his feudal rivals by 1615, but neither he nor his successors felt entirely secure, and took every possible precaution against rebellion by one or more of the powerful and semi-independent *tozama* (外様) families such as the Mōri (毛利) in Chōshū (長州) in western Honshū and the

*1*

Shimazu (島津) in Satsuma (薩摩) in southern Kyūshū.[2] The Tokugawa shoguns feared these great families might conspire with the Spanish or Portuguese, get their help in procuring artillery and ships, or even call upon them for military or naval support in an attempt to overthrow the Tokugawa regime.

European missionaries were either driven out or executed, and most Western traders were expelled as well because of their association with Catholicism. Japanese Christians were forced to renounce their beliefs or be executed. Japanese were prohibited from leaving the country, and those who were then abroad were not allowed to return to Japan for fear that they might come back contaminated with Christianity. It was forbidden to build ocean-going vessels. In the history of East–West relations, this was the most decisive rejection of an approach from the West by an Asian nation. Among the Europeans, only the Dutch, who were Protestant and eschewed missionary activity, were allowed to trade with Japan, but they were restricted to a tiny trading enclave at Nagasaki (長崎) with annual visits to Edo (江戸).

The objectives of the *sakoku* policy being political and not economic, the *bakufu* allowed trade with China and Korea to continue. Trade with China was put under official control in Nagasaki along with the Dutch trade. The *bakufu* also allowed the Shimazu in Satsuma to trade indirectly with China through the Ryukyu (琉球) Kingdom. Korean trade continued to be conducted by the Sō (宗) family in Tsushima (対馬) with the permission of the *bakufu*.

The types of merchandise traded during the isolation period were basically same as before. The major imports were silk and cotton textiles, sugar, spices, tea, medicines, and porcelain. The *bakufu* even ordered the daimyo of Satsuma and Tsushima to ensure that there would be no decrease in total silk imports as a result of the *sakoku* policy.[3] Japan exported mainly silver, copper, lacquerware, and pottery, among which silver was the main attraction for its early trading partners. As the 17th century progressed, however, Japanese silver mines became harder to work, and the *bakufu* had to curtail silver exports. Although copper replaced silver as the primary export in the 18th century, trade remained at low levels throughout most of the remainder of the Tokugawa era.[4] The increase in the domestic production of cotton, silk, and sugar also contributed to the decline in trade. In 1790 the *bakufu* reduced the number of Chinese vessels permitted to trade at Nagasaki from twelve to ten a year, and the annual voyages of the Dutch from two to one.[5]

Japan's population, which had increased from 12 million to 31 million during the first century of the Tokugawa period, reached Malthusian limits around 1720, when new additions of cultivated land became difficult.[6]

With limited natural resources and with virtually no economic benefit from foreign trade, the Japanese were forced to lead very frugal lives. By the end of the Tokugawa period, however, Japan had developed a highly commercial urban culture and sufficient small-scale industry. Edo, the capital, maintained standards of public health and infrastructure that supported a population of more than a million, one of the largest urban populations in the world at the time.

Japanese society was divided into four rigid categories: samurai, peasants, artisans, and merchants. In the late Tokugawa period peasants are estimated to have made up 85 percent of the population, merchants and artisans 8 percent, and samurai 6 percent.[7]

There is an estimate that Japan's per-capita GNP in 1820 was about 40 percent that of Britain and about half that of the United States.[8] The Japanese literacy rate in the mid-19th century was 40–50 percent for adult males, and 10–20 percent for adult females, which was comparable to that of the contemporaneous British. The *terakoya* (寺子屋 elementary schools), which existed in nearly every village throughout Japan in the 19th century, greatly increased levels of popular literacy.[9]

## 1.1.2. Tokugawa Ideologies

Before the Tokugawa period, Japan's religious history had been that of a syncretism of Shinto, Buddhism, and Confucianism, among which Buddhism had generally held the dominant position.[10] The Tokugawa government required all Japanese to register with a Buddhist temple, and ordered all temples to ensure that registrants did not become Christians. The registration functioned at the same time as a census record. The Buddhist temples were thus absorbed into the social control structure of the Tokugawa state.[11]

The *bakufu* adopted the Zhu Xi (朱熹) school of Confucianism as the official state ideology in 1634.[12] The *bakufu* considered the teachings of Zhu Xi (1130–1200) useful for establishing a rigidly hierarchical society based on ties of loyalty between lord and subject.[13] While Zhu Xi stressed the importance of benevolence, righteousness, faithfulness, wisdom, and loyalty, the *bakufu*'s version of Zhu Xi Confucianism, Shushigaku (朱子学), emphasized loyalty above the other virtues and very nearly shifted the objects of the old

Confucian value of filial piety from parents to feudal superiors.[14]

A scholarly family, the Hayashi, was given the responsibility of serving as the regime's Confucian ideologues, and was placed in charge of an academy in Edo responsible for nurturing the ideology. The last Hayashi head of the academy was the official chosen to negotiate with Commodore Mathew Perry in 1854 (see 2.1.1).

Despite the official sanction given to Shushigaku, a rival school of Confucianism soon found supporters. The philosophy of Wang Yang-ming (王陽明 1472–1528) became an important part of Japanese political culture as Yōmeigaku (陽明学) after having been thoroughly naturalized by a series of Japanese scholars. While Shushigaku placed special emphasis on *taigi meibun* (大義名分 doing one's duty to the lord in accordance with one's place in society), Yōmeigaku emphasized the importance of a person acting upon the truth as he individually perceived it. Yōmeigaku brought into its structure the ancient Japanese concept of *makoto* (誠 sincerity).[15] Given the syncretism of Japanese thought, when Yōmeigaku's emphasis on "action" and "sincerity" were mixed with the elements of xenophobia and nativism, the result could be dangerous, as was observed in the actual practice of *sonnō jōi* (尊皇攘夷 revere the emperor and expel the foreigners) activists in the late Tokugawa period (2.3.2). Yōmeigaku's teaching also had an influence on violent ultranationalist movements in the 1930s (14.1.4).[16]

There emerged, on the other hand, the Kokugaku (国学 National Learning) scholars, who argued that Japan should do away with the ideologies of China, and should turn to its native religion of Shinto and reexamine the historical chronicles such as the *Kojiki* (古事記) of the Nara era (710–784). Motoori Norinaga (本居宣長 1730–1801) argued that the great glory of Japan was its unbroken line of emperors, and its endurance was proof of Shinto's superiority.[17]

The Mito school (水戸学派) scholars placed Shintoism first in their allegiance as the Kokugaku scholars did, but, unlike them, the Mito school scholars accepted Confucianism. Aizawa Seishisai (会沢正志斎 1782–1863), the most influential leader of the school, embraced the Shinto concepts that the imperial family were descendants of the sun goddess, Amaterasu Ōmikami, and argued that the uniqueness of Japan's *kokutai* (国体 national polity) lay in the imperial line that had survived inviolate through the ages.[18] He had high regard for the Chinese Confucian sages as well, and lectured about their ethical viewpoints.[19]

Meanwhile, Dutch learning, or Rangaku (蘭学), developed as a window on the outside world after the *bakufu*'s relaxation of controls on the import of Western books in 1720. Japanese scholars could acquire works that did not contain Christian ideas through the medium of the Dutch trading station in Nagasaki. They could also have personal contact with Europeans in the Dutch factory there.[20] While these scholars' interest was primarily in science, their awareness of Japan's backwardness made many of them critical of the *bakufu*'s *sakoku* policy.[21] Their criticism of the *bakufu* often cost them their lives.[22] Nevertheless, the views of those scholars were valued by some enlightened *bakufu* leaders. Their sacrifices contributed to making Japan's modernization more rapid than it might otherwise have been.

Perhaps the most active intellectual in the 1850s was Yoshida Shōin (吉田松陰 1830–1859). He studied the Confucianism of Zhu Xi and the Wang Yang-ming school, and Dutch learning under Sakuma Shōzan (佐久間象山). His political thought was very much like that of the Mito school, as he was strongly influenced by Aizawa Seishisai of the Mito school.[23] Yoshida unsuccessfully tried to smuggle himself abroad on one of Perry's ships. He was put to jail, first in Edo and then in the Chōshū domain. When he was released, he was allowed to open a small private school, the Shōkasonjuku (松下村塾), where he taught many of the young Chōshū domain samurai who were to become the leaders of the Meiji Restoration.[24] He believed that the existing leadership was incapable of solving the national crisis, and he envisioned the establishment of a new order under the leadership of "grass-roots heroes." No less influential was Satsuma's official domain school, the Zōshikan (造士館), which had a longer history and larger facilities than the Shōkasonjuku.[25] Like the Shōkasonjuku, the Zōshikan produced many young leaders who played important roles in the Meiji Restoration and in the Meiji government.[26]

While all the teachings discussed above were basically the concern of the samurai class, there was an important moral education movement addressed to the common people, the Shingaku (心学), or Heart Learning, school which was begun by Ishida Baigan (石田梅岩 1685–1744). Robert Bellah emphasizes that the Shingaku played an important role in economic rationalization in the Tokugawa period, and had a significant influence on the growth of modern industrial Japan.[27]

Baigan's Shingaku was an amalgam of Shintoism, Buddhism, and

Confucianism.[28] Baigan did not oppose the samurai-centered value system of his age. Rather, he argued as a former merchant that merchants should be considered worthy of following the samurai's values. He took the ethics of the samurai as a model for the ideals of the merchants, and emphasized honesty, frugality, and diligence as the important virtues for the merchant class.[29] He also gave moral justification to merchants' occupation and to the profit derived from it, saying that the merchant's honest profit corresponded to the samurai's stipend for loyal service. Shingaku was spread throughout Japan by itinerant lecturers like Baigan himself and his followers. They used simple language that did not require the listener to have knowledge of difficult Chinese concepts and their complex Chinese characters. Though Shingaku as an educational movement ceased to exist with the start of the Meiji government, the ethics textbooks of the new public school system read much like a Shingaku lecture.[30]

Among the Tokugawa ideologies described above, the one that was most effectively used to bring about the Meiji Restoration was the Mito-school scholars' emperor-centered *kokutai* concept. At the end of Tokugawa period, when Japan was involved in the political crisis that led to the collapse of the *bakufu*, the anti-*bakufu* young leaders, emphasizing the divinity of the emperor as the Kokugaku and Mito school scholars did, effectively used the emperor and Shintoism as a unifying and constructive nationalist symbol. Thus, they successfully carried out the difficult job of demolishing the feudal system and creating new Meiji Japan.

In terms of its legacy to Meiji Japan, Confucianism was the most important. Being a philosophy rather than a religion, Confucianism was not in conflict with Shintoism or Buddhism. In fact, both Shintoism and Buddhism were strongly influenced by Confucianism in Japan. By the end of the Tokugawa era, the Japanese version of Confucianism, typically Shushigaku, had equipped the Japanese with the patterns of thought and discipline needed by soldiers in the modern army or workers in modern organizations. Morishima argues that without these Japanese disciplined by Confucian spirit, the Meiji government could not have carried out its policy of *fukoku kyōhei* (富国強兵 enrich the country, strengthen the army) so speedily and efficiently.[31]

## 1.2. Hegemonic Britain

### 1.2.1. Britain's Foreign Policy in the Mid-19th Century

Though Japan's reentry into world society in the middle of the 19th century was brought about by the United States, the hegemonic world power at that time was Great Britain. Britain held a predominant position in world politics and the global economy.[32] The Industrial Revolution in the late 18th century through the early 19th century made Britain dominant in industrial production and trade in the world. The formidable Royal Navy was the protector of the vast colonial territories of the British Empire. After the battle of Trafalgar in 1805, the Royal Navy was probably as powerful in actual fighting power as the next three or four largest navies combined.[33] The American navy was that of a second-rate power. The seven ships that Commodore Perry brought to Tokyo Bay amounted to one-fourth of the US Navy's total strength.

By the mid-19th century, with the intellectual underpinnings provided by its great political economists such as Adam Smith (1723–1790) and David Ricardo (1772–1823), Britain had just launched its crusade for "free trade." It embarked on unilateral free trade in the 1840s, expecting that the success of free-trading Britain would motivate other nations to follow its lead. This proved to be the case, at least in Europe. In 1860 Britain and France concluded the Cobden–Chevalier Treaty with a reciprocal most-favored-nation clause. It was subsequently followed by a network of free-trade agreements among other major European nations,[34] which lasted until 1890 when Germany started a protectionist trade policy.

In the mid-19th century, British free traders promoted the idea of withdrawal from colonies. "In the period from 1840 to 1870," writes Langer, "interest in the colonies reached its nadir in England."[35] In 1852 the young Benjamin Disraeli spoke of "these wretched colonies" as "a millstone 'round our necks."[36]

In Asia, the rule of India proved costly. The British involvement in India had started as a conventional mercantilist exercise in imperialism. By the early 19th century, Britain had nearly conquered all of India, yet controlling territories and suppressing rebellions continued to cost the British heavy losses of lives and treasure. By the 1810s, the private East India Company had reached the limits of its financial resources, and the British government began subsidization of the colony. These subsidies increased throughout the first half of the century and rose to very high levels with what the British called the "Great Mutiny" of 1857.[37]

With their experience in India, the British government leaders were becoming convinced that their policy with respect to China must not be dependent upon control of the territory and administration of that country. They concluded that Britain's primary interest was the retention of its commercial supremacy worldwide, and that this objective could best be achieved not by the conquering of additional territory, but through government support for the ideals of free trade, coupled with the safeguarding of the rights of British merchants by the making and enforcement of treaties with independent governments responsible for the expense of the actual administration of British export markets. Thus began the era of what some scholars have called Britain's "informal empire."[38] John Gallagher and Ronald Robinson argue that "British policy was trade with rule when necessary, but trade with informal control if possible,"[39] since the latter was more economical than the former.[40]

In contrast with the "formal empire" best typified by the British rule of India, "informal empire" used force only to maintain security for trade. Britain adopted this policy in many parts of the world, China being the outstanding example.[41] In 1855, the British had treaties with Siam (now Thailand) that preserved more of Siamese sovereignty than was the case with China,[42] and Japan's first foreign commercial treaty of 1858 with the United States (2.2.1) was basically patterned on the 1855 British–Siam treaty. As Japan soon concluded a similar treaty with Britain, Japan was incorporated into Britain's informal empire.[43]

## 1.2.2. The Opium Wars and the Treaty Port System

Driven by British demand for Chinese tea, and in the absence of any other British product demanded by the Chinese, exports to China of contraband opium from India by British merchants started to increase in the early years of the 19th century. Opium had been illegal in China since the early 18th century, but its illegality had not actually hampered imports. Local Chinese officials used "illegality" as a pretext for collecting bribes. In the 1830s, however, the increase in opium imports caused a heavy drain of silver from China and a rise in the price of silver in terms of copper. In those days, the Chinese public used copper currency for household purchases, while silver currency was used for large commercial transactions. The appreciation of silver currency against copper currency entailed great economic hardship for the Chinese public, because by law they had to pay taxes at the ratio of three parts copper to seven parts silver.

When the Chinese authorities launched decisive measures to stop opium smuggling, Britain waged the first Opium War in 1840. China was compelled to open five ports by the Treaty of Nanjing of 1842. This was also the treaty whereby Great Britain obtained a "perpetual" lease of the island of Hong Kong. A supplementary agreement in 1843 secured Britain extraterritoriality and the minimal tariff of 5 percent ad valorem on China's imports and exports, as well as a most-favored-nation clause.

The United States and France subsequently concluded treaties similar to the Treaty of Nanjing with China, enjoying the privileges of the most-favored-nation clause. It is noteworthy that the United States pledged that it would not import opium into China, thanks to the influence of missionaries in China and at home who opposed the opium trade.[44]

The Treaties of Nanjing did not, however, create as much trade as the British had expected. Trade failed to grow mainly because Chinese officials continued to be obstructive, and the newly opened ports were remote not only from the areas producing tea and silk, but also from the main population centers of the Yangtze valley.[45] In 1856–58, aiming for more favorable business conditions in China, Britain, along with France, waged the Arrow War (the second Opium War). The resulting Treaties of Tianjin of 1858, to which the United States and Russia also became signatories, did away with the Canton system of licensed Chinese intermediaries, opened ten additional treaty ports along the Yangtze River and on coasts of the Yellow Sea, and specified an import duty for opium, thus legitimizing the opium trade which the Nanjing Treaty had not made either legal or illegal.[46] The US government discontinued its opium trade prohibition policy in deference to Britain's tenacious opium trade policy.

The Qing government wanted the four powers to come to Beijing by land for the exchange of ratifications in carts, as had been the ancient rule for tribute missions. The United States and Russia observed the request, but the British and French refused it and moved up the Hai River with a large fleet, destroying the forts on the way. The Chinese took hostage thirty-nine foreigners, including Consul Harry Parkes, who was later to become the longtime British minister in Japan.[47] British and French forces occupied Beijing and

*9*

burned the Imperial Summer Palace. In the ensuing Convention of Beijing of 1860, China was forced to open the port of Tianjin, cede a part of Kowloon to Britain, and return to France all property confiscated from the Catholic Church since 1724.

The indemnities conceded by China to the powers were substantial. The Qing government was forced to pay $21 million by the Nanjing Treaty, $6 million by the Tianjin Treaties of 1858, and $16 million by the Convention of Beijing of 1860.

In terms of territorial gains, while the island of Hong Kong and the Kowloon Peninsula were colonized by the British, the Russians, formally neutral, profited the most. Taking advantage of the Qing government's preoccupation with the Arrow War and the Taiping Rebellion,[48] Russia secured the area north of the Amur through the Treaty of Aigun in 1858, and in return for its self-proclaimed mediation services to the British and French, it acquired the entire Manchurian seacoast, including the future site of Vladivostok, from the Amur to the Korean frontier, by the Treaty of Beijing of 1860.

To many British, freedom of trade and freedom for traders were so axiomatic as to justify the use of force when they were denied.[49] The Opium Wars, however, invited much criticism in Britain. Although there was no restriction on the domestic sale or use of opium in Britain,[50] it was recognized by many that these were morally questionable wars fought in defense of British smuggling in China.[51] In 1857, the British House of Commons passed a resolution sponsored by the Tory opposition denouncing the Second Opium War. The coalition government of Lord Melbourne with Lord Palmerston as foreign secretary fell. The Liberals were successful in the ensuing election, however, and the irascible Lord Palmerston returned to power, this time as prime minister.

The aim of the Opium Wars was not to conquer China, but to open the country to trade. They represented a short-term use of force to extract long-term concessions. By the treaties of Nanjing and Tianjin, Britain imposed a "free trade" regime on China, which, unlike the network of reciprocal free-trade agreements spread among European countries in the 1860s (1.2.1), was unilateral and unequal. These treaties also prescribed various measures to safeguard the rights of British merchants in China. Thus the Opium Wars established the so-called treaty port system, a typical form of informal empire.

The features of the treaty port system were: (1) Foreigners were to be

10

allowed to trade at specified ports; (2) They would pay low customs duties, which were specified in formal agreements the host countries could not change at will; (3) Foreigners would live in designated areas of the open ports, known as foreign settlements; (4) Foreigners would be subject only to their own national law, administered through consular courts; and (5) Treaty powers would be provided most-favored-nation treatment, but the host countries were not provided the same.

In the version of the regime enforced in China, troops of the foreign powers could be stationed in their settlements, and gunboats could patrol the Yangtze River and the territorial waters of China to enforce the treaty power rights. Moreover, the British in China had indirect control of the Chinese Imperial Maritime Customs Service, which, with Sir Robert Hart, the British nominee as head of the inspectorate of customs, turned into the Chinese government's only reliable and uncorrupt source of income and a source of great influence for British diplomacy.[52]

Meanwhile, the incorporation of China into its informal empire increased Britain's interest in Japan, but the belief that opening Japan would entail an extensive and expensive use of force made the British cautious about undertaking new initiatives. When the British foreign secretary learned that an American expedition was on its way to Japan, he expressed the view that if America succeeded, Britain could profit from it, and if it failed, it might be better to wait a while.[53]

# 1.3. America from Colonial Times

## 1.3.1. European Settlement and the Ideological Basis of the Independence

In 1630, just as Tokugawa Japan was moving toward its *sakoku* isolation, a group of four hundred ardent English Puritans led by John Winthrop, the first governor of the Massachusetts Bay Company, crossed the Atlantic to build the first successful large-scale colony in the New World.[54] In his famous lay sermon aboard the *Arbella* during the voyage to New England, Winthrop declared, "We shall find that the God of Israel is among us. . . . For we must consider that we shall be as a city upon a hill, the eyes of all people are upon us."[55] By the end of the 1630s, over 20,000 Puritan settlers had followed Winthrop.

Puritanism, a British variant of Calvinism, was such a potent and vital force that it precipitated the Puritan Revolution in Britain in the early 1640s, and in America it became an important element of American culture. Massachusetts, however, was an intolerant theocracy, and Rhode Island was founded as a refuge for those who had different beliefs. Pennsylvania was founded for the Quakers who were persecuted not only in Britain, but by the Puritans of Massachusetts and Connecticut. Maryland was founded for the Catholics disenfranchised both in Britain and certain other colonies. Both Pennsylvania and Maryland became havens for other sects, notably the wide variety of German and Swiss Protestant refugees who rapidly gave Pennsylvania a German-American majority. The final wave of immigration during the colonial period was made up of staunchly Calvinist Presbyterian Scots-Irish who had been moved by the British government from their original homes along the English–Scottish border to Northern Ireland to balance and control the Catholic Irish. By the time the Scots-Irish arrived in the mid-18th century, the more desirable and fertile coastal areas had already been filled up, and many were forced to take small holdings in the upland regions of the Appalachian mountain chain.

Early Puritan settlers believed that they were a chosen people who had a covenant with God to build a society governed by divine law. Thus they firmly rejected religious freedom, which was thought tantamount to allowing false religious ideas. In Britain, the Act of Tolerance was enacted in 1689, but in many colonies in America, religious intolerance continued for many years afterward.

As the 18th century progressed, however, religious intolerance began to be undermined. Firstly, European Enlightenment thought, which emphasized the use of reason in religion, weakened the rule of the established church and contributed to religious freedom in America.[56] No less important was the Great Awakening, a wave of religious enthusiasm which swept the American colonies in the 1730s and 1740s. Preachers of the Great Awakening emphasized the inner religious experience of the individual in achieving salvation, denouncing the Anglican Church,[57] which was still legally recognized as a tax-supported church in some colonies, as dogmatic and formalistic. The Great Awakening leaders aroused alarm that the Anglican leaders were attempting to establish an Anglican episcopate in America.[58] Being cross-denominational and intercolonial, the Great Awakening had a strong cultural influence upon colonists.[59]

Both the Great Awakening and Enlightenment thought, by challenging Anglican authoritative religious rule and contributing to religious freedom, prepared the ideological ground for the American Revolution (1.3.2).

In terms of political influence, no ideas contributed more to the American Revolution than those of John Locke, a prominent Enlightenment philosopher who declared that every human being possessed certain natural and inalienable rights (among which were life, liberty, and property), that people created governments to safeguard these rights, and that if a government failed to preserve such rights, people had the right to supplant the government with one that would protect those rights.[60] The Pietism of the Great Awakening and the rationalism of the Enlightenment joined forces to support the American Revolution.

## 1.3.2. The American Revolution

Confrontation between the American colonies and the British government began when the latter started to impose a series of taxes on colonists after the Seven Years' War, which ended in 1763.[61] Colonists strongly resisted the Stamp Act of 1765 in particular.[62] In 1773, the Boston Tea Party incident occurred,[63] which brought about punitive measures by the British including closure of the port of Boston. In 1774, the colonists held the first Continental Congress, and resolved that each province should have its own government and troops, and should suspend all commercial intercourse with Britain.[64] In 1775, the war started at Lexington between the colonist troops and the British regulars. When the colonists won the battle of Saratoga in 1777, the French declared war on Britain and sent a fleet that was key to bringing about a decisive American victory at the battle of Yorktown in 1781.

The Treaty of Paris in 1783 formally confirmed American independence from Britain.[65] The British acceptance of American independence was, however, grudging and incomplete. Resolution of the matter required a second conflict, the War of 1812. Though the Americans suffered the burning of their new capital at Washington, the British suffered a disastrous defeat at the hands of Andrew Jackson at the Battle of New Orleans.

Meanwhile, a year after the onset of the war, the Declaration of Independence was issued on July 4, 1776 proclaiming the rationale of the war for independence.[66] In 1777, the Continental Congress passed the Articles of Confederation, which established a union among the thirteen states. But it was a weak organization, having no authority to control each state. Efforts to create a strong central government continued, and in 1787 Alexander Hamilton and James Madison managed to convene a Constitutional Convention in Philadelphia.[67]

Thirty-nine delegates agreed on the framework of a new republic—the first republic since the brief British Puritan Commonwealth of Oliver Cromwell. The new government was given a strong executive: the president, who was both chief of state and head of government. The executive was constrained by two additional equal and independent branches: the legislative and the judicial.

A disagreement arose between small states and large states on how each state should be represented in the legislature. The compromise created a House of Representatives that was to be composed of delegates whose number was determined by state population, and a Senate that was to be composed of an equal number of representatives from all the states.[68]

The new constitution was ratified in June 1788. To meet the concerns of George Mason and other anti-federalists who feared the reach of an all-powerful central government, ten amendments to the Constitution enumerating civil rights were adopted as the Bill of Rights in 1791. The First Amendment prescribed separation of church and state by stating that Congress should "make no law respecting an establishment of religion or prohibiting free exercise thereof." The Second Amendment emphasized the necessity of the militias that patrolled to protect slaveholders from slave rebellions.[69]

### 1.3.3. Slavery and the Civil War

A major issue that divided the Convention members was slavery. As of 1780, there were well over 500,000 slaves in an overall population of just under four million. They were concentrated in the southern states.[70]

Slavery was becoming uneconomic in the northern states, and there was hope that it would die out in the southern states as well because of its inherent inefficiency. But this hope died with the invention of the cotton gin by Eli Whitney in 1793 (see 5.3.4, US Cotton Industry). With the gin, seeds could be quickly removed from raw cotton, and the large-scale economical production of raw cotton became possible. Suddenly cotton became a hugely profitable crop. Additionally, there were two events that made cotton plantation owners in the South rich. Firstly, the British cotton textile industry's

*14*

Table 1.3.3. American Raw-Cotton Production and Exports (million pounds)

|           | Average annual production | Average annual exports | Average annual exports to Britain |
|-----------|---------------------------|------------------------|-----------------------------------|
| 1790–1794 | 3.9                       | 0.5                    | 0.5                               |
| 1820–1824 | 190                       | 142                    | 94                                |
| 1850–1854 | 1,236                     | 931                    | 681                               |
| 1880–1884 | 2,944                     | 1,980                  | 1,248                             |

Source: S. J. Chapman, *The Cotton Industry and Trade* (London: Methuen & Co., 1905), 2.

development immensely increased demand for raw cotton. Secondly, in 1830, President Andrew Jackson removed Native American tribes from vast southeastern areas suitable for cotton production. These developments transformed the southern economy and changed the dynamics of slavery. US raw cotton production increased 320-fold from 1790–1794 to 1850–1854. Most of the raw cotton was exported, mainly to Britain (table 1.3.3). The number of slaves increased from 700,000 in 1790 to 1.19 million in 1810, 2.01 million in 1830, and 3.95 million in 1860.[71]

While slave labor had become vital for southerners, northerners believed that slavery was a disgrace to the new American experiment in freedom and human rights. It seemed a contradiction and hypocrisy for Americans to pride themselves that they had created the world's freest society. By the early middle of the 19th century, most of the northern states had outlawed slavery.[72] By the middle of the 19th century, the difference between North and South on slavery was so wide that the two regions were like two nations.

In 1860, when Abraham Lincoln was elected president, seven southern states seceded from the North, forming a new nation, the Confederate States of America. Four more states joined the Confederacy after the Civil War started in April, 1861.[73]

The victory of the North (the Union) in the four years of war preserved the United States as one nation and ended the institution of slavery.[74] But the war left 620,000 to 750,000 soldiers dead, a higher number than the number of American military deaths in all other wars combined.[75]

### 1.3.4. The Aftermath of the Civil War

The major questions facing the post-bellum North were what to do with the rebellious South and what to do with four million illiterate freed slaves in

Chapter 1

the South.

Lincoln had wanted a rapid restoration of normal relations with the South after the war. He had intended to grant amnesty to those who would take an oath of loyalty to the Union and allow any state to establish a new government as soon as it abolished slavery and complied with Union laws. He persuaded Congress to enact the Thirteenth Amendment that provided for the abolition of slavery, and Congress passed it in January 1865. But he did not live to see it adopted in December that year after the necessary ratifications by state governments.[76] Lincoln was assassinated on April 14, five days after the Grant–Lee surrender agreement in Virginia to end the war.[77]

Andrew Johnson, who succeeded Lincoln, followed Lincoln's policies. He granted the prewar southern leaders general amnesty and allowed them to recover political power. He was prepared to recognize the southern state governments upon ratification of the Thirteenth Amendment.

Johnson's conciliatory position was not shared by Congress, however, which was controlled by the so-called Radical Republicans. They were wary of the southern whites' possible counterrevolutionary movements.[78] Events in the South appeared to justify their apprehension. Encouraged by Johnson's lenient policies, the state governments in the South, while abolishing slavery, enacted a series of laws known as the "Black Codes," which had the consequence of relegating Black Americans to second-class citizenship.[79]

The Radical Republicans were convinced that the southern whites had not been sufficiently punished.[80] Having secured a two-thirds majority in both houses in the 1866 midterm elections, the Radical Republicans pushed through a series of "reconstruction" measures. When Congress passed the Fourteenth Amendment in January 1868, giving all Americans equal citizenship,[81] the Radicals placed the states which refused to ratify the Amendment under military government.[82] In March 1868 the Radicals in the House of Representatives impeached Johnson, but he was saved by one vote in the Senate. When the Fifteenth Amendment was passed in February 1869 providing for Black suffrage, they wanted the southern states to ratify it to be eligible to send delegations to Congress.[83]

The southern whites' resentment of the northern intervention grew. They were determined to reestablish the old order of white supremacy by resorting to terroristic methods. The Ku Klux Klan, a secret society of vigilantes which had been organized in 1866, started to terrify Black men into giving up their

16

voting rights. In 1969 President Ulysses Grant used federal troops to root out the Ku Klux Klan, but terrorism under ad hoc local white sponsorship continued.[84]

By the early 1870s, however, the North was beginning to weary of its attempt to impose its rule on the South.[85] In 1872, Grant instructed federal officers not to interfere any further in southern politics. Encouraged by the withdrawal of northern support for the state governments in the South, the southern "redeemers" stepped up their efforts to reestablish white supremacy.

A series of Supreme Court decisions in the late 1870s and early 1880s further assisted the cause of white supremacy. They established the principle that the federal government could not interfere where state laws imposed limitations on Black Americans' exercise of their civil rights. This opened the way to virtual disenfranchisement of Black people by applying special literacy tests and poll taxes in voting.[86]

As racial feeling became intensified rather than easing toward the close of the century, the southern states adopted the so-called Jim Crow laws, reviving principles of the 1865–1866 "Black Codes," and mandating racial segregation in all public facilities in states of the South.[87]

The Civil War brought about the ending of slavery, which in turn gave birth to an apartheid society. The simmering issue of the human and civil rights of Black Americans was left unresolved for many decades. It was not until the middle of the 20th century that the Civil Rights Movement gained strength.[88]

## 1.3.5. Exceptionalism and Manifest Destiny

In colonial times, the idea that Americans were charged by God with the task of reforming themselves for others to copy—with building a "City on a Hill"—was dominant. Many colonists believed that they had a divine mission or destiny, and would not follow Europe into a historical future. This sentiment, often termed American exceptionalism, constituted one of the important factors that led to the American Revolution.[89]

One strand of American exceptionalism was what has been called "isolationism" in US foreign policy. The classic expression of this position was George Washington's warning in his Farewell Address of 1796. By declaring, "The great rule of conduct for us in regard to foreign nations is in extending our commercial relations, to have with them as little political connection as possible,"[90] he cautioned that Americans should preserve their nation's unique position of aloofness from European imperialist politics. Washington's admonition is reread in Congress every year on the anniversary of his birth, and isolationism remained an important part of American attitudes in foreign policy until World War II.

After the American Revolution, meanwhile, as the Republic became stronger and more successful, Americans began to believe that they had a natural right to expand across adjacent lands in North America. They believed that it was America's clear destiny to provide less fortunate people under foreign governments with the blessings of the superior American political and social system.[91] Indeed, the drive to the West from the early decades of the 19th century through the 1840s was largely fueled by this idea of "manifest destiny."[92]

When the United States signed the Treaty of Paris with Britain in 1783, the western border of the United States was the Mississippi River, with the mouth of the Mississippi at New Orleans controlled by Spain. Over the next sixty-plus years, the United States spread its territory westward to the Pacific. It purchased the vast Louisiana territories from Napoleon in 1803,[93] acquired Florida from Spain by threatening war in 1819, obtained the Oregon territory from Britain after a near war and negotiation in 1846,[94] and gained Texas, New Mexico, Arizona, and California from Mexico by invasion and a war in 1845–46. By 1850 the American territorial domain had been tripled.

The ideas of manifest destiny, like those of American exceptionalism, derived from the belief that America was destined to be a "City on a Hill." When they reached the Pacific coast, the supporters of manifest destiny argued that expansion should not stop at the coastline, but should continue beyond. In the 1850s, this manifest destiny sentiment helped inspire the US government to send a historic naval expedition to Japan. Though the direct purpose of Commodore Perry's expedition was trade expansion with China and the protection of whalers (as discussed in 2.1.2), there was certainly in the background of this ambitious project the idea that awakening an Asian hermit nation was American manifest destiny.

## NOTES

### 1.1. Japan before Opening the Country

1　Yamamoto Takeo, *Nihonshi* (Tokyo: Obunsha, 1979), 252.

2　The *bakufu* classified local rulers in Japan into three categories according to their relationships to the *bakufu*: as kinsmen (*shinpan* 親藩), hereditary vassals (*fudai* 譜代), or less-trusted allies (*tozama* 外様).

3　Ronald P. Toby, *The State and Diplomacy in Early Modern Japan* (Stanford: Stanford University Press, 1984), 96.

4　Mitani Hiroshi, *Perī raikō* (Tokyo: Yoshikawa Kōbunkan, 2003), 3–4.

5　Mitani, *Perī raikō*, 7–8. Christopher Howe, *The Origins of Japanese Trade Supremacy* (Chicago: University of Chicago Press, 1996), 39.

6　The population of Japan grew from 12 million in 1600 to 31 million in 1720, and to 34 million in 1870. The cultivated land during this period increased from 2,065 million *chō* in 1600 to 2,927 million *chō* in 1720, and to 3,223 million *chō* in 1870. The strong growth in population between 1600 and 1720 was supported by the opening of new farmland during the period, but the difficulty in opening new arable land after 1720 put a limit to the population increase. Howe, *The Origin of Japanese Trade Supremacy*, 50.

7　The emperor and his family, the court nobles, priests, and doctors were not included in any of the four groups. Assignment to a particular caste was according to birth.

8　In 1820, GDP per capita of Britain, the United States, Japan, and China in 1990 international dollars were 1,707, 1,257, 669, and 600 respectively. Angus Maddison, *The World Economy: A Millennial Perspective Development Centre Studies* (Paris: Development Centre of the OECD, 2001), Table B-21, 264.

9　The *terakoya* were often established in Buddhist temples or Shinto shrines in villages. From the turn of the 19th century, nearly every village had a *terakoya*. There were some 63,000 villages in the late Tokugawa period. Nakane Chie and Ōishi Shinzaburō, eds., *Tokugawa Japan: The Social and Economic Antecedent of Modern Japan*, trans. Conrad Totman (Tokyo: University of Tokyo Press, 1990), 118, 230. The *terakoya* attendance rate reached 70 percent in Edo at the beginning of the 19th century. https://en.wikipedia.org/wiki/Terakoya.

10　Strong Buddhist influence is evident in the seventeen-article "constitution" of Prince Shōtoku promulgated in 604. During the Nara period (710–784) and the Heian period (794–1192), Buddhism was supported officially by the state and local lords. The Kamakura period (1192–1333) saw attempts by several Buddhist sects to return to pure Buddhism with each sect propounding its own persuasive theology. Prominent founders of those sects were Hōnen (1133–1215), Shinran (1173–1262), Eisai (1141–1215), Dōgen (1200–1253), and Nichiren (1222–1282). Confucianism was introduced to Japan at approximately the same time as Buddhism, but it did not develop philosophically in Japan until the Tokugawa period. H. Gene Blocker and Christopher L. Starling, *Japanese Philosophy* (Albany, NY: State University of New York Press, 2001), 63.

11　Robert Bellah, *Tokugawa Religion: The Values of Pre-Industrial Japan* (New York: The Free Press, 1957), 51.

Chapter 1

12  Hayashi Razan (1583–1657), an enthusiastic promoter of Zhu Xi philosophy, was instrumental in making Shushigaku the official ideology of the *bakufu*. Furuta Hikaru and Koyasu Nobukuni, eds., *Nihon shisōshi dokuhon* (Tokyo: Tōyōkeizai Shinpōsha, 1979), 86. Ishida Ichirō, *Nihon shisōshi gairon* (Tokyo: Yoshikawa Kōbunkan, 1963), 176.

13  Blocker and Starling, *Japanese Philosophy*, 79. Mikiso Hane, *Premodern Japan: A Historical Survey* (Boulder: Westview Press, 1991), 162–163.

14  Blocker and Starling, *Japanese Philosophy*, 75.

15  Ibid., 84. Hane, *Premodern Japan*, 162–163.

16  Ibid., 163.

17  Ishida, *Nihon shisōshi*, 214. Bellah, *Tokugawa Religion*, 100.

18  Bellah, *Tokugawa Religion*, 103–104. Komatsu argues that in Shinto there is no concept of an absolute deity that is the creator or Almighty God, and no clear distinction between *kami* (神) and human beings, and that the term *kami* is an honorific for noble, sacred sprits which all beings have. Keiichiro Komatsu, *The Origins of the Pacific War and the Importance of 'Magic.'* (London: Routledge, 1999), 278.

19  The Mito school grew out of a plan by Tokugawa Mitsukuni (徳川光圀 1628–1700), the daimyo of Mito and the grandson of Tokugawa Ieyasu, to compile a multivolume scholarly work, the *Dai Nihonshi* (大日本史 History of great Japan). Bellah, *Tokugawa Religion*, 102–103.

20  G. B. Sansom, *The Western World and Japan* (New York: Alfred A. Knopf, 1950), 203–206, 247–260. Johannes Hurschmeier and Tsunehiko Yui, *The Development of Japanese Business, 1600–1973* (London: George Allen & Unwin, 1975), 70–71.

21  Sansom, *The Western World and Japan*, 248–259.

22  Takano Chōei (1804–1850) and Watanabe Kazan (1793–1841), both well-known scholars of Dutch learning, were persecuted and driven to suicide as they expressed their disagreement with the *bakufu*'s policy of driving away all foreign ships approaching Japanese shores. Sakuma Shōzan (1811–1864), a scholar of Shushigaku and Dutch learning as well as an expert on Western gunnery, had a wide following as a teacher and influenced many young men, but was murdered by anti-foreign fanatics. Yokoi Shōnan (1809–1869), a well-known Shushigaku scholar and an advisor to Matsudaira Shungaku, lord of Echizen, was also assassinated for his pro-Western views by a reactionary samurai.

23  In 1851, Shōin traveled to Mito to see Aizawa Seishisai, whose works he had read earlier. Hane, *Premodern Japan*, 215–216. Albert M. Craig, *Chōshū in the Meiji Restoration* (Cambridge: Harvard University Press, 1961), 159.

24  They included Itō Hirobumi (伊藤博文), Kido Takayoshi (木戸孝允), Yamagata Aritomo (山県有朋), Yamada Akiyoshi (山田顕義), Takasugi Shinsaku (高杉晋作) and Kusaka Genzui (久坂玄瑞). Ibid., 157.

25  The Zōshikan was established in 1773. In a spacious enclosure with a Confucian temple, lecture halls, and dormitories, a faculty of sixty or more scholars taught a student body of four hundred to eight hundred boys. Haru Matsukata Reischauer, *Samurai and Silk* (Cambridge: Harvard University Press, 1986), 35–37.

26  They included Saigō Takamori (西郷隆盛), Ōkubo Toshimichi (大久保利通), Tōgō Heihachirō (東郷平八郎), Ōyama Iwao (大山巌), and Matsukata Masayoshi (松方正義).

*Notes*

27  Bellah argues that Ishida Baigan's Shingaku played an important role in economic rationalization in the Tokugawa period and had a significant influence on the growth of modern industrial Japan. He compares the role of the Shingaku ethic in Japan's modernization to Max Weber's Protestant ethic in Europe. Bellah, *Tokugawa Religion*, 158–161.

28  Ishida Baigan derived many of his arguments for merchant ethics and roles from works by Suzuki Shōsan (1579–1655), a Zen Buddhist priest and former warrior. Shōsan advocated that each and every occupation was Buddha-practice. He also wrote that the merchant must devote himself squarely to the acquisition of commercial gains, but he must have great reverence for the virtue of honesty if he hoped to reap any advantage. See Winston L. King, *Death Was His Kōan: The Samurai-Zen of Suzuki Shōsan* (Berkeley: Asian Humanities Press, 1986), 247, and Nakamura Hajime, "Suzuki Shōsan, 1579–1655 and the Spirit of Capitalism in Japanese Buddhism," *Monumenta Nipponica: Studies on Japanese Culture Past and Present*, vol. 22, no. I-2, ed. Joseph Pittau (Tokyo: Sophia University, 1967), 9.

29  Tōyama Shigeru, *Nihonjin no kinben: Chochiku kan* (Tokyo: Tōyōkeizai Shinpōsha, 1987), 39. Bellah, *Tokugawa Religion*, 158, 160–164.

30  Bellah, *Tokugawa Religion*, 173.

31  Morishima Michio, *Nihon wa naze seikōshitaka* (Tokyo: TBS Britannica, 1984), 86.

### 1.2. Britain's Foreign Policy in the Mid-19th Century

32  The Industrial Revolution in Britain in the late 18th through early 19th century immensely increased the British industrial production. The British share of world industrial production was 24 percent in 1820, 21 percent in 1840, and 21 percent in 1860, whereas that of the United States was 4 percent, 5 percent, and 14 percent respectively. W. W. Rostow, *The World Economy: History and Prospect* (Austin: University of Texas Press, 1978), 52.

Britain's share of world export trade in manufactures in the early 1850s was probably more than 40 percent. In the export trade of certain manufactures, such as textiles, British industry enjoyed a virtual monopoly position. Bernard Semmel, *The Rise of Free Trade Imperialism* (Cambridge: Cambridge University Press, 1970), 157. Albert H. Imlah, *Economic Elements in the Pax Britannica* (Cambridge: Harvard University Press, 1958), 72.

33  Paul Kennedy, *The Rise and Fall of the Great Powers* (London: Unwin Hyman, 1988), 154.

34  In 1861, Belgium signed a treaty with France. In 1862, Portugal and Denmark signed treaties with Britain. Between 1863 and 1866, many other European countries entered the network by means of treaties with France. Peter Mathias and Sidney Pollard, *The Cambridge Economic History of Europe*, vol. III (Cambridge: Cambridge University Press, 1989), 40–41.

35  William Langer, *The Diplomacy of Imperialism* (New York: Alfred A. Knopf, 1965), 70.

36  In the middle of the 19th century, Britain was dominantly competitive in the export of manufactures. Thus Britain did not feel it necessary to possess sovereignty over the lands with which it traded to the same extent as either in the preceding mercantilist

Chapter 1

days or in the period of neo-mercantilist imperialism which followed, starting in the 1870s. See John Strachey, *The End of Empire* (London: Victor Gollancz, 1959), 72.

37 This was a major but ultimately unsuccessful uprising in India against the rule of the British East India Company. The Indians term it their "First War of Independence."

38 W. G. Beasley, *Japanese Imperialism, 1894–1945* (New York: Oxford University Press, 1987), 3–4.

39 John Gallagher and Ronald Robinson, "The Imperialism of Free Trade," in *The Decline, Revival and Fall of the British Empire*, ed. Anil Seal (Cambridge: Cambridge University Press, 1982), 15.

40 Beasley, *Japanese Imperialism*, 15.

41 Ibid., 4–5.

42 George Woodcock, *The British in the Far East* (New York: Athenaeum, 1969), 68.

43 Beasley, *Japanese Imperialism*, 18.

44 Ping Chia Kuo, "Caleb Cushing and the Treaty of Wanghia, 1844," *Journal of Modern History*, vol. 5, no. 1 (March, 1933), 35.

45 Beasley, *Japanese Imperialism*, 17.

46 Peter and Pollard, eds., *The Cambridge Economic History of Europe*, vol. III, 156. Annual imports of opium into China increased by 2.5 times between 1839 and 1880. By the 1900s, opium exports from India amounted to 15 percent of the British government budget in India. Of the Chinese national tax revenues, those from the sales of both imported and domestically produced opium constituted 14 percent by the 1910s. In 1906, Britain finally agreed to an annual reduction of 10 percent in imports of opium from 1908 on.

47 Out of the thirty-nine hostages, only eighteen were eventually returned alive.

48 The Taiping Rebellion lasted from 1850 to 1864, taking an estimated toll of at least twenty million lives. The leader of the rebels was Hong Xiuquan (洪秀全), who had founded a religious group being inspired by elements of Christianity. Hong was an ethnic Hakka who sought to overthrow the Manchu-led Qing government. The Western powers were first sympathetic to the rebels, but turned supportive of the Qing government after the latter accepted the Beijing Treaty of 1860. In 1864, the Qing government finally won the civil war, albeit at great cost to its fiscal and political structure.

49 Beasley, *Japanese Imperialism*, 15.

50 In Britain there was no restriction on the purchase or consumption of opium until 1876.

51 Semmel, *Rise of Free Trade Imperialism*, 152–153.

52 In 1854, when the Taiping rebels held Shanghai and the customs officers were driven away, Great Britain, France and the United States set up an inspectorate of customs. This system proved advantageous to the Qing government also, since it secured stable customs revenue through an uncorrupted and efficient customs service. In 1858, by an agreement between the Chinese government and the Western powers, the new system was extended to all the ports. Robert Hart, who was appointed as inspector-general in 1863, served until 1908. John Fairbank, *Trade and Diplomacy on the China Coast* (Stanford: Stanford University Press, 1969), 462.

53 William L. Neumann, *America Encounters Japan* (Baltimore: Johns Hopkins Press,

*Notes*

1963), 51.

### 1.3. America from Colonial Times

54  In 1620, a group of 102 pilgrims (the "Pilgrim Fathers") sailed in the *Mayflower* and founded the colony of Plymouth, Massachusetts. But they were not so much anxious to build a strong colony as to have their religious freedom there. In fact, the colony in Plymouth grew very slowly, numbering scarcely three hundred by 1630. On the other hand, the Massachusetts Bay Company was established under a charter issued by Charles I to have a strong colonial establishment in America. Sydney E. Ahlstrom, *A Religious History of the American People* (New Heaven: Yale University Press, 1972), 106, 144. Nakanishi Terumasa, *Amerika gaikō no tamashii: Teikoku no rinen to honnō* (Tokyo: Shueisha, 2005), 106–107.

55  Ahlstrom, *A Religious History of the American People*, 147.

56  The European Enlightenment, starting primarily in the 17th century, revolved around the use of reason to discover and understand the laws that governed nature and society. This movement encompassed a range of thinkers, from those whose primary accomplishments were in the physical realm (e.g., Newton) to those whose primary contributions were in the philosophical realm (e.g., Locke). This approach to understanding all aspects of the universe—whether the laws of motion or the laws of God—was to use reason in order to study, analyze, and understand those aspects. Rationalists expected that their approach would lead to progress in improving the human conditions. Michael Corbett and Julia Corbett, *Politics and Religion in the United States* (New York: Garland Publishing, 1999), 46.

  The impact of the Enlightenment on religion was immense. Though some who were affected by Enlightenment currents did not question the utility of religious establishments, the general impact of the Age of Reason was against revealed orthodoxies and the privileges of establishments. The observable decline of churches in the last quarter of the 18th century was largely a consequence of Enlightenment thought. Robert Handy, *A Christian America: Protestant Hopes and Historical Realities* (New York: Oxford University Press, 1984), 17–18.

57  M. Corbett and J. Corbett, *Politics and Religion*, 57. Handy, *A Christian America*, 20. Carman and Syrett, *History of the American People*, 84.

58  The preachers of the Great Awakening raised the alarm that an Anglican episcopate would mean additional taxes, priest-controlled courts, and the assumption of secular functions by episcopal authorities. Carman and Syrett, *History of the American People*, vol. 1, 115.

59  Handy, *A Christian America*, 18.

60  Carman and Syrett, *History of the American People*, 114. M. Corbett and J. Corbett, *Politics and Religion*, 33–34.

61  Before the British defeat of France in the Seven Years' War, the British government had avoided imposing heavy taxes on colonies so as not to weaken them in their fight against the French and Indians.

62  The British government attempted to raise revenue through direct taxation of all colonial commercial and legal papers. The opponents of the Stamp Act claimed that it was a violation of the British constitution for Parliament to tax them, since British

Chapter 1

subjects could not be taxed without their consent, which came in the form of representation in Parliament, and the colonists elected no members of Parliament. The British government repealed the act in 1766. Carman and Syrett, *History of the American People*, 129–132.

63 In 1773, a band of men disguised as Indians dumped 18,000 pounds worth of tea into the water of Boston Harbor from the vessel of the East India Company, which had a monopoly on the tea trade in America. At that time, the East India Company was in financial difficulty, with huge amounts of tea stocks. The monopoly on the tea trade had been given by the British government to rescue the company. As the company sold tea directly to retailers through its own agents, angry tea merchants who had been deprived of business were behind the "Indians." Ibid., 140.

64 Ibid., 142–144.

65 The United States took possession of nearly all the territory east of the Mississippi River and south of the Great Lakes, with the British retaining control of Canada and Spain taking Florida.

66 The Declaration of Independence was drafted mainly by Thomas Jefferson. Its basic points are as follows: All men are created equal; men are endowed by their Creator with certain unalienable rights among which are life, liberty, and the pursuit of happiness; governments are created among men for the purpose of securing these rights; governments derive their powers from the consent of the governed; and if a government does not secure the rights of men, it is the right of people to alter it or to abolish it and to institute a new government. Jefferson borrowed heavily from John Locke in drafting the declaration. M. Corbett and J. Corbett, *Politics and Religion*, 61.

67 Paul Johnson, *A History of the American People* (New York: HarperCollins Publishers, 1999), 185.

68 Ibid., 208.

69 Carl T. Bogus, "The Hidden History of the Second Amendment," *University of California at Davis Law Review*, vol. 31, no. 2 (winter 1998), 311–407. The Second Amendment reads, "A well-regulated Militia being necessary to the security of a free state, the right of the people to keep and bear Arms shall not be infringed." Different interpretations of this amendment have fueled a long-running debate over gun-control legislation. Opponents of gun control, of which the National Rifle Association is the most visible, contend that this amendment protects the people's right to bear arms. In 2008 (in *District of Columbia v. Heller*) the Supreme Court handed down a decision that held that the amendment protects an individual right to possess and carry firearms, while also ruling that the right is not unlimited and does not prohibit all regulation of all firearms or similar devices. Supreme Court rulings in 2010 and 2016 were basically in line with the 2008 ruling. Despite these decisions, the debate between various organizations regarding gun control and gun rights continues. https://en.wikipedia.org/wiki/Second_Amendment_to_the_United States Constitution.

70 Ross Robertson and Gary Walton, *History of the American Economy* (New York: Harcourt Brace Jovanovich, 1979), 228.

71 US Department of Commerce, Bureau of the Census, *Historical Statistics of the*

*Notes*

*United States* (Washington, DC: US Government Printing Office, 1975), 14.

72 Robertson and Walton, *History of the American Economy*, 228–229.

73 By February 1, 1861, South Carolina, Mississippi, Florida, Georgia, Alabama, Louisiana had seceded. Texas soon followed. Virginia, North Carolina, Tennessee, and Arkansas left the Union after the war broke out in April 1861, when Confederates attacked Fort Sumter in South Carolina. Carman and Syrett, *History of the American People*, 597.

74 Ibid., 644–648.

75 Total US military casualties since the American Revolutionary War are estimated to be 1,354,664 or more. The five major wars ranked by total number of military deaths after the Civil War are WWII (405,399), WWI (116,516), the Vietnam War (58,209), the Korean War (54,246), and the Iraq/Afghanistan Wars (7,222).

The Civil War was a moral and religious contest as well as a political one. In fact, the second Great Awakening movement that had begun in the late 18th century had a significant influence on both sides. It provided northerners with a strong moral basis in New Testament Gospel texts for their quest to abolish slavery. Southerners argued their position, quoting Old Testament texts on patriarchal and Mosaic acceptance of servitude as well as the apostle Paul on obedience to one's masters. Ministers were among the most fanatical of the combatants on both sides, and southern clergymen were particularly responsible for prolonging the struggle, despite the Confederacy's huge disadvantages in terms of population and industry. James Stobaugh, *American History* (Green Forest, AR: Master Books, 2012), 166. Johnson, *History of the American People*, 470.

76 It was on December 6, 1865 that the necessary three-quarters of state legislatures ratified the Thirteenth Amendment. Section 1 of Thirteenth Amendment reads, "Neither slavery nor involuntary servitude, except as a punishment for crime whereof the party shall have been duly convicted, shall exist within the United States, or any place subject to their jurisdiction."

77 General Ulysses Grant and General Robert Lee had met at Appomattox in Virginia on April 9, 1865, to end hostilities.

78 Dulles, *The United States since 1865*, 8.

79 Ibid., 15. Johnson, *History of the American People*, 501.

80 Johnson, *History of the American People*, 501.

81 Section 1 of the Fourteenth Amendment reads: "All persons, born or naturalized in the United States and subject to the jurisdiction thereof, are citizens of the United States and of the State wherein they reside . . . "

82 Dulles, *The United States since 1865*, 20, 22. Johnson, *History of the American People*, 503.

83 Dulles, *The United States since 1865*, 22. Section 1 of the Fifteenth Amendment reads: "The right of citizens of the United States to vote shall not be denied or abridged by the United States or any State on account of race, color, or previous condition of servitude."

84 Dulles, *The United States since 1865*, 27. Johnson, *History of the American People*, 506.

85 Dulles, *The United States since 1865*, 28.

86 Ibid., 30.

87 Ibid., 30. "Jim Crow" laws provided for racial segregation in all public facilities such as transportation, schools, dining facilities, lodging establishments, toilets, and drinking fountains in southern states.

88 Segregation of public schools was declared unconstitutional by the Supreme Court in 1954. The remaining Jim Crow laws were overruled by the Civil Rights Act of 1964 and the Voting Rights Act of 1965.

89 M. Corbett and J. Corbett, *Politics and Religion*, 46.

90 Trevor B. McCrisken, "Exceptionalism," *Encyclopedia of American Foreign Policy*, vol. 2 (New York: Charles Scribner's Sons, 2002), 67. Manfred Jones, "Isolationism," *Encyclopedia of American Foreign Policy,* vol. 2 (New York: Charles Scribner's Sons, 2002), 338–339.

91 Carman and Syrett, *History of the American People*, 530.

92 It was John O'Sullivan who first used the phrase "manifest destiny" in an editorial in the *New York Morning News* in 1845. Thomas R. Hietala, *Manifest Design: American Exceptionalism and Empire* (Ithaca: Cornell University Press, 1985), 255.

93 Louisiana at that time was a territory of 828,000 square miles, as large as America itself. It included the present-day states of Louisiana, Arkansas, Oklahoma, Missouri, Kansas, Iowa, Nebraska, South Dakota, and most of North Dakota, Wyoming, and Montana, as well as part of Minnesota. America paid 15 million dollars to France for the purchase.

94 The Oregon territory included the present states of Washington, Oregon, Idaho, and parts of Montana and Wyoming.

# Chapter 2
# Japan's Opening of the Country and the Fall of the *Bakufu*

## 2.1. Japan's Opening of the Country

### 2.1.1. America's China Trade and Whaling in the Pacific

One important impetus for the Perry expedition came from the American hope that Japan would be a stepping stone to the Chinese market. Since Americans had been shut out of the British mercantile system in the western hemisphere in retaliation for the American Revolution, they felt a special need for new markets and new sources of supply. China seemed the perfect answer.[1] The first business voyage to China was made in 1784. It was a profitable journey, and was subsequently followed by many trips by American traders. They sailed mainly by clipper ships, but with advent of the steamship age in the mid-19th century, American entrepreneurs planned regular commercial sea routes between San Francisco and Shanghai, and they wanted to secure ports in Japan for resupplying coal.[2]

Another important purpose of the expedition to Japan was helping American whalers operating in the North Pacific. The Pacific Ocean was the hunting ground for the whales that supplied the oils for lubricating and illumination for America's industries and urban upper class until the petroleum industry's development starting from the 1860s. By the mid-1840s, American whalers constituted more than 75 percent of the world's whaling fleet, and by the late 1840s about 90 percent of all American whalers were in the Pacific.[3] By the early 1850s, the annual value of whales taken in the North Pacific reached $9 million, which was about $2 million more than the annual US imports from China and about four times as much as its exports to China at that time.[4]

Whaling voyages continued to become longer as whales were caught in larger numbers and were sought further north in the Pacific. Voyages that had taken two years or so in the 1830s took three, four, or even five years by the 1850s. This increased the importance of Pacific ports as supply and repair stations.[5] Hawaii provided an important launching point to American whalers, but the majority of usable ports in the North Pacific beyond Hawaii were in the Russian territory stretching from the Kamchatka Peninsula to Alaska.[6] The Russian government, however, closed their ports to American whalers on account of the crews' bad behavior.[7] Japan's location in the Pacific Ocean thus seemed all the more important for American whalers in the 1850s.

## 2.1.2. Perry and the Treaty of Kanagawa

On July 8, 1853, Commodore Matthew C. Perry anchored his flotilla of four warships off the town of Uraga (浦賀) at the mouth of Tokyo (then Edo 江戸) Bay.[8] The *bakufu* had been advised of this expedition by the Dutch at Nagasaki, yet its actual appearance caused consternation. Perry stayed for only ten days, but he impressed the Japanese with the strength of his squadron, which included two steamships—the first ever seen in Japanese waters—and with his own goodwill. He was dignified, firm, fearless, and yet polite. President Fillmore's letter addressed to the Japanese emperor was received respectfully by *bakufu* officials. Perry thereupon sailed away, warning that he would return the following spring to receive a reply.

The presidential letter requested friendship, commerce, supplies, and the protection of shipwrecked seamen. Perry returned to Edo Bay on February 13, 1854,[9] bringing seven ships this time, including three paddlewheel steamers.

The *bakufu* officials were aware of the violence that Britain inflicted on China in the Opium Wars through the Dutch and the Chinese. The *bakufu* decided not to test their chances with armed Western visitors, and opted to receive Perry and send him away with a minimum of concessions.[10] It is noteworthy that detailed information about America provided by John Manjirō, a

*28*

Japanese castaway who had returned to Japan in 1851 after having spent ten years in the United States, had considerable influence on the *bakufu*'s decision to conduct peaceful diplomacy.[11]

Perry had brought with him the text of the first American commercial treaty with China concluded in 1844, suitably emended to serve as a draft for consideration by the Japanese. The chief Japanese negotiator, Hayashi Daigaku no Kami (林大学頭),[12] was firm in rejecting the opening of trade relations, however, saying that it was impossible to discard the laws and customs of three centuries so precipitously. This apparently did not surprise Perry. Francis Hawkes writes, "[Perry] was not sanguine enough to hope that he could procure an entire adoption of the Chinese Treaty by the Japanese. He was not ignorant of the differences in national characteristics between the inhabitants of China, and the more independent, self-reliant, and sturdy natives of the Japanese islands."[13] Perry accepted the Japanese limitations on the type of treaty to be negotiated, and left the task of negotiating a commercial treaty to the diplomatic representative who might come later. Hayashi and his colleagues were prepared to open official relations with the United States and provide emergency facilities to American ships and crews.[14] Thus the actual negotiations took only a week. On March 31, 1854, just over a month after his return to Japan, Commodore Perry and the Tokugawa government signed the Treaty of Peace and Amity (the Kanagawa Treaty 神奈川条約), through which the *bakufu* agreed to open the port of Shimoda (下田) at once and Hakodate (箱館) a year later for supplies of water and fuel, and to assist ships and crews in distress (Article II). The treaty included a most-favored-nation clause for the United States (Article IX), and a clause stating that an American consul or agent might be sent to Shimoda after eighteen months, provided either government deemed it necessary (Article XI).[15] The Kanagawa agreement was thus a minimal arrangement, what was then called a "wood [for ship repair] and water treaty." The *bakufu* subsequently concluded similar treaties with Britain, France, Russia,[16] and the Netherlands.

Between Perry's first visit and his return some six months later, Abe Masahiro (阿部正弘), the *rōjū* (老中 senior councilor) of the *bakufu* in charge of foreign affairs, transmitted the president's letter to the emperor in Kyoto, and circulated copies to the major daimyo, including the *tozama*, asking for their opinions. The court's response was that the Americans should be driven away. The opinions of the feudal lords were divided, but many were violently anti-foreign. While the *bakufu* could have dealt with this situation on its own responsibility, Abe had intended to strengthen the *bakufu*'s position by letting them know about the crisis that Japan was facing. But his unprecedented action resulted in bringing the imperial court into the current controversy and giving potential opponents of the *bakufu* an opportunity to participate in the policymaking process.

During the two-year interval before an American diplomatic agent arrived (2.1.3), the xenophobic *sonnō-jōi* (revere the emperor and expel the foreigners) ideology (1.1.2) began to spread, weakening the political foundations of the *bakufu*.

### 2.1.3. Harris's Negotiations with the *Bakufu*

In August of 1856, Townsend Harris arrived at Shimoda as the first foreign diplomat to take up residence in Japan.[17] The Japanese initially declined to receive Harris, arguing that the Japanese government had not consented to the dispatch of a consul. The Japanese version of the Perry treaty read that a consul might be appointed only if both nations deemed it necessary.[18] But Harris overrode the objections of the *bakufu* officials assigned to deal with him in Shimoda, and was soon installed in a local temple as a residence.

Despite much early harassment by *bakufu* spies and petty restrictions, Harris established friendly relations with the government officials dispatched from Edo, who were impressed with his peaceful, if sometimes irascible, approach and sincerity.

With the assistance of his brilliant young secretary, the Dutch immigrant to the US Henry Heusken, Harris was first able to negotiate an expansion of the Perry Treaty of Kanagawa, concluding the Convention of Shimoda in June, 1857. This agreement opened the port of Nagasaki for the purchase of supplies by American vessels, permitted Americans to reside at Shimoda and Hakodate, granted extraterritoriality to the Americans, and provided for the exchange of coins by weight of bullion content, with an allowance of 6 percent for recoinage.[19]

In December 1857, Harris at last obtained an audience with the shogun Iesada (家定) to present his letter of credence from President Pierce. Taking the opportunity of this first visit by a foreign diplomat to Edo, he gave extended presentations to Hotta Masayoshi (堀田正睦), Abe's successor, and other *bakufu* officials. The *bakufu*'s internal memorandum of Harris' speech indicates that Harris's arguments were well understood by the Japanese. Harris emphasized the importance of foreign trade for a nation's economic development, and the advantages of reaching an agreement with an American envoy "unattended by military force" rather than negotiating with the British "who should bring fifty men-of-war to these shores."[20] He also stated that the United States would prohibit the trade of opium, though Britain was anxious to bring it to Japan.[21]

An extended quotation of Heusken's record of Harris's arguments on the benefit of trade will be in order, because they indicate Harris's awareness of the Japanese attitude toward trade.[22]

> Your Excellencies deceive yourselves, he said, if you think that commerce exists only for the acquiring of money by those engaged in it. . . .
>
> Commerce is the blood, the great source of life of an Empire; look at England. Without trade the people who live in that small country would starve. What is it that has made her the master of two hundred million human beings? Trade! What has made her the mightiest country of the world? Trade! Look at Holland, another country which occupies a land barely taken from the sea. Holland, that small parcel of land, constitutes a nation worthy of esteem. And why? Because of trade.
>
> For more than two hundred years Spain and Portugal were the most powerful nations of the world. Now they occupy a mediocre position. Why? Because they neglected trade! I therefore pray that your Excellencies will not believe that trade is conducive only to the sordid purpose of filling the coffers of a few individuals. No, commerce is conducive to a higher, more sublime purpose. It is the life, the great activity of nations, and if Japan in employing its resources is opened for commerce, there is no reason why it would not end in a most fortunate position, the England of Asia.

## 2.1.4. The Treaty of Amity and Commerce

Harris came to Japan after having negotiated a new commercial treaty with the Kingdom of Siam that was closely patterned on the British treaty with that kingdom (1.2.1). The draft Harris used in his negotiations with the Japanese was based on the Harris Siam treaty, which he had shown to the *bakufu* prior to the negotiations.[23]

An agreement was reached on July 29, 1858 in line with the draft treaty that Harris had prepared. The Treaty of Amity and Commerce (Nichibei shūkō tsūshō jōyaku 日米修好通商条約) provided for the opening of reciprocal diplomatic relations (Article I), and the opening for trade of five ports; Hakodate, Nagasaki, Kanagawa from July 4, 1859;[24] Niigata (新潟) from January 1, 1860; and Hyōgo (兵庫) from January 1, 1863; and the opening for residence of two cities: Edo from January 1, 1862 and Osaka (大阪) from January 1, 1863. It also conceded the right of Americans to trade freely with Japanese in the open port cities and to lease ground and own buildings in the open port cities (Article III). The distance Americans were able to go from open ports was set, generally at 10 *ri* or 24.4 miles (Article VII). There was a strict ban on trade in opium (Article IV) and a somewhat looser prohibition on the propagation of Christianity (Article VIII). Extraterritoriality was granted for American visitors and residents (Article VI).

The most-favored-nation status of the United States was not specifically mentioned in this treaty, but was carried over by incorporation from the 1857 Convention. Harris conceded the right to the Japanese to give one year's notice after July 4, 1872 of intent to renegotiate the Treaty (Article XIII), but in a decision that proved detrimental to Japan, set no date for the expiration of the treaty. Harris later wrote that he had hoped that the Japanese would have gained enough experience before 1872 to negotiate the treaty revision, but the third-party beneficiaries of an unequal treaty with no termination date proved unwilling to give up their privileges (4.1.1).[25]

A separate agreement, *Regulations Under Which American Trade Is to Be Conducted with Japan*, specified ad valorem tariffs on exports and imports. Exports were subject to a 5 percent duty, with the exception of gold and silver coins and copper in bars. Imports were divided into four classes. Class I enumerated articles which were nontaxable: silver and gold, coined and uncoined; wearing apparel in actual use; household furniture, and printed books for private use. Class II articles, which attracted a 5 percent duty, were all articles used for the purpose of building, rigging, repairing, or fitting out of ships; salted provisions, bread and breadstuffs; living animals; coal, zinc, lead, and tin; raw silk; whaling gear of all kinds; timber for building houses; rice and unthreshed rice; and steam machinery. Class III articles, which were subjected to a 35 percent duty, were all intoxicating liquors. Articles not mentioned in the above three classes, expected to be the majority of imports, were subject to a 20 percent duty. The treaty also provided the following: "Five years after the opening of Kanagawa, the import and export duties shall be subject to revision if the Japanese government desires it."[26]

The *bakufu* signed treaties that were basically identical to the Harris treaty with Britain, France, Russia, and the Netherlands. The tariff schedule of the British treaty, however, contained a modification. Lord Elgin, the plenipotentiary envoy to China who visited Japan to negotiate the British version, successfully moved cotton and woolen textiles from the 20 percent duty class to the 5 percent duty class.[27]

The terms of the Harris Treaty with Japan were much less severe than those of the treaties Britain forced on China. Japan lost no territory, while China lost Hong Kong and a part of Kowloon; the opium trade was prohibited in Japan, while it was legitimized in China; the propagation of Christianity was prohibited in Japan, albeit indirectly, while it was allowed in China; foreigners were not allowed to go beyond 10 *ri* limits from open ports in Japan, while foreigners were able to travel to all places of the interior of China; and patrolling of internal waters by foreign warships was not allowed in Japanese internal waters, while foreign warships and licensed foreign commercial vessels were permitted to patrol internal waters in China.

Nevertheless, Japan was unmistakably put into the British-style treaty port system.[28] Japan shared with China deprivations of its sovereignty over tariffs and jurisdiction over foreigners, as well as the denial of reciprocal most-favored-nation treatment.

# 2.2. The Aftermath of the Treaty of Amity and Commerce

### 2.2.1. Controversies over the Treaty

The Harris Treaty and Regulations were the first agreements by which the Japanese government conceded to the Japanese people the right of commerce with foreigners since Japan had withdrawn into isolation in the early 17th century. It naturally aroused much contention among the feudal lords. Hotta decided to seek the emperor's approval to allay the opposition.

Unfortunately for Harris and Hotta, the emperor and most of his courtiers were now in favor of the Mito policy of *jōi* (expelling the foreigners). After a month of hard bargaining in which monetary bribes were involved, Hotta managed to obtain from the imperial court a draft decree which recognized that decisions on foreign policy were for the *bakufu* to make, not the court. But even this compromise broke down when the court let it be known that they had been pressured into accepting it. In the furor that followed, the decree was withdrawn, and Hotta had to leave office.[29]

In this emergency, Ii Naosuke (井伊直弼) was appointed as *tairō* (大老 great councilor), a standing greater than that of *rōjū*. Ii signed the Treaty of Amity and Commerce in July 1858 on his own authority in the belief that it was the only way of avoiding the harsher terms that Britain would demand.

Ii's autocratic action gave rise to a chorus of disapproval among his opponents. The most influential opponent continued to be Tokugawa Nariaki (徳川斉昭), daimyo of the Mito domain. He contended that it was absurd of the *bakufu* to plead that they could not drive the foreigners away until the country had increased its military strength through the profits of foreign trade. Military preparations should come first, and commerce later. If foreigners attacked Japan, they could not penetrate far into the country, as they had no maps. If trade were permitted, they would soon learn all about the geography and internal conditions of Japan, and that would be dangerous.[30]

The expulsion argument was supported by not a few feudal lords and court advisors,[31] some because they had a genuine fear of foreign contacts, and others because they welcomed any support for their intrigues against the *bakufu*.[32] Ii suppressed his opponents mercilessly. A confrontation between Ii and his opponents over the question of succession to the shogunate made the confrontation more severe and the suppression more acrimonious.[33] Ii was assassinated in March 1860 by a group of samurai, mostly from Mito, in front of the Sakurada Gate (桜田門) of the shogun's Edo castle (now the Tokyo Imperial Palace).

It should be noted that the opposition to the treaties at that time was solely against the *bakufu*'s signing the treaties in disregard of the emperor's will, and the subjugation of the imperial will to foreign powers. No grievance was expressed by the opponents against the inequalities of the treaties, such as extraterritoriality, loss of tariff autonomy, or unilateral most-favored-nation treatment. As to extraterritoriality, though Harris confessed after his retirement that he had inserted the extraterritoriality clause against his conscience,[34] the Japanese side was not conscious of any infringement of their sovereign powers by the exemption of foreigners from their jurisdiction. Law and justice were regarded as personal rather than territorial in nature in Japan. Prior to *sakoku*, the *bakufu* had granted Europeans living in Japan extraterritoriality.[35]

As to the tariff, the *bakufu* negotiators first proposed a duty of 12½ percent on exports as well as imports, but taking into account Harris's recommendation against export duties, they accepted a 5 percent duty on exports, and sliding-scale duties on imports that Harris proposed, apparently without considering the protective effect import duties might have with respect to Japanese industry.[36] The Japanese remained ignorant of the use of tariffs for the protection of industry until Itō Hirobumi (伊藤博文), who had had a lengthy study tour in the United States, urged (unsuccessfully) the benefits of protection for nascent industry in an 1873 memorandum and the adoption by the new Meiji government of a push for tariff autonomy.

## 2.2.2. An Outflow of Gold

The opening of the three ports of Yokohama, Nagasaki, and Hakodate on July 1, 1859, shifted Japan from near autarky to the status of a free trading nation. It naturally had an enormous impact on the Japanese economy. A heavy outflow of gold was the first problems Japan faced.

While Japan had once had rich silver mines, they were very nearly exhausted by the early 1800s, and the *bakufu* was compelled to reduce the weight of Japan's silver currency. In later years, the recoinage of currency became an essential means of raising government revenue. Thus, in a world of bullion-based monetary systems, Japan was adopting a kind of a fiat currency system.

In those days, the currency widely used for the settlement of foreign trade accounts in Asia was the Mexican silver dollar. In keeping with the 1 to 15 gold–silver ratio that existed internationally, one Mexican silver dollar contained fifteen times as much silver as an equivalent value in gold.[37] At this ratio, one Mexican silver dollar could buy one *ichibu* (一分), which was one-quarter of one *ryō* (両).[38] However, the weight of a silver *ichibu* with a fiat value of one-quarter of one *ryō* was eventually reduced to one-third as a result of a series of recoinages, making the gold–silver ratio 1 to 5.[39] When trade started, this discrepancy and the treaty provision calling for coinage exchange by weight caused immediate large inflows of silver and outflows of gold, as one Mexican dollar could buy three *ichibu*, or three-quarters of an *ichiryō koban* in Japan, which was equivalent to three Mexican dollars outside Japan.

The *bakufu* officials had been aware of the risk of this type of transaction prior to the start of trade. The first negotiation on the exchange rate between Japanese currency and the Mexican dollar had been held in 1854 between the representatives of Perry and *bakufu* officials. While the Japanese wanted a one-*ichibu*-per-dollar exchange, the Americans proposed a weight-for-weight exchange, and no agreement was reached at that time. In 1857, Harris successfully persuaded *bakufu* officials to agree to the weight-for-weight exchange with a 6 percent allowance for recoinage. In the 1858 treaty negotiation, Harris wanted the same exchange formula as that in the 1857 Convention, and proposed prohibition of the export of Japanese currency.

Much to Harris's surprise, however, the *bakufu* proposed the free use of both foreign currency and Japanese currency by either Japanese or foreigners, and free exchange of silver and gold currency by weight, as well as the free export of Japanese currency abroad.[40] The *bakufu* had decided to mint new silver *nishu-gin* (二朱銀) weighing one and one-half of an *ichibu*, which were to be exchanged at the rate of two of *nishu-gin* to one Mexican dollar, making the gold–silver exchange ratio 1:15.[41] This decision had been reached after much debate within the *bakufu*. The treasury commissioner (*kanjō bugyō* 勘定奉行) proposed revaluation of gold coinage. The foreign affairs commissioners (*gaikoku bugyō* 外国奉行) opposed such a policy because it would bring about inflation, and proposed reduction of the purchasing power of silver *ichibu*. The *kanjō bugyō* insisted that the *bakufu* did not have enough bullion for such a measure. After an extended discussion, the proposal of the *gaikoku bugyō* was adopted.

This measure would have been effective if *nishu-gin* had been supplied in sufficient quantity, and the old *ichibu* had been completely withdrawn from the market in time for the start of foreign trade. But the *bakufu* left *ichibu* current in the marketplace because of the shortage of *nishu-gin*. The *bakufu* believed that it could prevent currency speculation by making *nishu-gin* available for foreign trade and restricting the use of *ichibu* to domestic transactions. Foreign traders, however, would not accept *nishu-gin*, and demanded *ichibu*, which were still in circulation among the Japanese.

Facing the outflow of gold, the *bakufu* ordered the suspension of the exchange of the Mexican dollar with *ichibu*. This measure greatly reduced foreign trade transactions.[42] Harris and Rutherford Alcock, the new British envoy to Japan, made strong protests and had the *bakufu* rescind the suspension order.

36

Harris and Alcock feared, meanwhile, that the heavy outflow of gold would undermine the Japanese gold standard system. They suggested that the *bakufu* appreciate gold against silver. In January 1860, the *bakufu* declared that all existing gold coinages were to be revalued by 170 percent to 230 percent depending on their actual bullion content, and in the next month minted new gold coins weighing one-third of the old ones. These measures restored the Japanese gold-silver exchange rate to approximately 1:15.[43] Additionally, to raise government revenue, the *bakufu* minted two new kinds of gold coins, *nibu-han* (二分判) and *nishu-kin* (二朱金), with inferior bullion content to the existing gold coinages in the amount of over 50 million *ryō*, which amounted to about 40 percent of the existing gold and silver coinages in circulation.[44]

Revaluation of gold and debasement of the gold coinages restored the 1:15 gold–silver ratio and stopped the outflow of gold. However, during the first eight months after the start of the trade, half a million to one million *ryō* of gold coins were exported, mainly through Mexican dollar–*ichibu–koban* exchange transactions.[45]

### 2.2.3. Inflation

The new issue of debased gold coinages in large amounts described above and the revaluation of the old gold coinages which increased the financial asset values of all gold coinage holders inevitably caused inflation. Inflation was also accelerated by the issuance of *hansatsu* (藩札 domain paper currency) by feudal lords in substantial amounts toward the end of the Tokugawa period. Originally, *hansatsu* issuance was permitted by the *bakufu* as a supplement to the *bakufu*'s coin currency. In the closing days of the Tokugawa period, however, feudal lords ignored *bakufu* regulations, and floated large issues of *hansatsu* to finance their increased expenditures. In fact, the feudal lords did not stop issuing *hansatsu* until the abolition of their domains in 1871. The total of *hansatsu* thus issued is estimated to have been something like 19 to 28 million *ryō*.[46]

In addition to the increase in currency issuance as above, the beginning of free trade also brought about big changes in commodity prices in Japan.[47] Japan in the mid-19th century was unique in its move from nearly complete autarky to full exposure to open trade.[48] In such a case, the prices of exports are expected to rise to international levels and the prices of imports to fall to international levels. In Japan's case, however, the prices of exports such as tea and raw silk went up rapidly as foreign trade began, while the prices of

Chapter 2

Table 2.2.3. Japan's Foreign Trade 1859–1868 (thousand Mexican $) and Price Indexes

|  | Exports | Imports | Trade balance | Cumulative trade surplus | General price indexes |
|---|---|---|---|---|---|
| 1859 | 891 | 603 | 288 | 288 | 100 |
| 1860 | 4,173 | 1,659 | 3,054 | 3,342 | 121 |
| 1861 | 3,787 | 2,365 | 1,422 | 4,764 | 136 |
| 1862 | 7,279 | 3,882 | 3,397 | 8,161 | 128 |
| 1863 | 12,208 | 6,199 | 6,009 | 14,170 | 137 |
| 1864 | 10,572 | 8,102 | 2,470 | 16,640 | 167 |
| 1865 | 18,490 | 15,144 | 3,346 | 19,986 | 221 |
| 1866 | 16,617 | 15,771 | 846 | 20,832 | 349 |
| 1867 | 12,124 | 21,673 | −9,550 | 11,282 | 380 |
| 1868 | 15,553 | 10,693 | 4,860 | 16,142 | 340 |

*Source:* Yamamoto Yūzō, "Meiji ishinki no zaisei to tsūka," in *Kaikō to ishin*, eds. Umemura Mataji and Yamamoto Yūzō (Tokyo: Iwanami Shoten, 1989), 124. Lawrence Klein and Kazushi Ohkawa, eds., *Economic Growth: The Japanese Experience since the Meiji Era* (Homewood, IL: Richard D. Irwin, 1968), 165–167.

imports such as textiles and sugar rose slightly in the early 1860s, and only began to decline in the second half of the 1860s.[49] Increases in import prices in the early 1860s might be attributable to the deficient distribution system.[50]

Additionally, Japan registered a trade surplus for eight consecutive years from 1959 to 1866 (table 2.2.3) generating a cumulative trade surplus of about 21 million Mexican dollars (about 16 million *ryō* at the conversion rate of four Mexican dollars to three *ryō*). The increase in money supply due to the trade surplus and price hikes of both exports and imports after the opening of trade contributed to raising the general price level in the 1860s.

Between 1860 and 1867, the price of rice rose more than tenfold, while the prices of other daily necessities showed similar, though smaller, increases. The general price level went up more than three times (table 2.2.3).

Inflation began to subside after 1870. The new Meiji government's anti-inflation measures finally took hold. A considerable amount of domain currency was written off at the loss of the holders, mostly wealthy merchants. The introduction of a new currency denominated in "yen" in 1871,[51] replacing the old currency, effectively reduced the total money supply. The increase in low-priced imports and an outflow of gold due to trade deficits that started from the late 1860s must have also helped to lower price levels.

However, the severe inflation that raged for the first several years of the 1860s inflicted great economic hardship on people's lives. The samurai, whose livelihood was dependent on fixed stipends, were hit especially hard. Their economic travails fueled their anti-trade sentiments, driving the *bakufu* into an ever more difficult political situation.

## 2.3. The Fall of the *Bakufu*

### 2.3.1. Moves to Close the Country

Few *bakufu* officials understood the positive economic benefits of foreign trade (except for revenues from customs duties and the purchase of military equipment). Many *bakufu* officials saw foreign trade as implying the loss of finite and valuable Japanese resources for no significant return.[52]

While the treaties had established free commercial transaction between foreigners and Japanese, the *bakufu* officials were reluctant to give up their control of commerce, and attempted to restrict foreign trade. In May of 1860, they issued a decree that exports of five selected items, including raw silk, must pass through the hands of certain designated wholesale houses in Edo, which were under *bakufu* patronage and supervision. In the first couple of years this measure decreased exports only minimally because of large-scale evasion by merchants in ports, but, as observed below, it reduced the exports of raw silk from Yokohama from the end of 1863, when the *bakufu* decided to apply this decree strictly.

In early 1860, the *bakufu* sought to postpone the opening of the ports of Niigata and Hyōgo (modern Kobe) and the cities of Edo and Osaka, which were to be opened not later than January 1, 1863 (2.1.4). Harris was sympathetic to the *bakufu*'s difficult position, and Alcock also judged that the concession would help the *bakufu* in its struggle against the opponents of the opening of trade. In the London Protocol, signed in June 1862, the powers agreed to postpone the opening of the two ports and two cities until January 1, 1868. This gave the *bakufu* breathing space, as it would limit expansion of foreign trade and thus alleviate the pressure from advocates of expulsion. The negotiations were mainly conducted between Britain and the *bakufu*. With the outbreak of the Civil War in the United States in 1861, and Harris's return to his home country in May 1862, Alcock was now the unchallenged leader among the treaty power representatives.

In the spring of 1863, meanwhile, proponents of *jōi* managed to have the court proclaim an imperial edict that intercourse with the West should end as of June 25, 1863. The *bakufu* was forced to endorse the edict, because it had bound itself, vis-à-vis the court, to "restore the old law of expulsion" at some appropriate date.[53] Tokugawa Yoshinobu (徳川慶喜), who was now a guardian during the minority of Shogun Iemochi and thus the de facto leader of the *bakufu*, supported the edict, believing that preserving relations with the court was vital to the survival of the shogunate. He did not believe that the court posed a more serious threat than the treaty powers, but he felt that some indication that the *bakufu* was moving toward eventual expulsion of the barbarians would have to be provided to the court. Thus the idea of closing the port of Yokohama was formulated as an alternative to the court's expulsion order. It would also effectively reduce the amount of "disruptive" foreign trade.

The idea was flatly rejected by all the treaty power representatives. The *bakufu* then decided to strictly apply the decree of 1860 toward the end of 1863. By strengthening the control on the designated wholesale houses, the *bakufu* effectively reduced raw silk exports from Yokohama.

In the meantime, on June 26, 1863, Chōshū, acting on its own initiative on the basis of the court edict, fired on an American vessel, and within a month, it fired on French and Dutch vessels. In retaliation, the United States sent a warship to Shimonoseki on July 13, and sank two Chōshū vessels and shelled the batteries. A few days later, French forces landed and damaged the batteries in Shimonoseki. Chōshū retaliated by closing the strait. Alcock, who had been on leave in Britain from March 1862 to March 1864, arranged a joint naval expedition of seventeen treaty-power warships in September 1864. The bombardment and landing forces destroyed all the batteries in Shimonoseki.[54]

The ensuing Shimonoseki treaties signed by the *bakufu* and the four powers that took part in the expedition provided for an indemnity of three million dollars to be paid in six installments, but it also provided that the powers would waive the indemnity if the *bakufu* opened Shimonoseki or some other equivalent port for foreign trade. The *bakufu* chose to pay the indemnity rather than open another port, but requested a delay in meeting the second and subsequent payments.

The British proposed remission of remaining two-thirds of the indemnity in return for the prompt opening of Hyōgo, the written ratification of the treaties by the emperor, and the reduction of the tariff to a uniform rate of 5 percent. In the negotiations conducted in Osaka with presence of an allied squadron in Osaka harbor, less than thirty miles from Kyoto, the *bakufu* told the powers that Hyōgo could not be opened until the date fixed by the London Protocol, but it would continue to pay the indemnity in default of opening the port, and that it would submit the emperor's ratification of the treaties and would agree to have tariff negotiations in Edo.

The negotiations on tariffs in Edo produced the Convention of 1866, which fixed the import duties on all dutiable articles at a maximum of 5 percent. Specific duties were quoted on eighty-nine articles. For each of these articles, 5 percent *ad valorem* duties were converted, item by item, to a weight-based or quantity-based duty. Specific duties made tariff assessment easy, whereas, in the case of *ad valorem* duties, importers often had to negotiate with customs officers who had the authority to assess the value of the articles. Efficient administration was an advantage of specific duties, but there was a big drawback for the Japanese. Since the duties thus fixed were not adjusted for inflation, the actual duties on some articles calculated on an *ad valorem* basis became as low as 1 percent as their prices went up.

The Japanese duties became lower than those of Britain, the world leader of free trade,[55] offering little protection to Japanese industry, which was technologically far behind that in the West. Except for partial revisions accepted by the treaty powers in 1894, most of those duties remained unchanged until 1911, when it became possible for Japan to set its own tariffs (4.3.2).[56]

At the Convention, Harry Parkes, who took over for Alcock in July 1865,[57] made two new demands: that trading in the treaty ports be completely open to all Japanese without official intervention, and that Japanese be allowed to travel abroad freely for business or academic research. These deregulatory measures, which were very important for Japan's development, were unwillingly accepted by the *bakufu*.[58]

## 2.3.2. Developments Leading to the Fall of the *Bakufu*

Ii's harsh measures and his assassination brought about major changes in national politics. The imperial court loomed larger in the political picture, and feudal lords opposing the *bakufu*'s policy became more assertive. Most importantly, anger against the *bakufu* spread political activity to the lower levels of samurai, from whom emerged political activists, called *shishi* (志士 men of

*41*

high spirit). The influence of Yōmeigaku, which emphasized the importance of a person acting on the truth as he believed it, was clearly observed (1.1.2). They envisioned themselves as saviors of Japan. And many of them at the time vehemently adopted the Mito cry of *sonnō-jōi* (revere the emperor and expel the foreigners). Ii had ignored the germination of the *kokutai* (国体 national polity) sentiment with its elevation of the emperor to a national symbol.

The steep inflation that began soon after the opening of trade caused a wide range of disaffected samurai to hate foreign trade and foreigners. There were many assassinations of foreigners, as well as a major attack on the British Legation. Among the senseless killings was that of Henry Heusken, Harris's sole assistant, in January 1861 (3.1.1).[59]

The leadership of the *sonnō-jōi* movements gradually shifted from Mito to Chōshū. It was Chōshū leaders in Kyoto who urged the court to issue the expulsion order in 1863 (2.3.1). After the retaliatory bombardment by the four powers in September 1864, however, Chōshū broke with the anti-foreign policy. They were now convinced that the military strength of the West was such that foreign pressures could only be challenged by a Japan equipped with the most modern weapons and techniques. In a similar way, Satsuma also underwent a kind of baptism by fire in August 1863, when British warships attacked Kagoshima in retaliation for the killing of an Englishman in the previous year (3.1.1).[60] In both cases, direct contact between Satsuma and Chōshū representatives and British diplomats led to the formation of ties of friendship and respect between them.[61]

As the rivalry between the *sonnō-jōi* group and the *bakufu* intensified, there emerged a third movement supported by some great feudal lords. They basically supported the *bakufu* and the opening of the country, but wished to reform the *bakufu* using their connections with the senior nobles in Kyoto. It was an effort to save the *bakufu* through the unity of the court and the *bakufu*, the idea of *kōbu-gattai* (公武合体).[62]

The struggle for power among these three factions often developed into armed clashes. Violence was, by and large, between Chōshū, a leading *sonno-joi* advocate, and Satsuma, the leading promoter of *kōbu-gattai*.

The *kōbu-gattai* project began to disintegrate, however, chiefly because of differences between the *bakufu* and Satsuma. While Satsuma wanted the effort to be jointly managed with the major feudal lords, the *bakufu* sought to retain its prestige as a leader by equipping itself with modern military forces with the help of France, which was willing to support the *bakufu* in competing with Britain in a fluid political situation.

Satsuma, disapproving of the *bakufu*'s moves, decided to join hands with Chōshū, its former foe. The alliance was realized early in 1866.[63] When the *bakufu* sent a punitive expedition to Chōshū in June 1866 (the second such expedition),[64] Satsuma sided with Chōshū, and Chōshū routed the *bakufu* army.

In September 1867 Yamauchi Yōdō (山内容堂), moderate but re-form-minded daimyo of Tosa, submitted a memo to Yoshinobu, who had be-come the shogun in January that year, urging him to resign. Giving up the hereditary office did not seem to him an unbearably high price if it would avert a civil war when Japan was under the threat of Western imperialism, and if the Tokugawa clan could retain some influence in the new regime (though this hope proved to be in vain).[65] In November of 1867, Yoshinobu formally restored the powers of government to the emperor.

Except for a few Tokugawa adherents who held out for a few months, the entire country submitted to a newly formed government led by court nobles and mostly young and vigorous samurai from the leading anti-*bakufu* do-mains. The youthful emperor Meiji, whose father, the bitterly anti-foreign emperor Kōmei (孝明天皇), had just died, took the *gokajō no seimon* (五箇条の誓文 the five-article charter oath), setting out the new government's broad in-tentions before the court nobles and leading feudal lords in April of 1868.[66]

The opening of Japan thus resulted in the downfall of the Tokugawa re-gime that had lasted some 250 years. But given the tolerance among the European powers for the use of force against "less civilized" countries and the derisible state of its coastal defenses, the *bakufu* had had little choice in the matter. It was fortunate for Japan that the country that asked Japan to open its door was the United States, which was critical of the diplomacy of the "Old World" of which Britain was the leader. It was doubly fortunate for Japan that it could, thanks to the timing of the Perry Expedition, complete its political and social reforms before the storm of Western imperialism resumed in the 1870s (1.2.1, 6.1.1).

Chapter 2

NOTES

2.1. Japan's Opening of the Country

1   James C. Thomson, Jr., Peter W. Stanley, and John Curtis Perry, *Sentimental Imperialism* (New York: Harper & Row, 1981), 9–10.

2   Japan had been a coal exporter until the middle of the 1920s, when its coal imports exceeded its coal exports.

3   John Curtis Perry, *Facing West: Americans and the Opening of the Pacific* (Westport, CT: Praeger Publishers, 1994), 92–93, 322.

4   Ibid., 93. Kōsaka Masataka, *Fushigino Nichibei kankei* (Tokyo: PHP Institute, 1996), 8–9.

5   Donald D. Johnson, *The United States in the Pacific* (Westport, CT: Praeger Publishers, 1995), 50.

6   Russia sold Alaska to the United States in 1867 for the price of $7,200,000.

7   Terry Burcin, "Commodore Perry's 1853 Japanese Expedition: How Whaling Influenced the Event that Revolutionized Japan," master's thesis submitted to the Graduate Faculty of the Virginia Polytechnic Institute and State University (May 2005), 14–17.

8   Matthew Calbraith Perry (1794–1858) was a member of a distinguished naval family and a veteran of forty years of naval service, which he began as a teenager in a battle against the British in one of the incidents that led to the War of 1812. His major command had been in the Mexican War in 1846–1848.

9   He heard rumors that French and Russian squadrons were planning to visit Japan, and he hastened his departure from Hong Kong, where he had docked after his first visit to Japan.

10  Mitani Hiroshi, *Perī Raikō* (Tokyo: Yoshikawa Kōbunkan, 2003), 53–56. Ishii Takashi, *Nihon kaikokushi* (Tokyo: Yoshikawa Kōbunkan, 2010), 76–88. Charles Ralph Boxer, *Jan Compagnie in Japan, 1600–1817* (London: Oxford University Press, 1968, reprint of the 1936 edition published in The Hague), 185–187. Haga Noboru argues that the *bakufu* leaders, after reading the Chinese descriptions of the Opium Wars and the Taiping Rebellion, were more afraid of domestic rebellion as a result of opening the country than the outside intervention itself. See Haga Noboru, "Ahen sensō, Taiheitengoku, Nihon," in *Chūgoku kingendaishi no shomondai*, ed. Tanaka Masami Sensei Taikan Kinen Ronshū Kankōkai (Tokyo: Kokusho Kankōkai, 1984), 87–123. Matsuda Wataru, Joshua A. Fogel, trans. and ed., *Japan and China: Mutual Representations in the Modern Era* (London: Curzon Press, 2000), 43–47.

11  As a boy of fourteen, Manjirō was shipwrecked with five companions while on a fishing trip and rescued by an American whaler in 1841. Following the end of the voyage in 1843, the captain of the whaler, William Whitfield, took him to his home in Fairfield, Massachusetts and sent him to school. Whitfield was a generous man and a religious one. Under the name "John Mung," Manjirō became a part of the Whitfield family and won the cordial respect and liking of the community. He joined a whaling voyage in 1846 and was elected first mate when the captain became insane. He then joined the 1849 Gold Rush to California, and acquired the funds to attempt a return to Japan. He landed on the coast of Okinawa in January 1851. He was arrested, and

*Notes*

underwent long and intensive interrogations in Kagoshima, in Nagasaki, and in his native domain of Tosa. In June, 1852, he was released, as his worth had been eventually recognized. His testimony was found to be very informative and valuable by the authorities, who had been forewarned of Perry's arrival. The record of his testimony was widely read within the *bakufu*. He was called many times to meetings with high *bakufu* officials, including Abe Masahiro and Tokugawa Nariaki. He was given the family name of Nakahama and made a samurai of the Tosa domain, and later of the *bakufu*. Several historians think that his report served to dispel unwarranted fears and suspicion of the intent of the Perry expedition. Nakahama Hiroshi, *Nakahama Manjirō* (Tokyo: Fuzambo International, 2005), 108–149. (Nakahama Hiroshi is a great-grandson of Manjirō.) Mitani, *Perī raikō*, 96.

12 His title, "Daigaku no Kami," meant "lord of the academy."

13 Francis L. Hawkes, abridged and edited by Sidney Wallach, *Narrative of the Expedition of an American Squadron to the China Seas and Japan Under the Command of Commodore M. C. Perry, United States Navy*, compiled at his request and under his supervision by Francis Hawkes, D.D., L.L.D. (New York: Coward-McCann, 1952), 209.

14 Ishii, *Nihon kaikokushi*, 110.

15 William Beasley, trans. and ed., *Select Documents on Japanese Foreign Policy, 1853–1868* (London: Oxford University Press, 1955), 159–165.

16 The Treaty of Peace and Amity of 1854 with the Russians provided in Article 2 for recognition of the four islands south of the Etorofu Strait—Etorofu, Kunashiri, Shikotan, and Habomai—as Japanese, and Uruppu and the islands to the north as Russian. Other provisions provided for assistance and non-confinement of castaways, the appointment of a Russian consul when this was thought "indispensable," and "reciprocal extraterritoriality." The territorial boundaries peacefully established by the 1854 treaty are the basis for the present Japanese claim for the return of the northern islands taken by Russia after World War II and never returned.

17 Harris, a lifelong bachelor, had been a New York china importer for many years, and had used his minor political connections to obtain a seat on the Board of Education; he founded a free school for the poor (it later evolved into the City University of New York). His business began to deteriorate in the late 1840s, and it seems he became something of an alcoholic. His mother's death in 1851 apparently affected him deeply. He gave up his New York business, bought a half-interest in a vessel sailing to San Francisco, and when that venture proved unprofitable, went on to China, taking occasional work as a supercargo on American vessels and also traveling extensively as a tourist in South and Southeast Asia over the next seven years. He appears to have given up alcohol, although there are some contemporary references that hint of occasional relapses. He attempted to join the Perry Expedition, but was refused. President Pierce had heard the stories of his drinking problem, and part of the delay in his appointment was caused by the time it took for his political friends in New York to provide evidence that he had reformed his habits. See: Carl Crow, *He Opened the Door of Japan* (Westport, CT: Greenwood Press, 1974, reprint of a 1939 edition from Harper Row).

18 The English version of the treaty read that a consul might be appointed if either

Chapter 2

party deemed it necessary, though the Japanese version read "both parties." It is thought that the discrepancy derived from a Japanese interpreter's mistake. Mitani, *Perī raikō*, 6–7, and 178–181. Mitani writes that it is highly probable that high officials of the *bakufu* already knew about the discrepancy before Harris arrived. Ibid., 198–202.

19  Mario Emilio Cosenza, *The Complete Journal of Townsend Harris: First American Consul General and Minister to Japan* (Garden City, NY: published for Japan Society, New York by Doubleday, Doran & Company, 1930), 571–573.

20  Beasley, *Select Documents*, 164. William G. Beasley, *The Rise of Modern Japan: Political, Economic and Social Change since 1850*, 3rd ed. (London: Phoenix, 2000), 31. Ohara Takashi, *Nichibei bunka kōshōshi* (Tokyo: Yōyōsha, 1954), 61.

21  According to the translation of the *bakufu's* internal memorandum published in US Congress, *Foreign Relations, 1879* (Series 1902), Harris said to Hotta, " . . . China has prohibited the importation of opium; but the English bring it in armed vessels and smuggle it in. The Chinese officials are aware of this practice, but they have no power to put a stop to it, and hence let it be carried on in the ports without opposition. It appears that the English think the Japanese too are fond of opium, and they want to bring it here also. If a man uses opium once he cannot stop it, and it becomes a life-long habit to use opium; hence the English want to introduce it into Japan. The President of the United States thinks that for the Japanese opium is more dangerous than war. The expense of a war could be paid in time; but the expense of opium, when once the habit is formed, will only increase with time. The President wishes the Japanese to be very prudent about the introduction of opium, and if a treaty is made, he wishes that opium may be strictly prohibited." Beasley, *Select Documents*, 162–163.

22  Henry Heusken, *Japan Journal, 1855–1861*, trans. and ed. by Jeannette C. van der Corfut and Robert A. Wilson (New Brunswick, NJ: Rutgers University Press, 1964), 173–174.

23  Harris sent a Dutch-language translation of the US–Siam treaty to the *bakufu's* foreign affairs department on October 25, 1856. Harris, *The Complete Journal*, 247. Michael R. Auslin, *Negotiating with Imperialism* (Cambridge: Harvard University Press, 2004), 24.

24  Kanagawa was later changed to Yokohama for security reasons.

25  Statler, *Shimoda Story*, 553–554.

26  Harris, *The Complete Journal*, 578.

27  Harris condemned Elgin's actions, which would reduce Japan's customs revenue by two-thirds. Ishii, *Nihon kaikokushi*, 380–381. Statler, *Shimoda Story*, 553. Cotton textiles (yarn and cloth) and woolen textiles were the two largest import items during the early decades after the opening of trade, and Britain was by far the largest supplier of both items to Japan.

28  William Beasley, *Japanese Imperialism, 1894–1945* (New York: Oxford University Press, 1987), 24.

2.2. The Aftermath of the Treaty of Amity and Commerce

29  Beasley, *The Rise of Modern Japan*, 33.

*Notes*

30  G. B. Sansom, *The Western World and Japan* (London: The Cressent Press, 1950), 293. The description is from the memorial addressed to Ii Naosuke by Tokugawa Nariaki and dated July 16, 1858.

31  About 15 percent of the daimyo advocated expulsion of foreigners in 1853, and 9 percent in 1857–58. Opponents of opening the country without war numbered about forty eight percent in 1853, and 12 percent in 1857–58. The opinions that the opening of the country was unavoidable amounted to 29 percent in 1853, and 59 percent in 1857–58. Tanaka Akira, *Kaikoku to tōbaku* (Tokyo: Shueisha, 1999), 70. The decrease in advocates of expulsion and the increase in supporters of opening the country in the second survey show that more daimyo correctly recognized the situation in which Japan was placed.

32  Sansom, *The Western World and Japan*, 309.

33  Shogun Iesada (家定), who died in the summer of 1858, had no direct successor. Nariaki's son, Yoshinobu, was supported as an heir by reform-minded feudal lords as well as by opponents of opening the country. Fearing that Yoshinobu's succession to the shogunate would mean the control of the *bakufu* by Nariaki, Ii made Iemochi (家茂), eight-year-old head of Kii family, the shogun. Ii placed Nariaki and Matsudaira Yoshinaga (松平慶永) under house arrest, forced Yoshinobu to retire, and prosecuted many supporters of the candidacy of Yoshinobu as well as opponents of opening of the country. Yoshida Shōin was executed for opposing opening the country.

34  Inazō Nitobe, *The Intercourse between the United States and Japan* (Wilmington, DE: Scholarly Resources, 1973, first published in 1891), 107.

35  F. C. Jones, *Extraterritoriality in Japan* (New Heaven, CT: Yale University Press, 1931), 2–6. Sakata Seiichi, "Nihon no kindaika to Ansei no Nichibei Shūkō Tsūshō Jōyaku," *Kaigai Jijō Area Study*, no. 7 (Tokyo: Takushoku University Institute of World Studies, 1971), 62–70.

36  Ohara, *Nichibei bunka kōshōshi*, 65. Treat, *Japan and the United States, 1853–1921*, 39.

37  Peter Frost, *The Bakumatsu Currency Crisis* (Cambridge: East Asian Research Center of Harvard University, 1970), 11.

38  The Tokugawa coinage denominations were based on a quaternary system. *Ichibu* (one *bu* 分) was one quarter of one *ryō* (両). (A *koban* 小判 was one *ryō*). One *shu* (朱) was a quarter of one *bu*. One Mexican silver dollar coin weighed 7.2 *monme* and its silver content was 90 percent (6.48 *monme*). One *koban* weighed three momme and its gold content was 57 percent (1.71 *monme*) and its silver content was 43 percent (1.29 *monme*). One gold *ichibu* coin weighed 0.75 *monme*. Its gold content was 0.43 *monme* and its silver content was 0.32 *monme*, its gold equivalent bullion weight being 0.451 (0.43 + 0.32 × 1/15) *monme*, which was about one-fifteenth of a Mexican silver dollar's silver bullion weight (6.48 × 1/15 = 0.432).

39  In the early Tokugawa era, the gold-to-silver exchange ratio was close to 1:15. But in the case of silver *ichibu* (called simply "ichibu"), its weight was reduced eventually to one-third (from 7.5 *monme* to 2.5 *monme*) in 1838, making the gold-to-silver ratio 1:5. Other silver coinages were also recoined, but the loss of bullion weight was smaller. The silver *ichibu* was the most widely circulated coin, and stands as an

Chapter 2

example of a coin debased to raise revenue for the *bakufu*. Ishii Takashi, *Bakumatsu kaikōki keizai kenkyū* (Yokohama: Yūrindō, 1987), 5–7. Frost, *The Bakumatsu Currency Crisis*, 5.

40 Ishii, *Bakumatsu kaikōki keizai kenkyū*, 22–23. Shimbo Hiroshi, *Kindai Nihon keizaishi* (Tokyo: Sōbunsha, 1995), 23.

41 Ishii, *Bakumatsu kaikōki keizai kenkyū*, 28–42. Frost, *The Bakumatsu Currency Crisis*, 21.

42 Ishii, *Bakumatsu kaikōki keizai kenkyū*, 53–56.

43 Frost, *The Bakumatsu Currency Crisis*, 36–37.

44 One *nibu-han* weighed 0.8 *monme* and one *nishu-kin* weighed 0.2 *monme*. Their bullion content was 22 percent gold and 78 percent silver. Shimbo, *Kindai Nihon keizaishi*, 23. In 1871, the Meiji government declared that the new yen would have the same gold weight as two *nibu-han*, which weighed 1.6 *monme* and had a bullion content of 0.435 *monme* gold [0.352 (1.6 × 0.22) + 0.083 (1.6 × 0.78 × 1/15)], because one American dollar had the same bullion content (1.5 grams of gold, which was 0.4 *monme*). Umemura Mataji and Yamamoto Yūzō, *Kaikō to ishin* (Tokyo: Iwanami Shoten, 1989), 127-128.

45 Ohara, *Nichibei bunka kōshōshi*, 127–128. There are widely varying estimates of gold coin export totals. Ishii estimates it to have been only about 100,000 *ryō*, having revised his previous estimate of 500,000 *ryō*. Ishii, *Bakumatsu kaikōki keizaishi kenkyū*, 114–122. Fujino estimates the outflow to have been over 10 million *ryō* from 1859 to 1869. Fujino Shōzaburō, "Bakumatsu kin no kaheiryō to sono ryūshutsuryō," *Discussion Paper Series A*, no. 206 (Tokyo: Institute of Economic Research, Hitotsubashi University, 1989), 10–11.

46 Shimbo, *Kindai Nihon keizaishi*, 32.

47 J. Richard Huber has compared relative commodity prices in Japan and the rest of the world before and after Japan entered world commerce, and has estimated Japan's gains from trade. According to Huber, between 1846–55 and 1871–79, the prices of Japan's main exportables increased by 33 percent on average, while those of importables fell to 39 percent of the relative prices which prevailed in isolation. The change in terms of trade is figured by dividing 133 by 39 to yield 3.4. J. Richard Huber, "Effect on Prices of Japan's Entry into World Commerce after 1858," *The Journal of Political Economy*, vol. 79, issue 3 (Chicago: University of Chicago Press, 1971), 614–627. "Exportables" are goods that are exported and are of the same sort as those that are produced domestically. Likewise, "importables" are goods that are imported and at the same time produced domestically.

48 Bernhofen and Brown state that Japan's move from near-complete isolation to being fully exposed to the forces of international competition provided a unique historical case that empirically validated the Heckscher–Ohlin–Ricardo theory of comparative advantage. Daniel M. Bernhofen and John C. Brown, "A Direct Test of the Theory of Comparative Advantage: The Case of Japan," Working paper (Worcester, MA: Clark University, August 10, 2001), 1–4.

49 Shimbo analyzes the movement of prices of twenty items, grouping them into exports (raw silk and silk cloth), imports (cotton fiber, cotton thread, cotton cloth, seed oil, and raw sugar), and domestic goods that were neither exported nor

imported (thirteen other items). The ratio of the price of exports to that of domestic goods climbed to reach 1.6 in 1862 and 1.61 in 1863, and then went down in the following years and stayed in the range of between 1.1 and 1.3 in the second half of the 1860s. On the other hand, the ratio of the price of imports to that of domestic goods also went up in the early 1860s and reached 1.12 in 1863, and then declined to 1.00 in 1866, and stayed between 1.00 and 0.80 in the second half of the 1860s. Shimbo, *Kindai Nihon keizaishi*, 26.

50　Yamamoto, "Meiji ishinki no zaisei to tsūka," in *Kaikō to ishin*, eds. Umemura and Yamamoto, 121.

51　The New Currency Act, proclaimed in May of 1871, adopted a gold standard. One gold yen coin weighed 1.7 grams, and contained 1.5 grams (0.4 *monme*) of gold, which was same amount of gold as in one US gold dollar. Ishii, *Bakumatsu kaikōki keizai kenkyū*, 214.

## 2.3. The Fall of the *Bakufu*

52　Christopher Howe, *The Origin of Japanese Trade Supremacy* (London: Hurst & Company, 1996), 74.

53　In October 1858, Ii sent one of the *bakufu* councilors, Manabe Akikatsu (間部詮勝), to Kyoto to get the emperor's approval for the treaties. With the emperor himself opposing the treaties, the approval was not easily obtained. In the lengthy discussions, Manabe declared that the treaties were temporary evils that could not be avoided, and that as soon as adequate armaments might be prepared, the barbarians would be expelled. In February 1859, the imperial reply was handed down acknowledging the inevitability of signing the treaties as temporary measures pending restoration of the old law of exclusion at some appropriate date in the future.

54　The fleet was composed of nine British, three French, and four Dutch warships. The single American representative was a small vessel leased from a Chinese firm. All US warships in the Pacific were involved with the search for Confederate raiders.

55　The Japanese tariffs on all dutiable goods averaged 3.7 percent in 1867, whereas the average British tariffs on all imports were 8.9 percent in 1866–70.

56　Modest upward revisions were made on a limited number of items. About forty items were now subject to duties ranging from 5 percent to 15 percent. Payson Treat, *Diplomatic Relations between the United States and Japan, 1853–1895* (Stanford: Stanford University Press, 1932), 432.

57　Alcock was transferred back to China. The British government considered Alcock's conduct in Japan too aggressive. Michael Auslin, *Negotiating with Imperialism* (Cambridge: Harvard University Press, 2004), 117.

58　Auslin, *Negotiating with Imperialism*, 134.

59　Heusken was out riding on January, 14, 1861, when he was assaulted and fatally wounded.

60　A British squadron leveled much of the city of Kagoshima in August 1963, in retaliation for the killing by Satsuma samurai of an Englishman who failed to give way to Shimazu Hisamitsu's entourage.

61　Beasley, *The Rise of Modern Japan*, 83.

62　In 1861 the *bakufu* leadership arranged the marriage of the shogun to the emperor's

Chapter 2

sister. Contrary to the *bakufu*'s expectations, this made the *sonnō-jōi* adherents more anti-*bakufu*, as they took it to be a crude plot to manipulate the court to the *bakufu*'s advantage.

63   The mediator between Satsuma and Chōshū was Sakamoto Ryōma (坂本龍馬), a *shishi* from Tosa. He had outgrown the narrow anti-Western position he had originally embraced, and now supported opening the country and reforming Japan at the national level. He arranged a meeting between Saigō of Satsuma and Kido of Chōshū in Osaka in March 1866. Saigō and Kido concluded a secret alliance.

64   The *bakufu* had sent its first punitive expedition in the fall of 1864 against Chōshū, which had attempted to enter Kyoto by force in the summer of that year. Satsuma had joined the *bakufu* forces in defeating Chōshū at that time.

65   Beasley, *The Rise of Modern Japan*, 52.

66   The charter oath proclaimed that policy would be decided only after wide consultation, taking account of the interests of all Japanese, "high and low," that "base customs of former times" would be abandoned; and that in the pursuit of national strength, "knowledge shall be sought throughout the world." The emperor Meiji was then sixteen years old.

## Chapter 3
# Early Mutual Impressions

## 3.1. Successful American Diplomacy

### 3.1.1. The Successful Diplomacy of Perry and Harris

When two countries start a new relationship, the impressions the people form of each other at the initial stage are important. They influence to a considerable extent the ensuing bilateral relationship well into the distant future. In this sense, the diplomacy of both Perry and Harris was markedly successful in creating a favorable image of America. Despite his squadron's warlike appearance, Perry was under strict orders not to use force except in self-defense and to conduct the mission not only with credit to the United States but without wrong to Japan. He carried out the directives very nearly to perfection. A secretary to Perry wrote: "Not a shot has been fired, not a man wounded, not a piece of property destroyed, not a boat sunk or a single Japanese to be found who is the worse off . . . "[1] Perry's statesmanlike diplomacy not only won the respect of the Japanese, but laid the foundation of the "historic friendship" between the two countries.[2] The Japanese erected an imposing monument in his honor at his landing place in Kurihama, dedicating it with appropriate ceremony in July, 1901, during the forty-eighth anniversary of Perry's arrival.

*51*

*Chapter 3*

Harris's diplomacy was even less threatening. With no naval force to back up his demands, he had little choice but to proceed peacefully and patiently, and his nonmilitant manner was much appreciated by the Japanese. He was in fact sympathetic to the *bakufu* in its difficulties created by the signing of the commercial treaties. When Heusken, Harris's valued assistant and sole colleague since 1856, was slain by *shishi* from Satsuma on January 14, 1861 (2.3.2),[3] and Secretary of State William H. Seward proposed a joint naval demonstration by the treaty powers to demand satisfaction for the murder, Harris dissuaded Seward, and only asked the *bakufu* to pay $10,000 to Heusken's widowed mother "for her support." The *bakufu* officials greatly appreciated the attitude taken by Harris.[4] While the other foreign representatives withdrew to Yokohama on the grounds that the *bakufu* was unable to guarantee the security of foreign lives and property, Harris alone refused to leave Edo. Harris kept his confidence in the *bakufu*'s good faith and willingness to ensure his protection.

Harris's attitude taken in this incident contrasted with the action the British took in the Namamugi Incident (生麦事件) in August 1862 (2.3.2), in which an Englishman who was leading a mounted sightseeing party was killed. The Englishman had tried to cross the path of the formal procession of Shimazu Hisamitsu, calling to his friends, "I know how to treat these people." According to Japanese customary law, he had committed an offense punishable by death. An order was given and he was slain on the spot. The British demanded an indemnity payment of 625,000—500,000 dollars from the *bakufu* and 125,000 dollars from Satsuma. The *bakufu* made the payment in the amount the British demanded, but Satsuma refused. The British resorted to naval operations and destroyed half of the town of Kagoshima.[5]

Harris wrote to Alcock, "I had hoped that the page of future history might record the great fact that in one spot in the Eastern world the advent of Christian civilization did not bring with it its usual attendants of rapine and bloodshed; this fond hope, I fear, is to be disappointed . . ."[6]

The Japanese have always believed that Harris gave much more consideration to their interests than they would have received if the first trade treaty had been with Britain.[7] In fact, he was held in such great respect by the Japanese government that, when he was about to leave Japan, a formal letter was addressed to the secretary of state asking that his stay might be prolonged.[8]

### 3.1.2. The Return of the Shimonoseki Indemnity

The US action of remitting the Shimonoseki indemnity to Japan also strongly impressed the Japanese with the goodwill of the Americans and the contrast between American and British diplomacy. The Convention of 1864 (2.3.1) had stipulated that the *bakufu* would pay a 3 million dollars indemnity for the Chōshū bombardment of foreign ships in the Straits of Shimonoseki in 1863. The indemnity was distributed, following a British suggestion, equally among the four powers after deducting 420,000 dollars from the total for compensation to the powers which had had vessels actually fired upon: the United States, France, and the Netherlands. Under this plan, 785,000 dollars ($420,000 × 1/3 + $2,580,000 × 1/4) was allotted to the United States.[9]

The amount was about forty times what the United States had paid to repair the vessel.[10] The State Department Examiner of Claims pronounced the whole affair an act of extortion, and put the money aside in an escrow account. Early in 1868, Secretary of State Seward first called the attention of Congress to this money which had been received "without substantial equivalent."[11] An organized campaign led by leading educators, including Professor David Murray of Rutgers University, appealed for the return of the money to Japan, and a number of American chambers of commerce joined in the campaign.[12] President Grant proposed using the money to finance a student exchange with Japan. Bill after bill was introduced in Congress, some passing one house and some the other.

Finally, in 1883, legislation requiring the return of the Shimonoseki indemnity monies to Japan reached the White House without any stipulation as to its use. The delay was primarily due to the difficulties inherent in the passage of such unprecedented legislation. The Japanese followed these moves by the Americans with deep interest, and the actual return of the money was welcomed as a "strong manifestation of the spirit of justice and equity which has always animated the United States in their relations with Japan."[13] The Japanese government used the money to make long-needed improvements to the harbor of Yokohama, where it might serve to perpetuate the goodwill of the United States.

None of the other recipients of the Shimonoseki indemnity restored monies to Japan. British consul-general to Japan Harry Parkes, who had sponsored the negotiations between the powers and the *bakufu*, expressed his contempt for the American concern regarding the return of the money.[14]

## 3.2. Japan's Ratification Embassy of 1860

### 3.2.1. Americans' Warm Welcome

The first official Japanese group to come into contact with American culture on its home ground was the embassy of seventy-seven members and an escort of ninety-six sent to the United States in 1860 to exchange the ratifications of the Harris treaty. The embassy, consisting of two ambassadors and an inspector,[15] seventeen officers, and fifty-seven attendants and servants, sailed from Yokohama on February 9, 1860, on board the USS *Powhatan* (Perry's flagship in 1854), and arrived in San Francisco on March 29, after calling at Honolulu for supplies.

The escort group left Uraga on February 4 on board the *Kanrin-maru* (咸臨丸), a corvette built in Holland, and arrived in San Francisco on March 17. The *Kanrin-maru*'s commander was Kimura Yoshitake, and the captain was Katsu Kaishū (勝海舟).[16] Other members were basically naval officers and sailors, but some non-navy men like Fukuzawa Yukichi (福沢諭吉) were included.[17] The voyage was assisted by Captain John Brooke of the US Navy.[18] Nakahama Manjirō (中浜万次郎) (2.1.2) was also on board as Brooke's interpreter, and he served as the actual sailing master of the vessel during its somewhat rough passage.[19]

The two groups were united for a while in San Francisco, until the *Powhatan* group resumed travel to Panama, where they crossed the isthmus by train and met a US frigate that took them to Washington. They arrived on May 14, and attended various state functions: a formal presentation to President Buchanan, a White House state banquet, and a ceremony for the formal exchange of treaty ratifications with Secretary of State Lewis Cass.

The escort group stayed in San Francisco until May 8, and returned home on June 23 via Honolulu. The embassy members, after visiting Baltimore, Philadelphia, and New York, headed home June 29 on board the US warship *Niagara*, taking the Atlantic route and arriving at Shinagawa on November 9. All expenses of the embassy were paid by the United States.

In the United States, the envoys were welcomed with a spectacular show of enthusiasm in the cities they visited as well as in the capital. In New York, hundreds of thousands filled the streets of Manhattan to watch the procession of the embassy escorted by seven thousand welcoming troops. In Baltimore, according to a press report, three-quarters of the population were out in the streets to catch a glimpse of the visitors from the Orient.[20]

For the Americans, the visit of the 1860 embassy was virtually their first encounter with Japanese people. The envoys' appearance and behavior were given full treatment in newspapers and magazines. The two-sworded, top-knotted samurai must have looked like creatures from another planet. The *New York Illustrated News* reported: "To speak honestly, they looked a comical group, and nothing but remembrance that they were strangers and persons of mark in their own country, unused to Western manners and habits, and that they had come here as the representatives of a great civilized nation . . . kept me from laughing heartily at their appearance . . . "[21] Most of the newspapers, however, were more polite. They noted favorably the ease and courtesy of the Japanese when besieged by curiosity seekers. *Frank Leslie's Illustrated Newspaper* reported: "The Oriental strangers were very affable, wrote autographs and gave their tobacco or other trifling objects with great liberality to those who begged from them, and in short, adapted themselves with great good nature to the barbarians who crowded around . . . " The same newspaper told its readers: "The Japanese civilization was obviously not the crude and unsophisticated one which had often been presented in American writings. Japan possesses a higher degree of culture and organization than any other of the Asiatic races."[22]

### 3.2.2. The Japanese Views of the Americans

The Japanese envoys' first impressions of America and the Americans are shown by their travel diaries and other records. Their observations were not uniform. While the older officials observed American culture critically, the younger members' views were overwhelmingly favorable.

The views of Vice-Ambassador Muragaki Norimasa, the oldest among the three leaders at forty-seven, were colored by his conviction that all foreigners were barbarians. After a jolly banquet in San Francisco, he remarked in his diary, "As a ceremonial expression of friendship, the dinner was perhaps sincere, but looked at critically, it was just like what I imagine to go on in an Edo restaurant when construction laborers have their drinking bouts." In Washington, he compared the Congressional debates on the Capitol Hill to fish sellers shouting in the fish market at Nihonbashi. He also considered open discussions before general audiences dangerous.[23]

Nonomura Ichinoshin, Muragaki's servant, was more approving: "For the most part, the people of this country are extremely generous, honest, and sincere. They do not despise foreigners. They trust even those whom they have never seen before. They are also somewhat naïve like our provincials who have never been to a big city."[24] Fukushima Keizaburō, at eighteen one of the youngest in the embassy, was also positive and frank: "High-ranking people do not look down on the lower class or oppress them . . . I believe that the lower classes in Japan would be eager for the American way of life if they ever tasted its freedom . . . Of seventy-seven of us, the majority were anti-foreign in sentiment when we left our country. Now we regret our misunderstanding. If Americans felt about us as we did about them, we would soon be insulted. It is a stupid way to behave, and I for one am determined to try and understand the sincere heart of America."[25]

The escort members saw only San Francisco, but were similarly impressed. Nagao Kōsaku, Commodore Kimura's servant, who was hospitalized in San Francisco and overwhelmed by the American doctors' care and friendliness, was totally enchanted with the new land.[26]

Even Muragaki changed his views of the Americans toward the end of the trip, and came to believe that the Japanese could learn much from them, though he did not leave any sign of such thoughts in his diary. Hattori Itsurō, a great-grandson of Muragaki, writes that Muragaki confided to his wife, after his return to Japan, that he was now ashamed to have called the Americans barbarians, and that the Japanese would never have treated the Americans with such kindness if the situation had been reversed.[27]

Among the Japanese mission members, those who had the greatest influence on the forthcoming developments in Japan were not the embassy leaders, but Katsu Kaishū and Fukuzawa Yukichi. Both praised the liberal and republican America, and their actions based on their impressions had a lasting impact in Japan.

Katsu was a reform-minded samurai well versed in Dutch learning,[28] and this intellectual background made him a keen observer of American culture during his stay in San Francisco. He was impressed with the social equality in America, and became more strongly convinced that Japan needed structural social reform, and that a feudal Japan under the control of the Tokugawa family would have no future. When he was promoted to acting commissioner of the navy in 1862, he founded the Kobe Naval Academy to train talented samurai from all over Japan regardless of their domain affiliations.[29] One of

*56*

his disciples was Sakamoto Ryōma. Katsu had Sakamoto recruit extremist *jōi* proponents as students to enlighten them and broaden their views.[30] Katsu had many sympathizers outside the *bakufu*. For example, Saigō Takamori (西郷隆盛) of Satsuma was greatly impressed by his first meeting with Katsu. When the final assault on Edo by the imperial coalition forces was to begin, Katsu met with Saigō, the commander of the enemy coalition forces, and surrendered Edo Castle, exempting the city from a devastating battle.[31]

As Katsu played an important role within the government in transforming a feudal Japan into a modern Japan, so did Fukuzawa outside the government. While Katsu's contributions were not so much by writing as by deeds, those of Fukuzawa were as a busy publicist of modern ideas. His visits to the United States in 1860 and to Europe in 1862 enabled him to gain direct knowledge of social, political, and economic affairs in the West.[32] In 1866, he published *Seiyō jijō* (西洋事情 Conditions in the West), which was an immediate success and was followed by sequels in 1868 and 1870.[33] In this "bible of overseas information," he wrote: "The United States of America is republican in the best sense of the word. This is the country in which real representatives of the people meet and discuss national politics without any private interests."[34] He also gave a translation of the Declaration of Independence, which had the effect of inspiring several young leaders to work for the overthrow of the Tokugawa regime.[35] Kamei argues that the Declaration of Independence had an important influence on the Japanese drafters of the *gokajō no seimon* (2.3.2).[36] In 1867 Fukuzawa went to the United States for a second time and brought back as many books as he could to be used as textbooks at his Keio Gijuku academy (now Keio University). With this impetus, American books became widely used in Japanese schools in the early Meiji era.[37]

The first decade of the Meiji era (1868–77) is called by Japanese historians the age of "civilization and enlightenment" (*bunmei kaika* 文明開化). The Japanese tried to become "enlightened" through serious study of the Western civilization of the day. Fukuzawa, a leader of this movement, described the United States as the foremost nation of "civilization and enlightenment," and popularized the image of America as the sacred land of liberty.[38]

Toward the end of the first decade of the Meiji era, however, Fukuzawa's admiration for America became somewhat reserved. He enumerated what he began to think were defects in American republicanism, and even saw a tendency toward mobocracy in his *Bunmeiron no gairyaku* (文明論之概略 An outline of a theory of civilization) published in 1875.[39] After the turn of the century, criticism of contemporary America began to spread in Japan. Nevertheless, the earlier image of America as an admirable incarnation of liberty—the image Fukuzawa had popularized—remained a deep undercurrent in the minds of many Japanese, and was handed down to their descendants.

# 3.3. The Iwakura Embassy of 1871

### 3.3.1. A Large-Scale Study Group

The new Meiji government sent a large-scale embassy to the United States and Europe from December 1871 to September 1873. The mission consisted of Iwakura Tomomi (岩倉具視), the *udaijin* (右大臣 deputy premier), as ambassador extraordinary and plenipotentiary, and four vice-ambassadors—namely Kido Takayoshi (木戸孝允), the *sangi* (参議 state council); Ōkubo Toshimichi (大久保利通), the *ōkura kyō* (大蔵卿 finance minister); Itō Hirobumi (伊藤博文), the *kōbu taifu* (工部大輔 vice-minister of industry); and Yamaguchi Naoyoshi (山口尚芳), the *gaimu shōyū* (外務少輔 assistant vice-minister of foreign affairs).[40] They were assisted by forty-three officials, including ten commissioners who were experts in their respective fields.[41] Fifty-nine students, including five girls, accompanied the embassy.[42] It was perhaps the first mission in world history to include such a large proportion of a government's leadership, sent abroad for such an extended period at such a critical point in national politics. Barely three years had passed since the unprecedented Meiji Restoration. The abolition of the feudal domains and the establishment of the prefecture system, one of the most crucial reforms, had just been carried out four months before. Many other reform measures were yet to be implemented, and many problems were known to be in the offing.

The objectives of the mission, as set forth in a letter from Sanjō Sanetomi (三条実美), the *dajō daijin* (太政大臣 prime minister) to Iwakura, were threefold: to improve Japan's image overseas following the Restoration; to have preliminary talks about revision of the commercial treaties in force at the time; and to investigate the social and economic conditions of the various powers and clarify the sources of their "enlightened civilization."

Since the first objective had been defined as being limited to courtesy calls on foreign governments, and since a request for a postponement of treaty negotiations had already been made to the powers concerned, the investigation

*Early Mutual Impressions*

of social and economic conditions was the most important objective for the mission. While the new government had so far carried out several reforms, they had been rather haphazard. There seemed to be a requirement for the establishment of a firm, long-range program for reforms—a blueprint for modernization. The Meiji leaders wanted to determine how the West had acquired its wealth and power, and how Japan could achieve the same levels. There was a firm intention to apply what would be learned from the West to the problems of Japan. Thus, the mission was in effect a large study group.

The embassy originally planned to be abroad for ten months, but their trip was extended to twenty-one months mainly because of a prolonged stay in Washington, where the mission became involved in treaty negotiations that they had not originally planned.[43] They had to send two members of the embassy back to Tokyo to obtain credentials to begin formal negotiations,[44] although in the event the pair's four-month round trip to Tokyo proved useless, as the treaty negotiations broke down.[45]

The mission members had very little understanding of international commercial agreements. The Americans opened by asking the Japanese to permit internal travel and residence as well as religious toleration and protection for Japanese Christians. Iwakura broke off the negotiations when he realized that, under the existing network of unconditional most-favored-nation agreements, all concessions made by Japan to the United States in exchange for American concessions would have to be conceded automatically to all other treaty powers without obligating those powers to make any concessions to Japan in return.

### 3.3.2. Hospitable Americans

Notwithstanding the failure of the treaty negotiations, the American government and people were very hospitable to the Japanese visitors throughout their long tour. This extended from the mission's arrival in San Francisco on January 15 to the long, wintry rail journey across the continent from January 31 to February 29,[46] the extended stay in Washington from February 29 to July 27 (there was an interlude of travel in New York and New England from June 9 to 22),[47] and through to their departure from Boston on August 6, 1872. Kume Kunitake (久米邦武), the embassy's diarist, describes in the *Tokumei zenken taishi Beiō kairan jikki* (特命全権大使米欧回覧実記, henceforth the *Jikki*):[48]

When our steamer arrived in San Francisco, city officials and representatives—public and civil, men and women—welcomed us, entertained us daily, and expressed their regret that our departure was so soon. In Sacramento and Chicago, because of the time which would have been needed to do full justice to the various sites, officials and citizens asked us to extend our stay by several days. When we prolonged our stay in Washington, we received, almost daily, letters and messengers with invitations from municipalities and companies and had almost no days free. In New York City, for instance, we were asked to extend our stay and our hosts felt quite offended when we could not do so.

In every city they visited, the media were eager to report on the mission's activities. This time the media coverage was not merely for the sake of novelty, as had been the case with the 1860 mission. The media interest derived from recognition and admiration of the Japanese success in launching a modern nation from the "fresh ruins of a feudal order."[49] *Daily Evening Bulletin* in San Francisco reported:[50]

Japan is today, all the circumstances of her previous condition considered, the most progressive nation on the globe. . . . Unlike the Chinese, its people readily make changes in clothing, food, manufactures, and mode of living, when they see improvement therein. They are, as a race, impulsive, highly intelligent, brave to rashness, cleanly in their habits, have a high sense of personal honor, and are universally polite, from the highest dignitary to the lowest in the land, and withal are kindly disposed towards foreigners, especially Americans.

### 3.3.3. Learning about American Industry and Society

The mission members visited schools, factories, government institutions, courts, insane asylums, dockyards and naval yards, workshops, military and naval academies, libraries, churches, and stock exchanges. Visits were often made in separate small groups.

Among such study tours, the most notable was the one conducted by Commissioner Hida Tameyoshi in Philadelphia at the invitation of the city's business community. As a mechanical engineer, Hida was assigned to observe advanced American industry and technology, and the Philadelphia side

*Early Mutual Impressions*

prepared a schedule that fitted that purpose. Hida and his party made intensive study visits to forty-three factories and places of interest between March 16 and April 6. Local press reported daily in approving terms and in detail how the Japanese visitors observed and eagerly learned about the facilities that the American hosts proudly showed them. Within the three weeks, they inspected two dockyards, five iron and steel works, and factories making locomotive engines, marine engines, various vehicles, machine tools, sawing machines, measurement devices, textile machinery, printing presses, gas lighting equipment, boilers, carpets, and bricks—as well as three mines, the Philadelphia Mint, two railroad companies, a printing shop, a newspaper company, and other facilities. Everywhere Hida's serious attitude pleased the hosts, many of whom gave him proprietary documents concerning their products.[51]

Education was another field in which the embassy had a keen interest. They visited several schools in different localities, and were particularly impressed with the public schooling they saw. Kido wrote in his diary that the schools maintained admirable discipline, and went on to discuss the need for an educated citizenry in Japan after he visited an elementary school in San Francisco: "We clearly must have schools if we are to encourage our country's development as a civilized country, improve ordinary people's knowledge, establish the power of the state, and maintain our independence and sovereignty. It is not enough to have a few able men make good. Nothing is more important than schools."[52] Kido also recorded his judgment about the role of education in building a strong Japan: "The creation of public morals and a sound national foundation depends on education, on education alone. Our people are no different from the Americans or Europeans of today; it is all a matter of education or lack of education."[53]

The Japanese travelers also learned of Christianity's powerful role in American society. Kume remarked with surprise on the importance of the Bible for the Americans. It was, he thought, the equivalent of the Confucian classics and Buddhist sutras put together. Every household seemed to have a Bible, and no one would travel far without taking one with him.[54]

The Meiji government's continuation of the *bakufu* ban on Christianity drew disapproval wherever the embassy traveled.[55] This made the embassy members more serious observers of Christianity in the United States. During the journey, they had heated discussions among themselves.[56] Kume's view in the *Jikki* is considered to reflect the general consensus.

*61*

There are many strange aspects in Christ's teachings. It would scarcely take an intelligent scholar to defeat the arguments advanced by the Christians and render them silent. However, when we compare the sincerity of their practice to ours, we cannot but feel ashamed. . . . Every week on the day of worship, rich and poor, carrying their Bibles with them, go to church to listen to sermons, pray and sing, and then return home. Parents teach the Bible to their children. . . . Even if their teachings are not lofty or profound, they are firm in their practice and in their faith. . . . I wonder whether it is in this aspect more than anything else that we cannot compete, because what is most treasured in religion is practice, not argument.[57]

While Bible tales such as the resurrection sounded unpersuasive to Kume, he recognized that the Americans' religious convictions lay behind their sincerity and hard work. He considered moral behavior to be the basic element in maintaining order in society, and thus in the enriching and strengthening of a country. He thought America's strength stemmed from a common belief in Christianity.

Alexis Tocqueville observed in the early 1830s that the Christian religion had greater influence in America than in other countries, and that the Americans derived from their own home the love of order which they carried with them into public affairs. It is interesting that Kume's observations were quite similar to Tocqueville's.[58]

# 3.4. Americans in Japan

### 3.4.1. Missionaries
Though Harris's treaty prohibited Americans from engaging in missionary activity, four American missionaries came to Japan immediately after the signing of the treaty to lay the groundwork for future proselytizing, expecting that the ban would sooner or later be lifted. As the open teaching of Christianity was proscribed, they had to engage in some secular profession. The careers of two of the first American missionaries, James Hepburn and Guido Verbeck, are illustrative of the important contributions the early missionaries made to the modernization of Japan.[59]

Hepburn, a graduate of Princeton and of Pennsylvania Medical School,

*Early Mutual Impressions*

had served as a missionary in Asia for several years and then practiced medicine in New York for over ten years before accepting an appointment from the Presbyterian Board of Foreign Missions to go to Japan. He set up a dispensary in Yokohama, and soon won the confidence of the Japanese through his dedication to their care. He treated thirty to forty patients a day at his dispensary and visited as many in their homes. Despite the dangers foreigners faced in those days, he was ready to go wherever he was called. He never flinched from any demand made on him. Meanwhile, his enthusiasm for his future teaching of Christianity soon led him to embark upon an ambitious undertaking: the preparation of an English–Japanese dictionary that might help to break down the language barrier between the missionary and his prospective converts. He devised a system for transliterating Japanese into Latin letters, which became the basis for his dictionary—a great contribution to the new international role of Japan.[60]

Verbeck, born in the Netherlands and educated as an engineer, immigrated to the United States in 1853 at the age of twenty-three. He studied theology in New York to become a missionary, and was chosen as a missionary-educator in Japan by the Dutch Reformed Church. He opened a school for teaching English in Nagasaki. He was a faithful, simple man, dedicated to his work and firm in his convictions. His school was so successful that in 1864 it was given official recognition and governmental status. He encouraged his students to study in the United States and assisted them in doing so. Many of them went to Rutgers College in New Brunswick, New Jersey, through the good offices of the Dutch Reformed Church.[61] After nine years at Nagasaki, Verbeck moved to Tokyo at the invitation of the Meiji government and became the principal of a new institution called the Nankō School, which would eventually develop into Tokyo Imperial University.[62] He also served the government in various capacities relating to education. He was a respected associate of many Meiji-era leaders as well as an intimate friend of Ōkuma Shigenobu (大隈重信) and Iwakura Tomomi. His proposal made to Ōkuma in 1869 led to the Iwakura embassy of 1871–73.[63] Verbeck resigned his advisory posts in 1879, and, after a brief trip back to the United States, returned to Japan to devote his entire time to missionary activities.[64]

Hepburn and Verbeck came to Japan as missionaries, but they could not preach their faith in the gospel until the ban was lifted in the mid-1870s. Thus, they engaged in their subsidiary roles. Through those contributions,

Chapter 3

however, they won the confidence of the Japanese. The Japanese were impressed with their dedication to their professions and their uprightness and sincerity. They won no converts to Christianity, at least before the toleration of Christianity, but they won many admirers for themselves.

### 3.4.2. Advisers and Educators

A major aspect of Japan's modernization process in the early Meiji era was the employment of foreign specialists by the government in virtually all areas of activity. The Ministry of Industry hired many British because many public works such as railroads, telegraph lines, and lighthouses were ordered from British firms.[65] The navy and army ministries hired many French advisers. In the medical field, the government largely turned to Germans. With regard to foreign affairs and education, the government depended mainly on Americans. Among the advisers to the foreign office, the achievements of Henry Willard Denison, who was awarded the Order of the Rising Sun, First Class,[66] were the most notable. He was with the Ministry of Foreign Affairs from 1880 until his death in 1914. He helped Japan to negotiate treaties after the Sino–Japanese War of 1894–1895 and the Russo–Japanese War of 1904–1905, as well as to negotiate revisions of the unequal treaties with the European powers in the 1880s and 1890s.

In terms of influence on young Japanese in the early Meiji era, the role of American educators was important. They also helped to improve Americans' perception of Japan. The contributions of three educators who came to Japan in the 1870s were especially important.[67]

In 1870, Rutgers received an inquiry from the daimyo of Fukui asking for the dispatch of an educator-teacher who would organize a scientific school in his domain and also teach at the school. The daimyo was Matsudaira Yoshinaga of Echizen (越前). He sent the invitation at the suggestion of Verbeck, who was anxious to have some Rutgers graduates carry on his own pioneering educational work in Japan. William E. Griffis, an 1869 graduate of Rutgers College and a postgraduate student majoring in theology, was selected by the Rutgers faculty for the assignment. Griffis had taught some of the first Japanese students in the Rutgers Grammar School and at Rutgers College, and was interested in Japan. In later years, he wrote of his Japanese students and the reason why he accepted the offer:

64

*Early Mutual Impressions*

(They) . . . were all young men brimming with a splendid samurai spirit. They were all of fine character, and studied with great diligence in their thirst for knowledge. They aspired to become famous men of the future. I had the greatest respect for them, and deeply admired their yearning for a new Japanese Imperial nationality. It was for this reason that I decided to go to Japan. I was especially friendly with Kusakabe, and had the highest respect for his character. I thus went joyfully to Fukui.[68]

Kusakabe Tarō was the first Japanese to be elected to Phi Beta Kappa. He died (and was buried) in New Brunswick; his degree was awarded posthumously. Griffis carried Kusakabe's gold ΦBK key to Fukui to present it to his father.[69] In Fukui, Griffis worked hard, and successfully launched a scientific curriculum. He won a great deal of respect from the domain leaders, as well as from his students.[70] Griffis was in Fukui for only eleven months (from March 4, 1871 until January 22, 1872), as he was called to Tokyo to teach chemistry and physics at the Nankō School. He stayed in Tokyo until July 18, 1874.

After returning to the United States, he resumed his study of theology at a seminary and entered the ministry in America, but he maintained a strong interest in Japan for the rest of his life, and he became one of the most influential writers of his day in providing images of the new Japan to his interested contemporaries.[71] Through his first book, *The Mikado's Empire*, which quickly went through twelve editions after its original publication in 1876, he became America's first "old Japan hand." Foster Rhea Dulles writes, "Perhaps no one exercised a greater influence at this time in encouraging a friendly attitude toward the people about whom he wrote with both authority and a deep appreciation of their native culture."[72]

On the occasion of the visit of the Iwakura mission, Minister Mori in Washington had sought advice from several prominent American educators on the construction of a school system in Japan, and he was particularly impressed with the comments he received from David Murray, professor of mathematics and astronomy at Rutgers.[73] Murray was a dedicated educator with a deeply religious mind. Kido, Itō, and Mori met Murray in Washington and were in agreement that Murray should be employed as an educational adviser and superintendent in charge of school administration. Murray accepted the offer and arrived in Japan in May 1873. During his stay in Japan for the next five and a half years, he made remarkable contributions to the modernization of the Japanese educational system, encouraging the education of girls, founding normal schools, and improving school curricula. At Murray's final imperial audience in 1879, the emperor awarded him the Order of the Rising Sun, Third Class.[74]

As an influential American educator in the early Meiji era, William Smith Clark must also be mentioned. When he signed a one-year contract in March 1876 to become the first president of the Sapporo Agricultural College, he was, as the president of the Massachusetts Agricultural College, a man of prominence in American national educational circles. He was actually present in Sapporo for only eight and a half months, from July 31, 1876 to April 16, 1877, but his enthusiastic personality made a strong impact on the lives of his students.[75] As a fervent Christian himself, he was convinced that the moral education of his students was quite as important as their training in agriculture.[76] Clark converted nearly all of his students and laid the basis for a nondenominational church in Sapporo, out of which came Uchimura Kanzō and other religious leaders.[77] His overall impression of Japanese life was extremely favorable. After his return to Massachusetts, whenever he spoke in public about what he had observed in Japan, he praised Japanese efforts toward modernization and the astonishing speed and success of these efforts.

Griffis, Murray, and Clark all came to Japan as educators. As teachers and educational administrators they accomplished much in their special fields, but they accomplished something more important than the improvement of education in Japan. By winning the respect of the Japanese, they greatly improved Japanese perceptions of America, and helped to make the early relationship between the two countries close and cordial at the grassroots level. What the three men had in common was a strong sense of mission: an anxiety to spread the idea of Christianity. The Japanese were not touched by the Bible tales, but they were impressed by the personalities of their teachers who were Christians. As upright, ethical teachers, they were impressive models for their students. Teaching was more effective than preaching in Japan for spreading understanding of Western mores.

*66*

## NOTES

### 3.1. Successful American Diplomacy

1   Inazō Nitobe, *The Intercourse between the United States and Japan* (Wilmington, DE: Scholarly Resources, reprint edition 1973; first published in 1891), 113. Francis L. Hawks supervised, Sidney Wallach abridged and edited, *Narrative of the Expedition of an American Squadron to the China Seas and Japan* (New York: Coward-McCann, 1952), introduction, xxi.

2   Thomas Bailey, *A Diplomatic History of the American People* (Englewood Cliffs, NJ: Prentice-Hall, 1980), 311.

3   Nitobe, *The Intercourse between the United States and Japan* (Wilmington, DE: Scholarly Resources, 1973), 76.

4   Ibid., 76.

5   Payson Treat, *The Far East* (New York: Harper & Brothers, 1928), 218.

6   William Neumann, *America Encounters Japan: From Perry to MacArthur* (Baltimore: Johns Hopkins Press, 1963), 57–58.

7   Robert Schwantes, *Japanese and Americans: A Century of Cultural Relations* (Westport, CT: Greenwood Press, 1955), 27.

8   Nitobe, *The Intercourse between the United States and Japan*, 115.

9   Payson J. Treat, *Japan and the United States, 1853–1921* (Boston: Houghton Mifflin, 1921), 110–111, and Neumann, *America Encounters Japan*, 60.

10   Nitobe, *The Intercourse between the United States and Japan*, 86.

11   Treat, *Japan and the United States*, 111. Neumann, *America Encounters Japan*, 60.

12   Neumann, *America Encounters Japan*, 70.

13   Treat, *Japan and the United States*, 112.

14   Neumann, *America Encounters Japan*, 70.

### 3.2. Japan's Ratification Embassy of 1860

15   The chief ambassador was Shinmi Masaoki (新見正興) and the vice-ambassador was Muragaki Norimasa (村垣範正). The group's inspector was Oguri Tadamasa (小栗忠順). Shinmi, a son of the daimyo of Bizen in western Japan, was a figurehead. Muragaki was a veteran foreign affairs officer. While both ambassadors remained inconspicuous after returning to Japan, Oguri, the youngest of the three senior members, was the most energetic. After the trip to the United States, he made great efforts to rebuild the military strength of the *bakufu*, eventually serving as the commissioner of the navy and the army. He was a staunch Tokugawa loyalist, but he could save neither the *bakufu* nor his own life. He was ousted by Yoshinobu at the last stage, since he strongly advocated all-out battle against the coalition forces. He was arrested in his home village and was beheaded along with his son. Miyoshi Masao, *As We Saw Them* (Berkeley: University of California Press, 1979), 154–155.

16   Kimura was the director of the Nagasaki Naval Academy, a *bakufu* naval school built in 1855. Kimura's orders called for him to proceed to Washington should any of the three leaders be incapacitated. Katsu was the head of the faculty of the academy.

17   Fukuzawa joined the party as a servant of Kimura.

18   Captain Brooke had been on the ocean survey mission when the ship grounded and

Chapter 3

broke up at Yokohama in a storm. While he was waiting in Japan for return transportation, he was offered the task of assisting Kimura and his crew in navigating the *Kanrin-maru* to San Francisco. He accepted the job, selecting ten out of his crew. The *Kanrin-maru*'s return cruise to Japan was assisted by five of Brooke's crew.

19 Brooke was impressed with Manjirō's fine personality and greatly appreciated his contribution to the voyage as a coordinator between Japanese and Americans on board the *Kanrin-maru*. Brooke wrote in his journal, "Manjirō is certainly one of the most remarkable men I ever saw." George Brooke, Jr., *John M. Brooke's Pacific Cruise and Japanese Adventure, 1858–1860* (Honolulu: University of Hawaii Press, 1986), 211, 222.

20 Miyoshi, *As We Saw Them*, 29–30.

21 Ibid., 67.

22 Neumann, *America Encounters Japan*, 63.

23 Miyoshi, *As We Saw Them*, 56.

24 Ibid., 56.

25 Lewis Bush, *Seventy-Seven Samurai* (Tokyo: Kodansha International, 1968), 176–177.

26 Miyoshi, *As We Saw Them*, 57.

27 Hattori Itsurō, *Shichijūshichi-nin no samurai Amerika e iku* (Tokyo: Kodansha, 1974), 357–359.

28 Matsuura Rei, *Katsu Kaishū to bakumatsu Meiji* (Tokyo: Kodansha, 1973), 2–9.

29 Miyoshi, *As We Saw Them*, 157.

30 Matsuura, *Katsu Kaishū*, 26–27.

31 Katsu was in the *bakufu*'s highest military position at that time. Katsu offered Saigō the surrender of Edo Castle in exchange for saving Yoshinobu's life and preserving the Tokugawa family as one of the major domain holders. Ishii Takashi, *Katsu Kaishū* (Tokyo: Yoshikawa Kōbunkan, 1974), 136–190.

32 He was recruited for the Japanese government mission in 1862, visiting France, Britain, Holland, Prussia, Russia, and Portugal as one of the specialists who conducted research on the social and political institutions of European countries.

33 Of the first edition, 150,000 copies were sold at once, and pirated editions quickly multiplied that number.

34 Kamei Shunsuke, "The Sacred Land of Liberty: Images of America in Nineteenth Century Japan," in *Mutual Images*, ed. Akira Iriye (Cambridge: Harvard University Press, 1975), 60.

35 Ibid., 60.

36 Ibid., 59.

37 Ibid., 60.

38 Ibid., 59–60.

39 Ibid., 61.

### 3.3. The Iwakura Embassy of 1871

40 The early Meiji government used ancient court titles for cabinet officers in line with its "restoration" ideology. The *udaijin* was the third-highest position in the administration next to the *sadaijin*, but with no one in the *sadaijin* position at the time,

Iwakura was next to *dajō daijin* (prime minister) Sanjō Sanetomi. Both were from the old court nobility. *Sangi* Kido was ranked next to the *udaijin* in the administration. Haga Tōru, "Meiji ishin to Iwakura shisetsudan," in *Iwakura shisetsudan no hikakubunkashiteki kenkyū*, ed. Haga Tōru (Kyoto: Shibunkaku, 2003), 6–7.

41  Haga, "Iwakura shisetsudan," in *Iwakura shisetsudan*, ed. Haga, 7–11. Eugene Sioviak, "On the Nature of Western Progress: The Journal of the Iwakura Embassy," in *Tradition and Modernization in Japanese Culture*, ed. Donald H. Shively (Princeton: Princeton University Press, 1971), 11.

42  The youngest of the girls was six-year-old Tsuda Umeko, who stayed in the United States until 1882. She became a pioneer in women's education in Japan, founding what became Tsuda Women's College.

43  The unscheduled entry into treaty negotiations came about because Itō and Mori Arinori (森有礼), the Japanese minister in Washington, buoyed by the warm and enthusiastic American reception, argued that they should take advantage of the favorable mood and go beyond the original plan. A move to substantive negotiations was also recommended by Secretary of State Hamilton Fish, who told Mori that, as 1872 was a presidential election year, the embassy might as well negotiate with the Grant administration as with a possible new and unfamiliar administration (Grant was, in the event, reelected). Michael R. Auslin, *Negotiating with Imperialism* (Cambridge: Harvard University Press, 2004), 180–182. The prolonged stay in Britain, where they had originally been scheduled to stay a month but they had to extend it due to the delay of an audience with Queen Victoria, also made their trip schedule longer.

44  They had a letter from Emperor Meiji to President Grant, which charged Iwakura with the task of substantive discussions regarding treaty renegotiation, but Fish judged that the authority of the embassy to sign formal agreements was ambiguous. Alistair Swale, "America: 15 January–6 August 1872," in *The Iwakura Mission in America and Europe*, ed. Ian Nish (London: Routledge, 1998), 20.

45  Ōkubo and Itō left Washington on March 20 and reached Tokyo on May 1, but the Tokyo government resisted giving them negotiating authority, insisting that the mission was going beyond the scope of its original purposes. Ōkubo and Itō managed to get credentials eventually, and left Yokohama on June 22, arriving at Washington on July 22. Izumi Saburō, *Meiji yonen no anbassadoru* (Tokyo: Nihon Keizai Shimbunsha, 1984), 108. Auslin, *Negotiating with Imperialism*, 192.

46  The mission took the newly completed (in 1869) transcontinental railroad. The US government chartered a train with sleeping cars for them. They were scheduled to arrive in Washington in seven days, but they were trapped in heavy snow in the Rocky Mountains. They had to evacuate to nearby Salt Lake City, where they spent seventeen days. On February 26 and 27 they stayed in Chicago, where they presented the mayor with a check for 5,000 dollars to aid the victims of the great fire in the previous year. This gesture was reported with widespread approval in the American and European press accounts of the embassy's progress across the United States.

47  In Washington, the embassy had an official audience with President Ulysses S. Grant on March 4, visited Congress on March 6, and had their first meeting with Secretary of State Hamilton Fish on March 11. While they waited for the two envoys to return from Tokyo with full powers, the US government arranged a trip to New York City,

West Point, Niagara Falls, Saratoga Springs, and Boston.

48 Kume Kunitake, ed., *Tokumei zenken taishi Beiō kairan jikki*, vol. 1 (Tokyo: Hakubunsha, 1878), 11. Kume was the official recorder of the embassy, and continued his research after the embassy's return to Japan. Before completing the *Jikki* in 1878, he apparently consulted with many of the other embassy members. The *Jikki* is therefore the collective expression of various points of view. The English edition of this book is titled *The Iwakura Embassy, 1871–73: A True Account of the Ambassador Extraordinary and Plenipotentiary's Journey of Observation Through the United States of America and Europe*, compiled by Kume Kunitake, vol. 1, *The United States of America*, trans. Martin Collcutt (Tokyo: The Japan Documents, 2002). The *Jikki* was written in old Japanese, but an edition translated into contemporary Japanese was published. Kume Kunitake, *Tokumei zenken taishi Beiō kairan jikki*, trans. Mizusawa Shū (Tokyo: Keio University Press, 2008).

49 Edwin O. Reischauer, *The United States and Japan* (Cambridge: Harvard University Press, 1950), 19.

50 Alistair Swale, "America: 15 Janurary–6 August 1872," in *The Iwakura Mission in America and Europe*, ed. Nish, 13.

51 Marlene Mayo, "A Story of Philadelphia," trans. Ido Keiko, in *Iwakura shisetsudan no hikakubunkashiteki kenkyū* (Kyoto: Shibunkaku Shuppan, 2003), 47–89.

52 Kido Takayoshi, *Kido Takayoshi nikki*, ed. Nihon Shiseki Kyōkai (Tokyo: University of Tokyo Press, 1967), vol. 2, 126–127. Also see Irokawa Daikichi, *Meiji no bunka* (Tokyo: Iwanami Shoten, 1970), 56. The English edition of this book is Irokawa Daikichi, *The Culture of the Meiji Period*, trans. and ed. Marius B. Jansen (Princeton: Princeton University Press, 1985).

53 Kido Takayoshi, *Kido Takayoshi monjo*, ed. Nihon Shiseki Kyōkai (Tokyo: University of Tokyo Press, 1971), vol. 4, 320. This statement is in the letter that Kido wrote to his colleague Sugiyama Takatoshi two days after his visit to three elementary schools in San Francisco. Irokawa writes, "In those days universal public school education was already established in the United States, and there were as many as 141,700 schools and 7,210,000 students in the United States. Kido's surprise is easily imagined, since he had known nothing beyond a few feudal domain schools and *terakoya*." Irokawa, *Meiji no bunka*, 54.

54 Kume, *Jikki*, trans. Mizusawa, 363–364.

55 In 1870 the Meiji government, which had continued the Tokugawa ban on Christianity, arrested about 3,000 suspected Catholics at Urakami in Nagasaki and shipped them to various parts of Japan for incarceration. Despite the protests of foreign representatives, the detention and exile of Christians continued until March, 1873. In that year, the government removed the edict against Christianity as an "evil sect" from public notice boards.

56 Kume, *Jikki*, trans. Mizusawa, 397–398.

57 Ibid., 363–367. Kume also discussed commonalities between Christianity and Confucianism, and deplored the tendency to dismiss Confucianism in Japan. Ibid., 367–368.

58 Alexis Tocqueville toured in the United States in 1831, and wrote in 1835, " . . . there is no country in the world where the Christian religion retains a greater influence

*Notes*

over the souls of men than in America. . . . There is certainly no country in the world where the tie of marriage is more respected than in America, or where conjugal happiness is more highly or worthily appreciated. . . . While the European endeavors to forget his domestic troubles by agitating society, the American derives from his own homes that love of order which he afterwards carries with him into public affairs." Alexis Tocqueville, *Democracy in America* (New York: Vintage Books, 1955), 314–315.

## 3.4. Americans in Japan

59 Foster Rhea Dulles, *Yankees and Samurai* (New York: Harper & Row, 1965), 139–140.

60 Ibid., 140–141.

61 Verbeck wrote a letter of introduction for his students to John M. Ferris, a leader of the Dutch Reformed Church in America. Ferris arranged to enroll them in Rutgers Grammar School and later in Rutgers College. The number of students who studied at Rutgers between 1866 and 1885 totaled about 300. The Japanese government sent a letter of thanks to Ferris through the Iwakura mission in 1872. Ishizuki Minoru, "Overseas Study by Japanese in the Early Meiji Period," in *The Modernizers: Overseas Students, Foreign Employees, and Meiji Japan*, ed. Ardath Burks (hereafter cited as *The Modernizers*) (Boulder, CO: Westview Press, 1985), 171.

62 Robert Schwantes, *Japanese and Americans* (Westport, CT: Greenwood Press, 1976), 157.

63 Marius Jansen, "Amerika ni okeru Iwakura shisetsudan," in *Iwakura shisetsudan no hikakubunkashiteki kenkyū*, ed. Haga Tōru (Kyoto: Shibunkaku Shuppan, 2003), 17–18.

64 With the appointment of David Murray as a new adviser on education, Verbeck, being a man of broad learning rather than an education specialist, was no longer needed. However, as the Japanese government officials appreciated his lofty character as well as his understanding of Japanese conditions and his facility with the Japanese language, he was asked to stay on as an adviser until 1879.

65 In 1868–1900, British employees in the Japanese government totaled 1,034, of whom 553 were hired by the Ministry of Industry for public works. The total government foreign employees during the same period numbered 2,400. Hazel J. Jones, "The Griffis Thesis and Meiji Policy toward Hired Foreigners," in *The Modernizers*, 226.

66 Denison alone, of all the foreign advisers employed by the Japanese government, was awarded the medal. Ardath Burks, "The West's Inreach: The Oyatoi Gaikokujin," in *The Modernizers*, 195.

67 Foster Rhea Dulles, *Yankees and Samurai* (New York: Harper & Row, 1965), 156.

68 Nagai Tamaki, *Kusakabe Tarō den* (Fukui: Fukui Hyōronsha, 1930), 76–77. Ishizuki, "Overseas Study by Japanese in the Early Meiji Period," in *The Modernizers*, 165.

69 William Elliot Griffis, *The Mikado's Empire* (Tokyo: Jiji Press, 1971), 430–431.

70 Griffis writes in *The Mikado's Empire*, " . . . As I walked [in the school], I wondered how long it would take to civilize such barbarians. Here were nearly a thousand young samurai. What was one teacher among so many? Could it be possible that

Chapter 3

these could be trained to be disciplined students? These were my thoughts then. A few months later, and I had won their confidence and love. I found they were quite able to instruct me in many things. . . . In pride and dignity of character, in diligence, courage, gentlemanly conduct, refinement and affection, truth and honesty, good morals, in so far as I know or could see, they were my peers." Griffis, *Mikado's Empire*, 434.

71  Ardath Burks, introduction to *The Modernizers*, 2.

72  Dulles, *Yankees and Samurai*, 160.

73  Kaneko Tadashi, "Contributions of David Murray to the Modernization of School Administration in Japan," in *The Modernizers*, 303.

74  Dulles, *Yankees and Samurai*, 161–162.

75  Clark's parting message, "Boys, be ambitious," which he gave to his students who gathered to bid farewell to him at his departure from Sapporo, made him widely known among the Japanese. The message was so much in keeping with the spirit of early Meiji Japan that it was picked up in new school textbooks and spread throughout Japan. Dulles, *Yankees and Samurai*, 186.

76  Ibid., 186.

77  Schwantes, *Japanese and Americans*, 55.

# Chapter 4
# Treaty Revision

## 4.1. Early Negotiations

### 4.1.1. Tariff Autonomy Rather than Judicial Autonomy

The greatest foreign policy question for the Meiji government was the revision of the treaties with treaty powers signed in 1858 (2.1.4) and revised in 1866 (2.3.1). The new government leaders now realized that two of their sovereign rights, tariff autonomy and jurisdiction over foreigners in Japan, were seriously impaired. The first attempt at revision was made in 1872 in Washington by the Iwakura mission members, but they accomplished nothing (3.3.1). The treaties had provisions that they could be revised by the mutual consent of both parties after July 4, 1872, but no treaty powers would give up their privileges given by the unequal treaties.[1] They were even anxious to gain additional concessions from Japan, such as religious toleration and the opening of more ports to trade.

Early in 1873, the Italian minister requested that Italian businessmen be given the right to travel outside the treaty port limits so that they might deal directly with Japanese raw-silk suppliers in the regional inland centers, bypassing the Yokohama go-betweens. In response, the Japanese government, on the

*73*

counsel of an American adviser in the foreign office, offered to agree to the Italian request, subject to the travelers "submitting to the protection and jurisdiction of the territorial authorities." The treaty powers, however, urged the Italian government not to conclude such an agreement, and the Italians acquiesced. The powers did not want Japan to apply its laws to Italian businessmen even outside the treaty port limits until Japan achieved an amelioration of its judicial system.[2]

The American government joined the other powers in prevailing upon Italy to desist. This was, however, the last instance of American participation in the "cooperative policy" of acting in East Asia in concert with the European powers—in reality, acceptance of British leadership in East Asian policy—which had long been the guiding principle of American policy in China and Japan.

The Japanese leaders had undertaken to have Western-style criminal and civil codes as well as a Western-style court system, but they were, at the same time, cautious about the dangers of hasty reforms. They were aware that reforms would fail unless the new system harmonized with Japanese social organization and personal relationships. The extraterritoriality question appeared to them to be more difficult than the tariff issue. In the 1870s, therefore, the Japanese government decided to devote its attention to the tariff question.

One strand of thought was that the economic problems arising from the treaty tariff would outweigh the temporary loss of national dignity of ceding extraterritoriality to the treaty powers. The Convention of 1866 (2.3.1) reduced all duties to 5 percent, and, on the basis of a 5 percent duty, quoted specific duties on eighty-nine items. As prices rose, the duty-to-price ratios of these items declined. The average duty on all imports on an *ad valorem* basis became 3.1 percent in 1870, whereas it was 44.9 percent in the United States in the same year and 8.9 percent in "free trading" Britain in 1866–70.[3] Such low Japanese tariffs gave little protection to the nascent Japanese industries. The most seriously affected were the cotton and sugar industries.

In Tokugawa-period Japan, cotton was the main textile for clothing, and cotton-growing and -weaving were important industries. However, the prices of raw cotton, cotton yarn, and cotton cloth in autarchic Japan were much higher than world prices.[4] The opening of foreign trade resulted in a large increase in imports[5] and a decrease in the prices of those commodities, causing great economic hardship to the Japanese producers. The damage might have

**Table 4.1.1-a. Customs Duty Share of Government Revenues, Japan, US, and UK**

|      | Japan | US    | UK  |
|------|-------|-------|-----|
| 1860 | —     | 94.9% | 35% |
| 1870 | 3.1%  | 47.3% | —   |
| 1880 | 4.1%  | 55.9% | 25% |
| 1890 | 4.1%  | 57.0% | —   |
| 1900 | 5.7%  | 41.1% | 21% |

*Source:* Nippon Ginkō Tōkeikyoku, ed., *Meiji ikō honpō shuyō keizai tōkei* (Tokyo: Namiki Shobō, 1999), 128–136. Alfred E. Eckles, Jr., *Opening America's Market* (Chapel Hill, NC: University of North Carolina Press, 1995), 49. Albert H. Imlah, *Economic Elements in the Pax Britannica* (Cambridge: Harvard University Press, 1958), 161.

been much worse without the Japanese currency's depreciation against the dollar in the 1870s,[6] the large increase in domestic demand for cotton textiles,[7] and the government support measures for the industry,[8] as well as the protection offered by various non-tariff barriers against imports.

Sugar was another major product whose imports increased drastically after the opening of trade. From 1868 to 1882, sugar imports rose by 10.4 times, and in the next five years by 1.7 times.[9] The import share of domestic demand rose from 13 percent in 1868 to 67 percent in 1882 and 82 percent in 1887. Domestic refined sugar prices, which were almost four times as high as world prices in the pre-trade years, dropped by half as they converged toward world market levels in the post-trade years.[10] Many sugar cane and sugar beet growers gave up their businesses and converted to other industries, such as mulberry growing for silkworm feed and salt production.[11]

Low tariffs also restricted the Japanese government financially. While about half of the federal revenue of the United States was derived from customs duties in the 1870s and 1880s, the contribution of customs duties to the central government budget in Japan was 2 to 4 percent in the early Meiji years. Even in Great Britain, about one-fourth of the government's annual revenue came from import duties in the late 19th century (table 4.1.1-a).

Denied the right to set its own import duties, the Meiji government relied heavily on the land tax, which accounted for over 80 percent of total tax revenue in most of the years in the 1870s and 1880s (table 4.1.1-b). This put a heavy burden on farmers,[12] causing many peasant riots. In the years 1868–73, 177 peasant revolts occurred, of which sixty-six were in opposition to the tax burden.

Chapter 4

**Table 4.1.1-b. Meiji Government Revenues (1,000 yen)**

| | Total government revenue | Tax revenue | | | Other revenue |
|---|---|---|---|---|---|
| | | Total | Land tax | Customs duty | |
| 1868 | 33,089 | 3,157 | 2,009 (63%) | 720 | 29,930 |
| 1870 | 20,959 | 9,323 | 8,218 (88%) | 648 | 11,636 |
| 1875 | 86,321 | 76,528 | 67,717 (88%) | 1,038 | 9,793 |
| 1880 | 63,367 | 55,262 | 42,346 (76%) | 2,624 | 8,105 |
| 1885 | 62,156 | 52,581 | 43,023 (81%) | 2,085 | 9,575 |
| 1890 | 106,469 | 66,114 | 40,084 (60%) | 4,392 | 40,355 |
| 1895 | 118,452 | 74,697 | 38,692 (51%) | 6,785 | 43,755 |
| 1900 | 295,854 | 133,926 | 46,717 (34%) | 17,009 | 161,928 |

*Note:* Figures in parentheses are land tax's share of government tax revenue.
*Source:* Nippon Ginkō Tōkeikyoku, ed., *Meiji ikō honpō shuyō keizai tōkei* (Tokyo: Namiki Shobō, 1999), 128–136.

## 4.1.2. The Bingham Treaty of 1878

John Bingham, the fifth US minister to Japan[13] and the most senior American political appointee to Japan in the 19th century, was convinced that the Japanese demand for tariff autonomy was "so reasonable, so just, and so much in the interest of Japan"[14] that from 1874 onward, he urged Washington to act unilaterally to give Japan tariff autonomy if other treaty powers would not. Though Secretary of State Hamilton Fish did not adopt Bingham's suggestion on the grounds that it would violate the US "cooperative" policy of acting in concert with the European powers,[15] as well as handicap American exports to Japan, William Evarts,[16] Fish's successor, concurred with Bingham and set aside the cooperative policy.

In November 1877, the Japanese government formally conveyed to Bingham its intention to enter negotiations for tariff autonomy in return for opening two or more ports and abolishing export duties. As the Japanese government's policy at the time was simultaneous individual negotiations at the foreign capitals, identical notes were sent to all the Japanese representatives stationed in treaty-power capitals.

Yoshida Kiyonari (吉田清成), the Japanese minister in Washington, presented the proposal to Evarts in January 1878. Negotiations soon started and proceeded smoothly. Final agreement was reached in late June, and signatures were affixed on July 25.

76

The Convention Revising Certain Portions of Existing Commercial Treaties annulled the existing tariffs and trade regulations (Article I), forbade discriminatory duties on imports and exports from and to either country (Article II),[17] removed export duties to the United States (Article III), retained consular jurisdiction (Article IV), and provided for opening Shimonoseki and one other port to citizens and vessels of the United States (Article VII). Finally, through Article X it was agreed, "The present convention shall take effect when Japan shall have concluded such conventions or revisions of existing Treaties with all the other Treaty Powers holding relations with Japan as shall be similar in effect to the present convention, and such new conventions or revisions shall go into effect."

When Bingham received a copy of the Convention in September 1878, he immediately requested that the Convention be modified to strike out the tenth article. He learned then, for the first time, that the tenth article had been recommended by Terashima Munenori (寺島宗則), minister of foreign affairs, to Yoshida in 1877, in consideration of Fish's objection to a separate treaty at that time.[18] Bingham argued that the convention without the tenth article would make an example to influence the other powers to move to release Japan from unfair tariff restrictions, while US exports to Japan would be protected from any unfair treatment by Article II and also by the most-favored-nation clause.[19] But his appeal was of no avail.

Britain manifested strong displeasure at the treaty, declaring it "contrary to all usage" for the United States to act secretly and independently.[20]

Ratifications were exchanged in Washington in April 1879, but the treaty never entered into force because of the tenth article. Britain refused to conclude a similar treaty with Japan. Italy and Russia showed some signs of willingness to look with favor on treaty revision, but Britain worked with Germany to dissuade the European powers from concluding revised treaties with Japan, thereby blocking any subsequent Japanese attempts to seek separate deals.

## 4.2. Extraterritoriality

### 4.2.1. Cases Involving Extraterritoriality

Bingham, while advocating unilateral US action to grant Japan tariff autonomy, shared with his counterparts of the other treaty powers the view that

Chapter 4

Japan needed to establish an effective judicial system before ending extraterritoriality. But he held a different interpretation concerning the extraterritorial privileges of foreigners under the terms of Article VI of the Harris treaty of 1858: "Americans committing offences against Japanese shall be tried in American consular courts, and when guilty shall be punished according to American law." He took the position that it only conferred on foreigners the right to be tried in their own courts, but did not relieve them from the obligation to obey the laws of Japan.[21] In 1871, the Japanese government tried to prevent hunting within game preserves, temple groves, and burial places, as well as within the limits of cities and other inhabited places. While his predecessor Charles DeLong had accepted the view of his Tokyo colleagues that such regulations affecting foreigners could be made only by the foreign powers, Bingham held that they could be made by the Japanese government, and that American citizens were bound by them. Bingham's view was confirmed by Fish.[22]

In 1878, an American citizen boarded a railway train from Kobe to Kyoto without a ticket. Bingham instructed the consul in Kobe to arrest and try the accused. The consul replied with a query as to where in American law he would find authority for the punishment for such an offense. Bingham replied that it was not American law, but the Japanese railway regulations that American citizens had to observe.[23]

Hostility to extraterritoriality would not have developed so widely in Japan if the system had worked in practice without serious friction. In fact, however, there were many ongoing instances of gross abuse of extraterritorial rights, evoking public anger and giving rise to demands for immediate abrogation.

In February 1878, a British subject, John Hatley, was brought into a British consular court on a charge by the Japanese authorities that he had smuggled twenty pounds of opium into the port of Yokohama on December 14 of the previous year, contrary to the British treaty and the laws of Japan. The British consular court held blandly that "medicinal opium is chargeable to 5 percent duty on original value," and the case was dismissed. This decision aroused much controversy, as the Japanese government had taken every precaution to protect its people from the curse that opium had been to China. Japanese law prescribed a year's imprisonment for smoking opium.

A serious instance of high-handed abuse of extraterritoriality occurred in the summer of 1879. A cholera outbreak in the cities of the Kansai area led the Japanese authorities to impose emergency quarantine regulations on ships arriving from infected areas. Bingham promptly issued the necessary notifications to the American consul-general. But the British minister in Tokyo, Sir Harry Parkes, took the position that the Japanese government had no right to make regulations affecting British subjects or British ships, and that only the British consul had the power to detain them. The first ship that arrived at Yokohama after the quarantine was the German steamer *Hesperia* from Kobe on July 11, and the German consul at Yokohama, Eduard Zappe, took the British line. The Japanese officials had at once sent the ship to the quarantine anchorage for a seven-day detention. Zappe and his chief staff-surgeon inspected the vessel the next day, and decided that it should not be held in quarantine. When the Japanese quarantine officer refused to accept his decision, Zappe sent a German gunboat to take the *Hesperia* out of quarantine and into the port of Yokohama.

The *Hesperia* incident was a shocking example of the Anglo–German interpretation of extraterritorial privilege in Japan driven to its most extreme limit. It created excitement at the time, and the anger of the Japanese public was raised to a fever pitch after the appearance of cholera in Kanagawa and Tokyo. The Japanese government could only issue a formal protest. General Grant, then on a visit to Japan, stated that if it had happened in America, the German gunboat would have been instantly sunk.[24] In October, Bingham reported to the department that there had so far been 86,644 fatalities due to the epidemic, and added, "I cannot resist the conviction that this roll of death would not have been nearly so great if the government of Japan had been aided and not resisted, as she was by certain foreign powers, in the laudable endeavor to prevent the spread of the contagion by land and maritime regulation."[25]

### 4.2.2. Extraterritoriality Negotiations in the 1880s

In the 1880s, with public demands for the restoration of judicial autonomy becoming stronger, the Japanese government judged that the extraterritoriality question should be given more urgency than tariff issues. In July 1880, a penal code, a code of criminal procedure, and a civil code were promulgated anew and scheduled to come into effect on January 1, 1882. With the introduction of the new codes, the Japanese government believed that it had made ample provision for the protection of the rights of foreign residents.

In January 1882, Inoue Kaoru (井上馨), the minister for foreign affairs of the Itō Hirobumi government, called a joint conference with the representatives of the treaty powers in Tokyo. He presented a proposal that for the transition period of five years, foreign judges were to sit in the Japanese courts to deal with criminal and civil cases involving foreigners, and at the end of that transition period, extraterritorial jurisdiction was to cease. A twelve-year life for the convention was also proposed. Bingham at once approved of the proposals, but Parkes rejected them, saying that Japanese judicial reforms had not yet advanced far enough. The conference was adjourned in July 1882, accomplishing nothing, but the Japanese government, having reviewed the exchange of views in the conference, completed a memorandum in August 1884 which clarified the positions of the individual powers as well as the Japanese counterarguments.[26]

After the failure of the 1882 conference, Bingham recommended to Washington a separate treaty with Japan along the lines proposed by Japan. But, with the treaty of 1878 remaining inoperative, the State Department judged that no good would be achieved by separate action. Meanwhile, the presidential election of 1884 was won by the Democrats for the first time since the end of the Civil War. Thomas F. Bayard was made the secretary of state in the new Grover Cleveland administration, and Richard B. Hubbard took over as Bingham's successor in Tokyo.[27]

In May 1886, a second conference of the Tokyo diplomatic representatives was called. Hubbard was instructed by Bayard to accept any acceptable compromise which might bring about a solution to the existing impasse. "The chief object of the United States," wrote Bayard, "is to secure to Japan, as far as practicable, complete autonomy. The speediest and most effectual way of accomplishing this end appears to be by cooperating with the other treaty powers, at the same time taking care not to depart from our settled policy of avoiding entangling alliances."[28] Bayard would not change the previous administration's policy on the treaty negotiations.

In the interval between these two diplomatic conferences, the United States had taken another step to support Japan by concluding a formal extradition treaty. While Great Britain took the position that it had the right to follow and seize fugitive subjects within the Japanese borders, the American government recognized that such actions were properly an exercise of Japanese domestic police powers, in no way authorized by the extraterritoriality provisions of the foreign treaties. The extradition treaty was promptly negotiated, and was signed on April 29, 1886. Ratifications were exchanged in Tokyo on September 27, while the second diplomatic conference was in session.[29]

At the start of the second conference, Inoue presented a draft convention formulated based on the memorandum of 1884. But during the conference, a revised version was presented by the British and German representatives, and after many sessions, which were carried over into 1887, a convention on jurisdiction was drafted basically in line with the Anglo–German proposal. It called for the following: The opening of the interior within two years; the codification of Japanese criminal, civil, and commercial laws within two years according to Western models; a "mixed court" system, with a majority of foreign judges sitting in courts dealing with foreigners; the continuation of consular courts for three years after the opening of the interior; and the duration of the convention for seventeen years.

The conference seemed to be heading for agreement when it was unexpectedly wrecked by a storm of hostile public reaction in Japan. Ever since the first conference on extraterritoriality in 1882, there had been growing irritation in Japan at the delay in the treaty powers' conceding what were regarded as the legitimate sovereign rights of the nation. The Japanese public had now become more familiar with the principles of international relations, which seemed to indicate that Japan had an unconditional right to autonomy.[30]

The anti-foreign clamor was strengthened by the unfortunate circumstance of the shipwreck of the British steamer *Normanton* in the Inland Sea while the conference was in session. All the British and other European passengers were saved, and the captain and all the crew escaped, but all the Japanese passengers drowned. And yet the British consul declared, after a formal inquiry, that the captain was not at fault.[31]

Some ministers in the cabinet also voiced opposition to the foreign proposals in the drafted convention.[32] They especially denounced the concept of mixed courts, and suggested that revision should be postponed until the first legislature was assembled in 1890.[33] In July 1887, Inoue adjourned the diplomatic conference *sine die*, and in September he resigned from the post he had held for eight years.

In January 1888, Ōkuma Shigenobu (大隈重信) became foreign minister.[34] He changed the Japanese negotiating pattern from multilateral conferences to bilateral negotiations. He turned first to Mexico, a state which had no residents in Japan and very little bilateral trade. Negotiations for a commercial treaty were conducted between Mutsu Munemitsu (陸奥宗光), the Japanese minister in Washington, and his Mexican counterpart in Washington; a Treaty of Amity and Commerce was concluded in November 1888. The treaty reciprocally provided both parties with freedom of commerce and residence and tariff and judicial autonomy, as well as a conditional most-favored-nation clause. Ōkuma and Mutsu expected that this treaty would improve Japan's position in its negotiations with the treaty powers.

Britain contended that the privileges that Japan had conceded to Mexico should be given to Britain as well because of the most-favored-nation clause in the treaty of 1858. Japan refused, invoking the treaty's conditional most-favored-nation clause, by which Japan had granted privileges to Mexico in exchange for equivalent privileges given to Japan by Mexico. The Japanese argued that, unless Britain gave similar privileges to Japan, Japan should not be obligated to give those privileges to Britain. The United States supported this Japanese position, but Britain would not agree to the interpretation, insisting that the most-favored-nation clause of the 1858 treaty was absolute. No agreement was reached between Japan and Britain.

The United States had already informed Japan, during the conference of 1886, of its readiness to conclude a separate treaty in case the multilateral conference failed to come to an agreement. As the election of 1888 elected Republican Benjamin Harrison as the next president, and a change in personnel in the State Department and in the foreign service was inevitable, Bayard and Hubbard were all the more anxious to conclude a new treaty with Japan before a new administration took office in March of 1889.

Pursuing his bilateral negotiation strategy, Ōkuma presented his proposals to Hubbard first, and then to the representatives of Great Britain, Germany, France, Russia, Austria-Hungary, and Italy. The United States was the quickest to respond. Hubbard sent Ōkuma's proposals to Washington by cable on December 27, 1888, with his comment that he considered the proposals satisfactory and his recommendation that the United States should be the first to conclude the treaty with Japan. On the very day that Hubbard's cable arrived, Bayard sent back an instruction fully agreeing with Hubbard. A new Treaty of Amity, Commerce and Navigation was signed between the two countries in February 1889.

It provided for the following: Reciprocal rights of entrance, of travel and residence, and of the possession of real and personal estates;[35] most-favored-nation treatment with respect to import duties; import duties to be levied conforming to the annexed tariff;[36] the continuation of American consular jurisdiction for five years; conditional most-favored-nation treatment in matters of commerce and navigation, travel and residence; the implementation of the treaty on February 11, 1890; and a duration of twelve years. In a separate note, the Japanese government announced that foreign judges would sit in the Supreme Court in all cases in which an American citizen was involved as a defendant,[37] and that the elaboration of the codes of law would be completed within two years.[38]

Hubbard wanted the signed treaty to be submitted to the Senate by the incumbent Democratic administration. But a delay occurred, as Ōkuma attempted to conclude similar treaties with the European treaty powers simultaneously. The new Republican administration in Washington[39] did not immediately submit the treaty to the Senate, reserving it for further consideration.

It seemed, however, that Ōkuma's strategy of negotiating individually would achieve success. His hard-line approach adopting the strategy of conditional most-favored-nation status and threat of the repudiation of treaties proved effective.[40] In June 1889, Ōkuma signed a commercial treaty with Germany that was similar to the US–Japanese treaty,[41] and in August he concluded a similar treaty with Russia without the side note concerning foreign judges and the codification of laws.[42]

Lord Salisbury, the British prime minister and foreign secretary, finally agreed to negotiate with Japan in June with proposals of some modifications to the Japanese draft.[43] While the negotiations were going on in London, however, the *Times* made the draft treaty public, and the Japanese people were for the first time informed of the nature of the treaties that were being concluded. Public opposition was aroused at the terms of the draft treaty. Britain had made some concessions from the position it had taken in 1886, but the general public in Japan, with the courage of ignorance, demanded more concessions.[44] Sharp differences of opinion divided the cabinet, also. Opponents alleged that both the presence of foreign judges in the Japanese courts and the Japanese government's commitment to the completion of the codes would contravene the constitution that had just been promulgated on February 11,

1889.[45] In October, a fanatic hurled a bomb at Ōkuma, seriously wounding him. The cabinet resigned, and the new treaties with the United States, Germany, and Russia were held in abeyance.

## 4.3. Negotiations in the 1890s

### 4.3.1. US Minister Swift's Hostile Position
John Franklin Swift, the new American minister to Tokyo, was critical of his predecessor's hasty conclusion of the treaty of 1889. He dismissed as unworthy the efforts of Bayard and Hubbard, who wanted to testify to America's traditional goodwill by leadership in the recognition of Japan's sovereign rights.[46] In June 1889, he wrote to James G. Blaine, the new secretary of state, "As to the supposed benefit of being the first to make a treaty or the disadvantage of being the last, I do not regard either as worthy of a moment's consideration."[47]

Swift was a product of the California environment of the day, which had exaggerated fears of white Americans being overrun by "Orientals." He had some other extraordinary opinions concerning the Japanese. He advised that great caution should be used in extending to Americans the privilege of doing business in direct competition with native Japanese, as it would only result in friction.[48] He did not believe that a treaty right of general residence throughout the country would be of such advantage to American merchants or manufacturers as would justify the risk of actions by US citizens that might cause trouble in Japan. Swift declared that Japanese merchants were seriously deficient in commercial integrity as measured by the standards of Europeans and Americans.[49]

Swift also recommended that before any negotiations with Japan, steps should be taken to communicate directly between Washington and the powers. Blaine was not at first negative about the 1889 treaty, but Swift eventually convinced Blaine to reject the work of Bayard and Hubbard,[50] and obtained Blaine's pledge that the treaty of 1889 would not be approved or submitted to the Senate by the president without serious modifications.[51]

In Japan, a new cabinet was organized in December 1889 with Yamagata Aritomo as prime minister and Aoki Shūzō (青木周蔵) as the minister for foreign affairs. It was now clear that negotiations on the lines laid down by Ōkuma would only provoke another domestic crisis. But it could hardly be expected that the treaty powers would make fresh concessions for which Japan had no equivalents to offer.[52] It was also apparent that negotiations with Swift would be unproductive in view of his obviously hostile stand. Meanwhile, in East Asia, the Russian project of the trans-Siberian railway was intensifying the Anglo–Russian rivalry.[53] The Japanese leaders felt that they might be able to take advantage of this new geopolitical development. They decided to turn from the United States to Great Britain as the key power to negotiate with.

### 4.3.2. Negotiations with Britain

Aoki met with Hugh Fraser, the British minister in Tokyo, on December 27, 1889, and stated to him that the domestic situation in Japan left the Japanese government no other alternative than withdrawing the proposal as to placement of foreign judges on the Supreme Court and the codification of the laws of Japan, and postponing the acquisition by foreigners of real estate until the date when consular jurisdiction should have ceased to exist.[54] Fraser replied that the proposed changes were so far beyond the range of his instructions that he could not enter negotiations, but he agreed to transmit the Japanese proposals to London.

Salisbury now knew that the Japanese were willing to sacrifice their reputation as a docile new member of the international community in order to get rid of consular jurisdiction, and might very well abrogate their treaty with Great Britain.[55] It is likely that Aoki had hinted of abrogation mildly, while Ōkuma had threatened it bluntly.

In June 1890, Salisbury accepted the Japanese proposals with only minor requests for modifications. He requested that consular jurisdiction should be retained for a period of not less than five years, and that the new Japanese codes should be in operation for at least one year before consular jurisdiction ended.

Japan could not take advantage of the new British proposals, however. The new Diet was opposed to the new codes that were scheduled to come into force in January 1893. The opponents alleged that those codes were unsuited to the popular customs of the country, and introduced a bill for the postponement of the codes for four years. In the meantime, in May 1891, an attack by a deranged policeman on the visiting Russian crown prince Nicholas Alexandrovich led to the resignation of the cabinet, including Aoki.

The new Matsukata administration failed in its efforts to halt the legislation delaying the new law codes, and the cabinet resigned. The second Itō cabinet was formed in August 1892, and Mutsu Munemitsu was appointed as the minister for foreign affairs. Mutsu was determined to succeed where so many predecessors had failed, and vowed to conclude revised treaties on lines acceptable to the Japanese people. He proposed that from the date the new treaty came into force, consular jurisdiction would be abolished, but that the treaty would not take effect until at least five years after being signed. Thus, he did not link the commencement of the treaty with the enforcement of the new Japanese legal codes.

Negotiations started in London in September 1893 between Aoki, who was at that time the Japanese minister in Berlin, and Fraser, the minister in Tokyo. Negotiations centered on the issues of the exact state of the new Japanese codes and the duration of the treaty. On the codification question, the British agreed to demand only the publication of an English translation of the codes, on which Aoki gave satisfactory assurances. As to the duration of the treaty, the British proposed twenty years, but they settled at twelve years. As to the Japanese import tariffs, duties on forty-seven items ranging from 5 percent to 15 percent were provided in the annexed protocol, the items not mentioned in the protocol being subject to statutory tariffs enacted by Japan.[56] Thus Britain chose to surrender extraterritoriality to save as many commercial advantages as possible.

An agreement on all questions was reached on July 13, 1894, and the Treaty of Commerce and Navigation that restored full judicial autonomy to Japan was signed on July 16. The ratifications were exchanged in Tokyo on August 25, 1894. The United States and eighteen countries followed Britain in concluding similar treaties with Japan.

### 4.3.3. The Treaty with the United States

The United States and Japan had had no discussions on treaty revision since December 1889 when Japan turned to Great Britain. The Japanese government felt that negotiations with the United States would be unproductive while Swift was in office (4.3.1). But in March 1891 Swift died of a heart attack, and Frank Coombs succeeded Swift as the US minister in Tokyo. Coombs sided with Bingham and Hubbard, but his tenure ended before he could make any contribution to the negotiations. In the meantime, the election of 1892 brought Democrat Cleveland back to the presidency, and Walter

Gresham became secretary of state.[57]

Mutsu was anxious to restore friendly relations with the United States, which had been most cooperative with the Japanese attempts to regain full sovereignty throughout most of the long negotiation process. In February 1894 Mutsu informed Gresham of the treaty terms Japan was proposing to Britain. Gresham was concerned, however, about Article I of the proposed treaty that granted nationals of the two contracting parties reciprocal liberty to enter, travel, and reside in any part of the territories of the other.[58]

Mutsu had no intention of letting the Japanese immigration issue threaten the successful conclusion of the revised treaty with the United States. He readily inserted an Article II that permitted the United States to regulate Japanese immigration in the American treaty.[59]

In the treaty with the United States, there was another provision which was not in the treaties with the other treaty powers. The United States inserted a provision that permitted Japan full tariff autonomy to demonstrate its goodwill toward Japan. But Japan continued to levy the same low treaty tariffs on imports from the United States as on imports from other powers, in accordance with the most-favored-nation clause.

In 1911, Japan eventually obtained full tariff autonomy from all the treaty powers, as the twelve-year duration period of the 1894 treaty, which had taken effect in 1899, finally ended. In the end, it took fifty-three years for Japan to restore tariff autonomy. It proved to be detrimental to Japan that the treaties of 1858 had no termination date.

NOTES

4.1. Early Negotiations

1 Article XIII of the 1858 treaty with the United States read, "After the 4th of July, 1872, upon the desire of either the American or Japanese government, and one year's notice given by either party, this Treaty, and such portions of the treaty of Kanagawa as remain unrevoked by this Treaty, . . . shall be subject to revision by Commissioners appointed on both sides for this purpose, who will be empowered to decide on, and insert therein, such amendments as experience shall prove to be desirable." The 4th of July was later changed to the 1st of July. The treaties with other countries had similar provisions for their revisions. Harris later wrote that he had believed that this article would enable the Japanese to revise the treaty, but the actual turn of events proved otherwise. It was Harris's mistake that he had failed to write a date for the expiration of the treaty. Had a treaty duration of, say, thirty years been set in the treaty, the Japanese would have regained full tariff and judicial autonomy in 1888. See Oliver

Chapter 4

Statler, *Shimoda Story* (New York: Random House, 1969), 553–554.

2　Shih Shun Liu, *Extraterritoriality: Its Rise and Its Decline* (New York: AMS Press, 1969), 199–200. Kajima Morinosuke, *Nihon gaikōshi II: Jōyaku kaisei mondai* (Tokyo: Kajima Kenkyūjo Shuppankai, 1970), 190. Another reason European businessmen were not eager to do business outside the treaty ports was that they had established such advantageous business practices inside the treaty ports that they saw no reason to venture beyond them. Inoue Kiyoshi, *Jōyaku kaisei: Meiji no minzoku mondai* (Tokyo: Iwanami Shoten, 1955), 50.

3　Nippon Ginkō Tōkeikyoku, ed., *Meiji ikō honpō shuyō keizai tōkei* (Tokyo: Namiki Shobō, 1999), 136, 280, US Department of Commerce, Bureau of the Census, *Historical Statistics of the United States* (Washington, DC: US Government Printing Office, 1975), 888, and A. H. Imlah, *Economic Element in Pax Britannica* (Cambridge: Harvard University Press, 1958), 160.

4　J. Richard Huber compares Japan's prices of ginned cotton, cotton yarn, and cotton cloth with world prices in 1846–55 and in 1871–79. In 1846–55, the Japanese prices were two to two and a half times as high as world prices, but in 1874–79, Japanese prices declined substantially as they converged toward world market levels in dollar terms. In 1846–55, the average price per pound of ginned cotton, cotton yarn, and cotton cloth was $0.231, $0.548, and $0.651 respectively in Japan, whereas in the international market it was $0.112, $0.199, and $0.250 respectively in the same period. In 1871–79, the price per pound was $0.156, $0.362, and $0.368 respectively in Japan, whereas in the international market it was $0.152, $0.239, and $0.278 respectively in the same period. J. Richard Huber, "Effect on Prices of Japan's Entry into World Commerce after 1858," *Journal of Political Economy*, vol. 79, issue 3 (May–June, 1971), 620.

5　Imports of raw cotton increased from 1,400 tons in 1870 to 22,000 tons in 1890 and to 152,500 tons in 1900; those of cotton cloth increased from 4,300 tons in 1870 to 6,800 tons in 1890, and to 15,550 tons in 1900. Nakamura Takafusa, *Meiji Taishōki no keizai* (Tokyo: University of Tokyo Press, 1985), 215.

6　One hundred yen equaled US$103 in 1874, US$94.50 in 1879, US$90.75 in 1884, US$78.75 in 1889, and US$55 in 1894. Japan went on the gold standard in 1896 at the rate of $1 = ¥2. The decline in the yen's exchange rate against the dollar was partly due to the fall in the world market price for silver in the 1870s.

7　Domestic demand for cotton cloth increased from 27,900 tons in 1870 to 62,100 tons in 1890, and to 107,550 tons in 1900. Nakamura, *Meiji Taishōki no keizai*, 215.

8　The government support measures for the cotton industry are discussed in 5.3.6.

9　Japan's sugar imports were 4.6 tons in 1868, 48.0 tons in 1882, 81.2 tons in 1887, and 118.9 tons in 1897. Higuchi Hiroshi, *Honpō tōgyōshi* (Tokyo: Diamond, 1935), 530–532.

10　Refined sugar was traded in Japan at $0.227 per pound on average in 1846–55, while its world price was $0.061 in the same period. In 1871–79, the Japanese price went down to $0.112, while the world price was $0.08 in the same period. Huber, "Effect on Prices of Japan's Entry into World Commerce after 1858," *Journal of Political Economy*, vol. 79, issue 3 (May–June, 1971), 620.

11　Some sugar producers continued their production. They were helped by the same

*Notes*

conditions that favored the cotton industry, particularly the strong growth of demand for sugar. Shadan Hōjin Tōgyō Kyōkai, ed., *Kindai Nihon tōgyōshi* (Tokyo: Keiso Shobo, 1962), 101–102.

12  In the land tax reform, the government first determined the entire country's land values based on crop yields, and collected land tax at 3 percent of the assigned land values. The landowners collected rents from tenant farmers on the basis of this land tax; these were often as high as 80 percent of their produce.

13  Bingham was born in Pennsylvania in 1815. He practiced law in Ohio from 1840 until 1854, when he was elected to Congress, where he served until 1873. He was defeated in 1862 and 1872. In 1864, he served as judge advocate of the army, which brought him into prominence during the trial of the assassins of President Lincoln. Bingham's service in Tokyo from 1873 to 85 was longer than that of any US minister or ambassador before or since. According to Tyler Dennett, Bingham deserves "equal rank with Townsend Harris among the determined and uncompromising American friends of Japan." See Jack L. Hammersmith, *Spoilsmen in a "Flowery Fairyland": The Development of the U.S. Legation in Japan, 1859–1906* (Kent, OH: Kent University Press, 1998), 106–108.

14  Payson J. Treat, *Diplomatic Relations between the United States and Japan, 1853–1895* (Stanford: Stanford University Press, 1932), 2–3.

15  Hamilton Fish became secretary of state in 1869 in the Grant administration.

16  The presidential election in 1876 was won by the Republican Rutherford Hayes, who nominated William Evarts, a distinguished lawyer and political leader from New York, as secretary of state. Bingham was retained as minister to Japan.

17  Article II read, "It is, however, further agreed that no other or higher duties shall be imposed on the importation into Japan of all articles of merchandise from the United States, than are or may be imposed upon the like articles of any other foreign country . . . "

18  Treat, *Diplomatic Relations*, 54. In February 1877, Yoshida asked the State Department if the United States would prefer to conclude a new treaty conditionally to take effect when all the treaty powers assented. The reply was a refusal on the grounds that it would change the relative position of the two governments, converting the United States into the party proposing the revision. Ibid., 28. Evarts, however, abandoned the policy of cooperation, and sent instructions to that effect to Bingham on June 21, 1877. Ibid., 30–31. It is not clear when or how well the Japanese government was informed of this policy change.

19  Ibid., 50–54. Though US interests might thus be protected by the use of most-favored-nation privilege, Japan would have to extend new concessions granted to the United States—such as the opening of Shimonoseki and one more port—to other treaty powers without being able to exercise the right to tariff autonomy.

20  Parkes wrote, "The Americans have made a Treaty with Japan—such a Treaty! But they have protected themselves from its consequences by stipulating that it is not to take effect until other nations agree to a similar treaty, which we, for one, are certainly not likely to do. They would throw themselves by it entirely into the hands of the Japanese. The object of the Americans is, of course, transparent—they wish to lead the Japanese to believe that they are willing to meet their wishes, and, if unable to do so, it

Chapter 4

is because other nations, notably England and Parkes, won't enable them to do so." F. C. Jones, *Extraterritoriality in Japan* (New Heaven, CT: Yale University Press, 1931), 89.

### 4.2. Extraterritoriality

21 Payson J. Treat, *Japan and the United States: 1853–1921* (Boston: Houghton Mifflin, 1921), 118.

22 Ibid., 119.

23 Ibid., 119.

24 Treat, *Japan and the United States*, 121.

25 Jones, *Extraterritoriality*, 88.

26 Inoue, *Jōyaku kaisei*, 94–95.

27 Richard Hubbard had had no diplomatic experience when he was offered the Tokyo post as a reward for his campaigning for Cleveland in 1884. He was governor of Texas in 1876–1879. Jack L. Hammersmith, *Spoilsmen*, 135–136.

28 Treat, *Japan and the United States*, 126.

29 Ibid., 127.

30 Jones, *Extraterritoriality*, 109–110.

31 The British steamer *Normanton* was wrecked in a storm off Kishū in the Inland Sea of Japan on its way from Yokohama to Kobe on October 24, 1886. Captain John William Drake rescued the British and other European passengers, and he and all the crew escaped from the sinking vessel, leaving all twenty-five Japanese passengers and the Indian firemen to drown. On November 1, the British consul held a hearing of the case, and on November 5 declared Drake without fault. Though it was not a criminal court but an administrative hearing, the Japanese public took it as a formal criminal court verdict and became enraged. The Japanese government did not want to allow this issue to affect its relationship with Britain, as revision negotiations were underway. They decided instead to resort to legal measures, and Home Minister Yamagata and Communications Minister Enomoto filed a lawsuit against Captain Drake. The British consular court in Yokohama eventually sentenced Drake to three months' imprisonment on a charge of neglect of duty in just two days' trial. Kajima, *Nihon gaikōshi*, 92–93.

32 Tani Tateki, minister of agriculture, took the initiative in presenting a memorial to the throne, which was supported by the minister of justice and two other government leaders. Treat, *Diplomatic Relations*, 252

33 The first national election was held in July 1890, and the first session of the House of Representatives and the House of Peers was convened in November 1890.

34 After Inoue had resigned in September 1887, Itō, the prime minister, held the position of foreign minister until Ōkuma, the head of the opposition Kaishin Party, agreed to join the cabinet as foreign minister in January 1888. In February 1888, Mutsu Munemitsu was appointed as the minister in Washington. In April that year, Itō resigned the premiership to assume the post of president of the Privy Council. Kuroda Kiyotaka succeeded Itō.

35 Treat, *Diplomatic Relations*, 289.

36 Duties on some 445 articles were enumerated in the annex. The *ad valorem* duties ranged from 5 to 20 percent, and a considerable number of specific rates were given.

*Notes*

Treat, *Diplomatic Relations*, 290–291.

37  The provision regarding foreign judges on the supreme court was not included in the treaties, but was put in a separate note to make it seem to be a voluntary promise by the Japanese government. Britain wanted, in the later negotiations with Japan, to make the notes as binding as the treaty itself. See Jones, *Extraterritoriality*, 125.

38  Treat, *Diplomatic Relations*, 291. The codification of laws "according to Western models" was not required in this convention, while it was called for in the Anglo–German proposals of 1886. See Inoue Kiyoshi, *Jōyaku kaisei: Meiji no minzoku mondai* (Tokyo: Iwanami Shoten, 1955), 142.

39  The secretary of state of the administration of Benjamin Harrison was James G. Blaine, and the successor of Hubbard was John Franklin Swift. Both Blaine and Swift were given their posts as a reward for their services to the Republican Party. Swift had been appointed one of the three commissioners sent to China in 1880 to negotiate a treaty which suspended Chinese immigration. Thomas A. Bailey, *A Diplomatic History of the American People* (Englewood Cliffs, NJ: Prentice-Hall, 1980), 8. Treat, *Diplomatic Relations*, 284–285.

40  Ōkuma was prepared to unilaterally declare termination of the treaty with Britain, if Britain refused treaty revision and yet demanded that privileges accorded to other countries that concluded new treaties with Japan should also be accorded to Britain based on the unconditional most-favored-nation clause of the old treaty. This repudiation strategy was recommended by Karl Friedrich Herman Roesler, legal adviser to the cabinet. He asserted that the treaties of 1858 could legally be abrogated on three grounds: 1) Sovereign states' international treaties could not be effective indefinitely; 2) The revision clause of the treaties of 1858 gave Japan the right to revise the treaties and, in the case of Japan's being denied the exercise of such right, Japan could justifiably abrogate the treaty and revise it by Japanese legislation; and 3) With the promulgation of the Meiji Constitution, the principle of "changed circumstances'" could be applied. Henry William Denison, an adviser to the ministry of foreign affairs (3.4.2), concurred with Roesler, and added that the British refusal in 1879 of Japan's request for a meeting to express Japan's desire to revise the treaty constituted a breach of contract and gave Japan the right to abrogate the treaty. Ōishi Kazuo, *Jōyaku kaisei kōshōshi* (Tokyo: Shibunkaku Shuppan, 2008), 152–179.

41  The German treaty was a surprise to Britain, which had led European resistance against Japan. Ōishi attributes this German move to: 1) Germany's intention to get ahead of Britain in treaty revision; and 2) the judgment by Germans, especially Theodor von Holleben, the German minister in Tokyo, that Ōkuma was serious about resorting to the strategy of repudiating treaties. Ōishi, *Jōyaku kaisei kōshōshi*, 25–70.

42  Ibid., 85. Germany and Russia wanted Ōkuma to give them assurances that Japan, unless it concluded a new treaty, would never let Britain enter the interior of Japan based on the most-favored-nation clauses of the old treaties. Ōkuma gave them such assurances. Inoue, *Jōyaku kaisei*, 145.

43  Britain's requests were: 1) That Japan should announce that it was now engaged in elaborating civil, criminal, and commercial codes in accordance with Western principles; 2) That foreign judges should be appointed in the appeals courts as well as in

the supreme court; 3) That a conditional most-favored-nation clause should be replaced with an unconditional one. Jones, *Extraterritoriality*, 118–120. Treat, *Diplomatic Relations*, 296.

44  Jones, *Extraterritoriality*, 122.
45  Inoue, *Jōyaku kaisei*, 154–155, 160–161.

### 4.3. Negotiations in the 1890s

46  Hubbard had given the Japanese government assurances that there would never be any restrictions on Japanese immigration into the United States; he had even advocated a convention to provide for reciprocal rights of naturalization. Treat, *Diplomatic Relations*, 297–298.

47  Ibid., 296.
48  Ibid., 324.
49  Ibid., 324.
50  Treat, *Diplomatic Relations*, 294.
51  Ibid., 309.
52  Jones, *Extraterritoriality*, 129.
53  Anglo–Russian rivalry in East Asia became apparent in the mid-1880s, when Russia attempted to build a military base in Korea. While Russia gave up the plan in the face of Britain's strong opposition, the rivalry was again heightened in the late 1880s when Russia decided to build the trans-Siberia railway.
54  Jones, *Extraterritoriality*, 130.
55  Ōishi argues that it was not so much the Anglo–Russian rivalry as the fear of Japan's repudiation of the treaties that eventually made Britain conciliatory toward Japan. Ōishi, *Jōyaku kaisei kōshōshi*, 153, 177. In fact, Fraser sent his comment to Salisbury on August 16, 1889, saying that now that Germany had signed its new treaty with Japan, the possibility of Japan's repudiating the existing Anglo–Japanese treaty had increased, and that it would not be wise for Britain to drive Japan to take such measures that would also adversely affect British treaties with other Asian countries. Ibid., 79–80.
56  Eleven items were dutiable at 5 percent; two at 7-1/2 percent; four at 8 percent; twenty-seven, including cotton manufactures and woolen manufactures, at 10 percent; and two at 15 percent.
57  Gresham succeeded John Foster, the successor of Blaine, who had retired in June 1892. In Tokyo, Coombs was succeeded by Edwin Dun. Dun had worked as an agricultural development expert in Hokkaidō from 1867–1871. He had been in the employ of the Japanese government some ten years before he joined the American Legation in Tokyo, where he served as minister from 1893 to 1897. He was pro-Japanese, but in terms of treaty revision negotiations, his contribution was limited.
58  Treat, *Diplomatic Relations*, 425.
59  Article II contained a clause stating, "It is, however, understood that the stipulations contained in this and the preceding Article do not in any way affect the laws, ordinances, and regulations with regard to trade, the immigration of laborers, police and public security which are now in force or which may hereafter be enacted in either of the two countries." Ibid., 432.

# Chapter 5

# The US and Japanese Economies, and Their Economic Relations in the 19th Century

## 5.1. The United States and Japan in the World Economy in the 19th Century

### 5.1.1. US Economic Developments in the 19th Century

The United States was a smaller economy than Japan in terms of GDP in the early 19th century because of its smaller population. According to Angus Maddison's estimation, which uses PPP (purchasing power parity) converters instead of exchange rates,[1] US GDP in 1820 was less than two-thirds of Japan's GDP (table 5.1.1-a). The US population being less than one-third that of Japan in 1820, its per capita GDP was twice that of Japan. In the next fifty years, the US economy grew almost eight times larger to become nearly four times the size of the Japanese economy. Population increased fourfold and GDP per capita twofold. By the eve of WWI, US GDP had expanded another fivefold to become seven times that of Japan.[2] Between 1870 and 1913, while the Japanese population increased by one and a half times and GDP per capita almost by two times, enlarging GDP almost by three times, the US population increased by 2.4 times and per capita GDP expanded by 2.2 times. In fact, the United States was the most spectacular example of rapid economic

*93*

Chapter 5

Table 5.1.1-a. US, Japan, and the World Population and GDP

|  | 1820 | | | 1870 | | | 1913 | | |
|---|---|---|---|---|---|---|---|---|---|
|  | US | Japan | World | US | Japan | World | US | Japan | World |
| Population (million) | 10.0 | 31.0 | 1,041 | 40.2 | 34.4 | 1,270 | 97.6 | 51.7 | 1,791 |
| GDP ($ billion) | 12.5 | 20.7 | 694 | 98.3 | 25.4 | 1,101 | 517.4 | 71.6 | 2,704 |
| Per capita GDP ($ thousand) | 1.25 | 0.67 | 0.67 | 2.44 | 0.74 | 0.87 | 5.30 | 1.38 | 1.51 |

*Notes:* 1. GDP and per capita GDP are in 1990 international dollars.
     2. GDP of Japan and the world are based on PPP converters of the International Comparison Program of the United Nations.
*Source:* Angus Maddison, *The World Economy: A Millennial Perspective* (Paris: OECD, 2001), 241, 261.

growth in the 19th and early 20th century.

In 1820, the US share of the world's industrial production was 4 percent, while that of Great Britain was 24 percent. By the end of the 19th century, however, while the British share had declined to 20 percent, that of the United States had risen to 30 percent. Japan's share was 1 percent at the end of the century.[3]

The industrial revolution in the United States began in the middle of the 19th century, and by the end of the 1880s, income from manufacturing exceeded that from agriculture (table 9.1.3-a).

US agriculture was far from a declining industry, however. Wheat production in the United States showed a strong increase through the 19th century.[4] Its share of the world output increased from less than 10 percent in the early 19th century to over 20 percent in the late 19th century. The United States was the world's biggest wheat producer from the 1870s through the 1920s (table 5.1.1-b), exporting 25 to 30 percent of its output from 1880s through the 1920s.[5]

Even more impressive was raw cotton production. US raw-cotton mill consumption and its exports combined to account for over 70 percent of world mill consumption in the 19th century, and over 60 percent in the early 20th century (table 5.1.1-c).[6]

In most of the 19th century, agricultural products accounted for about two-thirds of US total exports,[7] raw cotton being by far the biggest export item (table 5.1.1-d).

*94*

Table 5.1.1-b. World Wheat Production (million bushels)

|  | 1831–1840 | 1851–1860 | 1871–1880 | 1899–1904 | 1924–1929 | 1934–1939 |
|---|---|---|---|---|---|---|
| France | 190 (21.0) | 223 (18.6) | 275 (15.3) | 338 (11.1) | 280 (6.7) | 302 (6.3) |
| Russia | 110 (12.1) | 130 (10.9) | 224 (12.5) | 545 (17.9) | 757 (18.1) | 1257 (26.1) |
| US | 78 (8.6) | 137 (11.4) | 338 (18.8) | 714 (23.4) | 826 (19.7) | 716 (14.8) |
| World | 906 | 1,198 | 1,794 | 2,545 | 4,192 | 4,822 |

*Note:* Numbers in parentheses are percentages of each country's wheat production of global wheat production.

*Source:* W. W. Rostow, *The World Economy: History & Prospect* (London: Macmillan Press, 1978), 147, 164–165. Wilfred Malenbaum, *The Wheat Economy, 1885–1939* (Cambridge: Harvard University Press, 1953), 238–239.


Table 5.1.1-c. World and US Raw-Cotton Production and Consumption (million pounds)

|  |  | 1820–1831 | 1882–1884 | 1910–1913 | 1926–1928 | 1936–1938 |
|---|---|---|---|---|---|---|
| World | Mill consumption (A) | 420 | 4,000 | 10,500 | 12,200 | 14,000 |
|  | Imports (B) | 370 | 2,800 | 6,490 | 6,800 | 6,270 |
| US | Mill consumption (C) | 50 | 890 | 2,400 | 3,300 | 3,300 |
|  | Exports (D) | 280 | 1,900 | 4,520 | 4,390 | 2,420 |
| US / World | (D)/(B) | 76% | 68% | 71% | 65% | 39% |
|  | (C)+ (D) / (A) | 79% | 70% | 66% | 63% | 41% |

*Note:* Figures represent mill consumption of raw cotton. The raw cotton consumed in hand-spinning is not included.

*Source:* R. Robson, *The Cotton Industry in Britain* (London: Macmillan, 1957), 2


Table 5.1.1-d. US Major Export Items (million dollars)

|  | Total exports | Raw cotton | Leaf tobacco | Wheat | Meat products | Cotton products | Machinery |
|---|---|---|---|---|---|---|---|
| 1840 | 124 | 64 | 10 | 2 | — | — | — |
| 1860 | 334 | 192 | 16 | 4 | 14 | — | — |
| 1880 | 836 | 212 | 16 | 191 | 114 | 10 | 1 |
| 1900 | 1,394 | 242 | 29 | 73 | 114 | 24 | 88 |
| 1920 | 8,228 | 1,136 | 245 | 597 | 279 | 398 | 588 |

*Source:* US Department of Commerce, Bureau of the Census, *Historical Statistics of the United States* (Washington, DC: US Government Printing Office, 1975), 884–886, 898–899,

Agricultural development was greatly encouraged by the passage of the Homestead Act of 1862, which made the acquisition of farmland easy even for those with little capital. The act provided that any adult citizen (or person intending to become a citizen) who headed a family could qualify for grant of 160 acres of public land by paying a small registration fee and living on the land continuously for five years. More than 270 million acres of public land, or nearly 10 percent of total area of the United States, were given away to 1.6 million settlers this way. Between 1860 and 1880 alone, over 65 million acres of government land in the West were given away to homesteaders.[8]

Just as important in the development of the West was the extension of the railroad network (table 5.1.1-e), which, from the 1860s onward, played a critical role in bringing new land into production. The railroads built up the Western population, lowered transportation costs, and brought new supplies into national and international markets. The development of railroads had powerful and multiple effects on US economic development, stimulating the adoption of new technologies in the coal, iron and steel, and engineering industries. In fact, American railroads in the 19th century were the very symbol of the growth of the United States into the world's foremost industrial nation by the century's end.

"Yankee inventiveness" was fully demonstrated in the 19th century. The invention of the cotton gin in 1793 was followed by a flood of inventions and technical innovations including the telegraph (1832), the sewing machine (1846), the commercial exploitation of petroleum (1859),[9] the Remington typewriter (1874), the telephone (1874), the electric lamp (1879), hydroelectric power generation for commercial use (1882),[10] various steel-making processes, and numerous agricultural machines.[11] The development of "safety bicycles" in the 1890s, with their ball bearings and pneumatic tires, prepared the way for the development of the automobile industry in the next century.[12]

Table 5.1.1-e. World Railroad Mileage, 1840–1888

|        | 1840  | 1850   | 1860   | 1870    | 1880    | 1888    |
|--------|-------|--------|--------|---------|---------|---------|
| Europe | 1,879 | 14,465 | 31,885 | 63,300  | 101,720 | 130,000 |
| US     | 2,820 | 9,020  | 30,630 | 53,400  | 93,670  | 156,080 |
| Japan  | —     | —      | —      | —       | 75      | 910     |
| World  | 4,715 | 23,555 | 66,290 | 128,235 | 228,440 | 354,310 |

*Source:* W. W. Rostow, *The World Economy History & Prospect* (London: Macmillan Press, 1978), 53.

The maturing of the American system of mass production in the 19th century established the preconditions for the assembly lines of the 20th century.[13]

No less important was the development of the software of economic power in this century, such as new techniques for forming and managing very large corporate organizations, as well as new marketing and distribution methods.[14] Here again the importance of the great American railroads is observed, for they gave their executives, many of whom had gained experience in managing large organizations in the Civil War, the opportunity to develop and commercialize their management techniques.

## 5.1.2. The Meiji Government's Political, Social, and Economic Reforms

Being the offspring of Britain, the United States was a "modern" state from its birth in terms of its political and social systems, but Japan required a total transformation from its premodern feudal society into a modern state in order to achieve modern economic development. The Meiji government launched a series of fundamental reforms of Japan's political, social, and economic structure.

The four-tier societal rank system of *shi-nō-kō-shō* (士農工商) and restrictions on freedom of entry into new occupations (1.1.1) were abolished in 1869. Centralization of political power came about with the surrender by the feudal lords of their fiefs to the government—*hanseki hōkan* (版籍奉還)—in 1869, and with the abolition of the feudal domains and the creation of prefectures—*haihan chiken* (廃藩置県)—in 1871. In 1873, the government moved to replace the in-kind rice tax with a monetary land tax—*chiso kaisei* (地租改正). All arable land was assessed and a land tax of 3 percent was imposed. This land-tax reform took six years to complete, but it provided the government with a stable and predictable source of revenue. All these political, social, and economic reforms provided Japan with the prerequisites for economic growth from the 1870s onward.

In 1876, the government suspended all annual pension payments to former samurai, giving them instead commutation bonds totaling 173 million yen, an amount equal to 40 percent of Japan's 1876 national income. This bond issuance, the expenditures for the Seinan War of 1877 amounting to 42 million yen,[15] and the proliferation of banknotes of the national banks that had begun in 1876 combined to provoke serious inflation in the late 1870s.

The proliferation of banknotes was due to the decision by *Ōkura kyō* (大蔵 卿) Ōkuma Shigenobu (大隈重信) to allow the national banks to issue banknotes exchangeable for government paper currency but not redeemable in gold.[16] He made the decision because the provision of the National Banking Act of 1873 allowing the national banks to issue only notes that were redeemable in gold limited the volume of banknotes issued, causing economic stagnation.[17]

Matsukata Masayoshi (松方正義), who became *ōkura kyō* in 1881, set out to take a series of measures to bring down the inflation caused by Ōkuma's policy. He gave the right to issue banknotes only to the newly founded Bank of Japan, forbidding other banks to issue them. He also cut government spending and introduced additional taxes, thus achieving a budget surplus enabling the redemption of a large number of inconvertible notes.[18] Those measures brought about severe deflation, causing many bankruptcies and rural distress, but they left Japan with a stable financial base for future economic growth.

Given Japan's economic and industrial backwardness, the Meiji government was well aware of the importance of government initiative in building economic infrastructure and in nurturing modern industries with Western manufacturing technology. As early as 1871 the government instituted a postal service between Tokyo and Osaka. The first railway between Shinbashi (Tokyo) and Yokohama was built in 1872, and was subsequently followed by other railway construction throughout the country.[19] The government also built many model factories equipped with Western machinery, including silk-reeling filatures in Maebashi and Tomioka (5.3.3).[20] Though those establishments served to introduce Japanese entrepreneurs to Western manufacturing techniques and factory methods, few of them grew into profitable businesses, and they became the targets of Matsukata's fiscal economy drive. They were sold to private individuals or groups in the 1880s.

While most of the government-sponsored undertakings failed to generate profits, a purely private cotton mill founded in Osaka in 1882 realized profits from the start (5.3.5). The success of the Osaka Cotton Spinning Mill was followed by several other new cotton-spinners with similarly modern facilities. It is impressive that they all did well when the Japanese cotton-yarn market was depressed due to heavy inflows of foreign goods.[21]

The heavy industries—iron, steel, engineering, and chemicals—were slower to develop. These industries required more expensive capital equipment than the textile industry,[22] and the scarcity of capital in Japan was a handicap. Further, these industries required more scientific and technical support than textile manufacture. As late as 1896, practically all Japanese steel requirements were met by imports.[23]

Through the 19th century, Japan remained an agricultural economy in terms of its industrial structure. In the early Meiji era, over 80 percent of working Japanese were in agriculture. At the turn of the century, about 70 percent of the workforce was still made up of farmers, with manufacturing industries employing a little over 10 percent of the labor force. The textile industries, mainly the cotton-spinning and raw-silk reeling mills, employed the majority of Japanese factory workers.[24] The primary industry's share of the national income was still twice as great as that of the secondary industry at the turn of the century (9.1.3-b).

# 5.2. Early Japanese Foreign Trade

### 5.2.1. British Dominance in Early Japanese Trade

For all its initial success in opening Japan, the United States lagged far behind Great Britain in bilateral trade in the early years. The Civil War was undoubtedly responsible for the poor performance of American traders in the first half of the 1860s. According to the records of the port of Yokohama, which accounted for about 80 percent of Japan's trade in those days, American vessels shipped 26 percent of Japan's imports and 33 percent of its exports in 1860, but the percentage dropped to 1 percent and 2 percent respectively in 1865.[25]

With the opening of Japan, British firms located at Chinese treaty ports and in Hong Kong, such as Jardine Matheson & Co. and Dent & Co., moved staff and Chinese employees to Japan,[26] and quickly established a strong commercial presence in the Japanese treaty ports (table 5.2.1-a).

American merchants, notably Walsh, Hall & Co.,[27] were also active in establishing themselves in the ports, but they were far exceeded by British firms in the scale of their establishments.

At the early stage, cotton and woolen manufactures were Japan's major imports (table 5.2.1-b). Britain's cotton industry was by far the strongest in the world in the 19th century, and its woolen textiles were also highly competitive in world markets, although the traditional rank of woolens as Britain's top

Chapter 5

Table 5.2.1-a. Treaty Power Commercial Presence at Yokohama in 1863

|  | UK | US | Holland | Prussia | France | Others |
|---|---|---|---|---|---|---|
| Firms | 16 | 5 | 4 | 5 | 2 | — |
| Residents | 140 | 80 | 40 | 14 | 18 | 8 |
| Rent for land | $10,255 | $2,843 | $2,550 | $423 | $1,736 | — |

Source: Kaikoku Hyakunen Bunka Jigyōkai, ed., Nichibei bunka kōshōshi, vol. 2, Tsūshō sangyō hen (Tokyo: Yōyōsha, 1954), 86.

Table 5.2.1-b. Early Japanese Foreign Trade Commodity Structure (%, share)

| Imports | 1865 | 1868 –72 | 1878 –82 | Exports | 1865 | 1868 –72 | 1878 –82 |
|---|---|---|---|---|---|---|---|
| Cotton thread | 6.2 | 18.3 | 22.7 | Raw silk | 84.2 | 56.9 | 43.2 |
| Cotton fabrics | 30.6 | 16.4 | 15.7 | Tea | 10.5 | 24.5 | 22 |
| Woolens | 47.6 | 16 | 14.4 | Marine products | 0.5 | 5.9 | 6.3 |
| Sugar | 1.5 | 9.4 | 11.3 | Grains | — | — | 5.5 |
| Grains | — | 21.1 | 1.4 | Minerals (coal, etc.) | 0.1 | 1.6 | 3.3 |
| Metal products | 4.5 | 2.3 | 6 | Metals | — | 3.5 | 2.6 |
| Others | 9.7 | 16.5 | 28.5 | Others | 4.7 | 7.6 | 17.1 |

Notes: 1. Japan's grain imports in 1868–72 were mainly rice imported to cope with the poor harvest in 1869–70.
2. Besides the imports listed in the table, there were sizable imports of ships and arms made before the abolition of the feudal domains in 1871, which were not reported to the customs houses. The buyers of those unlisted imports were mainly the domains of Satsuma, Chōshū, and Tosa.
3. Raw-silk exports include silkworm eggs.
Source: Takahashi Kamekichi, Kindai Nihon keizai hattatsushi (Tokyo: Tōyōkeizai Shinpōsha, 1973), 218–219. Sugiyama Shinya, "Kokusai kankyō to gaikoku bōeki," in Kaikō to ishin, eds. Umemura Mataji and Yamamoto Yūzō (Tokyo: Iwanami Shoten, 1989), 192–195.

export item had been taken over by cotton textiles after the industrial revolution.[28]

Britain supplied about half of all Japanese imports in the 1870s, about 40 percent in the 1880s, and about 30 percent in the 1890s. Of Japanese exports, on the other hand, the British share was about 20 percent in the 1870s, about 10 percent in the 1860s, and about 6 percent in the 1890s (table 5.2.1-c).

Japan's biggest export item after the opening of trade was raw silk (table 5.2.1-b). It sold well in Europe, where raw silk was in short supply due to a silkworm disease. China had been a major European supplier, but its role was

100

**Table 5.2.1-c. Japan's Annual Imports and Exports with UK and US**

| | Imports (million yen) | | | Exports (million yen) | | |
|---|---|---|---|---|---|---|
| | Total | UK | US | Total | UK | US |
| 1873–1875 | 27.1 | 12.3 (45.4) | 1.32 (4.8) | 19.3 | 3.63 (18.8) | 6.19 (32.0) |
| 1876–1880 | 30.7 | 16.4 (53.5) | 2.28 (7.4) | 26.1 | 4.78 (18.2) | 7.93 (30.2) |
| 1881–1885 | 29.5 | 13.6 (46.0) | 2.68 (9.0) | 34.3 | 3.93 (11.4) | 13.4 (39.0) |
| 1886–1890 | 57.9 | 22.5 (38.9) | 5.06 (8.9) | 56.9 | 5.93 (10.4) | 22.1 (38.3) |
| 1891–1895 | 93.8 | 31.1 (33.1) | 7.81 (8.3) | 100.0 | 5.67 (5.7) | 38.5 (38.5) |
| 1896–1900 | 235.2 | 60.7 (25.8) | 36.8 (15.6) | 169.2 | 9.53 (5.6) | 49.8 (29.4) |
| 1901–1905 | 340.8 | 67.9 (19.9) | 59.9 (17.5) | 288.1 | 15.1 (5.2) | 86.0 (29.8) |
| 1906–1910 | 424.7 | 84.8 (20.0) | 59.1 (13.9) | 421.1 | 20.4 (4.8) | 130.8 (31.0) |

*Note:* Numbers in parentheses are percentages of Japan's imports or exports from or to UK or US of Japan's total imports or exports.

*Source:* Nippon Ginkō Tōkeikyoku, ed., *Meiji ikō honpōu shuyō keizai tōkei* (Tokyo: Namiki Shobō, 1999), 291, 294.

considerably reduced by the disorders of the Taiping Rebellion.[29] British merchants handled a substantial part of the Japanese raw silk and silkworm eggs destined for European markets.

## 5.2.2. Japan's Trade with the United States

Even after the Civil War, Americans were unable to shake off the Britain's dominance in exports to Japan. Cotton and woolen manufactures, Japan's major imports, were basically items that the United States imported rather than exported. Woolens produced in the United States were protected by high duties, and their prices were much higher than those of comparative products abroad.[30] The US cotton industry was apparently more competitive internationally than its woolen industry. Some cotton cloth was exported to China and Latin America, but they were mainly of coarse grades of the sort which Japanese consumers procured domestically from their traditional sources. Thus, American cotton-goods sales in the Japanese market remained negligible. The US share of Japanese imports remained below 10 percent until the mid-1890s (table 5.2.1-c).

In total Japanese exports, tea was the runner-up to raw silk (table 5.2.1-b), but it was Japan's biggest export item to the United States in the early stages (table 5.2.2-a).

Japan's exports to the United States surpassed those to Britain in the

Chapter 5

Table 5.2.2-a. Shipments for US at Yokohama in 1866–68 (thousand dollars)

| | April–June 1866 | July–Sept. 1866 | Oct.–Dec. 1866 | Oct.–Dec. 1867 | 1868 |
|---|---|---|---|---|---|
| Tea | 162.3 (55.0%) | 767.8 (93.4%) | 949.5 (57.1%) | 736.8 (75.3%) | 3,165.1 (82.0%) |
| Raw silk | 104.5 (35.4%) | 6.9 (0.8%) | 11.0 (0.7%) | 131.0 (13.4%) | 548.2 (14.2%) |
| Other items | 28.4 (9.6%) | 47.2 (5.7%) | 701.3 (42.2%) | 111.1 (11.3%) | 149.9 (3.9%) |
| Total | 295.2 | 825.0 | 1,661.8 | 978.9 | 3,863.2 |

Source: Ohara Takashi, Nichibei bunka kōshōshi (Tokyo: Yōyōsha, 1954), 110–111.

Table 5.2.2-b. US Trade with Japan and China (million dollars)

| | US trade with Japan | | US trade with China | |
|---|---|---|---|---|
| | Exports | Imports | Exports | Imports |
| 1860–69 | (1866–69) 4 (0.2%) | (1866–69) 10 (0.6%) | 55 (1.7%) | 104 (3.2%) |
| 1870–79 | 14 (0.2%) | 83 (1.6%) | 21 (0.4%) | 174 (3.3%) |
| 1880–89 | 31 (0.4%) | 149 (2.3%) | 52 (0.7%) | 188 (2.8%) |
| 1890–99 | 83 (0.9%) | 236 (3.1%) | 76 (0.8%) | 195 (2.6%) |

Note: Percentages in parentheses show those of US exports or imports to or from Japan or China of total US exports or imports.
Source: US Department of Commerce, Bureau of the Census, Historical Statistics of the United States (Washington, DC: US Government Printing Office, 1975), 903–907.

1870s, as Japanese tea exports to the United States increased (5.3.1). The US share of Japan's exports rose to as high as almost 40 percent on average in the 1880s and the first half of the 1890s (5.2.1-c). Adding to robust tea exports, an increase in raw-silk exports to the United States from the 1880s contributed to the high US share of Japanese exports. While the recovery of raw-silk production in Europe gradually reduced imports from Japan, Japanese raw silk found a new market in the United States.

While the US market was vital for Japan's exports, Japan was a very small market for US exports throughout the 19th century. Of total US exports, those to Japan stayed well below 1 percent in the early years of trade, and only came close to 1 percent in the 1890s (table 5.2.2-b). Of total US imports, the share of those from Japan increased to about 3 percent in the 1890s.

China was a larger trading partner to the United States than Japan both in exports and imports in the 1860s through 1880s, but the position was reversed in the 1890s, and it remained that way throughout the prewar years.[31]

## 5.3. The Tea, Raw-Silk, and Raw-Cotton Trade between the US and Japan

### 5.3.1. Japan's Tea Exports to the United States

In the United States, tea consumption increased after the Civil War, which was further encouraged by the abolition, in 1872, of a duty of 25 cents per pound on imported tea.[32]

In Japan, an innovative tea-processing method was developed in the 18th century, and by the time of Japan's opening to trade, Japanese green-tea production had reached highly competitive levels in terms of quality as well as productivity.

When Japanese green tea was first exported to the United States, the American green-tea market had been dominated by China. But Japan gradually increased its sales until it sold twice as much green tea as the Chinese, though total sales of all Chinese teas—black, green and Oolong combined—were greater than those of Japanese tea (table 5.3.1).[33]

Japan exported over 90 percent of its domestic tea production in the 1870s, about 80 percent in the 1880s and about 70 percent in the 1890s.[34] The United States absorbed over 90 percent of Japan's tea exports from the second half of the 1860s through the 1880s, and over 80 percent in the 1890s.[35] Of Japan's exports to the United States, tea accounted for 70 to 80 percent in the 1860s and about 90 percent in the 1870s,[36] and it remained the

Table 5.3.1. US Tea Imports by Country (million pounds)

|           | UK          | China        | Japan        | India     |
|-----------|-------------|--------------|--------------|-----------|
| 1861–65   | 2.8 (10.1%) | 24.0 (87.1%) | 0.3  (1.0%)  | —         |
| 1866–70   | 2.3  (5.5%) | 30.7 (72.6%) | 8.2 (19.3%)  | —         |
| 1871–75   | 3.5  (5.9%) | 36.4 (60.5%) | 16.2 (26.9%) | —         |
| 1876–80   | 3.0  (4.6%) | 31.6 (49.5%) | 28.4 (44.4%) | —         |
| 1881–85   | 1.4  (1.9%) | 38.9 (52.0%) | 33.8 (45.2%) | —         |
| 1886–90   | 3.8  (4.6%) | 42.6 (50.8%) | 36.5 (43.4%) | —         |
| 1891–95   | 3.3  (3.6%) | 47.6 (52.5%) | 38.5 (42.4%) | —         |
| 1896–1900 | 3.3  (3.7%) | 45.8 (52.3%) | 34.4 (39.3%) | 2.4 (2.7%)|

*Note:* Percentages in parentheses are those of US tea imports from each country of total US tea imports.

*Source:* Shinya Sugiyama, *Japan's Industrialization in the World Economy, 1859–1899* (London: Athlone Press, 1988), 148.

Chapter 5

biggest export item of Japan's exports to the United States until it was replaced by raw silk in the mid-1880s.

## 5.3.2. Japan's Raw-Silk Exports to the United States

Cultivation of silk was brought into the American colonies in the 17th century by the British, and it continued modestly with the encouragement of the colonial governments. But attempts to launch large-scale sericulture proved to be unsuccessful owing to the absence of the necessary sericulture experience and the lack of skilled labor.[37]

Meanwhile, American demand for silk fabrics grew steadily, and imports increased accordingly. While most of the demand was met by imports of finished fabric until the middle of the 19th century, a domestic silk manufacturing industry developed strongly after the Civil War, being assisted by the government tariff policy. While duties on general silk goods were maintained at 50 to 60 percent ad valorem, the import duty on raw silk was abolished in 1857.[38] While annual imports of silk manufactures remained at around $30 million, domestic production of silk manufactures using imported raw silk increased (table 5.3.2-a).

The introduction and rapid spread of the power loom, which swiftly replaced the hand loom, distinguished the development of the silk industry in the United States during this period from that of other countries. In 1880, 63 percent of all looms in operation were powered, and the ratio rose to 92 percent in 1890. In Japan, by the late Tokugawa period, raw-silk production was already well developed as a secondary occupation for farmers in Japan's mountainous areas. When Japan was opened to trade, raw silk was in short supply

Table 5.3.2-a. US Silk Manufacturing Industry, 1850–1910 (thousand dollars)

|      | Domestic production (A) | Imports of silk piece goods (B) | A/A+B (%) |
|------|-------------------------|---------------------------------|-----------|
| 1850 | 1,809                   | 17,640                          | 9         |
| 1860 | 6,608                   | 32,726                          | 17        |
| 1870 | 12,211                  | 23,904                          | 34        |
| 1880 | 41,033                  | 32,189                          | 56        |
| 1890 | 87,293                  | 38,686                          | 69        |
| 1900 | 107,256                 | 31,129                          | 78        |
| 1910 | 196,912                 | 32,888                          | 86        |

*Source:* Shinya Sugiyama, *Japan's Industrialization in the World Economy 1859–1899* (London: Athlone Press, 1988), 100.

in Europe due to an outbreak of silkworm disease, and demand for Japanese raw silk and silkworm eggs was high. As cocoon production gradually recovered in Europe, however, European silk merchants started to complain about the quality of Japanese raw silk, and prices started to fall.[39]

Meanwhile, the emergence of the United States as a major silk manufacturing country provided a favorable opportunity for Japanese raw-silk producers.[40] At an early stage, the US silk manufacturing industry was satisfied with lower-priced, coarser thread from China, but as the use of power looms spread, it began to require thread of superior quality, uniformity, and strength. Though Japanese raw silk was not necessarily of high quality, it moved comparatively well with the changing patterns of the American market, and its sales surpassed those of China in the early 1880s in the US market (table

Table 5.3.2-b. US Annual Raw-Silk Imports (thousand pounds)

|  | China | Japan | Italy | France | UK | Total |
|---|---|---|---|---|---|---|
| 1866–70 | 154 (22.6) | 49 (7.2) | — | 34 (5.0) | 316 (46.2) | 682 |
| 1871–75 | 424 (38.7) | 228 (20.8) | 1 (0.1) | 73 (6.7) | 194 (17.7) | 1,095 |
| 1876–80 | 1,007 (53.7) | 548 (29.2) | 1 (0.1) | 157 (8.4) | 143 (7.6) | 1,874 |
| 1881–85 | 1,172 (33.4) | 1,443 (41.1) | 402 (11.5) | 408 (11.6) | 45 (1.3) | 3,507 |
| 1886-90 | 1,126 (21.7) | 2,744 (52.8) | 956 (18.4) | 264 (5.1) | 37 (0.7) | 5,193 |
| 1891–95 | 1,932 (26.9) | 3,629 (50.6) | 1,223 (17.0) | 317 (4.4) | 15 (0.2) | 7,175 |
| 1896–1900 | 2,696 (28.7) | 4,542 (48.8) | 1,782 (19.0) | 316 (3.6) | 2 (0.0) | 9,384 |

*Notes:* 1. Numbers in parentheses show percentages of US raw-silk imports from each country of total US raw-silk imports.
2. Imports from UK presumably included Chinese, Japanese, and European raw silk.
*Source:* Shinya Sugiyama, *Japan's Industrialization in the World Economy, 1859–1899* (London: Athlone Press, 1988), 104.

Table 5.3.2-c. Japan's Annual Raw-Silk Exports and Its Main Destinations

|  | 1866 –70 | 1871 –75 | 1876 –80 | 1881 –85 | 1886 –90 | 1891 –95 | 1896 –1900 |
|---|---|---|---|---|---|---|---|
| Total (tons) | 612 | 683 | 1,004 | 1,484 | 1,998 | 3,089 | 3,150 |
| US (%) | 3.4 | 1.8 | 17.4 | 39.3 | 55.1 | 56.0 | 57.8 |
| France (%) | 37.2 | 41.5 | 46.5 | 48.6 | 38.4 | 37.7 | 33.8 |
| Britain (%) | 59.0 | 45.9 | 31.6 | 11.5 | 4.2 | 1.6 | 0.7 |
| Others (%) | 0.3 | 10.8 | 4.4 | 0.6 | 2.3 | 4.6 | 7.8 |

*Source:* Shinya Sugiyama, *Japan's Industrialization in the World Economy, 1859–1899* (London: Athlone Press, 1988), 80.

Chapter 5

**Table 5.3.2-d. Major Raw-Silk Producers' Shares of the Raw-Silk World Trade (%)**

|  | 1859 –62 | 1868 –72 | 1878 –82 | 1888 –92 | 1898 –1902 | 1908 –13 | 1921 –25 |
|---|---|---|---|---|---|---|---|
| China | 50.6 | 49.0 | 51.7 | 42.8 | 42.7 | 35.3 | 25.0 |
| Italy | 24.4 | 30.9 | 29.6 | 30.9 | 28.0 | 24.7 | 13.3 |
| Japan | 9.3 | 8.3 | 13.0 | 19.9 | 22.3 | 38.0 | 60.4 |
| Levant | 7.9 | 4.8 | 3.3 | 4.3 | 5.3 | 4.1 | 0.9 |
| India | 7.8 | 7.0 | 2.4 | 2.0 | 1.7 | 0.9 | 0.3 |

*Source:* Giovanni Federico, *An Economic History of the Silk Industry, 1830–1930* (Cambridge: Cambridge University Press, 1997), 200.

5.3.2-b).

In terms of geographical distribution of Japan's raw-silk exports, Europe's share was dominant at the early stage, but exports to the United States surpassed those to Europe in the second half of the 1880s. The US share kept increasing afterward (table 5.3.2-c).

In the world raw-silk market, China continued to be the largest exporter throughout the 19th century, with the runner-up being Italy. Japan took over China's position in the early 20th century (table 5.3.2-d),[41] and continued to be the leader in the remaining prewar years.[42]

### 5.3.3. The Story of Arai Ryōichirō

For many years after the opening of trade, Western merchants controlled almost the whole of Japan's foreign trade. As late as 1890, four-fifths of silk exports were still in foreign hands, though Japanese were by that time beginning to overcome the disadvantages of inexperience and inadequate credit by which they had at first been handicapped.

Among the Japanese businessmen who played a pioneering role in establishing direct foreign trade in the raw-silk business, Arai Ryōichirō was the true leader. He sailed for New York in early March 1876 at the age of twenty and almost single-handedly established direct sales of raw silk in the US market. In her book *Samurai and Silk*, Haru Reischauer describes how Arai, who was her grandfather, overcame various difficulties in his early career in New York, and eventually established himself as a trusted and respected figure in the American silk business.[43]

Ryōichirō was born in 1855 as the sixth son of the Hoshinos, an old and wealthy peasant family in Gunma, where the silk-reeling industry had

*The US and Japanese Economies, and Their Economic Relations in the 19th Century*

developed since the early 19th century.[44] At the age of twelve Ryōichirō was adopted by the Arais, a family of wealthy raw-silk wholesalers. The Hoshinos' raw-silk business was then carried on under the management of Hoshino Chōtarō, the enterprising eldest son. In 1875 Chōtarō was determined to launch direct exports of raw silk to the United States, and asked Ryōichirō, who was studying English in Yokohama, to go to New York to help materialize his plan.

Ryōichirō's first business was with B. Richardson & Sons, one of the most prominent silk brokers in New York. In early May of 1876, Ryōichirō received from Richardson an order for 400 pounds of raw silk for delivery in September. It was the first US–Japan direct raw-silk sale without intermediary merchants, and the first Japanese raw silk transported across the Pacific. But the sale turned out to be most unfortunate for Ryōichirō and Chōtarō. Trans-Pacific cable communications were not to start for another two years, and it took eight weeks for the order to reach Gunma by mail. By the time the order arrived by mail in early July, the market had risen by 80 percent. Chōtarō asked Ryōichirō to renegotiate the price, but Ryōichirō refused to budge from his promise to Richardson. Chōtarō had to pledge his entire family assets to cover the loss. When the order was delivered at the price Ryōichirō had quoted, Richardson, impressed with Ryōichirō's honest manner, increased the price by one dollar per pound when he made payment, which accounted for 20 percent of the loss.[45] The economic loss the Hoshino brothers incurred was large, but the reputation for honest dealing they gained was significant.

Arai's sales of raw silk in his second year in New York were ten times as great as his first year, and he then doubled sales in the third year.

As imports of Japanese raw silk increased, however, many unreliable suppliers entered into the business, giving grounds for complaints about the quality of Japanese raw silk. Ryōichirō was deeply concerned for the reputation of the Japanese silk industry as a whole. He often went to Japan to urge Japanese producers to keep production in line with American requirements.[46] It required a great deal of patience and firmness to convey the requirements and problems of American manufacturers to the Japanese producers, who had no knowledge of the high-speed spinning machines used in the US. Chōtarō, for his part, organized a company with his colleagues to work on the improvement of silk thread and to disseminate the information to silk producers all over Japan.[47] Ryōichirō's greatest contribution to the development of the

*107*

Japanese raw-silk trade with the United States was to bridge the gap in understanding between American manufacturers and the Japanese raw-silk producers. If he had been a short-term resident in the United States, he could never have established a continuous dialogue on problems of mutual concern between the Japanese exporters and American buyers.[48]

Ryōichirō moved into semi-retirement in 1927, when he passed on control of his company to a subsidiary of the Mitsubishi Shōji Kaisha, a trading company of the Mitsubishi group, although he continued to serve as an adviser.

When he died at the age of eighty-four in the winter of 1939, the American Commodity Exchange paid him the unusual tribute of pausing trade for a moment of silence while the funeral was in progress.[49] His good friend Paolino Gerli, a leading silk merchant and prominent member of the Japan Society of New York,[50] included in his eulogy the following words:

> A young man in your twenties, you came to us from Japan, to bring us tidings of good things to come, of friendships to be made; ambassador of an ancient art to a new industry, and you opened before our eyes the treasure box of silk . . . As the years passed, we came to know you intimately, and with this knowledge, there grew upon us an increasing appreciation of your great character as a man, of your industriousness, fairness, equity, sympathy, and deep understanding. You led in charity, and were always solicitous of the welfare of this, your adopted country, which you loved and served so well . . . May the sweetness of your nature, the loftiness of your spirit, abide with us.[51]

### 5.3.4. The US Cotton Industries and Trade

When the American Revolution cut off imports from Britain, the American colonists were compelled to supply themselves with clothing. The progress of the domestic cotton textile industry was greatly limited, however, by the British prohibition on the export of textile machinery.[52] It was not until the last decade of the 18th century that the manufacture of cotton textiles was begun on any considerable scale. After several ventures at different places in New England, the first modern cotton mill was started in 1790 in Rhode Island. The mill was set up by Samuel Slater, a young Englishman who came to the United States in response to an advertisement by a New England society for the promotion of industrial growth.[53] He had worked in a cotton mill in

Britain, and from memory he constructed duplicates of a water-frame spinning machine and other machines which were in use in Britain at the time.[54] Thus, American cotton-yarn production by machine was finally begun. Procurement of the necessary raw cotton was, however, another question.

By the late 1780s, the southern cotton planters had started growing long-staple or sea-island cotton from seeds brought from the Bahamas. But until about 1840, this cotton was raised only along the coast of South Carolina and Georgia. Having failed to grow long-staple cotton at any distance from the sea, the residents of the hill country cultivated short-staple or upland cotton, which grew inland. The problem with the upland cotton, however, was the difficulty in detaching the seeds from the lint. The 1793 invention of the cotton gin by Eli Whitney made this type of cotton a marketable commodity,[55] as "with it a negro was able to clean fifty times as much as he could do in the old-fashioned way."[56] With the subsequent improvements in the quality of both long- and short-staple cotton, American cotton culture showed steady growth. Throughout most of the 19th century, the United States raised half to three-quarters of the world output of raw cotton, and of US production, two-thirds to three-quarters were exported, Britain being by far the biggest buyer.[57]

Meanwhile, the American cotton manufacturing industry also showed strong growth after the turn of the 19th century, stimulated by expanding domestic consumption by a growing population that was becoming wealthier, as well as by the increasing supplies and the resultant reduction of prices of raw cotton. On the basis of the number of spindles, the American cotton manufacturing industry expanded by more than sixteen times between 1820 and 1850, and another 3.2 times in the subsequent thirty years. It accounted for about 10 percent of the world's cotton production capacity in 1850 and about 16 percent in 1885. In 1850, Great Britain had 5.8 times as many spindles as the United States, but in 1895 the difference was reduced to 2.8 times, and 1.9 times in 1910 (table 5.3.4).[58]

The US export of cotton cloth started in the 1820s; by the late 1890s, the United States had become almost the monopoly supplier in north China and Manchuria.[59] In 1901, US cotton-cloth exports to China accounted for 37 percent of total US cotton-cloth exports. Other major markets were South America (24 percent), the West Indies (14 percent), and Mexico and Central America (8 percent).[60]

Chapter 5

Table 5.3.4. Number of Spindles in US, UK, India, and Japan (thousand spindles)

|      | US           | UK           | India      | Japan      | World   |
|------|--------------|--------------|------------|------------|---------|
| 1845 | 2,500 (9.1)  | 17,500 (63.5) | —          | —          | 27,500  |
| 1850 | 3,600 (10.3) | 21,000 (60.3) | —          | —          | 34,800  |
| 1861 | 5,000 (11.0) | 30,300 (66.4) | 340 (0.7)  | —          | 45,640  |
| 1875 | 9,500 (14.1) | 37,500 (55.7) | 886 (1.3)  | —          | 67,390  |
| 1880 | 11,500 (15.7) | 39,750 (54.1) | 1,400 (1.9) | 12         | 73,460  |
| 1885 | 13,250 (16.3) | 43,000 (53.0) | 2,050 (2.5) | 60         | 81,050  |
| 1890 | 14,550 (16.7) | 43,750 (50.2) | 3,270 (3.8) | 278 (0.3)  | 87,030  |
| 1895 | 16,100 (16.8) | 45,400 (47.2) | 3,800 (3.9) | 581 (0.6)  | 96,040  |
| 1900 | 19,000 (18.1) | 46,400 (44.2) | 5,000 (4.8) | 1,268 (1.2) | 105,000 |
| 1910 | 27,400 (20.4) | 53,400 (39.9) | 6,360 (4.7) | 2,005 (1.5) | 134,000 |

*Notes:* 1. The number of spindles shown for the UK in 1900 is that in 1901, which is the nearest available figure.

2. Numbers in parentheses show each country's percentage of the total number of spindles worldwide.

*Source:* D. A. Farnie, *The English Cotton Industry and the World Market, 1818–1896* (New York: Oxford University Press, 1979), 180. Melvin Thomas Copeland, *The Cotton Manufacturing Industry of the United States* (Cambridge: Harvard University Press, 1912), 5, 7, 17. Thomas Ellison, *The Cotton Trade of Great Britain* (London: Frank Cass & Co., 1968), 35, 65. Sung Jae Koh, *Stages of Industrial Development in Asia* (Philadelphia: University of Pennsylvania Press, 1966), 367. James A. B. Scherer, *Cotton as a World power* (New York: Frederick A. Stokes Company, 1916), 349, 424. R. Robson, *The Cotton Industry in Britain* (New York: Macmillan & Co., 1957), 340. Seki Keizō, *The Cotton Industry of Japan* (Tokyo: Japan Society for the Promotion of Science, 1956), 311. Louis Bader, *World Developments in the Cotton Industry* (New York: New York University Press, 1925), 9.

## 5.3.5. The Japanese Cotton Industry and Trade

In Japan, by the middle of the Tokugawa era, cotton textiles were an established industry, as cotton fabrics had become the main material for the common people's clothing. However, when Japan was opened to trade, the Japanese cotton industry was no match for the Western industry, especially that of Britain, which had mechanized its production a century earlier. The inflow of foreign cotton textiles caused considerable economic damage to Japanese cotton producers. The Meiji government tried various measures to modernize the Japanese cotton industry, but all those attempts proved ineffective. Nevertheless, many domestic cotton producers managed to stay in business (table 5.3.5-a). They were saved largely by an overall increase in the consumption of cotton clothing in Japan, as well as by Japanese consumers' conservative preference for traditional fabrics. Imported cotton textiles mostly

*110*

The US and Japanese Economies, and Their Economic Relations in the 19th Century

Table 5.3.5-a. Japanese Cotton Production, Imports, and Exports (thousand tons)

| | Domestic production | | | Imports | | | Exports | |
|---|---|---|---|---|---|---|---|---|
| | Raw cotton | Cotton yarn | Cotton cloth | Raw cotton | Cotton yarn | Cotton cloth | Cotton yarn | Cotton cloth |
| 1870 | 21.3 | 18.2 | 23.6 | 1.4 | 5.4 | 4.3 | — | — |
| 1880 | 21.3 | 17.8 | 35.1 | 0.9 | 17.3 | 9.1 | — | — |
| 1890 | 23.0 | 36.0 | 55.3 | 22.0 | 19.3 | 6.8 | 0.0 | 0.0 |
| 1895 | 15.8 | 84.3 | 91.0 | 89.6 | 8.8 | 8.8 | 2.1 | 0.6 |
| 1900 | 7.4 | 127.9 | 95.5 | 152.5 | 5.5 | 15.6 | 37.9 | 3.5 |
| 1905 | 3.2 | 208.6 | 160.4 | 257.5 | 0.3 | 15.3 | 48.5 | 7.2 |
| 1910 | 1.5 | 235.9 | 174.9 | 293.4 | 0.2 | 11.4 | 61.2 | 14.7 |

Source: Nakamura Takafusa, *Meiji Taishōki no keizai* (Tokyo: University of Tokyo Press, 1985), 215.

filled new urban demands created by the availability of high-quality yet competitively priced imports. Most Japanese consumers, however, especially farmers, remained content with low-grade coarse-count homespun clothes. Additionally, a shortage of raw-cotton supplies in the international market caused by the Civil War gave the domestic industry some breathing room, albeit for a short period. Some raw cotton was even exported to Britain in the middle of the 1860s.

In the 1870s and even during the early years of the 1880s, homegrown raw cotton nearly filled the demand of Japanese cotton-yarn producers (table 5.3.5-a). But in the 1880s, domestic raw-cotton producers became unable to meet the needs of the rapidly expanding cotton-spinning industry. The first raw-cotton imports were from China; then came imports of Indian cotton. American cotton imports began from the mid-1890s (table 5.3.5-b). As the Japanese mills increased the export of the cotton goods of finer grades, they increased imports of long-staple American raw cotton from the mid-1890s.[61] In 1896, the government abolished import duties on raw cotton, abandoning the policy of protecting domestic cultivation of cotton.

Imports of cotton yarn started to increase as early as the late 1860s, as cotton-cloth manufacturers learned to use foreign cotton yarn to compete with imported cotton cloth. In the 1880s, however, the Japanese spinners started to produce internationally competitive cotton yarn, and their products gradually supplanted imported yarn (table 5.3.5-a). Export duties on cotton yarn were withdrawn in 1894, and by 1897 exports of cotton yarn exceeded its imports.[62]

*111*

Chapter 5

Table 5.3.5-b. Japan's Raw-Cotton Imports by Exporting Countries (thousand yen)

| | China | India | US | Others | Total |
|---|---|---|---|---|---|
| 1880 | 170 (100%) | — | — | 0 (0%) | 170 |
| 1885 | 750 (92.7%) | 59 (7.3%) | — | 0 (0%) | 809 |
| 1890 | 3,764 (70.2%) | 1,114 (20.8%) | | 134 (2.4%) | 5,365 |
| 1895 | 14,160 (57.0%) | 7,693 (31.0%) | 2,338 (9.4%) | 630 (2.5%) | 24,822 |
| 1900 | 12,448 (20.9%) | 17,864 (30.0%) | 27,010 (45.4%) | 2,149 (3.6%) | 59,471 |
| 1905 | 16,863 (15.2%) | 53,553 (48.4%) | 35,166 (31.8%) | 5,040 (4.5%) | 110,623 |
| 1910 | 34,133 (21.4%) | 101,218 (63.6%) | 17,193 (10.8%) | 6,677 (4.2%) | 159,221 |
| 1912 | 18,888 (9.4%) | 108,673 (54.1%) | 64,601 (32.2%) | 8,661 (4.3%) | 200,824 |

Source: W. A. Graham Clark, *Cotton Goods in Japan* (Washington, DC: US Government Printing Office, 1914), 10.

The first Japanese cotton-spinning mill equipped with imported machinery was the Kagoshima Cotton Spinning Works, erected in 1866 by the Satsuma clan. This mill was later purchased by the Meiji government under the government's program to promote the cotton textile industry.[63] The government also built model spinning mills,[64] and provided government funds to private concerns wishing to establish their own cotton mills.[65] However, none of these mills could earn their way, mainly owing to the lack of technical and management capability.

Meanwhile, a private enterprise without government support was launched successfully in Osaka. This was the Osaka Cotton Spinning Company, erected in 1882 by Shibusawa Eiichi and other capitalists, including several former feudal aristocrats.[66] To prepare the construction of the mill, in 1879 a Japanese engineer was sent to a British spinning company to study the operation of spinning machinery.[67] The Osaka Cotton Spinning Company started operations in 1883 with 10,500 spindles powered by steam engines at a time when most of the government-subsidized mills were being operated with water power and were on a scale of 2,000 spindles. The factory was lighted with electric lamps instead of oil lamps, and adopted double-shift, all-night operations to raise productivity per spindle. In scale of production, it was fully comparable with mills operating in England. From the outset, it was flooded with orders, and it paid a dividend of 6 percent in its first year, 18 percent in 1884, and 30 percent in 1887.[68]

The successful operation of the Osaka Cotton Spinning Company

112

encouraged other industrialists to build spinning companies with comparable modern equipment. Between 1887 and 1900, twenty such mills were built, including the Kanegafuchi Spinning Company, established in Tokyo in 1887 with 29,000 spindles, and the Ozaki Spinning Company (the predecessor of the Dai Nippon Spinning Company), built in 1900 with 9,216 spindles in Ozaki, Hyōgo prefecture.[69]

The first Japanese export of cotton goods was a shipment of a small quantity of cotton yarn to China in 1890. In the 1890s, China imported cotton yarn mostly from India and some from Britain. In 1894 India supplied 89.5 percent of China's demand for foreign cotton yarn, Britain's share being 8 percent. Japan's share of China's cotton-yarn imports in that year was 2.5 percent, but it increased to 33 percent in 1900;[70] Japan became the world's biggest supplier, surpassing India, in 1913.[71]

Cotton cloth in China was supplied by Britain and the United States. Lancashire cotton cloth had long dominated the South China markets, where finer cloth was much in demand. American manufacturers supplied coarse cloth to the northern parts of China, where people were too poor to buy fabrics made of costlier material. After the Russo–Japanese War, Japanese cotton cloth started to enter Manchurian markets. American cloth accounted for 98 percent of the Manchurian market in 1901, but in 1907 the American share declined to 29 percent, with the Japanese share increasing to 58 percent.[72] It was during this period that Japanese business practices were criticized by Americans as inconsistent with the principle of the Open Door.[73] The Japanese merchants' purchase of Manchurian beans also helped their cotton-cloth business, as they often settled accounts receivable for cotton cloth by receiving beans.[74]

There were some other factors that led to American cotton-cloth manufacturers' withdrawal from Manchuria. After the turn of the century, there were increases in the demand for cotton textiles in the US market and in exports to the South American markets, as well as a decrease in the demand in China for imported cotton cloth due to the development of the Chinese cotton industry.[75] The cotton weavers' demand for foreign cotton yarn increased in China, but American manufacturers did not show much interest in marketing their yarn products in the Chinese markets.[76] Transport costs, which formed a larger portion of the cost of yarn than that of cloth, might have been one of the reasons.

*113*

The United States exported some cotton goods to Japan, but its annual exports averaged only about 2 percent of its exports to China in the 1890s,[77] and also comprised only about 2 percent of Japan's imports of cotton goods during the same period. In 1890, for example, Britain supplied 97 percent of Japan's imports of cotton goods, with the United States and Germany supplying the rest.[78] The main US exports of cotton goods were coarse-grade cotton cloth, but these were also the chief products of the Japanese mills, with which they could successfully compete with the US mills in the Japanese market.

### 5.3.6. A Complementary US–Japanese Trade Relationship

When Japan started to trade with the United States, tea sold well at the initial stage, and then raw-silk exports followed. In the United States, domestic production of both tea and raw silk had long been given up. While Japanese tea exports gradually decreased as demand in the United States declined, raw-silk exports continued to increase through the 19th century and beyond.

Lockwood says that the rise of the silk industry in Japan was the most conspicuous instance of the adaptation and growth of a traditional industry in response to foreign demand.[79] In fact, Japanese raw-silk producers encountered severe competition in the international market, but through their efforts to beat the competition, they learned about quality control, production management, factory administration, and entrepreneurship. The manufacturing and business prowess thus attained was transferred to other industries.[80] In particular, the cotton textile industry owed its successful development after the 1880s to the early experience of the raw-silk industry.

Raw-silk production was enormously labor-intensive and required very attentive care. Japanese industriousness and cheap labor gave Japan a comparative advantage in raw-silk sales in the US market. Japan's narrow, mountainous lands were not disadvantageous, as mulberry-tree cultivation did not require flat, open lands. Raw-silk production did not require much capital, either. Raw-silk exports, which required no imported raw materials, were also valuable for Japan in that exports meant that much of foreign-exchange earnings, whereas cotton cloth exports required the importation of raw cotton, which cost at least half cotton-cloth exports, net foreign-exchange earnings being about half of cotton-cloth exports.[81]

The United States, meanwhile, had an advantage in raw cotton. Cotton cultivation required large, open lands with a tropical or semitropical climate.

The southern states provided these amply. Labor for cotton cultivation was first furnished by slavery. The Civil War legally abolished slavery, but African-Americans in the South continued to provide relatively low-cost labor for raw cotton production. It became the main US export to Japan from the late 1890s (table 9.2.4-c), when Japan started to increase its cotton manufactures exports. By then, in Japan, the import duty on raw cotton had been abolished and cotton cultivation had virtually ceased.

Basically, trade between the two countries was very complementary. It was especially beneficial to Japan. Japan's raw-silk exports to the United States greatly helped Japan modernize its industry by providing Japan with the lion's share of its foreign-exchange earnings. Japan kept increasing imports of American raw cotton after the turn of the century. The harmonious and comfortable relationship continued until the late 1930s (9.2.4, 16.2.2).

## NOTES

### 5.1. The United States and Japan in the World Economy in the 19th Century

1 The theory of purchasing power parity states that the exchange rate between two countries' currencies equals the ratio of the countries' price levels (the theory of absolute PPP). The theory of relative purchasing power parity states that the percentage change in the exchange rate between two currencies over any period equals the difference between the percentage changes in national price levels. Paul Krugman and Maurice Obstfeld, *International Economics* (Reading, MA: Adison–Wesley, 2000), 395–398.

2 Though the US GDP in 1913 of $517.1 billion in 1990 dollars was 7.2 times as large as the PPP-converted Japanese GDP in 1913 of $71.6 billion in 1990 dollars, the former at current prices was $39.6 billion and the latter at current prices was ¥4.73 billion which was $2.33 billion, if converted by the exchange rate in that year (¥100 = $49-3/8). The former was 17.0 times larger than the latter.

3 In 1896–1900, the United States accounted for 30 percent, Britain 20 percent, Germany 17 percent, France 7 percent, and Japan 1 percent of the world's industrial production. W. W. Rostow, *The World Economy: History & Prospect* (London: Macmillan Press, 1978), 52–53.

4 Wheat represented about 50 percent of the total value of grain crops in the United States in the late 19th century, corn being the runner-up with about one-half of the output of wheat. Of the total US agricultural output, grains accounted for about 20 percent. Raw cotton accounted for about 10 percent. Other major items' shares were as follows: potatoes, 3 percent; fruits, 3 percent; milk and milk products, 16 percent; poultry and eggs, 9 percent; and meat animals, 33 percent. Harold Barger and Hans H. Landsberg, *American Agriculture, 1899–1939: A Study of Output, Employment and Productivity* (New York: National Bureau of Economic Research, 1942), 27, 50.

5 Rostow, *The World Economy*, 150–151. Berger and Landsberg, *American Agriculture*,

53.

6   R. Robson, *The Cotton Industry in Britain* (London: Macmillan Co., 1957), 2. S. J. Chapman, *The Cotton Industry and Trade* (London: Methuen & Co., 1905), 6. M. B. Hammond, *The Cotton Industry: An Essay in American Economic History* (New York: American Economic Association, 1897), 345–346. Murayama Takashi, *Sekai mengyō hattenshi* (Osaka: Nihon Bōseki Kyōkai, 1961), 277.

7   Agricultural products accounted for about half of the total US exports in the 1910s, and about one-third in the 1920s (9.2.1-b).

8   Earnest Ludlow Bogart, *The Economic History of the United States* (New York: Longmans, Green & Co., 1907), 268.

9   When the commercial exploitation of petroleum began in 1859, kerosene was considered the most valuable fraction because of its suitability for oil lamps. Fractionating of other components developed in later years.

10   A Frenchman first succeeded in generating electricity by water power in 1873, but the world's first commercial hydroelectric power-generating plant was constructed in Wisconsin in 1882. Rondo Cameron, *A Concise Economic History of the World* (New York: Oxford University Press, 2016), 98.

11   By means of improved agricultural machines, the average amount of grain that could be harvested, threshed, and prepared for the market by a single man per day was increased from about four bushels in 1830 to about fifty bushels in 1880. Bogart, *The Economic History of the United States*, 270.

12   Many of the entrepreneurs of the American automobile industry, including Henry Ford, started in the bicycle business. John B. Rae, "The Bicycle Manufacturers," *American Automobile Manufacturers: The First Forty Years* (Philadelphia and New York: Chilton Company, 1959), 8–15.

13   The idea of machining parts to tolerances that would permit them to be used interchangeably in mass production was first applied to the manufacture of muskets during the American Revolution. The sewing-machine industry was the first to use the system commercially at mid-century. The development of the sewing-machine industry was stimulated by the requirement for uniforms for the Civil War, a requirement that also led to the first wide usage of ready-to-wear sizing. Vernon Ruttan, *Is War Necessary for Economic Growth?: Military Procurement and Technology Development* (Oxford: Oxford University Press, 2006), 21.

14   American giants such as Singer Sewing Machines and Standard Oil developed new domestic and foreign marketing and production techniques that put them in the vanguard of 20th-century multinational corporations.

15   The Seinan War, or the Satsuma Rebellion, was the last and the largest rebellion by dissidents against the new Meiji government. Suppressing the rebellion took the government six months. The ¥42 million expenditure was covered by a ¥15 million loan from the Fifteenth National Bank and a ¥27 million government note issue.

16   Umemura Mataji and Yamamoto Yūzō, *Kaikō to ishin* (Tokyo: Iwanami Shoten, 1989), 138–140, 154–155. Miyajima Shigeki and Warren E. Weber, "A Comparison of National Banks in Japan and the United States between 1872 and 1885," *Monetary and Economic Studies* (February 2001), 31–48. *Ōkura kyō* was the head of the finance ministry before the cabinet system started in 1885.

*Notes*

17  The National Banking Act of 1873 was drafted adopting Itō Hirobumi's (伊藤博文) recommendation that Japanese banking system should be modeled on the American system, which Itō had studied first hand in the United States in late 1870.

18  The new government paper currency was redeemable in silver. The silver standard thus established lasted until the switch to the gold standard in 1897.

19  In Tokyo, Osaka, and Kyoto, the railways that linked to the nearest ports were constructed in 1877. In 1899 the main trunk route connecting all three cities was completed.

20  Tomioka Filature was founded by the government in 1872 in Gunma as a pilot factory. French engineers provided technical assistance, and the plant was equipped with French steam-powered reeling machines. Tomioka Filature had the effect of disseminating improved methods and technologies in machine reeling among silk producers in Japan. Other government-financed factories included cotton mills at Hiroshima and Aichi, a cement plant at Fukagawa, a machinery factory at Akagawa, a glass factory at Shinagwa, and a shipyard at Hyōgo (Kobe).

21  The price index of cotton yarn in Japan—setting the 1934–36 prices as 100—was 41 in 1883–1890. Those of cotton cloth, raw silk, and silk fabrics were 54, 100, and 85 respectively in the same period. At the time, it was chiefly coarse Indian yarn that depressed the Japanese market. Shimbo Hiroshi, *Kindai Nihon keizaishi* (Tokyo: Sōbunsha, 1995), 105–106.

22  An up-to-date steel plant at the turn of the 20th century required an investment of at least 28–30 million dollars, whereas the Japanese cotton mill industry presented a gross investment of no more than 250,000 dollars per factory in 1900. William W. Lockwood, *The Economic Development of Japan* (London: Oxford University Press, 1955), 23.

23  G. C. Allen, *A Short Economic History of Modern Japan, 1867–1937* (London: George Allen & Unwin, 1946), 79.

24  Lockwood, *The Economic Development of Japan*, 462–463. Allen, *A Short Economic History of Modern Japan*, 195. Takahashi Kamekichi, *Nihon kindai keizai hattatsushi*, Vol. 3 (Tokyo: Tōyōkeizai Shinposha, 1973), 484, 638.

5.2. Early Japanese Foreign Trade

25  There are no official Japanese statistics on Japan's exports and imports by country between 1859 and 1872. Only the numbers of vessels that called at the treaty ports for import or export during the period were recorded. The administration of custom houses at open ports was transferred to the Ministry of Finance in 1872, and trade statistics began to improve. Trade records compiled by customs authorities at ports before 1872 lack uniformity and contain various irregularities. See Shinya Sugiyama, *Japan's Industrialization in the World Economy, 1859–1899* (London: Athlone Press, 1988), 44–45. Ohara Takashi, ed., *Nichibei bunka kōshōshi* (Tokyo: Yōyōsha, 1954), 85.

26  Yokohama Kaikō Shiryōkan, ed., *Zusetsu Yokohama gaikokujin kyoryūchi* (Yokohama: Yūrindo, 1998). This book shows all the foreign firms that moved to the Yokohama settlement and their activities, along with many photographs taken at that time.

27  Walsh & Co., the forerunner of Walsh, Hall & Co., was the first American trading

company to set foot in Japan. It was originally founded by the Walsh brothers, Thomas and John, in Nagasaki. Its Yokohama branch, located at lot 2 of the Yokohama Bund, was called Amerika Ichiban-kan (American number one house). In May 1862, the Walsh brothers formed Walsh, Hall & Co. with the participation of Francis Hall. Walsh, Hall & Co. quickly established its reputation as the leading American trading house. F. G. Notehelfer, *Japan Through American Eyes: The Journal of Francis Hall, Kanagawa and Yokohama, 1859–1866* (Princeton: Princeton University Press, 1992), 15–16, 29, 32–37.

28 Albert H. Imlah, *Economic Elements in the Pax Britannica* (New York: Russel & Russel, 1958), 104–107, and J. H. Clapham, *The Woollen and Worsted Industries* (London: Methuen & Co., 1907), 272.

29 The Taiping Rebellion was one of the most deadly and protracted rebellions in Chinese history. It lasted for fourteen years, from 1850 to 1864, raging over sixteen provinces and destroying more than 600 cities. It was led by a self-proclaimed convert to Christianity, Hong Xiuquan, who declared himself the Heavenly King of the Taiping Tianguo (太平天国 Heavenly Kingdom of Great Peace). For all Hong's ideological and military passion, the Taiping failed to overthrow the Qing, and were ultimately eliminated.

30 Alston H. Garside, *Wool and Wool Trade* (New York: Frederick A. Stokes, 1939), 2.

31 China's share of US exports in the 1910s, 1920s, and 1930s was 0.9 percent, 2.2 percent, and 2.2 percent respectively, whereas that of Japan in the same periods was 3.0 percent, 5.3 percent, and 7.6 percent respectively. Of US imports, China's share in the 1910s, 1920s, and 1930s was 3.0 percent, 3.8 percent, and 2.9 percent respectively, whereas that of Japan in the same periods was 7.4 percent, 9.3 percent, and 7.8 percent respectively. Japan was still a larger trading partner than China as late as 1940.

### 5.3. The Tea, Raw-Silk, and Raw-Cotton Trade between the United States and Japan

32 Tea can be roughly divided into three classes according to the different methods of processing: black or fermented tea, green or unfermented tea, and oolong or semi-fermented tea. Japan produced mostly green tea, which was produced by steaming, rolling, and firing with no fermentation. While the British usually consumed black tea, Americans preferred green tea. They boiled green tea and drank it with sugar and milk. In the 1880s and 1890s, about two-thirds of tea imports to the United States were green tea, the rest being black and oolong tea. Ohara, *Nichibei bunka kōshōshi*, 139.

33 China was the world's biggest tea exporter in the 19th century, though its lead narrowed toward the century's end. In 1896–1900, an average of 209 million pounds of tea were exported annually by China, 154 million pounds by British India, 125 million pounds by Ceylon, 44 million pounds by Japan, and 11 million pounds by the Dutch East Indies. In the same period, 279 million pounds of tea were imported by Britain, 107 million pounds by Russia, 80 million pounds by the United States, and 23 million pounds by Canada and Australia. See Sugiyama, *Japan's Industrialization in the World Economy*, 140–141.

## Notes

34  Ibid., 142. See also Matsuzaki Yoshirō, *Cha no sekaishi* (Tokyo: Yasaka Shobō, 2007), 312.

35  Sugiyama, *Japan's Industrialization in the World Economy*, 143.

36  Ohara, *Nichibei bunka kōshōshi*, 113–114.

37  Sugiyama, *Japan's Industrialization in the World Economy*, 98–99.

38  Ibid., 99.

39  Ibid., 111.

40  Ibid., 114.

41  Giovanni Federico, *An Economic History of the Silk Industry, 1830–1930* (Cambridge: Cambridge University Press, 1997), 198.

42  Japan's share of the world raw-silk trade increased to 80.0 percent in 1930–34 and 83.1 percent in 1935–38, while that of China decreased respectively to 12.6 percent, 10.7 percent. Ibid., 200.

43  See Haru Reischauer, *Samurai and Silk* (Cambridge: Harvard University Press, 1986),155–259.

44  Gunma had been the leading raw-silk-producing prefecture until the late 1880s, when Nagano started producing more raw silk than Gunma. Of the total raw-silk production in Japan, Gunma produced 17 percent in 1876, 25 percent in 1885, and 18 percent in 1895, whereas Nagano's production accounted for 12 percent, 11 percent, and 22 percent respectively. While the silk industry in Gunma developed through the improvement of traditional production methods, that in Nagano adopted relatively new silk-producing methods. Other districts that followed Gunma and Nagano in raw-silk production were Fukushima, Gifu, Yamanashi, and Saitama. Sugiyama, *Japan's Industrialization in the World Economy*, 115–119.

45  Haru Reischauer, *Samurai and Silk*, 208.

46  Ibid., 227–228. Arai Ryōichirō crossed the Pacific ninety times in his life. Ibid., 217.

47  Ibid., 224.

48  Ibid., 228.

49  Ibid., 258.

50  Gerli held the archives of the Japan Society during World War II, and was instrumental in reviving the Society after the war and interesting John Foster Dulles and John D. Rockefeller III in its leadership. His actions were purely altruistic, for at that time he had no business interests in Japan.

51  Haru Reischauer, *Samurai and Silk*, 258.

52  Seki Keizō, *The Cotton Industry of Japan* (Tokyo: Japan Society for the Promotion of Science, 1956), 12.

53  Melvin Thomas Copeland, *The Cotton Manufacturing Industry of the United States* (Cambridge: Harvard University Press, 1923), 4.

54  The water frame was invented by Richard Arkwright in 1769, improving the spinning jenny that James Hargreaves had invented in 1764. Samuel Crompton combined the spinning jenny and the water frame to make the mule by in 1779. Another important invention was the ring frame, patented by John Thorpe, an American, in 1828.

55  Eli Whitney was a young man from Massachusetts who had just graduated from a mechanical engineering course at Yale College. When he was travelling in the South,

one of cotton growers in Georgia happened to ask him to try to invent a machine for cleaning short-staple cotton. M. B. Hammond, *The Cotton Industry* (New York: Macmillan, 1897), 25–27. Besides the Whitney gin, major American inventions in the cotton machinery field include the power loom by Francis Lowell in 1814 and the ring-frame spinning machine by John Thorpe in 1828. Copeland, *The Cotton Manufacturing Industry of the United States*, 5. Seki, *The Cotton Industry of Japan*, 11.

56 Hammond, *The Cotton Industry*, 27.

57 Germany was second to Britain as a buyer of American raw cotton in the 1890s, with France being the third. Japan's share of US cotton exports was about 4 percent in the early 1900s, but it rose to about 10 percent in the early 1920s and about 30 percent in the middle of the 1930s. S. J. Chapman, *The Cotton Industry and Trade* (London: Methuen & Co., 1905), 7. Ohara, *Nichibei bunka kōshōshi*, 387.

58 Copeland, *The Cotton Manufacturing Industry of the United States*, 5, 7, 17, 19. Thomas Ellison, *The Cotton Trade of Great Britain* (London: Frank Cass & Co., 1968), 65.

59 The exporters were mainly mills in the southern states of the United States. Since they were not competitive with mills in the North in the better grades, they sought outlets for their products in foreign markets. Sung Jae Koh, *Stages of Industrial Development in Asia: A Comparative History of the Cotton Industry in Japan, India, China, and Korea* (Philadelphia: University of Pennsylvania Press, 1966), 233–234.

60 Chapman, *The Cotton Industry and Trade*, 154–155.

61 American cotton was the most expensive, and Chinese cotton the cheapest. Thus, American cotton was used only for producing finer cotton yarn. Ordinarily it was not used for yarns under 16s. For example, for making 20s, about one-fourth American, one-half Indian, and one-fourth Chinese cottons were used. For 24s the mix was frequently half-and-half American and Indian cottons. When American cotton was relatively cheap, its proportion was increased. W. A. Clark, *Cotton Goods in Japan* (Washington, DC: US Government Printing Office, 1914), 27.

62 Seki, *The Cotton Industry of Japan*, 19.

63 The Kagoshima Spinning Mill was built in Kagoshima in accordance with the will of Shimazu Nariakira with 3,468 spindles in 1866. Shimazu built another mill with 2,000 spindles in Osaka in 1871. These two mills were purchased by the government and designated as model mills, but were later put up for auction.

64 The Meiji government built two mills of 2,000 spindles each in Aichi and Hiroshima in 1878.

65 The Meiji government imported spinning machinery for sale to private individuals on favorable credit terms. Ten spinning mills of 2,000 spindles each were thus built in 1880 and shortly thereafter.

66 The Osaka Cotton Spinning Company became the Tōyō Spinning Company in 1914, when it merged with the Mie Spinning Company, one of the ten mills founded with loans from the government in the early 1880s.

67 The engineer was Yamanobe Takeo, who studied machinery at Kings College and worked at a spinning mill located in a small town called Blackburn, since no mill would accept him in Manchester. Takahashi, *Nihon kindai keizai keiseishi*, Vol. 3, 689.

68 Koh, *Stages of Industrial Development*, 38.
69 Ibid., 39.
70 Takahashi, *Nihon kindai keizai hattatsushi*, Vol. 3, 518.
71 D. A. Farnie, *The English Cotton Industry and the World Market, 1818–1896* (New York: Oxford University Press, 1979), 126.
72 Takahashi, *Nihon kindai keizai hattatsushi*, Vol. 3, 520.
73 The Open Door was proclaimed by the United States in 1899 and 1900 as its China policy. See 6.5.2.
74 Koh, *Stages of Industrial Development*, 240–241.
75 Ibid., 236–237.
76 Ibid., 237–238.
77 Ibid., 432, and *Clark, Cotton Goods in Japan*, 164.
78 Clark, *Cotton Goods in Japan*, 164–165.
79 Lockwood, *The Economic Development of Japan*, 27.
80 Rostow, *The World Economy*, 423.
81 Lockwood, *The Economic Development of Japan*, 94, 341–344.

# Chapter 6
# Imperialism in East Asia and the Japanese and American Responses

## 6.1. Imperialism in the Late 19th Century

### 6.1.1. A New Wave of Imperialism

In the middle of the 19th century, as observed in 1.2.1, free trade prevailed throughout Europe, and some British leaders even suggested the idea of withdrawal from the colonies. In fact, during this period, European interest in overseas expansion reached its lowest point. The age of colonial empire-building seemed to have come to an end at last.

It was a temporary recession, however, in the tide of the European powers' imperialist expansion.[1] Japan was fortunate that its opening came about during this period. Soon after the inauguration of the Meiji government, the storm of neo-mercantilist imperialism resumed with a vengeance.

The most dramatic example of this outburst was the partitioning of Africa. By the 1890s, nine-tenths of Africa was partitioned. Only a decade earlier it had been a mysterious and unexplored "dark continent." Between 1870 and 1900, Great Britain, which had had the largest empire to start with, acquired new territories of 4.75 million square miles, amounting to one-third of the British Empire's eventual peak area. During this period, France acquired an

*123*

Chapter 6

area of 3.5 million square miles, largely in Africa but also in Indochina. Belgium got 900,000 square miles in Africa (the "Belgian Congo"). Germany, newly united in 1871, began its colonial career in this period, annexing a million square miles of territory in Africa and the Pacific. Russia pushed out its boundaries eastward and southward over Asia.[2]

This wave of territorial expansion by the European powers was doubtlessly one of the great events in world history.[3] Its impact on both European and non-European nations, including Japan and the United States, was significant.

### 6.1.2. Factors that Drove Europe to Imperialist Competition

What drove the Europeans to imperialist competition at this time? Politically, the Franco–Prussian war (1870–71), which ended in the defeat of France, was an important factor. The creation of a united Germany set the stage for a bitter rivalry that would last for the next seventy-five years. The two rivals sought alliances with other nations on the continent to prepare for a renewal of their conflict. Thus all the continental states were drawn into competition that bore a strong resemblance to the old-fashioned mercantilist imperialism of the 17th and 18th centuries.[4] The European powers resumed the race for colonial expansion, inspired by the British possession of vast foreign territories through which, they believed, Britain had grown great.[5]

Great Britain, on the other hand, fearing that its lifeline to its greatest colony, India, was endangered, immediately responded by acquiring colonial interests in Cyprus, Egypt, the Sudan, and East Africa along the sea route to India, which had been newly established by the opening of the Suez Canal in 1869.[6] The discovery of diamonds and gold in South Africa then drew the British into the expansion of their Cape Colony northward, and eventually into the costly Boer War.[7]

Economically, the great European depression, which began in the middle of the 1870s,[8] made the continental states return to protectionist trade policies, giving additional impetus to the race for colonies.

Germany introduced the Bismarck tariff in 1879, restoring import duties on agricultural products and increasing duties on manufactured goods. Just as the Anglo–French treaty of 1860 had marked the beginning of the free-trade period (1.2.1), this new German tariff marked its end and the beginning of a gradual return to protectionism on the continent.[9] France—which had already begun to drift back toward a protectionist trade policy after the

124

downfall, in 1870, of the empire of Napoleon III, who had supported the Cobden–Chevalier Treaty[10]—turned fully back to protectionism in 1892 with the introduction of a dual tariff.[11] This move was also prompted by the protectionist post–Civil War trade policy of the United States.[12]

These continental and American moves to protectionist trade policies gave rise to opposition to free trade in Britain.[13] By the late 19th century, British industrial competitiveness was no longer what it had been in the middle of the century. Britain's position as the workshop of the world was seriously challenged by the rapidly industrializing countries of continental Europe, notably Germany, and by the United States. Britain, however, retained a competitive edge in maritime transportation as well as in international banking and insurance services, and it accordingly had no wish for the volume of world trade to shrink. The British government therefore continued its free-trade policy, but became increasingly dependent on colonies to make up for the loss of export markets in Europe and the United States.[14] This British move, in turn, added greater pressure in the race for territorial expansion among the powers.

Before the 1890s, the territorial ambitions of the powers were primarily directed toward Africa, South and Southeast Asia, and the islands of the Pacific Ocean. However, by the end of the century they were expanding their competition to East Asia, which was fast becoming an arena for imperialist politics. The powers vied fiercely with one another in East Asia, as if they could succeed in their rivalries in Europe by extending influence to that region.[15]

## 6.2. The Sino–Japanese War and Subsequent Developments

### 6.2.1. The Korean Question

The world with which the Japanese leaders were faced in the late 19th century being as described above, Japan had virtually no other choice but to attempt to join the group of imperialist powers. Tokutomi Sohō (徳富蘇峰) wrote, "There are two courses open for our country—self-reliance or dependency. The first course requires imperialism as our aim, whereas the second means that we will have to be prepared to accept the fate of annexation by, or become the protectorate or dependency of, another nation."[16]

The Japanese leaders' most serious concern was a Korea controlled by some

*125*

country or countries hostile to Japan.[17] Korea was then under a decayed and tottering dynasty that had come near to outlasting two Chinese dynasties, and it stubbornly refused to open the country to Western civilization. The Koreans seemed to be content with their centuries-old status as a tributary of China. Each time domestic disturbances became uncontrollable, they asked China to dispatch troops to suppress them. To Japanese leaders, such a Korea appeared likely to fall prey to some Western imperialist power, as China did not appear capable of protecting Korea from outside dangers. Thus it was quite important for the defense of Japan to draw Korea into the Japanese orbit before some other country intervened. Japan was most concerned about Russian control of Korea. Yamagata Aritomo (山県有朋) pointed out in a memorandum of 1890 that, in the event of the completion of Russia's contemplated railroad across Siberia, Russian power would readily come to weigh heavily in East Asia, and Japan's "line of independence" running through the Tsushima (対馬) Islands would be threatened by a Russian dagger.[18]

There had been a note of acrimony between Korea and Japan since the late 1860s, as a result of Korea's rejection of the Japanese government's announcement of the Meiji Restoration. The Koreans took offense to the language of the Japanese announcement, claiming that by implication it placed Japan's ruler at a level equal to China's emperor. When neither side would retreat from its position in subsequent contacts, a group within the Japanese government insisting on an armed confrontation with Korea gained strength. Military action also seemed attractive as a means for diverting the discontent of the samurai, whose stipends had been abolished in the Meiji reform program. The opponents of an armed conflict prevailed, however, arguing that war would be a dangerous waste of resources, diverting energies from reforms at home, and would also provide European powers with an opportunity to fish in troubled waters to Japanese disadvantage.

The pro-war party, led by Saigō Takamori (西郷隆盛), departed the government. The reform party, led by Iwakura Tomomi (岩倉具視), set about the task of securing concessions from Korea by methods short of war. They dispatched three warships to conduct a so-called survey of Korean coastal waters in July 1875. When a party was sent ashore for water at Kanghwa, it was fired on by the local defense forces. In the ensuing exchange, the Japanese destroyed Korean coastal batteries.

The Treaty of Kanghwa of 1876 which ensued made Japan the first country to open the "Hermit Kingdom."[19] The treaty was modeled on the treaty Japan had concluded with the United States in 1858. It opened three Korean ports to trade, and granted extraterritoriality to Japanese in Korea, but not to Koreans in Japan. Duties on Japanese imports into Korea were provided in separate trade regulations.[20] There was a clause in the treaty that read: "Korea, being an independent state, enjoys the same sovereign rights as Japan." This description of Korea's international status as "independent" was to be a subject of contention later between Japan and China.[21]

The treaty made it possible for Japan to begin establishing its influence in Korea by encouraging the growth of a pro-Japanese faction in Seoul. China and Korean conservatives reacted to this with considerable hostility. Li Hongzhang (李鴻章), the high Chinese official who had responsibility for China's relations with Korea, set out to weaken Japanese influence by strengthening China's links with the Korean royal family and also by mediating the conclusion of treaties between Korea and the Western powers.

The Korean king's father, known as the Daewongun (大院君), was bitterly hostile to foreigners and resentful of his pro-Chinese daughter-in-law Queen Min (閔), who had ousted him from the post of regent. In 1882, he staged an unsuccessful putsch attempt. China sent in a large military force and transported the Daewongun to China. The result was a strengthening of China's influence over Korean politics.[22]

In 1884, progressive Koreans, with the encouragement of the Japanese, staged another coup d'état. Their aim was to wipe out the pro-China faction then in power, and to build a new Korea on the model of Japan. The coup failed in the midst of a bloody melee in the palace involving Japanese legation guards. The Chinese resident-general, Yuan Shikai (袁世凱), used Chinese troops to quell the coup proponents.

In 1885 Itō Hirobumi (伊藤博文) and Li Hongzhang had a meeting at Tianjin and agreed that henceforth neither side would send troops to Korea without advance notice to the other.[23]

### 6.2.2. The Sino–Japanese War

In March, 1894, an anti-government rebellion by the nativist and social revolutionary Tonghak ("Eastern Learning" 東学党) sect broke out in south Korea. At the request of the Korean king, China sent troops and notified Japan accordingly. In the notification, however, it stated that troops were being sent "in order to restore the peace of our tributary state." Japan declared that it had never recognized that Korea was China's tributary, and dispatched Japanese troops to Korea. Before either force arrived, however, the rebellion had been suppressed by the Korean army, and the king asked both China and Japan to withdraw their troops. The Chinese refused to leave until the Japanese did. Japan took the position that the rebellion had been due to official corruption and oppression in Korea, and asked China to join Japan in inaugurating a set of reforms which would guarantee peace in the future.[24] China rejected the proposals, as Japan had expected. Hostilities followed at the end of July.

By the end of September 1894, the Japanese navy had command of the Yellow Sea and the Japanese army controlled most of Korea. In October, the Japanese army crossed into southern Manchuria; it captured Port Arthur in the Liaodong Peninsula (遼東半島) the following month. The occupation of Weihaiwei (威海衛) in February 1895 gave Japan outposts on both sides of the sea approaches to Beijing, forcing China to come to terms.

Li Hongzhang was sent to negotiate with Itō Hirobumi at Shimonoseki, and a peace treaty was signed in April. China recognized the independence of Korea, and ceded to Japan the Liaodong Peninsula, Taiwan,[25] and the Pescadores (the islands that lie between Taiwan and the Fujian coast). China also agreed to pay an indemnity of 200 million taels (about 300 million yen) within seven years with interest at 5 percent, and to open four additional treaty ports to Japanese trade and residence, as well as to all the treaty powers in China. A new treaty of commerce and navigation was to be negotiated, but until that time Japan was to be given most-favored nation treatment. The indemnity provided Japan with a gold reserve, allowing Japan to shift to the gold standard in 1897.

With the acquisition of Taiwan, Japan became a colonial power. The Japanese government was determined to make a success of the governance and development of its first colony. High-ranking and capable officials were selected as governor-generals and their assistants.[26] While some military measures were needed to suppress native insurgents at the early stage, the local Japanese authority's efforts proved successful in eventually transforming a backward territory into a modern, self-sufficient colony. At the outset, the Japanese ability to manage alien territory was watched with a skeptical eye abroad, but after its success, doubts turned to praise. The Japanese were fortunate to have the passive acquiescence of a submissive population. Most of the

*128*

Figure: Map of Manchuria in 1900

population had little sense of Chinese nationalism.[27]

## 6.2.3. The Triple Intervention and Its Aftermath

In waging the war, Japan took caution not to provoke the powers' intervention, but after the victory, Japanese demands went beyond the original aim of cutting Korea loose from Chinese tutelage. Russia saw the cession of Liaodong as a threat to its rail route to China through Manchuria, and, uniting with France and Germany, "advised" Japan to return it to China. Knowing that Russia would back the demand with force and seeing no indication of help from Britain or the United States, the Japanese government submitted. Though Japan negotiated with China and received an additional 30,000,000 taels as compensation, money could not wipe out the loss of honor. Half a century's work had still not put Japan in a position to reject the "advice" of one of the major powers. The shock was great. The immediate effect on Japan was its subsequent large-scale and rapid military buildup. Army expenditures rose from just under 15 million yen in 1893 to 53 million yen in 1896. The naval budget, which stood at 13 million yen in 1895, was increased nearly fourfold in 1898.

In Korea, the Japanese submission to Russia had a negative impact on Japan's Korean policy, as the reduction in Japan's prestige led to the increased influence of pro-Russian politicians in Korean politics. The Russians incited the Korean queen Min to expel the pro-Japanese politicians from the Korean government. In an attempt to restore the Japanese position, the new Japanese minister in Seoul, Miura Gorō (三浦梧楼), planned a coup attempt in October 1895.[28] The attempt was grossly mishandled. The Daewongun, whom Miura instigated to join the coup, broke into the palace together with some pro-Japanese Korean officials. Miura and some Japanese soldiers followed them. In the subsequent melee, the queen was murdered.[29] Conroy argues that, as the duly accredited Japanese minister was involved, it was a national crime that even the most loosely constructed laws of war could not excuse.[30] The incident seriously damaged Japan's international prestige, and Japanese influence in Korea declined further still.[31]

In China, the three powers that had participated in the intervention against Japan were fully resolved to make China pay for the help they had given it. They claimed spheres of influence in various parts of China: France in the southern provinces, Germany in Shandong, and Russia in Manchuria.

Figure: Map of China in 1920

Russia secured the right to build its trans-Siberian railway across Manchuria to Vladivostok in a secret treaty with China signed in June 1896.[32] In the treaty, both parties committed themselves to support each other with all the land and sea forces at their disposal against any aggression by Japan directed against Russian territory in eastern Asia, China, or Korea.[33]

In March 1898, Germany acquired the lease of Jiaozhou in Shandong, justifying it with a missionary outrage that had occurred in November 1897.[34] The German action prompted Russia's lease of Port Arthur and Dalian, which Russia had only recently denied to Japan.[35] This was soon followed by Britain's lease of Weihaiwei[36] and France's lease of Guangzhou (广州).[37] Then came Britain's expansion of its Hong Kong colony by the lease of the northern part of Kowloon in June 1898,[38] the last of the "vicious circle of demands upon China."[39]

## 6.2.4. The Boxer Uprising

China's humiliating experiences—first its defeat by Japan and then the aggressions by the European powers—gave rise to a movement among thoughtful Chinese for reforms. Many of them advocated reforms on the model of Japan. However, these attempts were unfortunately frustrated by the conservatives in the Qing government led by the empress dowager (西太后) and high court officials. They were overwhelmingly anti-foreign, and they overlooked and sometimes even encouraged anti-foreign outrages in many places in China.

One such movement, by a group called the Boxers (義和团), gained strength and swept through the northern provinces. In June 1900, the Boxers seized the legation quarter in Beijing, within which were 920 foreigners from eleven countries. An allied force organized by five powers entered Beijing and relieved the entrapped foreigners, who had endured the Boxers' assault for fifty-five days.

Japan provided the largest number of troops (38 percent of the allied forces),[40] and, as a result, incurred the heaviest casualties. And yet Japan received only 7.7 percent of the total indemnity of 450,000,000 taels ($333,000,000).[41]

Japanese troops won an international reputation for their courageous acts and disciplined behavior in the Boxer Uprising. Various reports of heroism were written by nationals of the allied powers about this rescue operation, but there was general agreement among them that Lt. Colonel Shiba Gorō (柴五郎)

was the bravest of the brave. After the fighting, rampant looting by foreign soldiers was observed. The Russians behaved the worst, while the Americans and British behaved somewhat better. The Japanese soldiers did not loot, being subject to strict discipline.[42]

During the Boxer Uprising, the Russians seized most of Manchuria on the pretext of protection of its railway installations, and then pressed China with various extraordinary demands as a condition of withdrawing its troops. Japan, together with Britain and the United States, warned China against entering an agreement which would grant special privileges to Russia. The warning had little weight, however, because none of the three was ready to back their claim with force. Britain was engaged in the Boer War. The United States could hardly be expected to engage in a war in Manchuria to secure its Open Door ideals. Japan, which had a vital interest at stake, could not enter lightly into a war with the greatest land power in Europe.

# 6.3. The Anglo–Japanese Treaty and the Russo–Japanese War

### 6.3.1. The Anglo–Japanese Treaty

It was the Anglo–Japanese Alliance that gave Japan the support necessary for a challenge to Russia. Ever since the Triple Intervention, the idea of an alliance with Great Britain, known to be concerned about the Russian threat to East Asia as well as to India, had been espoused by some Japanese. For the British part, while having traditionally prided itself on its isolation, with the increasing Russian threat to East Asia, the merits of an alliance with Japan became persuasive to leading British politicians.[43] As a result of a series of developments occurring after the Sino–Japanese War, Britain had found Japan positioned in the Anglo–American Open Door group standing against the Triple Intervention group. Russia's acquisition of Port Arthur further increased British concern about Russia. The Japanese army's efficiency and discipline shown at the time of the Boxer Uprising in 1900 also impressed the British (6.2.4).

In November 1901, Great Britain gave its first draft of the proposed treaty to Japan. Itō Hirobumi was cautious about the proffered alliance with Great Britain because he believed that it might lead to war with Russia. He was inclined instead toward a negotiated agreement with Russia. On the other hand,

*133*

Yamagata Aritomo, Prime Minister Katsura Tarō (桂太郎) and Foreign Minister Komura Jutarō (小村寿太郎) did not think any effort to come to terms with Russia would succeed; they believed a showdown with Russia to be inevitable.

The Yamagata–Katsura–Komura view prevailed, and negotiations with the British were pressed forward. A treaty of alliance was signed on January 30, 1902.[44] The treaty committed both signatories to maintaining the independence and territorial integrity of China and Korea, but it recognized that Japan was "interested to a peculiar degree politically as well as commercially and industrially" in Korea. It also provided that each signatory would remain neutral if the other became involved in a war in the Far East, except that they would act together if either were attacked by two powers or more.

### 6.3.2. The Russo–Japanese War

In April 1902, apparently in response to this pressure, Russia agreed to withdraw its forces from Manchuria within eighteen months in three six-month stages.[45] Though the first stage of withdrawal was conducted on schedule, the second stage, due on April 1903, was delayed without explanation. The Japanese government now decided to seek a more general settlement with Russia through direct negotiation. Japan proposed the following points to Russia:[46]

1. A mutual engagement to respect the independence and territorial integrity of China and Korea and to maintain the principles of equal opportunity for the commerce and industry of all nations in those countries.
2. Reciprocal recognition of Japan's preponderate interests in Korea and Russia's special interests in railway enterprises in Manchuria.
3. Reciprocal undertakings on the part of Russia and Japan not to impede development of industrial and commercial activities of Japan in Korea and of Russia in Manchuria.
4. Reciprocal engagements that in case Japan found it necessary to send troops to Korea or Russia found it necessary to send troops to Manchuria . . . the troops were in no case to exceed the actual number required, and were to be forthwith recalled as soon as their missions were accomplished.

*134*

5. Recognition on the part of Russia of the exclusive right of Japan to give advice and assistance in the interests of reform and good government in Korea.

The Japanese proposal was very simple, and might easily have been accepted by Russia in its entirety, but Russia proposed a neutral zone in northern Korea and removed China and Manchuria from the scope of the discussions. It would not even agree to the Open Door in Korea. Most vexatiously, it used every device to delay the discussions.[47] By the end of 1903, the Japanese leaders had accepted as inevitable the impossibility of reaching a compromise with Russia. War came in February 1904.

The Japanese army landed in Korea and moved north into Manchuria. In April, a naval victory outside Port Arthur gave Japan control of the seas across which it needed to move its reinforcements. In June, General Nogi Maresuke's (乃木希典) army laid siege to Port Arthur. In August, the Japanese army of 125,000 beat the Russian Grand Army of 158,000 in the Battle of Liaoyang. Meanwhile, Port Arthur was finally captured by Nogi's army in January 1905, after a fierce battle over half a year. Then came the Japanese victory in the Battle of Mukden in February, involving 250,000 troops under Ōyama Iwao (大山巌) and 370,000 under Aleksei Kuropatkin. In a final blow to Russian hopes, the Russian Baltic fleet, which had sailed halfway round the world, was met by Admiral Tōgō Heihachirō's (東郷平八郎) forces in the Tsushima Strait in May and decisively defeated.

President Theodore Roosevelt recognized Japan as an important counterweight in Asia, balancing the ambitions of Russia, and if the balance was to be tipped, Roosevelt preferred to see it tipped in the direction of Japan rather than toward Russia.[48] He thought of himself as an informal partner in the Anglo–Japanese alliance.[49] His support for Japan was also typical of his countrymen. As the war moved on from one Japanese victory to another, Americans gave loud cheers for its former pupil. They were also cheering for an underdog winning against odds by virtue of bravery.[50]

When Japan destroyed much of the tsar's Pacific fleet in April 1904, Roosevelt was pleased. "The Japs will win out," he told Hay. "The Japs have played our game because they have played the game of civilized mankind. . . . We may be of genuine service if Japan wins out, in preventing interference to rob her of the fruits of her victory."[51]

*135*

In August 1905, through the good offices of Roosevelt, a peace conference was held at Portsmouth, New Hampshire. By then, both sides had good reasons to end the struggle. Russia was facing revolutionary unrest at home, and Japan had strained its resources to the breaking point.[52]

Russia was represented by Finance Minister Sergei Witte and Minister Roman Rosen, minister in Washington, and Japan by Komura and Takahira Kogorō (高平小五郎), minister in Washington. In the treaty, Russia recognized Japan's freedom of action in Korea, and agreed to transfer to Japan the Liaodong leasehold and the Harbin–Port Arthur branch of the Chinese Eastern Railway (renamed the South Manchuria Railway).[53] Japan also secured the cession of the southern half of Sakhalin from Russia.[54]

In the financing of its war expenditures, Japan benefited from American Jews' strong hostility to Russia's anti-Semitism and pogroms. This antagonism prompted Jacob Schiff, senior partner of Kuhn, Loeb & Company, one of the richest and most powerful financiers in America, to join British bankers in raising a series of war loans for Japan. When the Japanese government sent Takahashi Korekiyo (高橋是清), then vice-president of the Bank of Japan, to London to raise 10,000,000 pounds (100 million yen), Schiff traveled to London and offered to underwrite half of the sum.[55] British bankers agreed to raise the other half. Ultimately, Schiff and other American bankers subscribed to Japanese government loans amounting to about 400 million yen, which were about half of the total of government bonds issued abroad for the war expenditure.[56]

# 6.4. Developments after the Russo–Japanese War

### 6.4.1. Some Signs of a Change in US–Japanese Relations

While relations between Japan and the US were quite friendly during the war, some signs of a change were observed after the war. The first was the Japanese public's unfavorable reaction to the peace terms reached at Portsmouth. They resented the loss of an indemnity, and held Roosevelt responsible for the loss.[57] Mobs assaulted the American embassy and destroyed several Christian churches. The Japanese people were not informed that Japan was in the state of near exhaustion financially as well as militarily, whereas Russia was ready to continue to fight if Japan did not withdraw its demand for an indemnity.[58] But the Japanese public's riotous acts compromised the American image of the

*136*

Japanese considerably.

In the United States, meanwhile, the San Francisco Board of Education ordered that Japanese children be excluded from regular schools and sent to an "Oriental school" to "relieve crowding" in October 1906 (8.2.1). The Japanese government protested to the Roosevelt administration, which prevailed upon the school board to withdraw its order. Though this incident was thus closed, similar anti-Japanese incidents occurred repeatedly in the Western states, growing increasingly more serious, and culminating in the federal government's Japanese Exclusion Law of 1924 (8.4).

The immigration disputes are discussed in detail in chapter 8, but it is important to note that the first serious immigration dispute occurred immediately after the Russo–Japanese War. There had been anti-Japanese movements as early as the 1890s, but they were related to concerns about cheap Japanese labor, and were the same in nature as the opposition to cheap Chinese labor that began in the 1850s. This time, however, they were related to the "Yellow Peril" alarm, which spread as a result of the Japanese defeat of Russia. Sensational articles appeared in the press, warning that Japan, which had just defeated what was supposedly the greatest military power of the West, would now attack the other powers in turn and wrest from the Europeans their territories in Asia, and then from the Americans the Philippines, Hawaii, and finally the entire Pacific coast.[59]

Sensible Americans paid little attention to those fanciful war scares, but many Americans were too little informed about the people across the Pacific to clearly distinguish between fact and fancy. In this respect, the Japanese were no better than the Americans. In fact, many Japanese were now beginning to feel that their relations with the United States might no longer be what they had been. There was a sense of insecurity caused largely by the intrusion of the racial factor into Japanese relations with the United States. Tokutomi Sohō wrote that Japan had no true friend in the world; there was no value in international sympathy or understanding, and thus Japan should carry out whatever actions it believed to be in its interests, regardless of other nations' attitudes. The school of Pan-Asian thought, which held that Japan should act unilaterally to safeguard its position in Asia, grew out of such a feeling.[60]

## 6.4.2. Disagreements among Japanese Leaders over the Manchuria Policy

In Manchuria there emerged new Japan–US frictions in the wake of the Russo–Japanese War. Notwithstanding the Japanese government's official announcement that Japan was scrupulously keeping its Open Door pledge, the conduct of some Japanese invited complaints from American merchants in Manchuria and protests from the US legation in Tokyo. The protests were made against such acts as the Japanese military exclusion of American merchants from some areas where Japanese merchants were admitted, the lack of evenhandedness by Japanese customs officers, and the South Manchuria Railway's low rates for transporting some items of Japanese merchandise.

Much of the problem stemmed from the lack of consensus among the Japanese leaders with respect to Manchurian policy. The civilian government leaders were aware of the danger of losing the confidence of the United States and Britain, to which they had promised equal opportunity in Manchuria, but their views were not shared by army leaders, notably those in the Kwantung headquarters, who believed that, given that Japan's interests in Manchuria were properly strategic, they should exercise military and administrative rights that were much broader than those commonly given to railway guards.

In 1906, Saionji, then the prime minister, convened a meeting of elder statesmen, senior members of the cabinet, and service chiefs of staff to discuss the Manchuria question. Kodama, the army's chief of staff, argued that the "management" (*keiei*) of militarily important Manchuria required special administrative powers. Itō, the resident-general in Seoul, declared that Manchuria was Chinese territory, and its "management" was not part of Japan's responsibility. He also insisted that any Japanese approach which would invite Chinese enmity should definitely fail. Itō prevailed over Kodama, and this line of reasoning led to the Root–Takahira agreement of 1908, which mutually recognized the status quo in the Pacific and proclaimed Japan's adherence to the Open Door principles.[61] So far as Japan's relations with the United States were concerned, the Manchurian issue ceased to be a cause of disputes for the time being, though the fundamental disagreements in Japan between the civilian government and the army were to remain and debates between them were to continue for a quarter of a century.[62]

### 6.4.3. The Annexation of Korea

Soon after Japan entered the war with Russia in February 1904, the Japanese government secured an agreement from the Korean government under which the Korean government promised to accept advice concerning administration reforms, to afford facilities for any action Japan found it necessary to take to protect Korea from external attack or internal disturbances, and to authorize Japanese occupation of such places as might be necessary from strategic points of view.[63] In August, the Korean government agreed to appoint advisors on finance and foreign affairs—the former a Japanese, and the latter an American who had long been employed by the foreign ministry in Tokyo. In December, the Japanese were given supervisory authority over Korean police at both national and provincial levels.[64]

These measures were sufficient for Japan's purposes while the war lasted, but a different legal framework seemed necessary once peace was concluded with Russia. In the fall of 1905, having sounded out Britain and the United States to make sure that they would not raise objections, Tokyo decided to make Korea a protectorate of Japan, establishing a Japanese resident-general there.

The resident-general was to be directly answerable to the Japanese government, and was to be given extensive powers, including the authority to use Japanese troops to maintain law and order,[65] to supervise Japanese officials and advisors in Korea, and to intervene directly in the decision making of the Korean government whenever he saw fit. The Japanese government appointed Itō Hirobumi to the post, turning over the direction of the whole Korean operation to him.

In the negotiations with Korea for the establishment of the resident-general, Japan had met a strong resistance from Korea, and even after the treaty had been signed on November, 17, 1905, the Korean resistance continued. In June 1907, the Korean king secretly sent envoys to the Hague peace conference to ask for an international declaration of Korean independence. The attempt was unsuccessful, and this incident provided Itō with the grounds for tightening Japan's grip still more.[66] The Korean government was forced to accept an arrangement by which the Korean army was disbanded except for a battalion of royal guards, and Japanese were introduced into several important administrative and judicial posts.

Starting with disaffected ex-soldiers, rebellion spread rapidly after the summer of 1907.[67] Attacks on Japanese civilians became frequent.[68] Many Japanese leaders now felt that the mechanisms of control were still inadequate, and the only measure that promised to make them stronger was outright annexation.

After the war with Russia, the Japanese government had taken pains not to provoke objections to Japan's Korea policy from the Western powers. Russia, which had agreed to leave Korea to Japan in the Portsmouth Treaty of September 1905, signed a secret convention with Japan in July 1907 concerning their respective ambitions in Korea, Manchuria, and Mongolia, in which Russia recognized Japan's desire to achieve "political solidarity" with Korea.[69] In April 1910, Russia conveyed to the Japanese ambassador in Moscow Russia's recognition of Japan's annexation of Korea.[70]

The Anglo–Japanese alliance, as renewed in August 1905, had recognized Japan's "paramount political, military, and economic interests" in Korea, together with its right "to take such measures of guidance, control and protection" as might be thought "proper and necessary to safeguard and advance those interests."[71]

The American signal to go ahead on Korea had virtually been given to Japan when Roosevelt had approved the Taft–Katsura memorandum in July 1905, in which Prime Minister Katsura Tarō disavowed any aggressive designs on the Philippines and Secretary of War William Taft approved Japan's "suzerainty" over Korea.[72] The United States had made no difficulties about the Korean protectorate when the treaty was concluded in November 1905, and it had shown no signs of doing so since. Nor was there much likelihood of public pressure on Korea's behalf in Washington. When the Korean king appealed to the Hague in 1907, the *New York Tribune* had commented in editorials on July 20 and 26, "Corea had been saved by Japan from Russian conquest and agreed to conduct its foreign affairs through the Japanese government . . ." Hence "the gravity of the offense of the Emperor of Corea in sending a delegation to La Hague unknown to Japan may be estimated if we imagine the Emir of Bokhara sending one to ask intervention between him and the Czar or the Annamese King against France or some Indian Maharajah asking La Hague to expel the British from Hindustan. The title of Japan to deal with Corea, as she has, is at least as good as that of Russia, France, England or any other Power to deal as they have with subject nations. . . . Corea has been a source of irritation . . . menace to peace . . . well to have the menace removed. The peace and progress of the world are more important."[73]

Given international understanding about Japan's Korean policy, the Tokyo government had two problems yet to be solved before annexing Korea: Korean resistance and division of opinion within the Japanese leadership. While the Yamagata–Terauchi military faction was in favor of annexation as the ultimate solution, Itō continued to resist demands for annexation. He insisted that the problem of Korean–Japanese relations should and could be solved in a way that would maintain Korea's separate identity.[74]

Prime Minister Katsura and Foreign Minister Komura at first supported Itō's policy, but gradually tilted toward annexation.[75] By 1909 they had become convinced that Itō's system was not sufficient to meet the requirements of Japanese security, as things had not worked out well. The Korean court remained hostile and there seemed to be no end of riots and unrest.

Itō himself was also disappointed at the situation. While remaining opposed to annexation, he showed some signs by the spring of 1909 that he was beginning to think that if things did not improve, annexation might be unavoidable.[76] In June 1909, he submitted his resignation as resident-general, accepting Katsura's ardent plea that he return to Japan as president of the Privy Council.[77] There was a view that Itō exacted a "secret pledge" from Katsura at the time of his resignation stating that there should be no annexation at least for another seven or eight years.[78] In October 1909, Itō visited Harbin, possibly to ensure that there would be no misunderstanding with Russia over what was being planned. While there, he was assassinated by a Korean patriot.

Itō's death removed the obstacle to annexation in terms of the collective Japanese government policy. The assassination also gave the Japanese government an excuse for solving the question of Korean resistance by force. In May 1910, Army Minister Terauchi Masatake (寺内正毅) was appointed as resident-general in Seoul, and concurrently a force was put at his disposal sufficient for maintaining order in whatever circumstances might arise.[79] A treaty of annexation was negotiated secretly and signed on August 22, 1910. During the subsequent decade, the governor-general under Terauchi developed into a powerful bureaucratic machine which was able to undertake the ruthless political, educational, and social transformation of Korea.[80]

Chapter 6

# 6.5. US Foreign Policy: Expansionism and the Open Door

## 6.5.1. Ambivalent Expansionism

Toward the end of the 19th century, the United States also embarked on an expansionist policy. In 1897 it annexed Hawaii, and in 1898 it fought with Spain, acquiring the Philippines as well as Cuba, Puerto Rico, and Guam.[81] With the Spanish–American War, the United States became generally recognized as having joined the group of imperial powers, and as having become an Asiatic power as a result of its acquisition of the Philippines.[82]

These were the first extensions of US sovereignty to important territories beyond the continental limits of North America. This expansionism represented a big change in US foreign policy. Prior to this time, the United States had generally acquired sparsely populated lands that would be filled with Americans in time.[83]

US expansionism in this period was undoubtedly influenced by the European nations' expansionism. However, unlike Japan, which emulated Western imperialism unhesitatingly and pursued it rigorously because there was no other choice left at that time, there was much ambivalence in the United States about adopting an expansionist policy.

The anti-imperialists argued that to acquire foreign territories and govern them without the consent of their populations would be utterly contrary to the sacred principles of the Declaration of Independence as well as to the spirit of the US Constitution.[84]

The expansionists advanced a variety of arguments. Some alleged that those territories were commercially indispensable; others argued that they were needed for the defense of the United States. A widely accepted argument was that of contingent necessity—the argument that unless the United States took those territories, somebody else would, and that this would be still worse.[85] Some expansionists advocated the concept of the manifest destiny of the United States (1.3.5). They maintained, "We, as an enlightened and a Christian nation, have a duty to regenerate the ignorant and misguided inhabitants."[86] "We should rejoice that Providence has given us the opportunity to extend our influence, our institutions, and our civilization into regions hitherto closed to us, rather than contrive how we can thwart its designs."[87]

The annexation of Hawaii was the first case that provoked major debate on the issue of imperialism among the American public. In January 1893, US

*142*

Minister in Hawaii Stevens and other annexationists intimidated Queen Liliuokalani into yielding her authority and signing a treaty of annexation.[88] Democratic president Cleveland, who suspected that the queen had been wronged, ordered a thorough investigation. The report of the investigation by a special commissioner appointed by the president stated that Stevens had improperly interfered with the event and that a majority of the voters opposed annexation.[89] Expansionists, including supporters of a "Big Navy," sugarcane growers, whalers, and traders, as well as missionaries, argued for the annexation on strategic, commercial, and humanitarian grounds. The expansionist press asserted that if the United States did not take the islands, the British or the Japanese might do so, and use them to America's disadvantage. But Cleveland withdrew the proposed treaty of annexation from consideration by the Senate, though he approved maintaining American naval forces in the islands. The annexation did not materialize until Republican McKinley assumed the presidency in 1897.[90]

More hotly debated was the issue of the acquisition of the Philippines. In waging the Spanish–American War, the McKinley administration had no intention of making the whole archipelago American territory. The American objectives were to attack and defeat the Spanish military and naval forces and possibly seize the city of Manila, which might be made a base for American naval and commercial activities in the western Pacific. Even after the naval victory, Theodore Roosevelt, the secretary of the navy, voiced his opposition to annexation because the islands were too far away. Admiral Mahan, the famous naval strategist, recommended taking Manila and possibly the island of Luzon, but nothing else. The leadership of the Democratic Party opposed taking anything at all.[91] The idealists argued that it would be incompatible with the spirit of the Constitution. Isolationists simply did not want to be involved in the imperialistic rivalries among the powers.[92]

Meanwhile, the Filipino forces under the command of Emilio Aguinaldo, whom the United States had backed, took control of virtually the entire archipelago outside Manila before American ground forces arrived. The United States might have given the Filipinos their immediate independence.[93] But with a German fleet off the shore of Manila, it did not appear that the Filipinos were prepared or organized enough to survive by themselves in that age of high imperialism. Taking only the island of Luzon and leaving the governance of the rest of the islands to the Filipinos seemed impractical, since it

Chapter 6

seemed likely that some European powers or Japan would seize the remaining islands. The moralists strongly argued that the Americans had a moral obligation not to wash their hands of all responsibility for the backward Filipinos. The church element also welcomed the "little brown brother" as one to whom the gospel should be carried.[94] McKinley finally decided to take all of the islands, paying 20 million dollars to the Spaniards. The Filipinos, when they knew that they had been denied independence, arose in revolt in February 1899. A full-scale war lasted for three years.

In 1916, the US Congress promised independence to the Filipinos at some unspecified date in the future, which was followed by the establishment of an autonomous commonwealth in 1935 and complete independence in 1946. The Philippines thus became the first major Western colony to reclaim its sovereignty.[95]

## 6.5.2. The Open Door: Hay's Declaration and the Open Door in Later Years

In China, the United States had been satisfied with securing equal commercial advantages with the European treaty powers through the most-favored-nation clause. However, the European powers' partitioning of China in the late 1890s seemed to pose a serious threat to US commercial opportunity in China. In September 1899, Secretary of State John Hay asked Germany, Russia, Britain, France, Japan, and Italy to declare that they each would not interfere with any existing interests inside leased territories, that Chinese treaty tariffs should apply within each power's sphere of interest, and that each power would not discriminate against the other in setting port and railway rates within each sphere of interest.[96] While replies came from all the nations addressed, each response contained some qualifications except Italy's, which had no sphere of interest in China and agreed unconditionally. But Hay proclaimed that the assent of all the powers was "final and definitive." Japan, which needed the backing of the United States and Britain against Russia in its China policy, had no choice but to accept it, though Japanese industry had not yet reached a level at which it could compete with that of Britain and the United States on equal terms.

In July 1900, Hay issued the second Open Door note, when the plan to send an international expedition to Beijing to rescue the besieged foreign legation was in progress (6.2.4). Hay was concerned that the powers would

*144*

attempt to seek to enlarge their territorial concessions after the suppression of the Boxers. The note proclaimed that the United States was invading China to restore order, defend legal rights under the treaties and international law, preserve the Open Door for foreign trade, and help to maintain China as a "territorial and administrative entity." Unlike the original notes, it did not call for an answer from the powers.[97]

The Open Door remained as America's China policy for the next four decades. During that period, however, the US position swung between assertiveness and withdrawal.[98] When Russia stayed in Manchuria after the Boxer Uprising (1899–1901), Hay retreated to the position of his first Open Door notes, giving up the insistence that Manchuria was an integral part of China.[99] In the Portsmouth treaty of 1905, Chinese sovereignty over Manchuria was affirmed by Japan and Russia, but in the Root–Takahira Agreement of 1908 and the Lansing–Ishii Agreement of 1917 (7.3.1), the Open Door principles were compromised by the recognition of Japan's special interests in China. The Nine-Power Treaty of 1922 reaffirmed the Open Door, confirming China's territorial and administrative integrity in Article I and equal opportunity in China in Article III (7.4.3), but when Japan openly defied Article I (China's integrity) in Manchuria in 1931, the United States only issued a statement condemning Japan, taking no further action (13.4.1).

### 6.5.3. Was the Open Door a Successful American China Policy?

The Open Door was at least a political success for the US government at home. The year 1900 was an election year in the United States. The McKinley administration had to show the American public that it was acting effectively to safeguard American economic interests and protect the lives of Americans in China, and yet it had to avoid the Democrats' criticism that its actions were imperialistic. The Open Door note of 1900 was a statement addressed not only to the foreign governments, but to the American people—both the anti-imperialists and the exponents of an aggressive China policy.[100] It virtually resolved the debate between the imperialists and the anti-imperialists in the United States.[101]

As to the effectiveness of the Open Door as US foreign policy, it is generally agreed that Hay's initiative saved China by moderating the powers' demands in the Boxer Incident. Without it, the indemnity might have been even larger, and further division of China might have taken place. The Boxer

Protocol concluded in 1901 contained no territorial cessions.[102] Some historians assert, however, that the main reason why the powers did not engage in further partition of China was that they were unwilling to compete with each other over the division of spoils at the time. They were so suspicious of one another that no one of them was in a position to challenge the others.[103] Griswold observes that the political stalemate was largely attributable to the effectiveness of Salisbury's diplomacy in staying the advance of Germany and Russia, the two most expansionist countries at the time, in China.[104]

Thompson, Stanley, and Perry give their version of the rationale behind the Open Door: "Given small American trade (in China) and limited American military and naval power, it suited the nation's interests to make as small a governmental commitment as possible. . . . What the United States needed most . . . was the markets—primarily for its economic output but also for its political and religious culture. . . . So an open door to trade and evangelization, with someone else paying the bills . . . for keeping order, was the ideal setting for American expansion, [since it] gave Americans everything they really needed at the lowest possible cost."[105]

Kennan, while recognizing that the Open Door was accepted by the American public as Hay's major diplomatic achievement,[106] points out that it was not a policy that Americans cared enough about to support in any determined way; nor, if implemented, were Americans prepared to accept any particular responsibility for it.[107] He also argues that the term "open door" was not clear or precise enough to usefully be made the basis of a foreign policy.[108] While it had meaning only in relation to specific situations in China, the circumstances surrounding China from 1900 on were so complex and fluid that the term could not possibly have had any comprehensive meaning.[109] Besides, China was not a nation with the necessary qualifications for national statehood in the modern international context.[110] Kennan also points out, "No one liked to receive suggestions for alterations of his behavior from someone who obviously has far less to lose than he has from the consequences of such an alteration. There was always a feeling, both among the Japanese and among the British, that we were inclined to be spendthrift with their diplomatic assets in China for the very reason that our own stake in China meant so much less to us than theirs did to them."[111]

Other critics argue that it introduced into American China policy a chronic disparity between ends and means.[112] Griswold contends that the

United States promised something that it could not deliver. When the Japanese, alarmed by Russia's encroachment in Manchuria, inquired in early 1901 if the United States would join Japan in using force to ensure the observance of the Open Door, Hay replied that the United States was "not at present prepared to attempt singly, or in concert with other powers, to enforce these views in the east by any demonstration which could present a character of hostility to any other power."[113]

No country was more perplexed by the Open Door policy's ambiguity, inconsistency, and erraticism than Japan, which had the greatest political stake in China. Most vexatious was that it was hard to know how serious the United States was about implementing the Open Door policy. So far as the US activities remained within the traditional framework of old big-power diplomacy like that of the Theodore Roosevelt administration, there was no misunderstanding on the Japanese side. When the United States went out of the framework in pursuit of the "new diplomacy" expanding the interpretation of the Open Door, however, it often went beyond the Japanese comprehension and caused bilateral friction.

According to William Williams, the Open Door was a strategy of non-colonial imperial expansion,[114] and an American version of British informal empire or imperialism of free trade.[115] He argues, "The policy of the Open Door was designed to clear the way and establish the conditions under which America's preponderant economic power would extend the American system throughout the world without the embarrassment and inefficiency of traditional colonialism."[116] He also contends that it was irrelevant to criticize the Open Door policy for not emphasizing extensive military readiness, because it "was conceived and designed to win the victories without the wars." He admits, however, that "the central drawback of the approach was the probability that it would, if undertaken with vigor and determination, lead to a war, as was the case with Japan."[117]

## NOTES

### 6.1. Imperialism in the Late 19th Century

1  John Strachey, *The End of Empire* (London, Victor Gollancz, 1959), 71, 79.
2  J. A. Hobson, *Imperialism: A Study* (London: Archibald Constable & Co., rev. ed. 1905), 14–16. Strachey, *The End of Empire*, 79–81.
3  Hobson charged in 1902 that industrialists and bankers had instigated imperialism

Chapter 6

to provide profitable investments for surplus capital. Likewise, Lenin argued in 1916 that imperialism was an inevitable byproduct of capitalism in its monopoly stage. This Hobson–Lenin concept in the early 20th century was criticized later by many writers on many grounds. For example, Schumpeter attributed the cause of imperialism to capitalist immaturity. Langer ascribed it to international rivalries. Gallagher and Robinson discussed the imperialism of free trade. William L. Langer, *The Diplomacy of Imperialism, 1890–1902* (New York: A. A. Knopf, 1935), 70–77. J. Gallagher and R. Robinson, "The Imperialism of Free Trade," in *The Decline, Revival and Fall of the British Empire*, ed. Anil Seal (Cambridge: Cambridge University Press, 1982), 1–18. Marius Jansen, "Japanese Imperialism: Late Meiji Perspectives," in *The Japanese Colonial Empire*, eds. Raman Myers and Mark Peattie (Princeton: Princeton University Press, 1984), 64–65. W. G. Beasley, *Japanese Imperialism, 1894–1945* (New York: Oxford University Press, 1989), 2–5.

4    D. K. Fieldhouse, "Imperialism," in *Economic Imperialism*, eds. Kenneth E. Boulding and Tapan Mukerjee (Ann Arbor, MI: University of Michigan Press, 1972), 117.

5    Langer, *The Diplomacy of Imperialism*, 74.

6    Disraeli, who had denounced colonial expansion twenty years before (1.2.1), now sounded a new note of imperialism in his famous Crystal Palace speech in 1872. He purchased on his own authority the French shares in the Suez Canal Company in 1876, and, in a move meant to confirm the new policy, made Queen Victoria empress of India. Ibid., 70.

7    The Boer War (October 1899–May 1902) was fought between Britain and two Boer states, the South African Republic and the Orange Free State, over Britain's influence in South Africa. British casualties numbered 22,000.

8    GNP growth per capita decreased from 1.1 percent per annum in 1850–70 to 0.2 percent in 1870–90 in continental Europe. Peter Mathias and Sidney Pollard, *Cambridge Economic History of Europe*, vol. III (Cambridge, Cambridge University Press, 1989), 45. One of the main causes of the depression was the decline in the prices of agricultural products caused by the influx of cheap grain from the United States. Farmers accounted for some 60 percent of the population of continental Europe, and the decline in their income had serious consequences for overall demand. Ibid., 48. Other factors include the end of the long railway construction boom, which resulted in excessive investment and financial failures, and steel industry overcapacity tied to the introduction of new production techniques such as the Bessemer and Thomas processes. Iwami Tōru, *Sekai keizaishi* (Tokyo: Tōyōkeizai Shinpōsha, 1999), 66.

9    Mathias and Pollard, *Cambridge Economic History of Europe*, 52. Largely in retaliation for American protectionism, Germany also signed a series of preferential commercial treaties with countries in Central and Eastern Europe. The treaty with Austria-Hungary in 1891 was followed by agreements with Italy, Switzerland, Romania, Belgium, and Russia. Ibid., 61, 731.

10   Mathias and Pollard, *Cambridge Economic History of Europe*, 45.

11   In the dual-tariff system, lower tariffs ware applied to imports from countries which offered special advantages to France, and higher tariffs were applied to imports from countries which did not offer any special advantages. Mathias and Pollard,

*Notes*

*Cambridge Economic History of Europe*, 731.

12 After the Civil War, the Republican Party—the party of protection—retained control of the executive and legislative branches for most of the next half-century, and import duties that had been raised for revenue purposes during the Civil War were maintained or even raised. Mathias and Pollard, *Cambridge Economic History of Europe*, 657.

13 Jagdish Bhagwati, *Political Economy and International Economics*, ed. Douglas A. Irwin (Cambridge: MIT Press, 1996), 87.

14 Langer, *The Diplomacy of Imperialism*, 75. Bhagwati and Irwin, *Political Economy and International Economics*, 91–92.

15 Akira Iriye, *Japan and the Wider World: From the Mid-Nineteenth Century to the Present* (London: Longman, 1997), 7, 14.

6.2. The Sino–Japanese War and Subsequent Developments

16 John D. Pierson, *Tokutomi Sohō, 1863–1957* (Princeton: Princeton University Press, 1980), 318.

17 Watanabe Toshio, *Shin datsua-ron* (Tokyo: Bungeishunju, 2008), 26–98.

18 Akira Iriye, *Across the Pacific: An Inner History of American–East Asian Relations* (New York: Harcourt, Brace & World, 1967), 65–66.

19 W. G. Beasley, *The Rise of Modern Japan* (London: Oxford University Press, 1987), 43. Michael Montgomery, *Imperialist Japan* (London: Christopher Helm, 1987), 121.

20 Since no treaties were concluded with Western countries until 1882, Japan enjoyed practically exclusive control over Korea's foreign policy for six years after 1876. Frederick Foo Chien, *The Opening of Korea: A Study of Chinese Diplomacy, 1876–1885* (New York: Shoestring Press, 1967), 54, 196.

21 The term translated as "independent" was *jishu* in Japanese and *tzuchu* in Chinese in the original text, both meaning "autonomous" or "self-governing." Neither Koreans nor Chinese believed that the description meant a change in Korea's political status at the time of the signing of the treaty. Chien, *The Opening of Korea*, 46.

22 Ibid., 94–113.

23 The Convention of Tianjin was a diplomatic victory for Japan. It placed China and Japan on equal terms with respect to the right to military intervention in Korea. Ibid., 168.

24 The reforms that Japan demanded of Korea included the effective control of administration, improvement of the judicial system, and revision of the tax structure. These were reforms which the Western powers had demanded of China at various times. Mutsu Munemitsu was confident that they were reforms that the powers would welcome and China would reject. Beasley, *Japanese Imperialism*, 47. There were several developments that caused the Japanese to act in a determined way at this time. The most crucial was the Russian construction of the trans-Siberian railway, which had started in 1891. It would pose a serious threat to Korean independence when it was completed. Beasley, *The Rise of Modern Japan*, 145.

25 Li Hongzhang resisted the cession of Taiwan, which Japan had not occupied. But the Japanese were adamant. They saw the acquisition of Taiwan as opening the way for a

*149*

Chapter 6

Japanese advance to the south, possibly through the Chinese province of Fujian.

26  Kodama Gentarō (児玉源太郎) served eight years (1898–1906) as governor-general, and instituted the measures that gained the Japanese a reputation for being good colonial administrators. He made the fortunate choice of Gotō Shinpei (後藤新平) as chief civil administrator. Gotō successfully reformed the political, social, and economic order in Taiwan through his "scientific" approach. Gotō was assisted by Nitobe Inazō (新渡戸稲造), who later became deputy secretary-general of the League of Nations. Mark R. Peattie, "Japanese Attitude toward Colonialism," in *The Japanese Colonial Empire, 1895–1945*, eds. Ramon H. Myers and Mark R. Peattie (Princeton: Princeton University Press, 1984), 19, 84–86. A Taiwanese author writes about the Japanese prewar colonial management of Taiwan quite approvingly. Sai Konsan, *Taiwanjin to Nihon seishin* (Tokyo: Shogakukan, 2001).

27  Peattie, "Introduction" to *The Japanese Colonial Empire*, eds. Myers and Peattie, 19.

28  As Russia and the Korean queen intensified anti-Japanese movements, the Japanese government replaced the minister in Seoul, Inoue Kaoru, with Miura Gorō. Miura, a former soldier, was sadly lacking in diplomatic experience.

29  Watanabe, *Shin datsua-ron*, 99.

30  Upon returning to Tokyo, Miura was arrested on a warrant charging him with murder and assembling a mob for seditious purposes. The emperor of Japan sent Inoue Kaoru to Seoul to convey his condolences to the Korean king. Miura was not convicted, however. Hilary Conroy, *The Japanese Seizure of Korea, 1868–1910* (Philadelphia: University of Pennsylvania Press, 1960), 306–307, 321.

31  Soon after the incident, the Korean king escaped from the palace, taking refuge in the Russian legation. Beasley, *Japanese Imperialism*, 71–72, and Payson J. Treat, *Diplomatic Relations between the United States and Japan, 1895–1905* (Gloucester, MA: Peter Smith, 1963), 10–11.

32  The originally planned route of the trans-Siberian railway lay entirely within Russian borders, and followed the Amur and Ussuri rivers to Vladivostok.

33  The treaty would remain in force for fifteen years after the railway contract was confirmed. Gaimushō, ed., *Nihon gaikō hyakunen shōshi* (Tokyo: Yamada Shobō, 1954), 51. Payson Treat, *The Far East* (New York: Harper & Brothers, 1928), 324–325. China did not fulfill its obligation under this treaty in the Russo–Japanese War, however, because Japan had asked China to remain neutral during the war.

34  In November 1897, two German priests were murdered by a Chinese mob at Jiaozhou in Shandong. The Germans occupied Jiaozhou and demanded a lease of the bay, which was granted for the term of ninety-nine years. Treat, *The Far East*, 328.

35  The treaty signed in March 1898 granted Russia the lease of Port Arthur and Dalian for twenty-five years and the right to construct a branch railway from the main trans-Manchurian line to Dalian and Port Arthur. Ibid., 329.

36  The term of the lease was "for as long as a period as Port Arthur shall remain in the possession of Russia." Ibid., 330.

37  The lease agreement of Guangzhou to France for ninety-nine years was signed in May 1898. Ibid., 330.

38  The southern part of Kowloon had been leased to Britain in 1860 (1.2.2).

39  Treat, *The Far East*, 331.

*Notes*

40   Russia opposed Japan's sending a large number of troops for fear the service would give Japan special privileges, but Britain overrode the Russian dissent and suggested that Japan dispatch a full army division. Ibid., 349.

41   The Boxer Expedition and Indemnities

| | Soldiers | | | Indemnity Proportion of total receipt |
|---|---|---|---|---|
| | Dispatched | Killed | Wounded | |
| Japan | 13,000 | 349 | 933 | 7.7% |
| Russia | 8,100 | 160 | 741 | 29% |
| Britain | 5,800 | 64 | 288 | 11.25% |
| France | 2,100 | 50 | 166 | 15.75% |
| US | 4,060 | 48 | 231 | 7.3% |
| Germany | 450 | 60 | 244 | 20% |
| Italy | 100 | 18 | 18 | 5.9% |
| Austria–Hungary | 140 | 8 | 33 | 0.9% |

*Source:* Hirama Yōichi, *Nichiei dōmei* (Tokyo: PHP Institute, 2000), 27. Payson Treat, *The Far East* (New York: Harper & Brothers, 1928), 358.

The total indemnity amount of 450,000,000 taels was twice as much as the reparation that Japan acquired from China as a result of the Sino–Japanese War of 1894–1895. It was believed that the powers other than Japan and the United States considerably overestimated their losses and expenses. Treat, *The Far East*, 357.

42   Treat, *The Far East*, 352. James C. Thompson, Jr., Peter W. Stanley, and John Curtis Perry, *Sentimental Imperialism* (New York: Harper & Row, 1981), 137.

6.3. The Anglo–Japanese Treaty and the Russo–Japanese War

43   For example, in March of 1898, Chamberlain suggested the idea of an Anglo–Japanese alliance to Katō Takaaki, then minister in London.

44   Itō was visiting Russia when the agreement was signed. British concerns about the possibility of Itō concluding an agreement with Russia also prompted Great Britain to sign the treaty with Japan.

45   Beasley, *The Rise of Modern Japan*, 150.

46   Treat, *The Far East*, 369–370.

47   Kurino, the Japanese minister in St. Petersburg, handed over the first Japanese proposal on August 12, 1903, after having been kept waiting for nine days to see Foreign Minister Lamsdorf. Russia wanted to have the negotiations in Tokyo, which would delay proceedings because Rosen, the Russian minister in Tokyo, could only transmit the dispatches he received. Seven and a half weeks passed before the Russian reply was presented in Tokyo on October 3. Japan replied on October 30, but the Russian response was delayed for forty days (until December 1). Japan's response was made on December 21, to which Russia replied on January 6, still holding out for a neutral zone in Korea. Japan replied on January 13, stating that it would recognize that Manchuria was outside of Japan's sphere of interest provided Russia would promise to respect the integrity of China in Manchuria. Japan kept pressing for an early reply, but to no avail. On February 5, Japan announced the termination of the

negotiations. During the negotiations, Foreign Minister Komura said to Lloyd Griscom, the American ambassador in Tokyo, "The only desire of the Russian government seems to be to delay matters." At another time he said, "Japan will not wait more than a reasonable time for a reply, as negotiations must not be protracted to the military advantage of Russia." Treat, *The Diplomatic Relations*, 177, 179. Treat, *The Far East*, 371–372.

48  William L. Neumann, *America Encounters Japan* (Baltimore: Johns Hopkins Press, 1963), 121.

49  Walter LaFeber, *The Cambridge History of American Foreign Relations, vol. II: The American Search for Opportunity, 1865–1913* (Cambridge: Cambridge University Press, 1993), 203.

50  Ibid., 122–123.

51  Ibid., 122.

52  By then the Japanese army had nearly run out of ammunition, and war deaths rose to over 110,000. The shortage of officers due to heavy casualties was a particularly serious problem for Japan.

53  The American railway magnate E. H. Harriman proposed joint management of the South Manchuria Railway with Japan as part of his grand scheme for an around-the-world railway service. Katsura had accepted the offer subject to agreement from Komura, who had not returned from Portsmouth. Komura opposed the joint venture scheme. Considering that the railway was the only valuable asset which Japan had won in the war, and that the Japanese public had already shown great indignation at the slight gains from the war, Komura might have been justified in his opposition to the scheme. Treat, *Japan and the United States*, 190, Beasley, *Japanese Imperialism*, 93.

54  On the Treaty of Portsmouth, George Kennan writes, "This arrangement . . . proved to have considerable stability, and one is moved to conclude that it must have borne a fairly accurate relationship to the power realities and requirements of the area. At any rate, there were no discernible alternatives to it that promised any greater stability . . . " George F. Kennan, *American Diplomacy, 1900–1950* (Chicago: University of Chicago Press, 1951), 43.

55  Richard J. Smethurst, *From Foot Soldier to Finance Minister: Takahashi Korekiyo, Japan's Keynes* (Cambridge: Harvard University Asia Center, 2007), 152–154.

56  Schiff confided to Takahashi, " . . . We pray for the fall of the Russian monarchy. Now Japan has gone to war with Russia. If Japan wins the war, a revolution will surely break out in Russia. Thus, the monarchy will be buried. Because I pray for this, I am lending money to Japan." Ibid., 156.

6.4. Developments after the Sino–Japanese War

57  Komura demanded an indemnity of 1,200,000,000 yen, but Witte had been instructed not to cede an inch of territory or pay a kopek in indemnities. When the discussion reached an impasse, Roosevelt warned Japan not to prolong the war for a monetary considerations alone. Komura agreed to give up the indemnity, receiving only 20,000,000 dollars (40,000,000 yen) for the net cost of maintaining prisoners of war (the Japanese had many more Russian prisoners than the Russians had

*Notes*

Japanese).

58 Hirama Yōichi, *Nichiei dōmei: Dōmei no sentaku to kokka no seisui* (Tokyo: PHP Institute, 2000), 64.

59 The *Coast Seamen's Journal* pointed out, "Never in history had the Caucasian won out in competition with the Orient. The Oriental might gain manners and technology, but he would always remain an Oriental. The Mongolian would never adopt the Judaic-Christian philosophy while, racially, the Aryan always disappeared before the Mongolian." Iriye, *Across the Pacific*, 105.

60 Ibid., 116. Iriye, *Japan & the Wider World*, 44–45.

61 On November 30, 1908, Takahira Kogorō, the Japanese ambassador in Washington, and Elihu Root, the secretary of state, exchanged notes affirming that both powers were: 1. To subscribe to the policy of maintaining the status quo in the Pacific area. 2. To respect each other's territorial possessions in that region. 3. To uphold the Open Door in China. 4. To support by pacific means the "independence and integrity of China . . . " Thomas Bailey, *A Diplomatic History of the American People* (Englewood Cliffs, NJ: Prentice-Hall, 1968), 526. The Root–Takahira agreement was not a treaty, but an exchange of notes that bound the executive departments that negotiated the agreement. It testified, however, to the commitment of the Japanese to the Open Door principle, and to the US belief in the good faith of Japan. Payson J. Treat, *The Far East* (New York: Harper & Brothers, 1928), 402–403.

62 W. G. Beasley, *Collected Writings of W. G. Beasley* (London: Japan Library, 2001), 183. Beasley, *Japanese Imperialism*, 95, and Iriye, *Across the Pacific*, 114.

63 Beasley, *Japanese Imperialism*, 86.

64 Ibid., 87.

65 Yamagata was opposed to Itō, a civilian, holding the power of the supreme military commander. But Itō insisted that he would not accept the post unless he had the power to command soldiers. Yamagata gave in as a special case for Itō. Conroy, *The Japanese Seizure of Korea*, 338.

66 Beasley, *Japanese Imperialism*, 88.

67 There were 324 riots in 1907, 1,450 riots in 1908, 950 riots in 1909, and 147 riots in 1910. Conroy, *The Japanese Seizure of Korea*, 368.

68 Beasley, *Japanese Imperialism*, 88.

69 Ibid., 89–90.

70 Moriyama Shigenori, "Nikkan heigō no kokusai kankei," *Nenpō Kindai Nihon Kenkyū, 7* (Tokyo: Yamakawa Shuppansha, 1985), 92.

71 Britain recognized Japan's annexation of Korea in 1910. Ibid., 92.

72 In July 1905, Secretary of War Taft, then on a mission to Manila, stopped off in Tokyo and drew up with Katsura the Taft–Katsura memorandum. Bailey, *A Diplomatic History*, 519. Roosevelt felt that he could not possibly interfere for the Koreans against Japan. Conroy, *The Japanese Seizure of Korea*, 329.

73 Conroy, *The Japanese Seizure of Korea*, 350.

74 Ibid., 334, 344.

75 On April 17, 1909, Katsura wrote to Yamagata, "The sooner the day of his (Itō's) replacement the better for the next step in our policy . . . " Ibid., 372.

76 Ibid., 380. When Katsura and Komura met Itō in April 1909 in Tokyo and showed

Chapter 6

him a paper prepared by Komura saying that at a suitable time Korean annexation should be carried out, Itō did not object. Ibid., 377.

77  Ibid., 372.

78  It is the Kokuryūkai's publication, *Nikkan gappō hishi*, that writes that at the time of resignation Itō exacted from Katsura a secret pledge that there should be no annexation of Korea for at least another seven or eight years. Ibid., 370. Conroy writes that it is not certain which idea Itō had in mind—acquiescing to annexation or buying time to get in better functioning order—alongside principles of his own, including the maintenance of Korea's separate identity. Anyway, with Itō's death, "Katsura deliberately forgot his pledge." Ibid., 371, 373–374.

79  Beasley, *Japanese Imperialism*, 90.

80  Mark Peattie, "Introduction" to *The Japanese Colonial Empire*, eds. Ramon Myers and Mark Peattie (Princeton: Princeton University Press, 1984), 20. Peattie writes, "Terauchi's procrustean efforts to make the populace conform to Japanese values and institutions created violent antagonisms which could not long be contained and which finally burst forth in an explosion of national resentment in March 1919." Ibid., 21.

### 6.5. US Foreign Policy: Expansionism and the Open Door

81  When a riot took place in Cuba in 1898 in an attempt to break away from Spain, McKinley dispatched the battleship *Maine* to Havana harbor. The ship was mysteriously blown up, killing 266 Americans. While the cause of the explosion was still unclear, the popular demand for war became louder in the United States. Notwithstanding the appeal for peace by the Pope and Spain's offer of peace, McKinley ordered a blockade of Cuban ports, and a war was on. The treaty of Paris provided for the independence of Cuba and the concession of Puerto Rico, Guam, and the Philippines to the United States. Scott Nearing and Joseph Freeman, *Dollar Diplomacy: A Study in American Imperialism* (New York: Monthly Review Press, 1966), 253.

82  Treat, *The Far East*, 321.

83  Kennan, *American Diplomacy*, 14.

84  Bailey, *A Diplomatic History*, 475.

85  Kennan, *American Diplomacy*, 16.

86  Ibid., 15.

87  Nearing and Freeman, *Dollar Diplomacy*, 255–256.

88  By the end of the 1870s, two-thirds of all sugar properties in Hawaii were held by Americans. Time after time, the plantation owners organized revolts against the weak monarchy to acquire de facto control of the islands. Their aim was the eventual annexation of Hawaii to the United States.

89  Bailey, *A Diplomatic History*, 432.

90  Ibid., 433–435.

91  Thompson, Jr., Stanley, and Perry, *Sentimental Imperialists*, 112.

92  Ibid., 114.

93  Bailey, *A Diplomatic History*, 472.

94  Ibid., 472.

*Notes*

95 Thompson, Jr., Stanley, and Perry, *Sentimental Imperialists*, 118–119.

96 Treat, *The Far East*, 333–334, and also Treat, *Diplomatic Relations between the United States and Japan*, 72. The Open Door policy was originally advocated by Britain to maintain its dominance in Chinese trade in the face of the strategic penetration of Chinese territory by Russia, Germany and France. Britain asked the United States to support the policy, but the United States showed little interest at first. When John Hay became the secretary of state, however, he declared it as US policy in East Asia. Kennan, *American Diplomacy*, 22–31.

97 Bailey, *A Diplomatic History*, 482.

98 Thompson, Jr., Stanley, and Perry, *Sentimental Imperialists*, 132.

99 Griswold, *The Eastern Policy of the United States*, 84.

100 Thompson, Jr., Stanley, and Perry, *Sentimental Imperialists*, 128, 131.

101 Bailey, *A Diplomatic History*, 482, Kennan, *American Diplomacy*, 37.

102 William Appleman Williams, *The Tragedy of American Diplomacy* (New York: W. W. Norton, 1959), 51. T. A. Bisson, *American Diplomacy in the Far East, 1931–1940* (New York: Institute of Pacific Relations, 1940), 8.

103 Bailey, *A Diplomatic History*, 482.

104 Griswold, *The Eastern Policy of the United States*, 81–82.

105 Thompson, Jr., Stanley, and Perry, *Sentimental Imperialists*, 133.

106 Kennan, *American Diplomacy*, 37.

107 Ibid., 36.

108 Ibid., 45.

109 Ibid., 40.

110 Ibid., 40.

111 Ibid., 48.

112 Thompson, Jr., Stanley, and Perry, *Sentimental Imperialists*, 132.

113 Kennan, *American Diplomacy*, 35.

114 Williams, *Tragedy of American Diplomacy*, 50.

115 Ibid., 97.

116 Ibid., 50.

117 Ibid., 147.

# Chapter 7
# Friction and Cooperation between Japan and the United States in the 1910s and Early 1920s

## 7.1. Dollar Diplomacy

### 7.1.1. The Taft Administration's Anti-Japanese Policy

While in office, Theodore Roosevelt had been determined not to allow China issues to aggravate US relations with Japan, and avoided any challenge to Japan's established position in China. The administration of William Taft, however, departed from the Roosevelt policy soon after it took office in March of 1909. Taft, together with Philander Knox, his secretary of state, embarked on a vigorous economic policy in China, which they labeled for domestic consumption as "dollar diplomacy." It was based on the belief that by pursuing American economic interests in China, they could attain the political end of helping improve Chinese economic welfare and breaking the Japanese hold in China.

The newly formed Division of Far Eastern Affairs in the Department of State undertook this aggressive China policy.[1] The division was started in March 1908 under the young third assistant secretary of state Huntington Wilson, who had returned from Tokyo in 1906 after a nine-year posting. Several disagreeable experiences, such as an assault by a Japanese mob at the

*157*

US embassy in protest of the Portsmouth Treaty, Japan's rejection of Harriman's joint management proposal of the South Manchuria Railway, and the Japanese army's discriminatory conduct against American businessmen in Manchuria must have affected his perception of Japan unfavorably. By the time he left Japan, he had become noticeably anti-Japanese.[2]

Another eager promoter of the aggressive China policy in the State Department was Willard Straight. Prior to his appointment as acting chief of the Division of Far Eastern Affairs in November 1908, he had worked as a war correspondent in Korea during the Russo–Japanese War and served as US consul-general at Mukden from June 1906 to November 1908. In both places, he was a close and critical observer of the Japanese.[3] Straight seemingly had even more antagonism toward the Japanese than Wilson.[4]

Wilson and Straight asserted that Roosevelt's willingness to subordinate American interests in China in a quest for Japan's goodwill was misguided, and that by forcing American capital into China, the United States could break the strong Japanese hold there. They expanded the applicability of the Open Door, and insisted that the Open Door principles assured Americans equal investment opportunities throughout China.[5] They supported the participation of the American financial community in the financing of Chinese railways and other enterprises.

In Manchuria, E. H. Harriman and Straight sought to purchase the Chinese Eastern Railway from the Russians. Their real aim was the eventual purchase of the South Manchuria Railway from Japan that Harriman had failed to secure in 1905. They thought that purchase of the Chinese Eastern Railway from Russia would drive the Japanese to sell their railway. In case this approach proved ineffective, Harriman planned to construct a railway between Jinzhou and Aigun. Harriman's death in September, 1909, however, left Straight as virtually the sole proponent of the scheme. Straight singlehandedly concluded a preliminary agreement with the Manchurian Provincial Government for the financing and construction of the Jinzhou–Aigun line. But the American bankers now grew cautious without Harriman to lead them.[6]

## 7.1.2. The Knox Proposal

In November 1909, Knox made a surprising proposal for the neutralization or internationalization of all Manchurian railroads. The success of this proposal hinged on British cooperation, French and German support, Russian willingness to sell the Chinese Eastern Railway, and Japanese consent to give up the South Manchuria Railway.[7] Britain was the first to respond, saying that it would do nothing until it had ascertained the views of the other governments concerned, and in particular "what measure of participation would satisfy the Japanese government in regard to this undertaking."[8] This reply reflected the high value Great Britain assigned to its alliance with Japan.[9] The Japanese and Russian rejections came in January 1910, after consultations that produced almost identical notes presented on the same day. The Japanese and the Russians had also gained British approval for their proposed course of action.[10] The French stood by their Russian ally, and the Germans were not prepared to challenge the world on behalf of American investment opportunities. Japan and Russia concluded a secret agreement—ironically on July 4, 1910—laying down a firm division of spheres in Manchuria and providing for cooperation between them if they were challenged by any third party.[11] Instead of dividing Russia and Japan and opening the door to American participation in the financial exploitation of Manchuria, Knox had converted the Russo–Japanese rivalry into solidarity, and "nailed that door closed with him on the outside."[12] Both Russia and Japan had something to offer Britain: security for India. Griswold writes, "For Knox to have thought that he could persuade (British foreign secretary Edward) Grey to gamble such priceless assets on an American promotional scheme directed against Grey's own allies was a naïve assumption, to say the least."[13]

Knox's Manchurian railway neutralization proposal openly ignored the rights secured by Japan in the Portsmouth Treaty. Japan responded to this challenge by signing the Russo–Japanese Agreement of 1910. Japan also showed its displeasure by switching the procurement of railway materials for the South Manchuria Railway from American to British suppliers in 1910, and by not giving American manufacturers a share of the orders for the Andong–Mukden railway in 1911.[14] Japan's reaction to the US challenge did not go beyond these acts, but the Taft administration's Chinese policy certainly disappointed pro-American Japanese and increased wariness and mistrust toward America among anti-American Japanese.

Theodore Roosevelt worried about the negative impact of Dollar Diplomacy on US–Japanese relations. In a December 1910 letter, Roosevelt reminded Taft that Japan's interests on the Asian continent were vital, whereas US interests there, especially in Manchuria, were "really unimportant, and not

Chapter 7

such that the American people would be content to run the slightest risk of collision about them."[15] Roosevelt warned that Japan could be a serious threat to the security of the United States, and that to challenge Japan in Manchuria required tremendous military power, equivalent to the combined strength of the British navy and the German army. Roosevelt advised recognition of Japan's special interests in Manchuria in return for Japanese cooperation in controlling their troublesome emigration to California.[16]

Despite Theodore Roosevelt's concern, no serious frictions occurred in Japan–US bilateral relations while Taft was in office. Assisted by Britain, Japan generally behaved discreetly. The diplomacy of the Taft administration matured in its latter period. Huntington Wilson first contended that China, which owned Manchuria, needed it more than Japan did. But he later changed his position and conceded Japan's special position in Manchuria. It might have been that Wilson's experience in handling the Panama Canal problems demonstrated to him that Japanese interests in China were analogous to American interests in Panama.[17]

### 7.1.3. The Hukuang Railway Loan and the Downfall of the Qing Dynasty

In May of 1909, after long and complex negotiations, a consortium of British, French, and German bankers signed a contract with the Chinese government for the construction of the Hukuang Railways.[18] The United States government, which had shown little interest in the project while the negotiations were going on, now demanded American participation on equal terms in the arrangement already concluded. With the prodding of the State Department, a grouping of American bankers was formed with the goal of joining the European consortium, and Straight was made the group's agent. The Europeans were in no mood to welcome the Americans, because they knew that admitting them would inevitably lead to the entry of Japan and Russia.[19] Undeterred, Taft personally cabled Prince Chun, the regent of China, insisting on "equal participation by American capital in the present railway loan."[20] But Chun dared not offend the European powers. Negotiations dragged on for two years until May 1911, when an agreement admitting the United States to the Hukuang railway loan was finally concluded. In the next year, the Russians and the Japanese entered the project.[21]

By the time the Americans were admitted to the consortium, however,

*160*

opposition to the Hukuang loan had developed throughout China. Opposition was especially strong in the provinces, where some work had already been done on these lines under provincial charters. The provincial governments and local shareholders resented the Beijing government's move to nationalize the railways in order to use them as security for the loan. There was also a "rights-recovery" movement that demanded that only Chinese capital and engineers build the vital lines. A revolutionary movement led by Sun Yat-sen to establish a republican government had by then undermined the already shaky Manchu regime. Under such circumstances, the consortium powers' pressure on the Qing government for acceptance of the Hukuang loan triggered widespread disorder in Sichuan province. In October, as efforts were underway to pacify Sichuan, a military revolt began in Wuchang. The revolt spread through south China, and within a few months, the era of Manchu rule ended (11.1.1).[22]

Dollar diplomacy aimed to weaken Japan's hold in China, but in fact it strengthened it instead by bringing Japan and Russia closer together. It aimed to defend the integrity of China and promote Chinese welfare, but it helped bring about disorder and revolution, leading to the downfall of the Qing dynasty.

# 7.2. The Twenty-One Demands

### 7.2.1. WWI and Japan's Presentation of the Twenty-One Demands

World War I started on July 28, 1914 when Austria-Hungary declared war on Serbia.[23] Germany supported Austria-Hungary, and Russia supported Serbia. Other European powers soon entered the war in accordance with their respective alliances and ententes. WWI was now fought between the Allied powers—including Russia, France, Britain, and Serbia—on one hand and the Central powers—including Germany, Austria-Hungary, and the Ottoman Empire—on the other.

Japan declared war on Germany on August 23 on the grounds of its alliance with Britain, and offered its assistance to Britain. Obviously concerned about Japanese ambitions in China, British foreign secretary Edward Grey proposed that Japan limit its military operations to a naval campaign against German vessels in the China Seas. But the Japanese government insisted on attacking Jiaozhou (膠州), a German leased territory in Shandong (山東), and the German islands in the Pacific.[24] Grey acquiesced. Grey suggested that the Japanese insert in the demand for the surrender of Jiaozhou the clause, "With a view to eventual restoration of the same to China."[25] The Japanese agreed to follow this suggestion. By December, Japan occupied the entire province of Shandong and most of the German islands north of the equator.

On January 18, 1915, Japan presented the Twenty-One Demands to China.[26] Some understanding with China over the occupied territory in Shandong was needed sooner or later, and it appeared to be a good time to resolve Japanese anxieties about its position in Manchuria. The Japanese leases of Port Arthur and Dalian (大連) were to expire in 1923, and the lease of the South Manchuria Railway would expire in 1940.[27]

Foreign Minister Katō Takaaki (加藤高明) had obtained Grey's understanding about negotiations with China for the extension of the leases in Manchuria in 1913, while he was in London as the Japanese ambassador.[28] However, the demands that Katō presented to China included several matters other than the Shandong and Manchuria questions. The demands consisted of five groups.

Group I referred to Shandong. Japan required China to recognize Japan's right to settle the disposition of German rights in Shandong with Germany (Article 1), not to cede or lease any portion of Shandong to any third party (Article 2), to grant to Japan the right to construct a railway from Yantai or Longkou connecting with the Jianzhou–Jinan line (Article 3), and to open additional treaty ports in Shandong (Article 4).

Group II concerned South Manchuria and Eastern Inner Mongolia. Japan requested that China recognize the extension of the leases of Port Arthur, Dalian, the South Manchuria Railway, and the Mukden–Andong Railway to ninety-nine years (Article 1);[29] Japan's right to own land, reside, travel and conduct business in South Manchuria and East Mongolia (Articles 2 and 3); Japan's right to acquire mining concessions in these regions (Article 4); Japan's right to consent to China's granting other nationals the right to construct any railways in these regions, or to receive loans from any other power (Article 5); Japan's right to consent to China hiring political, financial, or military advisors in these regions (Article 6); and Japan's control of the Jilin–Changchun Railway for a period of ninety-nine years (Article 7).

Group III dealt with the Hanyehping Company.[30] China was to agree that "when the opportune moment arrives," the Hanyehping Company was to become a Sino–Japanese joint venture (Article 1), and China was to permit no mines in the vicinity to be worked by any other interest without the company's consent (Article 2).

Group IV pledged that China would not cede or lease any harbor or bay or any island along the coast of China to any other power.

Group V differed from the preceding four groups in that it was categorized as "wishes," and it included some items that appeared to threaten the administrative integrity of China.[31] It asked that China employ "competent" Japanese as political, financial, and military advisers (Article 1); that China grant the right to own land to existing Japanese hospitals, temples, and schools (Article 2); that China agree to establish joint Sino–Japanese police forces in certain unspecified locations (Article 3); that China procure from Japanese suppliers a certain quantity of arms, or establish an arsenal in China under joint Japanese and Chinese management (Article 4); that China grant to Japan the right to construct railways in the Yangtze area connecting Wuchang with the Nanchang–Jiujiang line and railways between Nanchang and Hangzhou and between Nanchang and Chaozhou (Article 5); that China agree to consult Japan before negotiating any foreign loan for internal improvements in Fujian province (Article 6);[32] and that China grant to Japan the right to proselytize for Buddhism in China (Article 7).

Mystery surrounds the origins of Group V of the demands. Katō said, after he had resigned from office, that Group V was included as a result of concessions made to "internal politics," implying that he had deferred to the pressure from the army and nationalist groups like the Kokuryūkai (黒龍会).[33] It is also widely assumed that Group V had been inserted as bargaining chips either to be negotiated away entirely or to be modified drastically to make it easier for China to accept other demands that were vital to Japanese interests.[34]

### 7.2.2. British and American Reactions to the Twenty-One Demands

Japan informed Britain of the demands on January 22, when the Japanese ambassador in London delivered a Katō memorandum to the British Foreign Office. The memorandum was, however, missing Article 2 of Group III and the entirety of Group V. Grey commented only that he was anxious that Japan should not fall into bad relations with China.[35] A week later, however, the British minister in Beijing reported that the Japanese were demanding from China more than the memorandum had listed.[36] The Japanese had secured

*163*

from Yuan Shikai a pledge not to disclose the contents of the demands to any third party. But Beijing was not a place where secrets could be kept. Grey sent a telegram to Katō saying that he wished to support Japan, but could not do so unless he was satisfied that any demands made did not clash with the objectives of the alliance. This was a courteous but strong protest to Japan.[37]

The American reaction was quite different from that of Britain. On February 8, the Japanese government delivered in Washington the same memorandum as Japan had given Britain. The State Department, however, had already been informed of the Japanese demands on January 23 by a cable from the American minister in Beijing.[38] The cable strongly condemned the Japanese action, saying, "The demands are stated to be such as could not be granted without abandoning entirely the open door as well as independence in political and industrial matters."[39]

The American minister in Beijing, Paul Reinsch, was a scholar of political science, and had no diplomatic experience when he was chosen as minister in China in 1913 by President Wilson, a fellow political scientist. In Beijing, the inexperienced and moralistic Reinsch quickly came under the spell of American-educated Chinese officials, particularly the able young diplomat V. K. Wellington Koo.[40]

Reinsch's alarm produced an immediate reaction from E. T. Williams,[41] the chief of the Division of Far Eastern Affairs at the State Department in Washington. Williams was a former China missionary who had entered diplomatic service late in life. He was radically pro-Chinese.[42] He submitted a memorandum to Secretary William Jennings Bryan proposing that the United States intervene directly in the Sino–Japanese negotiations as the custodian of the Open Door in China.[43]

Bryan was a veteran politician, having dominated the Democratic Party for nearly twenty years before handing the 1912 presidential nomination to Governor Woodrow Wilson of New Jersey. He believed that the American national interest required friendly relations with both Japan and China.[44] He was concerned about President Wilson's vulnerability to Reinsch's emotional and exaggerated anti-Japanese reports.

In fact, on January 27, Wilson told Bryan that he thought the United States should side with China, and at the same time asked Bryan to have Lansing prepare a memo about Japan's position vis-à-vis the Open Door. Of Japan, Wilson knew practically nothing,[45] and of China he knew very little apart from what he had learned in church circles or directly from China missionaries.[46]

Robert Lansing was an international lawyer then serving as counselor of the State Department.[47] The Lansing memorandum reported that Japan had entered numerous agreements that ostensibly committed her to maintain the Open-Door principles.[48] Wilson was somewhat confused, and tried to obtain Britain's view about the Japanese demands, but to no avail. The British did not like to take the Americans into their confidence on so delicate a matter. They did not appreciate the Americans' "missionary-mind" diplomacy.[49]

After much debate within the US administration, a note was given to the Japanese ambassador on March 13. The note condemned Articles 1, 3, 4 and 6 of Group V, and refused to accept Group IV.[50] As to Groups I and II, however, the note said that the US government was "disposed to raise no question, at this time." Further, no objection was raised to Group III, or Articles 2, 5 and 7 of Group V. Though the tone of the note was not friendly, the Japanese government was relieved to find that the United States made no clear objection to Group I or II.[51]

Reinsch, however, immediately sent a blistering dispatch, insisting that the US note "would definitely set a term to the existence of China as a free country. Should they become aware that the American government favors an adjustment . . . I fear that such knowledge would produce in the minds of the Chinese a conviction that the United States had betrayed its historic friendship and its moral responsibility in respect to principles of China's administrative integrity and the open door."[52]

Reinsch's cable worked.[53] Wilson told Bryan that Bryan henceforth should "set the matter in the right light alike in Reinsch's mind and in the mind of the Chinese."[54] The US policy was now switched to wholesale rejection of the Japanese agenda. Now the Chinese suddenly became recalcitrant, refusing further concessions to the Japanese, and even reopening some points which had already been agreed upon. The change in the Chinese attitude perplexed the Japanese diplomats, who could not understand what had happened.[55] In Tokyo, Katō was under bitter attack. The militarists and nationalists condemned him for being too weak. The *genrō* (元老 senior statesmen), who were anxious to maintain friendship with the Western powers, condemned him for his aggressive policy.

After all, Japan made revisions as below, and on May 7 issued an

Chapter 7

ultimatum. All items of group V except the one related to Fujian province (item 6) were dropped. Fujian was considered a Japanese sphere of influence. As a quid pro quo, Japan offered to restore the leasehold of Jiaozhou to China. Regarding group II, the demand for the right to residence and ownership of land in East Inner Mongolia was dropped. Instead, the establishment of joint Japanese and Chinese agricultural and industrial enterprises was proposed. The demand regarding the Hanyehping Company's rights to mine development (Article 2 of group III) was dropped. China's pledge not to cede or lease any harbor or bay or any island along the coast of China (group IV) was now modified to permit China to make such a declaration on its own initiative.[56] China accepted the ultimatum, and the treaties embodying groups I–IV were signed on May 25, 1915.

The United States forwarded the so-called Bryan Note. It was drafted by Lansing, who suggested Bryan should send it to Japan. The note told Japan that any agreement forced upon China would become the subject of future discussion with the United States.[57] This stance led to the Lansing–Ishii negotiations of 1917 (7.3.1). The Bryan note was the first "non-recognition" declaration in US diplomatic history. This approach was again to be adopted by Secretary of State Stimson in 1932 (13.4.1).

The Twenty-One Demands were carefully drafted by the Japanese government so as to avoid material effects on the United States. So far as Groups I through IV were concerned, no articles clearly contravened the Japanese interpretation of the principles of the Open Door. However, the American missionary-mind diplomacy was too unorthodox and unfamiliar for the Japanese foreign-policy elites to deal with successfully. They were students of the traditional diplomacy of European-style imperialism.

The imperialist British were more accommodating toward the Japanese. In fact, after Japan had modified its demands, Grey instructed the British minister in Beijing to exert all his influence on China to accept Japanese demands. What disappointed Grey was not so much the presentation of the demands to China as Katō's failure to consult him before the presentation of the demands, and, in particular, Katō's concealment of Group V and Article 2 of Group III in his initial memorandum.[58] Katō's method contravened Article I of the Anglo–Japanese alliance, which referred to joint consultation on all matters of common concern.[59] Grey must have been rendered unsure of the viability of the alliance. Though the Japanese actions did not shatter the alliance, the

166

old basis of confidence was severely shaken.[60]

# 7.3. Japan's Relations with the Powers during WWI and the Paris Peace Conference

## 7.3.1. The Lansing–Ishii Agreement

Soon after the United States entered World War I in April 1917, Foreign Minister Ishii Kikujirō (石井菊次郎), who had taken over for Katō as the foreign minister in October 1915, approached Washington asking for a discussion on Far East affairs. Ishii, taking advantage of Japan's status as an ally of the United States, wished to have the US recognize Japan's special relations with China.[61] Lansing agreed to have extended discussions in Washington. While Lansing was prepared to make compromises concerning the Japanese claims to rights in South Manchuria and Eastern Inner Mongolia,[62] Wilson remained unchanged in his determination not to allow any Japanese encroachment on China's integrity.[63] Negotiations lasted for two months, but they could not narrow their differences. To avoid the breakdown of the talks, they chose to resort to the use of diplomatic ambiguity. On November 2, 1917, Lansing and Ishii affixed their signatures to a joint declaration that the United States recognized that "territorial propinquity creates special relations between countries, and, consequently, the government of the United States recognizes that Japan has special interests in China."[64] At the same time, Japan pledged, in a separate protocol, to adhere to a lengthy declaration of respect for the Open Door and the independence and territorial integrity of China. In a violation of Wilson's principle that henceforth international agreements should be open and openly arrived at, the Americans accepted Ishii's insistence that the protocol be kept secret.[65]

The Lansing–Ishii agreement was a stopgap measure covering up US–Japanese differences with a veneer of apparent harmony.[66] It ended, albeit temporarily, the bickering over China, helping to maintain the appearance of US–Japanese wartime cooperation. It represented, on the part of Japan, the Terauchi cabinet's desire to mend fences with the United States.[67] On the part of the United States, the belief that it pledged Japan to the Open Door and the integrity of China soothed Washington's concerns and facilitated concentration on the fighting in Europe.

The Lansing–Ishii agreement did not, however, stop Japan's expansive

*167*

moves in China. Its ambiguity allowed Japan to construe it to suit its own purposes.[68] In fact, Japan maintained its strong hold on South Manchuria and East Inner Mongolia as well as Shandong, and it continued the practice of obtaining concessions from the Beijing warlords in return for loans.[69]

### 7.3.2. The Four-Power Consortium

Great Britain and France, which were unable to spare funds for loans to China, were concerned about Japan's "yen diplomacy." Powerless to prevent it themselves, they urged the United States to return to the consortium from which Wilson had withdrawn soon after taking office.[70] In November 1917, Wilson approved the State Department's plan to form a new four-power consortium of Britain, France, Japan, and the United States.[71] It was a proposition that each national group of the consortium of banks should receive the support of its government, that all preferences and options in China held by the member banks should be pooled, and that the administrative integrity and independence of China should be respected.[72] For the Japanese, however, any such pooling of preferences and options amounted to the same thing as Knox's Manchurian railway neutralization scheme (7.1.2).[73] It would undermine Japan's strong financial position in China, which Japan had established through independent loans to the Chinese government. Prolonged Japanese–American negotiations ensued, in which Japan attempted to obtain the exclusion of Manchuria and Mongolia from the application of the scheme. An agreement was finally reached in March 1920 to exclude the South Manchuria Railway zone and a number of other specified railway projects, as well as their related mining and industrial privileges in Manchuria and Mongolia, from the scope of the scheme.[74] The Japanese sphere of interest in Manchuria and Mongolia thus specified and recognized by the consortium was endorsed later at the Washington Conference of 1921–22 by the four "Root principles," which recognized all the generally accepted spheres of interest in China (7.4.4).[75]

### 7.3.3. The Siberia Expedition

The American military intervention in Siberia was another attempt to limit Japanese expansion in East Asia. In Russia, after the October Revolution of 1917, civil war ensued between the provisional government and the Bolsheviks. While the former continued fighting against Germany, the latter called for ending the war. The Allies asked the United States and Japan to send

*168*

an expeditionary force to Russia to help the provisional government,[76] but Wilson refused the request, saying that it would constitute interference in Russian internal affairs. However, in June 1918, when there arose the need to rescue Czechoslovakian troops—some 50,000 men who had deserted from the Austrian forces to fight under the Russian flag[77]—Wilson agreed to send an expedition, and invited Japan to join it. Wilson's decision was not so much motivated by a wish to rescue the Czechs as by his realization that intervention would take place regardless of his views, and by his judgment, as in the case of the four-power consortium, that the US could impose greater restraint on Japan from within, rather than outside, the expedition.[78]

In July 1918, Wilson, dispatching a US force of about 7,000 for Vladivostok, suggested that Japan send a force of similar size to the same area. The Japanese government conveyed to the US government its plan to send 10,000 to 12,000 men to Vladivostok.[79] Once the expedition was begun, however, the Japanese army sent more than three and a half divisions into the Amur Basin,[80] and then proceeded to secure the railway network. This deployment caused a strong US protest and a request for reduction of the Japanese forces.

In September 1918, Seiyūkai president Hara Takashi took over the cabinet[81] and shifted the course of foreign policy toward one of cooperation with the United States. He began to reduce the number of troops in Siberia, and in February 1919, he signed an American-sponsored agreement to entrust the operation of the Trans-Siberia and Chinese Eastern railways to an inter-Allied commission.[82] Wilson did not respond favorably to Hara's cooperative posture, however. When Wilson withdrew the American forces in January 1920, he did not inform the Japanese government of his decision.[83] This was an affront to the Hara cabinet. The interventionists now called for an independent policy more strongly than before.[84] Japan kept its expeditionary forces in place until October of 1922.

### 7.3.4. The Paris Peace Conference

The peace conference in Paris, which began in January 1919, also became an arena where the diplomatic duel between the United States and Japan over China was fiercely contested. Wilson attended the conference in person. The principal members of the American delegation were Secretary of State Lansing; Colonel Edward House, Wilson's personal advisor; General Tesker

Bliss; and Henry White, a diplomat. In what many commentators regarded as a political blunder, Wilson did not include anyone from the Senate or any leading Republican Party members.[85] The Japanese delegation was headed by Saionji Kinmochi (西園寺公望), and the chief negotiator was Makino Nobuaki (牧野伸顕), the foreign minister before Katō and a member of the House of Peers. The Japanese were armed not only with the Anglo–Japanese Alliance and various faits accomplis in East Asia, but also with secret treaties with the European allies that bound them to support Japanese demands on the German concessions Japan had occupied, as well as agreements with China, both open and secret.[86]

The Chinese delegation was a combination of officials from the Beijing government and representatives of influential warlords in the southern provinces.[87] It was quickly dominated by two intensely patriotic young Western-educated members, Wellington Koo and C. T. Wang. They were determined to use the peace conference as an occasion to undo the offensive treaties with Japan. They took full advantage of Woodrow Wilson's moralistic arguments.[88] Indeed, they were greatly helped in Paris by the Americans, who encouraged them to resist the Japanese.[89]

Wilson, having succeeded in gaining acceptance of the League of Nations Covenant, tried to parry the Japanese thrust for Shandong and the German islands with the mandate principle, according to which the conquered German territories would become wards of the international community as mandates under the League Covenant. However, he met strong opposition from the European powers, which wanted direct control of conquered territories, and he had to accept modifications of his proposals. The German islands became a Japanese Class C League Mandate, in the class subject to integration into the mandatory power's own territory. Shandong was excluded from the mandate system at the insistence of the Japanese, who were supported by the European colonial powers.

Wilson was then confronted by a Japanese demand for international recognition of the principle of racial equality. Japan proposed that the League Covenant declare the following:

> The equality of nations being a basic principle of the League of Nations, the High Contracting Parties agree to accord, as soon as possible, to all alien nationals of States members of the League equal and

just treatment in every respect, making no distinction, either in law or in fact, on account of their race or nationality.[90]

Wilson was at first sympathetic to the Japanese proposition. After a short trip home, however, he recognized that the racist southern wing of his Democratic Party, with its power in the Senate, would never approve of such an international commitment. Moreover, the British dominions of Australia and New Zealand, with their restrictive immigration policies, were strongly opposed, and were supported in their opposition by London. The amendment was brought to a vote, and was agreed to by eleven of the nations and opposed by six.[91] Nevertheless, Wilson, who was presiding over the meeting, ruled against adopting it because it had failed to pass unanimously.

A few days after the defeat of the racial equality amendment, the Japanese delegates brought up their claim to Shandong with very evident determination to see it honored or to withdraw from the conference. Since January, when the claim had first been presented and attacked by the Chinese delegates, the possibilities of a compromise between the two sides had been steadily diminishing. With public opinion in China now being enthusiastically in support of the strong stand taken by Koo and Wang, the Chinese now demanded the complete abrogation of the offensive treaties with Japan. Wilson was faced with the choice of rejecting Japan's claim and seeing the Japanese quit the conference, or accepting it and having his acceptance become a target for his American enemies. Every other participant, including Britain and France, was supportive of Japan's position on Shandong.[92] On April 30, Wilson accepted the Japanese terms exactly as they had been stipulated by the Japanese delegates.[93]

In China, on May 1, the news reached Beijing that the Chinese delegates acknowledged their case as hopeless because of the prior agreements. This news triggered mass protests in Beijing on May 4, beginning what came to be called the May Fourth Movement, which were followed by demonstrations in cities all over China. When the Treaty of Versailles was signed, the Chinese delegates were not present. The Treaty of Versailles was finalized without China's acceptance.[94] In the United States, the Senate voted down ratification of the Treaty of Versailles definitively on March 19, 1920. The Senate opponents referred to the Shandong issue as one of their reasons for rejecting the treaty.[95]

# 7.4. The Washington Conference

### 7.4.1. The US and British Aims of the Washington Conference

A series of American efforts to restrain Japan in China, which had begun with Dollar Diplomacy and had been followed by the Four-Power Consortium, the Siberia Expedition, and the attempt to restore Shandong to China at the Paris Conference, culminated in the Washington Conference of 1921–1922. The Washington Conference discussed two more important issues, the Anglo–Japanese Alliance and naval disarmament.

After World War I, the major naval powers, especially the United States, Great Britain, and Japan, continued extensive naval construction programs that they had embarked upon at the close of the war, each being unwilling to stop while the others did not. The British still held naval supremacy, but they could now ill afford a gigantic naval race, having lost much blood in WWI; they were now prepared to accept parity with the United States, abandoning their traditional policy.[96]

Closely related to the naval disarmament issue was the question of the renewal of the Anglo–Japanese Alliance, whose existence or nonexistence would fundamentally alter the naval balance. The alliance was to expire in 1921, and the United States was unequivocally opposed to its renewal. It had always been in the way of the US attempts to restrain Japan's aggressive Chinese policy. British leaders were basically in favor of the renewal.[97] Though the defeat of Germany and the Russian revolution had invalidated two of the principal reasons for which the Alliance had originally been concluded, Japan could still be a bulwark against the spread of communism to China and India.[98] They also believed that the alliance was useful for checking reckless Japanese activities in Asia.[99] In the imperial conference at which British dominion leaders met in London in 1921,[100] the Pacific dominions of Australia and New Zealand supported the renewal for that reason, but Canada opposed continuation of the alliance for fear of being put in a difficult position as a result of any deterioration of Anglo–American relations that the renewal might cause.[101] In the end, the conference resolved that a Pacific and Far Eastern conference attended by countries with Pacific interests should be convened to review the Anglo–Japanese Alliance.[102] Foreign Secretary Lord Curzon sounded the opinion of the United States, Japan, and China about the idea of holding such a conference in London. Japan withheld a reply.

*172*

In the United States, meanwhile, despite the country's defection from the League of Nations and Wilson's defeat in the presidential election, there was a consensus in Washington about the need for arms reduction to prevent another world war. In December 1920, Republican Senator William Borah introduced a resolution calling for an Anglo–American–Japanese disarmament conference. By mid-1921, the resolution was approved unanimously in the Senate, and received only four dissenting votes in the House.[103] An invitation was sent by Secretary of State Charles Evans Hughes to London, Paris, Rome, and Tokyo for a naval disarmament conference in Washington.

Curzon then proposed holding a Pacific and Far Eastern conference to discuss the Anglo–Japanese alliance question in London in advance of the naval disarmament conference in Washington. Hughes opposed this idea, however, and insisted on discussing both subjects at one conference in Washington. Curzon deferred to Hughes.[104] Four more nations—Belgium, Portugal, the Netherlands, and China—were invited to Washington.

Japan received the proposals from Britain (on July 8) and then from the United States (on July 11) as something of a shock. Japanese newspapers sensationally described them as an Anglo–American conspiracy against Japan.[105] The Japanese government leadership reacted calmly, but they felt that Japan should have been consulted more properly before it received the invitations.[106] They especially considered insensitive and improper the fact that Curzon had directly approached China without first clearing the move with Britain's ally, Japan.[107] The internationalists in Japan argued, however, that Japan should participate positively in the conference and take advantage of it to improve Japan's international image, which had deteriorated since World War I.[108] These views were shared by Hara, but conservative leaders, including Foreign Minister Uchida Yasuya (内田康哉), were cautious. They wanted to be informed in advance of the agenda of the conference in Washington. Though the US reply to the Japanese inquiry was that it would not prearrange the agenda, the Japanese government accepted the invitation in late July on the understanding that matters that were regarded as accomplished facts and those relating primarily to individual powers would be excluded from the agenda of the open conference.[109]

Hara and Uchida selected as plenipotentiaries Admiral Katō Tomosaburō (加藤友三郎), the navy minister;[110] Shidehara Kijūrō, the ambassador in Washington;[111] and Tokugawa Iesato (徳川家達), the president of the House

*173*

of Peers.[112] Katō was the real head of the delegation, though Tokugawa, being highest in rank, was announced as chief delegate. Katō had presided over the naval expansion program during the war, advocating preparedness against the United States, but he was well aware that Japan could not financially continue an indefinite naval arms race with the United States.[113] He was also convinced that Japan's naval strength had to be seen in the context of political relationships. It seemed that there was no one else who could convince both the military party and the politicians to accept the result of disarmament negotiations in the conference. Shidehara was an automatic choice as Katō's partner in view of Katō's lack of diplomatic experience. Tokugawa was head of the delegation on a largely honorific basis. Japan later sent Hanihara Masanao (埴原正直), the incumbent vice foreign minister, to help Shidehara in dealing with Chinese issues.

The American delegation was headed by Charles Evans Hughes, who was as senior an American political figure as had ever negotiated with Japan. He had been governor of New York and an associate judge of the Supreme Court, and in the presidential election in 1916, as the Republican candidate, he had lost to Woodrow Wilson by a very narrow margin. Other senior members of the American delegation were former secretary of state Elihu Root;[114] Henry Cabot Lodge, chairman of the Senate foreign relations committee; and Senator Oscar W. Underwood, ranking Democratic member of that committee and the leading advocate of free trade. Britain's principal representative was former prime minister Arthur J. Balfour,[115] with the other plenipotentiaries being Arthur Lee, first lord of the admiralty, and Auckland Geddes, the ambassador to the United States.

## 7.4.2. Naval Disarmament and Abrogation of the Anglo–Japanese Treaty

The conference opened on November 12, 1921, with an address by Hughes in which he made a dramatic proposal for naval disarmament. He presented a program for reducing the tonnage of capital ships to 500,000 tons for the United States and Britain and 300,000 tons for Japan by scrapping many of the capital ships (warships weighing over 10,000 tons) already built or partially completed.[116] It also called for a ten-year moratorium on the building of those ships. The tripartite negotiations between Hughes, Balfour, and Katō started on November 19. With Britain having already accepted the principle of naval parity with the United States, Hughes's main task in the negotiations

*174*

was to obtain Japan's assent to his plan. Katō first insisted on a 10:10:7 ratio. The idea of 70 percent rested on the premise that the approaching enemy armada would need a margin of at least 50 percent superiority over the defending fleet. This ratio assured Japan of strength insufficient to attack but adequate for defense.[117] But he eventually accepted a 60 percent ratio on December 15,[118] after obtaining an agreement on the retention of the battleship *Mutsu*, then the world's most powerful battleship,[119] and US and British pledges to freeze the status quo of their fortifications and naval bases in the Pacific.[120] France and Italy accepted 35 percent as their capital ship strength, and the Five-Power Treaty was signed February 5, 1922.

The first of the achievements of the conference was the Four-Power Treaty signed on December 13. When this treaty, the successor to the Anglo–Japanese Treaty, was announced, the public was taken completely by surprise, as the subject had not been suggested anywhere in the agenda. The negotiations were conducted in private by a very few persons. Liberals in Japan who believed in the new diplomacy of Wilsonian ideals considered the alliance a symbol of the old diplomacy that might as well be discarded, but most of the Japanese leadership believed that Japanese interests were best served by keeping the status quo to the greatest extent possible. In view of US opposition to the Anglo–Japanese alliance, however, they conceded that they might have to accept some kind of substitute for the alliance, such as an Anglo–Japanese–American understanding.

The Japanese government's instructions to the delegates regarding the alliance were broad and ambiguous, reflecting the division of opinions between the liberal and conservative schools within the government.[121] Japan's instructions to its plenipotentiaries stated that, while the old alliance in amended form could continue, a triple entente would be welcome. If Britain favored replacing the alliance with the entente, Japan would agree. The instructions did not suggest, however, any voluntary termination of the alliance by Japan.[122]

The British delegates were given no detailed instructions except that they should place top priority on concluding a successful disarmament agreement and maintaining a good relationship with the United States. Concerning the Japanese alliance, Balfour was given a great deal of discretion, which he used to the fullest.[123] He drew up a draft of a triple entente during his voyage across the Atlantic and handed it to Hughes at his first meeting with him on November 11. It stated that the three powers should "consult fully and frankly with each other as to the best means of protecting" rights of each power in the Pacific and Far Eastern region (article I), and that if the said rights of any of the contracting parties were "threatened by any other Power or combination of Powers," any two of the contracting parties should "be at liberty to protect themselves by entering into a military alliance," which was defensive in character (Article II). Though it did not commit the US to military operations, it left it open to Britain to renew a defensive alliance with Japan. Hughes did not like the Balfour proposal, which must have seemed too close to a military alliance, and he asked Balfour not to pass it to the Japanese "for the present."[124]

It was not until November 22 that the Balfour draft was passed over to Japan. Shidehara recognized that it would not be acceptable to the United States. Although suffering from gallstones that kept him confined to bed, he prepared a counter-draft that did not include the military option clause.[125] Balfour agreed to it and suggested its submission to Hughes as a Shidehara–Balfour draft. Hughes basically accepted it, but requested some modifications. He confined the region of the treaty to the Pacific and included France among the contracting parties, in order to facilitate the passage of the treaty through the US Senate.[126]

Article I of the treaty provided that if a controversy should develop between the contracting parties involving their rights in the Pacific region, the parties would consult to solve them. Article II provided that if the said rights were threatened by the aggressive action of any other power, the contracting parties would communicate with each other fully and frankly in order to arrive at an understanding as to the most efficient measures to be taken, jointly or separately, to meet the exigencies of the particular situation. Article III provided that the treaty would remain in force for ten years. Article IV provided that the Anglo–Japanese alliance would be terminated with the ratification of the treaty.

How did the alliance come to be dropped by the British and Japanese negotiators? Balfour had been told by the cabinet that Britain needed disarmament more than it needed the Japanese alliance. Though he had conceived of a scheme to enable Britain to revive the alliance, he realized in Washington that adherence to the alliance would make it difficult to bring a disarmament agreement to a satisfactory conclusion.[127] He did not want to hurt the feelings of the Japanese by proposing an end to the alliance,[128] but he found that Shidehara did not appear to be reluctant to give it up. Shidehara believed firmly that Japan should now discard the old diplomacy. His act could be interpreted as a breach of the instructions that did not authorize a voluntary abrogation of the alliance,[129] but there was no policy alternative in his mind other than going along with the United States.[130] This was in accord with the policy that his recent superior, the late prime minister Hara, had advocated.[131]

### 7.4.3. The Nine-Power Treaty

Another important achievement of the Washington Conference was the Nine-Power Treaty on China discussed by the Committee on Pacific and Far Eastern Questions, which was signed by the conference on February 6, 1922. The Chinese participants in the committee were Alfred Sze, the ambassador to Washington; Wellington Koo; and C. T. Wang. The session started on November 16, 1921, with Sze's presentation of a ten-point "Bill of Rights," which demanded the ending of the unequal treaties and the abolition of all special rights claimed by the powers.

After delegates from other countries expressed their views,[132] Elihu Root was asked to formulate principles embodying the common understanding of the delegates.[133] The principles Root proposed were: the integrity and independence of China, a stable Chinese government; equal commercial opportunity in China, and international cooperation vis-à-vis China. These were incorporated as Article I of the Nine-Power Treaty.[134] Article II pledged the signatories to adhere the principles of Article I, and Article III defined the Open Door carefully—the first explicit definition since the notes of 1899 (6.5.2).

It is noteworthy that Root did not say that the vested rights of powers in China should be cancelled. The fourth clause of Article I (which was called the "security clause") was tantamount to an affirmation of the status quo in China. In one of the sessions, Root stated, in reply to a question from Katō, that the resolutions did not make any alteration to the special interests that the powers had already acquired from China.[135]

China, on the other hand, did not give up trying to obtain the repeal of all special rights of the powers at the Washington Conference. Prior to the conference, Japan had proposed to China to have bilateral negotiations, but China had rejected the Japanese overture.[136] The Chinese believed that President Warren Harding, who had attacked Wilson during his presidential campaign in 1920 for his failure to solve the Shandong question at the Paris

*177*

Conference, was now in a political situation that required his administration to find a solution favorable to China.

The United States persuaded the Chinese representatives to have direct meetings with Japan. The Chinese finally agreed; the bilateral meeting began on December 1 with two American and two British "observers" in the room to allay Chinese objections to direct negotiations with Japan.[137] The meetings were broken off twice, and at one point the three Chinese delegates tendered their resignations, which the Beijing government refused to accept. After considerable exhortation, persuasion, and mediation by the Americans and British,[138] an agreement was at length reached, and was signed on February 6, 1922. It provided for the restitution of the leasehold of Jiaozhou with the exception of the Jinan–Qingdao Railway, which China was to buy from Japan with money obtained from Japanese bankers in the form of a fifteen-year loan secured by a lien on the road, with Japanese technicians and accountants to share in its operation until the loan was repaid in full.

The Chinese delegate brought the Twenty-One Demands to the conference, though they were not on the agenda. China demanded their abrogation, and stipulated the return of Manchuria in particular. Hanihara defended Japan's rights in Manchuria, referring to the fourth clause of article I of the Nine-Power Treaty. Balfour supported Hanihara's contentions.[139]

### 7.4.4. The Achievements of the Washington Conference

On the question of China, having observed the failure of Wilson's overly idealistic attempt, Elihu Root took a pragmatic approach to reach an agreement. He sought to ensure stability in Asia, but he did not attempt to change what had already been achieved by the powers. Root's four principles protected China's sovereignty, but they permitted the powers to hold on to their existing interests in China. The approach that Root adopted was that of the old diplomacy of Theodore Roosevelt, rather than Wilson's new diplomacy. Root knew that the Japanese would not sign the treaties without being assured of the rights that they had already obtained through the treaties between Japan and China.

Hughes approved the cautious approach taken by Root concerning the Asia issues, but he adopted a more decisive approach concerning naval disarmament and the Anglo–Japanese alliance. He was successful in linking those two issues. His statement on naval disarmament received such enthusiastic

*178*

support in America as well as in other countries that it created an atmosphere in which the Japanese delegates felt hesitant to stick to the Anglo–Japanese alliance, which was closely connected to the question of the capital ships ratio. Shidehara was convinced that the usefulness of the Anglo–Japanese alliance was now quite limited because of Britain's close relationship with the United States. Hattori argues that Shidehara gave up very little by ending the alliance, considering the improvement in US–Japanese relations.[140]

The Washington Conference greatly reduced international tensions in Asia by achieving naval disarmament, terminating the imperialistic Anglo–Japanese alliance, and settling the Shandong problem.

In Japan, supporters of the new diplomacy in government leadership prevailed over proponents of the old imperialist diplomacy, but how long the former could control the latter would depend on the strength of the support for the new diplomacy by the Japanese public. It did not seem strong enough to withstand future difficulties.

There was one serious question pending between Japan and the United States which was not discussed in the Washington Conference; the question of the Japanese immigration to the United States. Hughes intentionally removed it from the agenda out of fear that it would derail the entire conference. As discussed in the next chapter, two years after signing the Washington treaties, the US Congress voted not to allow new Japanese immigrants into the United States. The 1924 Japanese Exclusion Act was to put severe strain on the relationship between the two countries (8.4).

## NOTES

### 7.1. Dollar Diplomacy

1    Kitaoka Shinichi, "Kokumushō Kyokutōbu no seiritsu" in *Kyōchō seisaku no genkai*, ed. Kindai Nihon Kenkyūkai (Tokyo: Yamakawa Shuppansha, 1989), 3–10.
2    Ibid., 7.
3    A. Whitney Griswold, *Far Eastern Policy of the United States* (New York: Harcourt, Brace & Company, 1938), 136–137.
4    In 1904 he confessed that he had found himself "hating the Japanese more than anything in the world." Walter LaFeber, *The Cambridge History of American Foreign Relations* (Cambridge: Cambridge University Press, 1993), 229.
5    Warren I. Cohen, *America's Response to China* (New York: Columbia University Press, 2010, 1st ed. 1971), 70–71.
6    Griswold, *Far Eastern Policy*, 153.
7    LaFeber, *Cambridge American Foreign Relations*, 229.

*179*

Chapter 7

8   Griswold, *Far Eastern Policy,* 155.

9   Cohen, *America's Response to China,* 73.

10   Griswold, *Far Eastern Policy,* 155.

11   LaFeber, *Cambridge American Foreign Relations,* 230, W. G. Beasley, *Japanese Imperialism 1894–1945* (Oxford: Oxford University Press, 1987), 99.

12   Griswold, *Far Eastern Policy,* 157, LaFeber, *Cambridge American Foreign Relations,* 230.

13   Griswold, *Far Eastern Policy,* 160.

14   Michael H. Hunt, *Frontier Defense and the Open Door* (New Haven: Yale University Press, 1973), 228.

15   Cohen, *America's Response to China,* 73.

16   Ibid., 73.

17   Kitaoka says that a question brought about by the purchase of a vast tract of land adjacent to the Panama Canal by a German businessman, which Wilson had had to solve as assistant secretary of state, might have changed his view of Japan's position in Manchuria. Kitaoka, "Kokumushō Kyokutōbu no seiritsu," in *Kyōchō seisaku no genkai,* 28.

18   The Hukuang Railways stretched from Hankou southward to Guandong and westward to Sichuan.

19   LaFeber, *Cambridge History of American Foreign Relations,* 230.

20   Griswold, *Far Eastern Policy,* 161. Taft said in the cable, "I have resorted to this somewhat unusually direct communication with Your Imperial Highness, because of the high importance that I attach to the successful result of our present negotiations. I have an intense personal interest in making the use of American capital in the development of China an instrument for the promotion of the welfare of China. . . ." Thomas A. Bailey, *A Diplomatic History of the American People,* 10th ed. (Englewood Cliffs, NJ: Prentice-Hall, 1980), 531.

21   Griswold, *Far Eastern Policy,* 163, 171. The Russian and Japanese participation was in June 1912.

22   Cohen, *America's Response to China,* 76–77. Jonathan D. Spence, *The Search for Modern China* (New York: W. W. Norton & Company, 1990), 262–267. LaFeber, *Cambridge American Foreign Relations,* 232.

## 7.2. The Twenty-One Demands

23   WWI was triggered by the Balkan crisis. When the heir to the Austrian throne and his wife were assassinated by a Serbian nationalist in Sarajevo, the capital of Bosnia, on June 28, 1914, Austria-Hungary saw a good opportunity to suppress the Slavic nationalist movement, and declared war against Serbia on July 28, starting WWI. On November 11, 1918, Germany (the new Weimar Republic) surrendered to the Allied powers, ending the war.

24   Griswold, *Far Eastern Policy,* 181.

25   Ibid., 182.

26   Though the Japanese proposals have commonly been labeled as "the Twenty-One Demands," the Japanese government did not use the word "demands." It started with: "The Japanese Government and the Chinese Government, being desirous to

*Notes*

maintain the general peace in the Far East and to strengthen the relations of amity and good neighborhood existing between the two countries, agree to the following:"

27  Masuda Hiroshi and Kimura Masato, *Nihon gaikōshi handbook* (Tokyo: Yūshindō Kōbunsha, 1995), 52.

28  Peter Lowe, *Great Britain and Japan, 1911–1915* (London: Macmillan St Martin's Press, 1969), 221.

29  Ninety-nine years were the terms of the leases of Kowloon (Britain), Jiaozhou (Germany), and Guanzhou (France). Japan wanted its railway concessions to be extended to the same term, cancelling China's right to repurchase them after thirty-six years. Beasley, *Japanese Imperialism*, 112–113.

30  The Hanyehping Company, formed in 1908, was the largest iron mine and ironworks in China at the time, though it was surpassed by the Anshan mine in Manchuria in the mid-1920s. From its inception, the company was heavily indebted, the principal source of loans being Japan. In the loan agreement of 1913 with the Japanese government, the company had undertaken to provide Japan with 17 million tons of iron ore and 8 million tons of crude iron over a period of forty years. Chi-ming Hou, *Foreign Investment and Economic Development in China, 1840–1937* (Cambridge, MA: Harvard University Press, 1956), 75–77. C. F. Remer, *Foreign Investments in China* (New York: Howard Fertig, 1968), 507–508.

31  Beasley, *Japanese Imperialism*, 113.

32  Japan intended to establish a new sphere of influence in Fujian Province because of its geographical closeness to Taiwan. However, competitive French and British interests were already active in the province, and American businesses also had some involvement there.

33  There was a growing view in Japan, among some politicians and Pan-Asiatic expansionist societies such as the Kokuryūkai and the Genyōsha, that Britain was hindering the rise of Japanese dominance in the Far East, and that the Japanese government was too compliant in responding to British pressures. Lowe, *Great Britain and Japan*, 31, 226–227.

34  Kitaoka Shinichi, "Nijūikka saikō" in *Nihon gaikō no kiki ninshiki*, ed. Kindai Nihon Kenkyūkai (Tokyo: Yamakawa Shuppansha, 1985), 124.

35  Grey told Inoue that he recognized the justification for certain of the demands—notably those dealing with south Manchuria, which Katō had spoken to him about before leaving London in 1913—but that he was very anxious that Japan should not get on bad terms with China, as Great Britain, being Japan's ally, would inevitably become involved. Lowe, *Great Britain and Japan*, 229. Article II of the Anglo-Japanese Alliance of 1911 read, "If by reason of unprovoked attack or aggressive action, wherever arising, on the part of any Powers, either High Contracting Party should be involved in war in defense of its territorial rights or special interests mentioned in the preamble of this Agreement, the other High Contracting Party will at once come to the assistance of its ally, and will conduct the war in common, and make peace in mutual agreement with it."

36  Ibid., 231.

37  Ibid., 235.

38  James Reed, *The Missionary Mind and American East Asia Policy, 1911–1915*

Chapter 7

(Cambridge, MA: Harvard University Press, 1983), 164.

39  Ibid., 164–165.

40  Ibid., 163. Reinsch was born the son of a Lutheran pastor, educated in a Lutheran school, and had been a professor at the University of Wisconsin.

41  E. T. Williams was chargé d'affaires in Beijing during the Republican Revolution in China. He became the chief of the State Department's Division of Far Eastern Affairs in 1913.

42  Reed, *Missionary Mind*, 165.

43  Ibid., 166.

44  Ibid., 167.

45  Ibid., 168–169.

46  Tien-yi Li, *Woodrow Wilson's China Policy, 1913–1917* (Kansas City, MO: University of Kansas City Press, 1952), 14–15. In the development of American perceptions of China, the influence of American missionaries in China was quite strong. Americans learned more about China from missionaries than they learned from any other sources. It was customary for individual congregations to receive reports and newsletters giving ongoing accounts of China, and to hear about China in person from missionaries on their septennial furloughs. James Thomson, Jr., Peter Stanley, and John Curtis Perry, *Sentimental Imperialists* (New York: Harper & Row, 1981), 45.

47  Lansing, like the president, was a devout Presbyterian. With respect to the Twenty-One Demands, he positioned himself to faithfully execute Wilson's wishes, providing a clear alternative to Bryan. Reed, *Missionary Mind*, 169–171.

48  Ibid., 171.

49  Ibid., 173.

50  Ibid., 181, Kitaoka, "Nijūikkajō saikō," 138–139.

51  On March 27, Bryan proposed, with Wilson's sanction, some plans for American good offices as mediator with reference to Articles 1, 3, 4 and 6 of Group V. Reed, *Missionary Mind*, 184–186. Kitaoka, "Nijūikkajō saikō," 141–142.

52  Reed, *Missionary Mind*, 186.

53  Wilson was also influenced by a twenty-page cable from a group of prominent missionaries in Beijing, denouncing the Japanese demands as "international highway robbery." The cable (which cost 7,000 dollars and was paid for by Chinese friends) asked Wilson to do his duty "in compliance with the high mandate of the Christian Civilization of the Twentieth Century." Ibid., 188.

54  Ibid., 186–187.

55  Wilson's lapse of memory is said to have also been responsible for his sudden change of attitude. In mid-April, Wilson asked Bryan, "Has Reinsch been told definitely that it is not true that we have acquiesced in any of Japan's demands?" Apparently Wilson did not remember what the United States had declared in the March 13 note. Kitaoka, "Nijūikkajō saikō," 145.

56  Peter Lowe, *Great Britain and Japan, 1911–15* (London: Macmillan, 1969), 264–265. Payson J. Treat, *The Far East* (New York: Harper & Brothers, 1928), 462–463. Reed, *Missionary Mind*, 191.

57  The Bryan note declared: "In view of the circumstances of the negotiations which

*Notes*

have taken place and which are now pending between the Government of Japan and the Government of China, and of the agreements which have been reached as a result thereof, the Government of the United States has the honor to notify the Imperial Japanese Government that it cannot recognize any agreement or undertaking which has been entered into or which may be entered into between the Government of Japan and China, impairing the treaty rights of the United States and its citizens in China, the political or territorial integrity of the Republic of China, or international policy relative to China commonly known as the Open Door policy." Griswold, *Far Eastern Policy*, 194–195.

58　Lowe, *Great Britain and Japan*, 257.

59　Ibid., 232.

60　Ibid., 258.

7.3. Japan's Relations with the Powers during WWI and the Paris Peace Conference

61　Griswold, *Far Eastern Policy*, 214. Burton F. Beers, *Vain Endeavor* (Durham, NC: Duke University Press, 1962), 111–112.

62　Beasley, *Japanese Imperialism*, 164.

63　Wilson even said to Ishii during the preliminary opening conversations that Japan should renounce its claims to "special interests" in China and bind itself not to reassert such claims in the future. Beers, *Vain Endeavor*, 111.

64　Griswold, *Far Eastern Policy*, 216.

65　Tokyo presumably objected to putting this secret understanding in the published notes for fear that such a concession would provoke an embarrassing uproar at home. Bailey, *A Diplomatic History*, 635.

66　Beers, *Vain Endeavor*, 118.

67　Ibid., 118. In October 1916, Terauchi succeeded Ōkuma, who stepped down because of the bitter attacks on him for his domestic and China policy. Terauchi advocated a more moderate line toward China to soften American opposition. Ian H. Nish, *Alliance in Decline: A Study in Anglo–Japanese Relations, 1908–23* (London: Athlone Press, University of London, 1972), 198.

68　Griswold, *Far Eastern Policy*, 216.

69　The so-called Nishihara loan of 1918 totaling over 140 million yen extended to the Duan Qirui regime in Beijing was a typical example of such loans. Beasley, *Japanese Imperialism*, 117.

70　Wilson withdrew US government support from the six-power consortium on March 18, 1913, because he judged that the consortium was a scheme to take advantage of China's weakness and infringe on its sovereignty. Edward M. Lamont, *The Ambassador from Wall Street* (Lanham, MD: Madison Books, 1994), 153.

71　Griswold, *Far Eastern Policy*, 223.

72　Ibid., 224.

73　Ibid., 225.

74　Ibid., 225. After negotiations between the US and Japanese governments had failed to produce an agreement, Thomas Lamont, the chief executive of J.P. Morgan, and Inoue Junnosuke, the governor of Bank of Japan, met in Tokyo and worked out the agreement, which was approved by the consortium. Lamont, *Ambassador from Wall*

*183*

Chapter 7

*Street*, 153–159. At this time, Prime Minister Hara noted, "While we have maintained rather vaguely that Manchuria and Mongolia fall within our sphere of influence, the settlement of the new consortium question can be said to have brought about the powers' recognition of those spheres, so the agreement will be of real benefit for us in the future." Akira Iriye, *Japan and the Wider World* (London: Addison Wesley Longman, 1988), 48.

75  Hattori Ryūji, *Higashi Ajia kokusai kankyō no hendō to Nihon gaikō, 1918–1931* (Tokyo: Yuhikaku Publishing, 2001), 95–96. Hosoya Chihiro, *Nichibei kankei tsūshi* (Tokyo: University of Tokyo Press, 1995), 96–99.

76  Britain suggested to Washington that Japan be invited as the mandate of the Allies to occupy the Trans-Siberian and Chinese Eastern Railways. Lansing promptly rejected the scheme. Griswold, *Far Eastern Policy*, 228–229.

77  Treat, *The Far East*, 449. Griswold, *Far Eastern Policy*, 233.

78  Griswold, *Far Eastern Policy*, 234.

79  Ibid., 307.

80  Ibid., 309. The expansionists' argument in the army that the size of the force and the area of its operations should be left to Japan's discretion prevailed over that of the internationalists. The Japanese forces ultimately exceeded 72,000.

81  This was the first party cabinet in Japanese history. About Hara, Iriye writes, "In 1908 Hara Kei, a prominent Japanese politician, visited the United States for the first time. He was deeply impressed with America's economic might and its latent but unmistakable influence in world politics. He felt that even Europe, which he had seen in 1886 and now revisited, had come under America's political, economic, and even cultural influence. He vowed that an understanding with the United States would be a basic prerequisite for Japanese policy." Akira Iriye, *Across the Pacific* (Chicago: Imprint Publications, 1967), 111.

82  The commission was to be advised by a technical board headed by John F. Stevens, an American business executive. Hattori writes that Hara's signing of the Siberia and East China Railway Agreement was his most important act of cooperation with the United States. Hattori, *Higashi Ajia kokusai kankyō*, 49.

83  Ibid., 50.

84  Ibid., 50.

85  Bailey, *A Diplomatic History*, 602. All delegates were Democrats except White, who was not a party politician, but a career diplomat.

86  Japan had secured the consent of the Allies to the transfer of the German rights in Shandong and the German islands north of the equator by the secret understandings of February and March 1917 with Britain, France, Russia, and Italy. Japan had done this because it knew that its European allies had, in 1915, made agreements as to the disposition of the prospective German spoils in Europe. Treat, *The Far East*, 450–451. Cohen, *America's Response to China*, 86.

87  The Chinese southern provinces had long been in open rebellion against Beijing, but an armistice was reached in November 1918, and a domestic peace conference was to be convened in February 1919 assembling the warring factions in Shanghai. The Chinese delegation sent to Paris represented a compromise between these factions.

88  Arthur Walworth, *Wilson and His Peacemakers: American Diplomacy at the Paris*

*184*

*Peace Conference, 1919* (New York: W. W. Norton, 1986), 364.

89  Griswold, *Far Eastern Policy*, 244.

90  Ibid., 247.

91  Countries which voted in favor of the amendment included China, France, Italy, Brazil, and Greece. The most stubborn opponents were Australia and New Zealand; Britain sided with them. The United States abstained. Ibid., 250.

92  Ibid., 256. Spence, *Search for Modern China*, 293.

93  Under the Treaty of Versailles signed on June 28, 1919, Japan received the German rights in Shandong, which consisted of the Jiaozhou leasehold, which Japan had promised to return to China; the Qingdao–Jinan Railway, which Japan had promised to turn into a Sino–Japanese enterprise; three mines, and all German public property. Since China refused to sign the treaty, however, the Shandong questions were among the troublesome issues left in the aftermath of the conference. Treat, *The Far East*, 453.

94  On May 1, the news reached Beijing that the Chinese delegates acknowledged their case as hopeless because of the prior agreements. This news triggered mass protests in Beijing on May 4, which were followed by demonstrations in cities all over China. While the government dithered, pressure on the Versailles delegates not to sign the treaty was unrelenting. With typical indecision, the Chinese president did at last telegraph an instruction not to sign, but the telegram was sent too late to reach Versailles before the June 28 deadline. However, Chinese students and demonstrators, by surrounding their nation's delegation in their Paris hotel, forcibly prevented the delegates from attending the signing ceremonies. The Versailles treaty ended up without China's acceptance. Spence, *Search for Modern China*, 293–294.

95  Griswold, *Far Eastern Policy*, 257.

### 7.4. The Washington Conference

96  Griswold, *Far Eastern Policy*, 283–284.

97  For example, Curzon was pessimistic about the use of the tripartite entente. He wrote, ". . . we shall certainly be left worse off than before. For we shall lose the advantages of the Anglo–Japanese Agreement, which have been and are considerable. I do not allude to the obligations of military support which are obsolete, but to the steadying influence which the Agreement has exercised in international politics. . . . I regard the loss of these advantages with no small apprehension and am not at all sure that they will be compensated by a temporary conquest of the beaux yeux of America." Nish, *Alliance in Decline*, 364–365.

98  Ibid., 287.

99  Ibid., 288.

100  Imperial conferences were periodically held in London for the discussion of affairs of state concerning the entire empire. The dominions were thus permitted to share in the formation of British foreign policy. Ibid., 288.

101  Nish, *Alliance in Decline*, 334.

102  Ibid., 338. Ian Nish, *Japanese Foreign Policy in the Interwar Period* (Westport, CT: Praeger Publishers, 2002), 26.

103  Bailey, *A Diplomatic History*, 638–639.

Chapter 7

104 Griswold, *Far Eastern Policy*, 294. Curzon informed Hughes, with considerable resentment, that Britain "wished to dissociate herself from responsibility for arranging the conference." Nish, *Alliance in Decline*, 350.

105 Asada Sadao, *Ryō-taisenkan no Nichibei kankei* (Tokyo: University of Tokyo Press, 1993), 101.

106 Nish, *Alliance in Decline*, 345, 347.

107 Ibid., 341–342. Nish writes, "Britain was so obsessed with resolving the problems created by the imperial conference that she had ignored the courtesies which had normally been extended to her ally." Ibid., 347.

108 Asada, *Ryō-taisenkan no Nichibei kankei*, 102–103. The proponents of the positive policy included Hayashi Gonsuke, the ambassador in London, and Ishii Kikujirō, the ambassador in Paris, as well as Shidehara Kijūrō, the ambassador in Washington. They believed that it was important for Japan to show that it was no longer the Japan of yesteryear at the coming conference, and suggested that Japan should seize the initiative by voluntarily proposing those things that the United States was expected to propose, thus turning the atmosphere of the conference in Japan's favor. Asada Sadao, *Japan and the United States, 1915–25*, Yale University, PhD dissertation, 1963 (Ann Arbor, MI: University Microfilms, 1966), 182.

109 When Shidehara, ambassador in Washington, met Hughes in July, Hughes told Shidehara that he could not accept the Japanese request for prior agreement over the agenda, but he promised to be fair and just regarding Japanese–Chinese relations. And he excluded from the draft agenda that he sent out to participants in September the Shandong question, as well as the question of the Anglo–Japanese alliance, apparently taking Japan's request into account that matters that were regarded as accomplished facts and those relating to individual powers should be exclude from the agenda. Nish, *Alliance in Decline*, 346, 357.

110 Katō was the chief of staff of Tōgō's squadron at the Battle of Tsushima of 1905. He had served as the navy minister of the Ōkuma and Terauchi cabinets before he assumed the same post in the Hara cabinet. Notwithstanding the fact that he was a career naval officer, he was a political leader with a civilian perspective. Hara put his full confidence in Katō. Asada, *Ryō-taisenkan no Nichibei kankei*, 75.

111 Shidehara had been the vice-minister for foreign affairs until his assignment to the US post in 1919.

112 Tokugawa Iesato was the adopted son of the last shogun, Tokugawa Yoshinobu, and was widely respected in Japan.

113 Iriye, *Japan and the Wider World*, 51. Katō's view was supported by the treaty school and the influential Admiral Tōgō, but was opposed by the fleet school, which argued for a large navy. Nish, *Alliance in Decline*, 321.

114 Root served as secretary of war (1899–1904) in the McKinley administration, secretary of state (1904–09) in the Roosevelt administration, and New York's Republican senator (1909–15). He received the Nobel Peace Prize in 1912. Root inherited his pro-Japanese outlook from an earlier age when America had more in common with Japan than czarist Russia, the kaiser's Germany, or Manchu China. He prided himself on the part he had played in concluding the Root–Takahira Agreement. He thought that the United States would have to grow out of its sentimental attitude of

*186*

*Notes*

protecting China and recognize the cold logic and necessity of Japan's position vis-à-vis China. Asada, *Japan and the United States*, 200.

115 Balfour was seventy-three years of age when he agreed to head the British delegation in the place of Prime Minister Lloyd George, who could not attend the conference because of his preoccupation with the Irish question. Nish, *Alliance in Decline*, 362. Balfour had served as chancellor of the exchequer (1891–92 and 1895–1902), prime minister (1902–05), navy secretary (1915–16), and foreign secretary (1916–19). He had been the principal representative of the British delegation to the League of Nations until the middle of October. He had played an active part in discussions on the alliance at the imperial conference. Senators Lodge and Underwood had a considerable regard for Balfour. Shidehara said of Balfour that "he was a world figure and Hughes could not receive him in his unduly blunt way. In fact he was a person of embarrassingly great prestige and character." Nish, *Alliance in Decline*, 362–363.

116 Hughes proposed that the United States, Britain, and Japan scrap a total of sixty ships with a combined tonnage of 1,878,073 tons, with the United States scrapping thirty ships totaling 845,740 tons, Britain twenty-three ships amounting to 583,375 tons, and Japan seventeen ships totaling 448,958 tons. Raymond Leslie Buell, *The Washington Conference* (New York: Russell & Russell, 1922), 153.

117 Asada Sadao, "From Washington to London: The Imperial Japanese Navy and the Politics of Naval Limitation, 1921–1930," in *The Washington Conference, 1921–22: Naval Rivalry, East Asian Stability and the Road to Pearl Harbor*, eds. Erik Goldstein and John Maurer (Ilford, Essex: Frank Cass, 1994), 148.

118 Asada, *Japan and the United States*, 251.

119 Hughes demanded the scrapping of the *Mutsu*, which was 98 percent complete according to American standards, but Japan insisted that it had been commissioned in September 1921 and was fully manned before the conference convened. The *Mutsu* had a great sentimental hold on the Japanese people because it had been built partly by the subscriptions of school children as well as the general public. It was the most powerful battleship afloat at the time, equipped with eight 16-inch guns that could fire projectiles of nearly 2,200 pounds in weight at a maximum range of 25 miles or 40 kilometers. It had a displacement of 33,800 tons and a speed of 23.5 knots an hour—2 knots more than the *Maryland*, the only superdreadnought the United States was to have retained under the original proposal. If Japan were allowed to retain the *Mutsu* along with another superdreadnought, the *Nagato*, which had been built in 1921, it would have twice as many superdreadnoughts as the United States and Britain. The question was finally settled with the United States completing two battleships that were 80 to 90 percent complete at the time of the conference, and Britain building two new superdreadnoughts. Buell, *The Washington Conference*, 159–161.

120 The United States excluded Hawaii from such a pledge, but included Guam, the Aleutians, and the Philippines. Britain excluded Singapore, but included Hong Kong. Japan was barred from further fortification of any but the home islands. With this fortification agreement, the operational strength of the US fleet in the Pacific was limited to de facto parity with Japan's sea power. Asada, *Japan and the United States*, 233, 240.

*187*

Chapter 7

121 Asada, *Ryō-taisenkan no Nichibei kankei*, 110–111, Nish, *Alliance in Decline*, 360–361.

122 Nish, *Japanese Foreign Policy*, 29.

123 No detailed instructions were prepared because it had been assumed that Premier Lloyd George would attend the conference. Nish, *Alliance in Decline*, 362–363.

124 Though Hughes wanted Balfour not to tell the Japanese about the draft, it was leaked by an official in the State Department to a counselor in the Japanese embassy in Washington. Shidehara, who was confined to bed at the time, could not understand why Balfour had given the draft to Hughes without any consultation with the Japanese. Shidehara was somewhat relieved to learn later that Balfour had talked about his idea to Tokugawa (who had failed to inform Shidehara) and that the draft was Balfour's personal one. Nish, *Alliance in Decline*, 372.

125 Asada, *Japan and the United States*, 251.

126 Nish, *Alliance in Decline*, 374. Hughes excluded East Asia because he wanted to avoid having to invite the Chinese to take part in the discussions. Ibid., 380.

127 Balfour wrote to Lloyd George soon after his arrival in Washington, "Adherence to the Alliance to its present form will be very unpopular in the United States, and render the conclusion of a satisfactory and enduring arrangement for the limitation of armaments extremely difficult to negotiate . . . " Ibid., 368.

128 Okazaki Hisahiko, *Shidehara Kijūrō to sono jidai* (Tokyo: PHP Institute, 2003), 245.

129 Ibid., 245.

130 Asada, *Ryō-taisenkan no Nichibei kankei*, 114, 120, 134.

131 Ibid., 246. Nish, *Alliance in Decline*, 381. Hara was assassinated in November 1921.

132 The Japanese delegate stated that Japan would be willing to agree to principles which would guide the future actions of the nations. Buell, *The Washington Conference*, 249.

133 It was Balfour who proposed that Root prepare the principles. Balfour had written his draft on the question of China and handed it to Hughes, together with his draft on the three-power entente, at his meeting with Hughes on November 11. Root revised Balfour's proposals "in phraseology rather than in principle." Griswold, *Far Eastern Policy*, 322. Hattori, *Higashi Ajia kokusai kankyō*, 95.

134 The four principles of article I were: (1) To respect the sovereignty, independence, and territorial and administrative integrity of China; (2) To provide the fullest and most unembarrassed opportunity to China to develop and maintain for herself an effective and stable government; (3) To use their influence for the purpose of effectually establishing and maintaining the principle of equal opportunity for the commerce and industry of all nations throughout the territory of China; and (4) To refrain from taking advantage of conditions in China in order to seek special rights or privileges which would abridge the rights of citizens of friendly states and from countenancing actions inimical to the security of such states. Griswold, *Far Eastern Policy*, 323.

135 Hattori, *Higashi Ajia kokusai kankyō*, 96.

136 The first approach was made from Japan to the Beijing government as soon as the Versailles Treaty became effective. On January 16, 1920, Japan conveyed to China its desire to open negotiations relative to the restoration of Jianzhou to China. Not receiving any response from China, Japan made a second approach on April 16, to

*Notes*

which China replied on May 22 that it was not in a position to negotiate directly with Japan. Japan presented a comprehensive plan of the restitution of the province to China on September 7, to which China responded on October 5 that the suggested terms of settlement fell far short of demonstrating the sincerity of Japan's desire to settle the question. Ichihashi Yamato, *The Washington Conference and After* (New York: AMS Press, 1928), 281–284.

137 Griswold, *Far Eastern Policy*, 326. Buell, *The Washington Conference*, 255.

138 Hughes, Lodge, Root, and Balfour first put pressure mostly on Japan, but they later concentrated their pressure on the obstinate Chinese. The main issue was the disposition of the Qindao–Jinan Railway. China kept refusing Japanese compromise propositions, including a joint management proposal (September 1921) and its sale to China by the payment of the Chinese government treasury notes (January 1922). Lodge wrote to Coolidge, "We have done everything, that is humanly possible. . . . If we do not settle Shandong, it will be wholly the fault of China and we shall be able to prove to the world that she prevented it." Asada, *Japan and the United States*, 327, 331–332. Ichihashi, *Washington Conference and After*. 282–283. Hughes once took Sze to see Harding, who said to Sze, "It would be a colossal blunder in statecraft if China were not to take advantage of the opportunity now afforded her for the settlement of the Shandong question as the alternative might involve the risk of losing the province." Griswold, *Far Eastern Policy*, 327.

139 Balfour likened the Japanese lease of Guandong to British lease of Kowloon. Hattori, *Higashi Ajia kokusai kankyō*, 103.

140 Ibid., 103.

# Chapter 8
# US–Japanese Immigration Disputes

## 8.1. The Roots of the Immigration Question in California

### 8.1.1. Characteristics of the Californians Contributing to Immigration Disputes

In the mid-19th century, California was an vast, underpopulated, resource-rich area. The land area of the state of California is equal to that of Japan, but its population was less than a two-hundredth of Japan's in 1850, and a thirtieth of Japan's as late as 1900. Until the opening of the transcontinental railways in 1869, its land accessibility was very poor. It was possible to travel by land from Missouri to California, but the journey was extremely dangerous owing to the natural obstacles of terrain and weather, disease, and attacks by marauding Native Americans. As late as the 1850s, the trip from a starting point in Missouri required four months' arduous travel. Many of the adventurers of the 1849 Gold Rush went to the Panama Isthmus by ship, boarded the American-owned Panama Railroad, and took ship for California on the Pacific side. This was the route, albeit in the opposite direction, that the Japanese Ratification Embassy of 1860 took when traveling from San Francisco to Washington, DC (3.2.1). Even after the transcontinental railroad

*191*

was completed in 1869, the connection between the eastern and western coasts was unreliable; in 1872, a heavy snowstorm in the Rocky Mountains delayed the Iwakura Embassy's trip by nineteen days (3.3.2).

Settlers who had passed through such trials in order to get to the bright opportunities promised by California seemed to have certain characteristics. The great majority had been in modest economic circumstances in their former homes, and were not likely well-educated. Eastern capitalists had bought up most of the large parcels of California land from Mexican ranchers, and the settlers coming over the deserts and mountains lacked the capital to participate in the California land rush. When they did manage to get some share of the wealth of the Golden State, no matter how small, they were fiercely possessive of their new homes and lands, and were often almost paranoid about losing them.

Many of the Californians came from the defeated and desolate southern states of the erstwhile Confederacy. Apparently many of them brought with them to California ideas of racial superiority, and when the issue of restrictions on Asian immigration became heated, they sometimes met with cooperation from Democratic Party congressional representatives from the southern states.

As California was far from the Washington, DC, and New York centers of American governance, when law and order broke down in the early years, vigilante justice was often employed to restore order.

### 8.1.2. Immigration Disputes with the Chinese and Japanese

The first major immigration dispute was the anti-Chinese movement that began in the 1850s. It was started by labor organizations in California objecting to cheap labor, and was later joined by groups other than labor organizations urging openly racist slogans calling for preservation of racial purity and Western civilization. It culminated in the Chinese Exclusion Act of 1882.[1]

Anti-Japanese immigration agitation in California began in the 1890s. It was largely a continuation of the anti-Chinese movement.[2] When Japanese immigration began to increase in the 1890s after the exclusion of Chinese laborers, agitation against the Japanese followed a similar pattern to that against the Chinese.

In the early 20th century, however, opposition to Japanese immigration assumed a different tone from the agitation against the Chinese in the previous century. The increase in Japanese immigrants coincided with Japan's emergence as an imperial power.[3] The underpopulated and largely undefended western coast of the United States was now faced with an Asian power that had defeated Russia, supposedly the greatest military power in the West at the time. As observed in 6.4.2, Japan's emergence as a strong military power and the contemporaneous increase in Japanese immigrants and their gradual establishment in the West provoked the "Yellow Peril" alarm against the Japanese. Unlike Northeast China, the West Coast was never in danger of open aggression. Unschooled Californians, however, could not understand geopolitical factors, and genuinely feared for the safety of their hard-won assets and hopeful possibilities.

Since the late 19th century, anti-Japanese articles had been seen in the newspapers like those of the Hearst chain, and with the outbreak of the Russo–Japanese war, the tone of the articles became increasingly sensationalistic. In February 1905, the *San Francisco Chronicle* launched a crusade against the Japanese. It warned of the dangerous effects of Japanese immigration on American society, carrying anti-Japanese articles almost daily for months under such menacing headlines as "The Japanese Invasion, the Problem of the Hour," "Crime and Poverty Go Hand in Hand with Asiatic Labor," and "The Yellow Peril—How Japanese Crowd Out the White Race."[4]

In March 1905, the California legislature adopted a resolution calling for limiting and diminishing the further immigration of Japanese. The resolution was more or less a summary of the newspapers' complaints. It included such statement as "the close of the war between Japan and Russia will surely bring to our shore hordes of the discharged soldiers of the Japanese Army, who will crowd the State with immoral, intemperate, quarrelsome men, bound to labor for a pittance, and to subsist on a supply with which a white man can hardly sustain life."[5] In May 1905, the Asiatic Exclusion League was formed in California, aiming to extend the Chinese exclusion laws to the Japanese.[6]

### 8.1.3. The Japanese Population and Their Farming in California

From 1890 to 1920, the Japanese population in California increased from 1,147 to 70,196; its percentage of the total population of California rose from less than 0.1 percent to 2.04 percent during this period (table 8.1.3-a). It is worth noting that Japanese in California comprised between 50 and 60 percent of the entire Japanese population in the continental United States

Chapter 8

Table 8.1.3-a. Japanese in California and the Continental United States

| | Japanese in California (a) | Population of California (b) | Japanese in the Continental United States (c) | (a)/(b) ×100 | (a)/(c) ×100 |
|---|---|---|---|---|---|
| 1880 | 86 | 864,694 | 148 | 0.0099 | 58.1 |
| 1890 | 1,147 | 1,213,398 | 2,030 | 0.095 | 56.2 |
| 1900 | 10,151 | 1,485,053 | 21,326 | 0.68 | 41.7 |
| 1910 | 41,356 | 2,377,549 | 72,157 | 1.73 | 57.3 |
| 1920 | 70,196 | 3,426,861 | 119,207 | 2.04 | 58.8 |

Source: Toyokichi Iyenaga and Kenoske Sato, *Japan and the California Problem* (New York: G. P. Putnam's Sons, 1921), 92–94.

throughout this period.[7] The high proportion of Japanese in that one state, as well as their tendency toward collective living, contributed to anti-Japanese sentiments among Californians.

Most of the Japanese in California were engaged in agriculture. They were first employed by American landowners as farm labors. But they gradually saved portions of their earnings and invested them to become owner-farmers or tenant farmers. From 1905 to 1920, farmland under Japanese ownership in California increased from 2,442 acres to 74,769 acres, while farmhand leased by Japanese increased from 54,831 acres to 331,150 acres; farmland under cropping contract to Japanese farmers rose from 4,775 acres to 70,137 acres (table 8.1.3-b).[8] A cropping contract was a type of sharecropping lease that entitled a contractee a designated share of the crops while giving him no legal rights over the land.[9] Total Japanese agricultural landholdings in California in the form of ownership, lease contract, and cropping contract equaled 458,056 acres in 1920, accounting for 1.64 percent of the total farmland in California, which was 27,931,444 acres that year.[10]

Most of the land secured by the Japanese was at first either untillable or of the poorest quality, but by dint of patient toil, the Japanese converted it into productive soil.[11] The most successful was George Shima, the "potato king," who began reclamation efforts in the Stockton–Sacramento delta region in 1899. By 1913, he had reclaimed 28,800 acres.[12]

Another important contribution by the Japanese farmers to the development of California agriculture was the production of vegetables and fruits which demanded careful and labor-intensive cultivation. In 1917, Japanese farmers produced $141 worth of crops per acre, whereas California produced

194

Table 8.1.3-b. Japanese Agricultural Landholding in California (acres)

|  | 1905 | 1909 | 1913 | 1920 | 1922 | 1923 |
|---|---|---|---|---|---|---|
| Owned | 2,442 | 16,449 | 26,707 | 74,769 | 51,000 | 62,769 |
| Leased | 54,831 | 137,233 | 205,983 | 331,150 | 152,000 | 131,991 |
| Cropping contract | 4,775 | 42,276 | 48,997 | 70,137 | 145,000 | 109,756 |
| Total | 62,048 | 195,958 | 281,687 | 458,056 | 349,000 | 304,520 |

*Source:* Eiichiro Azuma, *Between Two Empires: Race, History, and Transnationalism in Japanese America* (New York: Oxford University Press, 2005), 63.

$42 worth of farm products per acre.[13] By 1941 the Japanese were producing 30 to 35 percent by value of all commercial truck crops grown in California.[14]

# 8.2. The San Francisco School Incident and the Gentlemen's Agreement

## 8.2.1. The San Francisco School Incident of 1906–1907

The anti-Japanese movement had drawn little notice outside California and neighboring states until 1906, when there occurred an incident that attracted national and international attention: the San Francisco school-board crisis.

On October 11, 1906, the San Francisco Board of Education, under pressure from the Asiatic Exclusion League, ordered Japanese and Korean children to be excluded from the regular schools and sent to an Oriental school to join Chinese children. An old California law had empowered school boards to "exclude all children of filthy or vicious habits, or children suffering from contagious diseases, and also to establish separate schools for American Indian children, and for children of Mongolian and Chinese descent."[15]

A variety of charges were made against the Japanese in attempted justification of the order. They were alleged to be overcrowding the school, to be vicious, immoral, and above the normal age limits for the grades.[16] All of these charges were found on close investigation to have been greatly exaggerated. There were 25,000 students in all the twenty-three public schools in San Francisco, of whom only ninety-three were Japanese; just twenty-seven of those were above the normal age limits for their grades. Teacher testimony as to the conduct and general desirability of Japanese students completely vitiated charges of immorality.[17]

For Japanese who believed that they had finally obtained Great Power status after a half-century of desperate effort and their recent victory in the Russo–Japanese War, the segregation order was a terrible offense to national pride and an affront to national dignity.[18] In an imperialist world divided between rulers and the ruled, Japan had managed to move into the circle of rulers. It was an intolerable insult to the Japanese that the Americans intended to place them alongside the Chinese among the ruled.

After protests by the Japanese consul in San Francisco had come to naught, the Japanese ambassador lodged a formal protest with the Theodore Roosevelt administration on October 25, claiming that the right to education was a part of most-favored-nation rights of residence granted to the Japanese by the treaty of 1894.[19] The Department of Justice of the Roosevelt administration filed lawsuits against the San Francisco Board of Education on behalf of the Japanese children.[20] Roosevelt thought, however, that a more direct approach was needed. He did not foresee that the United States would fight Japan over Japan's China policy, but he could envisage a possible conflict with Japan over immigration disputes. He dispatched Secretary of Commerce and Labor Victor H. Metcalf to San Francisco for an on-the-spot investigation,[21] and wrote to his friend Kaneko Kentarō (金子堅太郎) that he would do everything possible to "protect the rights of the Japanese who are here."

On December 4, 1906, in his annual message to Congress, Roosevelt called attention to Japan's remarkable progress toward modern civilization, the economic and cultural ties between the two nations, and its generosity to the San Francisco earthquake victims.[22] He termed the segregation order a "wicked absurdity," and warned that he would use the US Army, if necessary, to protect the Japanese in California.[23]

According to US law, citizenship was granted only to "free white persons" or "persons of African nativity or descent." As for the Japanese, there had been both positive and negative court rulings in the past.[24] Roosevelt was an advocate of a legislation conferring on Japanese the right to become naturalized American citizens.

Roosevelt's strongarm tactics, however, did not calm the agitation in California. They made the agitation even more active, and many anti-Japanese bills and resolutions were presented to the California state legislature. Roosevelt became convinced that the only way to prevent immigration disputes with Japan was to stop immigration from Japan. In January 1907, he called the mayor and the entire Board of Education of San Francisco to the

White House, and promised that he would take measures to restrict Japanese immigration. In return for the promise, he secured the consent of the San Franciscans to rescind the segregation order.[25] The lawsuits against the board were withdrawn, and the 1907 session of the California legislature adjourned without passing any anti-Japanese measures.

In March 1907, Roosevelt issued an executive order that prohibited the immigration of Japanese laborers from Hawaii, Canada, Mexico, and other erstwhile "vestibules."[26] This was the first important measure to curtail Japanese immigration. The Japanese government did not object to the measure, as they knew that without it, the school segregation order would not be rescinded. The Japanese government could not legally object to it, either, since the 1894 treaty with the United States provided in Article II that stipulations in the treaty "do not in any way affect the laws, ordinances, and regulations with regard to trade, the immigration of laborers, . . . which are now in force or which may hereafter be enacted in either of the two countries."

## 8.2.2. The Gentlemen's Agreement of 1908

Roosevelt and Secretary of State Elihu Root then moved to restrict direct Japanese emigration to the United States. They could have gotten an exclusion law through Congress very easily, but unlike the California exclusionists, they wanted to accomplish this without the affront to Japan that such legislation would present. They sought to solve the issue through diplomatic channels. After a year and a half of detailed negotiations, an agreement which became known as the Gentlemen's Agreement of 1908 was reached, whose substance consisted of six diplomatic notes exchanged between the two governments in late 1907 and early 1908.[27] The Japanese government agreed to issue passports to the United States only to non-laborers, laborers returning from a visit in Japan, and the parents, wives, and children of domiciled laborers, as well as to laborers who already possessed a property interest in a farming enterprise in the United States.[28] Rather than a formal and open treaty, the Japanese pushed to make the arrangement an agreement between the two administrative governments; the exact stipulations were not to be made public.[29] They did not want it to be known to the world that they had accepted an immigration status that was not equal to that of Europeans.[30]

The Japanese government adhered to the agreement scrupulously. While the number of Japanese admitted to the United States was 9,948 in 1907 and

7,258 in 1908, it decreased to 4,288 on average annually during the years 1909–1913. Moreover, during the same years, more Japanese departed from the United States than were admitted. When the treaty of 1894 was supplanted by the treaty of 1911, the immigration clause (Article II) of the old treaty was dropped at Japan's insistence. In return for this, the Japanese government declared that it would maintain the control required by the Gentlemen's Agreement with the same effectiveness as it had exercised for the previous three years. The American acceptance of the Japanese position demonstrated that the Gentlemen's Agreement had been accepted by the US government as an effective method of regulating Japanese immigration.[31]

A problem did arise relating to the immigration of Japanese wives. Under the Gentlemen's Agreement, many "picture brides" immigrated to the United States after marriages by proxy, in which brides were selected for immigrant grooms by their families and other go-betweens in their native villages.[32] The practice was perfectly legal under Japanese law, but it was cited by the Californians as another example of Japanese treachery.[33] Bowing to strong objections in California, but only after much argument as to the validity of the marriages with the State Department, the Japanese government decided to stop the issuance of passports to picture brides in 1919.[34]

# 8.3. The Alien Land Laws in California

### 8.3.1. Roosevelt's Efforts to Block the Alien Land Bills

The school segregation incident caused a demographic change in Japanese immigrants in California. To avoid friction with white Americans, Japanese immigrants started to move from urban areas of the state to rural ones, where many of them cultivated undeveloped land or land deserted by whites. But exclusionists attempted to obstruct such Japanese efforts.[35] They introduced in the state legislature of 1907 an alien land bill that provided that no alien should hold real property for more than five years without obtaining citizenship.[36] Because of Roosevelt's efforts, however, the alien land bill failed enactment in the 1907 session along with several other anti-Japanese bills. Since regulating immigration was the exclusive right of the US Congress, the only means available to local exclusionists for discouraging Japanese immigration were by such indirect methods as land ownership restrictions, or the expulsion of Japanese students from public schools as discussed above.

198

An alien land bill similar to that of 1907 was introduced again in the 1909 session of the California legislature, along with other anti-Japanese measures.[37] Roosevelt intervened once more. He wired Governor Gillett that "passage of the proposed legislation would be of incalculable damage to the State of California as well as to whole Union."[38] The requested intervention of the governor and the speaker of the assembly brought about the defeat of the offensive bills.[39]

Roosevelt's intrusion into California state politics caused Japanese immigration to become a partisan political issue in California.[40] In the presidential campaign of 1908, the Democrats in California declared that only the president from their party could prevent "the Pacific slope from being overrun by Hordes of Japanese," and argued that "Labor's choice Bryan—Jap's choice Taft."[41] Despite this effort, the Democrats lost California by a large margin.[42]

Roosevelt left the White House in March 1909 with the uneasy feeling that, as Griswold writes, "He had scotched the snake but not killed it."[43] The formula that he bequeathed to William H. Taft, his successor, was "to insist on keeping out Japanese immigration; but at the same time to behave with scrupulous courtesy to Japan as nation and to the Japanese who are here; and also to continue to build up and maintain at the highest point of efficacy our navy."[44]

In the 1910 election, California Republicans kept their majority in the state legislature and made Hiram Johnson governor, but the Democrats, using the anti-Japanese issue, increased their vote considerably.[45] Johnson, on the other hand, refrained from using the Japanese question politically, doing Roosevelt's bidding.[46]

When the 1911 session of the California legislature convened, an alien land bill prohibiting aliens ineligible for citizenship from holding real property in the state was introduced; it passed the Senate by a vote of 29 to 3. Taft and Secretary of State Philander Knox brought pressure against the bill, and, thanks to Governor Johnson's cooperation, the bill was scuttled in the Assembly, though the Taft administration had to persuade Californians with the selection of San Francisco as the site for the Panama–Pacific Exposition scheduled to be held in 1915.[47]

In the election of 1912, California Democrats used presidential candidate Woodrow Wilson's message that he stood for Japanese expulsion to good effect (Wilson had made this statement at the California Democrats' request).

Chapter 8

They printed Wilson's message on a small card with Roosevelt's 1906 statement in favor of naturalizing Japanese on the reverse, and distributed the card in vast numbers.[48] This tactic helped them capture 44 percent of the vote in California—their best showing since Grover Cleveland had carried the state in 1892.[49]

## 8.3.2. The Discriminatory Alien Land Law of 1913

The year 1913 was a turning point for the anti-Japanese movement. With a Democratic president in Washington who supported Japanese expulsion and was pledged to respect states' rights criticizing the Republican administration's intervention in the California state government during the election campaign, the exclusionists in California were determined to pass an anti-Japanese law in the 1913 legislature. The session was flooded by more than thirty immigration-related measures, among which were several anti-Japanese land bills. Japanese ambassador Chinda Sutemi (珍田捨巳) made repeated requests to the new administration to check the hostile legislation as the bills proceeded through the legislative process.[50] The Wilson administration now had a major diplomatic problem to resolve.

In the previous session, Governor Johnson had acted at the request of the Republican Taft administration to block a discriminatory land bill, but this time he did not cooperate with the Democratic Wilson administration. In fact, he was to become the behind-the-scenes manager of the alien land bill in the legislature.[51] Wilson, mindful of his campaign pledges as well as Johnson's irascible character, was at first hesitant to communicate directly with Johnson, and tried to convey his messages to Johnson through his associates—an approach that displeased Johnson.[52]

Meanwhile, there was a large-scale protest rally in Tokyo on April 17. It was not until April 22, after having realized for the first time the full seriousness of the issue,[53] that Wilson sent a telegram directly to Johnson asking him to veto legislation that would be inconsistent with the US–Japanese treaty of 1911. He then sent Secretary of State William Jennings Bryan to Sacramento on April 24. By that time, however, Johnson had determined to challenge the federal government.

While Bryan was heading for California, Johnson, together with California State Senator Francis Haney, a leading Progressive, and Ulysses Webb, the state's attorney general, drafted a bill that was discriminatory, but legally not inconsistent with the US–Japanese treaty of 1911. Section 2 of Johnson's bill stated that aliens ineligible for US citizenship "may acquire, possess, enjoy and transfer real property, or any interest therein, in this State, in the manner and to the extent and for the purposes prescribed by any treaty now existing between the government of the United States and the nation or country of which such alien is a citizen or subject, . . . "[54] The US–Japanese treaty of 1911 gave the Japanese the right to own such structures as houses, manufactories, warehouses and shops, and to lease land for residential and commercial purposes, but it did not say anything concerning the ownership of land for any purpose or the lease of lands for agricultural purpose.[55]

Had Bryan offered some quid pro quo, as Roosevelt and Taft had done with regard to the restriction on Japanese immigration, his mission might have produced some positive results, but Bryan came to Sacramento empty-handed. In fact, Chinda had offered to Bryan prior to his trip to the West a concession which might have served to break the impasse: he suggested that Japan might be willing to curb the immigration of "picture brides." But Bryan ignored the offer. Bryan disappointed Johnson and Californians who had expected some return for their cooperation. Bryan said, "I have no program. I came here to confer."[56]

The bill was introduced in the Senate the day following Bryan's arrival and was pushed through both houses in less than four days, passing the Senate on May 2 by a vote of 35 to 2, and the Assembly by a vote of 72 to 3 on the following day.[57] Bryan left California on May 3, asking Johnson to postpone signing to give Washington time to consider its position on the bill. Johnson agreed, but after an inconclusive exchange of communications with Wilson, he signed the bill on May 19. This bill included an additional clause permitting ineligible aliens to lease farmland for periods not to exceed three years, making the law a little more accommodative,[58] but no amendment was made regarding the ownership of farmland. The Japanese government presented its formal protest against the law's discriminatory character,[59] but to no avail. The Wilson administration offered to "compensate Japanese for any loss which they might show to have been sustained on account of the statute,"[60] but the Japanese declined the offer. For them, it was not a matter of money, but of national dignity.

From 1914 to 1918, there was no significant anti-Japanese agitation, perhaps because of American preoccupation with World War I. There was also

Chapter 8

the factor of the Californians' appreciation of Japan's participation in the San Francisco Exposition, in which many European states were prevented from participating by the war. However, it gradually became known that there were loopholes in the alien land law of 1913. The Japanese continued buying and leasing land in the names of their children who were US citizens.

### 8.3.3. The Alien Land Law of 1920

In 1919, the anti-Japanese campaign in California revived. The instigators were politicians who wanted to use the campaign for their own narrow political purposes on the national stage.[61] James Phelan, a Democrat seeking reelection to the US Senate in 1920, appealed for more stringent state alien land legislation than the 1913 Alien Land Law.[62] In the same legislature, J. M. Inman, a Republican state Senator who was campaigning for a congressional seat, introduced an alien land bill designed to plug loopholes in the 1913 law.[63] Inman's fellow Republicans did not want the passage of the bill to help Democrat Phelan to win reelection to the Senate.[64] Governor Stephens did not like, however, the idea of either party using the California legislature for their political purposes in national politics. He managed to prevent those bills from being passed in the state legislature.

The only way left for the anti-Japanese forces to seek a more restrictive amendment to the 1913 law was to place the measure directly on the ballot of the forthcoming general election in the form of an initiative petition. While Hiram Johnson had been the governor of California, he had been successful in establishing a "direct democracy" measure whereby the voters could bypass the state legislature in referendums and thus enact legislation superior in force to laws emanating from the legislature. By strenuous effort, Inman and the anti-Japanese groups collected signatures necessary for the referendum.[65] Once the measures were on the ballot, the anti-Japanese forces in California united in their common purpose and conducted an emotional anti-Japanese campaign. The new Alien Land Law was approved by a margin of three to one (668,483 to 222,086) in the general election of November 2, 1920.[66]

The law provided that if aliens ineligible to citizenship furnished the funds to purchase land, and the title of such land was taken in the name of another person, such an act was presumed to be done with the intention to avoid the Alien Land Law and was void, and the land was subject to escheat to the state. The Japanese were thus barred from buying land in the name of their

202

children. While the 1913 law included a clause permitting ineligible aliens to lease farmland for three years, the new law did not have such clause.[67]

The 1920 law substantially decreased the total acreage controlled by Japanese farmers. Between 1920 and 1923, Japanese agricultural landholdings decreased from 458,058 acres to 304,520 acres (table 8.1.3-b).[68] Many Japanese farmers gave up farming, or became farm laborers. While Japanese farmland ownership and leaseholds decreased, cropping contracts increased, as they were regarded as legal under the 1920 law. In November 1923, however, the Supreme Court declared that the cropping contract was a form of lease and was therefore illegal.[69] The foreman system emerged as the most prevalent replacement for the cropping contract.[70] But foremen, as well as farm labors, were salaried workers employed by American landlords. Both were subject to unequal power relationships with their white landlords that reduced their share of the returns from their skills in the vegetable and fruit fields. The Issei farmers accepted these subordinated statuses in the hope that the following generation, the Nisei, as American citizens, would be able to achieve economic and social justice in the future.[71]

# 8.4. The Legislation of the Japanese Exclusion Law of 1924

### 8.4.1. Developments in 1921 through Early 1924

The passage of the Alien Land Law of 1920 meant that the Californians had exhausted what they could do at the state level to discourage Japanese immigration. Further restrictions would only be possible with an exclusion act passed by the US Congress. The goal of the Japanese exclusionists was the enactment of a law stipulating outright prohibition of Japanese immigration, as had been done with the Chinese since 1882, and had been done with almost all other Asiatic peoples through the Asiatic Barred Zone Act of 1917, which created a delineated geographical zone that included all of Asia except Japan, China, and the Philippines. Immigration from the Philippines was regulated by literacy tests,[72] and that from Japan by the Gentlemen's Agreement of 1908.

Toward the end of the 1921 session of Congress, a bill prohibiting immigration of aliens ineligible for citizenship was proposed by Representative Albert Johnson (Republican, Washington), chairman of the House Committee on Immigration and Naturalization, but the session was ad-

Chapter 8

journed before it was taken into deliberation.[73]

The year 1922 was an important year for the exclusionists. Their long-standing contention that Japanese were "aliens ineligible to citizenship" was validated by the US Supreme Court. On November 13, 1922, in the case of *Takao Ozawa v. the United States*, the court rejected Ozawa's petition for naturalization.[74] The contention of Ozawa's counsel, George Wickersham, former attorney general of the United States, was that the absence of any specific congressional prohibition against Japanese meant that they were eligible. The court ruled, however, that since Japanese were not specifically included in the statues governing naturalization, whose basic language dated from 1790, they could not be admitted to citizenship.[75] Though there had already been rulings in the lower federal courts that denied Japanese applicants' naturalization, the finality of this decision by the US Supreme Court greatly disappointed the Japanese.

When Congress met in December 1923, Representative Albert Johnson re-introduced the same bill that he had belatedly submitted in the previous session. The bill aroused no strong opposition in the House. It was expected that if Japanese exclusion were to be defeated, it would be in the Senate, which was traditionally more sensitive to the international implications of its acts.[76] In the Senate, David Reed (Republican, Pennsylvania) and several other Senators expressed willingness to put the Japanese under a quota. Reed also supported the Gentlemen's Agreement, and submitted a bill that exempted from the quota provisions aliens entitled to enter the United States under the provisions of an agreement relating to immigration.[77]

On the other hand, anti-Japanese immigration bills similar to the one proposed by Albert Johnson in the House were submitted in the Senate in early 1924 by Henry Cabot Lodge, Republican floor leader and chairman of the Senate Committee on Foreign Relations, and also by Samuel Shortridge, a Republican senator from California.[78]

### 8.4.2. The Hanihara Letter

Ambassador Hanihara Masanao (埴原正直) in Washington conveyed to Hughes the Japanese government's serious concern about the anti-Japanese immigration bills submitted to Congress in December 1923 through January 1924.[79] Saburi Sadao (佐分利貞男), counselor of the Japanese embassy, warned the Division of Far Eastern Affairs of the State Department that those bills,

*204*

if passed, would "definitely end" the influence of the "conciliatory party" in Japan.[80]

This sort of fear was also shared by the State Department officials. John Van Antwerp MacMurray, chief of the Division of Far Eastern Affairs, voiced his concern that the bills would "make difficult, if not impossible, that sympathetic and wholehearted cooperation, in the area of the Pacific Ocean, which the results of the Washington Conference have brought within the range of practical realization."[81]

Hughes, who was at first not inclined to take action to stay the hands of Congress, wrote a letter in mid-February to Albert Johnson and Senator LeBaron Colt, chairman of the Senate Committee on Immigration, expressing his opposition to the anti-Japanese legislative action. He stressed that it would largely undo the work of the Washington Conference, and expressed his strong support for the continuation of the Gentlemen's Agreement.[82]

Meanwhile, during the course of the debate in the Senate, complaints were voiced that the Gentlemen's Agreement was a secret document that no one had ever seen.[83] Though the terms of the agreement were generally known, Hughes suggested to Hanihara on March 27 that he write a letter to the secretary in which the Gentlemen's Agreement would be summarized in a brief and definite fashion that could be presented authoritatively.[84] With approval from Tokyo, Hanihara prepared such a letter, presented it to Hughes on April 10, and Hughes sent it to Albert Johnson and LeBaron Colt on the same day. The following day it was put in the congressional record and copies were distributed to all members of Congress.

The first part of the letter was a long and accurate exposition of the substance of the Gentlemen's Agreement and its workings. Then Hanihara addressed to the bills pending;

... To Japan the question is not one of expediency, but of principle. To her the mere fact that a few hundred or thousands of her nationals will or will not be admitted into domains of other countries is immaterial, so long as no question of national susceptibilities is involved. The important question is whether Japan as a nation is or is not entitled to the proper respect and consideration of other nations. . . .

The manifest object of the [exclusion clause] is to single out Japanese as a nation, stigmatizing them as unworthy and undesirable in the eyes of the American people. And yet the actual result of that particular provision, if the proposed bill becomes law as intended, would be to exclude only 146 Japanese per year. . . .

Relying on the confidence you have been good enough to show me at all times, I have stated or rather repeated all this to you very candidly and in a mot friendly spirit, for I realize, as I believe you do, the grave consequences which the enactment of the measures retaining that particular provision would inevitably bring upon the otherwise happy and mutually advantageous relations between our two countries.[85]

### 8.4.3. The Passage of the Japanese Exclusion Bill

Notwithstanding Hanihara's appeal, the House of Representatives passed the Johnson bill by a vote of 322 to 71 on April 12. In the Senate, with strong administration pressure, there was a possibility that the bill would fail to secure a majority, let alone the two-thirds majority necessary to override an expected veto by President Coolidge on foreign policy grounds.

There was no move in the Senate until April 14, when Lodge suddenly asserted that the phrase "grave consequences" was in fact a "veiled threat" against the United States, and that since no one could be permitted to threaten the United States with impunity, Japanese exclusion must become law. Other senators, including most of opponents of the Japanese exclusion bill, professed to agree with Lodge. Reed, a leader in the fight against the Japanese exclusion law, now said that he felt "compelled, on account of that veiled threat, to vote in favor of exclusion."[86]

A few Senators were not swept off their feet by Lodge. Senator George Moses from New Hampshire contended that the letter was never improper and the phrase "grave consequences" could hardly be interpreted as a veiled threat. Senator Thomas Sterling from South Dakota said it was wrong to "make the letter of the Japanese ambassador the pretext" for rejecting the Gentlemen's Agreement. Sterling also stated that he did not think the letter was "in any respect discourteous to or defiant of the American government or people . . . he [Hanihara] refers to the pride—and I think justly so—and to the sensitiveness of his people in this regard, their sensitiveness about being discriminated against."[87]

The Senate, however, voted down the amendment recognizing the Gentlemen's Agreement by a vote of 76 to 2,[88] and two days later passed the new amendment providing for the exclusion of aliens ineligible for citizenship by a vote of 71 to 4.

Astounded by the interpretation Lodge put on his letter, Hanihara immediately protested that he had not "in any part of his body" any feeling toward his beloved America.[89] He wrote to Hughes on April 17.

> Frankly I must say I am unable to understand how the two words read in their context could be construed as meaning anything like a threat. I simply tried to emphasize the most unfortunate and deplorable effect upon our traditional friendship which might result from the adoption of a particular clause in the proposed measure. . . . In using these words, I had no thought of being in any way disagreeable or discourteous and still less of conveying a "veiled threat."[90]

Hughes, who was no less surprised at the Senate action, replied, " . . . I had no doubt that these words were to be taken in the sense you have stated, and I was quite sure that it was far from your thought to express or imply any threat."[91]

Hughes forwarded Hanihara's letter to Congress without avail; the coup de grace had already been administered to the Gentlemen's Agreement. Coolidge belatedly intervened with the suggestion that the application of the exclusionist clause be postponed until 1926. The suggestion was rejected. Coolidge reduced the requested term of postponement to one year. Again he was rebuffed. On May 26, 1924, he signed the bill into law, to become effective on July 1.

The 1924 Japanese exclusion act represented the culmination of almost twenty years of persistent anti-Japanese campaigns in the United States. It was to govern American immigration policy for the next twenty-eight years, until the enactment of the Immigration and National Act of December 24, 1952, after the end of the American occupation of Japan.

### 8.4.4. The Domestic Political Background of the Enactment of the 1924 Law

Lodge's speech served to convert several opponents of the anti-Japanese bill to supporters. But conversion on much larger scale had already taken place even before Lodge's speech. With the 1924 presidential election near at hand, the

Chapter 8

Republican leaders were anxious to avoid the misfortune they had experienced in 1912. In that year, the Republicans lost the presidential election to the Democrats due to a split in their party. While the Republicans were successful in staying together to elect Harding in 1920, in 1924 they were again threatened by defection of the Progressives.[92] Robert La Follette, a Progressive Republican from Wisconsin, left the Republican Party to run for president as a candidate of the Progressive Party, as Theodore Roosevelt had done in 1912. There were signs that many Republicans inclined to the principles of progressivism would follow him.

Moreover, the Harding/Coolidge administration had been plagued with political scandals, the Teapot Dome scandal during Harding's time in office in particular.[93] Not only the opposition Democrats, but also the Progressive Republicans such as La Follette and Hiram Johnson had been severely critical of both the Harding and Coolidge cabinets with reference to the scandals.

Another issue that divided the Republican Party was the anti-lynching bill banning the extrajudicial hanging of African-Americans. The anti-lynching bill had been passed in the House and was under debate in the Senate. It was strongly opposed by senators from the southern states, and they were bitterly resentful of the western senators who promoted the bill. The southerners' resentment was so great that they opposed the anti-Japanese immigration bill that the westerners promoted.[94]

It was imperative for the Republicans to remove those issues that divided the party, and to form a united front against the Democrats. In order to achieve these goals, the party leaders decided to use the Japanese immigration question, which had been a divisive issue within the party. It was expected, however, that the president would veto an exclusion bill on foreign policy grounds, and it was therefore necessary to pass any exclusion bill by an overwhelming majority that could clearly provide the two-thirds majority necessary to override a presidential veto. By agreement with southern Democrats, southern congresspeople and senators were told to support the Japanese exclusion bill in return for the western Republicans dropping their support of an anti-lynching bill.[95] Hiram Johnson now agreed to drop his accusations concerning the Teapot Dome scandal in return for the party's all-out support for the Japanese exclusion bill, for the enactment of which he had given such sustained effort.[96]

By April 14, many opponents of the anti-Japanese immigration bill had

*US–Japanese Immigration Disputes*

turned into supporters. Lodge's speech provided those Senators with a pretext for their overnight conversion. Democratic Senator Thomas Heflin mockingly observed, "When Republican leaders discovered that they were whipped, . . . they had a hurried conference, . . . and now they come in and say that they take offense at something that a Jap ambassador has written upon the subject. . . . Why is it that this step is taken now, just preceding a presidential election, and Republican Senators pretending to get offended all of a sudden at something which the Japanese ambassador has suggested?"[97]

What happened in the Senate in April, 1924 was one of the cases often observed in the history of American lawmaking. When politicians have to choose between the interests of their party or their personal interests in domestic politics and the foreign policy interests of their country, they choose the former. While sacrificing the country's international interests costs no votes, doing otherwise risks defeat in elections. If the choice of the Japanese exclusion act would help avoid disintegration of the party, offending the Japanese might comparatively be a problem of much less importance.

There was also at that time a bitter rivalry between the Senate and the State Department. The Senate resisted the State Department's attempts to block the Japanese exclusion act as an unwarranted intervention by the executive branch in the constitutional treaty-making powers of the Senate.[98] Lodge was resentful in particular of the collaboration between the State Department and the Japanese ambassador. Though it was not known publicly that Hughes and Hanihara worked in concert, Lodge was too sophisticated not to be aware of such collaboration.[99] Lodge must have found satisfaction in embarrassing Hughes, whom he personally disliked.[100]

Lodge's action also reflected his personal conviction that the Japanese were at no higher stage of civilization than the Chinese and Indians, who had long been excluded from the United States. He argued that Chinese civilization was superior to Japanese civilization, that all Japanese civilization had been taken from China until the Japanese began to borrow from Western civilization, and that prospective Japanese immigrants should be classed in the same category with those from China and India. He therefore dismissed the Japanese resentment and sense of humiliation as being invalid.[101]

It was also unfortunate that there was antagonism between Hughes and Hiram Johnson,[102] who was at that point a leader in the Japanese exclusion movement in the Senate. The Senate actions might have been less severe otherwise.

*209*

# Chapter 8

## 8.5. The 1924 Law and US–Japan Relations

### 8.5.1. Repercussions in Japan

The Exclusion Act of 1924 had "grave consequences" concerning the Japanese view of Americans, if not any "grave consequences" in terms of any immediate break of relations with the United States.

When the bill became law, there was an outburst of denunciation in practically all the newspapers in Japan.[103] The *Osaka Asahi*, one of the two dailies enjoying a circulation of over a million copies, wrote that the law was a "glaring breach of international customs and a deliberate insult." The *Osaka Mainichi*, equally influential, said that the "national honor of Japan" had been seriously hurt.[104]

Mass rallies against the exclusion law took place throughout Japan. A convention held in Tokyo by an ultranationalist group on June 5 gathered 30,000 people.[105] On July 1, when the law went into effect, both houses of the Japanese Diet passed a resolution protesting against the discrimination embodied in the law. The day was designated a "National Humiliation Day" in Japan, and protests took place all over the country. In Osaka, four anti-American rallies took place, each attracting an audience of several thousand.

The law delivered a profound shock to pro-American liberal intellectuals such as Nitobe Inazō (新渡戸稲造), who had identified himself as a "bridge" between Japan the United States. He was so shocked that he swore that he would never set foot on US soil again unless the exclusion law was abrogated.[106]

Kaneko Kentarō resigned as president of the America-Japan Society, a position he had occupied since the organization's founding in 1917. He said in his resignation letter, " . . . When I learned the Immigration Bill was passed in so drastic a manner and with such an overwhelming majority, I felt as if the hope of my life were destroyed. . . . When my hope to serve my country and my second home—America—is frustrated, I cannot conscientiously occupy the post of . . . President of the Society any longer."[107]

The reactions of Japanese business leaders were calmer and more realistic. Shibusawa Eiichi (渋沢栄一), a Japanese business tycoon, suspected that the exclusion law was not supported by the majority of Americans, and believed that the Japanese should stay quiet.[108] Equally realistic but more enlightening and critical of the Japanese was a view expressed by Ishibashi Tanzan (石橋

*210*

湛山), the leading economic commentator.[109] He criticized the Japanese attitude that accepted American discrimination against other Asians so long as the Japanese themselves were treated as equals by whites as being Japan-centered and lacking in pan-Asian perspective. He argued that the Japanese should not focus on a token immigration quota but should speak on behalf of all Asians excluded by the United States.[110]

Reasonable as these views were, they did not find many supporters in Japan. An American diplomat in Tokyo noticed effects of the law even on government officials. Jefferson Caffery, chargé d'affaires at the American embassy, reported: "Prior to the passage of the Act, the younger officials in the foreign ministry were more than ready to grant favors or to supply information, whereas requests now are often acceded to with evident reluctance." He also explained that an atmosphere in the foreign ministry had been created in which friendly relations with Americans could work against the young Japanese diplomats' careers.[111]

### 8.5.2. Reactions in the United States

American reaction differed depending on the region. The West was largely supportive of the anti-Japanese legislation. However, in the rest of the country, many opposed the law.

Research conducted by the Japanese foreign ministry showed that among nineteen California newspapers, ten were in favor of the Japanese exclusion clause, five were against exclusion, and the rest were neutral. The East Coast was mostly sympathetic to the Japanese. Forty out of forty-four newspapers east of Chicago criticized the law.[112] In New York, only one out of eleven newspapers supported the exclusion clause.[113] The *New York Times* argued that the immigration act was a "rude means of obtaining an object which Japan was more ready to agree to diplomatically."[114] The *New York Herald Tribune* denounced the act as "an unnecessary affront to Japan."[115] In Boston, the *Christian Science Monitor* opposed the exclusion clause because Congress had chosen a "method . . . highly offensive to a Nation with whom the United States should take especial pains to remain on terms of peace and amity."[116]

Thirty college presidents, including Charles W. Elliot, president emeritus of Harvard, John G. Hibben of Princeton, and William H. P. Faunce of Brown, signed a message condemning "the 'Inconsiderate Action' of Congress." This message, drafted by President Elliot, stated that the action of

Chapter 8

Congress "does not represent the sentiments of the American people toward Japan." The signatories included two Californians: David Starr Jordan, president emeritus of Stanford University, and W. W. Campbell, president of the University of California.[117]

The National Chamber of Commerce and the World Peace Foundation passed resolutions criticizing the passage of the exclusion law. A group of twenty-four prominent New York business and professional men sent a cablegram to the America-Japan Society in Tokyo expressing regret.[118]

Religious groups were mostly sympathetic to Japan.[119] The Congregational Conference in New York urged Coolidge to veto the immigration bill, and the Congregational Committee on Friendly Relations with Japanese and Other Citizens in Los Angeles resolved that racial discrimination in the naturalization laws should be abolished.[120] The Federal Council of the Churches of Christ in America (FCCCA) called it a "needless and wanton act" and warned that the consequences would slowly appear in succeeding decades.[121] The driving force of these campaigns was clergymen who had formerly been missionaries in Japan. The central figure was Sydney Gulick, who had stayed in Japan for twenty-five years from 1888 to 1913. Gulick refused to accept the 1924 law and continued to work for its repeal until the outbreak of WWII.[122]

### 8.5.3. Actions Taken by the US and Japanese Governments

Five days after the passage of the bill in the Senate, Hughes wrote to Lodge; "It is a dangerous thing to plant a deep feeling of resentment in the Japanese people, not that we have need to apprehend, much less to fear war, but that we shall have hereafter in the East to count upon a sense of injury and antagonism, instead of friendship and cooperation. I dislike to think what the reaping will be after the sowing of this seed. I fear that our labors to create a better feeling in the East, which have thus far been notably successful, are now largely undone."[123] When President Coolidge signed the bill that contained the Japanese exclusion provision on May 26, 1924, he declared; "In signing this bill . . . I regret the impossibility of severing from it the exclusion provision which in the light of existing law affects especially the Japanese . . . We have had for many years an understanding with Japan, by which the Japanese Government has voluntarily undertaken to prevent the emigration of laborers to the United States . . . If the exclusion provision stood alone, I should disap-

*212*

prove it without hesitation if sought in this way at this time."[124]

In June 1924, Ambassador Cyrus Woods resigned from his ambassadorial post in Tokyo in protest against the law. On leaving Japan, he regretfully commented;

> We had all in our hand, and we have deliberately and wantonly thrown it away. Here was Japan in the most strategic position in the Orient— geographically, militarily, and politically. The only organized nation in the East . . . This nation has become and in complete sincerity wants to remain our friend, patterns her Occidental growth and more abundant life on us, believes in us, is looking forward to continuing relations of mutual benefit, and we chuck the whole thing overboard . . . I confess I'm utterly unable to see it.[125]

In Japan, Shidehara, who became foreign minister a month after the passage of the law,[126] believed that it was unwise to sacrifice the basic framework of understanding with the United States for the sake of vindicating the national honor.[127] He explained in the Diet that since in the United States the executive branch of the government could do nothing against the legislative branch, it was useless to protest to the former. He also argued that impatient speeches and actions in Japan were counterproductive, and remaining calm would bring about better results.[128]

The Japanese government presented its formal protest on May 31, 1924, but it was determined not to let the immigration issue harm US–Japanese relations. After the US reply on June 16,[129] and the Japanese response on September 11, there was no further correspondence on this subject between the two governments. In the September 11 letter, the Japanese government indicated that it would present no more letters of protest, and the US government expressed its sincere appreciation for the Japanese government's position.[130]

### 8.5.4. The Aftereffects of the 1924 Law on US–Japanese Relations

Ambassador Edgar Bancroft, who succeeded Woods, wrote to Hughes on January 5, 1925; " . . . My conclusions are that the Japanese people, with substantial unanimity, keenly felt that a humiliating slight was put upon their race by the form of the Immigration Act; that this feeling of insult was intensified by the friendship of the Japanese toward America, and their confidence that America was their friend . . . "[131] William Castle, chief of the Division of Western European Affairs of State Department and later the ambassador to Japan succeeding Bancroft, stated that it would leave to future generations "a heritage of hatred across the water which in future years might burst into flame."[132]

Hanihara, who had resigned from diplomatic service in July 1924, broke his long silence on May 23, 1930 at the farewell dinner given in honor of Ambassador Castle. He still refused to give an account of how the letter was prepared, and continued to assume full responsibility for the incident, but he clearly stated that the Japanese were still resentful of what had happened in 1924. He stated;

> I do not intend to go into the details of this matter on this occasion. But one thing must be said to dispel the popular misconception as to the true nature of that regrettable incident. It is not so much a question as to whether one nation should or should not exercise its sovereign rights in regulating matters relating to its domestic affairs, as it is often represented to be. More precisely, it is a question as to whether one people should treat another people sympathetically or unsympathetically, fairly or unfairly. In that incident the Ambassador of a friendly Power, whose warmth of friendship and high regard for the Government and people to whom he was accredited was everywhere widely known and accepted was gratuitously accused of the wanton act of using a "veiled threat" against that very country. The Secretary of State's categorical assurance to the contrary was brushed aside by that accusing party. Naturally the Japanese Government and people deeply resented this, and that resentment is felt now as it was then. Nor will it ever die out so long as the wound inflicted remains unhealed. Friendship once marred in this manner can with difficulty resume its wholesome growth unless some effective remedy is administered.[133]

After the 1924 law, many right-wing societies mushroomed in Japan protesting against US discrimination. There was inevitably a pan-Asianist strain in these movements.[134] They argued that since the United States had closed its door to the Japanese, it had no right to restrict Japanese activities in East

Asia.[135] Though there is no way of ascertaining how closely the Japanese exclusion law and Pearl Harbor were related, it is certain that the 1924 law provided the rightist groups and military hardliners with a potent weapon in their efforts to arouse hatred toward America.

A commander of one of the Japanese squadrons heading to Pearl Harbor wrote in his diary that since the Japanese had previously just endured the treacherous behavior of the Americans, such as the exclusion of Japanese immigrants, it was now time to teach them a lesson.[136]

Emperor Hirohito once said to his close aides after the war that the US rejection of Japanese immigrants was an indirect cause of the Pacific War.[137]

When the negotiations to avert war started in Washington in February 1941 (16.4.1), Secretary of State Cordell Hull confided to Ambassador Nomura Kichisaburō that he had once tried without avail to find a way to revise the 1924 law. Hull referred to his earlier attempt again when he handed the Japanese delegates the note of November 26 that led to the end of diplomatic efforts to avoid war.[138]

## NOTES

### 8.1. The Roots of the Immigration Question in California

1   The law provided for the suspension of immigration of Chinese laborers for ten years, and it also barred the Chinese from the privilege of naturalization. The law was then renewed three times, and in 1904 it was made permanent. It was in 1943 that the law was finally abrogated.

2   Toyokichi Iyenaga and Kenoske Sato, *Japan and the California Problem* (New York: G. P. Putnam's Sons, 1921), 79.

3   Hirobe Izumi, *Japanese Pride, American Prejudice* (Stanford, CA: Stanford University Press, 2001), 3.

4   Roger Daniels, *The Politics of Prejudice: The Anti-Japanese Movement in California and the Struggle for Japanese Exclusion* (Berkeley: University of California Press, 1962), 25–26.

5   Daniels, *The Politics of Prejudice*, 27.

6   A. Whitney Griswold, *The Far Eastern Policy of the United States* (New York: Harcourt, Brace & Company, 1938), 347.

7   Iyenaga and Sato, *Japan and the California Problem*, 92–94.

8   Eiichiro Azuma, *Between Two Empires: Race, History, and Transnationalism in Japanese America* (New York: Oxford University Press, 2005), 63.

9   Ibid., 65.

10  Iyenaga and Sato, *Japan and the California Problem*, 135.

11  Ibid., 136.

12  When he died in 1926, his estate was estimated at between $15 and $17 million. He

Chapter 8

attempted to give leadership to the Japanese-American community and enjoyed a certain amount of entrée into California political circles, but he was always subject to press criticism as an Oriental who had risen too far and too fast. Don Hata and Nadine Hata, "George Shima: The Potato King of California," *Journal of the West*, vol. 25, no. 1 (1986), 55–56.

13 Iyenaga and Sato, *Japan and the California Problem*, 125.

14 Masakazu Iwata, "The Japanese Immigrants in California Agriculture," *Agricultural History*, vol. 36, no. 1 (January, 1962), 25.

   8.2. The San Francisco School Incident and the Gentlemen's Agreement

15 Daniels, *Politics of Prejudice*, 32.

16 Griswold, *Far Eastern Policy*, 349.

17 Ibid., 350.

18 Hirobe, *Japanese Pride, American Prejudice*, 4.

19 Griswold, *Far Eastern Policy*, 350.

20 The Department of Justice instituted two lawsuits, one in the Federal Circuit Court and the other in the State Supreme Court, "for the purpose of enforcing the provisions of the 1894 treaty giving the Japanese an equal right of education." Yamato Ichihashi, *Japanese in the United States* (New York: Arno Press and The New York Times, 1969), 241–242.

21 Griswold, *Far Eastern Policy*, 350.

22 A strong earthquake hit San Francisco on April 14, 1906, and subsequent fires destroyed entire sections of the city. Japan donated $246,000, which was more than the combined contributions from all other nations.

23 Griswold, *Far Eastern Policy*, 352.

24 The Act of 1790 restricted eligibility for naturalization to aliens who were "free white persons." The criterion that one must be a "free white person" was modified by the Congress in 1870 after the Civil War, when "persons of African nativity or descent" were granted naturalization privileges. Though Chinese were denied naturalization after 1882, it was not certain whether Japanese could become naturalized in the United States. Federal court rulings had been mixed. In some cases Japanese had been admitted citizenship, but in other cases they were denied naturalization. There had been no decision by the Supreme Court until November 13, 1922, when Japanese were declared ineligible (8.4.1). Frank Chuman, *The Bamboo People: The Law and Japanese-Americans* (Del Mar, CA: Publisher's Inc., 1976), 65–66. Ichihashi, *Japanese in the United States*, 298.

25 Roosevelt also agreed to setting an age limit for each grade. Griswold, *Far Eastern Policy*, 353.

26 Roosevelt requested that Congress authorize the president to restrict Japanese immigration from intermediate points. Conveniently, an immigration bill was under consideration in Congress, and an amendment designed to check secondary Japanese immigration was added to the bill, which became the immigration law of 1907. Daniels, *Politics of Prejudice*, 41–44.

27 Ibid., 44.

28 Ichihashi, *Japanese in the United States*, 246.

*216*

*Notes*

29 Ibid., 245.

30 Minohara Toshihirō, *Hainichi imin-hō to Nichibei kankei* (Tokyo: Iwanami Shoten, 2002), 29.

31 It is noteworthy that on this occasion one Congressman made a speech touching upon the Gentlemen's Agreement, " . . . If such an agreement is in existence and it is pretended to have the force of law or to be binding in any way upon Japan, why not incorporate such an agreement in the treaty?" Ichihashi, *Japanese in the United States*, 256.

32 Daniels, *The Politics of Prejudice*, 44. Although it is difficult to determine how many married women came to the United States as "picture brides," there was a considerable increase in the number of married women in the 1910s. The census showed that there were 24,326 Japanese in 1900, of whom 410 were married women. In 1910 there were 72,157 Japanese, of whom 5,581 were married women. In 1920 there were 111,010 Japanese, of whom 22,193 were married women. Ichihashi, *Japanese in the United States*, 291.

33 Daniels, *Politics of Prejudice*, 44.

34 Griswold, *Far Eastern Policy*, 363–364.

## 8.3. The Alien Land Laws in California

35 Minohara, *Hainichi imin-hō*, 30.

36 Ichihashi, *Japanese in the United States*, 261.

37 Ibid., 261.

38 Griswold, *Far Eastern Policy*, 357.

39 Ichihashi, *Japanese in the United States*, 250. At this time Roosevelt told president-elect Taft that "the Republican machine finally came to my help." Daniels, *Politics of Prejudice*, 47.

40 Ibid., 46.

41 Ibid., 46.

42 Ibid., 47.

43 Griswold, *Far Eastern Policy*, 357.

44 Ibid., 357–358.

45 Daniels, *Politics of Prejudice*, 49.

46 Ibid., 50.

47 Minohara, *Hainichi imin-hō*, 35–37. Ichihashi, *Japanese in the United States*, 264.

48 Daniels, *The Politics of Prejudice*, 56.

49 Ibid., 56.

50 Ambassador Chinda met Wilson on March 5, the second day of the new administration. He then visited Bryan on March 13. He had another interview with Bryan on April 12, and one with Wilson on April 15. Ichihashi, *Japanese in the United States*, 271.

51 Daniels, *Politics of Prejudice*, 59.

52 Johnson pointed out to one of Wilson's messengers that Wilson should communicate directly with him if he had anything to say. Daniels, *Politics of Prejudice*, 60.

53 Taft had not passed on to Wilson detailed information about the immigration problem in California. Minohara, *Hainichi imin-hō*, 40.

*217*

Chapter 8

54 Minohara, *Hainichi imin-hō*, 41–45. Ichihashi, *Japanese in the United States*, 269. H. A. Millis, *The Japanese Problem in the United States* (New York: Macmillan Company, 1915; reprint, New York: Arno Press, 1978), 316. Citations refer to the 1978 edition.

55 Article I of the 1911 treaty read, "The subjects or citizens of each of the high contracting parties shall have liberty to enter, travel and reside in the territories of the other, to carry on trade, wholesale and retail, to own or lease and occupy houses, manufactories, warehouses and shops, to employ agents of their choice, to lease land for residential and commercial purposes, and generally to do anything incident to or necessary for trade, upon the same terms as native subjects or citizens, submitting themselves to the laws and regulations there established . . . " Millis, *Japanese Problem*, 313.

56 Daniels, *Politics of Prejudice*, 62.

57 Ibid., 62.

58 Minohara, *Hainichi imin-hō*, 46. Millis, *Japanese Problem*, 316.

59 Ichihashi, *Japanese in the United States*, 273.

60 Ibid., 273.

61 Hirobe, *Japanese Pride, American Prejudice*, 6.

62 Daniels, *Politics of Prejudice*, 81.

63 Chuman, *Bamboo People*, 77

64 Ibid., 77.

65 Ibid., 78.

66 The three-to-one majority was disappointing to the exclusionists, who had expected an overwhelming majority, perhaps ten to one. Daniels, *Politics of Prejudice*, 90. Phelan, one of the most active supporters of the Alien Land Law of 1920, was defeated in his bid for reelection to the Senate. Chuman, *Bamboo People*, 79.

67 The new law also forbid the three-year lease by ineligible aliens which was allowed by the old law. Iyenaga and Satō, *Japan and California Problem*, 141.

68 Azuma, *Between Two Empires*, 63.

69 Ibid., 71. Prior to the Supreme Court ruling, being pressed by exclusionists, the California attorney general declared that cropping contracts were a form of lease in the summer of 1921. Ibid., 69.

70 The 1929 statistic reported 104,560 foremen and no cropping contractees. Ibid., 63, 71.

71 Ibid., 73.

8.4. The Legislation of the Japanese Exclusion Law of 1924

72 Immigration from the Philippines was regulated by a literacy test in much the same way as voting by African-Americans was restricted in the South by literacy tests.

73 Minohara, *Hainichi imin-hō*, 89.

74 Ozawa had lived most of his life in the United States and Hawaii, was a graduate of Berkeley High School, and had attended the University of California. He was a Christian. Daniels, *Politics of Prejudice*, 98.

75 Ibid., 98.

76 Ibid., 99.

77 This was the so called Reed amendment, which was to be rejected later after Lodge's

*Notes*

speech. Minohara, *Hainichi imin-hō*, 143.

78 Ichihashi, *Japanese in the United States*, 300.

79 Asada Sadao, *Japan and the United States, 1915–25*, Yale University, PhD dissertation, 1963 (Ann Arbor, MI: University Microfilms, 1966), 387.

80 Ibid., 387.

81 Akira Iriye, *Across the Pacific* (New York: Harcourt, Brace & World, 1967), 152.

82 Ichihashi, *Japanese in the United States*, 300–301.

83 Daniels, *Politics of Prejudice*, 100.

84 Ibid., 100.

85 Ibid., 101.

86 Chuman, *Bamboo People*, 101.

87 Henry Taft, *Japan and America: A Journey and a Political Survey* (New York: Macmillan Company, 1932). 186.

88 Daniels, *Politics of Prejudice*, 101.

89 Asada, *Japan and the United States*, 393.

90 Taft, *Japan and America*, 172.

91 Ibid., 186.

92 In the 1908 election, Theodore Roosevelt chose Taft as his successor and did not run for the presidency. But Roosevelt was disappointed by Taft's conservative policies, and he once again sought nomination as the candidate of Republican Party. But since the party re-nominated Taft, Roosevelt formed the Progressive Party, and ran for the presidency with California governor Hiram Johnson as his running mate. He lost to Woodrow Wilson, though he received more votes than Taft.

93 Prior to the Watergate scandal, the Teapot Dome scandal was regarded as the greatest and most sensational scandal in the history of American politics. In 1922, Albert Fall, secretary of the Interior of the Harding administration, leased the Teapot Dome oil fields to Harry Sinclair of Sinclair Oil without competitive bidding. La Follette played an important role in the investigation of the matter. Fall was found guilty of bribery in 1929 and fined $100,000, and was sentenced to one year in prison.

94 One of the proponents of the anti-lynching bill was Samuel Shortridge, Republican senator from California, who was also a strong proponent of the anti-Japanese bill. The southerners contended that those who were bashing the Japanese had no right to oppose their bashing African-Americans. Minohara, *Hainichi imin-hō*, 145.

95 As evidence, Minohara refers to a letter written by Shortridge addressed to James Phelan, in which Shortridge pledged to stop promoting the anti-lynching bill. Minohara, *Hainichi imin-hō*, 148.

96 Before Roosevelt's death in 1919, Hiram Johnson had refrained from supporting anti-Japanese measures in deference to Roosevelt. But after his death, Johnson became a leader of Japanese exclusion movements, organizing the "Executive Committee of Western States," a committee for anti-Japanese measures, which was composed of one senator and one representative from each of eleven Western states, cutting across party lines. Daniels, *Politics of Prejudice*, 96.

97 Taft, *Japan and America*, 172.

98 Griswold, *Far Eastern Policy*, 376.

99 Both Hughes and MacMurrey testified that the inclusion of the phrase "grave

Chapter 8

consequences" had not been advised, suggested or approved by any member of the State Department (Asada, *Japan and the United States*, 390–391). But Minohara contends that there is little doubt that MacMurray suggested the use of the phrase and Hughes approved it. He refers, as evidence, to the following facts: 1) When Hanihara met MacMurray on April 15, MacMurray clearly stated to Hanihara that it was not Hanihara who was responsible. 2) Foreign Minister Matsui Keishirō said in answer to a question at a plenary session of the Privy Council that Hanihara had used the phrase "grave consequences" after consultation with Hughes. 3) There is a description in the letter from B. W. Fleisher, the owner of the *Japan Advertiser*, to Roland Morris, the ex-ambassador to Tokyo, that Hughes, when he received the letter from Hanihara, commented that the letter should be made "even stronger." 4) Nelson Johnson, the ambassador to China, wrote a letter to MacMurray on September 29, 1924, asking if a story that Johnson had heard from the American consul general in Seoul—that Hughes had sent the letter back to Hanihara a couple of times suggesting that it be "pepped up"—was true. MacMurray did not reply to Johnson. 5) William Castle, the ambassador in Tokyo, wrote in his diary on February, 25, 1930, that Eugene Dorman had heard from Taketomi Toshihiko, who had served in Washington as first secretary in the Japanese embassy in 1924, that the whole letter had been written by MacMurray, that Hanihara had expressed concern about the strong tone of the letter, and that he (Castle) could now understand why MacMurry was unpopular in Tokyo as a candidate for the post of ambassador to Japan. Minohara, *Hainichi imin-hō*, 194–197.

100  Frederick Moore, *With Japan's Leaders* (New York: C. Scribner, 1942), 72. Moore writes, "That Lodge did not like his fellow New Englander was well known . . . I was told on good authority that the Senator's denunciation of the Japanese at this time was largely due to personal politics."

101  Asada, *Japan and the United States*, 392.

102  The incident that destroyed the relationship between Hughes and Hiram Johnson occurred during the 1916 presidential election. Hughes, as the Republican presidential candidate, made a campaign tour of California. He happened to stay in the Hotel Virginia, where Hiram Johnson was also staying. Hughes did not attempt to meet Johnson while staying at the hotel. Johnson, being the governor of California, felt insulted. Hughes had expected Johnson to come to greet him, as he was the presidential candidate. Minohara, *Hainichi imin-hō*, 140–141.

103  Ichihashi, *Japanese in the United States*, 315.

104  Hirobe, *Japanese Pride, American Prejudice*, 23.

105  Ibid., 33.

106  Ibid., 29. After the passage of the law, Nitobe declined all requests for lectures or speeches in the United States, including an invitation from his old friend Nicholas Murray Butler, who was the president of Columbia University. Asada Sadao, *Ryō-taisenkan no Nichibei kankei* (Tokyo: University of Tokyo Press, 1993), 308. Nitobe wrote in a book published in 1931, "The repercussion of this legislative act on Japan was profound. She felt as though her best friend had, of a sudden and without provocation, slapped her on the cheek. She questioned the sanity of American legislators. At heart, however silent, she does not now and never will accede to this law, passed

in a manner so far from 'gentlemanly'—whatever may be the legal 'rights' of a country as regards its own enactments. Each year that passes without amendment or abrogation only strengthens and sharpens our sense of injury, which is destined to show itself, in one form or another, in personal and public intercourse. All talk of peace and goodwill is vain, so long as one nation sows in the heart of another the seeds of suspicion and resentment." Taft, *Japan and America*, 196.

107 Hirobe, *Japanese Pride, American Prejudice*, 29–30.

108 Ibid., 30.

109 He started as a journalist at the *Mainichi Shimbun* and later became the president of Tōyōkeizai Shinpōsha, a leading Japanese economic magazine publisher. He espoused a liberal political view advocating the "Small Japan" policy, the core of which was the abandonment of Manchuria. He was appointed as minister of finance in the first Yoshida cabinet in 1946, and as minister of industry in the Hatoyama Ichirō cabinet of 1953. He served as prime minister from December 1956 to February 1957.

110 Hirobe, *Japanese Pride, American Prejudice*, 30–31.

111 Ibid., 31.

112 Ichihashi, *Japanese in the United States*, 316.

113 Hirobe, *Japanese Pride, American Prejudice*, 52.

114 Ibid., 53.

115 Ichihashi, *Japanese in the United States*, 316.

116 Hirobe, *Japanese Pride, American Prejudice*, 53.

117 Ibid., 57.

118 Ichihashi, *Japanese in the United States*, 317. Hirobe, *Japanese Pride, American Prejudice*, 61.

119 Gulick's ardent campaign incurred the Japanophobes' wrath and the US intelligence agencies' suspicion of being a Japanese agent. Taylor, *Advocate of Understanding*, xiii, 78–89, 111–127.

120 Hirobe, *Japanese Pride, American Prejudice*, 60.

121 Taylor, *Advocate of Understanding*, 162.

122 Ibid., 136–148.

123 Akira Iriye, *After Imperialism* (Boston: Harvard University Press, 1965; reprint, Chicago, IL: Imprint Publications, 1990), 35. Citations refer to the 1990 edition.

124 Ichihashi, *Japanese in the United States*, 309–310. It was the Japanese government that wanted President Coolidge to declare that he was opposed to the Japanese exclusion provision when signing the bill. Minohara, *Hainichi imin-hō*, 209.

125 Asada, *Japan and the United States*, 395.

126 Shidehara was appointed as foreign minister by Katō Takaaki, who formed the cabinet on June 11, 1924, after the Kiyoura government.

127 Iriye, *After Imperialism*, 36.

128 It is widely known that Shidehara followed a piece of advice that British ambassador in Washington James Bryce had given him. Bryce said to Shidehara that he believed that the Americans had the sense of justice to rectify the situation in due course, that persistent protest might lead to a war, and that the immigration issue was not a problem over which Japan should fight a war with the United States. Minohara, *Hainichi*

*imin-hō*, 222. Hirobe, *Japanese Pride, American Prejudice*, 37.

129 The State Department replied that since Congress had exercised the power to regulate immigration as one of its prerogatives, the executive branch could do nothing about it. Ichihashi, *Japanese in the United States*, 314.

130 When Yoshida Isaburō (吉田伊三郎), who was appointed as the interim ambassador after Hanihara had resigned, met Hughes on September 15 to give him the September 11 letter from the Japanese government, he told Hughes that the Japanese government would not present any further protests, nor would it make public the text of the September 11 letter. Hughes repeated the words, "I certainly appreciate it," with his eyes filled with tears. Minohara, *Hainichi imin-hō*, 227.

### 8.5. The 1924 Law on US–Japanese Relations

131 Hirobe, *Japanese Pride, American Prejudice*, 88.

132 Ibid., 61.

133 Ichihashi, *Japanese in the United States*, 367. Minohara, *Hainichi imin-hō*, 199.

134 Iriye, *Across the Pacific*, 153.

135 Iriye, *After Imperialism*, 36.

136 The diary was written by Fujita Kikuichi, commander of the Eighth Squadron. Hirobe, *Japanese Pride, American Prejudice*, 1.

137 Terasaki Hidenari and Mariko Terasaki Miller, *Shōwa Tennō dokuhakuroku; Terasaki Hidenari goyōgakari nikki* (Tokyo: Bungeishunju, 1991), 19–21. Hirobe, *Japanese Pride, American Prejudice*, 243. Terasaki Hidenari, who served as one of the aides to Emperor Hirohito after WWII, recorded what the emperor said about the developments during the period from 1928 to 1941. The record was published as a book titled *Shōwa Tennō dokuhakuroku*. Terasaki Hidenari assisted Ambassador Nomura Kichisaburō in the negotiations with Cordell Hull in 1941 as first secretary in the Japanese embassy in Washington.

138 Asada, *Ryō-taisenkan no Nichibei kankei*, 315–316.

# Chapter 9
# The Economies of the US and Japan in the Early Decades of the 20th Century

## 9.1. The Economic Growth and Industrial Development of the US and Japan

### 9.1.1. US and Japanese Economic Growth

The population of the United States, which had increased dramatically in the 19th century and drawn even with that of Japan in the 1860s (table 5.1.1-a), continued its strong growth in the early 20th century, albeit at a decelerated pace. The expansion of the Japanese population, which had started to rise from the late 19th century, accelerated its pace after the turn of the 20th century (table 9.1.1).[1] In both countries, strong increases in population and industrial production expanded the GNP vigorously through the first three decades of the 20th century. In the 1900s, 1910s, and 1920s, the US GNP grew 57 percent, 34 percent, and 30 percent respectively (table 9.1.1), and Japan's growth was similarly strong. In the 1930s (1931–1940), while the Japanese economy continued to grow, the US economy suddenly stopped growing. The economic difficulties of the US are discussed in 12.1.1 and 15.1.1. The difference in economic scale between the two countries, in terms of GNP on a current foreign-exchange basis, narrowed in 1940, but the ratio

*223*

Chapter 9

Table 9.1.1. Population and GNP of Japan and US

| | Population | | GNP in current prices | | | GNP decade growth, constant prices | | |
|---|---|---|---|---|---|---|---|---|
| | US mil. | Japan mil. | US $ bil. | Japan ¥ bil. | Japan $ bil. | | US (%) | Japan (%) |
| 1890 | 63.1 | 39.9 | 13.1 | 1.06 | 0.89 | 1881–1890 | n.a. | n.a. |
| 1900 | 76.1 | 43.8 | 18.7 | 2.41 | 1.19 | 1891–1900 | 46.1 | 30.0 |
| 1910 | 92.4 | 49.2 | 35.3 | 3.93 | 1.94 | 1901–1910 | 56.7 | 22.6 |
| 1920 | 106.5 | 55.5 | 91.5 | 15.9 | 7.89 | 1911–1920 | 33.9 | 35.3 |
| 1930 | 123.2 | 63.9 | 90.4 | 14.7 | 7.24 | 1921–1930 | 29.9 | 35.6 |
| 1940 | 132.1 | 71.4 | 99.7 | 36.9 | 8.64 | 1931–1940 | 3.5 | 45.4 |

*Notes:* 1. Japan's GNP in current prices in dollars is based on $0.839 per ¥1 for 1890, $0.493 per ¥1 for 1900, $0.494 per ¥1 for 1910, $0.496 per ¥1 for 1920, $0.494 per ¥1 for 1930, and $0.234 per ¥1 in 1940.
2. GNP decade growth is the percentage by which growth of the average GNP during the indicated ten years exceeded the average GNP for the previous ten years. US GNP is based on 1958 prices, and Japanese GNP is based on 1934–36 prices.

*Source:* US Department of Commerce, Bureau of the Census, *Historical Statistics of the United States* (Washington, DC: US Government Printing Office, 1975), 8 (population), 224 (GNP); and Ōkawa Kazushi, Shinohara Miyohei and Umemura Mataji, "Kokumin shotoku" in *Chōki Keizai Tōkei*, eds. Yamazawa Ippei and Yamamoto Yūzō (Tokyo: Tōyōkeizai Shinpōsha, 1974), 178, 213 (GNP). Nippon Ginkō Tōkeikyoku, ed., *Meiji ikō honpō shuyō keizai tōkei* (Tokyo: Namiki Shobō, 1999), 12–13 (population), and, 318, and 320 (yen–dollar exchange rates).

was still 11.5:1 ($99.7:$8.64).

By 1890, the United States had displaced Britain as the world's major industrial power and continued its upward trajectory afterward. According to a League of Nations publication, during the period from 1896/1900 to 1926/1929, the US share of world manufacturing increased from 30.1 percent to 42.2 percent, whereas that of Britain declined from 19.5 percent to 9.4 percent, and that of Germany from 16.6 percent to 11.6 percent. Meanwhile, the Japanese share rose from 0.6 percent to 2.5 percent during the same period.[2]

## 9.1.2. US and Japanese Industrial Development

The United States was the world's largest producer not only of major manufactures but also of important raw materials and energy (table 9.1.2-a).

The United States took over from Britain by the end of 1890s as the world's leading producer of coal—the most important energy source since the Industrial Revolution—and maintained that position throughout the

*224*

The Economies of the US and Japan in the Early Decades of the 20th Century

Table 9.1 2-a. Major Industrial Products: US, Japan, and World

|  | 1913 | | | 1929 | | | 1938 | | |
|---|---|---|---|---|---|---|---|---|---|
|  | US | Japan | World | US | Japan | World | US | Japan | World |
| Coal (mil. tons) | 518 | 21.3 | 1,348 | 552 | 34.3 | 1,561 | 358 | 48.6 | 1,478 |
| oil (mil. tons) | 34.6 | 0.3 | n.a. | 136.1 | 0.3 | 206 | 164.1 | 0.3 | 273 |
| Steel ingots (mil. tons) | 31.8 | 0.2 | 76 | 57.3 | 2.3 | 121 | 28.8 | 6.5 | 110 |
| Copper (kilotons) | 574 | 67 | 920 | 974 | 75 | 1,894 | 506 | 102 | 1,947 |
| Electricity (bil. kWh) | 24.8 | 2.2 | n.a. | 116.8 | 15.1 | 287 | 142.0 | 32.4 | 459 |
| Automobiles (1,000 units) | 485 | 0 | n.a. | 5,358 | 28 | 6,288 | 2,489 | 22 | 4,002 |
| Cotton cloth (bil. sq. yds.) | 6.8 | 1.1 | 24.8 | 8.1 | 2.6 | 27.0 | 8.5 | 3.9 | 29.1 |
| Ships (numbers) | 276 | 52 | 3,333 | 112 | 164 | 2,740 | 160 | 451 | 2,976 |

*Notes:*  1. Japan's electric power generation in 1913 of 2.2 kWh is the figure for 1916, the nearest figure available.

2. Ships (numbers) represent the number of ships which are 1,000 gross tons and above.

*Source:* Statistics Division, OECD, *Industrial Statistics, 1900–1962* (Paris: OECD, 1964), 8, 38, 53, 74, 85, 106, 171–173. Miyazaki Saiichi, Okumura Shigeji, and Morita Kirirō, *Kindai kokusai keizai yōran* (Tokyo: University of Tokyo Press, 1981), 111. Nippon Ginkō Tōkeikyoku, ed., *Meiji ikō honpō shuyō keizai tōkei* (Tokyo: Namiki Shobō, 1999), 98–99, 125. Raymond Mikesell, *The World Copper Industry* (Baltimore: Johns Hopkins University Press, 1979), 10, G. C. Allen, *A Short Economic History of Modern Japan* (London: George Allen & Unwin, 1972), 209–210. Tsūshō Sangyō Daijin Kanbō Chōsa Tōkeibu, ed., *Honpō kōgyō no sūsei gojūnenshi* (Tokyo: Tsūshō Sangyō Chōsakai, 1963.3–1964.3), 311.

pre-WWII period.[3] Coal was one of the few raw materials in which Japan remained largely self-sufficient in the prewar days, though it imported some coal from its colonies and China in the 1920s and 1930s.[4]

In petroleum output, the United States displaced Russia as the world's largest producer by 1902.[5] Japan produced small amounts of low-grade petroleum, but domestic production provided less than 10 percent of Japanese consumption, the rest being imported, mostly from the United States—about 80 percent from the United States and about 10 percent from the Dutch East Indies.[6]

The rise of the iron and steel industry in the United States epitomized its emergence as the world's leading industrial power. By 1890, the United States had displaced Britain as the world's largest producer of pig iron and steel. The rich Minnesota ores, which accounted for over 80 percent of the ores mined

*225*

in the United States, contained 50–60 percent iron, compared to an average of 40 percent iron in the ores used by the rest of the world.[7] Japan's production of iron and steel fell far short of its consumption. As late as 1930, over one-third of the iron and steel materials consumed in Japan were still imports in the form of pig iron, scrap, and steel products.[8]

The United States also dominated world copper production until the 1930s, when new mines were developed in South America.[9] Copper was Japan's other important mineral. From the 1880s through the 1910s, Japan exported most of its copper output, but by the 1930s, the increase in domestic demand made Japan a net importer of the material.

The United States also led other industrial nations in the use of electricity for communications and lighting in the late 19th century, and as a power source after the turn of the century.[10] In this era, electricity was generated either by steam turbines that used coal or by water turbines that used flowing water; both coal and rapidly flowing water were abundant in the United States. These resources were not scarce in Japan, either. Japan's output of electricity was at nearly the same level as Britain's and Germany's in the 1930s.[11]

In terms of manufacturing, the most impressive event in the early 20th century was the development of the US automobile industry. The Americans speedily assimilated the European invention of the internal combustion engine, and they produced the first functional automobile with a gasoline engine in the United States in 1893.[12] By 1910, the US had twice as many cars as Europe. The advancement of the industry was led by Henry Ford, who introduced the Model T in 1908.[13] The US output of motor vehicles rose from 2.2 million in 1920 to 5.3 million in 1929.[14] By 1920, 8.2 million motor vehicles were registered in the United States, and the number increased to 23.1 million by 1925.[15] By 1927, nine-tenths of all passenger cars and four-fifths of all buses and trucks in the world were of American manufacture. Japan was almost totally dependent on American auto-makers, as observed in 10.3.4.

In 1929, the US motor vehicle industry produced 12.7 percent of the total national manufacturing output by value, and its employees constituted 7.1 percent of the total labor force of US manufacturing industries.[16] The US automobile industry played a leading role in the 1920s "decade of prosperity" enjoyed by the US economy.

By 1930, 60 percent of American households owned automobiles. The automobile was the most visible sign that the United States had become a consumer culture.[17] The wide spread of the automobile had an enormous impact on the US economy. By 1927, the industry accounted for 80 percent of the rubber, half of the plate glass, and 65 percent of the leather upholstery consumed in the country annually. By 1938, it was consuming 17 percent of all forms of steel and 90 percent of the gasoline produced in the United States.[18]

Japan shared with Britain the experience of economic development based on the production and export of textiles. In the case of Japan, raw silk, as well as cotton textiles, was of major importance.[19] Raw silk accounted for about 30 percent of Japan's total exports in the mid-1910s and about 40 percent in the mid-1920s. As late as 1930, it was still the chief source of foreign exchange to finance Japan's industrialization, as well as a major source of rural income supplementing the proceeds of rice cultivation.[20]

The cotton textile industry's development owed much to the early experience gained through raw-silk exports. When Japan was opened to foreign trade, the cotton industry could not compete with British imports, but by 1890 Japanese spinners were producing more cotton yarn than Japan imported, were exporting about one-quarter of their output by the early 1910s, and had exceeded British output (but not exports) by 1929 (table 9.1.2-b).[21] By 1933, Japan had surpassed Britain in cotton-cloth exports, becoming the world's largest exporter.[22]

In the 1910s, the Japanese textile industry accounted for one-third of the nation's total manufacturing output, and in the early decades of the 20th century it employed about 50 percent of the manufacturing labor force working in factories with more than five employees.[23]

In the United States, most large-scale cotton textile mills both spun and wove.[24] They expanded their cotton-cloth production at a pace fast enough to keep up with the increasing population. Their production represented about 30 percent of the world output in the 1910s through the 1930s,[25] but they marketed their products almost entirely in their protected domestic market.

In terms of its contribution to Japanese economic development, the shipbuilding industry played a very important role. Assisted by the government through a series of subsidy grants,[26] the industry developed rapidly from the late 19th century through the early 20th century, and especially during WWI.[27] Japanese shipbuilding's share of manufacturing output rose from 2.6 percent in 1912 to 7.3 percent in 1917.[28] The presence of the shipbuilding industry in Japan was larger than these figures indicate, as large Japanese

Table 9.1.2-b. Cotton Manufactures, Output and Exports: Japan, UK, and US

| | Japan | | | | UK | | | | US | |
| | Yarn (mil. lbs.) | | Cloth (mil. sq. yds.) | | Yarn (mil. lbs.) | | Cloth (mil sq. yds.) | | Cloth (mil sq. yds.) | |
| | Output | Exports | Output | Exports | Output | Exports | Output | Exports | Output | Exports |
|---|---|---|---|---|---|---|---|---|---|---|
| 1890 | 43 | 0.01 | 122 | 7 | 1,466 | 258 | n.a. | 5,125 | n.a. | 118 |
| 1913 | 794 | 187 | 1,050 | 235 | 1,983 | 210 | 8,050 | 6,913 | 6,800 | 445 |
| 1929 | 1,144 | 27 | 3,329 | 1,791 | 1,047 | 167 | 3,399 | 2,472 | 8,056 | 564 |
| 1936–38 | 1,396 | 46 | 4,232 | 2,423 | 1,358 | 159 | 3,806 | 2,023 | 8,530 | 252 |

*Notes:* 1. No published data exists on American cotton yarn production, as most American textile mills both spun and wove.

2. The figures shown for UK cotton yarn output and US cotton cloth output in 1890 are the available 1891–92 averages.

3. The figures shown for UK cotton yarn and cloth production in 1913, 1929, and 1936–38 are those of 1912, 1930, and 1937 respectively.

*Source:* R. Robson, *The Cotton Industry in Britain* (London: Macmillan & Co., 1957), 332–333, 342, 345, 358. Seki Keizō, *The Cotton Industry of Japan* (Tokyo: Japan Society for the Promotion of Science, 1956), 311. Murayama Takashi, *Sekai mengyō hatten shi* (Tokyo: Nihon Boseki Kyōkai, 1956), 578. Melvin Copland, *The Cotton Manufacturing Industry of the United States* (Cambridge, MA: Harvard University Press, 1912), 150.

shipbuilders diversified into industrial machinery, electrical machinery, and railroad cars.[29] By the mid-1920s, Japan had the third-largest mercantile fleet in the world, after Britain and the United States.[30] The fleet was an important foreign exchange earner, as 9.4.2-b shows.

Britain maintained world leadership in the shipbuilding industry throughout the pre-WWII period. Britain built two-thirds of the world's shipping annually during the pre-WWI period and one-third to one-half in the interwar years.[31] The US surpassed Britain in shipbuilding in 1918, 1919, and 1920, when the United States built an unprecedented tonnage of vessels to meet the Allies' urgent need for vessels to replace losses from the intensive German submarine campaign.[32] Though the high production was temporary, the extremely rapid stepping-up of ship construction by the United States during WWI demonstrated America's high capacity for wartime mobilization, which was demonstrated again during World War II.

Unlike other industrial powers, the United States was a great agricultural producer as well. The US dominance of the production and export of raw cotton and wheat in the world market is discussed in 5.1.1.

### 9.1.3. Income Disparity between Manufacturing and Agriculture

In both Japan and the United States, the development of the manufacturing sector entailed dramatic changes in the industrial structure and in income distribution. The disparity in labor incomes between manufacturing and agriculture in particular became a serious political issue in both countries.

In the United States, income from manufacturing exceeded income from agriculture by the end of the 1880s (table 9.1.3-a), but US agriculture stayed strong thanks to increased mechanization[33] and government assistance for agriculture.[34] The disparity in per capita incomes between agriculture and manufacturing, which had been at a ratio of 1:3 in manufacturing's favor in 1890, narrowed to 1:1.3 in 1910. However, the fall of farm prices in the 1920s widened the gap to 1:1.8 in 1930 (table 9.1.3-a). This situation gave rise to the controversy of "parity prices," which called into question the disparity between agricultural prices and nonagricultural prices.[35] Various remedial measures were suggested to help the agriculture sector. President Hoover's attempt to raise agricultural tariffs in 1929 was one of them. Unfortunately, however, his attempt led to the enactment of the infamous Smoot–Hawley Act (12.1.4).[36]

In Japan, the income disparity was bigger than in the United States, and the problem was much more serious. The workforce of the primary industries (about 95 percent of which were farm workers) accounted for 76 percent of the total workforce in 1889–1892 (table 9.1.3-b). By 1929–1932 it had decreased by 14 percent, but it still accounted for 51 percent of the total

Table 9.1.3-a. Workforce and Income of US Agriculture and Manufacturing

| | Workforce (millions) | | Income ($ millions) | | | Per capita income ($) | | |
|---|---|---|---|---|---|---|---|---|
| | Agriculture (a) | Manufacturing (b) | | Agriculture (c) | Manufacturing (d) | Agriculture (c)/(a) | Manufacturing (d)/(b) | (c)/(a): (d)/(b) |
| 1890 | 8.99 (42) | 4.04 (19) | 1889 | 1,519 (14) | 2,022 (19) | 169 | 501 | 1:3.0 |
| 1910 | 10.57 (30) | 7.68 (22) | 1907–1910 | 4,928 (19) | 4,648 (18) | 466 | 605 | 1:1.3 |
| 1930 | 10.09 (21) | 10.56 (22) | 1926–1929 | 8,678 (12) | 16,752 (22) | 860 | 1,586 | 1:1.8 |

*Note:* Numbers in parentheses are percentages of the total US workforce represented by the agriculture and manufacturing industries, and percentages of the national income represented by those industries.

*Source:* US Department of Commerce, Bureau of the Census, *Historical Statistics of the United States* (Washington, DC: US Government Printing Office, 1975), 240.

Chapter 9

Table 9.1.3-b. Workforce and Income of Japan's Primary and Secondary Industry

| | Workforce (millions) | | | Income (millions of yen) | | | Per capita income (yen) | | |
| | Primary Ind. (a) | Secondary Ind. (b) | | Primary Ind. (c) | Secondary Ind. (d) | | Primary Ind. (c)/(a) | Secondary Ind. (d)/(b) | (c)/(a): (d)/(b) |
|---|---|---|---|---|---|---|---|---|---|
| 1888–1892 | 17.18 (76) | 2.01 (9) | 1890 | 580 (63) | 91 (10) | | 34 | 45 | 1:1.3 |
| 1908–1912 | 16.48 (63) | 3.88 (15) | 1910 | 1,133 (39) | 666 (23) | | 69 | 172 | 1:2.5 |
| 1928–1932 | 14.77 (51) | 4.92 (17) | 1930 | 2,266 (20) | 3,239 (29) | | 153 | 659 | 1:4.3 |

*Notes:* 1. Numbers in parentheses are percentages.
2. The percentages show the proportion of the total Japanese workforce represented by the country's primary and secondary industries, and the percentages of the national income represented by those industries.

*Source:* Ōkawa Kazushi, ed., *Nihon keizai no seichōritsu* (Tokyo: Iwanami Shoten, 1955), 26 (workers), 160 (net domestic income).

workforce.[37] During the same period, the secondary industry's workforce (of which manufacturing's share was about 93 percent) increased by 2.4 times, and its income swelled by 35.6 times between 1890 and 1930, while during this period the primary industry's income increased by 3.9 times.[38]

In terms of per capita income, while that of the secondary industry grew by 14.6 times, that of the primary industry grew by 4.5 times during the period between 1890 and 1930. As a result, the disparity between the primary industry and the secondary industry widened from 1:1.3 to 1:4.3 by 1930.

With governmental measures to improve the rural economy being grossly inadequate, Japanese farmers were left worse off. This caused serious social problems as well as political ones. As discussed in 14.1.2, farmers' discontent about their disadvantaged state and grievances against the government policy gave rise to radical, antiestablishment agrarianism in rural areas.[39] Terrorism in the 1930s was closely related to the plight of the farmers. For example, the man who shot Inoue Junnosuke (井上準之助) on February 9, 1932, blamed Inoue for his negligence of the rural economic difficulties.[40] The terrorists who assaulted Inukai Tsuyoshi (犬養毅) on May 15, 1932 were also influenced by antigovernment agrarianism. With party politicians losing farmers' trust and big businesses incurring their enmity, the army was now increasingly regarded by them as a savior (12.2.3).

230

# 9.2. Foreign Trade in the US and Japan

## 9.2.1. US Foreign Trade

That the United States was the world's largest economy did not mean that it was the leader in international trade. In fact, the role of the United States in world trade in the early decades of the 20th century was quite different from that of Britain during the years when Britain was the world's largest economic power. During the century between the Napoleonic wars and WWI, Britain was the world's largest importer, in addition to being the world's leading exporter of manufactures.[41] Britain's imports accounted for 20 to 25 percent of its GNP. Britain consistently imported more than it exported in merchandise, covering the resultant deficit with income received from services such as banking, insurance, and shipping.[42] As discussed in 6.1.2, Britain continued to pursue a free-trade policy even after other powers returned to protectionist policies in the late 19th century. Britain also played somewhat of the role of lender of last resort in times of international financial difficulty.

On the other hand, through the early decades of the 20th century, US imports amounted to only 4 to 5 percent of GNP (table 9.2.1-a), and the US ran a large trade surplus.[43] The American economy's propensity toward self-sufficiency was largely attributable to an abundance of natural resources and the

Table 9.2.1-a. US and Japanese Exports and Imports and Their Shares of GNP

|  | US | | | | Japan | | | |
|---|---|---|---|---|---|---|---|---|
|  | Exports ($ mil.) | Exp/ GNP (%) | Imports ($ mil.) | Imp/ GNP (%) | Exports (¥ mil.) | Exp/ GNP (%) | Imports (¥ mil.) | Imp/ GNP (%) |
| 1889 | 742 | 5.9 | 745 | 6.0 | 70 | 10.1 | 66 | 9.6 |
| 1899 | 1,204 | 6.9 | 697 | 4.0 | 211 | 12.0 | 220 | 12.5 |
| 1904 | 1,461 | 6.4 | 991 | 4.3 | 319 | 13.6 | 371 | 15.8 |
| 1909 | 1,663 | 5.0 | 1,312 | 3.9 | 413 | 13.6 | 394 | 13.0 |
| 1914 | 2,330 | 6.0 | 1,894 | 4.9 | 591 | 15.0 | 596 | 15.1 |
| 1919 | 7,920 | 9.4 | 3,904 | 4.6 | 2,099 | 15.4 | 2,173 | 16.0 |
| 1924 | 4,592 | 5.4 | 3,610 | 4.3 | 1,807 | 13.9 | 2,453 | 18.9 |
| 1929 | 5,157 | 5.1 | 4,401 | 4.3 | 2,149 | 16.2 | 2,216 | 16.7 |
| 1934 | 2,133 | 3.3 | 1,655 | 2.5 | 2,172 | 16.2 | 2,282 | 16.2 |

*Source:* US Department of Commerce, Bureau of the Census, *Historical Statistics of the United States* (Washington, DC: US Government Printing Office, 1975), 884–885. Nippon Ginkō Tōkeikyoku, ed., *Meiji ikō honpō shuyō keizai tōkei* (Tokyo: Namiki Shobō, 1999), 290, 292.

Chapter 9

Table 9.2.1-b. Major Items of US Exports and Imports ($ million)

| Exports | 1899 | 1914 | 1929 | Imports | 1899 | 1914 | 1929 |
|---|---|---|---|---|---|---|---|
| Raw materials | 286 | 800 | 1,142 | Raw materials | 213 | 650 | 1,559 |
| Raw cotton | 210 | 610 | 771 | Raw silk | 32 | 98 | 427 |
| Leaf tobacco | 25 | 54 | 146 | Crude rubber | 32 | 71 | 241 |
| Foodstuffs | 538 | 430 | 754 | Foodstuffs | 222 | 476 | 963 |
| Wheat | 104 | 88 | 112 | Coffee | 55 | 111 | 302 |
| Fruits and nuts | 8 | 32 | 137 | Tea | 9 | 17 | 26 |
| Wheat flour | 73 | 54 | 80 | Sugar | 93 | 99 | 209 |
| Meat products | 109 | 68 | 79 | | | | |
| Semi-manufactures | 118 | 374 | 729 | Semi-manufactures | 92 | 319 | 885 |
| Iron and steel | 29 | 91 | 200 | | | | |
| Finished goods | 263 | 725 | 2,532 | Finished goods | 170 | 449 | 994 |
| Cotton goods | 24 | 49 | 135 | Cotton goods | 32 | 71 | 69 |
| Machinery | 61 | 168 | 604 | | | | |
| Autos, parts, engines | 10 | 35 | 541 | | | | |
| Total exports | 1,205 | 2,329 | 5,157 | Total imports | 697 | 1,894 | 4,401 |

Source: US Department of Commerce, Bureau of the Census, *Historical Statistics of the United States* (Washington, DC: US Government Printing Office, 1975), 884, 898–901.

country's self-sufficient production of foodstuffs and primary commodities, as well as its large domestic market, where American suppliers could have the benefit of economies of scale even without overseas markets. Its low import ratio was also to a considerable extent due to its traditional protectionist trade policy, as discussed below.

The merchandise composition of US exports and imports also reflected American trade characteristics as explained above, as well as the country's progress in industrialization. In 1899, raw materials (largely raw cotton), and foodstuffs (crude and manufactured) combined to make up 68 percent of total exports: finished manufactures accounted for 22 percent (table 9.2.1-b). In 1929, while the finished goods' share of exports increased to 49 percent, the share of raw materials and foodstuffs decreased to 37 percent. For imports, while the ratio of finished goods decreased from 24 percent to 21 percent between 1899 and 1929, that of crude materials increased from 31 percent to 35 percent.

Reflecting shifts as shown above, US exports to Europe decreased from 80 percent of total exports in 1890 to 48 percent in 1930, and imports from Europe dropped from 57 percent to 31 percent during the same period, while US exports to Asia and imports from Asia increased from 2 percent to 12 percent and from 10 percent to 28 percent of total exports respectively during the same period.[44]

## 9.2.2. Protectionist US Trade Policy

The US Constitution grants Congress sole power "to regulate commerce with foreign nations."[45] It grants the president no trade-specific authority.[46] In fact, until the mid-1930s it was the prime business of Congress to legislate a comprehensive tariff law, and the level of import barriers was one of the hottest issues between the Republican and Democratic parties.[47] The Democratic Party, which included delegates from export-oriented raw-cotton-producing southern states, was a comparatively lower tariff political party, whereas the Republicans were the party of a protectionist trade policy and higher tariffs. They contended that continuing the protective tariffs granted during the Civil War was an economic necessity,[48] that the tariff was a panacea for economic problems, and that the idea of free trade was a manifestation of British imperialism.[49] Democrats were less protectionist than Republicans, but even the most liberal Democrats' notion of trade was not based on comparative advantage but on a mercantilist view of trade. They shared the view with Republicans that America should be protected against cheap European imports.[50]

One of the traditional Republican trade policies was "reciprocity." The Republican Party's platform of 1896 declared " . . . Protection and Reciprocity are twin measures of American policies and go hand in hand."[51] Their idea of reciprocity was that—unlike the idea of reciprocity of the British, which was reciprocity of access—if foreigners restricted imports from the United States, they should be punished by higher American tariffs.[52] The first tariff law that incorporated the idea of "reciprocity" into American trade policy was the McKinley Tariff of 1890.[53] Its idea of reciprocity was inherited by subsequent Republican trade laws through the pre-WWII period and beyond.[54]

The McKinley Tariff's reciprocity provisions were repealed by Democrats in 1894, but Republicans returned them in 1897 with the Dingley Tariff.[55] The Underwood Tariff Act of 1913 during the Democratic Wilson administration got rid of the reciprocity clause and considerably reduced tariff levels. In 1921, the Republicans advocating a return to "normalcy" came back to power and enacted the Fordney–McCumber Tariff of 1922,[56] which restored the reciprocity clause (section 317) and gave the president discretion to raise or lower duties by a maximum of 50 percent to "equalize production cost

Chapter 9

**Table 9.2.2. US Trade Laws from the McKinley Tariff to the Smoot–Hawley**

| Trade law (period) and sponsoring party | Tariff rates (%) A | Tariff rates (%) B | President in office (period) and his party |
|---|---|---|---|
| McKinley Tariff (1891–1894), R | 23.0 | 48.4 | Harrison (1889–1893), R; Cleveland (1893–1897), D |
| Wilson Tariff (1895–1897), D | 20.9 | 41.3 | Cleveland (1893–1897), D |
| Dingley Tariff (1898–1909), R | 25.5 | 46.5 | McKinley (1897–1901), R; Roosevelt (1901–1909), R |
| Payne–Aldrich Tariff (1900–1913), R | 19.3 | 40.8 | Taft (1909–1913), R |
| Underwood Tariff (1914–1922), D | 9.1 | 27.0 | Wilson (1913–1921), D |
| Fodney–McCumber Tariff (1923–1930), R | 14.0 | 38.5 | Harding (1921–1923), R; Coolidge (1923–1929), R |
| Smoot–Hawley (1930–1934), R | 9.6 | 59.1 | Hoover (1929–1933), R |

*Notes:* 1. In the column of tariff law and president in office, R represents the Republican Party and D the Democratic Party.

2. Tariff rates A represents average duty on all imports. Tariff rates B represents average duty on all dutiable imports.

*Source:* US Department of Commerce, Bureau of the Census, *Historical Statistics of the United States* (Washington, DC: US Government Printing Office, 1975), 1083. Alfred Eckes, Jr., *Opening America's Market* (Chapel Hill, NC: University of North Carolina Press, 1995), 107.

differences" between the United States and competing nations (section 315).[57] Then came the high point in American protectionism with the passage of the Smoot–Hawley Tariff of 1930,[58] which raised average US tariffs on dutiable imports to the highest level in the 20th century.[59] The Smoot–Hawley had cost-equalizing provisions (section 336) as well as reciprocity provisions (section 338). As observed in 12.1.3, the Smoot–Hawley Tariff triggered a wave of retaliation, worsening the Depression.

Generally, a problem with free trade is that there is a chronic political imbalance between those who benefit from trade protection and those who pay the cost. It is an imbalance in intensity of interest. Suppliers who are threatened by imports tend to be concentrated, organized, and ready and able to press their interests in the political arena, whereas consumers who benefit from free trade will not take positive action because their interests are spread widely and thinly.[60] Usually, the aggregate benefit to the former, who are much fewer in the number, is smaller than the aggregate loss of the latter, who are much greater in number. Thus, protectionism reduces a nation's economic welfare as a whole. There is also a time factor. While damage from imports is suffered instantly, the benefits of free trade take time to be realized.

*234*

In the case of the United States, where the Constitution grants Congress the responsibility to regulate foreign trade, members of Congress were highly susceptible to protectionist pressure in their constituencies. Those who suffered from damages from imports appealed to Congressmen for import restrictions, while the public was indifferent and leave it at that.

The result was a high level of trade barriers, to the benefit of certain groups and the detriment of the nation as a whole.[61]

In 1934, in an attempt to free itself from one-sided pressure from producer interests, the Democrats enacted an entirely different sort of trade law, the Reciprocal Trade Agreement Act of 1934, which authorized the president to negotiate and implement pacts with other nations after obtaining reciprocal tariff reduction. With this authority, the president could reduce US tariffs by up to 50 percent without further recourse to Congress.[62] Thus Congress legislated itself out of the responsibility of making product-specific trade laws.[63] The Reciprocal Trade Agreement Act proved to be a harbinger of the postwar US free-trade policy.[64] But before the RTAA, Congress reigned supreme on trade.

### 9.2.3. Japanese Foreign Trade and Trade Policy

Japanese foreign trade showed remarkable growth after the turn of the century, as table 9.2.1-a shows. The ratio of combined Japanese exports and imports to GNP, which had started from almost zero in July 1859, reached about 20 percent by the end of the 1880s, about 30 percent in the 1910s, and over 30 percent in the 1920s and 1930s. This ratio was three times that of the United States, and was comparable to the ratios of Britain and Germany in those days.[65] It was higher than that of postwar Japan.[66]

Prewar Japan maintained a relatively moderate trade policy until 1937, when the Japanese government started to control foreign trade (15.3.5). When Japan regained tariff autonomy in 1911, the government, in framing the new tariffs, adopted the principles that industrial raw materials which could not be produced easily in Japan should be admitted free or at a low rate, that low duties should be imposed on semi-manufactured goods, and that moderate duties should be imposed on finished manufactured goods.[67] Excepting tariff increases after the Great Kantō Earthquake and also in the 1930s,[68] Japanese tariffs remained relatively low. For example, Japanese average duties on all imports of 5.6 percent in 1915, 4.2 percent in 1925, and 7.3 percent in 1930 were much lower than corresponding American tariff averages,

Chapter 9

**Table 9.2.3-a. Japanese Average Rates of Duties to Imports (percent)**

|                  | 1900 | 1905 | 1910 | 1915 | 1920 | 1925 | 1930 | 1935 | 1940 |
|------------------|------|------|------|------|------|------|------|------|------|
| All imports      | 5.8  | 7.0  | 7.7  | 5.6  | 3.1  | 4.2  | 7.3  | 6.1  | 4.3  |
| Dutiable imports | 8.3  | 11.6 | 15.3 | 17.2 | 8.2  | 12.5 | 19.3 | 20.0 | 14.3 |

*Source:* Yamazawa Ippei and Yamamoto Yūzō, "Bōeki to kokusai shūshi," Ōkawa Kazushi, Shinohara Miyohei, and Umemura Mataji, eds., *Chōki keizai tōkei 14* (Tokyo: Tōyōkeizai Shinpōsha, 1979), 252.

**Table 9.2.3-b. Major Items of Japanese Exports and Imports (¥ million)**

| Exports | 1899 | 1914 | 1929 | Imports | 1899 | 1914 | 1929 |
|---------|------|------|------|---------|------|------|------|
| Raw materials | 22 | 46 | 90 | Raw materials | 82 | 329 | 1,224 |
|   Coal | 12 | 15 | 17 |   Coal | 1 | 7 | 43 |
| | | | |   Crude oil | 8 | 11 | 93 |
| | | | |   Raw cotton | 62 | 219 | 573 |
| Foodstuffs | 27 | 64 | 160 | Foodstuffs | 44 | 79 | 271 |
|   Tea | 9 | 13 | 12 |   Rice | 6 | 25 | 71 |
| | | | |   Sugar | 18 | 22 | 64 |
| | | | |   Soybeans | 8 | 10 | 46 |
| Fabricated raw materials | 111 | 306 | 913 | Fabricated raw materials | 36 | 96 | 356 |
|   Raw silk | 63 | 161 | 781 |   Iron and steel | 10 | 23 | 77 |
|   Cotton yarn | 29 | 79 | 27 | | | | |
| Finished goods | 50 | 168 | 937 | Finished goods | 55 | 87 | 346 |
|   Cotton fabrics | 4 | 35 | 413 |   Machinery | 23 | 38 | 191 |
|   Silk fabrics | 17 | 34 | 150 | | | | |
| Total exports | 215 | 591 | 2,149 | Total imports | 220 | 596 | 2,216 |

*Notes:* 1. Figures shown as coal exports in 1929 are those available for 1928.

2. Figures shown as iron and steel in the category of fabricated raw materials are those of pig iron, iron/steel tape and bar, iron/steel shapes, and iron/steel plates. The figures for iron and steel shown in the 1929 column are those for 1928.

3. Total exports and imports include miscellaneous items.

*Source:* Nippon Ginkō Tōkeikyoku ed., *Meiji ikō honpō shuyō keizai tōkei* (Tokyo: Namiki Shobō, 1999), 280–289; Yamazawa Ippei and Yamamoto Yūzō, *Bōeki to kokusai shūshi* (Tokyo: Tōyōkeizai Shinpōsha, 1979), 176–183. Ōmichi Hiroo, ed., *Nihon keizai tōkei sōran* (Tokyo: Asahi Shimbunsha, 1930), 254–255.

which were 9.1 percent in 1915, 14.0 percent in 1925, and over 9.6 percent in 1930 (table 9.2.2, 9.2.3-a).

The merchandise composition of Japan's trade in these years reflected the Japanese economy's industrialization. In exports, finished goods expanded nineteen times in value between 1899 and 1929, while raw materials and

236

foodstuffs increased five times (table 9.2.3-b). In imports, while raw materials expanded fifteen times in value, finished goods increased six times.

The largest contributor to the expansion of Japan's exports was textiles. Exports of raw silk, cotton yarn, and cotton and silk fabrics combined to make up about half the value of Japan's exports in 1899 and two-thirds in 1929. Through these three decades, raw silk accounted for 50 to 60 percent of Japan's textile exports (table 9.2.3-b). Raw-silk exports were particularly valuable in that no imported material was required for production (5.3.6). Raw silk was mainly exported to the United States, while cotton fabrics and silk fabrics were chiefly sold to Asia.[69]

In its economic development, Japan drew heavily on overseas supplies of commodities that it could not produce more cheaply, as well as raw materials that were scarce in Japan. These Japan paid for with exports in which it had a comparative advantage.[70] Access to world markets enabled Japan to use its resources and skills most effectively, raising the overall productivity of the nation's economy. Japan reaped the fruits of international specialization on a large scale, thanks to the relatively free and multilateral structure of world trade in the early decades of the 20th century.[71]

No less important for Japan than the benefits of comparative advantage might have been the so-called dynamic effects of foreign trade brought about by increased competition and innovation. Foreign trade served Japan as an activator of change within the Japanese economy.[72] Trade with advanced industrial partners provided Japanese business with an incentive to seek new ways to export and compete with imports, as well as opportunities for gaining new technological and managerial know-how.

### 9.2.4. Close US–Japan Trade Relations

Through the early decades of the 20th century, notwithstanding the political frictions over China, which were becoming serious, and the incessant disputes over immigration (chapter 8), Japan and the United States maintained a close economic relationship that had continued since Japan's opening by Perry and Harris. Reciprocal visits by representatives of the chambers of commerce of both countries in 1908 and 1909 demonstrated the business leaders' determination to maintain close business relations and their refusal to permit the immigration disputes from adversely affecting expanding trade and investment ties.[73]

The United States continued to be Japan's biggest customer, taking about

Chapter 9

**Table 9.2.4-a. Japanese Trade with US and US Trade with Japan (five-year averages)**

| | Japanese trade with the US (millions of yen) | | US trade with Japan (millions of dollars) | |
|---|---|---|---|---|
| | Exports | Imports | Exports | Imports |
| 1900–04 | 69.6 (29.5%) | 51.7 (17.2%) | 22.9 (1.6%) | 38.6 (4.2%) |
| 1905–09 | 120.9 (31.7%) | 77.2 (17.3%) | 39.9 (2.3%) | 62.9 (5.0%) |
| 1910–14 | 167.2 (31.5%) | 96.3 (16.5%) | 43.3 (2.0%) | 84.5 (5.0%) |
| 1915–19 | 477.0 (31.8%) | 411.8 (33.4%) | 194.2 (3.4%) | 248.4 (8.9%) |
| 1920–24 | 629.7 (38.9%) | 645.2 (31.4%) | 273.4 (5.4%) | 340.3 (9.3%) |
| 1925–29 | 889.5 (42.5%) | 667.0 (28.9%) | 259.5 (5.2%) | 401.1 (9.4%) |
| 1930–34 | 452.9 (28.1%) | 536.8 (31.9%) | 161.2 (6.9%) | 172.4 (9.0%) |
| 1935–39 | 567.6 (19.4%) | 969.4 (33.2%) | 232.6 (8.1%) | 163.2 (6.9%) |

*Note:* The percentages show the proportion of Japan's total exports and imports represented by exports to or imports from the United States, and the proportion of all US exports and imports represented by exports to or imports from Japan.

*Source:* Nippon Ginkō Tōkeikyoku, ed., *Meiji ikō honpō shuyō keizai tōkei* (Tokyo: Namiki Shobō, 1999), 291, 293. US Department of Commerce, Bureau of the Census, *Historical Statistics of the United States* (Washington, DC: US Government Printing Office, 1975), 903–907.

**Table 9.2.4-b. Major Items of Japanese Exports to US**

| | | 1909 | 1919 | 1929 | 1934 |
|---|---|---|---|---|---|
| Exports to US (¥ million) | Raw silk | 86.8 (64.3) | 606.3 (73.4) | 759.7 (83.5) | 244.6 (61.8) |
| | Cotton and silk cloth | 4.8 (3.5) | 70.9 (8.6) | 27.3 (3.0) | 19.9 (5.1) |
| | Tea | 11.7 (8.6) | 15.8 (1.9) | 8.2 (0.9) | 4.7 (1.2) |
| | Ceramic ware | 2.9 (2.2) | 6.2 (0.7) | 14.8 (1.6) | 15.0 (3.8) |
| Total exports | | 134.9 | 825.6 | 909.4 | 395.6 |
| Exports to the world (¥ million) | Raw silk | 131.2 (34.4) | 643.5 (31.6) | 793.0 (38.3) | 288.2 (13.8) |
| | Cotton and silk cloth | 44.6 (11.7) | 486.0 (23.8) | 597.6 (28.9) | 744.6 (35.8) |
| | Tea | 13.1 (3.4) | 18.5 (0.9) | 12.0 (0.6) | 9.6 (0.5) |
| | Ceramic ware | 5.1 (1.3) | 22.6 (1.1) | 37.3 (1.8) | 42.9 (2.1) |
| Total exports | | 381.8 | 2,039.5 | 2,069.8 | 2,082.3 |
| Exports to US / Exports to the world (%) | Raw silk | 66.1 | 94.2 | 95.8 | 84.9 |
| | Cotton and silk cloth | 10.6 | 14.5 | 4.6 | 2.7 |
| | Tea | 89.5 | 85.8 | 68.3 | 48.8 |
| | Ceramic ware | 58.5 | 27.2 | 39.6 | 34.9 |

*Note:* Numbers in parentheses show percentages of Japanese exports to the US represented by each of these products, and percentages of global Japnese exports represented by each of these products.

*Source:* Shiozawa Kimio et al., eds., *Nihon shihonshugi saiseisan kōzō tōkei* (Tokyo: Iwanami Shoten, 1973), 190–254, 278–279, 306–317.

*238*

30 percent of Japanese exports in the 1900s and 1910s, and about 40 percent in the 1920s (table 9.2.4-a). The Japanese share of US imports rose from about 5 percent in the pre-WWI period to about 9 percent after the war. Japan moved up to become the third-largest supplier to the US market (after Canada and Britain) by the first half of the 1920s, and to the second position next to Canada by the second half of the 1920s.[74]

World War I expanded US exports to Japan. From 1910–14 to 1915–19, US exports to Japan increased by more than fourfold in current prices. The US share of Japan's imports went up to over 30 percent during the war and stayed at that level afterward. The Japanese share of US exports rose to over 5 percent in the 1920s, and well over 6 percent in the 1930s. Japan was the fourth-largest buyer of US exports in the second half of the 1920s, and third in the 1930s after Britain and Canada.

Raw silk made up 64 percent of Japan's export trade with the United States in 1909, 73 percent in 1919, and 84 percent in 1929 (table 9.2.4-b). Of Japan's raw-silk exports to the world, those to the United States accounted for 96 per-

Table 9.2.4-c. Major Items of Japanese Imports from US

|  |  | 1909 | 1919 | 1929 | 1934 |
|---|---|---|---|---|---|
| Imports from US (¥ million) | Raw cotton | 23.3 (43.4) | 286.1 (37.6) | 276.4 (42.6) | 400.9 (52.4) |
|  | Metal products | 5.4 (10.1) | 232.4 (30.5) | 64.9 (10.0) | 115.5 (15.1) |
|  | Machinery | 5.1 (10.6) | 94.5 (12.4) | 82.5 (12.7) | 72.8 (9.5) |
|  | Crude oil | 8.5 (15.8) | 26.5 (3.4) | 52.9 (4.1) | 72.5 (9.5) |
| Total imports |  | 53.7 | 760.7 | 648.9 | 765.3 |
| Imports from the world (¥ million) | Raw cotton | 106.6 (28.2) | 665.6 (31.3) | 572.6 (26.3) | 730.9 (25.2) |
|  | Metal products | 39.0 (10.3) | 341.2 (16.0) | 234.0 (10.7) | 283.9 (9.8) |
|  | Machinery | 29.0 (7.7) | 123.8 (5.8) | 184.5 (8.5) | 141.3 (4.9) |
|  | Crude oil | 14.1 (3.7) | 37.6 (1.7) | 94.6 (2.4) | 119.7 (4.1) |
| Total imports |  | 377.9 | 2,123.3 | 2,175.3 | 2,903.9 |
| Imports from US / Imports from the world (%) | Raw cotton | 21.9 | 43.0 | 48.3 | 54.6 |
|  | Metal products | 15.5 | 68.1 | 27.7 | 40.7 |
|  | Machinery | 19.6 | 76.3 | 44.7 | 51.5 |
|  | Crude oil | 60.2 | 70.7 | 52.4 | 60.6 |

*Note:* Numbers in parentheses show percentages of Japanese imports from the US represented by each of these products, and percentages of global Japanese imports represented by each of these products.

*Source:* Shiozawa Kimio et al., eds., *Nihon Shihonshugi saiseisan kōzō tōkei* (Tokyo: Iwanami Shoten, 1973), 190–254, 278–279, 306–317.

Chapter 9

cent in 1929.

The Japanese share of US imports of raw silk rose from 54 percent in 1904–1908 to 75 percent in 1920–24, 82 percent 1925–29, and 90 percent in 1930–34.[75] The United States levied no import duty on raw silk, but silk fabrics and cotton fabrics were subject to high tariffs, forcing these Japanese exports onto Asian markets.[76]

Tea, the leading Japanese export item to the United States until the mid-1880s, was now a minor export item. But the United States still bought the major share of Japanese exports of that commodity through the early decades of the 20th century. The United States was also an important market for Japanese ceramic ware.

Of Japan's imports from the United States, raw cotton accounted for 40 to 50 percent (table 9.2.4-c). Of Japan's raw cotton imports, the US share increased from 22 percent in 1909 to 55 percent in 1934. Of US raw-cotton exports, Japan's share was less than 4 percent in the first decade of the 20th century, but it exceeded 30 percent in the early 1930s. The United States was also the major supplier to Japan of metal products, machinery, and petroleum.

## 9.2.5. The Wartime Exchange of Japanese Shipping for American Steel

The exchange of Japanese shipping for American steel during WWI was a unique development that reflected the politically delicate but economically close relationship between the two countries at that time. When the United States imposed an embargo on iron and steel exports in July 1917 to preserve supplies for the US war effort, Japanese shipbuilders had outstanding purchase orders of 400,000 tons of steel plates with US mills, with delivery due in eighteen months.

Immediately after the US embargo, the Japanese shipbuilders appealed to the Japanese government to ask the US government to have them exempted from the embargo. They argued that the bulk of the steel in question was to be used to build vessels for the US and European allies' war effort. In addition to their American business associates, they also made their case directly to the relevant US government agencies and to the mass media in the United States.[77] Some American chambers of commerce and steel mills lobbied Washington in support of the Japanese campaign.[78]

The Allied nations had a severe shortage of shipping because of the heavy damage that the German submarines inflicted on their merchant vessel fleets.

240

In June 1917, Britain requested that Japan make its merchant ships available for Allied service. Japan in return asked Britain to supply materials for ship-building to Japan. Britain replied that, though it could provide Japan with a certain quantity of machine tools, it could not supply steel plates or other materials; Japan should ask the United States for those.[79]

Japan–US negotiations between the Japanese embassy and the State Department started in Washington, but little progress was made. There were many in the State Department who considered the embargo an excellent opportunity to restrict Japanese activities in Asia.[80] Secretary of State Lansing did not concur with them. He supported the goal of successful negotiations and agreed to a proposal by the Japanese ambassador in Washington to transfer the venue for negotiations to Tokyo in an attempt to break the impasse.[81] Negotiations in Tokyo between the Japanese shipbuilders and newly assigned US ambassador Ronald Morris, who had arrived in Tokyo in November 1917, proceeded smoothly.

An agreement was reached in late March 1918, under which fifteen ships aggregating 128,744 dead-weight tons were to be built of steel contracted before the embargo at the rate of one ton of steel for each dead-weight ton of shipping. The delivery of vessels was to be made from May to September 1918.[82] Another contract was subsequently signed for the supply of an additional thirty ships aggregating 245,850 dead-weight tons to be built at the rate of one ton of new steel supplies from the United States for each two dead-weight tons of shipping for delivery from January to June 1919.[83] The Japanese government, in the meantime, arranged to charter 150,000 tons of Japanese shipping to the United States for a period of six months. The tonnage represented about 12 percent of the total tonnage of Japanese ships over 5,000 dead-weight tons. This helped the Japanese shipbuilders and the US government to come to their agreement.[84]

After signing the contract, various problems arose, including delays in the delivery of steel plates from the United States and requests for alterations in specifications by the US side despite previous approvals. All those problems were solved amicably, however, through talks between representatives from each side, and the Japanese delivered all vessels within the dates promised.[85]

This deal gave both sides substantial economic benefits. One of the American government representatives stationed in Tokyo wrote to one of the Japanese shipbuilders later that all of the ships delivered were well thought of by the ship-owners in the United States.[86] The benefits to the Japanese ship-building industry were also large. They not only could avoid dockyard closures and worker layoffs due to shortages of materials, but also acquired big profits from the transaction.

One important aspect of this project was the fact that US government leadership showed a firm decision not to side with the views of Americans advocating confrontation, and instead pursued cooperation with Japan. It was also important that mutual respect and trust was established between the American and Japanese participants in this deal. They overcame difficulties through the spirit of cooperation and completed a project that proved beneficial to both sides. It was a plus-sum solution which would not have been reached had the views of the advocates of confrontation in Washington prevailed. The American representatives sent by the US Shipping Board to Japan to oversee the implementation of the contract were headed by John McGregor, an executive of a steel mill in San Francisco. The Japanese were impressed with the sincere and fair performance of the task by McGregor and his staff. The Japanese government awarded McGregor the Order of the Rising Sun (旭日章).[87]

# 9.3. Japan's Return to the Gold Standard after WWI

### 9.3.1. The Prewar Par or a New Parity?

After WWI, returning to the gold standard was the major trading nations' common goal. The United States returned to gold at the dollar's prewar par in 1919. The European nations and Japan had conferences in Brussels in 1920 and in Genoa in 1922, and agreed in principle to reestablish the gold standard at an early date.[88] Germany in 1924, Italy in 1927, and France in 1928 went back on gold at new parities. Britain reestablished the prewar gold parity of the pound in 1925, having effected severe deflationary policies. Under such circumstances, a return to gold was Japan's biggest trade and monetary policy issue in the 1920s.

After the war, the yen was pegged at close to the prewar gold standard par of $49.85=¥100, but Japanese price indexes were at much higher levels than those of the United States and Britain (table 9.3.1-a). There was no consensus among Japanese leaders as to whether Japan should let the yen fall to market levels and set a new gold parity, or lower domestic prices and return to the

242

*The Economies of the US and Japan in the Early Decades of the 20th Century*

**Table 9.3.1-a. Price Indexes of the US, Britain, and Japan**

|       | 1913 | 1919 | 1920 | 1921 | 1922 | 1923 | 1924 | 1925 | 1927 | 1929 |
|-------|------|------|------|------|------|------|------|------|------|------|
| US    | 100  | 199  | 221  | 140  | 139  | 144  | 141  | 148  | 127  | 138  |
| UK    | 100  | 242  | 307  | 197  | 159  | 147  | 166  | 159  | 142  | 137  |
| Japan | 100  | 236  | 256  | 200  | 196  | 199  | 206  | 202  | 170  | 166  |

*Source:* Hugh Patrick, "The Economic Muddle of the 1920s," in *Dilemmas of Growth in Prewar Japan*, ed. James William Morley (Princeton: Princeton University Press, 1971), 233.

gold standard at the prewar parity. Rivalry between the ruling Seiyūkai (政友会) party and the opposition Kenseikai (憲政会) party also made achieving a consensus difficult.

While the Kenseikai, a supporter of austerity and deflationary policies, argued for returning to gold at the prewar par as a "major nation" ranking with the United States and Britain, the Seiyūkai, a proponent of expansionary policies and industrial development, was cautious about an immediate lifting of the gold embargo. Finance Minister Takahashi Korekiyo (高橋是清) of the Hara Takashi (原敬) cabinet argued that what Japan now needed was economic expansion and the promotion of industry. He argued for an increase in the gold reserve for backing investment in China and the avoidance of the risk of gold outflow.[89] When Japan had an economic boom in 1919,[90] Takahashi allowed the boom to continue, opposing interest hikes by the Bank of Japan. Takahashi held firm in his "positive" position, notwithstanding the Kenseikai's claim that it was a bubble boom that should quickly be ended.[91]

In late 1919, Inoue Junnosuke, the governor of the Bank of Japan, was finally allowed to raise the Bank of Japan discount rate. He raised it to 8.03 percent, the highest level since 1907, and maintained that rate until 1925 (table 9.3.1-b). The economic boom ended, and being assisted by the following factors, a recession followed in 1920–1921. From late 1919 through early 1920, Britain raised interest rates to rein in inflation to prepare for returning to the gold standard, and the United States in turn raised rates to defend its gold standard.[92] The deflated economies of both countries had a deflationary impact on Japan. In addition, there was a worldwide fall in silver prices in 1920, which appreciated the yen's exchange rate against the tael, making Japanese goods less competitive with Chinese goods. By mid-1921, the Japanese stock index had fallen more than 60 percent from its peak in 1919.[93] Asset deflation created a large quantity of bad debts which were to be carried

*243*

Chapter 9

Table 9.3.1-b. Japanese GNP, Government Expenditures, Bond Issues, Discount Rates, and Exchange Rates, 1918–1930

| | Nominal GNP, ¥ mil. | Government budget (bond issues), ¥ mil. | Discount rates, % | Rates of specie reserve to note issue | $/¥100 rates High | $/¥100 rates Low |
|---|---|---|---|---|---|---|
| 1918 | 11,829 | 1,017 (n.a.) | 5.84 (9), 6.57 (11) | 0.62 | 52-1/8 | 50-7/8 |
| 1919 | 15,453 | 1,172 (n.a.) | 7.30 (10), 8.03 (11) | 0.61 | 51-7/8 | 49-7/8 |
| 1920 | 15,856 | 1,360 (n.a.) | 8.03 | 0.87 | 50/5/8 | 47-3/4 |
| 1921 | 14,886 | 1,490 (361) | 8.03 | 0.80 | 48-1/4 | 47-7/8 |
| 1922 | 15,573 | 1,430 (251) | 8.03 | 0.68 | 48-1/2 | 48-1/8 |
| 1923 | 14,924 | 1,521 (122) | 8.03 | 0.62 | 49 | 48-1/2 |
| 1924 | 15,776 | 1,625 (317) | 8.03 | 0.64 | 48-1/4 | 38-1/2 |
| 1925 | 16,265 | 1,525 (157) | 7.30 (4) | 0.65 | 43-1/2 | 38-1/2 |
| 1926 | 15,975 | 1,579 (214) | 6.57 (10) | 0.67 | 48-3/4 | 43-1/2 |
| 1927 | 16,293 | 1,766 (366) | 5.84 (3), 5.48 (10) | 0.63 | 49 | 45-5/8 |
| 1928 | 16,506 | 1,815 (458) | 5.48 | 0.61 | 48 | 44-3/4 |
| 1929 | 16,286 | 1,736 (194) | 5.48 | 0.65 | 49 | 43-3/4 |
| 1930 | 14,698 | 1,558 (80) | 5.11 (6) | 0.57 | 49-3/8 | 49 |

*Notes:* 1. Figures in parentheses in the government budget column are the government bond issue amounts.

2. Figures in parentheses following discount rates indicate the month when the discount rates were started.

*Source:* Ōkawa Kazushi, Takamatsu Nobukiyo, and Yamamoto Yūzō, "Kokumin Shotoku," in *Chōki keizai tōkei*, eds. Ōkawa Kazushi, Shinohara Miyohei, Umemura Mataji (Tokyo: Tōyōkeizai Shinpō-sha, 1974), 200 (GNP current prices), 213 (GNP 1934–36 prices). Emi Kōichi and Shionoya Yūichi, *Zaisei shishutsu*, ed. Ōkawa Kazushi (Tokyo: Tōyōkeizai Shinpōsha, 1966), 163 (government expenditures). Ōkurashō Shōwa Zaiseishi Henshūshitsu, ed., *Shōwa zaiseishi*, vol. 6, Kokusai (Tokyo: Tōyōkeizai Shinpō-sha, 1954), 3 (government bond issues). Nippon Ginkō Tōkeikyoku, ed., *Meiji ikō honpō shuyō keizai tōkei* (Tokyo: Namiki Shobō, 1999), 257 (discount rates), 320 (exchange rates). Mark Metzler, *Lever of Empire: The International Gold Standard and the Crisis of Liberalism in Prewar Japan* (Berkeley: University of California Press, 2006), 274.

over for years into the future.

In November 1921, Prime Minister Hara was assassinated, and Takahashi assumed the party presidency and premiership, continuing to retain the finance portfolio. He continued his expansionary policies, making up for the decline in tax revenue by issuing domestic bonds, helping to keep the economy from declining further (table 9.3.1-b).[94] The Kenseikai leaders criticized Takahashi's policy as loose. They contended that what the Japanese people needed was to economize on living expenses in a spirit of frugality.[95] It was

*244*

*The Economies of the US and Japan in the Early Decades of the 20th Century*

noteworthy that many business leaders supported this Kenseikai argument.[96] The National Federation of Chambers of Commerce called on the newly formed Takahashi cabinet to reduce fiscal spending. Takahashi reluctantly reduced the 1922 budget by 4 percent from that of 1921 (table 9.3.1-b).[97]

In the Seiyūkai party, meanwhile, a group of Takahashi opponents formed an anti-Takahashi faction, and the split led to the resignation of the Takahashi cabinet in April 1922.[98] Admiral Katō Tomosaburō (加藤友三郎) was chosen as successor; he formed a non-party "transcendent" cabinet. The finance minister of the new government, Ichiki Otohiko (市来乙彦), conducted a policy of general retrenchment, preparing for a return to gold.[99]

### 9.3.2. The Great Kantō Earthquake and the 1927 Financial Crisis

On September 1, 1923, the Great Kantō Earthquake (関東大震災) struck the Tokyo–Yokohama area. Over 140,000 people were killed or reported as missing. Damages reached 5.5 billion yen, amounting to over one-third of GNP in 1923 and over three times the central government's annual expenditures. The trade deficit expanded, dropping the exchange rate to a low of $38.5 per ¥100,[100] and ending any chance of restoring the gold standard in the immediate future.

After the formation and fall of two short-term nonparty cabinets (table 9.3.2),[101] Katō Takaaki (加藤高明), the president of the Kenseikai, was named premier in June 1924. He formed a cabinet based on a coalition of the Kenseikai, the Seiyūkai led by Takahashi, and the Kakushin Club led by Inukai Tsuyoshi. Though Takahashi held the post of agriculture and commerce minister, his influence in the fiscal and financial policies was limited.

Katō publicly launched a "Diligence and Thrift" campaign, emphasizing that it was the only way to solve the problem of the current account deficits and dependence on foreign borrowing.[102] Finance Minister Hamaguchi Osachi (浜口雄幸) pursued a fiscal policy of severe retrenchment.[103] The cabinet was clearly directed toward a return to the gold standard.[104]

The "Diligence and Thrift" campaign was well accepted by the public, as diligence and thriftiness were traditional Japanese virtues that had been taught in primary-school ethics classes through the Meiji, Taishō, and prewar Shōwa eras (1.1.2).

In April 1925, Takahashi retired from the post of Seiyūkai president and cabinet, and under the new presidency of retired general Tanaka Giichi (田中

*245*

Chapter 9

**Table 9.3.2. Japanese Elections, Cabinets and Economic Policy Directions in 1917–1930**

| House of Representative elections | | | Cabinet | | Economic policy directions |
|---|---|---|---|---|---|
| Date | Election returns | | Prime minister (in office) | Finance minister | |
| Apr. 20, 1917 | Seiyūkai Kenseikai Others | 165 121 85 | S: Hara (Sep. 1918–Nov. 1921) | Takahashi | Expansion |
| May 10, 1920 | Seiyūkai Kenseikai Others | 278 110 76 | S: Takahashi (Nov. 1921–Apr. 1922) | Takahashi | Expansion |
| | | | N: Adm. Katō (Apr. 1922–Aug. 1923) | Ichiki | Retrenchment |
| | | | N: Yamamoto (Sep. 1923–Jan. 1924) | Inoue | Recovery from earthquake damage |
| | | | N: Kiyoura (Jan. 1924–Jun. 1924) | Shōda | |
| May 10, 1924 | Kenseikai Seiyū Hontō Seiyūkai Kakushin Club Others | 151 111 103 30 69 | K: Katō (Jun. 1924–Jan. 1926) | Hamaguchi | Retrenchment |
| | | | K: Wakatsuki (Jan. 1926–Apr. 1927) | Kataoka | Retrenchment |
| Feb. 20, 1928 | Seiyūkai Minseitō Others | 217 216 33 | S: Tanaka (Apr. 1927–Jul. 1929) | Takahashi Mitsuchi (Aug. 1927–) | Expansion |
| Feb. 20, 1930 | Minseitō Seiyūkai Others | 273 174 19 | M: Hamaguchi (Jul. 1929–Apr. 1931) | Inoue | Retrenchment |
| | | | M: Wakatsuki (Apr. 1931–Dec. 1931) | | |

*Note:* In premier name columns, S stands for the Seiyūkai, K stands for the Kenseikai, N stands for non-party, and M stands for the Minseitō.
*Source:* Robert Scalapino, *Democracy and the Party Movement in Prewar Japan* (Berkeley: University of California Press, 1953), 212–237. Mark Metzler, *Lever of Empire: The International Gold Standard and the Crisis of Liberalism in Prewar Japan* (Berkeley: University of California Press, 2006), chapters 7 and 9. Nakamura Takafusa, *Shōwashi* (Tokyo: Tōyōkeizai Shinpō-sha, 1993), 56–60, 74–77.

義一), the Seiyūkai started to assert an aggressive new political course antago-nistic to the Kenseikai. In May, Inukai merged his party into the Seiyūkai. In July, 1925, the three-party coalition cabinet broke up over a disagreement among cabinet members, and Katō was asked to form a Kenseikai-only cabi-net.[105] The new government took concrete steps toward restoring the gold standard. In January, 1926, Katō died in office and was succeeded by Wakatsuki Reijirō (若槻礼次郎). Kataoka Naoharu (片岡直温), who took over

246

*The Economies of the US and Japan in the Early Decades of the 20th Century*

from Hamaguchi as the finance minister, continued the retrenchment policy.

Meanwhile, after the Great Kantō Earthquake, the Bank of Japan authorized Kantō-area banks and companies to issue special "earthquake bills" eligible for discount by the Bank of Japan.[106] This measure avoided immediate financial chaos, but became a hot political issue later, setting off a serious monetary panic in 1927. A substantial quantity of bad debts originating from the 1920–21 asset deflation later were converted into "earthquake bills."[107] As the settlement of these bills was postponed year after year, the opposition Seiyūkai hurled persistent accusations against the way the Kenseikai government had handled the matter.

In March 1927, Finance Minister Kataoka inadvertently and prematurely labeled a tottering bank as "failed" in response to a Seiyūkai representative harangue at the Diet session discussing the government's proposed bank bailout plan. The "misstatement" set off a bank panic, forcing many banks to close.[108]

In April, the Kenseikai government tried to provide relief funds to the Bank of Taiwan,[109] the largest holder of the earthquake bills, by obtaining an emergency imperial edict. This procedure required the Privy Council's consent.

At that time, the Seiyūkai and the Kenseikai were fighting fiercely in the Diet over Foreign Minister Shidehara's China policy (11.3.1).[110] The Privy Council was also opposed to Shidehara's China policy, and because of its opposition, it refused to approve the Wakatsuki cabinet's request for the issuance of the edict.[111] The Bank of Taiwan's branches on the Japanese mainland were forced to close, and Suzuki Shōten (鈴木商店), a very large trading firm to whom the Bank of Taiwan had made large loans, went bankrupt. On April 17, 1927, the Wakatsuki cabinet resigned.[112]

On April 19, 1927, Tanaka Giichi, the president of the Seiyūkai, was ordered to form a government. Tanaka, who had persuaded Takahashi to take the finance portfolio, obtained an emergency edict to impose a three-week moratorium on the repayment of debts, and then received the approval of a special session of the Diet for bailout measures for the Bank of Taiwan that the Seiyūkai had prevented the Kenseikai government from adopting.[113]

### 9.3.3. The Deflationary Atmosphere

In the 1920s, the Seiyūkai's expansionary policy and the Kenseikai's deflationary policy alternated, but the general political mood through the decade was

*247*

toward restriction. Though Takahashi had conducted expansionist economic policies while he was in office from September 1918 to April 1922, he could not pursue expansionist policies as freely as he wanted, as his forced reduction of the 1922 budget demonstrated (9.3.1).[114] He expanded fiscal expenditures in 1927 and 1928 by increasing bond issues, but the discount rates were maintained at high levels, and the decline of the yen was modest (table 9.3.1-b). So far as monetary policy was concerned, Inoue's contractionary line was firmly held. The ratio of the BOJ's specie reserves to its note issues during the 1920s was higher than any other period in Japan's modern monetary history (table 9.3.1-b).[115]

The movement for deflation was then international. It was a gold-centered worldwide stabilization movement based on bankers' vision.[116] The United States took the initiative for this movement. It encouraged other countries to return to the gold standard, extending "stabilization" loans when those countries decided to lift the gold embargo.[117] Benjamin Strong of the FRB of New York and Thomas Lamont of J. P. Morgan were leading figures in this movement. They were particularly eager for Japan's return to the gold standard. When Lamont came to Japan in October 1927, he strongly suggested that Japan take more vigorous deflationary policies,[118] and in the negotiations in 1930 for refunding the £25 million loan of 1905 that was coming due in January 1931, Lamont even suggested that Japan's return to the gold standard would be a precondition for any rollover loan.[119] Inoue's deflationary policies were conducted under such circumstances.

### 9.3.4. The Return to the Gold Standard at the Prewar Par

Tanaka resigned in July 1929, having lost the emperor's confidence over his handling of the case of Zhang Zuolin's assassination by the Kwantung Army. (11.3.4). The new cabinet was formed by Hamaguchi, now the head of the Minseitō (the successor of the Kenseikai). He and new finance minister Inoue lost no time in implementing a strong deflationary policy to prepare for returning to the gold standard at the prewar parity. Inoue ordered the Bank of Japan to tighten the money market,[120] reduced government expenditures by cutting spending on public works, and urged the Japanese public to reduce consumption and increase savings.[121]

The collapse of the New York stock market in October 1929 did not cause Inoue to change his plan to lift the gold embargo. He even considered the crash an auspicious sign for his policy objectives because it would probably reduce the danger of a large gold outflow from Japan.[122] Japan returned to the gold standard at the prewar parity on January 11, 1930, as scheduled. This was well supported by the media and the public, as the Minseitō's big victory in the House of Representatives election on February 20, 1930 showed (table 9.3.2).

The timing could not have been worse: the world's most serious and extended depression was to deliver a harsh blow to Japan, which had just appreciated the yen to the prewar level (12.2.1). The debacle was not necessarily Inoue's fault; no one expected that the recession that started in 1929 would turn into a record-breaking depression, largely because of the US Federal Reserve's policy blunders (15.1.2).

## 9.4. The International Financial Positions of the United States and Japan

### 9.4.1. US Financial Position

The United States had run chronic deficits on both merchandise trade and current account balances until 1874, when its merchandise trade balance turned positive. Until WWI, however, mainly because of large deficits in interest and dividend payments, tourism, and remittances by immigrants, its current account balances remained in deficit.[123] During WWI, however, the United States had a large current account surplus. The aggregate current account surplus during 1914–1919 was $15,337 million (table 9.4.1-a).

US assets abroad increased from $3.514 million in 1914 to $16,547 million in 1919 (table 9.4.1-b), including US government loans to foreign governments totaling $9,591 million. US liabilities abroad having decreased from $7,200 million to $3,985 million during the same period, net assets turned from minus $3,686 million to plus $12,562 million (table 9.4.1-b).

In the 1920s, the United States continued to have a current account balance surplus, and American assets abroad expanded from $16,547 million in 1919 to $28,694 million in 1929. Despite US liabilities' increase from $3,985 million to $8,931 million during the same period, the US net assets increased by $7,201 million to $19,763 million at the end of 1929.

In the 1930s, the movement of US long-term capital was sharply reversed. US investments abroad declined to $11,400 million in 1939, and with the

Chapter 9

**Table 9.4.1-a. US Balance of Payments ($ million)**

|  | 1897–1913 | 1914–1919 | 1920–1929 | 1930–1939 |
|---|---|---|---|---|
| Merchandise trade balance | 7,673 | 16,716 | 10,621 | 4,633 |
| Net other current transactions | −8,709 | −1,379 | −478 | −1,821 |
| Freight receipt | −571 | −362 | −182 | −850 |
| Tourism | −3,020 | −50 | −2,327 | −1,910 |
| Interest & dividends | −2,220 | 1,890 | 5,270 | 3,604 |
| Immigrant remittances | −2,390 | −1,200 | −3,069 | −1,614 |
| Other transactions | −508 | −1,657 | −170 | −1,051 |
| Current account balance | −1,036 | 15,337 | 10,143 | 2,812 |

*Note:* Figures are aggregate amounts during the period indicated.

*Source:* Cleona Lewis, *America's Stake in International Investments* (Washington, DC: Brookings Institution, 1938), 451, 553–554. US Department of Commerce, *The United States in the World Economy* (Washington, DC: US Government Printing Office, 1943), 216.

**Table 9.4.1-b. US Assets and Liabilities Position ($ million)**

|  | 1897 | 1914 | 1919 | 1929 | 1939 |
|---|---|---|---|---|---|
| Assets | 685 | 3,514 | 16,547 | 28,694 | 11,400 |
| Securities | 50 | 862 | 2,576 | 7,839 | 3,800 |
| Direct investments | 635 | 2,652 | 3,880 | 7,553 | 7,000 |
| Short-term credits |  |  | 500 | 1,617 | 600 |
| War loans to the allies |  |  | 9,591 | 11,685 |  |
| Liabilities | 3,395 | 7,200 | 3,985 | 8,931 | 9,600 |
| Securities | 3,145 | 5,440 | 1,623 | 4,304 | 4,300 |
| Direct investments | | 1,310 | 900 | 1,400 | 2,000 |
| Sequestrated properties |  |  | 662 | 150 |  |
| Short-term credits | 250 | 450 | 800 | 3,077 | 3,300 |
| Net assets | −2,710 | −3,686 | 12,562 | 19,763 | 1,800 |
| Gold stock |  | 1,526 | 2,707 | 3,997 | 17,800 |

*Note:* Figures for 1914 are those on July 1, 1914. Other figures are those on December 31 in each year.

*Source:* Cleona Lewis, *America's Stake in International Investments* (Washington, DC: Brookings Institution, 1938), 445–454, 553–554 (for 1897–1929 except gold stock). US Department of Commerce, *The United States in the World Economy* (Washington, DC: US Government Printing Office, 1943), 123 (for 1933–1939 except gold stock). US Department of Commerce, *Historical Statistics: Colonial Times to 1970* (Washington, DC: US Government Printing Office, 1975), 995 (gold stock).

increase in foreign investments in the United States to $9,600 million, US net assets drastically declined to only $1.8 million at the end of 1939. This was largely because of a massive capital flight from Europe caused by the increasing likelihood of war in Europe (15.1.4).[124] The US current account being in surplus, the capital inflow on a large scale meant a massive accumulation of gold in the United States. Between 1929 and 1939, US gold stocks increased by $13,803 million, from $3,997 million to $17,800 million.

### 9.4.2. Japan's Financial Position
During the Russo–Japanese War, the Japanese government issued bonds abroad to finance war expenditures (10.3.1, table 10.3.1-a, table 10.3.1-b). These Japanese government borrowings are reflected in table 9.4.2-a (long-term capital transactions in 1904–1913) and in table 9.4.2-b (portfolio liabilities in 1914).

The First World War gave Japan a windfall opportunity to improve its international balance of payment, as it did to the United States. The merchandise trade balance turned from a cumulative deficit of ¥553 million in 1904–1913 to a cumulative surplus of ¥1,334 million in 1914–1919. Additionally, earnings from shipping expanded enormously. Japan's cumulative current account balance turned from a deficit of ¥923 million in 1904–1913 to a surplus of ¥3,081 million in 1914–1919 (table 9.4.2-a).

Japan used its wartime current account surpluses for loans to the Allied powers for their war efforts and to China for Japan's political purposes, as well as for increasing its foreign exchange reserves. Britain received ¥283 million, France ¥131 million, Russia ¥240 million, and China ¥385 million, including the Nishihara loans.[125] These loans helped to increase Japan's assets as of 1919 to ¥1,911 million (table 9.4.2-b). Britain and France repaid their loans by the mid-1920s, but China and Czarist Russia defaulted.

Unlike the United States, however, Japan's current account balances returned to a deficit in the 1920s. Its merchandise trade registered a large deficit, mainly because of the overvalued yen. Large imports for reconstruction purposes after the 1923 earthquake also affected the trade balance. At the end of 1924, Japan's net asset position turned to minus ¥71 million (table 9.4.2-b).

In the 1930s, Japan's trade deficits decreased, but the improvement was largely due to the increase in exports to the yen-bloc areas. Japan had large trade deficits with the non-yen-bloc countries, for which settlements had to be

Chapter 9

Table 9.4.2-a. Japan's International Balance of Payments (¥ million)

|  | 1904–1913 | 1914–1919 | 1920–1929 | 1930–1936 |
|---|---|---|---|---|
| Merchandise trade balance | −553 | 1,334 | −4,424 | −700 |
| Net current transactions | −371 | 1,747 | 2,063 | 1,239 |
|   Interest and dividends | −490 | 8 | 506 | 357 |
|   Freight | 267 | 1,372 | 1,457 | 1,012 |
|   Government payments | −326 | 142 | −417 | −735 |
|   Other current transactions | 178 | 225 | 517 | 606 |
| Current account balance | −923 | 3,081 | −2,361 | 538 |
| Long-term capital transactions | 1,255 | −1,669 | −1,084 | −2,310 |
| Foreign reserve changes | 234 | 1,755 | −583 | −950 |

*Note:* Figures are aggregate amounts during the period indicated.
*Source:* Yamazawa Ippei and Yamamoto Yūzō, "Bōeki to kokusai shūshi," in *Chōki keizai tōkei 14*, eds. Ōkawa Kazushi, Shinohara Miyohei, and Umemura Mataji (Tokyo: Tōyōkeizai Shinpōsha, 1979), 62–63.


Table 9.4.2-b. Japan's Foreign Assets and Liabilities Position (¥ million)

|  | 1914 | 1919 | 1924 | 1930 | 1936 |
|---|---|---|---|---|---|
| Assets | 627 | 1,911 | 1,812 | 2,779 | 5,300 |
|   China and Manchuria | 439 | 1,163 | 1,386 | 2,599 | 4,686 |
|     Portfolio | 54 | 418 | 793 | 1,545 | 832 |
|     Direct | 385 | 745 | 593 | 1,054 | 3,854 |
| Liabilities | 1,979 | 1,722 | 1,883 | 2,466 |  |
|   Portfolio | 1,950 | 1,687 | 1,861 | 2,353 | 1,883 |
|   Direct | 29 | 35 | 22 | 114 |  |
| Net assets | −1,352 | 189 | −71 | 313 | 3,417 |

*Source:* Ishizaki Teruhiko, "Nihon no gaishi," Katō Eiichi, "Shihon yushutsu," in *Gendai Nihon no dokusen shihon*, ed. Miyazaki Giichi (Tokyo: Shiseidō, 1965), 7, 37, 167, 170, 172, 176. Chiming Hou, *Foreign Investment and Economic Development in China, 1840–1937* (Cambridge, MA: Harvard University Press, 1965), 225.


made in international currencies or in gold. Foreign reserves decreased in the 1920s and 1930s (table 9.4.2.-a). In its assets and liabilities position as well, though Japan increased its assets abroad in the 1930s, the bulk of Japan's investments abroad were made in yen-bloc areas like Manchuria and parts of China (table 9.4.2-b).

## NOTES

### 9.1. The Economic Growth and Industrial Development of the US and Japan

1   US Department of Commerce, Bureau of the Census, *Historical Statistics of the United States* (Washington, DC: US Government Printing Office, 1975), 8. Nippon Ginkō Tōkeikyoku, ed., *Meiji ikō honpō shuyō keizai tōkei* (Tokyo: Namiki Shobō, 1999), 12–13.

2   Economic, Financial and Transport Department, League of Nations, *Industrialization and Foreign Trade* (Geneva: League of Nations, 1945), 12–13.

3   Britain had long been the world's largest producer of coal. In 1880, Britain's coal production was 149.0 million tons, whereas that of the United States was 64.8 million tons. Statistics Division, OECD, *Industrial Statistics, 1900–1962* (Paris: OECD, 1964), 8. Britain was surpassed in the 1890s by the United States in the output of coal, but it did not lose competitiveness in the international market. For example, in 1913, Britain exported 98.3 million tons of coal, which accounted for one-third of its total output of coal and one-tenth of the value of its total exports. US exports of coal in 1913 were 24 million tons. Graeme Holmes, *Britain and America: A Comparative Economic History, 1850–1939* (Newton Abbot, Devon: David & Charles, 1976), 77.

4   Japan's coal imports started to become larger than its exports from the middle of the 1920s, but the net imports were only about 10 percent of domestic production even in the late 1930s.

5   Russia had been the world's largest oil producer until 1901. Russian production was 12.09 million tons in 1901, whereas that of the United States was 10.63 million tons. In 1902, while Russian production was 11.48 million tons, that of the United States was 13.59 million tons. The United States kept the lead throughout the prewar period. Vagit Alekperov, *Oil of Russia: Past, Present and Future* (Minneapolis, MI: East View Press, 2011), 80.

6   Daniel Yergin, *The Prize* (New York: Simons & Schuster, 1991), 307.

7   T. H. Burnham and G. O. Hoskins, *Iron and Steel in Britain, 1870–1930* (London: George Allen & Unwin, 1943), 295. In 1928, the United States produced 43 percent of the world's pig iron, but it consumed only 36 percent of the world's iron ore due to the higher quality of the Minnesota ores. Ibid., 295.

8   Japan had to depend on imports, not only of raw materials for iron and steel production, but also of high-grade steel products, which the Japanese steel mills could not produce. William Lockwood, *Economic Development of Japan* (Ann Arbor, MI: University of Michigan Press, 1993, published originally by the Princeton University Press, 1954), 47.

9   Britain lost its position as the world's largest producer of copper to the United States in the 1890s. Peter Jones, *An Economic History of the United States since 1873* (London: Routledge & Kegan Paul, first published 1956; reprinted 1964), 105. In the 1930s, new copper mines developed in South America and Africa increased their production. In 1938, the United States produced 506,000 tons of copper, Chile 351,000 tons, Zambia 255,000 tons, and Zaire 124,000 tons. Raymond Mikesell,

Chapter 9

*The World Copper Industry: Structure and Economic Analysis* (Baltimore: Johns Hopkins University Press, 1979), 10.

10 By 1919, 55 percent of all power used in manufacturing came from electric motors in the United States. Willis and Primack, *Economic History of the United States* (Englewood Cliffs, NJ: Prentice-Hall, 1989), 274.

11 In 1929, 1933, and 1938, British output of electricity was 17.0 billion kWh, 21.2 billion kWh, and 33.8 billion kWh; that of Germany was 18.4 billion kWh, 15.4 billion kWh, and 31.1 billion kWh. OECD, *Industrial Statistics*, 74.

12 Karl Friedrich Benz first successfully manufactured an automobile equipped with an internal combustion engine in 1885. Gilbert Fite and Jim Reese, *An Economic History of the United States* (Boston: Houghton Mifflin, 1959), 327. In 1900, 3,700 cars were made in the United States, but most of them were steam-driven; 500 were electric carriages; only 300 were gasoline motorcars. Jones, *Economic History of the United States*, 108.

13 When Ford formed his company in 1903, the Olds Company, which R. E. Olds had established in 1897, dominated the industry, accounting for 25 percent of automobile production. Ford decided to make a standard model of motorcar in a single color (black) in a vertically integrated manufacturing structure, and pass the savings in manufacturing onto the customer. Some of the margin he also passed to his labor force. In 1914, he doubled wages to $5 a day. The Model T, which he introduced in 1908, was an instant best seller. In 1917, he sold 730,041 cars at $350, which was half of the 1910 price. Ford reduced the price to $295 in 1923, when Model Ts accounted for 46 percent of national sales of 3,480,000 cars. The Ford moving assembly line was a final step, integrating numerous earlier related innovations into the massive River Rouge plant that had raw materials entering at one end and automobiles exiting at the other. In 1927, however, General Motors captured 43 percent of the market, and replaced Ford as the leading automaker. Ronald Seavoy, *An Economic History of the United States: From 1607 to the Present* (New York: Routledge, 2006), 260–261. Steven Tolliday, "The Foundations of the Ford System," in *Between Imitation and Innovation: The Transfer and Hybridization of Productive Models in the International Automobile Industry*, eds. Robert Boyer, Elsie Charron, Ulrich Jürgens, and Steven Tolliday (Oxford: Oxford University Press, 1998), 58, citing David Hounshell, *From the American System to Mass Production, 1800–1932* (Baltimore: Johns Hopkins University Press, 1984).

14 Francis Wallet, *Economic History of the United States* (New York: Barnes & Noble, 1955), 199.

15 Ibid., 199.

16 Jones, *Economic History of the United States*, 221.

17 Seavoy, *Economic History of the United States*, 260.

18 W. W. Rostow, *The World Economy: History & Prospect* (Austin: University of Texas Press, 1978), 211, Fred Albert Shannon, *America's Economic Growth* (New York: Macmillan Company, 1940), 608.

19 Rostow, *The World Economy*, 422.

20 Lockwood, *Economic Development of Japan*, 16. Giovanni Federico, *An Economic History of the Silk Industry, 1830–1930* (Cambridge: Cambridge University Press,

*254*

1997), 204–205. Nippon Ginkō, *Honpō shuyō keizai tōkei*, 280–284. At the end of the 1920s, two of every five farm households were engaged in the supply of cocoons as a supplementary occupation. Lockwood, *Economic Development of Japan*, 45.

21 The pace of Japanese mechanization of cotton weaving was slower than that of cotton spinning. As late as the early 1910s, three-quarters of the output from the spinning mills was woven on hand looms, and a fair amount of the hand-loom production was exported. As large spinning mills equipped with power looms started weaving operations in the 1910s, Japanese cotton cloth exports began to increase. W. A. Graham Clark, *Cotton Goods in Japan* (Washington, DC: Department of Commerce, Bureau of Foreign and Domestic Commerce, 1914), 116. Shimbo Hiroshi, *Kindai Nihon keizaishi* (Tokyo: Sōbunsha, 1995), 193–195.

22 In cotton cloth exports, Japan surpassed the United States in 1917, exporting 794 million square yards of the goods, whereas the US exports amounted to 765 million square yards. In 1933, Japan exported 2,090 million square yards, whereas Britain exported 2,031 million square yards. Murayama, *Sekai mengyō hattenshi*, 396, 423, 479.

23 Andō Yoshio, ed., *Kindai Nihon keizaishi yōran* (Tokyo: University of Tokyo Press, 1975), 11.

24 Most large textile mills spun and wove. The practice of combining yarn production and weaving was established in the early 19th century, when it was difficult to obtain a regular supply of yarn since producers were scattered and the means of communication was crude. Melvin Copland, *The Cotton Manufacturing Industry of the United States* (Cambridge, MA: Harvard University Press, 1912), 150.

25 Murayama, *Sekai mengyō hattenshi*, 611.

26 The Shipbuilding Encouragement Law of 1896, which granted subsidies to builders of iron and steel vessels of over 700 gross tons, was followed by the Navigation Subsidy Law of 1899, which entitled owners of Japanese-built ships to claim twice the amount of subsidy granted to owners of foreign-built ships. In 1909, revised subsidy laws came into force and gave further stimulus to the industry. G. C. Allen, *A Short Economic History of Modern Japan* (London: George Allen & Unwin, 1972), 82.

27 The gross tonnage of steamships launched annually had been less than 10,000 tons on average until the late 1890s, but it rose to over 50,000 tons in 1909–13. During WWI, Japanese shipbuilding capacity expanded enormously. Output increased to 144,000 tons in 1916; 338,000 tons in 1917; and 689,000 tons in 1918. Allen, *A Short Economic History*, 83. While in 1913 there were six shipyards capable of building vessels of more than 1,000 tons with a workforce of 26,000 men, by 1918 such shipyards increased to fifty-seven, employing a total of 97,000 workers. US Department of Commerce, *Shipping and Shipbuilding Subsidies* (Washington, DC: US Government Printing Office, 1932), 330. With the end of the war boom and the return of foreign competition, the tonnage of ships built in Japan declined for some years. The annual average gross tonnage of ships launched in Japan after WWI was 182,000 tons in 1920–24; 84,000 tons in 1925–29; 103,000 tons in 1930–1934; and 334,000 tons in 1935–38. OECD, *Industrial Statistics*, 124, 174.

28 Shimbo, *Kindai Nihon keizaishi*, 106.

255

Chapter 9

29  Ibid., 112.

30  Historically Britain had been the largest commercial fleet owner, followed by the United States. Japan rose to the fourth position in 1920 (France being the third), and to the third position in 1925, when Japan possessed 3,919,807 gross tons of shipping, with the United States and Britain owning 15,313,552 gross tons and 19,440,711 gross tons respectively. Japan remained the third-largest commercial fleet owner afterward. US Department of Commerce, *Shipping and Shipbuilding Subsidies*, 47.

31  Holmes, *Britain & America*, 78. Britain's annual average production of ships was 1,342,000 (gross) tons in 1920–24; 1,184,000 tons in 1925–29; 552,000 tons in 1930–34; and 777,000 tons in 1935–39. World production was 3,312,000 tons in 1920–24; 2,266 tons in 1925–29; 1,319 tons in 1930–34; and 2,293 tons in 1935–39. OECD, *Industrial Statistics*, 124, 174. Britain had an advantage over the United States in nautical engineering and labor costs, which were often from a third to a half of the total cost. Chester Wright, *Economic History of the United States* (New York: McGraw-Hill Book Company, 1949), 644.

32  In 1913, while Britain built 2,000,000 gross tons of merchant vessels, the output of the United States was 276,000 gross tons. In 1918, while the British output was 1,580,000 gross tons, the United States constructed 2,200,000 gross tons of vessels. In 1919, US output reached 3,326,000 gross tons. US Department of Commerce, *Shipping and Shipbuilding Subsidies*, 47.

33  In the 1880s and 1890s, steam tractors were used to draw combine harvesters. After 1910, gasoline-driven tractors replaced these large machines. The new type of tractor-drawn combines enabled two men to harvest about thirty acres a day. In 1914, over 17,000 tractors were manufactured in the United States and 32,000 in 1916. This total doubled within a year to 67,000 in 1917, and then more than doubled again within the following year to 161,000 in 1918. By 1929 there were well over 820,000 gasoline models in use. Jones, *Economic History of the United States*, 224.

34  For example, in 1862 the Morrill Act gave federal land to individual states for the purpose of setting up agricultural and mechanical colleges. In 1887 the Hatch Act provided $15,000 a year for each state to establish agricultural research stations. Willis and Primack, *Economic History of the United States*, 214.

35  Ibid., 341.

36  Judith Goldstein, *Ideas, Interests, and American Trade Policy* (Ithaca, NY: Cornell University Press, 1993), 124.

37  Umemura Mataji and others, "Rōdōryoku," in *Chōki keizai tōkei 2*, eds. Ōkawa Kazushi, Shinohara Miyohei and Umemura Mataji (Tokyo: Tōyōkeizai Shinpōsha, 1985), 202–203.

38  Ōkawa and others, "Kokumin shotoku," in *Chōki keizai tōkei 1*, eds. Ōkawa, Shinohara, and Umemura, 205–206. The ratio of per capita income of agricultural households to that of nonagricultural households hit bottom in 1930 and improved somewhat during the 1930s. After WWII it improved markedly, mainly because land reforms drastically reduced the tenant farmers. Additionally, the ruling Liberal Democratic Party adopted agricultural policies which were favorable to farmers. Very protectionist trade policies on agricultural imports were among those politically

oriented measures. According to Mizoguchi, the ratio of per capita income of agricultural households to that of nonagricultural households changed as follows (setting nonagricultural household per capita income at 100). 1890: 87, 1900: 52, 1910: 47, 1920: 48, 1930: 32, 1940: 49, 1955: 70, 1960: 76, 1970: 87, 1980: 108. Mizoguchi Toshiyuki, "Nihon no shotoku bunpu no chōki hendō," *Keizaikenkyū*, vol. 37, no. 2 (Tokyo: Institute of Economic Research, Hitotsubashi University, April 1986), 152–158.

39  Thomas Havens writes, "... agrarianism in Japan has taken its form as *Nōhon shugi* (農本主義), literally "agriculture-as-the-(national) essence-ism ... As the plight of the countryside grew steadily more serious, popular *Nōhon shugi* took on antiestablishment overtones that held a strong attraction for the young military officers involved in the May 15 Incident of 1932 and other political upheavals ... " Thomas R. H. Havens, *Farm and Nation in Modern Japan Agrarian Nationalism, 1870–1940* (Princeton, NJ: Princeton University Press, 1974), 7, 10–11. Ōuchi Tsutomu, *Nihon no rekishi 24: Fashizumu eno michi* (Tokyo: Chuokoronsha, 1974), 242–245.

40  Ōuchi, *Nihon no rekishi 24*, 337.

## 9.2. The US and Japan's Foreign Trade

41  Rostow, *The World Economy*, 70, League of Nations, *Industrialization and Foreign Trade*, 157–161. B. R. Mitchell and Phyllis Deane, *Abstract of British Historical Statistics* (London: Cambridge University Press, 1962), 298–302.

42  Albert H. Imlah, *Economic Elements in the Pax Britannica* (Cambridge, MA: Harvard University Press, 1958), 70–75, 133, 166.

43  Ibid., 160–161.

44  Barry Poulson, *Economic History of the United States* (New York: Macmillan Publishing, 1981), 499–500.

45  Section 8 of Article 1 of the United States Constitution reads, "The Congress shall have power to lay and collect taxes, duties, imposts and excises, ... To regulate commerce with foreign nations, and among the several States, and with the Indian tribes; ... "

46  I. M. Destler, *American Trade Politics* (Washington, DC: Institute for International Economics and New York: The Twentieth Century Fund, 1995), 14.

47  Ibid., 4–5.

48  Goldstein, *Ideas, Interests*, 92.

49  Ibid., 128.

50  Ibid., 129.

51  Ibid., 112.

52  Ibid., 113. The term "reciprocity" was first used in Britain in the 1870s when a change in the British unilateral trade policy toward requiring reciprocity of access was discussed as a means of opening the markets of other European countries that were returning to protectionism. Britain decided in the end not to adopt a reciprocity or "fair trade" policy. Free traders such as Gladstone, Cobden, and Peel prevailed. They condemned such a policy as old-fashioned protectionism. Jagdish Bhagwati, edited by Douglas Irwin, *Political Economy and International Economics* (Cambridge, MA: MIT Press, 1991), 88–91.

Chapter 9

53  Goldstein, *Ideas, Interests*, 105. The McKinley Tariff was named after William McKinley, then chairman of the House Ways and Means Committee, who later became president of the United States.

54  Reciprocity provisions in section 3 of the McKinley Tariff were succeeded by the Dingley Tariff of 1897 (section 3), by the Fodney–McCumber Tariff of 1921 (section 317), and by the Smoot–Hawley of 1930 (section 338). After WWII, the Trade Expansion Act of 1962 had a reciprocity provision (section 252) basically for agricultural products. Then came the strong reciprocity provision of section 301 of the Trade Act of 1974. It was succeeded by the Trade Agreement Act of 1979 (sections 301–306), the Trade and Tariff Act of 1984 (sections 301–307), and the Omnibus Trade and Competitive Act of 1988 (sections 301–310). Goldstein, *Ideas, Interests*, 105, 111–112, 126. Thomas O. Bayard and Kimberly Ann Elliot, *Reciprocity and Retaliation in U.S. Trade Policy* (Washington, DC: Institute for International Economics, 1994), 24–25.

55  The Dingley Tariff was originated by Nelson Dingley, chair of the House Ways and Means Committee, in response to President McKinley's call for a higher tariff. Goldstein, *Ideas, Interests*, 111. Alfred Eckes, Jr., *Opening America's Market* (Chapel Hill, NC: University of North Carolina Press, 1995), 75, 107.

56  Goldstein, *Ideas, Interests*, 123. The Fordney–McCumber tariff took its name from Representative Joseph Fordney, chairman of the Ways and Means Committee, and Senator Porter McCumber, chairman of the Senate Finance Committee.

57  Sasaki Takao, *Amerika no tsūshō seisaku* (Tokyo: Iwanami Shoten, 1997), 25. Of the thirty-eight changes that Harding and Coolidge made, thirty-three were upward and five were downward. Sasaki argues that the idea of production cost equalization denied the benefits of trade, because the benefits of trade were to take advantage of differences of production costs among trading nations. Ibid., 21.

58  The Smoot–Hawley Tariff took its name from Representative Willis Hawley, chairman of the Ways and Means Committee, and Senator Reed Smoot, chairman of the Senate Finance Committee.

59  Smoot–Hawley did not, contrary to popular belief, establish the highest tariff schedule in American history. Average ad valorem tariffs on dutiable imports in the Smoot–Hawley Act were 44.9 percent when enacted in June 1930. Those in the Tariff of Abominations of 1828 were 61.7 percent, and those in the McKinley Tariff of 1890 were 48.4 percent. In the case of Smoot–Hawley, however, price declines during the Depression pushed up the average ad valorem equivalent of specific duties that were fixed duties per quantity. Average ad valorem tariffs on dutiable imports as a result rose to 53.2 percent in 1931 and to 59.1 percent in 1932. Eckes, Jr., *Opening America's Market*, 106–107.

60  Destler, *American Trade Politics*, 4–5.

61  Ibid., 4–5.

62  Ibid., 13. From the Reciprocal Trade Agreement Act of 1934 through the Trade Expansion Act of 1962, the means by which Congress delegated authority for trade negotiations remained basically the same. Successive statutes authorized executive officials to negotiate (within specified numerical limits) reductions in US tariffs in exchange for reduction by its trading partners. When a deal was finally struck, it could

*Notes*

be implemented by presidential proclamation, without further recourse to Capitol Hill. Ibid., 71.

63 Ibid., 13–14.

64 The Truman administration participated in the GATT negotiations under the mandate given by an extension law of the Reciprocal Trade Agreement Act. Subsequent US administrations also followed suit in their trade negotiations until the 1962 Trade Expansion Act was enacted.

65 Lockwood, *Economic Development of Japan*, 316.

66 The aggregate amount of exports and imports of Japan accounted for 17.9 percent of its national income in 1962, 24.0 percent in 1980, 17.3 percent in 2000, and 25.8 percent in 2020.

67 Allen, *A Short Economic History of Modern Japan*, 128–129.

68 After the Great Kantō Earthquake, a duty of 100 percent ad valorem was imposed on 120 luxury items. There were also upward tariff revisions in the 1920s and 1930s to protect important manufacturing industries such as the steel, chemical, and woolen products industries, as well as mineral oil products and some agricultural products. High duties continued on luxuries. G. C. Allen, "Japanese Industry: Its Organization and Development to 1937," in *The Industrialization of Japan and Manchukuo, 1930–1940*, ed. E. B. Schumpeter (reprinted, London: Routledge, 2000; first published, London: Macmillan Company, 1940), 736–740. Hugh Patrick, "The Economic Muddle of the 1920s," in *Dilemmas of Growth in Prewar Japan*, ed. James William Morley (Princeton, NJ: Princeton University Press, 1971), 237–238.

69 Exports of silk fabrics to the United States increased substantially during the 1880s and 1890s, but further growth in this trade was checked by the increase in American tariffs just before the turn of the century. Allen, *A Short Economic History of Modern Japan*, 71. Until WWI, Japan exported more silk fabrics in value than cotton fabrics, but after the war exports of cotton fabrics exceeded those of silk fabrics by the ratio of 1:2 in 1919, 1:2.5 in the 1920s, and 1:3 in the 1930s. After the war, Asia took 60 to 70 percent of fabrics (both silk and cotton). Nihon Tōkei Kenkyūsho, *Nihon keizai tōkeishū* (Tokyo: Nippon Hyoron Shinsha, 1958), 180–181.

70 Lockwood, *Economic Development of Japan*, 319.

71 Ibid., 319.

72 Ibid., 319.

73 In 1908, representing the chambers of commerce of Seattle, Tacoma, Spokane, Portland, Eureka, San Francisco, Oakland, Los Angeles, San Diego, and Hawaii, a group of fifty-four people, including sixteen wives, came to Japan. They stayed in Japan for twenty-four days, visiting several major cities as well as the tourist attractions of Nara and Nikkō. The leader of the group was F. W. Dohrmann, chairman of the San Francisco Chamber of Commerce. In the following year, a fifty-one-member Japanese group, headed by Shibusawa Eiichi, representing the chambers of commerce of Tokyo, Osaka, Kobe, Kyoto, and Nagoya, and including four wives and ten staff, visited fifty-three cities in the United States over the course of three months.

74 US Department of Commerce, Bureau of the Census, *Historical Statistics*, 906.

75 Federico, *Economic History of the Silk Industry*, 214.

76 The US tariff rate on silk fabrics was 45 percent under the Underwood Tariff Act.

Chapter 9

The Fordney–McCumber Tariff raised the duty to 55 percent, and the Smoot–Hawley Tariff maintained it at that level. On cotton cloth, the Fordney–McCumber Tariff and the Smoot–Hawley Tariff levied specific duties, and, as a rule, the duties were made progressively higher as the yarns used in weaving them became finer. For items subject to specific duties, there were minimum ad valorem tariffs enforced to take into account the possibility of the specific duties becoming less meaningful. The minimum ad valorem rates on the finest cloth were 45 percent under the Fordney–McCumber Tariff; under the Smoot–Hawley Tariff, the rates—for example, on finely woven handkerchiefs—were as high as 67.5 percent. F. W. Taussig, *The Tariff History of the United States* (New York: G. P. Putnam's Sons, 1905), 466, 513.

77  The shipbuilders' associations sent cables to President Wilson and Secretary Lansing, to chambers of commerce in New York, Chicago, San Francisco, Seattle, Pittsburgh, Cleveland, Boston, and Washington, and to Japanese special envoy Ishii Kikujirō (石井菊次郎) and Ambassador Satō Yoshimaro (佐藤愛麿) in Washington. Nichibei Sen-Tetsu Kōkan Dōmeikai, *Nichibei sentetsu kōkan dōmeishi* (Tokyo: Sanseidō, 1920), 38–53, 77–83.

78  Chambers of commerce in San Francisco and Seattle conveyed the Japanese requests to their Senatorial and Congressional representatives in Washington, and a director of the US Steel Corporation cabled to the Kobe Chamber of Commerce that he would interview officials in Washington. Ibid., 41–42, 49.

79  War Trade Board, *Japanese Steel and Shipping Negotiations* (Washington, DC: US Government Printing Office, 1919), 7. Nichibei Sen-Tetsu Kōkan Dōmeikai, *Nichibei sentetsu kōkan dōmeishi*, 86.

80  Jeffrey Safford, "Experiment in Containment: The United States Steel Embargo and Japan, 1917–1918," *Pacific Historical Review*, vol. 39, no. 4 (Los Angeles: University of California Press, 1970), 441–442.

81  War Trade Board, *Japanese Steel and Shipping Negotiations*, 13.

82  The prices of steel averaged about eight cents per pound. The prices of ships varied from $265 per ton (May delivery) to $225 per ton (September delivery), War Trade Board, *Japanese Steel and Shipping Negotiations*, 22–23.

83  The new steel was to be supplied at American government prices averaging three cents per pound. Ships were to be delivered at $175 per dead-weight ton. Ibid., 22–23.

84  Safford, "Experiment," *Pacific Historical Review*, vol. 39, no. 4, 448. Nichibei Sen-Tetsu Kōkan Dōmeikai, *Nichibei sentetsu kōkan dōmeishi*, 221.

85  Nichibei Sen-Tetsu Kōkan Dōmeikai, 164–176, 192, 214.

86  Ibid., 214–215.

87  Ibid., 164–176, 192.

9.3. Japan's Return to the Gold Standard after WWI

88  David Flath, *The Japanese Economy* (New York: Oxford University Press, 2000), 52. At the Genoa meeting, Japanese representatives made informal commitments to British and American representatives that Japan would return to the gold standard when Britain did. Mark Metzler, *Lever of Empire: The International Gold Standard and the Crisis of Liberalism in Prewar Japan* (Berkeley: University of California Press,

*Notes*

2006), 141.

89 It was Takahashi's view that China needed funds for investment in railroads and industry, and if Japan did not lend China the funds, the United States and Britain would, and that whoever lent China funds would be able to dominate China. Patrick, "The Economic Muddle," in *Dilemmas of Growth*, ed. Morley, 232. Metzler, *Lever of Empire*, 123.

90 The 1919 economic boom in Japan was brought about by (1) an increase in Japanese exports to Europe, where there were strong reconstruction needs and the release of pent-up consumer demand after the war, and (2) the substantial amount of the gold inflow to Japan in settlement of wartime debts that increased the money supply in Japan. Metzler, *Lever of Empire*, 119, 121.

91 Hamaguchi Osachi (浜口雄幸), Diet representative, speaking for the opposition Kenseikai party, launched a vigorous attack that established his reputation as the leading critic of the Seiyūkai cabinet's loose spending policies. Ibid., 129.

92 Ibid., 131.

93 Ibid., 138–139.

94 Ibid., 137.

95 Ibid., 139.

96 Dan Takuma, the managing director of the Mitsui zaibatsu, declared that all Japanese must eliminate luxuries and "wasted expenses." Even Ishibashi Tanzan, who later gained fame for championing Keynesian policies, argued for a retrenchment policy at the time. Ibid., 140.

97 Ibid., 139–140.

98 The anti-Takahashi group later led their faction out of the Seiyūkai, forming the Seiyū Hontō with 149 Diet members (leaving the Seiyūkai with only 129 members), and eventually joined the rival Minseitō. Nakamura Takafusa, *Shōwashi* (Tokyo: Tōyōkeizai Shinpōsha, 1993), 56–57, 60. Metzler, *Lever of Empire*, 141, 147. Robert Scalapino, *Democracy and the Party Movement in Prewar Japan* (Berkeley: University of California Press, 1953), 227.

99 Metzler, *Lever of Empire*, 141, 165.

100 Nakamura Takafusa, *Meiji Taishō-ki no keizai* (Tokyo: University of Tokyo Press, 1985), 159.

101 One was led by Yamamoto Gonnohyōe (山本権兵衛), the retired navy admiral, and another by Kiyoura Keigo (清浦奎吾), the president of the Privy Council. The Yamamoto cabinet resigned when an anarchist attempted unsuccessfully to kill Crown Prince Hirohito on December 27, 1923. The Kiyoura cabinet resigned when the Seiyū Hontō, which was the only party that supported the Kiyoura cabinet, suffered a defeat in the general election in May 1924. Kitaoka Shinichi, *Nihon no kindai 5: Seitō kara gunbu e* (Tokyo: Chuokoron Shinsha, 2013), 37, 42–43.

102 Metzler, *Lever of Empire*, 154.

103 Hamaguchi proposed a 17 percent cut of the 1925 budget, though it was scaled down to a 6 percent cut in the face of resistance by Takahashi, Inukai, and Army Minister Ugaki. Ibid., 155.

104 Ibid., 153–154.

105 Saionji, the *genrō* (元老), did not like the Seiyūkai's political machinations, and

*261*

Chapter 9

believed that he should not follow the past practice of changing the prime minister when a cabinet fell. He recommended Katō again as the next prime minister of a Kenseikai-only cabinet. Nakamura, *Shōwashi*, 77. Kitaoka, *Nihon no kindai 5*, 50.

106 Ōuchi, *Nihon no rekishi 24*, 64–65. Metzler, *Lever of Empire*, 146. Patrick, "The Economic Muddle" in *Dilemmas of Growth*, ed. Morley, 246.

107 After the earthquake, the Bank of Japan rediscounted 430 million yen of the "earthquake bills." About 230 million yen had been paid off by November 1924, and about 200 million yen remained outstanding as of early 1927, almost half being held by the Bank of Japan. Patrick, "The Economic Muddle," in *Dilemmas of Growth*, ed. Morley, 246. Nakamura, *Shōwashi*, 81. Kitaoka, *Nihon no kindai 5*, 57.

108 When Kataoka was fending off questions made by a representative from the Seiyūkai in the Diet, he said, based on a note handed to him by one of his assistants, something to the effect that a bank in Tokyo was in a difficult condition, and mentioned the name of the bank. Though the bank was still open when he said this, it had to close its doors as a result of Kataoka's careless statement. A wave of bank runs followed. Miwa Ryōichi, *Gaisetsu Nihon keizaishi* (Tokyo: University of Tokyo Press, 1993), 112–113.

109 The Bank of Taiwan did business both as Taiwan's central bank and as a commercial bank in Taiwan and the Japanese mainland. During the WWI boom, the bank's lending on the Japanese mainland came greatly to exceed its lending within Taiwan. Metzler, *Lever of Empire*, 179.

110 The Seiyūkai criticized Shidehara's conciliatory China diplomacy as being weak-kneed. Its criticism of Shidehara was especially strong when he decided not to join the British and American bombardment of the Kuomintang army as a reprisal for the Nanjing Incident in March 1927 (11.1.2).

111 Nakamura, *Shōwashi*, 80–81.

112 Ōuchi, *Nihon no rekishi 24*, 78.

113 Ibid., 181.

114 Metzler, *Lever of Empire*, 138.

115 Under the terms of the Convertible Banknotes Law of 1884 and later revisions, the Bank of Japan's note issue followed a fiduciary model of the Bank of England. The formal "rules of the game" were as follows: The note issue was to be entirely covered by a specie reserve of silver and gold coins and bullion (later exclusively gold coins and bullion), but further issue could be made, backed by a fiduciary reserve consisting of government bonds and other securities, up to a limit fixed by law at ¥70 million in 1888, ¥85 million in 1890, ¥120 million in 1899, and raised by Takahashi Korekiyo to ¥1 billion in 1932. An additional issue against securities (the excess fiduciary issue) could also be made. If the excess issue extended over fifteen days, it required the finance minister's approval and was taxed at a minimum rate of 5 percent (reduced to 3 percent in 1932).

During the era of the gold embargo from 1917 to 1929, the ratio of the BOJ's specie reserves to its note issue never fell below 60 percent. In this way, although the Japanese government restricted gold exports, it continued to operate a kind of "shadow" gold standard in the 1920s. The relationship between the gold reserve and the note issue actually broke down when Inoue restored the gold standard, and huge gold outflows forced the ratio down to 35 percent in 1931. The average ratios of the BOJ's note issue to specie reserves were 42 percent in the 1900s, 60 percent in the 1910s, 69 percent in the 1920s and 30 percent in the 1930s. Metzler, *Lever of Empire*, 223, 250–251, 275.

116 Ibid., 131, 260.

117 Ibid., 190.

118 Lamont attributed the banking panic in the spring of 1927 not to the financial after-effects of the 1923 earthquake, but to Japan's failure to deflate after the war, because it had allowed the continuation of many enterprises that ought to have been liquidated in the recession of 1920–1921. Ibid., 185.

119 Ibid., 220. When Japan finally announced its decision to lift the gold embargo in November 1929, the American banking group extended to Japan a credit amounting to $25 million for defense against speculative attack against the yen. In London the British group simultaneously established a credit of £5 million. Ibid., 215. Metzler compares the gold standard that the United States strongly suggested Japan join with the US-sponsored Washington system of 1922. The former was a system by which the United States intended to monetarily confine Japan to a worldwide monetary stabilization system, while the latter was a system by which the United States intended to diplomatically contain Japanese expansionism in China. Ibid., 259–260.

120 The Bank of Japan of those days was not an institution that pursued monetary policies independently of the Japanese government. Kōzō Yamamura, "Then Came the Great Depression: Japan's Interwar Years," in *The Interwar Economy of Japan*, ed. Michael Smitka (New York: Garland Publishing, 1998), 287.

121 Nakamura, *Shōwashi*, 57.

122 Yamamura, "Then Came the Great Depression," in *The Interwar Economy*, ed. Smitka, 278.

9.4. The International Financial Positions of the United States and Japan

123 Cleona Lewis, *America's Stake in International Investments* (Washington, DC: Brookings Institution, 1938), 441. The United States had registered current account surpluses in 1898–1901, but otherwise it was a net capital importer until WWI. United Nations, Department of Economic Affairs, *International Capital Movements during the Inter-War Period* (Lake Success, NY: United Nations, 1949), 3.

124 US Department of Commerce, *The United States in the World Economy* (Washington, DC: US Government Printing Office, 1943), 120–123.

125 Harold G. Moulton, *Japan: An Economic and Financial Appraisal* (Washington: Institute of Economics of the Brookings Institution, 1931), 282–283. The Nishihara loans, totaling ¥145 million, were made from January 1917 to September 1918. The loans were made to Duan Qirui, warlord premier of the Beijing government, to persuade him to favor Japanese interests in China. The loans were named after Nishihara Kamezō (西原亀三), Prime Minister Terauchi's secretary. Charles Remer, *Foreign Investments in China* (New York: Howard Fertig, 1968), 540–541.

## Chapter 10

# Foreign Investments in the US and Japan and by the US and Japan in the Pre-WWII Period

## 10.1. Foreign Investments in the United States

### 10.1.1. British *Investments in US Railways*

Britain had historically been by far the largest foreign investor in the United States (table 10.1.1-a). Before World War I, of total foreign investments in the United States (portfolio and direct investments combined),[1] Britain's accounted for 60 to 80 percent.

British investment in the United States was heavily concentrated in railways. In 1908, British investments in American railways amounted to $2.85 billion,[2] which represented 81 percent of the $3.5 billion British investment in the United States in that year. The British investments in American railways were primarily portfolio investments (table 10.1.1-b). Other countries' investments in American railways were also basically portfolio investments, except for Canada's. Canada's investments in 1914, for example, included $82 million in direct investments in railway construction across the border by the Canadian Pacific Railway.

Railroad construction was a driving force for American economic development from the post–Civil War decades through the early 20th century

*265*

Chapter 10

Table 10.1.1-a. Foreign Investments (Portfolio and Direct) in US ($ million)

|      | Britain | Germany | Holland | France | Others | Total |
|------|---------|---------|---------|--------|--------|-------|
| 1899 | 2,500   | 200     | 240     | 50     | 155    | 3,145 |
| 1908 | 3,500   | 1,000   | 750     | 630    | 120    | 6,000 |
| 1914 | 4,250   | 950     | 635     | 410    | 845    | 7,090 |
| 1929 | 1,560   | 400     | 400     | 400    | 1,940  | 4,700 |
| 1937 | 2,388   | 125     | 823     | 452    | 2,332  | 6,112 |

*Note:* Investment figures represent the cumulative levels at the end of each year.
*Source:* Mira Wilkins, *The History of Foreign Investment in the United States to 1914* (Cambridge, MA: Harvard University Press, 1989), 159. Mira Wilkins, *The History of Foreign Investment in the United States 1914–1945* (Cambridge, MA: Harvard University Press, 2004), 72.

Table 10.1.1-b. Foreign Investments in US Railways as of 1914 ($ million)

|                                          | Britain | Germany | France | Holland | Canada |
|------------------------------------------|---------|---------|--------|---------|--------|
| Portfolio investments in railways        | 2,800   | 300     | 290    | 300     | 48     |
| Other portfolio investments              | 850     | 350     | 75     | 200     | 95     |
| Direct investments in controlled enterprises | 600 | 300     | 45     | 135     | 132    |
| Total                                    | 4,250   | 950     | 410    | 635     | 275    |

*Source:* Cleona Lewis, *America's Stake in International Investments* (Washington, DC: Brookings Institution, 1938), 546. Mira Wilkins, *The History of Foreign Investment in the United States to 1914* (Cambridge, MA: Harvard University Press, 1989), 165, 167, 169, 171, 173.

(5.1.1). It accounted for about 20 percent of US gross capital formation in the 1870s, and about 15 percent in the 1880s.[3] As of 1900, 25 percent of the total outstanding railway bonds in the United States were held by foreigners, mostly the British.[4] The British contributed much to the economic development of the United States through its investments in American railroads.[5]

## 10.1.2. Foreign Direct Investments in the Major US Industrial Sectors

In terms of FDIs in major US industries in pre-WWII America, those in the textile and chemical industries were conspicuous. In textiles, the British J. & P. Coats group, along with an Anglo-American joint venture in which the British had a controlling share, dominated the American cotton and linen thread industry by the mid-1890s.[6] One of the important factors that prompted their direct investments in the American textile industry was the high import duties (9.2.2). British and other European textile manufacturers

266

Table 10.1.2. Immigration from Europe to US, 1850–99 (in thousands)

|  | 1850–59 | 1860–69 | 1870–79 | 1880–89 | 1890–99 | 1850–99 |
|---|---|---|---|---|---|---|
| Britain | 444 | 533 | 579 | 811 | 329 | 2,696 |
| Ireland | 1,029 | 427 | 422 | 674 | 406 | 2,958 |
| Germany | 976 | 724 | 752 | 1,445 | 579 | 4,476 |
| Italy | 9 | 10 | 46 | 268 | 604 | 937 |
| Other nations | 356 | 184 | 452 | 1,443 | 1,675 | 4,110 |
| European total | 2,814 | 1,878 | 2,251 | 4,641 | 3,593 | 15,177 |

Source: US Department of Commerce, Bureau of the Census, *Historical Statistics of the United States* (Washington, DC: US Government Printing Office, 1975), 105–106.

chose to invest in production behind the tall American tariff wall.[7]

In investment in the chemical industry, German enterprises' technological advantage over their European and American competitors led to active German direct investments in the United States.[8] Bayer started producing dyes in Rensselaer, New York, in the 1880s. By 1914, many other German chemical companies operated in the United States, Bayer being the leader.[9] During WWI, however, production facilities and patents belonging to German enterprises were confiscated by the US government. Most of them were associated with chemicals.[10] In the 1920s, German chemical firms started to reenter the United States, but their total investments in production facilities in the United States were much smaller than their pre-WWI investments.

Besides the technological advantages typically shown in the chemical industry, Germans' large-scale immigration to the United States was another important factor in active German direct investment in the United States. During the five decades between 1850 and 1899, German immigrants to the United States were much more numerous than those from other European nations (table 10.1.2).[11] Those immigrants wrote home about opportunities in the United States and discussed them when they returned home. They were information providers, and they often became partners in American ventures.

In industries other than textiles and chemicals, American industries were fairly competitive, and foreign investors in the United States found themselves limited to filling niche markets or unable to stay in the market over the long term. In such fields, American manufacturers were actively engaged in overseas activities, as discussed in 10.2.1.

In telephony and electric machinery, American manufacturers were highly competitive internationally from the days of Bell and Edison. The German firms Siemens and AEG made some aggressive investments in the late 19th century, but they turned out to be short-lived. The US electrical industry continued to be dominated by two diversified giants: General Electric and Westinghouse.

In automobiles, French, German, and Italian manufacturers came to the United States in the early 20th century,[12] but all those makers' productions were short-lived. For example, Daimler did not rebuild its Long Island plant, originally built in 1905, after it burned down in 1913.[13] Rolls Royce, which started producing in Massachusetts in 1921, stopped production in 1929. By 1933, not a single foreign car company had a direct investment in the US automobile industry, which was controlled by Ford and GM.[14]

In the iron and steel industry, American mills had grown strong enough to control the US domestic market by 1914, though there were foreign contributions in niche markets such as crucible steel.[15]

In the oil industry, because of Standard Oil's dominant position, FDIs in the United States were minimal until the early 1910s, when the Royal Dutch Shell Group started vigorous investments in the United States.[16] By the end of the 1920s, it was conducting business in all forty-eight states and employed 35,000 workers. Yet it ranked fifth in asset size behind four American oil companies.[17]

## 10.2. US Foreign Direct Investments

### 10.2.1. US Enterprises' Direct Investments Abroad

Singer Sewing Machine was the first American multinational. Singer had its first overseas sales outlet in London in the early 1860s, when no other major American businesses had made any serious attempt to establish stakes abroad. During the 1860s, Singer built manufacturing plants in Canada and Austria, as well as Britain. By the 1880s, Singer had completed an international business system with a worldwide network of manufacturing plants and sales offices.[18]

The American multinationals that followed Singer abroad were electrical enterprises. The Bell and Edison interests made energetic efforts to introduce their telephony outside the United States; for this purpose, the Edison Telephone Company was formed in London in 1879,[19] and the International

Table 10.2.1. US Foreign Direct Investments by Sector ($ million)

|               | 1897 | 1908  | 1914  | 1924  | 1929  | 1935  |
|---------------|------|-------|-------|-------|-------|-------|
| Trade         | 62   | 89    | 179   | 314   | 378   | 345   |
| Utilities     | 22   | 85    | 133   | 224   | 1,025 | 1,088 |
| Manufacturing | 94   | 296   | 478   | 1252  | 1,821 | 1,870 |
| Agriculture   | 77   | 187   | 356   | 918   | 986   | 587   |
| Railroads     | 143  | 161   | 255   | 347   | 309   | 261   |
| Mining        | 134  | 445   | 720   | 967   | 1,227 | 1,218 |
| Petroleum     | 86   | 224   | 343   | 967   | 1,341 | 1,382 |
| Others        | 18   | 153   | 189   | 401   | 467   | 469   |
| Total         | 635  | 1,639 | 2,652 | 5,389 | 7,553 | 7,219 |

Source: Cleona Lewis, *America's Stake in International Investments* (Washington, DC: Brookings Institution, 1938), 605.

Bell Telephone Company was set up in Antwerp in 1880. Western Electric, a subsidiary of the American Bell Telephone Company, had factories in almost all major European countries and Canada by 1897.[20] With these facilities, these companies could sell to foreign governments that did not buy equipment made outside their country. The General Electric Company was incorporated in 1892, merging the Edison General Electric Company and the Thomson–Houston Electric Company. By 1919, GE had plants in Europe, Latin America, Japan, Australia, and South Africa as well as Canada. By the end of 1930, GE's worldwide investments equaled $111.6 million.[21]

The first American automobile manufacturing outside the United States was in Canada by Ford in 1904. Oldsmobile (1906) and Buick (1907) soon followed (General Motors later took over these plants). In 1911, Ford built an assembly plant in Britain, where by 1914 the Model T (9.1.2) had become a bestseller.[22] In the 1920s, Ford built assembly plants in Latin America, Japan, and Turkey. General Motors similarly established manufacturing facilities worldwide.

In addition to the companies mentioned above, other American multinational manufacturing companies were active in foreign investments from the late nineteenth century through the 1930s. They invested in such fields as metal products (American Radiator, Babcock & Wilcox, etc.),[23] office equipment (NCR, IBM, Remington, etc.),[24] and farm equipment (International Harvester, etc.).[25]

In the oil industry, Standard Oil established its overseas sales organization

Chapter 10

in the middle of the 1880s. Until then it had exported oil through export merchants or foreign importers. By 1907, it had fifty-five subsidiaries abroad. Some had refineries and some had transportation facilities.[26] In 1911, the US Supreme Court decided that Standard Oil was a monopoly and ordered its breakup. Of the thirty-four companies into which Standard Oil was split, Jersey Standard obtained the largest foreign assets in Europe, Latin America, Canada, and other areas. East Asia was allocated to New York Standard. In 1927, of the total consumption of refined products outside America's boundaries, Jersey Standard provided 23 percent, Royal Dutch Shell 16 percent, Anglo-Persian 11.5 percent, and Russian-owned refineries 6.5 percent, while the remaining 43 percent came from other companies, in large part US-controlled enterprises.

## 10.2.2. US Direct Investments in Latin America and the Middle East

Geographically, about half of US business investments were made in Latin America, about one-quarter in Canada, and about one-fifth in Europe in the pre-WWII decades (table 10.2.2-a). In the Middle East, US investments in oil resources started in the mid-1930s.

Latin America was the largest recipient of US investments in the fields of mining, petroleum, agriculture, and utilities (table 10.2.2-b). In mining, Chile was the largest recipient of American capital by virtue of its copper mines in the Andes.[27] In Mexico, US mining companies invested in silver, lead, and copper mining, political uncertainties notwithstanding.[28] Of the US mining investments in Latin America of $802 million in 1929, Chile received $382 million, Mexico $240 million, and Peru $79 million.[29]

Agricultural investments in Latin America were mainly made in the Caribbean (particularly in Cuba) and Central America. By 1929, Americans had invested $544 million in sugar production in Cuba, and $128 million in fruit growing in Central America.[30] The largest American investor in agriculture was the United Fruit Company, which was active principally in the banana business.[31]

United Fruit invested vigorously in railroads and public utilities in the West Indies, Central America, and Mexico.[32] It cut down forests, created plantations, and established company towns in places that had never been developed.[33] United Fruit's aggressive investment often drew criticism as being exploitive, but it undeniably had a large impact on the economic development

*270*

Table 10.2.2-a. US Direct Foreign Investment by Area ($ million)

|  | 1897 | 1908 | 1914 | 1924 | 1929 | 1935 |
|---|---|---|---|---|---|---|
| Latin America | 308 | 754 | 1,281 | 2,819 | 3,705 | 3,261 |
| Canada | 160 | 405 | 618 | 1,081 | 1,657 | 1,692 |
| Europe | 131 | 369 | 573 | 921 | 1,340 | 1,370 |
| Asia, the Middle East | 23 | 75 | 120 | 267 | 447 | 488 |
| Rest of the world | 3 | 15 | 30 | 176 | 279 | 283 |
| Banking | 10 | 20 | 30 | 125 | 125 | 125 |
| Total investments | 635 | 1,639 | 2,652 | 5,389 | 7,553 | 7,219 |

Source: Cleona Lewis, *America's Stake in International Investments* (Washington, DC: Brookings Institution, 1938), 606.


Table 10.2.2-b. US Direct Investments by Industries and Areas as of 1929 ($ million)

|  | Manufacturing | Mining | Petroleum | Agriculture | Utilities | Total |
|---|---|---|---|---|---|---|
| Latin America | 230 | 802 | 784 | 884 | 806 | 3,705 |
| Europe | 637 | 37 | 239 | – | 138 | 1,340 |
| Canada | 820 | 318 | 55 | 30 | 318 | 1,657 |
| Asia, the Middle East | 77 | 10 | 151 | 63 | 71 | 447 |
| Rest of the world | 57 | 60 | 113 | 8 | 2 | 279 |
| Total investments | 1,821 | 1,227 | 1,341 | 986 | 1,334 | 7,428 |

Notes: 1. Utilities comprise telephone systems, railroads, and other public utilities.
2. Total includes miscellaneous investments.
Source: Mira Wilkins, *The Maturing of Multinational Enterprise: American Business Abroad from 1914 to 1970* (Cambridge, MA: Harvard University Press, 1974), 182.

of the host countries.

The American oil majors first went to Mexico, but upon encountering strong nationalistic challenges, shifted their oil workers and money to Venezuela. By the end of the 1920s, Venezuela was producing more oil than Mexico.[34]

US oil investments in the Middle East were not obstructed by the host nations, but by Britain out of strategic considerations. In the early 20th century, only Iran had oil production in this region, and it was under the control of the Anglo-Persian Oil Company, in which the British government held a majority interest. Try as Americans would, they failed to enter the Iranian oil industry.[35] In 1928, after long negotiations aided by the US State Department, a group of American oil companies managed to obtain a 23.75 percent interest in the Turkish Petroleum Company (TPC), whose 50 percent shareholder was the British-controlled Turkish National Bank.[36] The agreement of 1928 enabled US oil companies to acquire their first oil concession in the Middle East, but it pledged the signers to operate only through TPC within an area delineated by a red line drawn around the former Ottoman Empire boundaries (with the exception of Kuwait).[37]

Gulf Oil, one of the signers of the 1928 agreement, faced a dilemma, because it had purchased options on concessions in Bahrain, Saudi Arabia, and Kuwait in 1927.[38] It sold the Bahrain concession to Standard Oil of California (Socal) which was outside the TPC agreement. The Saudi Arabia concession was allowed to lapse.

Socal set up a Canadian company, Bahrain Petroleum Company (Bapco), to hold the concession, as it was faced with the British government insistence that oil development in the Gulf region should be entrusted only to British concerns.[39] After long negotiations, in 1930 Britain approved Bapco's rights in Bahrain,[40] where it struck oil in 1932. In Kuwait in 1934, Gulf Oil formed a 50-50 joint venture, Kuwait Oil Company (KOC), with the Anglo-Persian Oil Company to evade British interference. In that year, the sheikh of Kuwait granted KOC an exclusive concession.[41] It struck oil in 1936. In the meantime, in 1933, Socal obtained a concession in the eastern part of Saudi Arabia from King Ibn Saud.[42] Socal's subsidiary, the California Arabian Standard Oil Company (renamed Aramco in 1944),[43] discovered oil in commercial quantities in Saudi Arabia in 1938.[44]

With Socal and Gulf Oil's activities in the Gulf, the United States established a firm foothold in the Middle East, which had been the British preserve.

## 10.3. Foreign Investments in Japan

### 10.3.1. Foreign Portfolio Investments in Japan

For some time after the opening of the country, Japan was not a debtor country to any appreciable extent.[45] Japan was a good student of Ulysses Grant, who advised against heavy reliance on foreign loans when he came to Japan in 1879.[46] But the Japanese victory in the Sino–Japanese War (1894–95) and the adoption of the gold standard in 1897 changed the situation. The wariness of foreign lenders diminished considerably, and Japan's position in international

Table 10.3.1-a. Major Foreign Borrowings by the Japanese Government

| Amount (millions) | Interest | Place of issue | Issue date | Maturity | Repaid, or outstanding as of 1947 |
|---|---|---|---|---|---|
| £10 (98) | 4% | UK | Jul. 1899 | Dec. 1953 | Outstanding £6.9 mil. |
| £10 (98) | 6% | UK, US | May 1904 | Apr. 1911 | Repaid Sep. 1907 |
| £12 (117) | 6% | UK, US | Nov. 1904 | Oct. 1911 | Repaid Sep. 1907 |
| £30 (293) | 4.5% | UK, US | Mar. 1905 | Feb. 1925 | Repaid Oct. 1924 |
| £30 (293) | 4.5% | UK, US, G | Jul. 1905 | Jul. 1925 | Repaid Oct. 1924 |
| £25 (244) | 4.0% | UK, US, G, F | Nov. 1905 | Jan. 1931 | Repaid May 1930 |
| £23 (225) | 5.0% | UK, F | Mar. 1907 | Mar. 1947 | Outstanding £17.9 mil. |
| £11 (107) | 4.0% | UK | May 1910 | Jun. 1970 | Outstanding £7.2 mil. |
| F450 (174) | 4.0% | F | May 1910 | May 1970 | Outstanding F15.5 mil. |
| F200 (77) | 5.0% | F | Apr. 1913 | May 1923 | Repaid May 1923 |
| £25 (244) | 6.0% | UK | Feb. 1924 | Jul. 1959 | Outstanding £10.5 mil. |
| $150 (301) | 6.5% | US | Feb. 1924 | Feb. 1954 | Outstanding $11.8 mil. |
| $71 (142) | 5.5% | US | May 1930 | May 1965 | Outstanding $9.6 mil. |
| £12.5 (122) | 5.5% | UK | May 1930 | May 1965 | Outstanding £5.6 mil. |

*Notes:* 1. The figures in parentheses are equivalent yen values in millions.
2. G stands for Germany and F stands for France.

*Source:* Ōkura-shō, Nippon Ginkō, eds. *Zaisei keizai tōkei nenpō* (Tokyo: Ōkura-shō Zaimu Kyōkai, 1948), 324–325. Harold Moulton, *Japan: An Economic and Financial Appraisal* (New York: AMS Press, 1969, reprinted from the 1931 edition), 488–489.

financial markets improved markedly. Japan could now obtain foreign loans much more advantageously than before. The first major foreign loan was in London in 1897, when the Bank of Japan sold Japanese government bonds amounting to ¥43 million that had been floated at home.[47] In 1899, £10 million (¥98 million) worth of government bonds were issued in London (table 10.3.1-a).

With the outbreak of war with Russia in 1904, bond issues to finance war expenditures began in earnest (6.3.2). In 1904, £10 million in bonds went on sale in May and £12 million bonds in November; both issues were sold half in London and half in New York. In 1905, £30 million in bonds were floated in May in London and New York, and another £30 million in July in London, New York, and Germany.[48] The loans subsequently floated were mostly for refunding the old loans, or for redeeming past domestic bonds that had higher interest rates. The credit rating of Japanese government bonds improved remarkably with the military successes during the Russo–Japanese War, and

*273*

Chapter 10

Table 10.3.1-b. Outstanding Japanese Foreign Indebtedness (¥ million)

|  | 1899 | 1905 | 1914 | 1919 | 1929 | 1936 |
|---|---|---|---|---|---|---|
| National government | 141 | 1,395 | 1,606 | 1,374 | 1,479 | 1,348 |
| Municipal government | 0.25 | 4 | 177 | 147 | 246 | 211 |
| Private corporations | 0 | 10 | 167 | 165 | 466 | 324 |
| Total | 141 | 1,409 | 1,950 | 1,687 | 2,190 | 1,883 |

*Note:* Private corporations' indebtedness does not include foreign direct investments made in Japan.
*Source:* Ishizaki Teruhiko, "Shikin chōtatsu (ge): gaishi" in *Gendai Nihon no dokusen shihon 7,* ed. Miyazaki Giichi (Tokyo: Shiseidō, 1965), 7, 37.

with Japan's subsequent economic growth.

Between 1899 and 1930, government bonds floated abroad amounted to £204.4 million, F650 million, and $221 million, equivalent to ¥2.69 billion.[49] At the end of 1914, outstanding government foreign loans amounted to ¥1.606 billion (table 10.3.1-b), which accounted for 64 percent of total outstanding government borrowings of ¥2.506 billion, and 41 percent of the GNP of ¥3.948 billion in that year. By 1936, the percentage of the former declined to 12 percent, and the latter to 8 percent.[50]

The city of Kobe issued the first municipal bond abroad in 1899; this was followed by international bond issues by Yokohama, Osaka, Tokyo, Kyoto, and Nagoya. Between 1899 and 1927, local governments borrowed a total of £18.1 million, F150.9 million, and $40.4 million, equivalent to ¥316 million altogether, including Tokyo and Yokohama's borrowings for reconstruction after the Great Kantō Earthquake.[51] Municipal foreign borrowings accounted for 70 percent of the total municipal borrowings at the end of 1914.[52]

After the Russo–Japanese War, private Japanese companies—mainly semigovernmental companies such as the South Manchuria Railway Company and the Oriental Development Company—raised foreign loans.[53] After WWI, borrowings by electric power companies increased.[54] The total of pre-WWII corporate borrowings amounted to £30.9 million, F50.6 million, and $251.4 million, equivalent to ¥826 million in all.[55]

All foreign portfolio investments in the Japanese government, the municipal governments, and private corporations (excluding foreign direct investments) outstanding as of 1929 totaled ¥2,190 million (table 10.3.1-b).

After the Manchurian Incident of 1931, no foreign loans were floated. However, Japan's capital imports on a large scale from the late 1890s until

*274*

1930 enabled Japan to run large budget deficits, to import more merchandise than it exported, and to make positive investments abroad as well as in Japan, exceeding the nation's savings by a considerable sum. Foreign borrowing not only helped Japan to cope with crises such as the war with Russia and the Great Kantō Earthquake, but also accelerated its economic expansion in an era when there were no international development lending institutions.[56]

### 10.3.2. Major Foreign Direct Investments in Japan before WWI

In 1899, the revised treaties of 1894 with the powers as well as the correspondingly revised Japanese civil legislation came into effect, enabling foreigners to conduct business throughout Japan and participate with equity in Japanese companies (4.3.2).[57] Until then, foreign business investments in Japan had been confined to the treaty settlement areas.

A Japanese newspaper reported on July 5, 1903 that foreign capital participation in Japanese companies had reached ¥24,226,500.[58] The newspaper also named several joint venture companies, including the Nippon Electric Company, the Murai Brothers Company,[59] and the Osaka Gas Company (table 10.3.2).[60]

Nippon Electric (日本電気 NEC) was the first joint venture with foreign capital after the Treaty of Commerce and Navigation of 1894 with the United States went into effect on July 17, 1899. It was 54 percent owned by the Western Electric Company, and 46 percent owned by five Japanese promoters led by Iwadare Kunihiko (岩垂邦彦).[61]

When Western Electric's overseas division manager, Henry Thayer, visited Japan in 1896,[62] he wanted to ascertain the advisability of choosing Japan as the eighth country for his company's overseas operations.[63] Through discussions with Iwadare, who was then Western Electric's agent in Japan,[64] and other people, Thayer was convinced of the potential of the Japanese telephone market. Western Electric's overseas expansion strategy was centered on joint ventures with local telephone manufacturers. With the help of Iwadare, Western Electric first negotiated with Oki Shōkai (沖商会), the only telephone manufacturer in Japan at that time. However, the negotiations failed. Oki Kibatarō (沖牙太郎), the founder and owner of the company, was overly afraid of being taken over by Western Electric.[65] Western Electric thus decided to form a new company with Iwadare.[66]

Starting up NEC's operations was not easy. The major problem was the

Chapter 10

**Table 10.3.2. Early Major Foreign Direct Investments in Japan**

| Starting year | Japanese organization | Foreign investor | Products or service | Capital (1,000 yen) | Foreign share |
|---|---|---|---|---|---|
| 1899 | Nippon Electric | Western Electric (US) | Telephones, switchboards | 200 | 54% |
| 1900 | Murai Brothers | American Tobacco (US) | Tobacco | 10,000 | 50% |
| 1902 | Osaka Gas | Anthony Brady (US) | Gas supply | 4,000 | 52.5% |
| 1905 | Tokyo Electric | General Electric (US) | Light bulbs | 400 | 51% |
| 1907 | Teikoku Seishi | J. & P. Coats (UK) | Cotton yarn | 3,000 | 60% |
| 1907 | Nihon Seikōsho | Vickers (UK), Armstrong (UK) | Special steel, arms | 10,000 | 50% |
| 1908 (1917) | Dunlop Far East (Nihon Dunlop) | Dunlop Rubber (UK) | Tires | (1,800) | branch (100%) |
| 1908 (1928) | Senwa Wilcox (Tōyō Babcock) | Babcock & Wilcox (UK) | Boilers | (1,750) | 100% (71.25%) |
| 1910 | Shibaura | General Electric (US) | Heavy electric equipment | 2,000 | 24% |

*Source:* Ishizaki Akihiko, "Nihon no gaishi" in *Gendai Nihon no dokusen shihon*, ed. Miyazaki Giichi (Tokyo: Shiseidō, 1965), 24–26, 29. Nihon Kōgyō Ginkō Gaiji-bu, *Gaikoku kaisha no honpō tōshi* (Tokyo: Nihon Kōgyō Ginkō, 1948), 53–61, 139–151, 231–239. Horie Yasuzō, *Gaishi yunyū no kaiko to tenbō* (Tokyo: Yuhikaku Publishing, 1950), 74–87, 115–128.

inexperience of the newly recruited factory workers. Though Western Electric trained NEC technical personnel in the United States and sent several staff members from Western Electric to key posts in NEC,[67] its output of telephone equipment in 1901–1904 was only half that of Oki. By the early 1920s, however, NEC was producing three times as much equipment as Oki.[68] For Western Electric, NEC proved to be a very successful investment. In 1918–1922, while Western Electric's investment in all foreign locations yielded average annual returns of 11 percent, NEC's figure stood at almost 25 percent.[69]

General Electric's affiliations with Tokyo Electric (東京電気) and Shibaura Seisakusho (芝浦製作所) were also important to the development of the Japanese electrical products industry. Tokyo Electric, a pioneer in electric bulb manufacturing in Japan,[70] faced financial difficulties in 1903–1904 due to tough competition from imports,[71] and sought financial and technological assistance from General Electric.[72] GE recognized the prospective capabilities of the company and decided to invest in Tokyo Electric. GE also saw the strategic advantage of local production over exporting to Japan in competition with its European rivals. Having become a 51 percent shareholder of Tokyo Electric,

276

GE sent three resident directors to the five-member board of the company. John Geary, one of the directors, stayed with Tokyo Electric for thirty years, and assumed the post of president of the company from 1921 to 1927.[73] With GE's participation, Tokyo Electric's performance improved remarkably.[74]

In 1909, GE agreed to make its technology available to Shibaura Seisakusho, a leading Japanese electrical machinery manufacturer, in exchange for a 24 percent share in the company.[75] GE's motive was basically same as had been the case with Tokyo Electric. Shibaura, like Tokyo Electric, was having an uphill battle against imports. GE sent John Geary to Shibaura's board. Some thirty years later, in 1939, Tokyo Electric and Shibaura Seisakusho merged into Tokyo Shibaura Denki (now Toshiba) capitalized at ¥87 million, in which GE held a 32.8 percent interest as a top shareholder.[76]

The Japanese victory in the Russo–Japanese War encouraged British investment in Japan. In 1907, J. & P. Coats formed Teikoku Seishi (帝国製糸), a 60-40 joint venture with Murai Katanito Seizōsho (村井カタン糸製造所) in Osaka.[77] In the same year, Vickers, Sons & Maxim, and Armstrong Whitworth joined with the Mitsui group to create Nihon Seikōsho (日本製鋼所 Japan Steel Works), a 50-50 (UK–Japan) joint venture in Hokkaidō. It became Japan's largest manufacturer of forged iron products and the main supplier of armaments to the Japanese navy.[78] In 1908, Dunlop Rubber built a branch factory in Kobe to manufacture bicycle tires, which was reorganized in 1917 to form Nihon Dunlop Gomu (日本ダンロップ護謨), a subsidiary company incorporated under Japanese law, capitalized at ¥1.8 million.[79] It continued to be the largest supplier of bicycle tires in the Japanese market until the late 1930s. British Babcock & Wilcox established a subsidiary factory in Yokohama in 1908 to manufacture boilers and auxiliary equipment. In 1928, Babcock reorganized it into a joint venture with Mitsui & Co. in view of the Japanese government's "buy Japanese" policy. The company remained the leading boiler maker in Japan through the pre-WWII years.[80]

### 10.3.3. Major Foreign Direct Investments in Japan from 1917 to 1937

In 1917, when the war in Europe was still going on, B. F. Goodrich, an American automobile tire manufacturer, entered into a joint venture with Yokohama Densen (横浜電線) on a fifty-fifty basis to establish Yokohama Gomu (横浜ゴム) in 1917 (table 10.3.3-a). Of the paid-up capital of ¥1 million, Yokohama Densen paid ¥800,000 and ceded ¥300,000 worth of shares to Goodrich in exchange for patents and technical know-how.[81] Soon after the start of production, the Great Kantō Earthquake almost completely destroyed Yokohama Gomu's newly built factories. Given the destruction, Goodrich initially considered withdrawal from Japan, but the enthusiasm of the Japanese side for reconstruction caused the Goodrich people to change their minds.[82] During WWII, Goodrich could not provide Yokohama with technical assistance, but Yokohama kept reserving on their books "technical fees" payable to Goodrich based on royalties on sales established in the original contracts with Goodrich. The royalties were duly paid when some foreign exchange restrictions were lifted after the war. The difficulties the two partners coped with deepened their mutual trust. After the war, they desired an early return to their prewar relationship. Yokohama Gomu was the first among the prewar joint ventures to get government approval for restoring prewar business ties. Nakagawa Suekichi (中川末吉), chairman of Yokohama Gomu, kept saying during the war, "War is a fight between governments, not between peoples. Therefore, we should keep confidence in Goodrich people."[83]

Western Electric, which had established a firm position in the Japanese telephone industry, collaborated in 1920 with Sumitomo in the manufacture of electric cable for telephones.[84] Sumitomo created Sumitomo Electric Wire and Cable Works Limited (住友電線) with capital of ¥10 million, in which NEC acquired a 25 percent interest in exchange for Western Electric's transfer of patents on electric cable production to Sumitomo Electric Wire.[85] Sumitomo Electric Wire acquired, in turn, 5 percent of NEC's shares. In the heavy electrical machinery industry, Westinghouse concluded a license agreement with Mitsubishi Denki (三菱電機 Mitsubishi Electric) in 1923. It obtained 4.8 percent of Mitsubishi Denki's paid-up capital of ¥45 million in return for providing Mitsubishi Denki with electrical machinery technology.[86] In the same year, Siemens and Furukawa Denki (古河電工 Furukawa Electric) jointly formed Fuji Denki (富士電機 Fuji Electric). Siemens acquired a 30 percent stake in the new company. It provided all its patents and know-how to the new company in exchange for receipt of a cash payment equal to one-fifth of the new company's paid-in capital of 7.5 million yen.[87]

In 1924, the German chemical firm VGF joined with Nihon Chisso (日本窒素) to form Asahi Kenshoku (旭絹織), acquiring a 20 percent interest in exchange for its patents and know-how with regard to production of viscose rayon yarn.[88]

*Foreign Investments in the US and Japan and by the US and Japan in the Pre-WWII Period*

**Table 10.3.3-a. Major Manufacturing Joint Ventures in Japan, 1917 to 1932**

| | Joint venture firm | Foreign investor | Products | Capital (¥1,000) | Foreign share |
|---|---|---|---|---|---|
| 1917 | Yokohama Gomu | Goodrich (US) | Tires | 2,500 | 50% |
| 1918 | Nichibei Itagarasu | Libbey–Owens (US) | Sheet glass | 3,000 | 33% |
| 1920 | Sumitomo Densen | Western Electric (US) | Electric wire | 10,000 | 25% |
| 1923 | Mitsubishi Denki | Westinghouse (US) | Heavy electric equipment | 9,800 | 4.8% |
| 1923 | Fuji Denki | Siemens (Ger.) | Heavy electric equipment | 10,000 | 30% |
| 1924 | Asahi Kenshoku | VGF (Ger.) | Rayon | 2,000 | 20% |
| 1927 | Nihon Chikuonki Shōkai | Columbia (UK) | Phonographs, records | 2,100 | 67% |
| 1927 | Daido Match | Sweden Match (Sweden) | Matches | 6,000 | 50% |
| 1928 | Kyōsan Seisakusho | Union Switch & Signal (US) | Railroad signals | 1,000 | 29.5% |
| 1929 | Nihon Bemberg Kenshi | J. P. Bemberg (Ger.) | Rayon | 10,000 | 20% |
| 1930 | Tōyō Carrier | Carrier (US) | Air-conditioning equipment | 300 | 46% |
| 1931 | Mitsubishi Sekiyu | Associated Oil (US) | Refined petroleum products | 5,000 | 50% |
| 1931 | Sumitomo Aluminium | Aluminium Ltd. (Canada) | Aluminum sheet, foil | 3,500 | 50% |
| 1932 | Tōyō Otis Elevator | Otis Elevator (US) | Elevators | 1,000 | 60% |

*Source:* Ishizaki Akihiko, "Nihon no gaishi" in *Gendai Nihon no dokusen shihon*, ed. Miyazaki Giichi (Tokyo: Shiseidō, 1965), 51–53. Yuzawa Takeshi and Udagawa Masaru, eds., *Foreign Business in Japan before World War II* (Tokyo: University of Tokyo Press, 1990), 6–12. Nihon Kōgyō Ginkō Gaiji-bu, *Gaikoku kaisha no honpō tōshi* (Tokyo: Nihon Kōgyō Ginkō, 1948), 79–88, 113–123, 125–138, 153–168, 181–194, 211–221, 223–230, 255–266, 282–296, 309–312, 327–338.

In 1930, the Carrier Corporation and Sanki Kōgyō (三機工業), a Mitsui & Co. subsidiary, formed the Tōyō Carrier Corporation, an air-conditioning equipment manufacturing joint venture in which Mitsui interests held a majority stake. With no competing manufacturers in Japan, most major buildings built in Japan in the 1930s were equipped with Tōyō Carrier's air-conditioning systems and equipment.[89] In 1932, in view of rising Japanese

Chapter 10

**Table 10.3.3-b. Major Foreign Companies' Subsidiaries in Japan, 1924–1937**

| Starting year | Japanese company's name | Foreign company | Note |
|---|---|---|---|
| 1924 | Ford Japan | Ford Motor (US) | Ford formed a subsidiary with a capitalization of ¥4 million. |
| 1925 | General Motors Japan | General Motors (US) | General Motors formed a subsidiary with a capitalization of ¥8 million. |
| 1927 | Victor Talking Machine of Japan | Victor Talking Machine (US) | Victor's subsidiary became a US–Japan joint venture in 1929. |
| 1934 | Nihon Kinsen Tōrokuki | National Cash Register (US) | NCR made its subsidiary a joint venture with a Japanese competitor in 1935. |
| 1937 | Nihon Watson Tōkei Kaikeiki | International Business Machine (US) | Nihon Watson Tōkei Kaikeiki was a marketing subsidiary capitalized at ¥500,000. |

*Source:* Ishizaki Akihiko, "Nihon no gaishi" in *Gendai Nihon no dokusen shihon*, ed. Miyazaki Giichi (Tokyo: Shiseidō, 1965), 51. Nihon Kōgyō Ginkō Gaiji-bu, *Gaikoku kaisha no honpō tōshi* (Tokyo: Nihon Kōgyō Ginkō, 1948), 195–210, 313–326, 339–347. Nissan Jidōsha Kabushiki Kaisha Sōmubu Chōsaka, *Nissan Jidōsha sanjūnenshi* (Tokyo: Nissan Motor Co., 1965), 14. Mark Mason, *American Multinationals and Japan* (Cambridge, MA: Harvard University Press, 1992), 134–135.

nationalism, Otis Elevator, which had been exporting elevators to Japan since the early 1890s, formed Tōyō Otis Elevator jointly with Mitsui & Co.[90]

Some foreign companies established wholly owned subsidiaries in Japan after WWI (table 10.3.3-b). Some remained the sole owner of their Japan-based organization; some found Japanese partners later in response to Japanese government pressures in the 1930s.

Ford and General Motors established wholly-owned subsidiaries in Japan to manufacture passenger cars in the 1920s. Ford had started exporting to Japan as early as 1905, and by the early 1920s, Model Ts had become a familiar sight in the major cities in Japan. The Great Kantō Earthquake in 1923, which necessitated the urgent import of large numbers of motor vehicles,[91] caused Ford to decide upon local manufacture. Ford started assembling cars in Yokohama from December 1924, creating a subsidiary with a capital of ¥4 million.

Ford's production in Japan prodded GM to launch a similar operation in 1925. GM chose to build a plant in Osaka, where the municipality, backed up by local business interests, warmly embraced the GM venture. GM was

*280*

_Foreign Investments in the US and Japan and by the US and Japan in the Pre-WWII Period_

**Table 10.3.3-c. Supply of Motor Vehicles in Japan, 1925–1935 (units)**

| | Domestically made | CBU imports | Imported knocked-down kits | | | |
| --- | --- | --- | --- | --- | --- | --- |
| | | | Total | Ford | GM | Kyōritsu |
| 1925 | 376 | 1,769 | 3,437 | 3,437 | | |
| 1927 | 302 | 3,895 | 12,668 | 7,033 | 5,635 | |
| 1929 | 437 | 5,018 | 29,338 | 10,640 | 15,745 | 1,251 |
| 1931 | 436 | 1,887 | 20,199 | 11,505 | 7,478 | 1,201 |
| 1933 | 1,681 | 491 | 15,082 | 8,156 | 5,942 | 978 |
| 1935 | 5,094 | 943 | 30,787 | 14,865 | 12,492 | 3,612 |

_Notes:_  1. CBU stands for completely built-up units.
　　　 2. Kyōritsu Jidōsha Seisakusho assembled knocked-down kits imported from Chrysler and other makers.
_Source:_ Udagawa Masaru, "The Prewar Japanese Automobile Industry and American Manufacturers," in _Japanese Yearbook on Business History: 1985_ (Tokyo: Japan Business History Institute, 1985), 82.

exempted from all city taxes for four years.[92] In 1927–1931, American automobiles—locally produced in Japan and imported combined—accounted for over 97 percent of total sales of passenger cars in the Japanese market (table 10.3.3-c). It was not until 1933 that Japanese makers' production exceeded 10 percent of the annual sales of passenger cars in Japan.

Victor Talking Machine, which had started exporting its products to Japan in 1903, formed a subsidiary, Victor Talking Machine of Japan, in 1927, to manufacture records, phonographs, and related accessories.[93] In 1929, Mitsubishi and Sumitomo each acquired a 16 percent stake in Nihon Victor. From its inception, Nihon Victor provided a phenomenal return on its partners' investments.[94]

In 1934, National Cash Register, which had exported cash registers to Japan since the early 1910s, established National Kinsen Tōrokuki (ナショナル金銭登録機), a marketing subsidiary. In 1935, it merged with a Japanese competitor, Nihon Kinsen Tōrokuki, into Nihon National Kinsen Tōrokuki. NCR owned 70 percent of the company. The new company almost monopolized the Japanese market, and exported extensively to Asia.[95]

In 1937, International Business Machine, whose early export performance in Japan was quite poor,[96] established a subsidiary for marketing its tabulating machines. But it was forced to discontinue sales of IBM machines at the end of 1940, when the government halted the issuance of licenses to import machines.[97]

In the oil industry, Standard Oil had had a sales outlet in Yokohama as early as 1893, and the Rising Sun Petroleum Company, the Japanese affiliate of Royal Dutch Shell, started selling Borneo oil in Japan in 1900.[98] Standard Oil started producing and refining oil in Niigata in 1900, but it sold all the facilities to Nihon Sekiyu (日本石油 Nippon Oil) in 1907.[99] Rising Sun built a refinery in Fukuoka in 1909, but it ceased operations in 1915.[100] Both Standard Oil and Rising Sun, however, continued as major exporters of crude and refined products to Japan until the oil embargo in 1941.[101] In 1929, the Associated Oil Company, headquartered in San Francisco, and Mitsubishi established Mitsubishi Sekiyu (三菱石油 Mitsubishi Oil), a fifty-fifty oil refining joint venture.[102] Mitsubishi Sekiyu continued to supply about 10 percent of Japan's oil demand until 1941.[103]

### 10.3.4. The Effect of Foreign Direct Investments on the Japanese Economy

There are no systematically compiled Japanese statistics on pre-WWII foreign direct investments, but the level of inward direct investment can be estimated from the payment of "income on foreign enterprises' undertakings and services." Lockwood estimates FDI at ¥70 million in 1913 and ¥200 million in 1933.[104] The scale of this foreign participation was decidedly small compared to foreign portfolio investment, which stood more or less at ¥2 billion in the 1910s through the mid-1930s (table 10.3.1-b). It is also much smaller than Japan's direct investment abroad (table 10.4.3-a).

Modest in amount as it was, the effect of direct investment on the Japanese economy was substantial. The technological capabilities of Japan's manufacturing industry were greatly improved thanks to foreign business investments. Yamamura cites the case of Mitsubishi Electric, whose company history candidly admits that the company's level of technological competence at the start was clearly far below that of its American and European competitors.[105] Thanks to the agreement with Westinghouse, however, Mitsubishi Electric "began to succeed in making machines which can be compared with those made by the best producers in the world."[106]

What Japanese gained from foreign businesses in Japan was not limited to manufacturing technology. They learned about business management in general. Japanese who worked for Ford and GM in Japan learned how sales,

*282*

accounting, and distribution management were done in the American automobile industry, and Japanese parts makers serving American automobile assembly plants received grounding in inventory and quality control. Western Electric's policy was to transfer the same system it used for managing its domestic operations to its overseas operations.[107] Western Electric inculcated, among other things, cost accounting and production control into its NEC partners. Nihon Watson's Japanese employees were thoroughly indoctrinated in IBM founder Thomas Watson's business philosophy.[108]

Managing a joint venture with personnel of different cultures is not easy. Labor relations in subsidiaries and branch offices in foreign lands also bring problems deriving from cultural differences. The success of FDI depends on how these problems are solved. In the case of NEC, Iwadare took pains to solve issues between American resident managers and Japanese employees.[109] Mutual trust is essential for successful FDI, but Singer did not consider it important. Singer refused to change its straight commission compensation to a system of fixed pay plus commission in the belief that its sales personnel would slack off in their efforts if they had fixed pay. A bitter labor dispute caused Singer to lose market share.[110] On the other hand, Nihon Watson was one of the successful cases in which management and employees overcame cultural differences with mutual trust and confidence. Watson's indoctrination was severe, but his management philosophy was based on trust in employees. Prewar and postwar IBMers in Japan had a reputation of being highly motivated and proud of their company.

# 10.4. Japan's Foreign Direct Investments

## 10.4.1. Japan's Investments in Business Bases Abroad

For many years after the opening of the country, Japanese export and import transactions were almost exclusively controlled by foreign merchants stationed in Japan. In the early 1880s, direct export sales still accounted for only 10 percent of the total value of Japan's exports.[111] It was an urgent task for Japan, which drew on foreign trade for its economic development, to have its own infrastructure to carry on export and import trade directly with foreign countries. Early Japanese foreign direct investments were mostly for establishing business bases abroad in service-sector enterprises such as trading companies, banks, and shipping companies.

While large American businesses in the manufacturing and other industries had their own business bases for marketing their products abroad or for securing supplies of foreign raw materials, in the case of Japan, trading firms assumed the task of marketing Japanese merchandise abroad and securing foreign materials and equipment for their clients. They played an important role in the economic development of Japan, as many Japanese businesses, especially small firms, were incapable of handling extensive foreign trade by themselves.

Mitsui & Co. (三井物産 MBK) opened its first overseas outlet in Shanghai in 1877, just a year after the founding of the company. The new office was established mainly for the purpose of selling Japanese coal in China. Purchasing Chinese raw cotton for Japanese spinners was soon added as a major business of this branch office. Before long, MBK had offices throughout China and in Hong Kong.[112]

MBK opened an office in New York in 1879, in London in 1877, in Paris in 1878, and in Lyon and Milan in 1880. The London office was mainly used to export rice to Europe. The New York, Paris, Lyon, and Milan branches principally handled raw silk and silkworm egg-cards.[113]

In New York, some fourteen Japanese trading companies followed MBK in opening branches in the early 1880s.[114] In Texas, three Japanese companies opened branches in the early 1910s to facilitate their purchases of raw cotton.[115]

In banking, the Yokohama Specie Bank (横浜正金銀行) established its New York office in 1880, the same year that the company was incorporated in Japan.[116] The Japanese trading companies in New York used the Yokohama Specie Bank for trade financing, foreign-exchange transactions, and as a source of general information.[117] The Yokohama Specie Bank later set up branches in the West Coast.[118] It opened new offices in any major cities where Japanese companies had opened new offices. After MBK and Nihon Yūsen (日本郵船 NYK) opened branches in Bombay to handle Indian raw cotton in 1893, the Yokohama Specie Bank opened its office there in 1894.

In marine transportation, Japanese shipping companies first established routes to Shanghai in the 1870s.[119] Regular services to the US West Coast ports were established in the 1890s.[120] By 1913, 52 percent of Japanese exports were carried on Japanese ships, and 47 percent of Japanese imports arrived on Japanese ships.[121]

Japan's FDIs in the United States were centered on services directly linked

*284*

Table 10.4.1. FDIs in US by Nationality and Industry, as of Mid-1937 ($ million)

| | Manufacturing | Transportation | Petroleum | Finance | Trade | Others | Total |
|---|---|---|---|---|---|---|---|
| Britain | 367 | 30 | 93 | 277 | 30 | 37 | 833 |
| Canada | 131 | 216 | 35 | 46 | 11 | 25 | 463 |
| Netherlands | 28 | 1 | 143 | 1 | 5 | 1 | 179 |
| Switzerland | 24 | 0 | 2 | 28 | 13 | 6 | 74 |
| Belgium | 66 | 0 | | 1 | 4 | 1 | 71 |
| France | 24 | 2 | 10 | 12 | 7 | 2 | 57 |
| Germany | 46 | 3 | | 0 | 6 | 0 | 55 |
| Japan | 1 | 2 | | 22 | 17 | | 42 |
| Latin America | 2 | | 0 | 2 | 14 | 1 | 18 |
| Others | 41 | 4 | 0 | 24 | 13 | 10 | 92 |
| Total | 729 | 257 | 283 | 412 | 119 | 82 | 1,883 |

*Source:* Mira Wilkins, *The History of Foreign Investment in the United States, 1914–1945* (Cambridge, MA: Harvard University Press, 2004), 389, 391.

with its trade with the United States. In dollar amounts, its FDIs in trade in the United States were second among the other investors after Britain, and those in finance were fourth (table 10.4.1). Though the total amount of Japanese investments in the United States was much smaller than those of its European competitors, Japanese FDIs related to trade and finance contributed greatly to the expansion of its exports and imports with the United States.

## 10.4.2. British, American, and Japanese Investments in China

Britain had long been the largest investor in China, but the Japanese reached about half the British level in direct investments by 1914, almost caught up with the British by 1930 in both direct investments and loans to the Chinese government, and took over the British position as the leading investor in China in the mid-1930s (table 10.4.2-a).

The United States remained a modest investor in China throughout the pre-WWII years, though there were various ambitious attempts both by business and government, such as Harriman's railway scheme, the Taft–Knox "dollar diplomacy" (7.1.1, 7.1.2). Noteworthy, however, were the American missionary property holdings in China. Remer estimates that the property held by American missionaries in China (importantly in educational and medical institutions) was valued at $43 million in 1930, twice that of

Chapter 10

**Table 10.4.2-a. Foreign Investments in China by Country ($ million)**

| | 1900 | | 1914 | | 1930 | | 1936 | |
|---|---|---|---|---|---|---|---|---|
| | Direct | Indirect | Direct | Indirect | Direct | Indirect | Direct | Indirect |
| Britain | 150 | 110 | 400 | 208 | 963 | 226 | 1,059 | 162 |
| Japan | 1 | 0 | 193 | 10 | 874 | 224 | 1,118 | 241 |
| US | 1 | 2 | 42 | 7 | 155 | 42 | 245 | 54 |
| Russia | 220 | 26 | 237 | 33 | 273 | 0 | 0 | 0 |
| France | 30 | 62 | 60 | 111 | 95 | 97 | 142 | 92 |
| Germany | 85 | 79 | 136 | 128 | 75 | 12 | 59 | 89 |
| Others | 5 | | 30 | | 167 | | 222 | |
| Total | 788 | | 1,610 | | 3,243 | | 3,483 | |

*Notes:* 1. "Direct" stands for direct investments. "Indirect" represents loans to the Chinese governments and to Chinese private corporations.
2. Figures include investments in Manchuria.
3. Figures shown as British and French investments at the end of 1900 are those at the end of 1902. Figures shown as Russian investments at the end of 1900 are those at the end of 1903. Figures shown as German investment at the end of 1900 are the average of those at the end of 1902, 1903, and 1904. Figures shown as German and French investments at the end of 1930 are those at the end of 1931.

*Source:* Chi-ming Hou, *Foreign Investment and Economic Development in China, 1840–1937* (Cambridge, MA: Harvard University Press, 1965), 13, 225.


**Table 10.4.2-b. Japan's Investments in China by Industry ($ million)**

| | End of 1914 | End of 1930 | End of 1936 |
|---|---|---|---|
| Transportation | 68.3 (64.3) | 204.5 (194.5) | 558.7 |
| Manufacturing | 10.6 (3.7) | 165.2 (49.2) | 328.3 |
| Mining | 29.1 (29.1) | 87.4 (82.5) | 22.2 |
| Import-export | 42.6 (5.0) | 182.7 (58.8) | 45.5 |
| Banking, financing | 6.4 (3.7) | 73.4 (40.4) | 95.7 |
| Real estate | 8.5 (8.5) | 73.4 (73.4) | 8.6 |
| Public utilities | 3.4 (3.4) | 15.7 (15.7) | 3.9 |
| Sundry | 23.7 (14.9) | 71.6 (35.4) | 55.0 |
| Total | 192.6 (132.6) | 873.9 (549.9) | 1,117.9 |

*Note:* Figures in parentheses are investments in Manchuria. Figures for investments in Manchuria in 1936 are not available, but total investment figures (direct investments plus loans) were $564.1 million for China and $829.9 million for Manchuria.

*Source:* Chi-ming Hou, *Foreign Investment and Economic Development in China 1840–1937* (Cambridge, MA: Harvard University Press, 1965), 225–226. Charles Remer, *Foreign Investments in China* (New York: Howard Fertig, 1968; first published in 1933), 430–431, 506.

*286*

runner-up France. Though these were not business investments (and are there-fore not included in table 10.4.2-a), American holdings in this field—as well as the number of American missionaries in China, which was far larger than those from any other foreign country[122]—represented a strong American at-tachment to China, and had considerable political influence on the China policy of the United States (7.2.2, 11.2.1).

Japan invested more in the transportation sector than in any other indus-try in China (table 10.4.2-b). But in this field, Russia, the builder of the Chinese Eastern Railway (CER), was the leading investor until the early 1930s. By 1904, the Russians had invested $208 million in the CER.[123] In 1905, as a result of the Russo–Japanese War, Japan acquired most of the southern branch of the CER,[124] and, as discussed in 10.4.3, it formed the South Manchuria Railway Company (SMR) to manage the railways and other interests acquired under the peace terms. In 1935, Japan bought the CER from Russia for ¥170 million,[125] becoming by far the largest owner of railroads in China among the powers.[126]

The first successful Japanese investment in manufacturing abroad was a purchase of cotton-spinning mills in China. The Treaty of Shimonoseki of 1895 permitted the Japanese (and foreign powers as well, because of the MFN clause in their bilateral treaties with China) to undertake manufacturing in the open ports.[127] After unsuccessful attempts by two Japanese spinners to produce cotton yarn in Shanghai, Mitsui & Co. bought a Chinese cotton mill in Shanghai in 1902, and put its operation under the management of its Shanghai branch manager.[128] In 1906, Mitsui acquired another Chinese cotton mill, and in 1908, combining the two mills, formed a new subsidiary, the Shanghai Cotton Manufacturing Company. This undertaking proved profitable. In 1909, the Naigaimen (内外綿) Company, a Japanese cotton mill, decided to build a spinning mill in Shanghai that was equipped with the newest machin-ery and managed by an experienced Japanese staff sent from Japan. Prior to the start-up of operations, the company trained thirty Chinese workers for a year in Japan.[129] Production, which started in 1911, was extremely successful.

Before long, prompted by the Naigaimen feat, several other Japanese spin-ners entered China. They all performed well, the mounting anti-Japanese feel-ings among the Chinese public notwithstanding. In fact, the successful Japanese cotton textile ventures in China were harbingers of subsequent im-portant Japanese investments in other industries in China. The textile

Chapter 10

**Table 10.4.2-c. British and Japanese Cotton Textile Mills in China, 1897–1936**

| | Spindles (in thousands) | | | Power looms | | |
|------|---------|----------|---------|---------|----------|--------|
| | British | Japanese | Total | British | Japanese | Total |
| 1897 | 80.5 | 0.0 | 160.5 | 0 | 0 | 0 |
| 1913 | 138.0 | 111.9 | 339.0 | 800 | 886 | 1,986 |
| 1919 | 244.1 | 332.9 | 577.0 | 2,353 | 1,486 | 3,839 |
| 1924 | 250.5 | 932.7 | 1,183.2 | 2,863 | 3,929 | 6,792 |
| 1929 | 153.3 | 1,462.2 | 1,615.5 | 1,900 | 11,467 | 13,367 |
| 1932 | 183.2 | 1,790.7 | 1,973.9 | 2,891 | 17,592 | 20,483 |
| 1936 | 233.5 | 2,167.1 | 2,400.6 | 4,021 | 28,915 | 32,936 |

*Note:* Total includes other foreign mills in China.
*Source:* Chi-ming Hou, *Foreign Investment and Economic Development in China* (Cambridge, MA: Harvard University Press, 1965), 88. Higuchi Hiroshi, *Nihon no taishi tōshi kenkyū* (Tokyo: Seikatsu-sha, 1939), 264.

industry accounted for 84 percent of Japanese investments in manufacturing in China proper (not including Manchuria) in 1936.[130] Before WWI, the British, Americans, Germans, and Japanese had invested in cotton textile manufacturing in China, but after the war, the German mills were sold to the British and the American mills to the Japanese, making the British and Japanese the sole foreign investors in the Chinese cotton textile industry.[131] By 1919 the Japanese mills had more spindles and by 1924 more power looms than their British rivals (table 10.4.2-c). By 1936, the Japanese mills had nine times as many spindles and six times as many power looms as the British mills.[132] The Japanese mills' main competitors were now the Chinese mills, which possessed one million more spindles than the Japanese in 1936.[133] The productivity of the Japanese mills was higher, however, turning out 35 percent of the yarn and 55 percent of the cloth in China while employing 31 percent of the workers in the industry.[134]

The Hanyehping iron and steel combine, which was located just south of Hankou, represented one of the most important Japanese investments in China.[135] From this firm's mines came the bulk of iron ore for the Japanese government-owned Yawata Iron Works in Kyūshū. Though the Japanese investments in Hanyehping were in the form of loans, the Japanese were given, by agreement, a "considerable degree of control, which was exercised through the Yokohama Specie Bank."[136] Hanyehping was the largest iron-ore mining operation and ironworks in China until it was surpassed by the Anshan mine in

*288*

Manchuria in the mid-1920s. Hanyegping's decline was partly attributable to the hostile Chinese attitude toward the Twenty-One Demands.[137] The Anshan iron mine was first run by a joint venture between the South Manchuria Railway (SMR) and Chinese interests,[138] but in 1934, the SMR bought the Chinese share of the company, making it a wholly-owned subsidiary.[139] By the early 1930s, Japanese-controlled iron-ore and pig-iron production reached three-fourths of the total iron-ore and pig-iron production in China.[140]

The SMR also owned coal mines at Fushun and Yentai. By 1931, the railway's investments in these two mines totaled ¥118 million.[141] By 1937, the Fushun colliery grew to become the greatest open-cut coal mine in China, producing one-fourth of all the coal produced in China.[142] The Japanese-controlled coal mines turned out about half of the total coal production in China in the late 1930s.[143]

### 10.4.3. The South Manchuria Railway Company

Of all Japanese foreign direct investments, over 80 percent were made in China in the mid-1910s through the mid-1930s, and of all Japanese investments in China, over 60 percent were located in Manchuria in the mid-1910s through 1930 (table 10.4.3-a). Between 1931 and 1941, investments in Manchuria expanded by 5.2 times, while those in the rest of China grew by 4.4 times at current yen values at that time.[144]

The bulk of Japan's investments in Manchuria were related to the SMR. The SMR owned a great variety of properties in addition to the railway and repair shops. The company was the owner of business property in Manchuria with a value of ¥474.4 million in 1921 and ¥758.7 million in 1931 (table 10.4.3-b).

Particularly important was the so-called railway zone, a land corridor along the railway track and the railway towns adjacent to important stations.[145] It had been the Russian-held real estate over which Russia had exercised extraterritorial rights, which were derived from the Sino–Russian railway contract agreements of 1896 and 1898.[146] In the railway zone, the SMR ran hotels, hospitals, and schools; collected taxes; and managed public utilities.[147] The SMR made Changchun, the northern terminal town of the railway (and the capital of Manchukuo after 1932), the first city in Asia in which all residential, commercial, and industrial buildings were equipped with water closets.[148]

Table 10.4.3-a. Japan's Foreign Direct Investment Outstanding

|  | End of 1914 | | End of 1930 | | End of 1936 | |
|---|---|---|---|---|---|---|
|  | ¥ mil. | $ mil. | ¥ mil. | $ mil. | ¥ mil. | $ mil. |
| China | 385 | 192 | 1,748 | 874 | 3,854 | 1,118 |
| Mainland China | 120 | 60 | 648 | 324 |  |  |
| Manchuria | 265 | 133 | 1,100 | 550 |  |  |
| United States | 50 | 25 | 90 | 45 | 141 | 41 |
| Others | 40 | 20 | 130 | 65 | 600 | 174 |
| Total | 475 | 237 | 1,968 | 984 | 4,595 | 1,333 |

*Note:* Figures for the United States listed in the 1930 column are those as of 1929, and figures listed in the 1936 column are those as of 1937.

*Source:* Charles Remer, *Foreign Investment in China* (New York, Howard Fertig, 1968; first published in 1933), 430–431, 470. Chi-ming Hou, *Foreign Investment and Economic Development in China, 1840–1937* (Cambridge, MA: Harvard University Press, 1965), 225. Yamazawa Ippei and Yamamoto Yūzō, "Bōeki to kokusai shūshi," Ōkawa Kazushi, Shinohara Miyohei, and Uemura Mataji, eds., *Chōki keizai tōkei* (Tokyo: Tōyōkeizai Shinpōsha, 1979), 56. Mira Wilkins, "Japanese Multinationals in the United States: Continuity and Change, 1879–1990," *Business History Review*, winter 1990, vol. 64 (Boston, MA: Harvard Graduate School of Business Administration, 1990), 586.

Table 10.4.3-b. South Manchuria Railway Company Properties by Sector (¥ million)

|  | 1906 | 1911 | 1921 | 1931 |
|---|---|---|---|---|
| Railways and workshops | 24.9 | 98.4 | 190.1 | 278.7 |
| Ships and harbors | 6.1 | 15.9 | 38.0 | 85.1 |
| Mines and ironworks | 45.7 | 54.7 | 149.5 | 145.0 |
| Electric and gas utilities | 0.4 | 5.7 | 17.1 | n/a |
| Railway zone properties: hotels, etc. | 3.1 | 10.6 | 38.3 | 188.9 |
| Miscellaneous | 7.6 | 17.9 | 41.4 | 60.9 |
| Total | 87.8 | 203.2 | 474.4 | 758.6 |

*Source:* Yoshihisa Tak Matsusaka, *The Making of Japanese Manchuria, 1904–1932* (Cambridge, MA: Harvard University Asia Center, 2001), 413.

The SMR was established in 1906 by Imperial Ordinance with an authorized capital of ¥200 million.[149] The articles of incorporation mandated a 50 percent share of all stocks to the Japanese government, with an additional 1 percent reserved for the Imperial Household, guaranteeing the state a majority interest. The remaining 49 percent was offered for public subscription.[150] The public was offered preferred stock on which a return of 6 percent was guaranteed,[151] while the government held common stock and control.

The SMR was legally a commercial joint-stock corporation, but it was managed by the Japanese government as an instrument of its Manchurian policy, or a government agent for Manchurian management.[152] The SMR's railway zone in particular, together with the Kwantung Leased Territory, was an important colonial possession administered as part of Japan's growing formal empire, while Japan's influence remained informal in the rest of Manchuria, which was under the Chinese government's jurisdiction.[153]

As observed in 6.4.2, there were serious debates among Japanese government leaders about the question of expanding formal control of Manchuria. The debates were to continue until 1931.

## NOTES

### 10.1. Foreign Investments in the United States

1   Foreign direct investment is a foreign investment that carries with it ownership and control (or the potential for control). Foreign portfolio investment is a foreign investment in stocks or bonds, government or corporate, or other long-term financial instruments. Mira Wilkins, *The History of Foreign Investment in the United States, 1914–1945* (Cambridge, MA: Harvard University Press, 2004), 616.

2   Cleona Lewis, *America's Stake in International Investments* (Washington, DC: Brookings Institution, 1938), 531.

3   James Willis and Martin Primack, *An Economic History of the United States* (Englewood Cliffs, NJ: Prentice-Hall, 1989), 245.

4   Ross Robertson and Gary Walton, *History of the American Economy* (New York: Harcourt Brace Jovanovich, 1979), 260.

5   W. W. Rostow, *The World Economy History and Prospect* (Austin, TX: University of Texas Press, 1978), 392.

6   Mira Wilkins, *The History of Foreign Investment in the United States to 1914* (Cambridge, MA: Harvard University Press, 1989), 362–365.

7   Wilkins, *Foreign Investment to 1914*, 356–357.

8   Ibid., 385.

9   Ibid., 395–396. Wilkins, *Foreign Investment, 1914–1945*, 48–49.

10   Wilkins, *Foreign Investment to 1914*, 384, 390.

11   There was a great flood of well-educated German refugees into the United States after the failure of the revolution of 1848; they were followed by many German immigrants in the following decades. Ethnic Germans were a vital part of early American life. Wilkins, *Foreign Investment to 1914*, 170.

12   As early as 1901–02, a French car brand, C.G.V., was manufactured in Rome, New York. Daimler Manufacturing Company built the first "American Mercedes" in Long Island in 1905. In 1910, Fiat started to manufacture luxury cars in Poughkeepsie, New York. Those cars sold at very high prices. A Mercedes sold for $7,500 in 1905. The price of a Model-T Ford was $500 in 1913), and $345 in 1916. Ronald Seavoy,

Chapter 10

*An Economic History of the United States: From 1607 to the Present* (New York: Routledge, 2006), 261. Wilkins, *Foreign Investment to 1914*, 419–420.

13   Wilkins, *Foreign Investment to 1914*, 420.

14   Ibid., 336–337.

15   Wilkins, *Foreign Investment to 1914*, 417. Ibid., 254–256.

16   In 1912, Royal Dutch Shell built its ocean terminal in Seattle to bring in Sumatra gasoline for sale on the West Coast, and purchased oil fields in Oklahoma and California to start oil production on American soil. Royal Dutch Shell's move was in response to Jersey Standard's decision to invest in an oil concession in Sumatra. Wilkins, *Foreign Investment to 1914*, 285–290. Royal Dutch Shell was created in 1907 through the merger of the Royal Dutch Petroleum Company and Shell Transport and Trading Company Ltd. of Britain. It was 60 percent owned by the Dutch and 40 percent owned by the British.

17   In 1929 the Royal Dutch Shell Group had assets of $677 million, and ranked eleventh in asset size among all American enterprises. But it was behind Standard Oil of New Jersey, Standard Oil of Indiana, Gulf Oil, and Standard Oil of New York, but ahead of Standard Oil of California and Texaco. Wilkins, *Foreign Investment, 1914–1945*, 265.

### 10.2. US Direct Investment

18   Mira Wilkins, *The Emergence of Multinational Enterprise* (Cambridge, MA: Harvard University Press, 1970), 39–47. Andrew Gordon, "Selling the American Way: The Singer Sales System in Japan, 1900–1938," *Business History Review*, vol. 82 (Boston, MA: Harvard Graduate School of Business Administration, 2008), 673.

19   Edison's other inventions such as the phonograph, megaphone, and microphone were sold in Europe by the Edison Telephone Company in London. The incandescent lamp was marketed by Edison Electric Light Company in London. Wilkins, *Emergence of Multinational Enterprise*, 52.

20   In 1899, AT&T, a subsidiary of the American Bell Telephone Company, acquired the assets of the parent company, including Western Electric. Wilkins, *Emergence of Multinational Enterprise*, 51. Mira Wilkins, *The Maturing of Multinational Enterprise: American Business Abroad from 1914 to 1970* (Cambridge, MA: Harvard University Press, 1974), 28.

21   Wilkins, *Maturing of Multinational Enterprise*, 67.

22   Wilkins, *Emergence of Multinational Enterprise*, 97.

23   In 1891, the Babcock & Wilcox Company established a British company, Babcock & Wilcox Ltd., with its sphere of operations to include the world outside of the United States and Cuba, which were already covered by the American company. American Radiator had had a branch in London since 1895, and built many factories in Europe before WWI. Wilkins, *Emergence of Multinational Enterprise*, 77.

24   National Cash Register had manufacturing plants in Europe and Australia from the 1890s. International Business Machine's predecessor companies started their foreign enterprises before WWI. E. Remington and Sons started production of the first typewriter in 1873, introducing the QWERTY layout. Remington had sales outlets in Germany and France in 1884, in Russia in 1885, in Britain in 1886, and so on

*Notes*

throughout Europe. Remington was also one of the world's most successful gun manufacturers. Ibid., 209, 212, 262.

25 The leader in this industry was International Harvester. By 1911, it had plants in Canada, Sweden, France, Germany and Russia. Ibid., 102–103.

26 Ibid., 62–64, 83.

27 In 1929, Anaconda bought the Chuquicamata mine—the world's largest deposit, which the Guggenheims had developed—becoming the largest copper producer in Chile. Wilkins, *Emergence of Multinational Enterprise*, 178–182. Wilkins, *Maturing of Multinational Enterprise*, 105.

28 US investors in Mexican mining included the American Smelting and Refining Company (ASARCO), the American Metal Company (later American Metal Climax), the Guggenheims, and Anaconda. Wilkins, *Maturing of Multinational Enterprise*, 103.

29 Lewis, *America's Stake*, 584. Paul Dickens, "American Direct Investments in Foreign Countries," in *Estimate of United States Direct Foreign Investment, 1929–43 and 1947* (reprinted from US Department of Commerce, Bureau of Foreign and Domestic Commerce, *Trade Information Bulletin*, no. 731) (New York: Arno Press, 1976), 18–19.

30 Lewis, *America's Stake*, 590.

31 Wilkins, *Maturing of Multinational Enterprise*, 94.

32 By 1914, United Fruit owned 669 miles of railroad in Central America and the West Indies. Wilkins, *Emergence of Multinational Enterprise*, 160. It also built telegraph and telephone facilities throughout Central America. Ibid., 129–130.

33 Ibid., 160.

34 In 1921, when Mexican oil output peaked at 193 million barrels, Venezuela produced 1.4 million barrels. By 1928, Venezuela produced 106 million barrels; Mexico, 50 million barrels. Ibid., 114–115. In 1929, the ten top-ranking oil-producing countries in the world were the United States, Venezuela, the USSR, Mexico, Iran, the Dutch East Indies, Romania, Colombia, Peru, and Argentina. Ibid., 121.

35 Ibid., 118.

36 The Turkish Petroleum Company was formed in 1912 to explore oil in Mesopotamia (now Iraq). Half of the TPC's share was owned by the Turkish National Bank, and a quarter each by Deutsche Bank and Royal Dutch Shell. The Turkish National Bank was a British-controlled bank set up in Turkey. Thirty percent of the Turkish National Bank was owned by Caluste Gulbenkian, an Armenian businessman who had put the TPC deal together in 1912. As a result of WWI, a new composition of the company's shareholding was to be negotiated. French participation was readily agreed, but it took eight years for Americans to finally be permitted to buy into the TPC share. Under the agreement signed in July, 1928, a consortium of US oil companies, Anglo-Persian Oil Company (which became the Anglo-Iranian Oil Company in 1935 and British Petroleum Company in 1954), Royal Dutch Shell, and Compagnie Française des Pétroles (CFP, which became Total in 1991) each obtained a 23.75 percent interest in TPC; the remaining 5 percent went to Gulbenkian. In October 1927, the TPC struck oil at Kirkuk. In fact, the discovery hastened the negotiations over the composition of the TPC that had been ongoing since 1920.

Chapter 10

Daniel Yergin, *The Prize* (New York: Simon & Schuster, 1992), 185, 204–205, 282. The American group comprised Jersey Standard, New York Standard, Atlantic Refining, Gulf Oil, and Pan American Petroleum & Transport. Wilkins, *Maturing of Multinational Enterprise*, 119.

37    The Red Line Agreement was to hold the field for the period of twenty years.

38    Gulf Oil purchased those options from New Zealand mining engineer Frank Holmes. Between 1923 and 1925, he acquired oil concession from the rulers of Saudi Arabia and Bahrain. They were more anxious to obtain water than oil. Holmes drilled for water and struck it, in exchange for which the rulers rewarded him with an oil concession. Yergin, *The Prize*, 280–282. Wilkins, *Maturing of Multinational Enterprise*, 119.

39    Before WWI, Britain made agreements with the sheikhs in the Gulf region that Britain would afford them protection from outside aggression; in return, oil development would be entrusted only to British concerns. Yergin, *The Prize*, 283.

40    The British government backed off because it felt that the entry of American capital would encourage more rapid development of oil in the Middle East; also, it would be to the benefit of both local rulers, who always needed money and might ask Britain for further subsidies, and the Royal Navy, which needed reliable oil supplies. Ibid., 283.

41    The Kuwait Oil Company was granted a seventy-five-year concession for an up-front payment of £35,700 and royalties of £7,150 a year until the discovery of oil. After oil was found, a minimum annual royalty of £18,800 would be paid. Ibid., 297–298.

42    The King Ibn Saud was heavily in debt at the time. Socal agreed to loan Ibn Saud £30,000 in gold and pay an annual royalty of £5,000 in advance until the discovery of oil. If the agreement were not terminated in eighteen months, Socal was to make a second loan of £20,000. In addition, Socal would make another loan of £100,000 on the discovery of oil. The total loan was to be repaid only out of any oil royalties, which were four shillings per ton of oil production. In deference to Muslim practice, the loans carried no interest. The concession was good for sixty years. Ibid., 291. Wilkins, *Maturing of Multinational Enterprise*, 214.

43    Socal also agreed to share ownership of the California Arabian Standard Oil Company with Texaco in 1936. The California Arabian Standard Oil Company was renamed Aramco in 1944. Wilkins, *Maturing of Multinational Enterprise*, 216–217.

44    The British had at first been skeptical about the petroleum potential in Saudi Arabia and were in no mood to make any large commitment to the Saudi government. Realizing their misjudgment, they obtained a concession in the western part of Saudi Arabia in 1936, but never found oil there. Yergin, *The Prize*, 291–292, 299.

10.3. Foreign Investments in Japan

45    Two small loans were issued in the 1870s. One was £1,000,000 in 9 percent bonds issued in 1870 for twelve years. In 1873, £2,400,000 of 7 percent bonds went on sale with payment in twenty-four years. Both were repaid at maturity. Harold Moulton, *Japan: An Economic and Financial Appraisal* (New York: AMS Press, 1969; reprinted from the 1931 edition), 488–489.

46    Donald Keene notes, "Grant's warning against foreign loans was probably the part of

*Notes*

the conversation [with the youthful emperor] that exerted the greatest effect." Donald Keene, *Emperor of Japan: Meiji and His World, 1852–1912* (New York: Columbia University Press, 2002), 316–317.

47  Gaimushō Tokubetsu Shiryōbu, ed., *Nihon ni okeru gaikoku shihon* (Tokyo: Kasumigasekikai, 1948), 9.

48  The foreign loans of £82,000 million accounted for 65 percent of the total government bond issues of ¥1,280 million to finance war expenditures. Ishizaki Teruhiko, "Shikin chōtatsu (ge): gaishi" Miyazaki Giichi, ed., *Gendai Nihon no dokusen shihon 7* (Tokyo: Shiseido, 1965), 13.

49  Moulton, *Appraisal*, 488–489.

50  Ishizaki, "Shikin chōtatsu" in *Dokusen shihon*, ed. Miyazaki, 41. Nippon Ginkō Tōkeikyoku. *Meiji ikō honpō shuyō keizai tōkei* (Tokyo: Namiki Shobō, 1992), 32. In 2021, the Japanese government's total outstanding borrowing (¥1,421 trillion) represented 262 percent of the Japanese GDP (¥541 trillion), and foreigners' holdings of government bonds accounted for 13.6 percent of the total government borrowings. The important difference between the Japanese government's international position in 2021 and that in 1914 is that in 2021, Japan's net external assets (¥411 trillion) were the world's largest, and Japan had been the top creditor for thirty-one years in a row, whereas Japan's net foreign assets in 1914 were in deficit. Excepting some years during WWI and immediately after the war, Japan's net external assets were in deficit in the 1910s and 1920s.

51  Moulton, *Appraisal*, 490–491.

52  Ishizaki, "Shikin chōtatsu," 42–43. By 1935, the percentage of municipal foreign borrowings of total municipal borrowings declined to 11 percent. Ibid., 42.

53  Foreign loans by private corporations excluding electric companies before WWI amounted to £18.5 million and ₣50.6 million, which were equivalent to ¥200 million. After WWI, they borrowed £4 million and $61.8 million, equivalent to ¥163 million. Moulton, *Appraisal*, 492–493.

54  Between 1923 and 1929, the five biggest electric companies borrowed in the aggregate £8.4 million and $189.6 million, equivalent to ¥462 million. Their foreign loans outstanding at the end of 1931 were ¥340 million, which accounted for 43 percent of their total bond issues. Ishizaki, "Shikin chōtatsu," 48. Moulton, *Appraisal*, 492–493.

55  Moulton, *Appraisal*, 492–493.

56  William Lockwood, *The Economic Development of Japan* (Ann Arbor, MI: Center for Japanese Studies, University of Michigan, 1993), 254–268.

57  Article I of the Treaty of Commerce and Navigation of 1894 with the United States provides that the subjects or citizens of each of the two contracting parties "shall have full liberty to enter, travel, or reside in any part of the territories of the other party ... " Article II stipulates that the subjects or citizens of each of the contracting parties "may trade in any part of the territories of the other by wholesale or retail in all kinds of produce, manufactures and merchandize of lawful commerce ... "

58  The Japanese newspaper was the *Nihon Shinbun*. It wrote, "Assuming that the total foreign direct investment in Japanese enterprises would be twice as much and a return on such investments would be 10 percent, the annual payment abroad of the

profits on them would be ¥4,845,300." Horie Yasuzō, *Gaishi yunyū no kaiko to tenbō* (Tokyo: Yuhikaku Publishing, 1950), 81.

59  Murai Brothers Co. was a joint venture between Murai Kichibē (村井吉兵衛), a cigarette manufacturer in Kyoto, and American Tobacco. The joint venture was bought by the Japanese government in 1904 when the Tobacco Monopoly Act was enacted. Ohara Keiji, *Nichibei bunka kōshōshi* (Tokyo: Yōyōsha, 1954), 428–429.

60  When Osaka Gas increased its capital from ¥350,000 to ¥4 million in 1902, Anthony Brady, an American investor, acquired a majority stake in Osaka Gas by investing ¥2.1 million. This investment aroused much controversy as to whether foreign capital should own a majority share of a Japanese utility company. The municipality of Osaka opposed it, and business circles supported it. The *Asahi Shimbun* sided with the former, and the *Mainichi Shimbun* with the latter. Brady withdrew the capital in 1925. Ibid., 429.

61  An episode about the relationship between Iwadare and GE management illustrates Iwadare's personality and the mutual trust and respect that developed between the GE leadership and the young Japanese businessman. Iwadare went to the United States at his own expense in 1886, quitting the Ministry of Industry where he had worked after graduation from Kōbu Daigakkō (工部大学校 today's Faculty of Engineering of Tokyo University) in 1882. He was employed at Edison Machine Works in New York, and his hard work was known to the top management. He left the job in 1888, however, as he was asked by the Osaka Electric Lighting Company to become its chief engineer. At that time, the choice of direct or alternating current for distribution was intensely debated in the United States and Europe. Edison Machine was a leading advocate of direct current against the alternating-current technology promoted by Westinghouse and Thomson Houston. Iwadare saw more potential in alternating current, and despite his two years' work at Edison Machine, he chose to equip Osaka Electric with an alternating-current generator, which he ordered from Thomson Houston. This outraged Edison Machine. Their wrath was so great that the company subsequently refused to accept any Japanese visitors. Edison General (Edison Machine became Edison General in 1889), however, later admitted the advantages of alternating current and merged with Thomson Houston, forming the General Electric Company in 1892 (10.2.1). The GE leadership dropped its criticism of Iwadare and even praised him as a man with the courage of his convictions. GE granted its Japanese agency to Osaka Electric Lighting, and when Iwadare left the company in 1895 in protest against Osaka Electric's management decision to develop a new product without consulting with GE, GE transferred the agency from Osaka Electric to Iwadare himself. When GE was affiliated with Tokyo Electric, GE asked Iwadare to be a board member of Tokyo Electric. Okamoto Shūkichi, *Iwadare Kunihiko* (Kamakura: Iwadare Kōtoku, 1964), 1–42. Suzuki Yoshitaka, trans. Thomas I. Elliott, *NEC Corporation 1899–1999* (Tokyo: The Japan Business History Institute, 2002), 8–9.

62  Thayer became vice president of Western Electric in 1902, president in 1909, and president of AT&T in 1919.

63  Okamoto, *Iwadare Kunihiko*, 59–60. Western Electric had already had seven plants abroad.

*Notes*

64  In 1888, when Iwadare was leaving for Japan, he was asked by Thayer, then Western Electric's New York branch manager, to recommend someone as Western Electric's Japanese agent. Iwadare had been unable to fulfill the request while he was with Osaka Electric, however. Having quit Osaka Electric in 1895, he then thought he would become the agent himself. His application for the job was readily accepted by Western Electric. Ibid., 42–43.

65  Oki was of the opinion that, from the viewpoint of national security, the telephone industry should keep its independence from foreign influence. Nihon Denki Kabushiki Kaisha Shashi Hensanshitsu, *Nihon Denki Kabushiki Kaisha nanajusshūnenshi* (Tokyo: Nihon Denki Kabushiki Kaisha, 1972), 26–27. Oki's telephones proved very useful in the Sino–Japanese War, and Oki won the trust of the Japanese army. Okamoto, *Iwadare Kunihiko*, 76–77.

66  In August 1898, Iwadare formed Nippon Denki Gōshi Kaisha, a limited partnership firm, for the purpose of transforming it into Nippon Electric Company Ltd., a joint stock company, with the participation of Western Electric. NEC's board consisted of three members: Iwadare, W. T. Carlton, and an American residing in Tokyo. Iwadare was elected as the managing director. Carlton was Thayer's most trusted secretary who came to Japan in 1897, and first negotiated with Oki and then worked with Iwadare to establish NEC. Nihon Denki, *Nanajūsshūnenshi*, 35–36, 43–47. Okamoto, *Iwadare Kunihiko*, 82–85. Carlton left Japan with his wife and their new-born son in May 1900, but became seriously ill two months later and died at the age of thirty-three. Suzuki, trans. Elliott, *NEC Corporation*, 9, 15–16.

67  Ibid., 18.

68  NEC's annual output of telephone equipment during the period from 1901 to 1903 was ¥136,000 on average, whereas Oki's corresponding figure was ¥253,000. In 1921, however, NEC produced 58.6 percent of Japan's total telephone equipment, whereas Oki's share was 17.6 percent. Nihon Denki, *Nanajusshūnenshi*, 51, 99.

69  Mark Mason, *American Multinationals and Japan* (Cambridge, MA: Harvard University Press, 1992), 34–35.

70  The first incandescent lamp was manufactured in Japan by Fujioka Ichisuke (藤岡市助) in 1890. He graduated from Kōbu Daigakkō in 1881 and taught at the school until 1886, when he became the chief engineer of the Tokyo Electric Lighting Company, the precursor of today's Tokyo Electric Power Company. After his success in electric bulb manufacture, he left Tokyo Electric Lighting and launched Tokyo Electric with his colleagues in 1899 to produce electric bulbs commercially. Tokyo Shibaura Seisakusho Sōmubu, *Toshiba hyakunenshi* (Tokyo: Tokyo Shibaura Denki Kabushiki Kaisha, 1977), 20–23.

71  Major foreign suppliers were GE (US), Siemens (Germany), Allgemeine (Germany), Phillips (the Netherlands), Three Stars (UK), and Sunbeam (UK).

72  Fujioka inquired of John Geary, GE's representative in Tokyo, if his company could get GE's financial and technological assistance. Geary, who knew Fujioka well and recognized his capability, proposed to GE's management that they invest in Tokyo Electric. Yasui Shōtarō, *Tokyo Denki Kabushiki Kaisha gojūnenshi* (Tokyo: Tokyo Shibaura Denki, 1940), 97–98.

73  Geary was awarded the Fourth Class Order of Merit for his contribution to the

*297*

Japanese electric industry's development. Shibaura Seisakusho, *Toshiba hyakunenshi*, 25–30.

74 In 1903 the company reported a loss of ¥8,000, but it reported a profit of ¥38,000 in 1906, ¥67,000 in 1908, ¥127,000 in 1910, and ¥378,000 in 1912. Ibid., 28.

75 Shibaura Seisakusho's predecessor, Tanaka Seisakujo, was incorporated in 1875. It was a main supplier of electric machines to the Japanese navy. In 1893, when business conditions went bad, the company was put under the management of Mitsui and was made a division of Mitsui Mining under the name of Shibaura Seisakusho. In 1904 it became an independent company in the Mitsui group. In 1907, when Masuda Takashi (益田孝), president of Mitsui & Co., visited GE, he and GE president Charles Coffin initialed a basic agreement about Shibaura's affiliation with GE. Ibid., 2–19.

76 Ibid., 38–41.

77 Nippon Kōgyō Ginkō Gaijibu, *Gaikoku kaisha no honpō tōshi* (Tokyo: The Industrial Bank of Japan, 1948), 231–239.

78 Ibid., 139–151.

79 Ibid., 169–178.

80 Ibid., 266–279. The joint venture's capital increased from ¥1.75 million in 1928 to ¥3 million in 1936. Mitsui's share increased from 28.75 percent in 1928 to 33.33 percent in 1936. Ibid., 276.

81 Yokohama Gomu Yonjūnenshi Hensan Iinkai, *Yokohama Gomu Seizō Kabushiki Kaisha yonjūnenshi* (Tokyo: Yokohama Gomu Seizō Kabushiki Kaisha, 1959), 6–14. The new company's board was composed of six directors, three from each side. Ibid., 10. Yokohama Densen later became Furukawa Denki Kōgyō (古河電気工業).

82 Ibid., 63–84.

83 Ibid., 444–452. Nakagawa Suekichi (中川末吉), chairman of Yokohama Gomu, kept saying during the war, "War is a fight between governments, not between peoples. Therefore, we should keep confidence in Goodrich people." Ibid., 445.

84 It was Iwadare who recommended Sumitomo as the Japanese partner in the joint venture. He knew Sumitomo from his days as chief engineer of Osaka Electric Lighting Company. In view of the public nature of the telephone business, for which sound and dependable management was required, he felt that Sumitomo was most appropriate. Nihon Denki, *Nanajusshūnenshi*, 100–104.

85 Sumitomo Denki Kōgyō Kabushiki Kaisha, *Shashi Sumitomo Denki Kōgyō Kabushiki Kaisha* (Osaka: 1961), 353–386. Suzuki, trans. Elliot, *NEC Corporation*, 35–36.

86 Kōgyō Ginkō, *Gaikoku kaisha*, 79–88.

87 Ibid., 125–137.

88 In 1929, Nihon Chisso and German J. P. Bemberg jointly created Nihon Bemberg. In 1933, Nihon Chisso, Asahi Kenshoku, and Nihon Bemberg merged into Asahi Bemberg Kenshoku, which was later renamed Asahi Kasei (旭化成). Kōgyō Ginkō, *Gaikoku kaisha*, 241–254.

89 Sanki Kōgyō held a 46 percent interest in the joint venture, and a former Mitsui man who was Carrier's agent in Japan held an 8 percent interest. Tōyō Carrier Kabushiki Kaisha, *Tōyō Carrier yonjūnenshi* (Tokyo: Tōyō Carrier Kabushiki Kaisha, 1970),

*Notes*

44–55, 100–102.

90 Otis had been represented in Japan by the American Trading Company since the early 1890s, and it had supplied 300 of the 386 electric elevators in use in Japan as of 1922. However, Otis went into a joint venture with Mitsui & Co. in 1925. Nippon Otis Erebēta Kabushiki Kaisha, *Nippon Otis Erebēta gojūnen no ayumi* (Tokyo: Nippon Otis Elevator Co., 1982), 12–14. Mason, *American Multinationals*, 134–136.

91 The city of Tokyo ordered 1,000 truck chassis from Ford. These arrived in Yokohama the following January and were quickly converted for use as buses in the Tokyo area. Ibid., 66

92 Nissan Jidōsha Kabushiki Kaisha Sōmubu Chōsaka, *Nissan Jidōsha sanjūnenshi* (Tokyo: Nissan Motor Co., 1965), 14.

93 Nihon Victor Gojūnenshi Henshū Iinkai, ed., *Nihon Victor gojūnenshi* (Tokyo: Nihon Victor, 1977), 46, 51.

94 Nihon Victor paid dividends of 40 to 50 percent on average of paid-in capital during the early years. Ibid., 206.

95 Nihon Kinsen Tōrokuki was formed with capital of ¥2 million by Fujiyama interests in 1920 to manufacture cash register domestically. In 1935, it sought affiliation with NCR to get financial and technological assistance from NCR. NCR obtained ¥1,400,000 worth of Nihon Kinsen Tōrokuki's shares, of which ¥900,000 worth was ceded by Nihon Kinsen Tōrokuki in exchange for NCR's patents, know-how, and technical assistance. Kōgyō Ginkō, *Gaikoku kaisha*, 314–319.

96 IBM's poor business performance in Japan was mainly because IBM was represented by Morimura, a company that had no experienced personnel to install and maintain the equipment. Mitsui & Co was marketing an IBM competitor's tabulating machine. Mason, *American Multinationals*, 116–117.

97 Nihon Keieishi Kenkyūsho, *Nihon Aibīemu gojūnenshi* (Tokyo: IBM Japan, 1988), 43–46.

98 Udagawa Masaru, "Business Management and Foreign-Affiliated Companies in Japan before World War II," in *Foreign Business in Japan before World War II*, eds. Yuzawa Takeshi and Udagawa Masaru (Tokyo: University of Tokyo Press, 1990), 5.

99 Standard Oil sold the entire oil production and refining facilities to Nihon Sekiyu for ¥1.75 million, though Standard Oil's investments on the facilities amounted to ¥6.5 million. Ibid., 5, 12. Nihon Sekiyu Kabushiki Kaisha Shomuka, ed., *Nihon Sekiyu-shi* (Tokyo: Nippon Oil Co., 1917), 347–359.

100 The rise of transportation costs during WWI made the operation unprofitable. Udagawa, "Business Management," in *Foreign Business*, eds. Yuzawa and Udagawa, 12.

101 Through the 1930s, Standard Oil and Rising Sun held 60 percent of the Japanese market. Yergin, *The Prize*, 307.

102 Mitsubishi Shōji (MSK) became a sole sales agent of Associated Oil in Japan in 1923, but it could not increase sales on account of Standard Oil and Rising Sun's aggressive sales activities. As a way to compete with them, MSK proposed and Associated Oil agreed to jointly have a refinery in Japan. Associated Oil continued to supply Mitsubishi Sekiyu with crude oil until the US government oil embargo in

*299*

Chapter 10

1941. Kawabe Nobuo, *Sōgō shōsha no kenkyū* (Tokyo: Jikkyō Shuppansha, 1982), 52–70.

103 Kōgyō Ginkō, *Gaikoku kaisha*, 212.

104 Lockwood, *The Economic Development of Japan*, 258, 323. The figures shown in table 9.4.2-b are much smaller than Lockwood's estimation. The author of "Nihon no gaishi" in *Gendai Nihon no dokusen shihon*, on which table 9.4.2-b is based, admits that he might have underestimated the amount of FDI in Japan. Ishizaki, "Nihon no gaishi," in *Gendai Nihon no dokusen shihon*, ed. Miyazaki, 10.

105 Yamamura Kōzō, "Japan's Deus ex Machina: Western Technology in the 1920s," *Journal of Japanese Studies*, vol. 12, no. 1, winter 1986 (Seattle, WA: University of Washington, 1986), 73–75.

106 Mitsubishi Denki Kabushiki Kaisha Shashi Henshūshitsu, ed., *Kengyō kaiko* (Tokyo: Mitsubishi Electric Co., 1951), 72.

107 Suzuki, trans. Elliott, *NEC Corporation*, 18–19.

108 Nihon Keieishi Kenkyūsho, *Nihon Aibīemu gojūnenshi*, 54–56.

109 Iwadare often had to tell resident American staff that too much detailed instruction to Japanese workers, who had willingness to work and pride, would be counterproductive. Suzuki, trans. Elliott, *NEC Corporation*, 18.

110 Andrew Gordon, "Selling the American Way: The Singer Sales System in Japan, 1900–1938," *Business History Review*, vol. 82 (Boston: The Graduate School of Harvard University, 2008), 694.

10.4. Japan's Foreign Direct Investments

111 Japan Business History Institute, ed., *The 100 Year History of Mitsui & Co., Ltd., 1876–1976* (Tokyo: Mitsui & Co., 1977), 27.

112 Mira Wilkins, "Japanese Multinational Enterprise before 1914," *Business History Review*, vol. 60, 1986, ed. Harvard University Graduate School of Business Administration (Boston: Harvard Business School, 1986), 217.

113 In 1890, of all MBK sales, rice accounted for 26.2 percent, coal 12.6 percent, and raw cotton 11.0 percent. In that year raw silk's share was 3.0 percent, but in 1914 raw silk became the most important commodity for the company. In that year MBK held a 33.6 percent share of all Japanese raw-silk exports to the United States. Japan Business History Institute, *The 100 Year History of Mitsui & Co., Ltd.*, 37, 71–72.

114 Wilkins, *Business History Review 60*, 218.

115 The three trading companies were Nihon Menka, Mitsui & Co., and Gōshō. Wilkins, *Business History Review 60*, 221.

116 Hijikata Susumu, *Yokohama Shōkin Ginkō* (Tokyo: Kyōikusha, 1980), 67. In New York it was joined by the Bank of Taiwan in 1917, Sumitomo Bank in 1918, the Bank of Chosen in 1919, Mitsubishi Bank in 1920, and Mitsui Bank in 1921. Mira Wilkins, "Japanese Multinationals in the United States: Continuity and Change, 1879–1990." *Business History Review*, vol. 64, winter 1990 (Boston, MA: Harvard Graduate School of Business Administration, 1990), 587.

117 Wilkins, *Business History Review 60*, 218.

118 The Yokohama Specie Bank set up branches in San Francisco in 1899, in Los Angeles in 1913, and in Seattle in 1917. In the United States, each state had its own laws on

commercial banking. For example, New York state law did not allow foreign banks to take deposits, but the state of California did not have such regulations, and the Yokohama Specie Bank and Sumitomo Bank took deposits in their branches in California. Regarding foreign trade and foreign exchange, Japanese banks were not subject to any regulations. Mira Wilkins, "American–Japanese Direct Foreign Investment Relationships, 1930–1952," *Business History Review*, vol. 56 (Boston, MA: Harvard Graduate School of Business Administration, 1982), 508. Wilkins, *Foreign Investment, 1914–1945*, 286.

119 In 1875, with a subsidy from the Japanese government, the Mitsubishi Gōshi Kaisha (三菱合資会社) bought four ships from the Pacific Mail Steamship Company for $810,000. Pacific Mail relinquished its Yokohama–Shanghai service to its Japanese rival. William Wray, *Mitsubishi and the N.Y.K., 1870–1914: Business Strategy in the Japanese Shipping Industry* (Cambridge, MA: Harvard University Press, 1984), 84–85. In 1898, Osaka Shōsen (大阪商船 OSK) opened the Shanghai–Hankou line penetrating into the interior of China. Wilkins, *Business History Review 60*, 216.

120 Tōyō Kisen (東洋汽船) opened a route to San Francisco in 1898. NYK established a Shanghai–Seattle line in 1899. OSK started a line to Tacoma in 1908. The Mitsui Line, Kawasaki Kisen, the Yamashita Line, and Kokusai Kisen later participated in marine transportation operations to the United States. Wilkins, *Business History Review 60*, 217.

121 Wilkins, *Business History Review 60*, 218–219.

122 In the mid-1920s, of the 8,300 Protestant missionaries in China, Americans numbered about 5,000. There were about 2,000 Catholic missionaries, mostly from European nations. Michel Oksenberg and Robert Oxnam, eds., *Dragon and Eagle— United States–China Relations: Past and Future* (New York: Basic Books, 1973), 139.

123 Ibid., 564.

124 The following sections of Chinese Eastern Railway were turned over to Japan: The trunk line between Changchun and Dairen (Dalian), 437 miles; the Port Arthur branch line, 28 miles; the Yingkou branch line, 9 miles; and the Fushun branch line, 28 miles. These made for a total of 515 miles. Remer, *Foreign Investment in China*, 574. Total railroad mileage in China was 2,708 miles in 1903. Hou, *Foreign Investment*, 126.

125 Soviet Russia's price was ¥625 million, whereas Japan offered ¥50 million. After negotiations lasting over a year, they agreed on ¥170 million, including a retirement allowance of ¥30 million for Russian employees. Harada Katsumasa, *Mantetsu* (Tokyo: Iwanami Shoten, 1981), 163.

126 The mileage of the foreign-owned railroads in China in 1911 was as follows: Chinese Eastern Railway (Russia), 1,073 miles. South Manchuria Railway (Japan), 709 miles. Yunnan Railway (France), 289 miles. Kiaochow–Tsinan Railway (Germany), 284 miles. Canton–Kowloon Railway, British section, 22 miles. Hou, *Foreign Investment*, 65. Between 1932 and 1937, Japan built thirteen lines in Manchuria with a total length of 2,030 miles. Ibid., 65. Remer's estimation of the foreign powers' investments in railways by 1931 is as follows: Russian Chinese Eastern, $210.5 million; Japanese South Manchuria, $138.3 million; Japanese Tientu Light Railway, $2.2 million; Japanese Chinchow–Pitzuwo Railway, $2.0 million; British

Chapter 10

Canton–Kowloon (British portion), $7.8 million; French Yunnan Railway, $32.0 million. Remer, *Foreign Investment in China*, 88.

127 Article 6 of the Treaty of 1895 stipulated that "all Japanese subjects may freely engage in any sort of manufacturing industry in the open ports of China." Jardine, Matheson & Co. in Shanghai first formed a cotton spinning and weaving company in Shanghai in 1897; another British textile firm, an American one, and a German one followed. These four firms had a total of 160,548 spindles. With the exception of the German firm, a substantial portion of their capital stock was held by Chinese. The operations of the four mills did not make large profits, and there was no new entry in later years. Chi-ming Hou, *Foreign Investment and Economic Development in China, 1840–1937* (Cambridge, MA: Harvard University Press, 1965), 8, 86. Even before the Shimonoseki Treaty, there had existed factories built by foreign merchants at the treaty ports opened by the Treaty of Nanjing of 1842. Their operations included manufacturing of such products as matches, paper, soap, and drugs that had previously been imported, as well as ship repairing and processing for exports. All this was done illegally. Mitsui & Co.'s Shanghai office formed a joint venture with British and German investors called the Shanghai Cotton Cleaning and Works Co., Ltd, which started operations in 1889. This was not a legal entity either. Mitsui sold its interest in 1899. Ibid., 7.

128 The manager was Yamamoto Jōtarō, who later became the president of the South Manchuria Railway Company.

129 Motoki Mitsukuni, *Naigaimen Kabushiki Kaisha gojūnenshi* (Tokyo: Naigaimen Kabushiki Kaisha, 1937), 37.

130 In 1936, Japanese investments in the textile industry in mainland China (including Hong Kong, but not including Manchuria) accounted for 83.8 percent of Japanese investments in manufacturing in China and 61.7 percent of the four major countries' total investments in the textile industry. Hou, *Foreign Investment*, 81.

131 Ibid., 86.

132 In 1936, fourteen Japanese cotton textile companies had fifty-three factories in Shanghai, Tientsin (Tianjin), Tsingtao (Qingdao), and Hankou, compared to Jardine Matheson & Company's three factories in Shanghai. Higuchi Hiroshi, *Nihon no taishi tōshi kenkyū* (Tokyo: Seikatsu-sha, 1939), 264–267.

133 Ibid., 264–265.

134 Remer, *Foreign Investment in China*, 497.

135 When the Hanyehping iron works was built in 1893, it was the most modern plant in the Far East. From 1902 to 1930, Japan made thirty-one loans to this company totaling ¥40 million. Hou, *Foreign Investment*, 76. Japan required in Group III of the Twenty-One Demands that Hanyehping be made a Sino–Japanese joint venture company "when the opportune moment arrived." (7.2.1)

136 Wilkins, *Business History Review 60*, 214.

137 Remer, *Foreign Investment in China*, 508–510. The Hanyehping complex employed 23,000 workers, and it was here that Mao Zedong and other Chinese Communist Party members gained their first significant experiences in labor organization. Jonathan Spence, *The Search for Modern China* (New York: W. W. Norton, 1990), 325.

302

*Notes*

138 Japan participated in the Anshan mine operation as a result of the Twenty-One Demands, which required that Japan be granted mining rights in South Manchuria and Eastern Inner Mongolia (Article 4 of Group II).

139 Remer, *Foreign Investment in China*, 491.

140 Ibid., 495. Hou, *Foreign Investment*, 231.

141 Remer, *Foreign Investment in China*, 490.

142 Ibid., 490. Hou, *Foreign Investment*, 69.

143 Remer, *Foreign Investment in China*, 495.

144 W. G. Beasley, *Japanese Imperialism, 1895–1945* (New York: Oxford University Press, 1987), 214–215.

145 Yoshihisa Tak Matsusaka, *The Making of Japanese Manchuria, 1904–1932* (Cambridge, MA: Harvard University Press, 2001), 87. Louise Young, *Japan's Total Empire* (Berkeley, CA: University of California Press, 1998), 25.

146 C. Walter Young, *Japanese Jurisdiction in the South Manchuria Railway Areas* (Baltimore: Johns Hopkins Press, 1931), 79.

147 L. Young, *Japan's Total Empire*, 31.

148 Gotō Shinpei, the SMR's first president, was particularly intent on the problem of public health and the need for adequate sewage systems. Ibid., 249.

149 The capital was increased to ¥440 million in 1920, to ¥800 million in 1933, and to ¥1,400 million in 1939, with the Japanese government continuing to hold half the shares. E. B. Schumpeter, *Japanese Economic History, 1930–1960* (London, Routledge, 2000), 384.

150 C. W. Young, *Japanese Jurisdiction*, 87–88.

151 Matsusaka, *Making of Japanese Manchuria*, 90.

152 Remer, *Foreign Investment in China*, 482.

153 C. W. Young, *Japanese Jurisdiction*, 87–88. Matsusaka, *Making of Japanese Manchuria*, 90. L. Young, *Japan's Total Empire*, 25. The question of formal empire and informal empire is discussed in 1.2.1.

*303*

# Chapter 11
# The New China and the Powers

## 11.1. China in the 1910s and 1920s

### 11.1.1. Political Developments after the Fall of the Qing Dynasty

When revolt spread in southern China in the fall of 1911 (7.1.3), the Qing (清)
government recalled Yuan Shikai (袁世凱) from involuntary retirement as its
military commander.[1] Yuan defeated the rebel forces, but he used the opportunity to solidify his own power. He talked with the rebel leaders and agreed
to the establishment of a republican government. He then persuaded the
Manchu rulers to abdicate.

Meanwhile, in January 1912, the Revolutionary Alliance, a broad spec-
trum of revolutionaries, convened the National Council in Nanjing (南京) and
elected Sun Yat-sen (孫逸仙) the provisional president of the Chinese
Republic.[2] However, Sun relinquished the title to Yuan Shikai, since Sun's
military power was no match for Yuan's. In his letter of resignation, Sun
requested the National Council to prepare a new draft of a provisional constitution. The provisional constitution was promulgated in March 1912, stipulating that a parliamentary system should be in place within ten months. The
election was held in December 1912, and the result was a clear victory for the

*305*

Kuomintang (国民党), a political party transformed from the Revolutionary Alliance.[3]

Sun had placed the party management in the hands of the young leader Song Jiaoren (宋教仁).[4] Song was expected to be named premier in the new parliament, but he was assassinated on March 20, 1913. It was widely believed that Yuan was behind the deed.[5] Soon afterward, a civil war broke out.[6]

Having crushed the Kuomintang troops, Yuan now forced the parliament to elect him president, and then evicted Kuomintang members from the parliament, calling the party a seditious organization. In January 1914, he dissolved the parliament and replaced the provisional constitution with a "constitutional compact," which gave him virtually unlimited power.[7] He devoted much of the next two years to preparing the way for a restoration of the empire, with himself as emperor. Opposition to his imperial aspirations grew, however, and a succession of provincial warlords declared their independence from Yuan's regime. In March 1916, Yuan declared that he would drop his plans to become emperor, but his prestige was now shattered. He died in June.[8] The Beijing government stayed in office, but it had no control over the provincial warlords. A kind of age of the warlords began.[9]

Sun Yat-sen spent three years in Japan while Yuan outlawed the Kuomintang. He returned in 1916 to Guangzhou (広州), and formed the Kuomintang government there. But his attempts to launch a national unification drive were twice frustrated by warlords who did not want Sun to use Guangzhou for such a project.

Sun's fundamental problem was a lack of funding. Thus, when a Comintern agent approached Sun in 1921 and offered him financial and military aid, Sun responded eagerly. In the early 1920s, the Soviet Union's anti-imperialist propaganda was quite active and gaining great influence in China. The Chinese leaders were greatly encouraged by the Soviet criticism of the Versailles Treaty and the Washington Treaties as nothing more than the division of the spoils of imperialism. Many Chinese intellectuals accepted Lenin's anti-imperialist arguments enthusiastically.[10] The alliance between the Kuomintang and the Soviet Union was formed in these circumstances.

In 1923, Adolf Joffe, the Soviet representative in Beijin, and Sun issued a joint statement of alliance between the Kuomintang and the Soviet Union.[11] In that year, the Comintern sent Michael Borodin to Guangzhou as Sun's special advisor, and the Kuomintang sent Chiang Kai-shek (蒋介石) to Moscow for military training. After his return, Chiang became superintendent of the newly created Whampoa Military Academy, where the officers of the Kuomintang army were to be trained. In 1924, the Chinese Communist Party (CCP), which had been inaugurated in 1921, joined the Kuomintang, forming a bloc within that party.[12]

Sun Yat-sen's death in early 1925 brought to the surface the fundamental ideological split within the Kuomintang. The Kuomintang left wing sought to continue the party's Soviet orientation. The party's right wing, while recognizing the importance of Soviet aid, did not want to move the Kuomintang ideology so far to the left as to alienate landlords and industrialists, an important segment of party supporters. The landlords were not sympathetic to peasant demands for lower rents. The industrialists were not sympathetic to the calls by urban strikers for higher wages. Though the leftists seemed to have the situation well in hand, there were some indications of a countertrend.[13] Most important was an incident in Guangzhou on March 20, 1926, which showed the fragility of the Communist position. On that day, Chiang Kai-shek suddenly arrested a number of senior Communist military officers and deprived them of all military authority, contending that they had plotted to gain control of the army. By this maneuver, Chiang seized effective control of Nationalist military power. Borodin had no recourse but to reach a "compromise" with Chiang.[14]

### 11.1.2. The Northern Expedition

With a centrist position now staked out politically, Chiang and the Kuomintang leaders developed plans for a military campaign to unify China: the Northern Expedition. The broad purpose of the expedition was defined as follows.

> The hardship of workers, peasants, merchants and students, and the suffering of all under the oppressive imperialists and warlords; the peace and unification of China called for by Sun Yat-sen; the gathering of the National Assembly ruined by Duan Qirui—all demand the elimination of Wu Peifu and completion of national unification.

Duan Qirui (段祺瑞) was a warlord who controlled Henan (河南) and Hebei (河北). He served as premier of the Beijing government intermittently in 1913–1918, and was chief of the Beijing government in 1924–1926. In 1918,

Chapter 11

while premier of the Beijing government, he received the controversial "Nishihara loans" from the Japanese government.[15] Wu Peifu (吳佩孚), a warlord in the south, controlled Hubei (湖北) and Hunan (湖南).[16]

The official mobilization order was issued on July 1, 1926. Chiang was named commander in chief of the National Revolutionary Army. By mid-December 1926, the Nationalists controlled seven provinces, with a population of around 170 million.[17]

In mid-March 1927, Chiang's army took Shanghai (上海) without serious incident, but on arrival at Nanjing (南京) in late March, Nationalist soldiers attacked foreigners and foreign property, including the American, British, and Japanese consulates. Several foreigners were murdered. The violence was the work of Communist provocateurs. Nevertheless, the foreign powers demanded of the Nationalist government punishment of those responsible, a written apology from Chiang, assurances that such incidents would not occur in the future, and reparations for damages and loss of life.[18] On April 12, 1927, the day after the diplomatic notes were presented by the powers, Chiang ordered the arrest of several hundred Communists and labor leaders. Arrests and executions continued over the next several weeks. Chiang bested the Comintern by squeezing the Communists out before they could eliminate him.[19]

Chiang formed his own government in Nanjing on April 18, independently from the government in Wuhan (武漢) led by Wang Chao-ming (汪兆銘).[20] The Northern Expedition suffered from the effects of the split between the Wuhan and Nanjing regimes. In August, Chiang relinquished his posts to help the reunification of the Kuomintang. Wang followed suit to facilitate the reunification of the Kuomintang.[21] Though the party was reunited, the Northern Expedition remained suspended.

During his temporary retirement, Chiang made a trip to Japan from the end of September until early November in 1927. The purpose of his trip was matrimonial rather than political, though he had two brief meetings with Prime Minister Tanaka Giichi (田中義一) during his stay in Japan. He met Song Jiaoren's widow in Kobe to get her permission to marry her youngest daughter, Soong Mei-ling (宋美齡).[22]

In January 1928, Chiang was once again named commander in chief, and the Northern Expedition resumed in early April. In early July, the Nationalist forces entered Beijing. Having achieved national unification, the Nanjing government made its foreign-policy goal clear. On July 7, it declared that all un-

308

equal treaties should be replaced with new arrangements.[23]

In Manchuria, Zhang Xueliang (張学良), who had succeeded to his murdered father's position, pledged allegiance to the Nationalist government. At the end of 1928, the Kuomintang flag, with its white sun on a blue and red ground (青天白日旗), flew from Guangzhou (広州) to Mukden (奉天).

## 11.2. US and British China Policy

### 11.2.1. The Sympathetic American Response to New China

The "awakening" of China became a popular notion in America in the 1910s, just as the awakening of Japan had fascinated Americans of earlier generations.[24] Many Americans pictured China as a land of great promise, where the people were dedicating themselves to the cause of modernization. They shared a view of the Chinese revolution as a worthy imitator of the American Revolution—a thoroughly praiseworthy quest by the Chinese for the freedom to determine their own future.[25] The idea that the United States had much to contribute to a new China was accepted as axiomatic by many Americans.[26]

American press editors and church leaders in particular created a naïve image of China. They wanted to believe in the ideal China that they pictured.[27] They hoped that China would modernize itself without becoming another Japan, which had become an imperialist country practicing European-style diplomacy. It would be the mission of a moral America to rescue the victim from the amoral imperialists, especially from what appeared to be an increasingly aggressive Japan.

President Wilson came to the presidency precisely at this juncture.[28] For Wilson, the international situation surrounding China was most unnatural. The Chinese were being denied their rightful sovereignty by the European powers, who were settling Chinese affairs among themselves. For example, Wilson regarded the international banking consortium as an immoral imposition on China.[29] Rather, the United States would employ more unilateral tactics to do what it could to help China. A week after the withdrawal from the consortium in May 1913, Wilson decided to recognize the Yuan Shikai regime, though Japan and Britain were skeptical about Yuan and had held off from the recognition of his government.[30]

The episode of Yuan's appeal to Christian churches for prayers for his new government epitomizes the tendency of Wilson and other Americans to give

*309*

priority to missionary concerns rather than to the facts on the ground. Yuan was no Christian, but he was clever enough to play on American devotion to Christian ideals. On April 17, 1913, Yuan asked some Protestant churches in China to pray for his administration and the parliament. The Associated Press in Beijing cabled the news home, where editors placed it on the front page the next morning. The president's cabinet meeting on that day began with Secretary of State Bryan noting the *Washington Post* headline reading "China Asks for Prayers." Wilson, who was the son of a Presbyterian minister and had family and personal ties of long standing with missionaries in China, emphasized that he did not know when he had been so stirred, and uplifted as when he read the report of the Yuan request in the press. Secretary of Commerce William C. Redfield apparently expressed his skepticism about Yuan's sincerity, but Wilson said, "We ought to accept the official appeal of wishing the prayers of Christians as honest and earnest and join with the Christian people in China in praying for the peaceful organization of the Republic of China."[31] For a week, the news received wide notice, especially in the religious press.[32] On Sunday, April 27, Americans prayed. Special services for China took place at churches throughout the United States. There were no signs of prayers in the churches in American Chinatowns.[33]

As discussed in chapter 7, Wilson sided decisively with China when Japan presented the Twenty-One Demands (7.2.4). At the Versailles Peace Conference, he tried earnestly to block Japan's acquisition of German rights in Shandong, albeit without success (7.3.4).

The Wilsonian goal of checking Japanese imperialist policy in China, however, seemed to have been fairly well realized at the 1922 Washington Conference, where President Harding's secretary of state, Charles Evans Hughes, took the initiative (7.4). The Nine-Power Treaty pledged that the contracting parties would not undertake further expansion at the expense of China; the Anglo–Japanese alliance and the Lansing–Ishii Agreement were abrogated; and Japan agreed to give up its claim to the old German rights in Shandong, with China buying out the Japanese-owned Jinan–Qingdao Railway using loans from Japan. However, most of the foreign spheres of influence remained undisturbed, and the restoration of tariff and jurisdictional autonomy was put off into the future.[34] Thus the Chinese hope of full restoration of their sovereignty was not fulfilled. Nevertheless, the Washington Conference seemed to be an important step toward a solution to the China question in line with the tenets of American idealism.

## 11.2.2. Kellogg's Unilateral Approaches

For a few years after the Washington Conference, the United States conducted its China policy in harmony with the other Washington powers. For example, in 1923, the United States participated in the joint naval demonstration designed to thwart Sun Yat-sen's attempt to gain a share of the income from customs duties collected at the Guangzhou port.[35] On the questions of tariff autonomy and extraterritoriality as well, the US position was not different from that of Britain and Japan. John V. A. MacMurray, the chief of the Far Eastern Affairs Division of the State Department,[36] insisted that the Chinese should bring order to their own affairs before asking the Americans to surrender their privileges under the treaty system.

However, the US China policy began to take an independent course from 1925, when the new secretary of state Frank Kellogg took office. Kellogg proved himself much less bound by the treaty provisions concerning China of the Washington Conference.[37] He was clearly more conciliatory toward China than his predecessor. When the Beijing government requested early revision of the unequal treaties in the summer of 1925, after a series of clashes that culminated in the Shanghai Incident on May 30 in which many Chinese were killed in Shanghai and later in Guangzhou,[38] Kellogg quickly supported the Chinese appeal.

At the urging of the United States, a tariff conference was convened in Beijing in October, 1925. Kellogg stated in his instructions to the American delegation that the conference "ought to go beyond the strict scope of its activities as defined in the [Washington] Customs Treaty and enter into a discussion of the entire subject of the conventional tariff, even including proposals looking toward ultimate tariff autonomy."[39] Kellogg also stated, "[Y]ou should retain your complete independence and avoid the possibility of any charge that the American government is taking sides for or against any other government represented at the Conference." Such an independent US stance could be compared to that taken by the United States toward Japan in the 1870s and 1880s, when the United States departed from cooperation with the European powers and unilaterally sought to assist Japan in its efforts to restore Japan's tariff and Judicial autonomy as discussed in 4.1.2 and 4.2.2.

The Tariff Conference negotiations failed to produce any agreement,

*311*

Chapter 11

however, firstly because of the differences in attitude among the great powers, and more detrimentally because of the confused political situation in China. The United States proposed an increase in tariff rates up to 12.5 percent in return for an abolition of *likin* (internal transit taxes).[40] Britain was at first negative, but softened its stance, and came close to the US proposal on the tariff rates.[41] Japan, however, refused to depart from the Washington formula of 2.5 percent surtax rates on ordinary goods and 5 percent on luxuries.[42] While the tariff negotiations were ongoing, the Beijing government's position became increasingly unstable. In February, 1926, when the conference reconvened after a New Year's holiday recess, a new civil war started in the north of China.[43] In April 1926, the Beijing government headed by Duan Qirui fell, and no further sessions of the conference were now possible.

Kellogg, being anxious to show American goodwill to China, but unable to do so because of the absence of a central government, issued a statement on January 27, 1927, stating that the United States was willing to enter into negotiations for the grant of tariff autonomy "with any government or delegates who can represent or speak for China."[44]

When Chiang and his colleagues achieved the military conquest of Beijing in early July 1928, and declared their intention to revise treaty relations with all countries (11.1.2), the United States was the first to respond favorably. On July 11, Kellogg sent telegraphic instructions to MacMurray, minister in Beijing, stating that " . . . understandings should be effected with the Nationalist government, which apparently is demonstrating a capacity to establish itself in China as the accepted government . . . "[45] With exceptional speed, a new tariff treaty was negotiated in Beijing and was signed on July 25 between MacMurray and Sung Tzuwen ("T. V.") (宋子文), the finance minister of the Nationalist government.[46] It granted tariff autonomy to China and provided for mutual most-favored-nation treatment.[47] Thus, the United States recognized the new Nationalist government ahead of the other Washington powers.[48] The conclusion of the treaty came as a complete surprise to the other Washington powers. Kellogg had not given them any notice of what was in progress in Beijing. He was determined to maintain the US lead in terms of support for the new Chinese government.[49]

It was undeniable that the new treaty greatly strengthened China's hand in dealing with the other powers, notably Japan.[50] MacMurray writes, in his historic 1935 memorandum *How the Peace Was Lost*, "The effect of our attitude

312

would be to condone the high-handed behavior of the Chinese and encourage them to a course of further recalcitrance." The US government was pressed, writes MacMurray, by pro-Chinese popular opinion in the United States into the hasty renunciation of its rights under the unequal treaties.[51]

On July 19, the Nationalists communicated a note to the Japanese minister in Beijing, Yoshizawa Kenkichi (芳沢謙吉), abrogating the treaties of 1896 and 1903. Yoshizawa, irritated by the US "popularity-courting policy," cabled to Tokyo that the conclusion of the US–Chinese treaty would amount to a unilateral abrogation of the Washington treaties,[52] and it should serve as a precedent for Japan, when, in the future, it decided not to abide by the Washington treaties.[53]

The policy that Japan followed in China after the summer of 1928 was, however, not unilateral, but one of seeking understanding with the powers. Tanaka instructed Uchida Yasuya (内田康哉), who had been named as the Japanese representative at the signing of the Kellogg–Briand Pact in Paris in August 1928,[54] to communicate Japan's position on China to the United States and Britain and solicit their cooperation in dealing with China. But Japan's effort proved to be a failure. Neither country was inclined to cooperate with a nation whose recent interventionist policies (11.3.3, 11.3.4) had worsened its relations with China.

In London, Uchida was told that the two countries' interests in China differed considerably, and all Britain would do for Japan was to agree to an ongoing exchange of views. A cooler reception awaited Uchida in Washington when he met Kellogg on September 29. Uchida conveyed to Kellogg Japan's position with regard to China, and straightforwardly inquired about the US goals in China.[55] Kellogg expressed his great sympathy toward China, but evaded answering Uchida's inquiries. The United States was not willing to forego the supposed diplomatic advantages that it had recently gained in China.[56]

MacMurray writes, "[Kellogg's] responses did not give Uchida anything but the impression that the United States was pro-Chinese to the extent that [it] wanted to advance [its] own interests by siding with the Chinese in their national aspirations, regardless of the effects upon the interests of our collaborators."[57] The US reply was, according to MacMurray, "disquieting to the Government of the nation which was most intimately and vitally and inescapably concerned with Chinese affairs . . . the effect [of Kellogg's chilly reception

*313*

of Uchida] upon the Japanese was that of a rebuff: to them it signified that the American Government had taken a position in favor of China and against Japan."[58]

### 11.2.3. Britain's Conciliatory Policy on the Nationalist Revolutionary Diplomacy

Whether the Washington system would successfully provide a workable alternative to the old diplomacy as a mechanism to harmonize the divergent interests of the powers in China depended on the degree to which they would cooperatively meet the challenges they would subsequently encounter. The Soviet-inspired, anti-imperialist nationalism of the Chinese Nationalists' radical "revolutionary diplomacy" was not what the three powers had expected when they were meeting in Washington in 1921–22. Unable to frame a common response to the unexpected developments in China, each of the powers started to act independently.

The boycott subsequent to the May 30 Shanghai Incident in 1925 was first targeted against both Japan and Britain,[59] but soon the Chinese started to concentrate their pressure on the British, dropping the Japanese from their boycott. For example, the slogan of the demonstration in Hunan in the fall of 1926 was "Fight the British, be friendly to the Americans, and ignore the Japanese!"[60] Under the circumstances, Britain started seeking an understanding with the Nationalists in the south. In the middle of July 1926, British officials in Hong Kong approached the Nationalists and offered them a loan in return for the cessation of the Hong Kong strike, the anti-British boycott, and all unfriendly acts in the Nationalist-controlled provinces.[61] Though no loan deals materialized, the British decided to acquiesce when the Nationalists started to collect surtaxes at Guangzhou outside the authority of the British-sponsored Maritime Customs Administration. In making this concession, the British tolerated the diversion of resources to the Nationalists for their military purposes as quid pro quo for putting an end to the boycott. Japan and the United States resented Britain's approval of the Nationalist collection of the surtax, but had no alternative to accepting it.[62]

All these developments led to a British declaration of its China policy on Christmas Day in 1926—the so-called Chamberlain Christmas message. It declared, "[T]he situation which exists in China today is . . . entirely different from that which faced the powers at the time they framed the Washington

*314*

treaties . . . " Accordingly, the British proposed that the powers should declare "their readiness to negotiate on treaty revision and all other outstanding questions as soon as the Chinese themselves have constituted a Government with authority to negotiate . . . " The message also stated that the authority of the Beijing government had diminished to a vanishing point, while in the south "a powerful Nationalist government at Canton [Guangzhou] definitely disputed the right of the government at Beijing to speak on behalf of China . . . "

The Christmas message was issued without prior consultation with the other Washington powers.[63] The British government leaders knew that the practice of unilateral actions did not conform to the spirit of the Washington system of cooperation.[64] But in view of the great changes in the situation in China, as well as widened differences in the powers' positions, they considered that Britain might as well declare its China policy independently.

On December 20, 1928, Britain recognized the Nationalist government and concluded a tariff autonomy agreement, five months after the United States had done so.

# 11.3. Japan's China Policy in the 1920s

## 11.3.1. Shidehara's China Policy

While the British judged that their national interest in China was chiefly economic gain, Japan considered that China was crucially important for its security as well as for its natural and agricultural resources. US China policy, on the other hand, seemed, to a considerable degree, to be under the influence of the sentimental regard that the American people had toward the Chinese people.[65]

About three weeks after the Chamberlain Christmas message (11.2.3) and nine days before the Kellogg announcement on January 27, 1927 (11.2.2), Foreign Minister Shidehara Kijūrō (幣原喜重郎) delivered a speech in the Diet on Japan's China policy. He pledged Japan's pursuance of noninterventionism, work toward Sino–Japanese coexistence, and support for reasonable Chinese demands.[66] The Shidehara message was more favorably received by the Nationalists than those by Chamberlain and Kellogg. Chamberlain's memorandum offended them because of its expressions suggestive of the old power-politics diplomacy. Kellogg's announcement was not appreciated because it was not clear to whom it had been addressed, and it conveyed nothing new or

315

practical. The Shidehara message was clearer, and the Nationalists knew to whom it was addressed.

Shidehara had been fairly well informed about the Nationalists. In November 1926, Saburi Sadao (佐分利貞男), director general of the Commerce Bureau of the Foreign Ministry and a delegate to the Beijing Tariff Conference, had a meeting with Chiang Kai-shek and other leaders of the Nationalist government in Guangzhou.[67] Saburi learned that the left–right rift within the Nationalists was serious, and that the right-wing Nationalists were quite reasonable people. Despite their public professions, they wished to effect revision of unequal treaties by "rational means" rather than by total repudiation. Saburi was also told that the Nationalist government well understood the Japanese position in Manchuria.[68] In December 1926, a group of Japanese businessmen in Shanghai sent letters to the Foreign, Navy, and Army Ministries in Tokyo. The letters read, "[I]t is urgently needed for the interest of Japan and China . . . to cause the Nationalist left to be replaced by the right which represents China's national aspirations," and hoped that the government would take proper steps toward this end.[69] The Japanese military in China, also noticing the internal factionalism within the Nationalists, began to approach the rightists. Supporting such a move, Consul General Yada Shichitarō (矢田七太郎) at Shanghai telegraphed early in January 1927 that "the opportunity seems near when we can approach the rightists, come to some understanding with them, and [help them] eliminate the Communists and Soviet Russia from the revolutionary army."[70] All this served to form Shidehara's policy of supporting the moderate Nationalists.

In the Nanjing Incident of March 1927 (11.1.2), Shidehara refused to participate in the joint naval bombardment. Military actions in China were not congruent with his idea of Sino–Japanese coexistence. Following the Nanjing Incident, he also opposed Britain's idea of applying sanctions against the Nationalists in case they failed to give satisfaction to the powers' demands. When violence broke out in Nanjing, he received a telegram from Morioka Shōhei (森岡正平), consul at Nanjing, definitely attributing the violence to Communist instigation.[71] Shidehara told the American ambassador in Tokyo that the incident was a Communist plot to embarrass Chiang Kai-shek in the eyes of foreigners, and that by applying sanctions the powers would play into the hands of the Communists. With Japan and the United States opposing the idea of sanctions, Chamberlain in the end dropped the idea.[72] Chiang showed real interest in reciprocating the Japanese initiative at this time, but he could not risk appearing too conciliatory toward any foreign government until his supremacy was ensured.[73]

### 11.3.2. Tanaka's China Policy

Shidehara's conciliatory Chinese policies were criticized in Japan as weak-kneed by the opposition Seiyūkai (政友会) and most Japanese military leaders. The China question was one of the most prominent issues dividing the political parties. On April 17, 1927, the Kenseikai's (憲政会) Wakatsuki Reijirō (若槻礼次郎) cabinet fell as a result of the refusal of the Privy Council to sanction a government plan to save the Bank of Taiwan from financial collapse (9.3.2). It was the obvious intention of some privy councilors to use the bank issue in order to force the downfall of the cabinet.[74]

A new cabinet was formed by Prime Minister Tanaka Giichi, president of the Seiyūkai, who concurrently held the post of foreign minister. Despite his criticism of Shidehara's China policy, Tanaka considered that Japan should support the moderate Nationalists and refrain from intervening in China's internal warfare. But Tanaka departed from his predecessor's policy against the use of force in May 1927, when he decided to send 2,000 troops from Dalian (大連) to Qingdao (青島) to defend Japanese nationals and their property (the first Shandong expedition).[75] Tanaka bowed to the argument within the Seiyūkai that he should show that he was different from his weak-kneed predecessor.[76] The expedition aroused Chinese resentment, but attention was diverted to Wuhan, where in July there was a historic purge of the Communists from the Wuhan government.[77] The Comintern instructed Russian advisors to flee from China,[78] and the Chinese Communists to deepen the revolution in the countryside. Mao Zedong (毛沢東) was among those who were assigned this task.[79]

Tanaka convened the "Eastern Conference" (東方会議) in Tokyo between June 27 and July 7, 1927, to discuss China policy. The participants included Minister Yoshizawa, Consul General Yoshida Shigeru (吉田茂) of Mukden, Yada of Shanghai, the commander of the Kwantung Army, officials from the ministries of foreign affairs, army, navy, and finance, and the army and navy general staff. In the conference, Yada argued that since the Nationalist forces had a popular base, eventually they would dominate the whole of China proper.[80] Though more cautious views were expressed by other participants, it

317

is significant that the conference adopted the views presented by Yada.[81]

On his way back to Beijing, Yoshizawa visited Nanjing on August 9 and 10, where he was given an overwhelming reception. Yoshizawa was the first foreign envoy to visit Nanjing, where Chiang had formed his government in April that year (11.1.2). The welcoming party commenced with the singing of the Japanese anthem. Chiang Kai-shek called Yoshizawa his "dear friend" and expressed his confidence that Japan would assist in the Nationalist revolution—as he understood the Eastern Conference had decided.[82]

Toward the end of September, Chiang visited Japan (11.1.2). During his stay, he twice met Tanaka, first in Hakone and then at his residence in Aoyama.[83] Chiang appealed for Japan's assistance in the revolution and asked him not to aid the corrupt warlords. Tanaka expressed his support of Chiang's efforts, but Chiang somehow became wary of Tanaka's China policy.[84] No agreement or understanding was brought about at either meeting.[85]

## 11.3.3. The Jinan Incident

When the Nationalists resumed the Northern Expedition in early April 1928, it was decided that the Chiang forces would head for Beijing through Shandong Province, taking the route along the Nanjing (南京)–Tianjin (天津) Railway. On the route was the city of Jinan (済南), where two thousand Japanese resided. Tanaka was cautious about proposals to dispatch a military force to protect Japanese nationals and property in the area, since Chiang Kai-shek had expressed his strong opposition to any such Japanese moves. Chiang communicated to Tanaka his assurances that he would do his utmost to see Japanese nationals and their property protected. The general staff of the Japanese army was also of the opinion that Chiang should be trusted, and should not be obstructed by the dispatch of a Japanese expedition.[86]

The war minister, on the other hand, insisted that Chinese soldiers could not be trusted, and the Seiyūkai was also supportive of an expedition because of the pledge the party had made in the previous election to stand for the principle of "protecting nationals on the spot" instead of evacuating them from places of danger.[87] The Foreign Ministry in Tokyo was in receipt of telegrams from its representatives in Qingdao and Jinan urging an expedition as an unavoidable necessity to protect Japanese nationals. Mainly due to pressure from the army minister and in consideration of party politics, Tanaka decided on April 19 to dispatch five thousand troops of the Sixth Division in

Kumamoto (the second Shandong expedition). In announcing the dispatch, the government twice repeated assurances that Japan had no intention of intervening in the civil war in China, and promised that the troops would be withdrawn as soon as their presence was no longer needed for the protection of Japanese nationals.[88]

The vanguard of the Japanese expedition entered Jinan on April 26, and the main body of the Sixth Division, commanded by Lieutenant General Fukuda Hikosuke (福田彦助), arrived in early May. Chiang Kai-shek entered Jinan on May 2, the day after Nationalist troops reached the city. Chiang Kai-shek requested that the Japanese troops withdraw from the inner city, as the Nationalist army would pledge to maintain order there. The Japanese accepted the request and took up positions in the commercial area outside the city center.

At nine o'clock in the morning of May 3, Nishida Kōichi (西田畊一), the acting consul general, and several Japanese officers visited Chiang Kai-shek at his headquarters. Nishida remarked that he was impressed with the good discipline of the revolutionary army and said he felt the Japanese forces could at any moment be withdrawn. Chiang Kai-shek said that the Northern Expedition would be continued and that he hoped Sino–Japanese ties would become closer.[89] Around nine-thirty, on his way back from the interview, Nishida learned that fighting had broken out between Chinese and Japanese soldiers in the commercial area.

Concerning the origin of the fight, Japan and China later presented different accounts.[90] A cease-fire was somehow brought about in the middle of the night.[91] But the truce was short-lived. Fukuda and other generals later admitted that the incident of May 3 had impressed them as evidence of a deep-seated anti-Japanese feeling on the part of Nationalist troops, and they felt that the prestige of the imperial army would be at stake if the Chinese "insult" were allowed to go unrebuked. It is believed that Fukuda's acceptance of the truce on the night of May 3 was designed to gain time.[92]

On May 7, Fukuda presented Chiang with a twelve-hour ultimatum with conditions the Nationalists could not possibly have been expected to accept. Chiang replied, accepting most of Fukuda's demands,[93] but Fukuda refused to regard the Chiang reply as satisfactory. On May 8, fighting was resumed. The Chinese offered stubborn resistance, but were finally expelled. Some 3,600 Chinese died,[94] and a harsh Japanese occupation of the city continued until

Chapter 11

March 1929, when the Nationalist and Japanese governments finally signed an agreement for the settlement of the incident (11.3.5).

The Jinan incident was in fact a watershed in the relations between the Nationalist and Japanese governments.[95] It frustrated all attempts at further Sino–Japanese rapprochement.[96] Chiang told Colonel Sasaki, who was attached to Chiang's army as a military adviser, in an unusually emotional fashion that the May incident had foreclosed any future possibility of his shaking hands with the Japanese military. Cohen argues, "In a few days the Japanese army succeeded in demolishing the edifice of goodwill that Japan's statesmen had so carefully endeavored to construct since they first conceived of Chiang Kai-shek as a moderate nationalist."[97]

The incident revealed the weakness of the chain of command in the Japanese military.[98] The Tokyo government's policy of nonintervention in the Chinese civil wars and its restriction of Japanese military actions to protection of Japanese nationals was not adhered to by the Japanese military officers in the field. The lesson of the Jinan incident was that the army leadership in Tokyo should have had field commanders strictly adhere to its policies. Fukuda's insubordination should have been sternly punished. However, Fukuda was not only not punished, but welcomed back to Tokyo with honors.[99] The *dokudan senkō* (独断専行 the discretionary right entrusted to the Japanese field commanders; see 14.1.1) practice of the Japanese army was to be repeated on several later occasions, as observed below (11.3.4) and in subsequent chapters.

### 11.3.4. The Assassination of Zhang Zuolin

The Japanese policymakers' chief concern in 1928 was safeguarding Japan's interests in Manchuria in case fighting between the Nationalists and Zhang Zuolin's (張作霖) forces extended to Manchuria. In January, when Zhang Qun (張群), Chiang Kai-shek's special envoy then in Tokyo, met Tanaka, he informally suggested to Tanaka that if Japan could persuade Zhang to withdraw from Beijing to Mukden, the Nationalists would agree not to move the Nationalist army beyond the Wall.[100] In May, the cabinet reached a decision that (1) Zhang Zuolin should be urged to withdraw immediately beyond the Wall, and if Zhang's troops should return to Manchuria in an orderly fashion, they need not be disarmed; and (2) the Japanese army would refuse the passage of Nationalist soldiers north beyond the Wall.[101]

*320*

On May 18 the army minister telegraphed the above cabinet decision to the Japanese military commanders in China and Korea. Commander Muraoka Chōtarō (村岡長太郎) of the Kwantung Army assembled all Japanese forces at Mukden to await the word to execute the army minister's order to move his troops to the strategic gateway of Shanhaiguan (山海関), where the Great Wall ends at the North China Sea.[102] Specific instructions were sent to Yoshizawa and Yada to communicate the above Japanese policy to Chinese leaders. In Beijing, Yoshizawa told Zhang that Japan wanted him to retreat promptly to Manchuria before the southerners reached the Beijing area, as his army was going to lose the war with the southern army. Zhang refused to take Yoshizawa's advice at the meeting, but his lieutenants were inclined toward retreat if the Nationalists agreed not to pursue them into Manchuria. After a series of conferences, Zhang decided to depart from Beijing late on the night of June 2. In Shanghai, Yada conveyed the cabinet decision to Huang Fu (黄郛) and Wang Chengting ("C. T.") (王正廷), who was soon to succeed Huang as Nationalist foreign minister. Both complained that Japan was intervening in Chinese internal affairs, but suggested that the Nationalist army would not pursue Zhang's troops beyond the Wall.

The Kwantung Army had treaty rights authorizing it to move freely throughout the Southern Manchuria Railway corridor and the Kwantung Leased Territory, but moving troops to Shanhaiguan was not within Japan's rights as guaranteed by the treaties. The Japanese government therefore sought to have an imperial command for the troop movement. However, now that the Nationalists suggested that they would not move their troops north of the Wall, it did not seem necessary to take any legally dubious measures. On May 31, Tanaka decided against dispatching troops to Shanhaiguan.

Exasperated by what they took to be Tanaka's indecision, Muraoka and Colonel Kōmoto Daisaku (河本大作) decided to assassinate Zhang Zuolin to create disorder so that they could have a pretext for military actions outside the treaty limitations and hopefully expand their control throughout Manchuria.[103] On the morning of June 4, when Zhang's train crossed the iron landbridge outside of Mukden, the explosives that were hidden on the landbridge were ignited. The car was blown up, killing Zhang. The assassins' hope that Zhang's death would lead to military action was, however, doomed to disappointment. Higher authorities both in Japan and China were determined not to precipitate a crisis. Coming on the heels of the Jinan incident, the assassination of Zhang Zuolin demonstrated the instability and confusion in Japan's decision-making and policy-executing bodies.

The assassination shattered Tanaka's plan to let Zhang Zuolin govern Manchuria while keeping a special and cooperative relationship with him.[104] Indeed, the problem of how to handle what had happened in Mukden troubled the Tanaka cabinet for its remaining days.[105] Tanaka considered that the culprits should be court-martialed. Genrō Saionji Kinmochi (西園寺公望) encouraged Tanaka to take this course of action, and strongly suggested that Tanaka inform the emperor of his decision.[106] The army minister, other officers in the ministry, and the general staff officers insisted that the case should be handled administratively. Some cabinet members and Seiyūkai officials sided with the army.[107] They argued that making public the Japanese military's involvement in the murder would make Japan's position in China extremely difficult. While a court-martial would require open presentation of evidence and formal accusations, administrative punishment would restrict the release of information embarrassing to the Japanese army.

On December 24, Tanaka went to the emperor and said that the Japanese military was involved in the case, and that the guilty parties would be severely punished.[108] The emperor replied by instructing him to uphold military discipline strictly.[109] The military leaders, meanwhile, strengthened their opposition to Tanaka. They now insisted on closing the case by announcing that the Japanese military was not involved in the assassination, and that the responsible officers would be administratively punished for having failed to prevent the incident. In June 1929, Tanaka finally bowed to the military. When Tanaka went to the emperor on June 27 to report about his decision to accept the military's idea, the emperor, who was so displeased with Tanaka's attitude, said to him, "This is different from what you told me. Is it not?" And the emperor suggested to Tanaka that he resign.[110] Tanaka resigned on July 2.[111]

### 11.3.5. The Recognition of the Nationalist Government

When the United States recognized the Kuomintang government in July 1928 (11.2.2), and Britain did so five months later (11.2.3), Japan had a serious problem left to be negotiated with the Chiang government: the settlement of the Jinan incident (11.3.3). In October 1928, Yada and C. T. Wang reached a set of agreements which included Japan's promise to withdraw troops and China's promise to protect Japanese lives and property. But the Japanese

*The New China and the Powers*

military refused to accept the troop withdrawal clause. In January 1929, Yoshizawa and Wang restarted negotiations, and they reached an agreement in March. Japanese troops were to withdraw within two months, and a joint Sino–Japanese committee was to be set up to investigate the question of compensation for damages. Though the Japanese military again raised objections, Yoshizawa and Tanaka managed this time to silence the military. The final documents, in which both countries jointly declared regrets over the incident and determination to wipe it out of memory, were signed on March 24, 1929.[112] The settlement of the Jinan incident paved the way for Japan's recognition of the Nationalist government, which came on June 3, a month before the fall of the Tanaka cabinet.

When Shidehara took over from Tanaka as foreign minister of the Minseitō's (民政党) Hamaguchi Osachi (浜口雄幸) cabinet in July 1929,[113] Japan had not granted tariff autonomy to China. Without this, China could not enjoy tariff autonomy vis-à-vis other countries, including the United States and Britain, because of the most-favored-nation clause in their agreements with China.[114]

Shidehara entrusted the negotiations to Saburi Sadao, now the newly appointed minister to China.[115] Saburi had been a popular figure among the Nationalists ever since he had visited them in the south in November, 1926 and reported his good impression to the Tokyo government. As soon as he arrived at Nanjing in early October 1929, he and Chiang Kai-shek agreed to "improve the general atmosphere" between the two countries.[116] Shidehara might well have felt that his policy of rapprochement with China was proving a success. But the tariff talks were suspended because of Saburi's mysterious death in a Hakone hotel while visiting Japan in late November. His death was officially judged to be suicide, but many, including Shidehara, suspected murder.[117]

Negotiations were resumed in January 1930 between Shigemitsu Mamoru (重光葵), the chargé d'affaires in Shanghai, and C. T. Wang. After some hard bargaining, they reached a compromise in mid-March, by which Japan recognized China's tariff autonomy. Though China agreed to set aside more than 40 percent of Japanese export items and impose the graduated tariff schedule on them for three years till 1933, China was at last granted tariff autonomy by all treaty powers.[118]

## 11.4. The London Naval Conference and Its Unfortunate Consequences

### 11.4.1. The London Naval Conference

Hamaguchi and Shidehara intended to pursue their East Asia policy on the basis of solid understanding and harmony of interests with the United States and Britain. The strategy was best exemplified by the signing of the London Naval Treaty in 1930. After the conclusion of the Washington Naval Treaty of 1922 pertaining to capital ships (7.4.2), the leading navies had concentrated on the building of auxiliary craft. In particular, Japan and Britain led the way by constructing 10,000-ton eight-inch-gun heavy cruisers, the so-called treaty cruisers.[119] By the end of 1929, Japan would possess twelve of them, Britain fifteen, and the United States one. The United States and Britain had agreed between themselves to have eighteen each of this type of ship, present a united front against Japan, and demand of Japan a 5:5:3 ratio, the ratio the Washington Treaty had adopted for capital ships.[120] Japan, on the other hand, had decided to insist on a 70 percent ratio for heavy cruisers,[121] submarine tonnage of 78,000,[122] and a 70 percent ratio in total auxiliary tonnage.

At the first roundtable discussion on February 17 in London, Wakatsuki Reijirō, the head of the Japanese delegation, explained the reasons why Japan demanded a 70 percent ratio.[123] With a 70 percent ratio Japan could guard against a US naval attack, but it could not attack the United States, whereas with a 60 percent ratio Japan could not defend against a US attack.[124] Wakatsuki also stated that the Japanese people could not understand why Japan should not be given a 70 percent ratio, unless the United States harbored the idea of engaging in a war with Japan.[125] With no clear challenge being made to Wakatsuki's statement, negotiations in London reached an impasse.

William Castle, who arrived in Tokyo as American ambassador during the London negotiations,[126] appreciated the fact that the Japanese concern about naval ratios was prompted by Japanese apprehension that Japan and the United States might one day come into conflict over a matter affecting the mainland. Castle stated:

> Opinion is virtually unanimous among Japanese that the only possibility of war occurring between the United States and Japan lies in the present state of China. . . . Until China is prepared to give serious

considerations to the vested rights of foreign powers in China, it is felt that the possibilities of serious trouble ... must be at all times guarded against. ... There is no doubt whatever that if China should attempt to wrest the South Manchurian Railway from Japan, Japanese opinion would force the government to resist the attempt by all means at its command. In such an event, it is likely the Chinese would appeal for sympathy to the United States. ... The Japanese feel no assurance that the United States would not be obliged by an inflamed American public to take the part of China.[127]

In London, a compromise formula was eventually produced in mid-March. It conferred on Japan (1) an overall naval ratio of 69.75 percent; (2) a 60 percent ratio in heavy cruisers, with a promise by the United States not to begin construction of the final three cruisers until 1934, 1935, and 1936 so that Japan could have a de facto 10:7 ratio until 1936; and (3) parity in submarine tonnage set at 52,700 tons. The compromise denied the Japanese demand with respect to the 70 percent principle regarding heavy cruisers and the submarine tonnages of 78,000. It did not allow Japan to build even a single heavy cruiser, while the United States could construct fourteen heavy cruisers between 1930 and 1936 and lay the keels for three additional cruisers in the final three years of the period.[128]

Nevertheless, the Japanese government decided to accept the compromise. A threat by Henry L. Stimson, the head of American delegation, was effective. Stimson stated baldly that Japan's refusal of the compromise would rupture the tri-power negotiations, and the United States and Britain would make a two-power agreement against Japan.[129]

## 11.4.2. The Unfortunate Consequences of the London Naval Agreement

The London naval disarmament agreement might have been a victory for the American delegation, but it caused a major crisis in Japan. It brought about a bitter confrontation between the government and the naval general staff, and a serious split within the navy between the pro-treaty camp (the treaty faction 条約派) and the anti-treaty camp (the fleet faction 艦隊派).

The fleet faction was led by Katō Kanji (加藤寛治), the chief of the navy general staff, and Suetsugu Nobumasa (末次信正), the vice-chief of the navy general staff. They were determined to wage a public campaign against the treaty. Their contentions were that Japan was being forced to lose its traditional naval superiority in Japanese waters by the United States, which sought its domination of China without hindrance by binding Japan to an inferior naval ratio.[130] They also argued that negotiations on the naval defense question were matters for which the head of navy general staff was responsible directly to the emperor, but the Japanese government had infringed the emperor's right of supreme command by concluding the London Naval Treaty.[131]

In 1925, Japan had instituted universal manhood suffrage. The bulk of newly enfranchised people did not have enough knowledge about the naval defense strategy or the constitutionality of the government action. The spirited and determined arguments Katō and Suetsugu developed fascinated them.[132] Hamaguchi and Shidehara's argument—that the worsening of relations with the United States would do more to compromise Japan's China policy than a 60 percent naval ratio—did not.[133] Many Japanese believed that the Japanese delegation had been coerced by the Anglo–American alliance to accept a treaty that seriously compromised the Japanese defense capability.

It was also unfortunate that Shidehara's economically oriented and cooperative foreign policy suddenly faced the disaster of the Great Depression that began in late 1929, as discussed in chapter 12. This turn of events made his economic internationalism look weak and ineffectual in contrast to the realism of the military.

The struggle within the navy between the treaty faction and the fleet faction ended in the victory of the latter, and this brought about changes in the leadership of the imperial navy. All ranking officers who had supported the treaty were cashiered,[134] and positions of influence within the Navy Ministry and the general staff were monopolized by members of the fleet faction.[135]

The Hamaguchi government managed to have the London Naval Treaty approved though the Japanese parliamentary procedures. But the opposition Seiyūkai, seizing the political opportunity, joined with the navy radicals in accusing the Hamaguchi cabinet of violating the right of supreme command,[136] despite the fact that the majority opinion of Japanese constitutional scholars was that the London Naval Treaty regulated the scale of naval forces, which was a matter for which the government, not the navy, was responsible to the emperor.[137]

It was most ironic and tragic that the Seiyūkai's partisan politics in

*326*

accusing the Hamaguchi government weakened the position of the civilian government vis-à-vis the military, effectively undermining the foundations of Japan's parliamentary cabinet system. Amidst the political turmoil, a young right-wing radical fatally wounded Hamaguchi on November 14,[138] and the prime minister died half a year later.

## NOTES

### 11.1. China in the 1910s and 1920s

1   In 1910, Yuan was told to retire by the Qing ruler, who feared that Yuan's influence on the army had become too strong.

2   Sun Yat-sen is commonly written as 孫文 in Japan.

3   In the House of Representatives, the Kuomintang won 269 of the 596 seats. In the Senate, of the 274 incumbents, 123 were Kuomintang members. Jonathan Spence, *The Search for Modern China* (New York: W. W. Norton, 1990), 280.

4   Sun Yat-sen, while remaining the party's leader, placed day-to-day management in the hands of Song Jiaoren (who was also called Charlie Soong). Warren Cohen, *America's Response to China* (New York: Columbia University Press, 5th ed., 2010), 77. Charlie Soong had six children. His first child (daughter) Ai-ling married wealthy industrialist (and YMCA director) H. H. Kung; his second child (second daughter) Ching-ling married Sun Yat-sen; his third child (first son), T. V. Soong, became an influential member of Chiang's Nationalist government; and his fourth child (third daughter), Mei-ling, married Chiang Kai-shek. His second and third sons became bankers.

5   Spence, *Modern China*, 281.

6   Cohen, *America's Response*, 79–81.

7   Spence, *Modern China*, 281–284.

8   He died of uremia—compounded, many thought, by anger and humiliation—in June 1916. Ibid., 287.

9   These men, known as "warlords," had a wide range of backgrounds and maintained their power in different ways. Some of them had risen through the ranks of Yuan's army, and some had served in the provincial armies and had risen to positions as military governor or senior officer. Some dominated whole provinces and financed their armies with local taxes collected by their own bureaucracies. Others controlled only a handful of towns and got their money from "transit taxes." Ibid., 288. After Yuan's death, Li Yuanhong, the Yuan regime's vice-president, succeeded him, but he had been in office only just over one year when Zhang Xun, a fanatical supporter of the Qing and a field marshal and inspector general of Yangzi province, led his army into Beijing in 1917 and declared the restoration of the abdicated Qing emperor Puyi, a boy of eleven. The restoration never got off the ground. The troops of rival generals stormed Beijing and defeated Zhang Xun. Spence writes that with the collapse of Zhang's insurrection, an age of warlords and regionalism began. Ibid., 287–288.

10   In 1917, Lenin wrote a book which he titled *Imperialism*. Combining the Marxist

theory (capitalist societies inevitably become imperialist because of their inherent inability to dispose of their products at home) with his own interpretation of colonialism and war among capitalist countries (war for repartition of colonies inevitably ensues between latecomer capitalists and older empires as the latecomers find the largest and most promising areas have been preempted as the colonies of the older empires), Lenin defined the situation in Asia as an integral part of the worldwide struggle against imperialism. Akira Iriye, *After Imperialism* (Cambridge: Harvard University Press, 1965), 11. John Strachey, *The End of Empire* (London: Victor Gollancz, 1959), 103–108.

11 Spence, *Modern China*, 335.

12 Ibid., 322–325. Iriye, *After Imperialism*, 41.

13 For one thing, among the Whampoa cadets there was a group whose members were strongly anti-Communist, though they were nationalists and anti-imperialists. Another indicator was the fact that the strongly leftist flavor of Guangzhou drove many businessmen out of the city to reestablish themselves in Shanghai or Beijing in the mid-1920s. Spence, *Modern China*, 343.

14 Borodin was instructed by the Comintern, which wanted to avoid a complete eviction of Communists from Guangzhou, to offer continued Soviet aid, and to keep restraints on Communist agitation in return for Chiang's willingness to contain the Kuomintang right wing. Spence, *Modern China*, 344. Cohen, *America's Response*, 107.

15 The "Nishihara loans," totaling nearly 90 million dollars, were made by the Japanese government to Duan Qirui to persuade him to favor Japanese interests in China. Though they were nominally loans for railway and industrial development, the entire sum was misappropriated for special military and political purposes. Some Nationalist leaders advocated a total repudiation of these loans, but the Nationalist government agreed in 1930 to pay Japan $5 million yearly toward the principal sums involved. Iriye, *After Imperialism*, 289. Spence, *Modern China*, 329. See note 134 of chapter 9 (9.4.2).

16 Spence writes that the omission of the name of Zhang Zuolin, the Manchurian warlord who then controlled Beijing, from the declaration was presumably an invitation to that crafty general to attack Duan from the north while the Kuomintang advanced from the south. Spence, *Modern China*, 346.

17 The seven provinces were Guangdong (広東), Hunan (湖南), Hubei (湖北), Jiangxi (江西), Fujian (福建), Guangxi (広西), and Guizhou (貴州).

18 Cohen, *America's Response*, 108. Iriye, *After Imperialism*, 131.

19 Cohen, *America's Response*, 108.

20 The Kuomintang government had been moved from Guangzhou to Wuhan in February, 1927. At that time the Nationalist government was under a heavy Communist influence. Chiang, who had become definitely anti-Communist, remained at Nanchang (南昌) to gather anti-Communist followers. Iriye, *After Imperialism*, 92. Wang Chao-ming (汪兆銘), or Wang Ching-wei (汪精衛), who had been Sun's most trusted lieutenant and was the leader of the left wing of the party, led the Wuhan government. He later became increasingly anti-Communist, but he lost a political struggle with Chiang Kai-shek for control over the Kuomintang.

Spence, *Modern China*, 336. In 1939 Wang accepted an invitation from Japan to form a Japanese-supported collaborationist government. The Wang Ching-wei scheme is discussed in 16.2.3.

21  When Chiang relinquished his post, Wang followed suit to facilitate the reunification of the Kuomintang. Cohen, *America's Response*, 109.

22  Spence, *Modern China*, 297, 362. Chiang promised Mrs. Soong that he would eventually convert to Christianity, and he was baptized in the Methodist church in 1929, a year after his marriage to Mei-ling.

23  Ibid., 228. Hosoya Chihiro, "Washinton taisei no tokushitsu to henyō," in *Washinton taisei to Nichibei kankei*, eds. Hosoya Chihiro and Saitō Makoto (Tokyo: University of Tokyo Press, 1977), 32.

## 11.2. US and British China Policy

24  Akira Iriye, *Across the Pacific* (New York: Harcourt, Brace & World, 1967), 118.

25  Cohen, *America's Response*, 105.

26  Ibid., 119.

27  Ibid., 127.

28  Wilson became the twenty-eighth president of the United States in 1913. He stayed in office until 1921.

29  Woodrow Wilson withdrew the United States from the six-power consortium in March 1913, because he judged that it was a scheme to take advantage of China's weakness and infringe on its sovereignty (7.3.2).

30  The British minister in Beijing considered the American action "outrageous," since Yuan had not yet given formal guarantees on the preservation of foreign rights and investments. Spence, *Modern China*, 282. The Japanese government called Wilson's attention to the facts: (1) The Chinese Republic was on the verge of civil war; (2) Yuan had usurped power; (3) Sun and the Kuomintang were disputing Yuan's claims to the presidency and preparing to fight; and (4) Recognition at this time would practically amount to interference in favor of Yuan. While the Wilson cabinet discussed the decision, Song Jiaoren was assassinated and Yuan was implicated in the murder. But Wilson did not give these discordant notes serious consideration. Cohen, *America's Response*, 79.

31  James Reed, *The Missionary Mind and American East Asia Policy, 1911–1945* (Cambridge: Harvard University Press, 1983), 36–37.

32  The influential *Christian Herald*, a nondenominational paper edited in New York, interpreted Yuan's move as a world-historical event: "It reminds one of the acts of Constantine that made Christianity the religion of the Great Roman Empire . . . or of the zeal of Charlemagne in subjecting pagan nations to the yoke of Christ." Ibid., 37.

33  Ibid., 37–38.

34  The powers promised in the Washington customs treaty to hold a tariff conference to implement an interim tariff increase of 2.5 percent on ordinary imports and 5 percent on luxury items in addition to the existing 5 percent duty on all imports, and to have subsequent discussions on tariff autonomy. On the extraterritoriality question, the powers agreed to set up a commission to study the problem further. Cohen,

Chapter 11

*America's Response*, 97.

35 In September 1923, the Guangzhou government presented a note to the diplomatic corps in Beijing stating that foreign obligations charged on customs revenues would be paid, but that part of the remainder collected in the southwestern provinces should be turned over for expenditures by the Guangzhou government. The diplomatic corps in Beijing refused the request and dispatched war vessels to Guangzhou with a view to impressing the Guangzhou government with the determination of the powers. The Guangzhou customs episode convinced Sun Yat-sen of the futility of counting on the support of the Washington powers, and moved him closer to the Soviet Union. Iriye, *After Imperialism*, 40. Hosoya, "Washinton taisei," in *Washinton taisei*, eds. Hosoya and Saitō, 9.

36 John Van Antwerp MacMurray was chief of the Division for Far Eastern Affairs in 1919–24, assistant secretary of state in 1924–25, and minister to China in 1925–29.

37 The Nine-Power Treaty provided, in Article VII, that " . . . there shall be full and frank communication between the Contracting Powers concerned" whenever circumstances seemed to require the application of the treaty.

38 On May 15, 1925, when a group of Chinese laborers broke into a Japanese cotton-spinning mill and smashed some of the machinery, Japanese guards opened fire and killed one of the laborers. This incident was followed by a wave of public outrage. The situation grew tense on May 30, when several hundred demonstrators attacked the police station in the Shanghai concession, where British police officers fired at the demonstrators, killing eleven and wounding twenty. A nationwide movement of protest against Japan and Britain began, and boycotts against British and Japanese goods were declared. The disturbance culminated in the massacre of June 23 in Guangzhou, where British troops fired at a huge rally, killing fifty-two demonstrators and wounding over a hundred. Anti-British and anti-Japanese boycotts spread in the south and Hong Kong. The Beijing government was placed in a difficult position. It did not want to antagonize the powers, but it decided to turn the nationwide outburst of indignation to its own advantage by supporting the militant movements. The Beijing government demanded of the powers early revision of the unequal treaties, as well as a formal apology and an indemnity. Iriye, *After Imperialism*, 60–62. Spence, *Modern China*, 340.

39 Iriye, *After Imperialism*, 73–74.

40 Ibid., 74.

41 Ibid., 73.

42 Ibid., 76.

43 The war was between the forces of Duan Qirui, who controlled Beijing at the time, and the combined forces of Zhang Zuolin and Wu Peifu.

44 Iriye, *After Imperialism*, 107.

45 Ibid., 228.

46 MacMurray was less sanguine about the Nationalists than was Kellogg, and likewise far more concerned about the repercussions that unilateral American recognition would have on cooperation among the powers. Nevertheless, once Kellogg and Coolidge had set the policy, MacMurray worked with T. V. Soong to conclude the treaty. John Van Antwerp MacMurray, *How the Peace Was Lost*: "Developments

*Notes*

Affecting American Policy in the Far East" (Stanford: Hoover Institute Press, 1992), 109.

47  Iriye, *After Imperialism*, 229.

48  Spence, *Modern China*, 381. MacMurray, *How the Peace Was Lost*, 109. Iriye, *After Imperialism*, 229. The United States formally recognized the Nationalists as the government of China on November 3, 1928. British recognition of the Nationalist government was on December 20, 1928, and that of Japan was June 3, 1929. Satō Motoei, *Shōwa shoki tai-Chūgoku seisaku no kenkyū* (Tokyo: Harashobo, 2009), 361.

49  MacMurray, *How the Peace Was Lost*, 120.

50  Ibid., 109.

51  Ibid., 119.

52  Ibid., 110.

53  Ibid., 110. Iriye, *After Imperialism*, 239.

54  In 1927, Aristide Briand, the French foreign minister, announced that France was prepared to enter into a pact with the United States for the mutual outlawing of war. Kellogg first showed little enthusiasm for the bilateral French proposal, but being prompted by American public opinion supporting the idea of outlawing war, proposed that the projected pact be expanded to include the other powers. Briand consented to the enlargement and the pact outlawing war as an instrument of national policy but permitting defensive war was signed by fifteen nations in Paris on August 27, 1928. In succeeding months it was approved by practically all remaining governments.

55  At the meeting with Kellogg, Uchida stated that "Japan, by geographical necessity, is more dependent upon China, economically and ergo politically, than any of the other powers: that she had in the past yielded to the temptation to smash through all obstacles and impose her will on China: that the Washington Conference had then given reason and occasion for her to realize that her own best interest would be served by the policy of live and let live which the American government postulated . . . that the Japanese government, recognizing the American government as the sponsor of the idea of cooperation with regard to Chinese problems, wished to know whether or not we would throw its undoubted influence toward bringing China back into the scheme of cooperation." Uchida meant, MacMurray says, that "the Japanese wanted to know indeed whether the moral influence the United States so far effectively asserted at the Washington Conference was, in practice, to prove discerning and just, or whether it was to prove vacuous and (as they considered it) hypothetical in that it curried favor with the Chinese by encouraging their obduracy against everybody but ourselves." MacMurray, *How the Peace Was Lost*, 118.

56  Iriye, *After Imperialism*, 243.

57  Ibid., 118–119.

58  Ibid., 118–119.

59  See note 38.

60  Iriye, *After Imperialism*, 67, 98.

61  Ibid., 98. The British–Nationalist dispute following the May 30 Incident reduced Hong Kong's trade by 40 percent and British exports to China by 25 percent in 1925. Ibid., 82.

Chapter 11

62   Ibid., 104.

63   Ibid., 99.

64   Kawai Hidekazu, "Hokubatsu eno Igirisu no taiō," in *Washinton taisei to Nichibei kankei*, eds. Hosoya Chihiro and Saitō Makoto (Tokyo: University of Tokyo Press, 1977), 166. Hosoya Chihiro, "Britain and the United States in Japan's View of the International System, 1919–37, in *Anglo–Japanese Alienation*, 1919–1952, ed. Ian Nish (Cambridge: Cambridge University Press, 1982), 12.

## 11.3. Japan's China Policy in the 1920s

65   Kawai, "Hokubatsu," in *Washinton taisei*, eds. Hosoya and Saitō, 165.

66   Iriye, *After Imperialism*, 110.

67   Ibid., 120.

68   Ibid., 120.

69   Ibid., 120.

70   Ibid., 121.

71   Morioka was shot twice at the Japanese consulate and was in peril for three hours. The commander of seventh division of the Nationalist forces, which stopped the violent acts by the soldiers, expressed his regrets to Morioka and told him that the violence had been committed by "bad soldiers" instigated by Communists. On the same day, Chiang Kai-shek, who had been at Wuhan when the incident broke out, arrived at Nanjing. Though he stayed only a few hours, he killed whomever he saw plundering, and closed the Nanjing branch of the Communist Party. Ibid., 128–129.

72   Ibid., 142.

73   Ibid., 133.

74   Ibid., 142.

75   Ibid., 144. Chamberlain, who had been resentful of Shidehara's refusal on several occasions to join Britain in its military operations in China, welcomed Tanaka's decision as one that followed British policy. Kawai, "Hokubatsu," in *Washinton taisei*, eds. Hosoya and Saitō, 182–183. This Shandong expedition epitomized Tanaka's tendency to be easily swayed by those around him. Ibid., 147.

76   Ibid., 147.

77   A conflict started in July 1927 between Hunan warlords on the one hand and Soviet advisers and Communists on the other. They had been allied against Chiang Kai-shek, but the Hunan warlords turned against the alliance when peasant leaders began carrying out agrarian reforms beyond the originally agreed plan which had provided that the only lands of major landlords would be confiscated. Warlords, joined by the recently humiliated landowners, raided the major leftist organizations and peasant associations. Thousands of leftist and peasant forces were killed. Realizing the weakness of their position, Wang Ching-wei and the Wuhan government leaders decided to side with the warlords, and began to try to heal the rift with Chiang. This resulted in an exodus of Russian advisers and Chinese Communists from the revolutionary center in Wuhan. Ibid., 147–148. Spence, *Modern China*, 357.

78   Borodin and other Comintern agents began the long trek back to the Soviet Union by car and truck across the Gobi Desert. Ibid., 358.

79   Ibid., 359.

## Notes

80 Iriye, *After Imperialism*, 153.

81 Ibid., 153, 155.

82 Ibid., 157.

83 Chiang was attended by Huang Fu, foreign minister of the Nationalist government, at both meetings. Mori Tsutomu, vice foreign minister, was present at the Hakone meeting.

84 Chiang wrote in his diary that he got an impression that Tanaka was insincere and was not very supportive of the Nationalist revolution. Hattori Ryūji, *Naze Nichibei kaisen wa sakerarenakattanoka* (Tokyo: NHK Publishing, 2012), 208.

85 Iriye, *After Imperialism*, 157–158.

86 Ibid., 195.

87 Ibid., 197.

88 Ibid., 197.

89 Iriye, *After Imperialism*, 199.

90 The Japanese version stated that about thirty southern soldiers entered the premises of a Japanese resident and started looting. The Japanese was beaten, but he managed to report to the consular police. Two policemen came to the house, but were insulted and threatened by the Chinese soldiers. A few minutes later, a group of thirty Japanese soldiers arrived and chased the Chinese soldiers, who fled to a military barracks two hundred yards away. Shooting started between the Japanese and Chinese soldiers. The Chinese account reported that public-relations officers of the Chinese Fourth Army were pasting some posters up around the house in question. They were interfered with by the Japanese, and fighting broke out. At the same time, a Chinese barracks was attacked by Japanese soldiers, but, under orders, the Chinese did not resist. Ibid., 199–200.

91 Ibid., 200.

92 The supply of food and munitions had been dwindling, and communications between units of the Japanese army were entirely cut off. Consequently, the military leaders felt that they should consent to a truce in order to resupply, regroup, and devise a systematic plan for resumption of fighting. Ibid., 201–202.

93 William Morton, *Tanaka Giichi and Japan's China Policy* (New York: St. Martin's Press, 1980), 118.

94 Japanese casualties at the fighting on May 3 totaled sixty-three, which included ten soldiers killed, forty-one soldiers wounded, and twelve civilians killed. On the Chinese side, war prisoners totaled 1,179. At the fighting that started on May 8, Japanese casualties were twenty-five soldiers killed and 157 soldiers wounded. Chinese casualties were 3,600 soldiers and civilians killed, and 1,400 soldiers and civilians wounded. Satō, *Tai-Chūgoku seisaku*, 244.

95 Morton, *Tanaka Giichi*, 122.

96 Ibid., 204. Chiang Kai-shek stated at the military academy on May 3, 1929, that May 3 was the most humiliating anniversary in history for the Chinese, as the Japanese imperialists had attempted to obstruct the Northern Expedition at Jinan on May 3, 1928, killed many of the revolutionary army soldiers, and occupied the city. Hattori Ryūji, *Higashi Ajia kokusai kankyō no hendō to Nihon gaikō, 1918–1931* (Tokyo: Yuhikaku Publishing, 2001), 209.

Chapter 11

97  Cohen, *America's Response*, 110.

98  Iriye, *After Imperialism*, 204.

99  Morton, *Tanaka Giichi*, 122.

100  Iriye, *After Imperialism*, 207.

101  Ibid., 209.

102  Ibid., 211.

103  The generally accepted explanation about the assassination was that it was Kōmoto's and some of his subordinates' independent action. Kōmoto, however, wrote in 1953 from China, where he had been detained since the end of the war, that it was Muraoka who first decided to kill Zhang Zuolin, and that Kōmoto, having learned about the scheme, conferred with Muraoka and other staff officers (with the exception of Chief of Staff Saitō) about the best way to kill Zhang Zuolin. Hattori, *Higashi Ajia*, 213–215.

104  At one point, he allegedly said, "My life's work is finished." Morton, *Tanaka Giichi*, 132.

105  The Kwantung Army first denied its involvement in the murder, fabricating an account that partisans from the south were the culprits. But the report from the commander in chief of the military police whom Tanaka had sent to Mukden for the investigation of the incident implicated the Kwantung Army. In October, Army Minister Shirakawa and Chief of Staff Suzuki finally told Tanaka the truth. Ibid., 134.

106  Satō, *Tai-Chūgoku seisaku*, 285.

107  Morton, *Tanaka Giichi*, 132.

108  Satō, *Tai-Chūgoku seisaku*, 288.

109  Morton, *Tanaka Giichi*, 150.

110  Satō, *Tai-Chūgoku seisaku*, 283–313. The emperor was advised later by Saionji that he might as well withhold his objection to the government decision lest the emperor should become involved in politics. The emperor henceforth followed Saionji's advice. Ibid., 311. Terasaki Hidenari and Mariko Terasaki Miller, *Shōwa tennō dokuhakuroku: Terasaki Hidenari goyōgakari nikki* (Tokyo: Bungeishunju, 1991), 22–23.

111  Tanaka died a few months after his resignation.

112  Iriye, *After Imperialism*, 249–250.

113  The Kenseikai (憲政会) was renamed as the Minseitō in 1927, when Hamaguchi took over from Wakatsuki as president of the party.

114  Iriye, *After Imperialism*, 241–242, 246–248. Satō, *Tai-Chūgoku seisaku*, 361.

115  Saburi became minister in Beijing in August 1929, accepting Shidehara's request, though he had been expected to be named ambassador to Russia. Saburi had worked under Ambassador Shidehara as counselor of the Japanese embassy in Washington, and attended the Washington Conference as a member of the Japanese delegation in 1921–22. His wife, daughter of Komura Jutarō, died in Beijing while Saburi was attending the Beijing Tariff Conference.

116  Iriye, *After Imperialism*, 263.

117  Ibid., 263.

118  Ibid., 271–272.

*334*

*Notes*

11.4. The London Naval Conference and Its Unfortunate Consequences

119 The emergence of 10,000-ton cruisers carrying eight-inch guns—the maximum allowed under the Washington Treaty—changed the notion of auxiliary ships. The world's navies placed special importance on the superiority of these high-speed "semi-capital ships" with great striking power (eight-inch guns had twice the firepower of six-inch guns). Asada Sadao, *Ryō-taisenkan no Nichibei kankei* (Tokyo: University of Tokyo Press, 1993), 178. Ian Nish, *Japanese Foreign Policy in the Interwar Period* (Westport, CT: Praeger Publishers, 2003), 66.

120 James Crowley, *Japan's Quest for Autonomy* (Princeton, NJ: Princeton University Press, 1966), 48–50.

121 The idea of a 70 percent ratio as Japan's minimum defense requirement vis-à-vis the United States rested on the premise that the approaching (US) armada would need a margin of at least 50 percent superiority over the defending fleet. This spelled a 70 percent ratio for the Japanese navy. This ratio assured Japan of "a strength insufficient to attack and adequate for defense." "The idea of a 70 percent ratio was crystallized into a firmly held consensus—even an obsession—within the Japanese navy." Asada, *Ryō-taisenkan*, 150. At the Washington Conference, Japan accepted a 60 percent ratio for capital ships, but Japan judged that the British and American non-fortification clause in the Five-Power Treaties and the absence of a restriction on auxiliaries would assure Japan of its naval superiority in the Western Pacific.

122 The Japanese navy's "attrition strategy" placed great stress on the absolute tonnage (rather than ratio) of large high-speed submarines, as the submarine squadrons were to engage in relentless attacks on the enemy's approaching main fleet. Asada, *Ryō-taisenkan*, 165.

123 Crowley, *Japan's Quest*, 48.

124 All ranking American naval officers who testified at Senate hearings on the London Naval Treaty admitted: (1) a 10:7 ratio would guarantee the security of the Hawaiian Islands; (2) this ratio would not permit the American navy to wage offensive operations in Japanese waters. Crowley, *Japan's Quest*, 46.

125 Ibid., 49.

126 William Castle had been assistant secretary of state for three years prior to his assignment as ambassador to Japan. He was regarded as pro-Japanese in the State Department. He was sent to Tokyo to help the US naval negotiators in London. During his stay in Japan, he made several speeches in major cities in Japan explaining the US position in the naval disarmament negotiations. Hattori Ryūji, *Shidehara Kijūrō to nijusseiki no Nihon* (Tokyo: Yuhikaku Publishing, 2006), 147–159.

127 Crowley, *Japan's Quest*, 50, 81.

128 Stimson commented with pride to one of his colleagues that the American delegation was "asking a nation greatly superior to us in existing young ships to stop active construction and to accept a position of inferiority to our potential program." Crowley, *Japan's Quest*, 55.

129 Ibid., 54.

130 Asada, *Ryō-taisenkan*, 181.

131 As to the right of supreme command, see chapter 14 (14.1.1).

132 Akira Iriye, *Origin of the Second World War in Asia and the Pacific* (London: Longman Group UK, 1987), 5–6.

133 Seki Shizuo, *Rondon kaigun jōyaku seiritsushi* (Tokyo: Minerva Shobo, 2007), 2.

134 The so-called Ōsumi purge forced out or prematurely retired Vice-Minister Yamanashi Katsunoshin, Vice-Admiral Sakonji Seizō, and Rear-Admiral Hori Teikichi, and others who were committed to naval limitation. Ōsumi, who was navy minister from 1933 to 1936, was a stiff opponent of naval limitation. Ōsumi was a protégé of Katō Kanji. Asada, *Ryō-taisenkan*, 190–191.

135 Ann Waswo, *Modern Japanese Society* (Oxford: Oxford University Press, 1996), 86.

136 Nish, *Interwar Period*, 69. Hattori Ryūji, "Chūso funsō to Rondon kaigun gunshuku kaigi," in *Nichibei kankeishi*, ed. Iokibe Makoto (Tokyo: Yuhikaku Publishing, 2008), 106.

137 Professor Minobe Tatsukichi of Tokyo Imperial University argued that the conclusion of the London Naval Treaty that regulated naval strength was a matter of Article 12, for which the government was responsible to the emperor. Article 12 of the Meiji Constitution prescribed: "The emperor determines the organization and peace standing of the army and navy." Seki, *Rondon kaigun jōyaku*, 244–245.

138 The assassin was a right-wing twenty-three-year-old civilian, apparently acting alone. His motive was a combination of opposition to the treaty and protest against the suffering caused by depression.

# Chapter 12
# The Great Depression, the Impasse in China, and the Road to Mukden

## 12.1. The Great Depression

### 12.1.1. US Economic Contraction in 1929–1933

The New York stock market, after having doubled in the preceding two and a half years, dropped sharply on October 24, 1929,[1] and kept on falling until it hit bottom in June 1932 at a level one-sixth of its peak in September 1929 (table 12.1.1-a). The stock market crash was preceded by a business slowdown that had started earlier, but after October 1929 the stock market drop in turn exacerbated the downturn in the real economy. Industrial production hit a peak in June 1929, dropped almost 40 percent by the end of 1930, and after recovering slightly in early 1931 tumbled steadily until it hit bottom in July 1932 at a level that was half its peak (table 12.1.1-a).

From early 1928 through the middle of 1929, the Federal Reserve Board implemented a tight money policy to stem the speculative fever on Wall Street. The open market sales of securities were conducted from January through August 1928 and discount rates were raised three times in 1928 from 3.5 percent to 5.0 percent, and to 6.0 percent in August 1929.[2] These measures caused some interest-sensitive industries to cool off in 1928. For

*337*

Chapter 12

**Table 12.1.1-a. US Security Price and Industrial Production Indices**

| | Security price indices (1926=100) | | | | | | |
|---|---|---|---|---|---|---|---|
| | 1927 | 1928 | 1929 | 1930 | 1931 | 1932 | 1933 |
| March | 109 | 141 | 196 | 163 | 112 | 54 | 42 |
| June | 114 | 148 | 191 | 142 | 87 | 34 | 77 |
| September | 129 | 162 | 216 | 139 | 76 | 56 | 81 |
| December | 136 | 178 | 147 | 102 | 54 | 45 | 79 |
| | Industrial production indices (1923–1925=100) | | | | | | |
| March | 113 | 112 | 124 | 106 | 89 | 68 | 60 |
| June | 107 | 108 | 125 | 99 | 83 | 59 | 91 |
| September | 106 | 116 | 123 | 92 | 77 | 67 | 85 |
| December | 96 | 109 | 96 | 77 | 68 | 60 | 69 |

*Source:* Lionel Robbins, "1914–1933," in *The Great Depression: Crucial Concepts in Economics,* eds. Geoffrey Wood and Forrest Capie (London: Routledge, 2011), 50 (security price indices), 59 (industrial production indices).

**Table 12.1.1-b. US GNP, Consumption and Private Investment**

| | GNP ($ bil.) | | Consumption ($ bil.) | | Private investment ($ bil.) | | Foreign trade ($ mil.) | |
|---|---|---|---|---|---|---|---|---|
| | Current | 1929 prices | Current | 1929 prices | Current | 1929 prices | Exports | Imports |
| 1927 | 96.3 | 97.3 | 72.6 | 73.2 | 14.7 | 15.2 | 4,982 | 4,240 |
| 1928 | 98.2 | 98.5 | 74.9 | 74.8 | 14.5 | 14.9 | 5,279 | 4,159 |
| 1929 | 104.4 | 104.4 | 79.0 | 79.0 | 14.6 | 14.6 | 5,347 | 4,463 |
| 1930 | 90.4 | 95.1 | 69.9 | 74.7 | 10.6 | 11.0 | 3,949 | 3,104 |
| 1931 | 75.8 | 89.5 | 60.5 | 72.5 | 6.7 | 7.5 | 2,494 | 2,120 |
| 1932 | 58.0 | 76.4 | 48.6 | 66.0 | 3.3 | 4.1 | 1,667 | 1,343 |
| 1933 | 55.6 | 74.2 | 45.8 | 64.6 | 2.9 | 3.7 | 1,736 | 1,510 |
| 1934 | 65.1 | 80.8 | 51.3 | 68.0 | 3.9 | 4.6 | 2,238 | 1,763 |

*Source:* US Department of Commerce, Bureau of the Census, *Historical Statistics of the United States* (Washington, DC: US Government Printing Office, 1975), 224, 229, 263, 319, 964. John Kendrick, *Productivity Trends in the United States* (Princeton: Princeton University Press, 1961), 294–297.

example, new automobile registrations peaked in November 1928, and building permits for new construction peaked in 1928.[3] Private investment figures in 1927–1929 in table 12.1.1-b reflect these moves.

Between 1929 and 1933, the GNP fell by almost half in nominal terms

338

and real GNP declined by about 30 percent (table 12.1.1-b). The fall in output was largely due to a decline in consumption and private investment. The rapid decline in stock prices made consumers and businessmen uncertain about their future income, causing them to cut their spending.[4] Consumption fell by 18 percent and private investment by 75 percent in real terms between 1929 and 1933. Deducting depreciation, net nominal private investment remained negative from 1931 to 1935.[5] The value of exports and imports shrank drastically (table 12.1.1-b), but with US exports accounting for only 3 to 5 percent of its GNP, their impact on its total demand was limited, though the drop in US imports seriously affected the economies of the countries exporting to the United States.

## 12.1.2. The Worldwide Depression

After WWI, European countries were dependent on American capital inflows to repay the war debt to the United States as well as to stay on the gold standard. When US lending to Europe was curtailed in 1928 as a result of the tight US monetary policy,[6] European countries were forced to tighten their monetary policies to maintain service on their external debts as well as to defend their gold standard. European economies started climbing down earlier than the US economy, and after the autumn of 1929, they showed rapid downturns similar to the US economy (table 12.1.2-a).

In Germany, industrial production and wholesale prices leveled off in 1927–1928 and started to decline rapidly from 1929. The German declines were as large as those in the United States. The British business falloff was milder than those in the United States and Germany. British industrial production hit bottom in 1931, a year earlier than the United States and Germany.

The stock-market collapse was communicated to commodity prices. International commodity price indices had plunged to half of their pre-crash levels by the end of 1930. By June 1932, the prices of some items had fallen to levels of one-quarter or less of their previous highs (table 12.1.2-b). In addition to declines in actual demand in the real economy, speculative selling in the commodity market pushed down commodity prices. Bank credit squeezes on commodity buyers in the United States were also a factor.[7] Many Latin American countries, which depended heavily on the US market for their exports of commodities, incurred immense damage.[8] Japan, whose raw silk exports had accounted for 36 percent of its total exports in 1929, was hit

Chapter 12

Table 12.1.2-a. Economic Indicators in US, UK, and Germany

| | Stock price indices | | | Industrial production indices | | | Wholesale price indices | | |
|---|---|---|---|---|---|---|---|---|---|
| | US | UK | Germany | US | UK | Germany | US | UK | Germany |
| 1927 | 60 | 87 | 116 | 89 | 96 | 102 | 99 | 104 | 101 |
| 1928 | 77 | 101 | 113 | 93 | 95 | 99 | 101 | 102 | 102 |
| 1929 | 100 | 100 | 100 | 100 | 100 | 100 | 100 | 100 | 100 |
| 1930 | 75 | 79 | 83 | 81 | 92 | 86 | 91 | 88 | 91 |
| 1931 | 46 | 74 | 51 | 68 | 84 | 68 | 77 | 77 | 81 |
| 1932 | 18 | 52 | 35 | 54 | 84 | 53 | 68 | 75 | 70 |
| 1933 | 40 | 72 | 53 | 64 | 88 | 61 | 69 | 75 | 68 |

*Source:* Charles Kindleberger, *The World in Depression, 1929–1939, Revised and enlarged edition* (Berkeley: University of California Press, 1986), 111–112. Nippon Ginkō Tōkeikyoku, ed., *Meiji ikō honpō shuyō keizai tōkei* (Tokyo: Namiki Shobō, 1999), 395, 397.


Table 12.1.2-b. Declines in Commodity Prices

| | | Coffee (¢ per lb.) | Cotton (¢ per lb.) | Raw silk ($ per lb.) | Wheat ($ per bushel) | Rubber (¢ per lb.) |
|---|---|---|---|---|---|---|
| 1929 | June | 23.50 | 18.04 | 4.96 | 1.50 | 20.56 |
| | December | 15.50 | 16.64 | 4.68 | 1.32 | 16.06 |
| 1930 | June | 13.38 | 13.21 | 3.56 | 1.05 | 12.38 |
| | December | 10.50 | 9.16 | 2.69 | 0.77 | 8.94 |
| 1931 | June | 9.50 | 8.42 | 2.40 | 0.76 | 6.38 |
| | December | 8.38 | 5.78 | 2.18 | 0.74 | 4.63 |
| 1932 | June | 10.10 | 4.99 | 1.27 | 0.64 | 2.69 |
| | December | 10.50 | 5.72 | 1.60 | 0.49 | 3.25 |

*Source:* Charles Kindleberger, *The World in Depression, 1929–1939. Revised and enlarged edition* (Berkeley: University of California Press, 1986), 139, 186.


severely (12.2.2).

The shrinkage in foreign trade was remarkable. Between 1929 and 1934, the value of world trade fell by two-thirds. The falloff in prices contributed greatly to the decline in trade values (table 12.1.2-c). Import restrictions by the United States and other countries in the early 1930s (12.1.4) also contributed to the contraction of world trade, and thus the world economy.

Unemployment worldwide rose to historic levels. It was particularly high in the United States and Germany (table 12.1.2-d). The impact of the depression on livelihoods was even more severe than these figures indicate. Destitute

**Table 12.1.2-c. Shrinkage in World Trade**

| | | 1929 | 1932 | 1934 | 1936 |
|---|---|---|---|---|---|
| Value in millions of dollars | Imports | 35,595 | 13,968 | 11,981 | 13,142 |
| | Exports | 33,021 | 12,885 | 11,333 | 12,581 |
| Price and quantum movement (imports + exports) | Price | 100 | 52.5 | 42.5 | 43.5 |
| | Quantum | 100 | 74.5 | 78 | 86 |

*Source:* The League of Nations, *Economic Statistical Series, 1910–1945* (Tokyo: Far Eastern Booksellers, 1987. Reprinted with permission of United Nations Publications Board), 8.

**Table 12.1.2-d. Unemployment in Selected Countries, 1929–1936 (percent)**

| | 1929 | 1930 | 1931 | 1932 | 1933 | 1934 | 1935 | 1936 |
|---|---|---|---|---|---|---|---|---|
| US | 3.9 | 9.7 | 17.4 | 25.9 | 26.4 | 22.5 | 20.8 | 18.2 |
| UK | 10.4 | 16.1 | 21.3 | 22.1 | 19.9 | 16.7 | 15.5 | 13.1 |
| Germany | 9.3 | 15.3 | 23.3 | 30.1 | 26.3 | 14.9 | 11.6 | 8.3 |
| Canada | 4.2 | 12.8 | 17.4 | 26.0 | 26.5 | 20.6 | 19.0 | 16.7 |
| Japan | n.a | 5.3 | 6.1 | 6.8 | 5.6 | 5.0 | 4.6 | 4.3 |

*Note:* There was considerable underemployment in the Japanese agricultural sector, which accounted for half of the total working population.
*Source:* US Department of Commerce, Bureau of the Census, *Historical Statistics of the United States* (Washington, DC: US Government Printing Office, 1975), 126. International Labour Office, *Yearbook of Labour Statistics, 1941* (Montreal, Geneva: International Labour Office, 1942), 50–51.

farmers were not considered unemployed, and neither were people who had given up seeking work. In the United States, total hours worked in mid-1932 were about 40 percent of those worked in 1929.[9]

## 12.1.3. Financial Crises and British Withdrawal from the Gold Standard

There were three waves of bank failures in the United States, starting with the one in October 1930. The second wave came in the spring of 1931, and the third one from late 1932 through early 1933. By the spring of 1933, the number of banks that had closed their doors reached almost 11,000, representing over 40 percent of the banks that had been in business in 1929 in the United States.

In Europe, the first major bank failure occurred in May 1931, when the Credit-Anstalt in Vienna, one of the largest and most important banks in central Europe, collapsed.[10] In June, German banks faced a rash of bank runs. At this juncture, President Hoover proposed a one-year moratorium on all intergovernmental payments of war debts and reparations,[11] but it was too late to stem the panic. In July 1931, the pound sterling was attacked, since it was widely deemed to be overvalued at $4.86. The Bank of England strived to support the pound, obtaining credits in New York and Paris, but new bank failures in Germany and the Netherlands led to withdrawals of funds from London. On September 21, 1931, Britain left the gold standard, which it had maintained for 77 months at the pre-WWI par.[12] Twenty-five countries followed Britain off gold.[13] Japan at first resisted suspension of the gold standard, to which it had returned as recently as January 11, 1930. But it quit the gold standard on December 14, 1931.[14]

Depreciation of the pound and other currencies applied strong deflationary pressures to countries adhering to the gold standard. In the United States, the Federal Reserve raised the discount rate to discourage gold outflows from 1.5 percent to 3.5 percent in October 1931.[15] The German government, which was more tenacious than the American authorities in clinging to the gold standard, kept the discount rate well above the rates in London and New York. In the fiscal policies as well, both the United States and Germany maintained very contractionary budgets (15.1.1). The global depression drew much of its force from the reinforcing deflationary policies of the United States and Germany to maintain the gold standard.[16]

### 12.1.4. The Smoot–Hawley Tariff and Moves toward Regionalism

Just as the depression was getting under way, President Hoover signed the Smoot–Hawley Tariff Act in June 1930, ignoring the protests of other countries and the dire warnings of economists in the United States.[17] Hoover had proposed in his 1928 presidential campaign tariff hikes limited to agricultural products, but the House Ways and Means Committee chose to consider non-agricultural products as well,[18] and the vote trading among committee members pushed tariffs up.[19] The House passed the bill in May 1929, and the debate in the Senate Finance Committee, with the onset of the economic decline, became more protectionist in tone. When the Senate passed the bill in March 1930, the average US tariff on dutiable imports turned out to be the highest in the 20th century.[20]

The signing of the bill triggered a wave of retaliation. Within two months,

342

all the major trading partners had raised tariffs, and by 1931, 26 countries had quantitative restrictions or exchange controls or both.[21] The Smoot–Hawley Tariff Act, taking retaliation into account, was definitely a deflationary force.[22] Kindleberger asserts that the signing of the bill made it clear that "in the world economy there was no one in charge."[23] He criticizes, from the standpoint of the "theory of hegemonic stability,"[24] the US action as irresponsible on the part of the world's largest economy, with the largest trade surplus and the largest gold reserves.[25]

Before the First World War, Britain maintained an open market for imports from any country, provided countercyclical, or at least stable, long-term lending, and acted as a lender of last resort in international financial crises. After WWI, however, while Britain continued its free-trade policy, it lost its ability to act as a stabilizer in international finance. The United States, on the other hand, remained protectionist in its trade policy, and showed no willingness to function as a lender of last resort.[26] Kindleberger argues that if a country acts as prewar Britain acted, and "especially if a country serves as a lender of last resort in financial crisis, the economic system is ordinarily capable of making adjustments to fairly serious dislocations by means of the market mechanism."[27] But in the early 1930s, contends Kindleberger, " . . . [E]very country turned to protect its national private interest, the world public interest went down the drain, and with it the private interests of all."[28]

In February 1932, Britain, long a bastion of free trade, enacted the Import Duties Act, which accorded British industry and agriculture their first general tariff protection in nearly a century by establishing a 10 percent ad valorem tariff on most imports. In July 1932, the representatives of Britain, the Dominions, India, and the Colonies met in Ottawa, and set up special trade relations within the British Empire, known as the Imperial Preference System.[29] This meant Britain made a fundamental trade policy change from free trade based on the reciprocal most-favored-nation principle to discriminative preferential trade.

Britain, meanwhile, did not give up hope of having an international agreement to stabilize exchange rates and lower tariff levels, and took the initiative to hold the World Economic Conference in London in June 1933. However, the Roosevelt administration, which was in the process of devaluing the dollar (15.1.2), declared, while the conference was in session, that it would oppose any intergovernmental arrangement for currency stabilization. This US announcement dashed all hopes of compromise.

Britain's response was to formalize the sterling area. Empire countries signed the British Empire Currency Declaration, pledging to fix their currencies to the pound sterling and to hold most of their foreign exchange reserves as sterling balances in London. By 1934, France and Germany had respectively formed their own trading zones with their own currency systems. France formed the "gold bloc" with Switzerland, the Netherlands, Italy (until 1934), Belgium, and Luxembourg (until 1935). Germany had barter trade agreements with countries in Central and South Eastern Europe as well as in Latin America, setting artificial parities between partner currencies and requesting them to accept payment in the form of German exports whenever possible.[30] Japan formed, with its colonies and Manchukuo, the yen bloc, which was extended to include portions of north China in 1936 (14.2.1).[31]

For its part, the United States enacted the Reciprocal Trade Agreement Act in 1934, authorizing the president to reduce tariffs by up to 50 percent.[32] The United States concluded reciprocal trade agreements with several Latin American countries, Canada, and some European countries.[33] It was a promising reversal of the traditional US protectionist trade policy that had lasted since the Civil War. In practice, however, the act resulted in the creation of a discriminatory trading group. While the countries with which the United States concluded trade agreements could enjoy reduced tariff rates, those countries outside the trade agreement network remained subject to the Smoot–Hawley tariffs. It was only after World War II that the Reciprocal Trade Agreement Act contributed to the establishment of an open world trading system.[34]

## 12.2. Japanese Economy and Society before the Manchurian Incident

### 12.2.1. The Shōwa Depression

When the stock prices plunged in New York in October 1929, the Japanese economy was subject to a severe deflationary policy that the Hamaguchi Osachi (浜口雄幸) cabinet, with Finance Minister Inoue Junnosuke (井上準之助), had embarked on in July that year to prepare for returning to the gold standard at the prewar parity (9.3.3, 9.3.4). Some economists and business leaders argued that Japan should not hasten to lift the gold embargo. Others

*The Great Depression, the Impasse in China, and the Road to Mukden*

Table 12.2.1-a. The Japanese Government Fiscal and Monetary Policies (¥ million)

|  | 1928 | 1929 | 1930 | 1931 | 1932 | 1933 | 1934 |
|---|---|---|---|---|---|---|---|
| Government expenditures | 1,815 | 1,736 | 1,558 | 1,477 | 1,950 | 2,255 | 2,163 |
| Government bond issues | 458 | 194 | 80 | 213 | 834 | 920 | 866 |
| Specie reserve | 1,062 | 1,072 | 826 | 469 | 425 | 425 | 466 |
| Bank of Japan note issue | 1,739 | 1,642 | 1,436 | 1,330 | 1,426 | 1,544 | 1,627 |
| Money supply (M1) | 13,977 | 14,151 | 13,461 | 12,921 | 13,410 | 14,179 | 15,063 |

*Note:* Government expenditures are not those of the general government, but those of general accounts (一般会計).

*Source:* Nippon Ginkō Tōkeikyoku, ed., *Meiji ikō honpō shuyō keizai tōkei* (Tokyo: Namiki Shobō, 1999), 133 (Government expenditures), 167 (Money supply), 170, 172 (Specie reserve and note issue), 252–253 (Stock prices), 395 (Wholesale prices). Mark Metzler, *Lever of Empire* (Berkeley: University of California Press, 2006), 277 (Money supply). Emi Kōichi and Shionoya Yūichi, *Zaisei shishutsu*, ed. Ōkawa Kazushi (Tokyo: Tōyōkeizai Shinpōsha, 1966), 163 (Government expenditures). Ōkura-shō Shōwa Zaiseishi Henshūshitsu, ed., *Shōwa zaiseishi, vol. 6, Kokusai* (Tokyo: Tōyōkeizai Shinpōsha, 1954), 3 (Government bond issues).

insisted that if Japan were to return to the gold standard, it should do so at a new devalued parity.[35] Inoue insisted, however, that Japan, being a major nation ranking with the United States and Britain, should return to gold at the old parity, and that the appreciated yen and deflationary policies to maintain it would make the Japanese economy stronger in the long run, eliminating inefficient and uncompetitive firms.[36] He ordered the Bank of Japan to tighten the money market, and reduced expenditures of the 1929 fiscal year budget, which had already been in force, by 79 million yen, or 4.6 percent. The fiscal 1930 budget was further reduced by 11 percent (table 12.2.1-a).[37]

Wholesale prices and commodity prices started to decline soon after the implementation of these retrenchment measures, and the declines were accelerated by the Wall Street stock-market crash in October 1929, as well as the government announcement in November of the return to the gold standard on January 11, 1930.[38] By the end of 1929, the yen/dollar rate had risen close to the prewar par. The export market shrinkage and the appreciated yen combined to decrease the value of Japan's exports by 44 percent in 1930 and another 20 percent in 1931. Domestic consumption fell by 8 percent in 1930 and 9 percent in 1931. Private investment dropped by 14 percent in 1930 and 26 percent in 1931. Nominal GNP decreased by 18 percent between 1929 and 1931 (table 12.2.1-b).

Inoue's policy was based on David Hume's classic theory of the price-

*345*

Chapter 12

**Table 12.2.1-b. Japan's Major Economic Indicators**

|  | 1928 | 1929 | 1930 | 1931 | 1932 | 1933 | 1934 |
|---|---|---|---|---|---|---|---|
| Wholesale prices | 100 | 97 | 80 | 68 | 75 | 85 | 87 |
| Stock price indeces | 100 | 88 | 60 | 45 | 61 | 87 | 103 |
| $/¥100   high | 48 | 49 | 49-3/8 | 49-3/8 | 37-1/4 | 31-1/4 | 28-1/2 |
|       low | 44-3/4 | 43-3/4 | 49 | 34-1/2 | 19-3/4 | 20-1/2 | 20-3/8 |
| Exports (¥ mil.) | 2.0 | 2.6 | 1.5 | 1.1 | 1.4 | 1.9 | 2.2 |
| Imports (¥ mil.) | 2.2 | 2.7 | 1.5 | 1.2 | 1.4 | 1.9 | 2.3 |
| Consumption (¥ mil.) | 12.7 | 12.3 | 11.3 | 10.2 | 10.2 | 11.2 | 12.5 |
| Private investment (¥ mil.) | 0.9 | 1.1 | 0.9 | 0.7 | 0.6 | 0.9 | 1.2 |
| Nominal GNP (¥ mil.) | 16.5 | 16.3 | 14.7 | 13.3 | 13.7 | 15.3 | 17.0 |

*Source:* Nippon Ginkō Tōkeikyoku, ed., *Meiji ikō honpō shuyō keizai tōkei* (Tokyo: Namiki Shobō, 1999), 200 (Nominal GNP), 252–253 (Stock prices), 281 (Exports), 292 (Imports). 320 (Yen/dollar rates), 395 (Wholesale prices). Nakamura Takafusa, *Senzenki Nihon keizai seichō no bunseki* (Tokyo: Iwanami Shoten, 1971), 333 (Consumption, private investment). Ōkawa Kazushi, Takamatsu Nobukiyo, and Yamamoto Yūzō, "Kokumin shotoku," in *Chōki keizai tōkei*, eds. Ōkawa Kazushi, Shinohara Miyohei, and Umemura Mataji (Tokyo: Tōyōkeizai Shinpōsha, 1974), 200 (GNP).

specie-flow mechanism, which held that under the gold standard system, domestic price deflation was supposed to increase exports, bringing gold into the country, increasing money supply, and improving the economy. In the early 1930s, however, amidst general deflation in the gold bloc, it was necessary to out-deflate other countries to increase exports. But prices in Japan were still higher than those in the United States and other European countries. Japan's trade balance continued to be in deficit.

Speculative selling of the yen led to a massive outflow of the gold. The gold reserve decreased from 1,072 million yen in 1929 to 469 million yen in 1931. The ratio of the BOJ's specie reserves to its note issue was now lowered to 35 percent (table 9.3.1-b).[39] The money supply (M1) fell by 5 percent in 1930 and 4 percent in 1931 (table 12.2.1-a).

Coming on top of the decade-long tight monetary policy (9.3.1), the triple effects of the harsh deflationary measures that started in July 1929, the onset of the World Depression in the fall of 1929, and the return to the gold standard at the prewar par in January 1930 made the Japanese depression, known as the Shōwa Depression (昭和恐慌), very severe.

## 12.2.2. Distress in Rural Communities and Businesses

The impact of the Shōwa Depression was most seriously felt in rural communities and small and medium businesses. In 1930, there were 823 business dissolutions, mostly small and medium enterprises, with total liabilities of 218 million yen.[40] Labor disputes resisting wage cuts and layoffs hit their prewar peak in 1930. Labor disputes took place in many large businesses also, including Kanebō, a leading textile mill, which suffered a strike on an unprecedented scale, though it had prided itself on its good labor relations record.[41]

As for rural depression, a survey conducted by a government agency on rural economic difficulties showed that tenant farmers' average annual income per household halved from 945 yen in 1928 to 462 yen in 1931 (table 12.2.2-a), and that 58.6 percent of owner farmers and 76.4 percent of tenant farmers were in deficit in 1930.[42]

Farmers' indebtedness averaged 830 yen per household in 1929 and 846 yen in 1932. Only 27 percent of those loans were made by banks; the rest came from private moneylenders with high interest.[43] Banks were unwilling to lend to small farmers. In 1932, loans for farmers aggregated 4,546 million yen, of which over 57 percent carried interest over 10 percent.[44]

In terms of agricultural products, rice, the Japanese staple food, accounted for about 50 percent of the value of the main agricultural crops (table 12.2.2-b).

Market prices of rice in Japan were determined by yearly crops in Japan proper and also by imports from Korea and Taiwan. Though imports accounted for 12 to 19 percent of the Japanese rice production (table 12.2.2-c), they represented about 22 to 35 percent of the Japanese market, since only 55

Table 12.2.2-a. A Survey of Farmers' Household Finances

| | Farmer type | 1928 | 1929 | 1930 | 1931 | 1932 | 1933 | 1934 |
|---|---|---|---|---|---|---|---|---|
| Income per household (yen) | Owner | 1,525 | 1,509 | 961 | 723 | 777 | 914 | 918 |
| | Tenant | 945 | 901 | 601 | 462 | 552 | 631 | 628 |
| Farmers in deficit (%) | Owner | 39.2 | 42.0 | 58.6 | 55.6 | 30.2 | 21.2 | 22.6 |
| | Tenant | 32.6 | 51.7 | 76.4 | 51.6 | 30.0 | 24.7 | 41.7 |
| Number of households surveyed | Owner | 31 | 37 | 51 | 54 | 29 | 21 | 22 |
| | Tenant | 17 | 30 | 42 | 44 | 27 | 22 | 38 |

*Source:* Kawai Ichirō et al., eds., *Kyōkō kara sensō e, Kōza Nihon shihonshugi hattatsushi-ron*, vol. 3 (Tokyo: Nippon Hyoron Sha, 1968), 349.

Chapter 12

**Table 12.2.2-b. Relative Importance of Principal Agricultural Products in Japan**

| | Value in million yen | | | Percentage of total | | |
|---|---|---|---|---|---|---|
| | 1926 | 1931 | 1936 | 1926 | 1931 | 1936 |
| Rice | 1,836 | 913 | 1,865 | 49 | 46 | 53 |
| Silkworm cocoons | 662 | 276 | 387 | 17 | 14 | 11 |
| Wheat, barley, oats | 302 | 155 | 331 | 8 | 8 | 9 |
| Vegetables | 252 | 168 | 231 | 7 | 8 | 7 |
| Other cereals | 229 | 127 | 219 | 6 | 6 | 6 |
| Meat and eggs | 161 | 133 | 177 | 4 | 7 | 6 |
| All others | 326 | 238 | 314 | 9 | 12 | 9 |
| Total | 3,769 | 2,010 | 3,525 | 100 | 100 | 100 |

*Source:* E. F. Penrose, "Japan, 1920–36," in E. B. Schumpeter, ed., *The Industrialization of Japan and Manchukuo, 1930–40* (London: Routledge, 2000. First published 1940 by Macmillan), 131.

percent of the domestic crop was marketed in Japan, the rest being consumed by farmers and their families.[45] Rice from Korea and Taiwan pushed down Japanese rice market prices (table 12.2.2-c), but the Japanese government did not take any restrictive measures against it, because such action would raise the cost of living of industrial workers. The welfare of industrial workers was regarded as more important than that of farmers. It was also considered that imposing tariffs or establishing a quota system on rice from Korea and Taiwan would be inconsistent with the Japanese government's colonial policy of treating Korea and Taiwan as integral Japanese territories.[46]

The most damaging consequence of the Great Depression to Japan's agricultural economy was the collapse of the raw-silk market. The world market price of raw silk dropped from $4.96 per pound in June 1929 to $2.69 in December 1930 and to $1.27 in June 1932 (table 12.1.2-b). In terms of value of Japanese agricultural output, cocoons were second to rice (table 12.2.2-b). More than two million farm households, or roughly 40 percent of Japan's agricultural population of some five and a half million households, raised silkworms in 1930.[47] In the mountainous districts of central Honshū, where paddy land was relatively scarce and commercial rice production difficult, upwards of 80 percent of local farm households raised silkworms. In these areas, sericulture was their major, or sole, source of income. In other areas, sericulture was an adjunct to the cultivation of rice and other crops. For both groups, the fall in prices of raw silk and cocoons proved devastating.

In 1929, of Japan's raw-silk production, 91 percent was exported, and of

*348*

The Great Depression, the Impasse in China, and the Road to Mukden

Table 12.2.2-c. Rice in Japan—Production, Imports and Prices

| | Domestic production (1,000 *koku*) | Imports quantities (1,000 *koku*) | | Percentage of imports of domestic production (%) | | Prices (¥ per *koku*) |
|---|---|---|---|---|---|---|
| | | Korea | Formosa | Korea | Formosa | |
| 1926 | 59.7 | 5.1 | 2.2 | 8.5 | 3.6 | 38.4 |
| 1927 | 55.6 | 5.2 | 2.6 | 9.3 | 4.7 | 35.9 |
| 1928 | 62.1 | 7.0 | 2.4 | 11.3 | 3.9 | 31.4 |
| 1929 | 60.3 | 5.3 | 2.2 | 8.7 | 3.7 | 29.2 |
| 1930 | 59.6 | 5.1 | 2.2 | 8.5 | 3.7 | 27.3 |
| 1931 | 66.9 | 8.0 | 2.7 | 11.9 | 4.0 | 18.5 |
| 1932 | 55.2 | 7.2 | 3.3 | 13.0 | 6.0 | 20.7 |
| 1933 | 60.4 | 7.5 | 4.2 | 12.4 | 7.0 | 21.4 |

*Note:* One *koku* is equivalent to about 180 liters of rice.
*Source:* E. F. Penrose, "Rice Culture in the Japanese Economy," in *Japanese Economic History, 1930–1960*, vol. III, ed. E. B. Schumpeter (London: Routledge, 2000. First published 1940 by Macmillan), 151–152.

Table 12.2.2-d. Japan's Raw-Silk Production and Exports

| | 1929 | 1930 | 1931 | 1932 | 1933 | 1934 |
|---|---|---|---|---|---|---|
| Raw-silk exports (mil. yen) | 781 | 417 | 355 | 382 | 391 | 287 |
| Index | 100 | 53 | 46 | 49 | 50 | 37 |
| Raw-silk exports / Raw-silk production (%) | 91 | 78 | 83 | 84 | 80 | 72 |
| Raw-silk exports to US / Japan's raw-silk exports (%) | 97 | 95 | 97 | 94 | 91 | 84 |
| Raw-silk exports / Japan's total exports (%) | 36 | 28 | 31 | 27 | 21 | 13 |

*Source:* Nippon Ginkō Tōkeikyoku, ed., *Meiji ikō honpō shuyō keizai tōkei* (Tokyo: Namiki Shobō, 1999), 284 (Raw-silk exports). E. F. Penrose, "Japan, 1920–36," in *The Industrialization of Japan and Manchukuo, 1930–40*, ed. E. B. Schumpeter (London: Routledge, 2000. First published 1940 by Macmillan), 220–221 (Raw-silk production). Mitsubishi Economic Research Bureau, *Japanese Trade and Industry* (London: Macmillan, 1936), 508 (Raw-silk exports to the United States).

Japan's raw-silk exports, 97 percent was shipped to the United States (table 12.2.2-d). Between 1929 and 1934 raw-silk exports to the United States fell from 758 million yen to 241 million yen. The US share of Japanese raw-silk exports declined a little from 97 percent to 84 percent. Japan's share of the US raw-silk market remained at over 90 percent during this period.[48]

Though the prices fell, cocoon production was maintained almost at the

*349*

Chapter 12

previous level. The price declines were rather accelerated by farmers' tendency to try to compensate for the income decrease by producing more cocoons. Silk being a luxury item, raw-silk demand was elastic to income rather than price. In 1931, the market price of cocoons was about 20 percent lower than the estimated cost of cocoon production.[49]

### 12.2.3. Anti-Government/Zaibatsu and Pro-Army Sentiment

Facing economic difficulties in rural communities and businesses, Inoue had no intention of changing his basic stance of implementing retrenchment policies. He was a firm believer in the liquidationist view that deflation would perform a necessary cleansing function by eliminating uncompetitive and inefficient suppliers and thus make the nation stronger in the long run.[50] Though Inoue agreed to provide emergency loans to farmers and small and medium businesses in distress,[51] the loans, totaling some 200 million yen in 1930–1931, were far short of the amount needed to alleviate the hardship and grievance of farmers and small businesses.

Historically, the prewar Japanese government was quite merciless toward farmers.[52] The heaviest burden of national and local taxation had been borne by the farming classes. In the mid-1930s, farmers paid 31.36 percent of their income in taxes on average, whereas commercial and industrial people paid 13.53 percent.[53] High taxes on farmland raised rents for tenants and caused incessant tenant–landowner disputes.[54] As observed above, the Japanese government's colonial rice policy also made Japanese farmers' economic life difficult. In addition, a large inflow of unemployed urban workers returning to the villages in the 1930s as a result of declines in demand for urban labor exacerbated the depressed conditions in the farm villages.[55] The difference in per capita income between the primary sector and the manufacturing sector, which had been 1:2 in favor of the latter in 1920, widened to 1:4 in 1930. The severe rural distress and the government's pitiless policies as above helped to give rise to anti-government agrarianism as observed below.

The episode of large-scale dollar buying by zaibatsu banks in the fall of 1931 after the British withdrawal from the gold standard also contributed to the general populace's anti-establishment feeling. As Inoue did not restrict the sale of dollars through the Yokohama Specie Bank, a large amount of dollars was bought forward. As the end-of-December settlement date approached, the hopes of the speculators who had sold the yen short against the dollar

350

grew steadily dimmer.[56] On December 11, however, the Minseitō (民政党) cabinet collapsed (13.1.4), and on December 13, the day when the Seiyūkai (政友会) cabinet of Inukai Tsuyoshi (犬養毅) was inaugurated, Finance Minister Takahashi Korekiyo (高橋是清) abandoned the gold standard. By the end of the month, the yen had dropped by 30 percent, bringing huge gains to the speculators. A newspaper report that the dollar purchases by the zaibatsu banks were speculative in nature caused a furor in public opinion, despite explanations by the banks that these dollars were needed for future international trade.[57]

As discussed in 15.3.1, thanks to Takahashi's reflationary policies, Japan's recovery from the Great Depression was faster than other major economies. But it was too late to avoid the unfortunate political developments that took place in Japan in the 1930s. Japanese society had become increasingly unstable through the wrenching economic adjustments in the 1920s, and, in particular, severe deflationary policies in 1929–1931. The accumulation of grim economic conditions gave rise to widespread and open dissatisfaction with the government. It was a grievance against the entire social and political system.[58] The discontent was particularly strong in economically distressed rural communities, where political activism, which had existed since the early 1920, became active in the early 1930s.[59] The activists asserted that party politicians and the zaibatsu leaders were corrupt, dishonest, selfish, and uncaring about the plight of farmers.[60]

The farmers' resentment was now communicated to the army.[61] The young officers assigned to the regiments in the countryside learned from newly recruited soldiers about the impoverishment of their families, and those officers were now acutely aware of the seriousness of the social and political implications of the problem.[62] Now that the political parties and the zaibatsu were discredited as elite groups in the eyes of the farmers, the army could present itself as an alternative force that had at heart the interests of the nation, and could offer hope for a solution to the hardships of the rural depression.[63] The army on its part moved to gain rural support. The war minister toured famine-stricken areas, and the army started its own public works schemes to provide rural employment.[64] Tokutomi Sohō commented that the villages were now "the army's electoral constituency."[65]

One of the solutions offered by the army involved Japanese control of Manchuria, which supposedly would allow successful export of Japan's surplus

Chapter 12

population, the growing of more foodstuffs for those at home, opportunities for small and medium-sized Japanese businesses to thrive, and other benefits.[66]

For a group of young officers who were planning a bold scheme in Manchuria, the distress of rural communities provided a useful justification for their action, and they were now fairly sure that their action would have public support.

## 12.3. The Impasse in Japan's China Policy

### 12.3.1. Unfavorable Developments after the Washington Conference

As observed in 7.4, the Japanese government committed itself to the new international order in East Asia that the United States proposed at the Washington Conference in 1921–1922. But support in Japan for this government decision was weak. Many Japanese felt that Japan should pursue its China policy independently of the United States.

The US initiative and the Japanese government commitment to it might have achieved a successful outcome, (a) had the two nations not faced bitter immigration disputes in the mid-1920s; (b) had the American economy continued to be prosperous; (c) had the United States continued to pursue a reasonably free trade policy; and (d) had China become a stable nation with administrative integrity, having a good relationship with the powers as the Nine-Power Treaty had expected.[67]

The realities that unfolded were, however, quite different. (a) The Japanese immigration exclusion act of 1924, being enacted two years after the Washington Conference, severely shook US–Japanese relations. Japanese rightists argued that since Americans discriminated against the Japanese because of their Asian ethnicity, they had no right to restrict Japanese activities in Asia (8.5.4).[68] (b) The American capitalism that had been a paradigm for Japanese businessmen now looked permanently depressed and hopeless (12.1.1).[69] (c) Just when the Great Depression was getting under way, the United States enacted protective tariffs that triggered retaliation by other countries and a consequent shrinkage in world trade (12.1.4). The United States appeared too preoccupied with protecting its own narrow interests to pay attention to the requirements of a functioning system of world trade. (d) China remained split until the late 1920s, and the Kuomintang, which achieved national unification in 1928, started a revolutionary diplomacy

*The Great Depression, the Impasse in China, and the Road to Mukden*

declaring that all unequal treaties should be replaced with new arrangements (11.1.2). Meanwhile, the United States, under the strong influence of the missionary community, continued to be pro-Chinese and severely critical of Japan's China policies (11.2.1, 11.2.2).

Those Japanese who had been critical of their government's policy of following the lead of the United States now found opportunities to express their discontent more loudly. The Japanese army and rightists became more assertive in advocating a unilateral China policy.

## 12.3.2. Japan's Position in Manchuria

Since 1905, when Japan had acquired the Kwantung Leased Territory from Russia, along with the South Manchuria Railway (SMR) and the so-called railway-zone (10.4.3), Japan's traditional Manchurian policy had been one of safeguarding these rights and strengthening Japan's influence in the rest of Manchuria that remained under the authority of the Chinese government. With a vast land area and rich natural resources, Manchuria was regarded as the key to Japan's economic development, and was often labeled in the media as the "lifeline" of Japan.[70] The area designated later as Manchukuo's territory—the four provinces of Liaoning (遼寧), Jilin (Kirin 吉林), Heilongjiang (黒竜江), and Rehe (Jehol 熱河), plus some parts of Inner Mongolia—covered an area of 1.3 million square kilometers, which was 3.4 times that of Japan, with an arable land area 2.8 times that of Japan.[71] During the first three decades of the twentieth century, the population grew at an average rate of about 4.2 percent a year to reach 31 million in 1930–31, with heavy immigration of Han Chinese from below the Great Wall.[72] Manchuria was the world production center of soybeans,[73] and the Fushun (撫順) colliery in Liaoning province was the world's largest open-cut coal mine.[74] Japan's direct investment in Manchuria in 1930 amounted to $550 million, equivalent to 56 percent of Japan's total foreign direct investment (table 10.4.3-a).

Japan's rights in Manchuria began to be undermined, however, from December 1928, when Zhang Xueliang (張学良) pledged allegiance to the Kuomintang government at Nanjing (11.1.2). With support from the Kuomintang leadership and Zhang Xueliang, a comprehensive and systematic anti-Japanese movement was launched throughout Manchuria.

A double tariff on goods entering and leaving the Japanese-controlled port of Dalian threatened to cripple the city. A hefty hike in the export levy on raw

*353*

materials shipped from various parts of China to Japan's Kwantung Leased Territory would suffocate Japanese industry there.[75] The construction of projected Japanese railways was opposed, expansion of the Fushun mining district was protested, pressure was brought to bear on Chinese house owners and landlords to raise the rents of Japanese and Korean tenants or to refuse renewals of rental contracts, and Chinese railways were encouraged to stage a fierce freight-rate competition with the South Manchuria Railway. The competition with Chinese railways and the decline in world demand for soybeans, the major freight item of the South Manchuria Railway, combined to reduce South Manchuria Railway profits substantially.[76]

Technically, the protocol annexed to the Sino–Japanese Treaty of Beijing of 1905 barred China from building any railway lines parallel to the South Manchuria Railway or from constructing any lines which might endanger the commercial viability of the Japanese lines.[77] Zhang Xueliang, however, harbored a plan to build a great Chinese railway network in Manchuria with financial help from the Nanjing government. In April 1931, C. T. Wang (Wang Zhengting 王正廷), Nanjing's foreign minister, announced that China would demand that all leased territories and all railroad and other communication rights, as well as jurisdiction over foreigners, be given back to China.[78]

### 12.3.3. An Impasse in Shidehara's China Policy

Foreign Minister Shidehara, who succeeded Tanaka in August 1929, tried to deal with these challenges through peaceful negotiations with the Chinese government. He requested negotiations citing the Treaty of Beijing of 1905, which recognized the Japanese rights in Manchuria which had been ceded to Japan by Russia by the 1905 Portsmouth Peace Treaty.[79] The Chinese side reluctantly agreed to participate in "technical talks," and negotiations were scheduled to commence in late May 1931 between former foreign minister Uchida Yasuya, who had recently been appointed president of the South Manchuria Railway, Zhang Xueliang, and Kao Chiyi, the representative of the Nationalist government in Manchuria. But on the eve of the conference, both Zhang and Kao were "taken ill" while in Nanjing, and the negotiations were suspended.[80] The interruption in diplomatic communications between the two countries was overtaken by a crisis created mainly by two developments that occurred in June: a general boycott of Japanese goods in Shanghai as a result of a clash between Chinese and Korean farmers in the Wanpaoshan region in Manchuria, which were followed by subsequent clashes between Chinese and Koreans in Korea;[81] and the murder of Captain Nakamura Shintarō, an intelligence officer, while he was on a secret mission in north Manchuria.[82]

On the Chinese side, Chiang was not in the position to take a moderate stance vis-à-vis Japan. There were still several warlords who were hostile to Chiang and seeking opportunities to topple the Nanjing government. Any compromises made by Chiang through negotiations with Japan would make him politically vulnerable to attacks by those warlords. He had to maintain a strong stance against Japan.[83]

By midsummer of 1931, Shidehara's China policy seemed to have reached an impasse. The Chinese anti-Japanese movement showed no sign of abating, and the United States, with which Shidehara had endeavored to maintain friendly relations, remained sympathetic toward China and totally uncooperative with Japan's China policy (11.2.2). In Manchuria, Japanese resident businessmen, being directly exposed to Chinese anti-Japanese activities, formed organizations to protect their rights and interests in Manchuria.[84] They claimed that if the Chinese anti-Japanese policy was left to take its natural course, it would leave no place for the Japanese in Manchuria, and strongly urged the Japanese government to take more vigorous and effective measures to protect them. In Japan, members of the opposition Seiyūkai, which had attacked the Minseitō government in the uproar following the London Naval Conference (11.4.2), now renewed their attacks on the government, contending that so long as Shidehara continued his pledge not to resort to force in negotiations with the Nationalist government, none of the problems in China would be solved.[85]

The army's China specialists believed that the Nationalist government responded only to the threat or actual use of force, and viewed Shidehara diplomacy with open contempt and increasing concern.[86] They were now convinced that no means other than direct action could solve the Manchuria problem. Given the political and economic situation in Japan at the time, they were confident that they could obtain the Japanese public's support for military action in Manchuria.[87]

## 12.4. The Road to Mukden

### 12.4.1. The Young Officers' Informal Groups in the Army

In the late 1920s, there emerged within the army informal groups of young officers who believed that Japan should prepare for a "total war" for which radical changes were needed in political, economic, and institutional structures. In foreign policy, they advocated a more aggressive Japanese policy toward Manchuria, which they believed was vitally important for Japan's economic expansion as well as for its defense against Soviet Russia. The precursor of such groups was the Futabakai (二葉会), which was formed in 1927 by some twenty military academy graduates of the fifteenth to the eighteenth classes.[88] In late 1927, the Mokuyōkai (木曜会) was inaugurated by a group of younger officers.[89] The Mokuyōkai and the Futabakai often had joint meetings under the name of the Issekikai (一夕会). In 1930, the Sakurakai (桜会), a new grouping consisting of officers below the rank of lieutenant colonel, was formed.[90] It was a group of radical young officers who believed that revolutionary means would be necessary to accomplish their aims.

The dire economic situation in Japan and undesirable developments in China and Manchuria convinced those officers of the need for the urgent implementation of their schemes. In March, 1931, the Sakurakai members plotted a coup d'état aiming to establish a government under the leadership of the army.[91] They were, however, dissuaded by senior members of the Issekikai, such as colonels Nagata Tetsuzan (永田鉄山) and Okamura Yasuji (岡村寧次),[92] who judged that a coup at the time would disrupt the unity of the army as well as that of the nation. Nagata and Okamura, in restraining the Sakurakai, stated their opinion that internal reform should be preceded by external action, and that internal reform measures should be undertaken within legal bounds.[93]

Activist army officers, especially those of the Sakurakai, were strongly influenced by civilian "restructuring" movement leaders like Kita Ikki (北一輝) and Ōkawa Shūmei (大川周明). Both were nationalist, socialist, and revolutionary. Kita's book *Nihon kaizō hōan taikō* (日本改造法案大綱 A general outline of measures for the reconstruction of Japan) was read by many young militarists and radicals as a gospel of national reform. Ōkawa, a scholar of Indian philosophy who lectured in the military staff colleges, was instrumental in spreading "restructuring" ideology through his contacts in high military and bureaucratic circles.[94] Both Kita and Ōkawa argued as socialists that the political and economic inequalities of contemporary Japan had been produced by the selfish actions and interests of a few privileged groups—the political parties, capitalists, and the court nobility. As nationalists and revolutionaries, they argued that Western thought had weakened the traditional Japanese spirit, and that Japan should be renovated through a coup d'état by the military, which was the only element of society that remained loyal to traditional Japanese values.[95]

Kita argued that revolutionary changes were needed in existing institutions, and that internal change should precede external expansion. Ōkawa, on the other hand, emphasized the instrumental role of an external crisis that would arouse the broad support necessary to accomplish domestic change.[96] This question of priority between internal action and external action was, more specifically, whether a coup d'état in Japan should precede or follow action in Manchuria. The "Manchuria first" view was promoted in the army by such officers as colonels Nagata and Okamura of the Ministry of the Army, as well as Colonel Itagaki Seishirō (板垣征四郎) and Lieutenant Colonel Ishiwara Kanji (石原莞爾) of the Kwantung Army.[97]

### 12.4.2. The Army's Manchurian Policy and the Kwantung Army's Moves

In June 1931, the senior officers of the Ministry of the Army and the General Staff adopted a document, "Manshū mondai kaiketsu hōshin no taikō" (満州問題解決方針の大綱 A general outline of a solution for the Manchurian problem), the first army document of major importance concerning the army's Manchurian policy.[98] The outline was prepared by a joint committee composed of five section chiefs of the Ministry of the Army and the General Staff. It read as follows:[99]

1) The alleviation of the anti-Japanese activities of the Zhang regime shall continue to be undertaken primarily through negotiation by the Foreign Office.

2) In spite of the above-mentioned efforts, should anti-Japanese activities be intensified, military action might become necessary.

3) Internal as well as international understanding are absolutely necessary for the settlement of the Manchurian problem. The Ministry of the Army . . . and the General Staff . . . shall make careful preparations . . .

so that, in the event of military action, public opinion will support the measures and the powers will not take opposing or suppressive steps.

4) The General Staff shall make plans concerning necessary forces in the event of military action.

5) Measures with regard to cultivation of internal and international understanding shall be undertaken with a view to achieving results in approximately one year; that is, by the spring of 1932.

6) The army shall maintain close contact with the Kwantung Army in order to make them act with discretion.

While they recognized the possibility of military action in Manchuria, they intended to continue to seek a negotiated settlement with China and to engage in public relations at home and abroad for about a year to obtain broad understanding regarding a direct and forceful solution in Manchuria. Considering the increasingly tense Sino–Japanese relationship, the outline sounded cautious. The senior Japanese military leaders' prime concern in Manchuria was Russia's military intervention. It is possible they may have thought that coming to an understanding with powers other than Russia would discourage adverse Russian moves in Manchuria.[100] It is also noteworthy that they were wary of possible rash actions by the Kwantung Army.

Ishiwara and Itagaki, meanwhile, had developed their own Manchurian policy. They were convinced that military action should be taken sooner than the spring of 1932, and it should be an operation designed to seize all Manchuria. They had made careful estimates of the capabilities of the Chinese troops in Manchuria and drafted a systematic and detailed plan of operations which would enable the Kwantung Army to extend its control throughout Manchuria.[101]

Their plan of operations was not submitted to central army authorities, but it is believed that Itagaki, when he went to Tokyo in July 1931, showed it to a limited number of officers of the Army Ministry and the General Staff, including Nagata, director of the military affairs section of the Army Ministry,[102] and Major General Tatekawa Yoshitsugu (建川美次), director of the strategic department of the General Staff.[103] Most likely Itagaki also told them that the action would be executed in late September.[104]

On September 1, Ishiwara briefed new Kwantung Army commander and lieutenant general Honjō Shigeru (本庄繁) on the plan of operations. Honjō

358

*The Great Depression, the Impasse in China, and the Road to Mukden*

had been appointed to the post on August 1, 1931, and arrived at Port Author in late August. He approved the plan as the one to be implemented "in the event of any major crisis."[105] Though Ishiwara did not reveal the whole Itagaki–Ishiwara scheme, he felt that he would be able to implement the plan under Honjō. Honjō's deputy, Chief of General Staff and Major General Miyake Mitsuharu (三宅光治), had previously received the plan and put his seal on it without having looked at so much as a page of it, saying, "It would be fine if we could use this later, wouldn't it?"[106] He did not, however, approve the idea of deliberately creating the crisis when Itagaki and Ishiwara hinted at such a possibility.[107]

Meanwhile, Miyake felt the need to confer with central headquarters about the increasingly tense situation. He sent a cable on September 14 urging Tatekawa and Major General Koiso Kuniaki (小磯国昭), director of the military affairs department of the Ministry of the Army, to come to Manchuria for "extensive talks."[108] Army Minister Minami Jirō (南次郎) and Chief of General Staff Kanaya Hanzō (金谷範三) decided to send Tatekawa with specific orders to caution Honjō against any rash action.

Tatekawa sent a confidential cable to Itagaki on September 15, letting him know of the purpose of his mission. Itagaki and Ishiwara decided to execute their plan before Tatekawa's meeting with Honjō. Tatekawa arrived at Mukden (奉天) on September 18, where Itagaki received him. He was scheduled to meet Honjō at Port Arthur (Lushun 旅順) the next day to convey his message.[109] Around 10:00 p.m. on the 18th, a small detachment of the Kwantung Army, at the instruction of Itagaki, ignited an explosive along the South Manchuria Railway a few miles north of Mukden to support the fiction of a Chinese attack. Fighting between the Kwantung Army troops and Chinese troops followed. Kwantung Army Headquarters at Port Arthur received the news of the clash a little after 11:00 p.m.

Miyake immediately summoned all staff officers. Ishiwara stressed the need for full-scale operations. Other staff officers supported Ishiwara. Honjō now decided to order a general assault. By the end of the next day all the major towns adjacent to the South Manchuria Railway were in Japanese hands.[110]

*359*

Chapter 12

## NOTES

### 12.1. The Great Depression

1   On October 24, the Dow Jones industrial average had fallen to 198 from 381 on September 3. It ended the year at 250. Ibid., Charles Kindleberger, *The World in Depression, 1929–1939*. Revised and enlarged edition (Berkeley: University of California Press, 1986), 105.

2   The discount rate was raised three times in 1928 from 3.5 percent to 5.0 percent. It was kept at 5.0 percent from July 1928 until August 1929. In an environment of rapidly rising stock prices, this pace of raising the rates did not keep pace with the rise in market rates, giving banks a strong incentive to borrow from the FRB. Milton Friedman and Ann Schwartz, *A Monetary History of the United States, 1867–1960* (Princeton: Princeton University Press, 1963), 289.

3   Christina Romer, "The Nation in Depression," in *The Great Depression Crucial Concept in Economics*, vol. II, eds. Geoffrey Wood and Forrest Capie (London: Routledge, 2011), 274–275.

4   Romer, "The Nation in Depression," in *The Great Depression*, eds. Wood and Capie, 277.

5   James Wills and Martin Primack, *The Great Depression of the 1930s* (Englewood Cliffs, NJ: Prentice-Hall, 1980), 359–360.

6   Table: US Capital Exports ($ million)

|  | 1928 1–6 | 1828 7–12 | 1929 1–6 | 1929 7–12 | 1930 1–6 | 1930 7–12 |
|---|---|---|---|---|---|---|
| Europe | 459.4 | 143.5 | 87.6 | 54.4 | 197.9 | 35.0 |
| Germany | 200.5 | 76.6 | 21.0 | 8.5 | 156.8 | 10.0 |
| Other areas | 382.4 | 245.8 | 370.3 | 159.0 | 370.7 | 171.4 |
| Total | 841.8 | 389.3 | 457.9 | 213.4 | 568.6 | 206.4 |

*Source:* Charles Kindleberger, *The World in Depression, 1929–1939, Revised and enlarged edition* (Berkeley: University of California Press, 1986), 56.

7   Kindleberger, *The World in Depression*, 113.

8   Introduction, *The Great Depression*, vol. I, eds. Wood and Capie, 11.

9   Thomas Cochran, *The Great Depression and World War II* (Glenview, IL: Scott, Foresman and Company, 1968), 16.

10  The Austrian government sought a loan for $21 million from major countries to rescue the Credit-Anstalt, but the French government interposed the condition that the Austrian government should abandon its customs union with Germany. The Austrians refused, and the rescue scheme failed. The idea of an Austrian–German customs union was promoted by Bruning, the German chancellor, as a policy to divert the electorate from the Nazis, who had recorded alarming gains in the election in September 1930. France opposed the customs union as being contrary to the Treaty of Versailles that required Austria to uphold its political independence. Kindleberger, *The World in Depression*, 146–147.

11  The moratorium was announced on June 20, 1931. It was hailed in Berlin and endorsed in London as "a very great gesture on the part of the United States." But France, which was owed 52 percent of the total of reparation payments, refused to

*Notes*

accept. Hoover stated that the French stood to lose only $100 million in reparations from the moratorium, while the United States would lose $250 million, and threatened to isolate France by dealing separately with each country over the moratorium. France eventually agreed in July. Ibid., 150–151. Barry Eichengreen, *Golden Fetters* (New York: Oxford University Press, 1995), 277.

12  The pound fell to $3.75 within a few days and reached a low of $3.25 in December.

13  They were largely countries in the British Empire, Scandinavia, Eastern Europe, and such traditional trading partners as Argentina, Egypt, and Portugal.

14  The dollar–yen rate went down from $48.375 per ¥100 in 1931 to $20.688 at the end of 1932. The average rate in 1932 was $28.120 per ¥100.

15  Peter Temin, *Lessons from the Great Depression* (Cambridge: MIT Press, 1991), 29.

16  Ibid., 34.

17  A total of 1,028 economists in the United States asked President Hoover to veto the legislation, and 34 protests were lodged with the State Department from foreign countries.

18  More than 1,100 people gave testimony before the Ways and Means Committee and almost 11,000 pages of testimony were published. Judith Goldstein, *Ideas, Interests, and American Trade Policy* (Ithaca: Cornell University Press, 1993), 124–125.

19  The committee members supported tariff hikes on products in other industries in return for support for tariff hikes on products in their own constituents' industries.

20  Smoot–Hawley did not, contrary to popular belief, establish the highest tariff schedule in American history. Average ad valorem tariffs on dutiable imports in the Smoot–Hawley Act were 44.9 percent. Those in the Tariff of Abominations of 1828 were 61.7 percent, and those in the McKinley Tariff of 1890 were 48.4 percent. In the case of Smoot–Hawley, however, price declines during the depression pushed up the average ad valorem equivalent of specific duties that were fixed duties per quantity. The overall average rate as a result rose to 53.2 percent in 1931 and 59.1 percent in 1932. Alfred Eckes, Jr., *Opening America's Market: US Foreign Trade Policy since 1776* (Chapel Hill, NC: University of North Carolina Press, 1995), 106–107.

21  Goldstein, *American Trade Policy*, 125.

22  Kindleberger, *The World in Depression*, 125. Temin, *Lessons from the Great Depression*, 81.

23  Kindleberger, *The World in Depression*, 126.

24  Eichengreen, *Golden Fetters*, 4. Hegemonic stability theory argues that an open, liberal, and stable world requires the existence of hegemonic or dominant power. Robert Keohane first used the term "hegemonic power." A similar line of thought is expressed by other scholars, including Robert Gilpin and Steven Krasner, as well as Charles Kindleberger. R. J. Barry Jones, ed., *Routledge Encyclopedia of International Political Economy* (London: Routledge, 2001), 406–408, 661–664.

25  Kindleberger, *The World in Depression*, 291. Throughout the interwar period, Britain remained the world largest trading nation, followed by the United States. Britain had a chronic merchandise trade deficit, though the deficit was more or less covered by surpluses in service revenues. The United States, on the other hand, ran a chronic and large trade surplus in goods. It had a chronic service-trade deficit, but the amount was only about half as much as the merchandise trade surplus. In 1929, the

*361*

Chapter 12

United States held 37.7 percent and France 15.8 percent of the world gold reserves.

26　Kindleberger, 290–291.

27　Ibid., 289. Temin disagrees with Kindleberger's assertion. Temin argues that the financial crisis of 1931 was not attributable to the absence of a hegemonic power, but to the fact that all the powers, including Britain and the United States, moved in the same direction, pursuing deflationary policies to recreate prewar monetary arrangements. Temin, *Lessons from the Great Depression*, 36. Eichengreen also expresses skepticism about Kindleberger's hegemonic stability argument. He emphasizes that international cooperation among the powers, rather than the existence of a hegemonic power, had held the gold standard in place in the pre-WWI years, but after the war there was no such cooperation. Eichengreen, *Golden Fetters*, 9.

28　Kindleberger, *The World in Depression*, 291.

29　League of Nations, *Commercial Policy in the Interwar Period: International Proposals and National Policies* (Geneva: League of Nations, 1942), 75. John Rothgeb, Jr., *U.S. Trade Policy: Balancing Economic Dreams and Political Realities* (Washington, DC: CQ Press, 2001), 39.

30　League of Nations, *Commercial Policy*, 69–71.

31　Between 1935 and 1938, the share of Japan's exports going to Korea, Formosa, Manchuria, and north China rose from 41 percent to 63 percent. League of Nations, *Economic Statistical Series, 1910–1945*, 22 (Geneva: League of Nations, 1948, Reprinted in Tokyo by Far Eastern Booksellers with permission of United Nations Publications Board), 35.

32　The main provisions of the Reciprocal Trade Agreements Act of 1934 were as follows: The president might negotiate on a reciprocal basis to lower or raise American tariffs by up to 50 percent of their Smoot–Hawley levels; negotiations were to be conducted on a product-by-product basis; any agreements reached with foreign governments could take effect without any further action by Congress; negotiations were to be conducted using the unconditional most-favored-nation approach; and the president's authority to negotiate was limited to three years. Rothgeb, *U.S. Trade Policy*, 46.

33　The United States concluded the first Reciprocal Trade Agreement with Cuba in August 1934. Cuba lowered tariffs on US-made textiles, automobiles, and farm products in exchange for lower US sugar tariffs. Additional agreements followed in 1935 with Belgium, Brazil, Canada, Colombia, Haiti, Honduras, the Netherlands, and Sweden, and in 1936 with Costa Rica, Finland, France, Guatemala, and Switzerland. By 1939, the United States had negotiated agreements with 21 countries, including Britain, but Japan and Germany remained outsiders through the prewar period. Ibid., 47.

34　The Reciprocal Trade Agreement Act was extended in 1937, 1940, 1943, and 1945, and the Truman government used the 1945 version to establish the General Agreement on Tariffs and Trade in 1947.

12.2. Japanese Economy and Society before the Manchurian Incident

35　Oppositions to returning to the gold standard at the prewar parity were voiced, for example, by economic journalists like Ishibashi Tanzan (石橋湛山) and Takahashi

*362*

Kamekichi (高橋亀吉), and by business executives of manufacturing industries like Mutō Sanji (武藤山治), the president of Kanebō (鐘紡). Ishibashi and Takahashi insisted that Japan should let the value of the yen fall to a realistic level against the dollar to decide the yen's parity with the dollar. Mutō warned that returning to the gold standard would cause great hardship to the medium and small manufacturing industries. On the other hand, Inoue had not a few supporters in the academic and business circles, especially big banks. They were of the view that Japan needed rationalization of industries, and returning to the gold standard at the prewar parity would give Japan a chance to implement it. Nakamura Takafusa, *Shōwa kyōkō to keizai seisaku* (Tokyo: Kodansha, 1994), 81–88. Nakamura Takafusa, *A History of Shōwa Japan, 1926–1989*, trans. Edwin Whenmouth (Tokyo: University of Tokyo Press, 1998), 70.

36  Nakamura Takafusa, "Depression, Recovery, and War, 1920–1945," in *The Economic Emergence of Modern Japan*, ed. Kōzō Yamamura (Cambridge: Cambridge University Press, 1997), 129.

37  Kawai Ichirō et al., eds, *Kyōkō kara sensō e, Kōza Nihon shihonshugi hattatsushiron*, vol. 3 (Tokyo: Nippon Hyoron Sha, 1968), 170–171. Nakamura, *A History of Shōwa Japan*, trans. Whenmouth, 71.

38  Mark Metzler, *Lever of Empire* (Berkeley: University of California Press, 2006), 222.

39  Under the terms of the Convertible Banknotes Law of 1884 and later revisions, the Bank of Japan's note issue followed the fiduciary model of the Bank of England. The formal "rules of the game" were as follows: The note issue was to be entirely covered by a specie reserve of silver and gold coins and bullion, later exclusively gold coins and bullion, but further issue could be made, backed by a fiduciary reserve consisting of government bonds and other securities, up to a limit fixed by law at ¥70 million in 1888, ¥85 million in 1890, ¥120 million in 1899, and raised by Takahashi Korekiyo to ¥1 billion in 1932. An additional issue against securities (the excess fiduciary issue) could also be made. If the excess issue extended over 15 days, it required the finance minister's approval and was taxed at a minimum rate of 5 percent (reduced to 3 percent in 1932).

During the era of the gold embargo from 1917 to 1929, the ratio of the BOJ's specie reserves to its note issue never fell below 60 percent. In this way, although the Japanese government restricted gold exports, it continued to operate a kind of "shadow" gold standard in the 1920s. The relationship between the gold reserve and the note issue actually broke down when Inoue restored the gold standard, and huge gold outflows forced the ratio down to 35 percent in 1931. Metzler, *Lever of Empire*, 223, 250–251, 275.

40  Kawai et al., eds, *Kyōkō kara sensō e*, 174.

41  Nakamura, *A History of Shōwa Japan*, trans. Whenmouth, 73.

42  Kawai et al., eds, *Kyōkō kara sensō e*, 349.

43  Ibid., 350–351.

44  Fumin Kyōkai, *Nihon nōgyō nenkan* (Tokyo: Fumin Kyōkai, 1942), 66. Andō Yoshio, *Kindai Nihon keizaishi yōran* (Tokyo: University of Tokyo Press, 1975), 122.

45  E. F. Penrose, "Japan, 1920–36," in *The Industrialization of Japan and Manchukuo, 1930–40*, ed. E. B. Schumpeter (London: Routledge, 2000. First published 1940 by

Macmillan), 138.

46  Ibid., 145.

47  Ann Waswo, "Japan's Rural Economy in Crisis," in *Economics and Finance, 1931–1945, Imperial Japan and the World, 1931–1945*, vol. III, ed. Antony Best (London: Routledge, 2011), 182.

48  Giovanni Federico, *An Economic History of the Silk Industry* (Cambridge: Cambridge University Press, 1997), 214.

49  Waswo, "Japan's Rural Economy in Crisis," in *Imperial Japan*, ed. Best, 182. The Mitsubishi Economic Research Bureau reported that the average cost of producing cocoons in 1931 was ¥3.62 per *kwan* (one *kwan* is equivalent to 3.75 kilograms), whereas the market price was ¥3.02 per *kwan*. Mitsubishi Economic Research Bureau, *Japanese Trade and Industry* (London: Macmillan, 1936), 257.

50  Nakamura Takafusa, *Shōwa kyōkō to keizai seisaku* (Tokyo: Kodansha, 1994), 93. Wakatabe Masazumi, "Ushinawareta jūsannen no keizai seisaku ronsō," in *Shōwa kyōkō no kenkyū*, ed. Iwata Kikuo (Tokyo: Tōyōkeizai Shinpō-sha, 2004), 90, Nakamura Muneyoshi "Kin kaikin o meguru shinbun media no ronchō," in *Shōwa kyōkō no kenkyū*, ed. Iwata Kikuo (Tokyo: Tōyōkeizai Shinpōsha, 2004), 119.

51  The loans were made through a program of fiscal investment and loans (財政投融資計画). By using this program, Inoue avoided depending on fiscal spending from the general account. The use of this scheme in such way as this was started by Inoue at this time. Kawai et al., eds., *Kyōkō kara sensō e*, 176.

52  The very strong protections for Japanese farmers today contrast with historical harsh treatment of farmers.

53  Shigeichi Mayeda, "Our Stricken Agriculture," in *Imperial Japan and the World, 1931–1945*, ed. Antony Best (London: Routledge, 2011), 6–7.

54  The number of tenancy disputes was 1,866 in 1928, but increased to 2,478 in 1930, and by 1934 to 5,828. Mathias and Polland, eds., *Cambridge Economic History, III*, 1132. Penrose, "Japan, 1920–36," in *The Industrialization of Japan and Manchukuo*, ed. Schumpeter, 138.

55  Kōzō Yamamura, "Then Came the Great Depression," in *Interwar Economy of Japan*, ed. Michael Smitka (New York: Garland Publishing, 1998), 280.

56  Many speculators bought the dollar forward at a premium for delivery at the end of December. If Japan were to go off the gold standard by the end of December, the spot price of the yen would plunge (the spot price of the dollar would rise sharply). Speculators would gain much at the end of December, fulfilling their forward contracts. However, if Japan were to stay on the gold standard, the spot dollar price at the end of December would probably be at the same level as in September. Speculators would lose the difference between the spot dollar price and the contracted price.

57  For example, Mitsui Bank purchased British government securities. When those funds were frozen by the British government, Mitsui Bank bought dollars to cover them, but this was erroneously reported as dollar-buying speculation. Nakamura, "Depression, Recovery, and War," in *The Economic Emergence*, ed. Yamamura, 131. Inoue criticized the forward dollar buying, but economists like Takahashi Kamekichi and Ishibashi Tanzan argued rightly that it was inappropriate for Inoue, who had

*Notes*

lifted the gold embargo, to criticize the forward buying of the dollar. Wakatabe, "Ushinawareta jūsannen," in *Shōwa kyōkō*, ed. Iwata, 104.

58  Nakamura Takafusa, *Shōwashi I* (Tokyo: Tōyōkeizai Shinpōsha, 1993), 128.

59  While farmers' unions with strong links to the socialist political parties had existed since the early 1920s, the early 1930s brought a rise of right-wing activism in rural communities. Nakamura, *A History of Shōwa Japan*, trans. Whenmouth, 78, 91.

60  Sandra Wilson, *The Manchurian Crisis and Japanese Society, 1931–33* (London: Routledge, 2002), 128–129.

61  G. C. Allen, *A Short Economic History of Japan* (London: George Allen & Unwin, 1972), 117.

62  Nakamura, *History of Shōwa Japan*, trans. Whenmouth, 78.

63  Wilson, *The Manchurian Crisis*, 129.

64  R. Dore and Ōuchi Tsutomu, "Rural Origins of Japanese Fascism," in *Dilemmas of Growth in Prewar Japan*, ed. James Morley (Princeton; Princeton University Press, 1971), 197.

65  Ibid., 197.

66  Wilson, *The Manchurian Crisis*, 129.

### 12.3. The Impasse in Japan's China Policy

67  Article 1 of the Nine-Power Treaty provided that the "Contracting Powers, other than China, agree . . . to respect the sovereignty, independence, and the territorial and administrative integrity of China" (section 1), and "to provide the fullest and most unembarrassed opportunity to China to develop and maintain for herself an effective and stable government" (section 2).

68  Minohara Toshihiro, *Hainichi iminhō to Nichibei kankei* (Tokyo: Iwanami Shoten, 2002), 236.

69  Kimura Masato, "The Zaikai's Perception of and Orientation towards the United States in the 1930s," in *Tumultuous Decade: Empire, Society, and Diplomacy in 1930s Japan*, eds. Kimura Masato and Minohara Toshihiro (Toronto: University of Toronto Press, 2013), 6.

70  The term "lifeline" was coined by Matsuoka Yōsuke in a Diet speech in January 1931. Louise Young, *Japan's Total Empire* (Berkeley: University of California Press, 1998), 88.

71  Table: The Japanese Empire's Land Area and Arable Land Area in 1936

|  | Total area (1,000 km$^2$) | Arable land (% of total area) |
|---|---|---|
| Japan | 383 | 60.5 (15.8) |
| Korea | 221 | 43.3 (19.6) |
| Formosa | 36 | 8.1 (22.6) |
| Manchukuo | 1,303 | 168.1 (12.9) |

*Source:* E. B. Schumpeter, *The Industrialization of Japan and Manchukuo, 1930–1940* (New York: Macmillan, 1940), 75.

72  Japanese residents in the Kwantung Leased Territory numbered 153,905 in 1920, and those in Manchukuo 376,036 in 1936. Schumpeter, "Industrialization of Japan and Manchukuo," in *Japanese Economic History*. ed. Schumpeter, 78.

Chapter 12

73  Chi-ming Hou, *Foreign Investment and Economic Development in China, 1840–1937* (Cambridge: Harvard University Press, 1965), 84.

74  C. F. Remer, *Foreign Investments in China* (New York: Howard Fertig, 1968), 490.

75  William Fletcher III, *The Japanese Business Community and National Trade Policy, 1920–1942* (Chapel Hill, NC: University of North Carolina Press, 1989), 75.

76  The South Manchuria Railway's profit as a percentage of capital dropped to 3.3 percent in 1931 from 11.8 percent in 1929, notwithstanding postponement of repairs to trains and rails as well as dismissal of employees in 1931. Sadako Ogata, *Defiance in Manchuria: The Making of Japanese Foreign Policy, 1931–1932* (Berkeley: University of California Press, 1964), 18. Young, *Japan's Total Empire*, 38. W. G. Beasley, *Japanese Imperialism, 1894–1945* (Oxford: Clarendon Press, 1987), 191.

77  Hattori Ryūji, *Manshū jihen to Shigemitsu Chūka kōshi hōkokusho* (Tokyo: Nihon Tosho Center, 2002), 107–108. James Crowley, *Japan's Quest for Autonomy* (Princeton: Princeton University Press, 1966), 103.

78  Marius Jansen, "The Manchurian Incident, 1931," in *Japan Erupts*, ed. James Morley (New York: Columbia University, 1984), 137.

79  Hattori, *Manshū jihen to Shigemitsu*, 107–108.

80  Crowley, *Japan's Quest for Autonomy*, 104.

81  The Japanese government encouraged Japanese and Korean farmers to settle in Manchuria by granting loans to them. While few Japanese responded to this policy, many Koreans emigrated across the border. In June 1931, Chinese farmers in Wanpaoshan region attempted to eject an entire Korean community from the region, and clashed with Japanese police. While there were no fatal casualties, Korean–Chinese antagonism, probably abetted by Japanese propagandists, spread to Korea. Several hundred Chinese residents were attacked, killed, or injured. In retaliation, the Chinese in Shanghai initiated a comprehensive boycott of Japanese goods. Crowley, *Japan's Quest for Autonomy*, 104.

82  Captain Nakamura Shintarō, an intelligence officer attached to the general staff of the Kwantung Army, had set out on a secret mission in the interior of Manchuria in June and mysteriously disappeared. Investigations conducted by the Kwantung Army produced evidence that he was arrested by Chinese troops and shot to death. The foreign and war ministries rejected the Kwantung Army's proposals for determined reprisal. Negotiations for settlement started in September between Minister Shigemitsu and Nationalist Finance Minister T. V. Soong, but the Mukden Incident occurred before they were able to work out a settlement. Akira Iriye, *After Imperialism* (Chicago: Imprint Publications, 1990), 291, 297.

83  Ibid., 295–296.

84  The largest of the Japanese resident groups in Manchuria was the Manshū Seinen Renmei (満州青年連盟 Manchuria Youth League), which had been formed in 1928 with three thousand members joining in the first year. It dispatched representatives to Japan in the summer of 1931, and asked the Japanese government to "strike a blow at the Chinese government." Ogata, *Defiance in Manchuria*, 38–39, 49–50. Crowley, *Japan's Quest for Autonomy*, 105.

85  Crowley, *Japan's Quest for Autonomy*, 105.

86  Ibid., 96.

*Notes*

87   Iriye, *After Imperialism*, 284.

### 12.4. The Road to Mukden

88   The Futabakai was organized by Colonel Nagata Tetsuzan, Colonel Okamura Yasuji, Colonel Obata Toshirō, and their classmates of the sixteenth class at the military academy. Nagata, Okamura and Obata were all graduates of the Army War College with honors. Its membership was soon enlarged to include military academy graduates from the fifteenth class to the eighteenth. Among the members were Itagaki Seishirō (sixteenth class) and Tōjō Hideki (東条英機) (seventeenth class). Kawada Minoru, *Manshū jihen to seitō seiji* (Tokyo: Kodansha, 2010), 9–13.

89   The Mokuyōkai mainly consisted of military academy graduates from the twenty-first to the twenty-fourth classes. The leader was Lt. Colonel Suzuki Teiichi (鈴木貞一) (twenty-second class). Among the members was Ishiwara Kanji (twenty-first class). Ibid., 9.

90   The Sakurakai was a grouping coalescing around Lieutenant Colonel Hashimoto Kingorō (橋本欣五郎) (twenty-third class), who was chief of the Russian section of General Staff Headquarters. Hashimoto was strongly influenced by Kita Ikki. Seki Hiroharu, "The Manchurian Incident, 1931," in *Japan Erupts*, ed. James William Morley (New York: Columbia University, 1984), 158.

91   Ogata, *Defiance in Manchuria*, 32. The March Incident was a plot to bring about the formation of a military government under Army Minister Ugaki.

92   Nagata was then director of the military affairs section of the Ministry of the Army and Okamura was director of the personnel section of the Ministry of the Army.

93   Ogata, *Defiance in Manchuria*, 32.

94   Ibid., 23.

95   Ibid., 25.

96   Ibid., 25.

97   Ibid., 33. Ishiwara was of the opinion that though internal reform was extremely difficult, a military conflict on the continent would create favorable conditions for sweeping political and economic reform at home. Ibid., 48–49. Ishiwara had known Itagaki since the day when both were students at a military preparatory school in Sendai. In 1921–22, they renewed their close connections when both were attached to the Expeditionary Forces in Hankou. In October 1928, Ishiwara was assigned to Kwantung Army staff headquarters in Port Arthur as second senior staff officer. Itagaki was assigned to Kwantung Army staff headquarters in May 1929 as senior staff officer replacing Kōmoto Daisaku. Probably there were Issekikai maneuvers behind this personnel change. Seki, "The Manchurian Incident, 1931," in *Japan Erupts*, ed. Morley, 143. Kobayashi Michihiko, *Seitō naikaku no hōkai to Manshū jihen* (Tokyo: Minerva Shobo, 2010), 177. The Itagaki–Ishiwara team led the Kwantung Army ideologically, politically, and strategically, with the commander-in-chief and the chief of staff providing merely nominal leadership. Ogata, *Defiance in Manchuria*, 55. Marius Jansen writes, "The Manchurian Incident was the joint product of Ishihara's conception and Itagaki's implementation or perhaps of Ishihara's ingenuity and Itagaki's influence." Seki, "Manchurian Incident," in *Japan Erupts*, ed. Morley, 139.

98   Ogata, *Defiance in Manchuria*, 53–54.

Chapter 12

99   Kawada, *Manshū jihen*, 33–34, 37.

100  Kobayashi, *Seitō naikaku no hōkai*, 155.

101  Crowley, *Japan's Quest for Autonomy*, 114. At that time the Chinese had at their disposal about 20,000 men in and around Mukden, and close to 250,000 troops in Manchuria as a whole. To deal with these, the Kwantung Army had one integrated division as a nucleus plus six battalions guarding the railway lines for a total strength of slightly more than 10,000 men. It was a strategic necessity for the Kwantung Army to make "a lightning strike" in order to destroy the numerically far superior Zhang forces. Seki, "The Manchurian Incident," in *Japan Erupts*, ed. Morley, 144. Ishiwara believed that with his plan the Kwantung Army might conquer the territory with minimum reinforcement. If necessary, he believed it possible to accomplish the task without the support of the home authorities. Ogata, *Defiance in Manchuria*, 42. Satō Motoei, *Shōwa shoki tai-Chūgoku seisaku no kenkyū* (Tokyo: Harashobo, 2009), 377–378. Yoshihisa Tak Matsusaka, *The Making of Japanese Manchuria, 1904–1932* (Cambridge : Harvard University Asia Center, 2001), 382.

102  In November, 1930, Nagata had long talks with Ishiwara and Itagaki in Mukden about military solutions to the problems of Manchuria. Nagata told Ishiwara that, while he was well aware of the need for Ishiwara's project for taking over Manchuria, if he expressed formal approval of it, implementation of the plan would become impossible. Nagata, however, accepted Ishiwara's request to obtain two 24-centimeter-caliber cannons from Japan. Seki, "The Manchurian Incident," in *Japan Erupts*, ed. Morley, 162.

103  Kobayashi Tatsuo, Kobayashi Yukio, and Seki Hiroharu, *Manshū jihen zenya* (Tokyo: Asahi Shimbunsha, 1987), 399.

104  Ibid., 399. Ogata, *Defiance in Manchuria*, 55–56.

105  Crowley, *Japan's Quest for Autonomy*, 117.

106  Seki, "The Manchurian Incident," in *Japan Erupts*, ed. Morley, 153. Miyake had been chief of staff of the Kwantung Army since July 1928.

107  Itagaki and Ishiwara argued to Miyake that central headquarters would extend ex post facto approval of the military action once it was taken. Miyake did not agree, and told them that he would not approve any actions that might produce significant diplomatic problems for the government. Crowley, *Japan's Quest for Autonomy*, 119. When Miyake went to Tokyo in June 1931, he was cautioned by Army Minister Minami against rash actions. Seki, "The Manchurian Incident," in *Japan Erupts*, ed. Morley, 176.

108  Iriye, *After Imperialism*, 298.

109  Tatekawa knowingly allowed the fatal night to elapse before transmitting the orders from the war minister and the chief of the general staff in order to cooperate with the Itagaki–Ishiwara plot. Ogata, *Defiance in Manchuria*, 59.

110  The occupied towns included, besides Mukden, Changchun (長春), Andong (安東), Fengcheng (鳳凰城), and Yingkou (営口). Mukden and Changchun were towns along the South Manchuria Railway. Andong, Fengcheng, and Yingkou were towns along the railways owned by the Chinese but constructed with Japanese capital. Kawada, *Manshū jihen*, 19.

# Chapter 13
# Developments after the Mukden Explosion

## 13.1. The Japanese Government, Army Leadership, and the Kwantung Army

### 13.1.1. The Government's Non-expansion Policy

At the cabinet meeting on the morning of September 19, 1931, when Army Minister Minami Jirō (南次郎) stated that fighting had started in Mukden as the result of Chinese provocation (he had not been informed otherwise), Foreign Minister Shidehara presented reports from the consul general in Mukden indicating that the incident was a premeditated action of the Kwantung Army,[1] and insisted that further military actions should be strictly forbidden. Prime Minister Wakatsuki concurred with Shidehara, and ruled that the crisis should be settled promptly as a local issue. Minami first learned then that what he had feared had occurred in Mukden, and he "lost courage" to propose the reinforcements to the Kwantung Army that had been decided at a joint meeting of the Army Ministry and the General Staff held prior to the cabinet meeting.[2] Minami promised to abide by the cabinet decision of non-expansion "with some anguish."[3] Chief of Staff Kanaya Hanzō (金谷範三) made a similar pledge at his imperial audience on the afternoon of the 19th.

*369*

Kanaya could not behave otherwise before the emperor, who firmly supported the cabinet decision.[4] Except for the expedition to Jilin (吉林) on September 21, to which he gave reluctant ex post facto consent,[5] Kanaya managed to prevent any further Kwantung Army military operations until the Qiqihar invasion in November (discussed below).[6]

Kanaya could not, however, stop Korean Army commander Hayashi Senjūrō (林銑十郎) from sending reinforcements to Manchuria to help the Kwantung Army's Jilin expedition.[7] Hayashi's act created the problem of violation of the right of supreme command (14.1.1), as he defied Kanaya's order prohibiting the troop dispatch. The Korean Army commander also ignored the rule that troop moves across borders should first be approved by the cabinet.[8] The Army Ministry and the General Staff demanded ex post facto cabinet approval, threatening withdrawal of the Army Minister from the cabinet. Wakatsuki gave in, as the alternative was the resignation of the whole cabinet.[9] With the cabinet approval, the chief of staff obtained a retroactive imperial sanction.

General Hayashi won media fame as the "border-crossing general."[10] Sir Francis Lindley, the British ambassador in Tokyo, observed, "Any action they may take to defend her [Japan's] interests in Manchuria will receive unanimous public support."[11] In fact, the army's successful operations in Manchuria received enthusiastic support from the public at large. Sick of the depression and the pervading sense of insecurity, the Japanese were eager for any kind of change, and they had the naive belief that Japanese control over Manchuria would usher in some kind of bright future for the whole of Japan. The army's military achievements fostered such optimism among the Japanese people.[12]

## 13.1.2. Division within the Army and the Kwantung Army's Initiatives

In Mukden, meanwhile, having received the order from Tokyo prohibiting further military actions, the Kwantung Army staff officers had a conference on the night of September 19 with the director of the Operations Department of the General Staff, Tatekawa, who had arrived at Mukden on the previous day (12.4.3). At the conference, the staff officers tried to convince Tatekawa of the necessity of pursuing their program of outright occupation and annexation of all Manchuria. Tatekawa told them, however, that the thinking in the Operations Department of the General Staff was neither occupation of Manchuria nor building a new state of Manchuria severed from China, but establishing a pro-Japanese regime in South Manchuria under the former Qing emperor Puyi (溥儀) through political maneuvering.[13] It fell far short of their expectations, but after a long, heated debate, Ishiwara and Itagaki decided to follow Tatekawa, who was a leader of their comrades (12.4.3). They revised their plan along the lines of Tatekawa' guidance, and sent it to central headquarters with Honjō's approval.[14]

The responses from central headquarters were divided, however. Vice-Chief of Staff Ninomiya Harushige (二宮治重) immediately expressed his support, while Kanaya kept his non-expansion position.[15] Director of the Military Affairs Department of the Army Ministry Koiso expressed his support,[16] but the minister and vice minister of the Army ordered the Kwantung Army not to engage in any activities to establish a new regime.[17] There was a clear division between the top leadership of the army and its junior officers. The former was more unwilling to defy the government decision of non-expansion, and the latter was more openly supportive of the Kwantung Army.[18]

This division within central headquarters, however, did not hinder the subsequent Kwantung Army activities. It rather prompted the Kwantung Army to push forward its own program and to make Tokyo comply with it.[19] On September 22, staff officers of the Kwantung Army discussed a concrete program to establish a new government in Manchuria. A memorandum titled "On the Settlement of the Manchurian Question" (*Manshū mondai kaiketsu-saku-an* 満州問題解決策案) was drawn up, which proposed establishing a pro-Japanese Chinese government headed by Puyi over four provinces in Manchuria and Mongolia, where Chinese local leaders would be charged with maintaining public order in their respective regions. Then the Kwantung Army immediately started underground activities to implement the program.[20] Five pro-Puyi local leaders were earmarked, and they were induced to declare independence from the Nationalist government.[21]

In early October, when the top army leadership in Tokyo was still keeping the non-expansion position, abiding by the government policy (13.1.1), the Kwantung Army decided to act more boldly, taking advantage of the *dokudan senkō* prerogative—a time-honored discretionary authority entrusted to the Japanese army field commanders (14.1.1).[22] Following the Kwantung Army's declaration on October 2 that it would seek to establish a new state in Manchuria severed from China proper,[23] and its announcement on October 4 that it would destroy the forces of Zhang Xueliang (張学良),[24] on October 8 the Kwantung Army bombed Jinzhou (錦州), where Zhang Xueliang had recently established a military headquarters.[25] The bombing, which caused not a few civilian casualties, shocked the world. The Kwantung Army was aware of the bombing's negative effect on the Japanese government's international relations. It intended to use the shock of the bombing to make the top army leadership in Tokyo more resolute against the "weak policy" of the cabinet.[26] Meanwhile, the Kwantung Army attempted to move its forces toward Jinzhou twice during November,[27] but Tokyo managed to stop both attempts.[28]

In the meantime, in early November an incident took place that could be used as an excuse for the Kwantung Army's military intervention in north Manchuria. Hostilities occurred near Qiqihar (斉斉哈爾) between Zhang Haipeng (張海鵬), one of the five pro-Japanese warlords, and Ma Zhanshan (馬占山), a warlord who was then loyal to the Nationalist government.[29] When the Ma forces destroyed a bridge bearing a railway constructed with Japanese capital, the Kwantung Army sought central headquarters' approval for dispatching troops to repair the bridge. Tokyo consented, with orders that the troops should return to Mukden as soon as the repair work ended. Central headquarters were wary of Russian intervention. The Kwantung Army troops defeated the Ma forces, which offered a heroic resistance, chased them to Qiqihar, occupied the town, and decided to stay there. At the strong urging of the chief of the general staff, the Kwantung Army finally agreed in late November to withdraw the main force, but it retained a small detachment at Qiqihar.[30] As the Kwantung Army had expected, there was no Russian reaction. The Russians were preoccupied with implementation of the first Soviet five-year plan that they had started in 1928, and they did not want a war with Japan at this juncture.

In mid-December, with the start of the new army leadership in Tokyo (13.1.4), which was more cooperative toward the Kwantung Army than its predecessor the Kwantung Army decided to mount an all-out attack on Jinzhou. When the reinforced Kwantung Army forces advanced to Jinzhou, however, they met little resistance from the Zhang army. Chiang Kai-shek was then in retirement as a result of internal political conflict (13.2.1),[31] and Zhang Xueliang could not count on the support of the Nanjing government. Zhang Xueliang decided not to fight with the Kwantung Army. In early January 1932, Jinzhou was placed under Japanese control.

### 13.1.3. A Shift in the Government Position

The Kwantung Army's moves after September 18 drew criticism from some quarters in Japan. Several scholars of international law criticized the actions as unjustified intervention.[32] Liberal journalists opposed any military solution to Manchurian issues and warned against the Japanese war fever.[33] Some business associations expressed opposition to taking strong measures in Manchuria at the cost of antagonizing the Western powers.[34] However, these voices were drowned out by the nationalistic reports trumpeted daily by the radio and the leading newspapers. They featured the military achievements in Manchuria with splashy headlines that raised the spirits of the populace.[35]

Under these circumstances, as well as heavy pressure from their subordinates, the army's top leaders who had once promised to follow the cabinet's non-expansion decision gradually changed their position. Army Minister Minami began to speak in favor of forming a new regime in Manchuria and against the withdrawal of troops.[36] Shidehara strongly contended that such a course would put Japan into extreme difficulties in terms of its international relations. Minami held firm, and Chief of Staff Kanaya now concurred with Minami. Wakatsuki, Shidehara, and other major cabinet members conferred among themselves, and decided in mid-October to shift their stance toward that of Minami and Kanaya.[37] The alternative was a head-on collision with the army, which would have meant Minami's resignation and the fall of the cabinet.

Crucially, the government could not ignore the fact that the army was enthusiastically supported by the general public. The public's anti-Chinese sentiments inspired by the army and the media presented the government leaders with an impossible quandary. Public feelings were so intense that the government clearly could not hope to control them. The government was well aware that it had to prevent the radicalization of the public, but it feared that "should it resort to indiscriminate suppression, the anti-Chinese sentiment of the people would immediately change its direction, and blow up internally."[38]

There was a coup attempt in October by a group of radical young officers in the Army General Staff.[39] It was abortive, as had been the March Incident (12.4.1). But it undoubtedly had a certain effect on the Wakatsuki cabinet policy shift. Wakatsuki and the other ministers now considered it necessary to narrow down their differences with the army leadership to prevent the explosion of social unrest in Japan.[40] They decided that they would not oppose the establishment of a new regime in Manchuria by cooperative Chinese, and that they would tolerate quiet assistance by the Kwantung Army.[41]

### 13.1.4. The Inukai Cabinet and Creation of Manchukuo

On December 11, 1931, the Wakatsuki cabinet collapsed due to a disagreement over the question of a coalition with the opposition Seiyūkai, which Home Minister Adachi proposed.[42] Adachi was opposed to Shidehara's China policy. On December 13, Inukai Tsuyoshi (犬養毅) of the Seiyūkai (政友会) was appointed as the prime minister, and Shidehara was replaced by Yoshizawa Kenkichi (芳沢謙吉).[43] Shidehara's diplomatic career came to an end at this point.[44] The post of war minister was taken by Lieutenant General Araki Sadao (荒木貞夫), who was popular among the young officers of the army. He made Lieutenant General Masaki Jinzaburō (真崎甚三郎) vice chief of General Staff. The new chief of General Staff was Field Marshal Prince Kan'in Kotohito (閑院宮載仁). Mori Tsutomu (森恪) was appointed chief cabinet secretary. His participation in the cabinet, as well as that of Araki, marked the cabinet's shift toward acquiescence to the Kwangtung Army's actions.[45] Mori was an advocate of a very radical Manchurian policy. He believed in the need to sever Manchuria from China by means of military force in order to keep the area under complete Japanese control.

Inukai, as the head of the Seiyūkai, publicly proclaimed a strong China policy, but he had no intention of going along with such radicals as Mori. He considered Chinese cooperation essential for settling the Manchurian question.[46] His prescription for settlement was recognition of Chinese sovereignty over Manchuria and negotiations with the Nanjing government. Shortly after the formation of the cabinet, Inukai secretly sent an agent to Nanjing; the agent reached an agreement in principle with Head of the Executive Yuan Sun Fo (孫科), son of Sun Yat-sen. But Mori and the army were opposed to what they had agreed. The Ministry of Foreign Affairs also complained about this kind of secret diplomacy.[47] A compromise plan was worked out by the Ministries of Army, Navy and Foreign Affairs in mid-January.[48] The plan was titled "Policy for settlement of the China problem" (*Shina mondai shori hōshin* 支那問題処理方針). It proposed, "For the time being, the region of Manchuria–Mongolia will be under the administration and control of a regime which is separate and independent from the regime in China proper, and it will gradually be directed toward possessing the form of a state."[49] The plan was adopted by the cabinet on March 12.[50]

In Manchuria, meanwhile, three pro-Japanese governors—Xi Qia (熙治) of Jilin (吉林), Zang Shiyi (藏式毅) of Liaoning (遼寧), and Zhang Jinghui (張景惠) of Heilongjiang (黒竜江)—agreed in mid-February on the establishment of a new state according to the process that the Kwantung Army had laid out,[51] and on March 1 they formally decided to make Puyi the head of state and call the new state Manchukuo.[52] On March 9, notification of the establishment of Manchukuo was sent to the powers, together with a request for recognition.[53]

The Inukai government could not prevent the establishment of Manchukuo, but it withheld granting of de jure recognition to Manchukuo, which contravened the Nine-Power Treaty.[54] Inukai was anxious to avoid further complications with the powers, and more significantly, he was determined to stop arbitrary actions by the Kwantung Army and restore discipline in the army.[55] This firm stance cost him his life on May 15, 1932 (14.1.2).

# 13.2. The Reactions of China

### 13.2.1. The Nationalist Government's Problems

The Mukden Incident took place when the Nanjing government was beset with serious internal strife and conflict with the Communists and regional warlords. When the Northern Expedition ended, having achieved something like national unification in July 1928, many of the anti-Nationalist warlords had been wiped out, but several powerful warlords remained independent.[56] They recognized Nanjing as the central government, but when their interests were harmed by a Nanjing government policy, they rebelled against Nanjing, often allying with dissident politicians within the Nationalist Party.

The most powerful dissident politician in the Nationalist Party was Wang Ching-wei (汪精衛), the leader of the left-wing group. He was in constant conflict with Hu Hanmin (胡漢民), the leader of the right-wing element in the Kuomintang leadership.[57] Junior to both Hu and Wang in party status, Chiang Kai-shek tried to chart his course by alternately favoring one or the other with his support according to the dictates of political necessity.[58] After Hu was made president of the Legislative Yuan, however, Wang often defied party decisions. In July 1930, Wang refused to accept party policies on military and financial reorganization, and, allying with warlords based in the northern and northwestern provinces, created a separatist Nationalist government in Beijing. At this time, Zhang Xueliang quickly sent his troops, and after fierce fighting, drove the dissidents out of the city.[59] In May 1931, when Nanjing called a party congress to consider the provisional constitution, Wang protested again, and backed by an anti-Chiang warlord, created a separatist government at Guangzhou, thus provoking a new civil war. The young marshal once again came to Chiang's aid and dealt a crushing blow to the warlord. Despite the defeat in the battle, the Guangzhou regime continued its opposition. Confronted by a split government, Chiang Kai-shek resigned as president of the Nanjing government in December 1931. Wang then agreed to dissolve the Guangzhou regime, and the two agreed to resume the leadership positions in the Nanjing government in January 1932.[60]

It was during Zhang Xueliang's expedition to the south that the Japanese launched the attack in Mukden. It should also be noted that the Mukden Incident occurred at a time when much of central China was covered by the floodwaters of the Yangtze and Huai rivers, which caused as many as four million deaths. Chiang Kai-shek was at this time in Fuzhou (福州), leading a force of 300,000 troops in his third campaign against the Communists.[61] Embroiled in his fight with the Communists, Chiang was not in a position to deal effectively with issues in Manchuria.[62] Chiang's instructions to Zhang were not to resist the Japanese.[63] It had been his conviction that he could not fight foreign powers—especially Japan—without first achieving internal unity. In terms of domestic strife, he believed that problems with the Communists were much greater than those with defiant Nationalists and warlords.[64]

Indeed, Chiang believed that the Communists were more dangerous to China than the Japanese.[65] In the summer of 1931, he concluded that a Japanese attack was imminent in Manchuria. At that time, he decided on a policy of nonresistance, and warned Zhang not to engage the Japanese. In the middle of September, just before the Kwantung Army putsch, he ordered Zhang to transfer the bulk of the northeastern forces out of Manchuria.[66] On September 18, when hostilities broke out, Zhang asked for instructions and was told again by Chiang not to resist.[67]

The wisdom of the policy of nonresistance taken by Chiang is questioned by Immanuel Hsu. Hsu writes, "If [Chiang] had authorized the northeastern army to resist the invader, the glamour of aggression might have been dimmed, thus providing a chance for the more moderate civilian government in Tokyo to have a greater voice in the China affair."[68]

## 13.2.2. China's Appeal to the League of Nations and the Powers' Reactions

Right after the Mukden Incident, the Nanjing government appealed to the League of Nations and the United States. It did not expect any effective intervention from either of them, but it had no other source of support. It had a faint hope that the appeal to the League might bring about a favorable turnabout in Japanese domestic politics.[69] The deliberations at the Council formally started on September 21,[70] but the Council, which was controlled by Britain and France, was unfriendly to China. The two powers were more cooperative with Japan than China. They regarded China as weak and disorganized, and incapable of protecting foreign rights and interests within its borders.[71] They felt that, considering that Japan's interests had long been threatened by the Chinese, the Japanese action was by no means entirely unjustified.[72] They saw a greater threat from a chaotic China than from a rightist Japan. They saw Japan as a bulwark against the danger of bolshevism in China.[73] The British and French were inclined to allow Japan to work out its own solution in Manchuria.[74] They might have wished to establish a precedent for the same treatment by the League if they were to be involved in a similar case with countries or regions over which they had political or economic influence. Some British saw a parallel between the Japanese problems with China and those of Britain with India. In France there was even an expectation that if Japan could pull Manchuria away from China, France could do the same for Yunnan.[75] The Council adjourned on September 30, accepting Japan's promise of troop withdrawal from occupied areas with no established deadline.[76]

The US ambassador Cameron Forbes in Tokyo, meanwhile, was convinced that civilian control in Japan had been firmly established and any military action in defiance of the civilian authorities would not be condoned. The assault on Mukden did not shake his confidence. Forbes did not change his home leave plans, and left Tokyo for the US on September 19. He believed that the departure would demonstrate his confidence in Shidehara's promise that military action would be halted. Secretary of State Henry Stimson expected the civilian government to control "a mutiny" by the Kwantung Army. Stimson said, in often-quoted words, that he had "to let the Japanese know we are watching them and at the same time to do it in a way that will help Shidehara, who is on the right side . . ."[77]

The Jinzhou bombing of October 8 (13.1.2), however, brought about a

Chapter 13

change in American policy in Manchuria. Stimson was dismayed that Shidehara did not voice any severe indictment of the army for the bombing.[78] Stimson now felt that he should turn to the League of Nations as a channel through which to warn Japan against aggression in Manchuria. President Hoover was wary, however, that the Europeans might dump the problem in America's lap.[79] Stimson insisted, "If we lie down . . . nothing will happen, and in the future the peace movement will receive a blow that it will not recover from for a long time."[80] Thereupon Hoover approved of Stimson's idea of closer relations with the League.

Stimson worked to have the United States invited to participate in the debates of the League Council. The US participation was decided on October 15 by a vote of thirteen to one, with Japan casting the single dissenting vote. Unanimity was necessary for a resolution to be effective, but Japan's objection that the United States, which was not a member of the League, had no right to participate in the discussion of the Council was overruled on the grounds that the question was a matter of procedure and did not require a unanimous vote.[81] On October 17, the United States took part in the Council debates that led to the resolution calling for settlement of the dispute by peaceful means invoking the Kellogg Pact, to which the United States was a party. The US partaking in the Council resolution, and more importantly, joining the Lytton Commission as discussed below, marked the end of its decade of isolation from the League.[82] On October 24, the Council passed the resolution that called for withdrawal of the Japanese troops by November 16. Japan's opposition deprived the resolution of legal validity, but Briand, the Council chairman, asserted that it retained its "full moral force."[83]

The League Council reassembled on November 16. Faced with the necessity of justifying the prolongation of military occupation, Japan decided to propose dispatching a team of investigators from the League to show them the realities of the area and to demonstrate the impossibility of early withdrawal of troops.[84] Subsequent negotiations between the Japanese delegate and the Council members resulted in the Council resolution of December 10, 1931, which established a commission consisting of five representatives from Britain, France, Italy, Germany, and the United States, later to be called the Lytton Commission, to conduct an investigation on the spot in Manchuria.[85] The resolution also called for withdrawal of Japanese troops, with no specific time limit, to the treaty railway zone. The Council also accepted Japan's declaration

*378*

reserving the right to "subjugate bandits" in Manchuria and declared that the League was to drop the Sino–Japanese dispute in Manchuria from its agendas until it received the report of the commission of inquiry. Thus, Japan gained time for settling the Manchurian question on its own terms.[86]

## 13.3. The Shanghai Incident

### 13.3.1. The Anti-Japanese Boycott and the Onset of the Conflict

Shanghai had been a center of an anti-foreign movement through the 1920s. In the summer of 1931, this hatred of foreigners was focused on the Japanese, and with the outbreak of the Mukden Incident, the intensity of anti-Japanese agitation increased as antipathy toward Japan increased. A vigorous economic boycott led by the Chinese Shanghai Chamber of Commerce nearly destroyed Japanese business. Of Shanghai's total imports, 29 percent came from Japan in 1930, but by December 1931 the ratio had dropped to 3 percent.[87] By the end of 1931, 90 percent of Japanese-operated factories in Shanghai had closed. Many anti-Japanese volunteer corps were organized in Shanghai under the guidance of the Nationalist government, and many Chinese were arrested and held in confinement for having dealt in Japanese goods.

The Shanghai international settlement was legally under the control of the Municipal Council, the top administrative organization consisting of nine foreign and nine Chinese councilors.[88] But it had no control over the Chinese in the settlement, who had a sort of extraterritoriality of their own.[89] Shigemitsu Mamoru (重光葵), the Japanese minister in China, warned the Nationalist government that it had sole responsibility for controlling the anti-Japanese boycott. The Chinese government's response was that it could not be expected to suppress the people's right to choose commodities, and ultimate responsibility for the boycott lay in the unfriendly acts Japan had committed over the years.[90] Japanese residents in Shanghai organized a committee, held several meetings, and at every meeting adopted a strongly worded resolution. They often clashed with Chinese, causing injuries on both sides. Given the severity of the anti-Japanese activities and Japanese residents' excitement, an open clash between China and Japan appeared to be only a matter of time.[91]

On January 28, 1932, the municipal council judged that tension had reached a point of imminent danger, and declared a state of emergency. It requested that the powers' military commanders deploy their troops to occupy

*379*

the sectors of the settlement assigned to them for defense in accordance with the prearranged plan.[92] It was during the Japanese occupation of its assigned part of the settlement that conflict broke out with the Chinese forces.[93]

Shanghai was a center of international business. Most of the powers' investments in China were in Shanghai,[94] and among the major cities of China, the largest numbers of foreigners lived in Shanghai. Hostilities there directly threatened their holdings and their own security. While foreign consuls and military officers in the settlement were sympathetic to the Japanese position in Shanghai, their home governments openly blamed Japan for the outbreak of hostilities in the settlement. The powers' criticism of Japan increased as the fighting escalated.

The Chinese forces stationed at Shanghai were the 19th Route Army, with some 33,500 men, which was one of the most capable components of the Chinese Revolutionary Army.[95] The Japanese navy sent reinforcements during January, but on the eve of hostilities, the Japanese land forces at Shanghai comprised only 1,833 marines.[96] The Japanese navy had grossly underestimated the strength of the Chinese army.[97] It belatedly asked the army for support. The army dispatched one division in early February and two more divisions in late February. The Japanese forces finally drove the Chinese army into a general retreat on March 2. On that day, General Shirakawa Yoshinori (白川義則), the commander of all the army expeditionary forces, declared a unilateral truce. Since the League Assembly was scheduled to meet on March 3, he judged that it would be best to cease hostilities before the Geneva meeting.[98]

When the Shanghai Incident occurred, it was viewed by many contemporary observers in the world as part of a grand design of the Japanese army to control northern and central China. In fact, however, unlike the Kwantung Army's actions in Manchuria, which had been carefully prepared, what happened in Shanghai on January 28 was an "incident" if not an "accident." Surprise and consternation were the dominant reactions in Tokyo official circles to the outbreak of hostilities in Shanghai. The army's China experts did not see any strategic usefulness in the Shanghai Incident.[99] They wanted to end hostilities as quickly as possible. They were particularly anxious to forestall any unfavorable effects of the Shanghai Incident on the Manchurian situation. They sent reinforcements because they wanted to avoid losing face by being defeated in a fight with the Chinese.[100]

*380*

*Developments after the Mukden Explosion*

### 13.3.2. The Truce

Whereas the Japanese government had no intention of accepting any third-party intervention with regard to the Manchurian question, it sought to use the good offices of the major powers for the settlement of the Shanghai Incident. In early February the United States presented a settlement plan consisting of five conditions. Four points referred to the Shanghai crisis, but the fifth called for settlement of "all outstanding controversies between the two nations . . . "[101] Stimson intended a settlement linking the Shanghai crisis to the Manchurian problem. The Japanese government requested that the two problems be delinked, but Stimson would not agree. Japan declined the US overture.[102]

In Shanghai, the two combatants had truce talks on several occasions through the good offices of the British and American consuls general, and Admiral Sir Howard Kelly, commander of the British China squadron. Though none of these talks produced an agreement, they encouraged the League of Nations to sponsor truce talks.

At the League Council, China proposed that the Shanghai problem should be taken up at the Assembly. In the Assembly, the smaller states were sympathetic to China, as they imagined themselves as a potential China in the hands of one of the great European nations.[103] On March 4, the Assembly resolved to open truce negotiations in Shanghai under the auspices of the League. The negotiations started on March 24 with the participation of three representatives each from Japan and China, as well as the ministers of Britain, the United States, France, and Italy (the six-power committee).[104] But the negotiations deadlocked. At the request of China, the disputes were again referred to the Assembly in Geneva. The Assembly adopted a proposal, but it was totally unacceptable to Japan. The negotiations were again deadlocked. British minister Miles Lampson and secretary-general of the League Eric Drummond worked out a compromise plan, which China readily accepted.[105] With major forces having already returned to Japan, Japan had no choice but to accept the plan. The agreement was signed in Shanghai on May 5.[106] The truce negotiations were clearly a victory for China, which obtained the intervention of the League Assembly. A "victorious" Japan watched in amazement as Chinese diplomacy chose the best possible timing and methods in appealing to the League.[107]

While the Japanese military operations were confined to Manchuria, the

*381*

Chapter 13

powers, excepting the United States, withheld open accusations of Japan. But the attitude of the European powers toward Japan in the Shanghai Incident was quite different. They were all critical of the Japanese military's actions, notwithstanding the fact that the Chinese anti-Japanese boycott was the direct cause of the hostilities and despite Japan's unilateral cease-fire and subsequent sincere participation in the truce talks. The incident undoubtedly brought about an unfavorable effect on the Manchurian situation, which Japan had earnestly tried to avoid.

## 13.4. Stimson's Challenge to Japan

### 13.4.1. The January 7 Note, the Open Letter to Borah, and the August Speech

By December 1931, Stimson was beginning to think that the United States should take more direct measures to stop the Japanese conquest of Manchuria. But Hoover was unwilling to take any military or economic action against Japan. He had stated as early as 1929, in an Armistice Day speech, that "neither our obligations to China nor our own interests or dignity require us to go to war" over Japan's violations of China's sovereignty. He had not changed his position. He would fight to defend United States territory, but he saw it as folly to get into a war with Japan over Chinese questions.[108]

With any resort to force or sanctions ruled out, Stimson came up with the idea of issuing a note of nonrecognition, the method that Secretary of State Bryan had used in 1915 in his China policy (7.2.4).

On January 7, 1932, Stimson sent a diplomatic note to Japan, China, and the other parties of the Nine-Power Treaty, stating that the United States "does not intend to recognize any situation, treaty, or agreement which may be brought about by means contrary to the covenants and obligations of the Pact of Paris of August 27, 1928 [the Kellogg–Briand Pact]."[109]

The Japanese government answered politely but with some sarcasm on January 16, 1932, stating that Japan would certainly observe the principle of the Pact of Paris and the Open Door, which were "the cardinal features of Japan's Asia policy."[110] It stated also that Japan had no designs on Chinese territory and no wish to exclude the citizens of other powers from their commercial opportunities in Manchuria, and that the object of the military actions had been to restore order in the province.[111] In fact, Japan had been

*382*

*Developments after the Mukden Explosion*

encouraged by the British government response issued on January 9, a week earlier than the Japanese answer.[112] It announced that no protest from London would be issued against Japan, and it made no reference to the matters to which Stimson attached most importance: the principle of nonrecognition of the fruits of unlawful aggression of the Kellogg–Briand Pact.[113]

Stimson was annoyed at the British uncooperativeness. He had believed that British and American interests in the Far East were identical. At the London Naval Conference in 1930, Stimson had used with good effect his diplomatic trump card, the threat of an Anglo–American accord directed against Japan (11.4.1). He had expected that he could use it again this time.

Stimson was not daunted, however. He tried another approach in February, when there appeared to be no immediate prospect of a truce in Shanghai (13.3.1). On February 24, Stimson wrote a public letter to William Borah, chairman of the Senate Foreign Relations Committee. It stated that the treaties signed in Washington in 1922 were all interrelated, and any modification of the terms dealing with the integrity of China in the Nine-Power Treaty (7.4.3) automatically introduced the possibility of modifying the disarmament agreements of the Five-Power Treaty (7.4.2).[114]

In Tokyo, the threat of American rearmament and refortification created deep concern. Additional American capital-ship tonnage and the erection of bastions in Guam and Philippines would constitute a grave threat to Japanese hegemony in the western Pacific.[115] The Washington Treaties could no longer be viewed as an adequate guarantee of Japan's naval security.[116] The navy's "fleet" faction, which had been opposed to the Washington and London agreements, now stressed more strongly than before the irreconcilability of the national objectives of Japan and the United States. Ambassador Cameron Forbes reported that both the French and British ambassadors in Tokyo felt the letter to Borah had "done a great deal of harm."[117]

Stimson found himself isolated again diplomatically. But he believed that he had done what had to be done.[118] On August 8, 1932, Stimson delivered a speech in New York, his third attempt. He said that, as a signatory of the Kellogg–Briand Pact, the United States was committed to consulting with other signatories to voice disapproval of a violation of the pact, and that consulting meant that the United States would take sides against the transgressor. The United States would not remain a neutral bystander.[119]

The speech created a great stir in Japan. The press called the speech

*383*

"malicious propaganda," and "vile and provocative." Ambassador Grew attributed such offensive remarks by the press to the foreign office spokesman Shiratori Toshio's (白鳥敏夫) provocative interpretation of the speech, and reported that Shiratori had intentionally aroused anti-American feeling among the Japanese to rally their support for a forward policy on the continent.[120]

## 13.4.2. Domestic and International Repercussions on Stimson's Actions

In the United States, interventionists, including church organizations and peace groups, viewed the letter to Borah as forthright, lucid, courageous, and logical.[121] They hailed Stimson's speech on August 8 as the end of isolation and a contribution to world stability.[122] In London, liberals rejoiced at the apparent renunciation by America of its traditional isolationist position. In Geneva, the speech caused elation, as the link between the United States and the League of Nations seemed to be forged at last.[123]

Stimson met criticism and opposition as well. In Britain, while liberals criticized the government position of choosing Japan over the United States, Foreign Secretary John Simon and the Tory leaders of the coalition MacDonald cabinet were disinclined to act against Japan out of the conviction that British interests in the Far East would best be served not by Anglo–American but by Anglo–Japanese cooperation.[124] They believed that stability was what the British needed to secure their vast holdings and huge investments in China. Japan represented the great imperial tradition which the Tories admired. Japan alone could act, they believed, as the bulwark against the extension of Communism in China.[125]

In the United States, President Hoover did not agree with any suggestion that the United States was ready for sanctions against Japan.[126] Other critics stated that Stimson was getting the nation into a dangerous situation by playing moral policeman for the world.[127] President Lowell of Harvard pointed out the risks of a policy which provoked and irritated but did not achieve its objective. He assailed mere expressions of disapproval as idle threats, ineffective and dangerous.[128] Grew warned, "When a nation is beset with a war psychology, moral obloquy of the rest of the world is a negligible force, except that it tends to strengthen, not to weaken, that nation's warlike temper, as witness the situations in Japan."[129] Shidehara observed that the series of Stimson statements simply produced feelings among the Japanese that were exactly

384

what their military leaders wanted.[130]

# 13.5. Japan's Withdrawal from the League of Nations

### 13.5.1. The Japanese Government's Recognition of Manchukuo

The Inukai government decided, for the time being, not to grant recognition to Manchukuo "within the meaning of international law." It merely acknowledged the receipt of the notification of the establishment of Manchukuo on March 18, 1932. As Ogata notes, the postponement of recognition, under the circumstances, was a "significant act."[131]

After Inukai's assassination on May 15, the Saitō Makoto (斎藤実) government was formed on May 22. Admiral Saitō was a liberal, civilian in attitude, and an independent.[132] His cabinet consisted of moderates from both major parties, but he compromised with the army by retaining Araki as the army minister and appointing Uchida Yasuya (内田康哉), who had the support of the army, as foreign minister. Uchida was a proponent of a vigorous Manchuria policy.[133]

Strong pressure on the Saitō government for recognition of Manchukuo came not only from the army but from almost all quarters. The Japanese newspapers, which had at an early stage advocated the need for government control of the military, now started to urge early recognition of Manchukuo.[134] From Manchuria, the Manshū Seinen Renmei (満州青年連盟 the Manchuria Youth League) dispatched its mission to Japan to pressure the government and mobilize public opinion toward immediate recognition.[135] The Diet on June 14 unanimously passed a resolution in favor of extending immediate recognition to Manchukuo.[136] The Saitō cabinet finally decided to approve recognition of Manchukuo, and the cabinet decision was announced on August 25 at an extra session of the Diet.[137] On September 15, 1932, the Japan–Manchukuo Protocol was signed and recognition was formally extended to Manchukuo.[138]

Japan's formal recognition of Manchukuo without awaiting publication of the Lytton Report, which was due in early October, shocked the League member countries as well as the United States, as they had withdrawn final judgement on the situation in Manchuria pending the issuance of the report.[139] Even the French conservatives, hitherto so decidedly pro-Japanese, bitterly attacked the action. *Le temps*, in an editorial, labeled the act discourteous, likening it to contempt of court. Even British Tories branded the action as a challenge to the League.[140]

### 13.5.2. The Lytton Report

On October 2, 1932, the Lytton Report was published. Headed by Lord Lytton of Britain, the Commission had spent more than four months from the end of February through June in Japan, China, and Manchuria. The Commission concluded that "the military operations of the Japanese troops" during the night of September 18–19, which started the Mukden Incident, "cannot be regarded as measures of legitimate self-defense," and that the present regime in Manchuria "cannot be considered to have been called into existence by a genuine and spontaneous independence movement."[141]

The report stated that, though "a mere restoration of the status quo ante would be no solution . . . the maintenance and recognition of the present regime in Manchuria would be equally unsatisfactory." The former would invite repeated troubles; the latter would be incompatible with the fundamental principle of existing international obligations." The prescription the Commission offered was the "constitution of a special regime for the administration of the Three Eastern Provinces" which would be consistent "with the sovereignty and administrative integrity of China," but would possess "a large measure of autonomy designed to meet the local conditions and special characteristics of the Three Provinces."[142] The Japanese rights and interests in Manchuria were to be assured by a Sino–Japanese treaty providing "free participation of Japan in the economic development of Manchuria, which would not carry with it a right to control the country either economically or politically."[143]

Japan had pursued a policy of establishing an independent state in Manchuria not under Chinese suzerainty. The Kwantung Army had declared its aim to establish a new state in Manchuria in October 1931, and had since endeavored to implement this policy (13.1.2). The Wakatsuki government and the Inukai government had, step by step, accommodated its policy to the changing political situation initiated by the Kwantung Army. The agreement that the Saitō government signed with Manchukuo on September 15 gave Japan a status that went far beyond the "free participation of Japan in the economic development of Manchuria." Japan was to have a complete control of the state of Manchukuo, militarily, economically, and politically.[144]

*386*

### 13.5.3. International Reactions to the Lytton Report

The Lytton Report met a favorable reception in the United States. Stimson judged it comprehensive and intelligent, but he drew back from openly demanding Japan's acceptance of the report.[145] In Britain, the Laborites and Liberals, as well as their chief, Prime Minister MacDonald, were supportive of it, but the Tories, who believed that a Japanese regime in Manchuria was better than a Chinese one, were rather embarrassed by the report.[146] The Chinese had at the outset objected to the Lytton Report because it did not recommend a return to the pre-September 18, 1931 situation, but they soon decided to accept the recommendations as a basis for settlement.[147]

Japan requested a six-week delay "for a careful review of the report" before its consideration by the League Council. At the Council meeting that started deliberations on November 21, Matsuoka Yōsuke, the Japanese chief delegate,[148] spoke passionately, reviewing the chaotic conditions in Manchuria in justification of Japan's actions there, and criticized the Lytton Commission for its unrealistic and unhistorical approach to the situation.[149] He stressed that the Japanese government could not consider China to be an organized state within the meaning of the League of Nations Covenant. He claimed, "The people of Manchuria suffered too long under the oppression of ruthless dictators, and seeing the opportunity to organize a civil government, they [local leaders] lost no time in taking advantage of [the situation] . . . Our action to recognize the State of Manchukuo was the only and surest way for us to take in the present circumstances."[150] Matsuoka then stressed that no solution which did not take the existence of Manchukuo into account would be acceptable to Japan.[151]

Wellington Koo, the Chinese chief delegate,[152] refuted Matsuoka's assertion, stating that "the bulk of the population in the Three Eastern Provinces were against the new order," and that "previous Chinese administrations could have been healthier and stronger, but even these they were not willing to barter away for a condition of virtual slavery." He asserted, "Never has there been a greater mockery of the principle of self-determination than in the so-called independence movement in the Three Eastern Provinces and establishment of Manchukuo." The doors of the Three Eastern Provinces, he contended, were "closed, and all this [Japanese] gibberish about the Open Door meant nothing."[153]

An impasse developed in the debate at the Council, and the matter was shifted to the Assembly on December 6, despite Japanese opposition. As in the case of the Shanghai Incident, the smaller states in the Assembly were severely critical of Japan. They urged immediate adoption of the Lytton Report, censure of Japan, and nonrecognition of Manchukuo.[154] With rising political tensions in Europe, those countries found themselves increasingly reliant on the League's collective security system.[155] The Chinese representatives' sophisticated anti-Japanese lobbying had also hardened the smaller nations' attitude toward Japan.[156]

While Simon wished to support Japan, he was well aware of the importance of securing the support of the smaller states in Europe. He could not afford to alienate them in the disquieting European political situation. Nevertheless, he felt that he had to apply a brake to the rising emotions of the lesser powers, which he felt could lead only to punitive measures and to Japan's withdrawal from the League.[157] On December 7, Simon made a speech which drew attention to those parts of the Lytton Report favorable to Japan.[158] The speech considerably dampened the smaller nations' criticism,[159] and he was able to shift the debates from the Assembly to the Committee of Nineteen.[160] The Japanese appreciated Simon's support, but the Chinese were bitter and frustrated, and they threatened an anti-Britain boycott.[161]

### 13.5.4. Japan's Withdrawal from the League of Nations

The committee could not come to an agreement within the year 1932, and it resumed debates on January 16. Just before the session in Geneva opened, the Japanese started new military operations in Manchuria. The Kwantung Army moved south, occupied Chengde (承徳), the capital of Rehe (Jehol 熱河) province, and in February commenced a full-scale offensive in Rehe province.[162] The Saitō government had succumbed to the army, which had argued that Manchuria would not be secured until the army controlled Rehe province. Stimson was greatly upset by the Japanese move, and even suggested to Ambassador Debuchi that Japan should get out of the League.[163] Simon was put into a difficult position, but decided not to take diplomatic notice of the Japanese operation. He was anxious to prevent the League from invoking Article 16 of the Covenant, which entailed economic sanctions against Japan.[164]

On February 14, the Committee of Nineteen voted unanimously to recommend to the Assembly the adoption of the Lytton Commission Report as the basis for settlement. The recommendation was based on Article 15, paragraph 4 of the League Covenant,[165] the provision to be applied when disputes were not settled through negotiations by the parties concerned. On February 24, the Assembly adopted the committee's recommendation by 42 of the 44 nations present—Siam abstained, and Japan voted no. In his speech rejecting the report, Matsuoka stated that the members of the Assembly did not understand the true situation in Asia, did not appreciate the chaos in China and Japan's difficulty in conducting negotiations with such a disorganized state, and had ignored Japan's good work in bringing peace and order to Manchuria. After the address, the entire Japanese delegation left the room.[166] On March 27, 1933, Japan formally notified the League of its withdrawal.

Matsuoka had been sent to Geneva in November 1932 under instructions not to make any compromise on Manchukuo, but to keep Japan in the League. The Japanese government's stance was that the League Assembly could censure Japan, but it could not legally expel Japan from the League. In fact, Britain and France, whose rights and interests in the Far East were similar to those of Japan, did not wish Japan's departure from the League.[167] In mid-February, however, when it became clear that the committee would invoke Article 15, paragraph 4 of the Covenant, Japan decided to leave the League. The Ministry of Foreign Affairs judged that the escalation of military operations in Rehe that the army would soon begin would most probably be regarded as "war" in the meaning of Article 16, entailing economic sanctions against Japan.[168] Japanese leaders felt that only by withdrawing from the League could Japan evade sanctions and preserve national dignity.[169]

In late January 1933, there were two last-minute conciliatory attempts by the British. One was Simon's effort to realize direct negotiations between China and Japan along the lines of paragraph 3 of Article 15 of the Covenant.[170] The other was the "Drummond–Sugimura formula," a compromise between the interests of Japan and those of the League, which was worked out by Secretary-General Eric Drummond and Undersecretary Sugimura Yōtarō.[171] Both attempts failed, largely because of Japan's unaccommodating response. After all, having decided on the full-scale Rehe campaign to be launched in mid-February, Japan was not in a position to accept any conciliatory proposals.[172]

Japan chose military success in Manchuria at the cost of any peaceful solution to the Manchurian problem. By withdrawing from the League, Japan

Chapter 13

ended decades of cooperation with the international community. After WWI, Japan had strengthened international cooperation by joining the League and signing the Washington Treaties and the London Naval Disarmament Treaty. There had, however, been groups in the imperial army and navy which had long insisted that Japan should adopt a more independent foreign policy. Withdrawal from the League meant a victory for those elements. They were now resolved to commit Japan to a new course in foreign policy.

NOTES

13.1. The Japanese Government, Army Leadership, and the
Kwantung Army

1   Shimada Toshihiko, *Manshū jihen* (Tokyo: Kodansha, 2010), 258.
2   The joint meeting was attended by Vice Army Minister Sugiyama and Head of Military Affairs Bureau Koiso from the Army Ministry, and Vice-Chief of General Staff Ninomiya and Chief of Operations Section Imamura, acting for Chief of Operations Division Tatekawa, who was then in Mukden, from the General Staff, and others. Koiso declared, "The Kwantung Army's action is entirely just," and stressed the need to send reinforcements, which everyone agreed on. He also said at the meeting that public opinion might suspect a plot. Kawada Minoru, *Manshū jihen to seitō seiji* (Tokyo: Kodansha, 2010), 28. Shimada Toshihiko, "The Extension of Hostilities, 1931–1932," trans. Akira Iriye, in *Japan Erupts*, ed. James Morley (New York: Columbia University Press, 1984), 246.
3   James Crowley, *Japan's Quest for Autonomy: National Security and Foreign Policy, 1930–1938* (Princeton: Princeton University Press, 1966), 123.
4   Shimada, *Manshū jihen*, 258.
5   There was a report of unrest in Jilin (Kirin), a town along the railway built with Japanese financial aid. The Kwantung Army sent troops there to "protect Japanese and Korean residents." The unrest was deliberately created by a Japanese army officer. Ogata Sadako, *Defiance in Manchuria: The Making of Japanese Foreign Policy, 1931–1932* (Berkeley: University of California Press, 1964), 63.
6   The Kwantung Army's projected invasion of Harbin in late September was determinedly prevented by the chief of staff. Harbin was located along the Russian-built Chinese Eastern Railway, and central headquarters was wary of Soviet army interference with Japanese action. Ibid., 67–68.
7   Immediately after the outbreak of hostilities in Mukden, Korean Army Commander Hayashi Senjūrō started preparing to send troops to Manchuria to assist the Kwantung Army. Kanaya forcefully prohibited the dispatch of reinforcements. Hearing of the Kwantung Army's Jilin expedition on the 21st, however, Hayashi defied Kanaya's order and moved the troops across the border. Shimada, *Manshū jihen*, 253–259.
8   Kawada Minoru, *Shōwa rikugun zenshi 1: Manshū jihen* (Tokyo: Kodansha, 2014), 71–75.

*390*

# Notes

9 The prewar army and navy could overthrow the cabinet by withdrawing the army or navy minister by invoking the rule that army and navy ministers must be military officers. Regarding this rule, see note 5 of chapter 14. Itō Takashi and Momose Takashi, eds., *Jiten Shōwa senzenki no Nihon: seido to jittai* (Tokyo: Yoshikawa Kōbunkan, 1996), 258–259.

10 Shimada, *Manshū jihen*, 262.

11 Crowley, *Japan's Quest for Autonomy*, 126.

12 Nakamura Takafusa, *A History of Shōwa Japan, 1926–1989* (Tokyo: University of Tokyo Press, 1998), 110.

13 Ogata, *Defiance in Manchuria*, 74–75. The General Staff had prepared a paper titled "The Situation Estimate, 1931" (*Shōwa rokunendo jōsei handan* 昭和六年度情勢判断) in April 1931 under Tatekawa's direction, which proposed three alternatives for the Manchuria settlement: Replacing the Zhang Xueliang regime with a pro-Japanese government in Manchuria with China retaining sovereignty (Plan One), building a new state severed from China (Plan Two), and the outright seizure and annexation of Manchuria (Plan Three). Shimada, *Manshū jihen*, 263. Kawada, *Shōwa rikugun zenshi 1*, 96–97. Seki Hiroharu, "The Manchurian Incident, 1931," trans. Marius Jansen, in *Japan Erupts*, ed. James Morley (New York: Columbia University Press, 1984), 173–174. What Tatekawa proposed to the Kwantung Army staff officers on the 19th was Plan One. "Manshū mondai kaiketsu hōshin no taikō" (General Outline of a Solution for the Manchurian Problem 満州問題解決方針の大綱) adopted in June 1931 (12.4.2) was prepared while taking this "Situation Estimate" into account. Kawada, *Shōwa rikugun zenshi 1*, 98.

14 Shimada, "The Extension of Hostilities," trans. Iriye, in *Japan Erupts*, ed. Morley, 255.

15 Notwithstanding Chief of Staff Kanaya's non-expansion order, the Operation Section of the General Staff prepared a memorandum titled "The settlement of the current crisis of Manchuria," which called for speedy execution of Plan One, and obtained the approval of Vice-Chief of the General Staff Ninomiya. Kawada, *Shōwa rikugun zenshi 1*, 115–116. Kawada, *Manshū jihen to seitō seiji*, 46.

16 Ogata, *Defiance in Manchuria*, 78.

17 Ibid., 79.

18 Ogata argues that the division between the top leadership and its junior officers was caused by a serious lack of communication and confidence between them. Ibid., 79. Iriye observes that it was rather due to the fact that the former was more sensitive to the nonmilitary aspects of military action (such as international implications) and more unwilling to defy the cabinet. Akira Iriye, introduction to *Japan Erupts*, ed. James Morley (New York: Columbia University Press, 1984), 237.

19 Ogata, *Defiance in Manchuria*, 80.

20 The Kwantung Army staff officers argued that, though the Nine-Power Treaty and the Covenant of the League did not permit Japan to resort to direct action to sever Manchuria from China proper, it was not against the spirit of the international agreements for the Chinese to break up internally. Yokota criticized the Kwantung Army's argument, however, by postulating the legal principle that when a region or subdivision attempted to secede from a state, any action by another state in support

*391*

Chapter 13

of the secession would be intervention in the first state's internal affairs and therefore a violation of general international law. Mitani Taichirō, "Changes in Japan's International Position and the Response of Japanese Intellectuals; Trends in Japanese Studies of Japan's Foreign Relations, 1931–41," trans. Cameron Hurst, in *Pearl Harbor as History: Japanese–American Relations, 1931–1941*, eds. Dorothy Borg and Shumpei Okamoto (New York: Columbia University Press, 1973), 178.

21 Those local leaders were Xi Qia (Hsi Hsia 熙洽) of Jilin, Zhang Haipeng (Chang Hai-p'eng 張海鵬) of Taonan, Tang Yulin (T'ang Yu-lin 湯玉麟) of Rehe (Jehol), Yu Zhishan (Yu Chih-shan 于芷山) of Tungpientao, and Zhang Jinghui (Chang Ching-hui 張景惠) of Harbin. They were all in support of former emperor Puyi, and had been in contact with the Kwantung Army. Ogata, *Defiance in Manchuria*, 76–77. Shimada, "The Extension of Hostilities," trans. Iriye, in *Japan Erupts*, ed. Morley, 257.

22 Ogata, *Defiance in Manchuria*, 81.

23 While the "Manshū mondai kaiketsusaku-an" of September 22 proposed establishing a pro-Japanese Chinese regime in Manchuria under Chinese suzerainty, the plan declared on October 2 proposed establishment of a new independent state in Manchuria severed from China proper. Kobayashi Michihiko, *Seitō naikaku no hōkai to Manshū jihen* (Tokyo: Minerva Shobo, 2010), 187. Inoue argues that Ishiwara believed that, although the annexation would make it impossible to have rapprochement with the Nationalist government, in the case of the creation of an independent state, a complete deterioration of the relationship with the Nationalist government could be avoided. Inoue Toshikazu, *Kiki no nakano kyōchō gaikō* (Tokyo: Yamakawa Shuppansha, 1994), 4.

24 Ogata, *Defiance in Manchuria*, 81.

25 Ibid., 79–82. It was estimated that Zhang Xueliang had gathered about 200,000 Chinese troops in Jinzhou by early October. Shimada, "The Extension of Hostilities," trans. Iriye, in *Japan Erupts*, ed. Morley, 288.

26 Ogata, *Defiance in Manchuria*, 81–82. Shimada, "The Extension of Hostilities," trans. Iriye, in *Japan Erupts*, ed. Morley, 288–289. Kobayashi, *Seitō naikaku no hōkai*, 188–189.

27 There were two shooting incidents between the Chinese and the Japanese in Tientsin in November. Both were instigated by Colonel Dohihara Kenji (土肥原賢二) of the Kwantung Army. He machinated the first incident on November 9 to abduct the former Manchu emperor Puyi and take him to Dalian during the confusion (13.1.5). The second Tientsin Incident was caused on November 26 to support the Tientsin Army's demand for reinforcements of its forces.

28 In both the first and second Tientsin incidents the Kwantung Army moved its forces toward Jinzhou in an attempt to occupy the city, but the General Staff in Tokyo managed to stop them. In the second incident it resorted to the "delegated right of supreme command" to overrule the field commanders' right to report direct to the emperor and act independently from the Chief of the General Staff (see 14.1.1). This delegation was called *Rinji sanbōsōchō inin meirei* (臨時参謀総長委任命令 or 臨参委命 the temporary delegation of the emperor's right of the supreme command to the Chief of the General Staff). This measure was initiated during the Russo–Japanese

*Notes*

war, and had never been applied until this time. Kawada, *Manshū jihen*, 172. Shimada, "The Extension of Hostilities," trans. Iriye, in *Japan Erupts*, ed. Morley, 294.

29  The Muslim general Ma Zhanshan's heroic battle against the Kwantung Army made him a hero to supporters of Chinese nationalism. But he later joined the Manchukuo government as the head of its military, accepting the Japanese offer. Having received public condemnation as a traitor, however, he soon resigned from the Manchukuo government. Shimada, *Manshū jihen*, 378.

30  Kawada, *Manshū jihen*, 172–175. Fujiwara Akira, *Nihon kindaishi, III* (Tokyo: Iwanami Shoten, 2007), 45.

31  Immanuel Hsu, *The Rise of Modern China* (New York: Oxford University Press, 1970), 639.

32  Professor Yokota Kisaburō wrote in the *Tokyo Imperial University News* that he believed that it would constitute an unjustified intervention to occupy cities located hundreds of kilometers away from Mukden "within a mere six hours after the blowing up of a few meters of railway track." Kakegawa Tomoko, "The Press and Public Opinion in Japan, 1931–1941," in *Pearl Harbor as History: Japanese–American Relations, 1931–1941*, eds. Dorothy Borg and Shumpei Okamoto (New York: Columbia University Press, 1973), 538–539. Yoshino Sakuzō and Rōyama Masamichi, both professors of Tokyo Imperial University, also expressed their opposition to the Kwantung Army's actions. Many other scholars, however, took the position that the Mukden Incident and the ensuing actions of the Japanese military did not violate the existing international legal order. For example, Tachi Sakutarō, professor of Tokyo Imperial University, viewed the actions as an exercise of the right of self-defense against an imminent violation of Japan's interests. Mitani, "Changes in Japan's International Position," trans. Hurst, in *Pearl Harbor as History*, eds. Borg and Okamoto, 576–578.

33  The journal *Chuokoron*'s October 1931 editorial opposed sending troops to Manchuria, stating that Japan's ultimate goals could not be gained by force. Another journal *Kaizō*, criticized the *Asahi* and the *Mainichi* for their servile attitude toward the military. Ishibashi Tanzan argued that the idea that Japan "will die without Manchuria" was "completely mistaken." He also contended that Japan should "abandon special rights and interests in Manchuria" rather than "turning China and the Western powers into Japan's enemies." Louise Young, *Japan's Total Empire: Manchuria and the Culture of Wartime Imperialism* (Berkeley: University of California Press, 1998), 85–87.

34  William Fletcher III, *The Japanese Business Community and National Trade Policy, 1920–1942* (Chapel Hill, NC: University of North Carolina Press, 1989), 77.

35  The *Asahi*, for example, stated that the Japanese had too long endured Chinese hostility, and that "[i]n the face of this clear violation of our vital rights and interests in Manchuria and Mongolia, the stern reality is that Japan must defend its rights even at great sacrifice." Kakegawa, "Press and Public Opinion" in *Pearl Harbor as History*, eds. Borg and Okamoto, 537.

36  Kawada, *Manshū jihen*, 154–156.

37  Ibid., 157.

38  Ogata, *Defiance in Manchuria*, 106.

Chapter 13

39 Ibid., 95–97. Nakamura Takafusa, *A History of Shōwa Japan, 1926–1989*, trans. Edwin Whenmouth (Tokyo: University of Tokyo Press, 1998), 85–86. Robert Scalapino, *Democracy and the Party Movement in Prewar Japan* (Berkeley: University of California Press, 1953), 367–368.

40 The same group that had planned the March Incident (12.4.1) planned the plot again in October 1931, and this time the plot was larger in scale. The entire cabinet was to be assassinated at once during a cabinet meeting, and the Metropolitan Police Board Headquarters was to be occupied. The Army Ministry and the Chief of General Staff was to be isolated until a military government could be installed under General Araki. Scalapino, *Democracy and the Party Movement*, 367–368. Ogata, *Defiance in Manchuria*, 96–97. Kawada, *Manshū jihen*, 164–167.

41 Kawada, *Manshū jihen*, 157.

42 Ibid., 192–193.

43 He had been the minister in China from 1923 to 1929, and the ambassador in France for two years before assuming the position of foreign minister.

44 Shidehara did not come back to politics until October 1945, when he became premier. He was in office till May 1946.

45 Shimada, *Manshū jihen*, 310–311.

46 Scalapino writes, "Inukai played a double line. In private, he worked to control military power and prevent a further expansion of the Chinese War. . . . In public, however, he continued to voice a 'strong' foreign policy stand which was in line with his own past and that of his party . . . " Scalapino, *Democracy and the Party Movement*, 368.

47 Ogata, *Defiance in Manchuria*, 139–140. Ian Nish, *Japan's Struggle with Internationalism: Japan, China and the League of Nations, 1931–33* (London: Kegan Paul International, 1933), 65.

48 Nish, *Japan's Struggle with Internationalism*, 66.

49 Shimada Toshihiko, "Manshū jihen no tenkai," in *Taiheiyō sensō eno michi II, Manshū jihen*, ed. Nihon Kokusai Seiji Gakkai (Tokyo: Asahi Shimbunsha, 1962), 177–178.

50 Ogata, *Defiance in Manchuria*. 141–142.

51 Those governors organized a supreme administrative council which would ostensibly decide all matters concerning the new state, and its decisions would be presented to the popular representative bodies to be formed in each province for their agreement. Representatives of Rehe (Jehol) and Mongolia were expected to be invited later to participate in the new state. Ibid., 129.

52 Puyi, who had been living in Tianjin, was taken to Lushun by Colonel Dohihara on November 9 during the first Tianjin Incident. Shimada, *Manshū jihen*, 302.

53 Ogata, *Defiance in Manchuria*, 129–130.

54 Ibid., 145.

55 Inukai even pondered the idea of proposing to the emperor "dismissal of about thirty young officers" with the approval of Chief of General Staff Prince Kan'in. Ibid., 150–151.

*394*

*Notes*

## 13.2. Reactions of China

56  Among them, most powerful were Li Zongren (李宗仁), Feng Yuxiang (馮玉祥), and Yan Xishan (閻錫山). Li Zongren dominated the provinces of Guangxi, Guangdong, Hunan, and Hubei. Feng Yuxiang controlled the provinces of Shandong, Henan, Shanxi, Gansu, Qinghai, and Ningxia. Yan Xishan had established a strong base in Shanxi, reaching out into Hubei, Suiyuan, and Chahar. Hsu, *Rise of Modern China*, 636.

57  Ibid., 637. Hu and Wang had been Sun Yat-sen's long-time supporters. In 1922, Sun asked the two to draft a manifest for reform of the Kuomintang. Jonathan Spence, *The Search for Modern China* (New York: W. W. Norton, 1990), 334–336.

58  Hsu, *Rise of Modern China*, 637.

59  Wang fled to Hong Kong and continued his opposition. Ibid., 638.

60  Ibid., 638–639.

61  From 1930 to 1935 Chiang launched a total of five campaigns against the Communists. The first campaign started in December 1930 and the second in April 1931. Both ended quickly in failure. The third campaign started on July 1931, but Chiang cut it short in September when the Japanese launched their invasion in Manchuria. After the fourth ended in failure in April 1933, the Nationalists scored a victory in their fifth attempt in November 1935. Mao Zedong lost the chairmanship of the Council of People's Commissars during the fifth campaign, but after the end of the fight in defeat he regained the chairmanship, holding the new leadership responsible for the defeat. Hsu, *Rise of Modern China*, 656–659.

62  Ibid., 646.

63  Edwin Pak-wah Leung, *Historical Dictionary of Revolutionary China, 1839–1976* (New York: Greenwood Press, 1992), 34. Hsu, *Rise of Modern China*, 646.

64  Hsu, *Rise of Modern China*, 656.

65  I Kenseki et al., *Kyū-ichihachi jihenshi—Chūgoku gawa kara mita Manshū jihen*, trans. Hayakawa Tadashi (Tokyo: Shinjidaisha, 1986), 251. Hsu, *Rise of Modern China*, 649.

66  There were 190,000 troops in three provinces in Manchuria in the summer of 1931; 60,000 in Liaoning, 80,000 in Jilin, and 50,000 in Heilungkiang. Immediately before the Mukden Incident, 50,000 men in Liaoning were transferred to North China. I Kenseki et al., *Kyū-ichihachi jihenshi*, trans. Hayakawa, 236. Hsu, *Rise of Modern China*, 646.

67  Chiang forbade Zhang to tell anybody that Chiang had ordered Chang to follow a policy of nonresistance. The public blamed Zhang for not fighting against the Japanese. He earned the ignominious title of "no-fight general." Zhang bore the criticism, but when he was put before a Kuomintang court-martial after the Xian Incident, he presented to the court Chiang's telegram dispatched on the night of September 18, 1931, which forbade him to resist the Japanese. I Kenseki et al. *Kyū-ichihachi jihenshi*, trans. Hayakawa, 250.

68  Hsu, *Rise of Modern China*, 647.

69  Ibid., 646–647.

70  The League of Nations Council consisted of five permanent members and nine

Chapter 13

non-permanent members in 1931. The five permanent members were Britain, France, Italy, Japan, and Germany. The non-permanent members were selected by the Assembly from time to time.

71 Armin Rappaport, *Henry L. Stimson and Japan, 1931–33* (Chicago: University of Chicago Press, 1963), 18. Sir Edward Grey, former foreign secretary, was among those who attributed the crisis to the anarchic conditions prevailing in China. R. Basset, *Democracy and Foreign Policy, A Case History: The Sino–Japanese Dispute, 1931–33* (London: Longmans, Green and Co., 1952). 38.

72 Basset, *Democracy and Foreign Policy*, 31–32, 38. The British newspapers were for the most part sympathetic to Japan. The exception was the *Manchester Guardian*, which was against Japan from the start. Ibid., 28, 31. In France as well, most of the press were sympathetic to Japan. Rappaport, *Stimson and Japan*, 20.

73 Ibid., 18, 20.

74 Ibid., 18.

75 Ibid., 20. The *Journal de Geneve*, looking upon Japan's position in Asia as analogous to France's in Europe, in its editorial of November 19, 1931, stated that China claimed duress in the treaty of 1915 and failed to carry out its treaty obligation; so did Germany in the one in 1919; and Japan had to send army into Manchuria; France had to do the same in the Ruhr in 1923. Ibid., 21.

76 Ogata, *Defiance in Manchuria*, 71.

77 Ibid., 72.

78 Rappaport, *Stimson and Japan*, 30.

79 David Schmitz, *Henry L. Stimson: The First Wise Man* (Wilmington, DE: Scholarly Resources, 2001), 105.

80 Ibid., 105–106.

81 Ogata, *Defiance in Manchuria*, 88. Henry L. Stimson, *The Far Eastern Crisis Recollections and Observations* (New York: Howard Fertig, 1974), 66.

82 Dorothy Borg, *The United States and the Far Eastern Crisis of 1933–1938* (Cambridge: Harvard University Press, 1964), 4.

83 Ogata, *Defiance in Manchuria*, 88. Stimson, *The Far Eastern Crisis*, 67–68.

84 The Japanese government had objected the dispatch of inspectors from the League to Manchuria in September, but having received later a report from Hayashi, the Consul General at Mukden, suggesting acceptance of an inquiry commission because many of foreign visitors who saw the actual situation seemed to understand the impossibility of rapid withdrawal of Japanese troops. Tokyo decided to propose the dispatch of the investigation team. General Honjō did not object the idea either. Ogata, *Defiance in Manchuria*, 116.

85 The five members of the Lytton Commission were Victor Bulwer-Lytton, the head of the commission; General Henri Edouard Claudel of France; Count Luigi Aldrovandi of Italy; Dr. Heinrich Schnee of Germany; and Major General Frank R. McCoy of the United States. Lytton, second earl of Lytton, was a distinguished Briton both by lineage and accomplishments. He was the son of a viceroy of India. He had served in the Admiralty, the India Office, as governor of Bengal, and briefly as viceroy of India. Rappaport, *Stimson and Japan*, 179. The appointment of McCoy was made with an eye to Japanese sensibilities. McCoy had been the representative in

*396*

*Notes*

Tokyo coordinating American relief efforts after the Great Kantō Earthquake of 1923, and he was known to many top Japanese officials. Stimson, *The Far Eastern Crisis*, 81. Nish, *Japan's Struggle with Internationalism*, 57.

86  Ibid., 117.

### 13.3. The Shanghai Incident

87  Shimada, "Extension of Hostilities," trans. Iriye, in *Japan Erupts*. ed. Morley, 305.

88  The nine foreign councilors were five British, two Japanese, and two Americans. The French settlement had its own council. Shimada, "Manshū jihen no tenkai," in *Taiheiyō sensō eno michi II*, ed. Nihon Kokusai Seiji Gakkai, 389.

89  Shimada, "Extension of Hostilities," trans. Iriye, in *Japan Erupts*, ed. Morley, 305.

90  Ibid., 306. Shimada, *Manshū jihen*, 323.

91  Shimada, "Extension of Hostilities," trans. Iriye, in *Japan Erupts*, ed. Morley, 308. Shimada, *Manshū jihen*, 328.

92  Ogata, *Defiance in Manchuria*, 142–143. The powers' military commanders in the settlement had since 1850 organized a defense committee, and in times of civil strife the powers had defended the sections assigned to them. Shimada, "Extension of Hostilities," trans. Iriye, in *Japan Erupts*, ed. Morley, 305.

93  Ogata, *Defiance in Manchuria*, 143.

94  In 1929, of British business investments in China, those in Shanghai accounted for 76.6 percent. Of American investments in China, those in Shanghai represented 64.9 percent. C. F. Remer, *Foreign Investment in China* (New York: Howard Fertig, 1968), 282, 395.

95  Shimada, "Extension of Hostilities," trans. Iriye, in *Japan Erupts*, ed. Morley, 308.

96  Shimada, *Manshū jihen*, 327–328.

97  At the early stage the navy did not consider that it needed support of the army, despite the fact they were vastly outnumbered by the Chinese army. The navy was anxious to gain a reputation equal to that of the Kwantung Army. Shimada, *Manshū jihen*, 332.

98  Shimada, "Extension of Hostilities," trans. Iriye, in *Japan Erupts*, ed. Morley, 314. The General Staff in Tokyo wanted Shirakawa to chase the 19th Route Army, but Shirakawa declared the truce, taking advantage of the field commander's autonomous right.

99  Crowley, *Japan's Quest for Autonomy*, 166.

100 Robert Ferrell, *American Diplomacy in the Great Depression* (London: Oxford University Press, 1957), 174.

101 Crowley, *Japan's Quest for Autonomy*, 163.

102 Elting Morison, *Turmoil and Tradition: A Study of the Life and Time of Henry L. Stimson* (Boston: Houghton Mifflin, 1960), 389. Crowley, *Japan's Quest for Autonomy*, 163. Rappaport, *Stimson and Japan*, 128.

103 Ibid., 132.

104 Shimada, "Extension of Hostilities," trans. Iriye, in *Japan Erupts*, ed. Morley, 316–317.

105 The compromised plan was that the six-power committee was to be given the right to call the attention of Japan or China to a violation of specific terms of the truce. Ibid.,

*397*

Chapter 13

317–318.
106 There was a terrorist attack in Shanghai on April 29. A Korean nationalist threw a bomb into the gathering of Japanese officials celebrating the emperor's birthday. General Shirakawa and the chairman of the Japanese residents' committee in Shanghai were killed. Admiral Nomura, Lt. General Ueda, Minister Shigemitsu, and Consul-General Murai were seriously wounded. But the incident did not interrupt negotiations, and the agreement was signed by Shigemitsu, who had his right leg amputated after the signing.
107 Shimada, "Extension of Hostilities," trans. Iriye, in *Japan Erupts*, ed. Morley, 317–318.

### 13.4. Stimson's Challenge to Japan

108 Schmitz, *Stimson*, 106, 108, 110.
109 Stimson, *The Far Eastern Crisis*, 96–97. Morison, *Turmoil and Tradition*, 387. Saitō Takashi, "Bei, Ei, Kokusai Renmei no dōkō," in *Taiheiyō sensō eno michi II, Manshū jihen*, ed. Nihon Kokusai Seiji Gakkai (Tokyo: Asahi Shimbunsha, 1962), 364.
110 Rappaport, *Stimson and Japan*, 99.
111 Ibid., 100.
112 In his memoir, Stimson held Britain responsible for encouraging Japan to maintain a defiant attitude toward the United States. Stimson, *The Far Eastern Crisis*, 105.
113 Basset, *Democracy and Foreign Policy*, 88. Saitō, "Bei, Ei, Kokusai Renmei no dōkō," in *Taiheiyō sensō eno michi II*, ed. Nihon Kokusai Seiji Gakkai, 365.
114 Morison, *Turmoil and Tradition*, 396.
115 Rappaport, *Stimson and Japan*, 141.
116 Crowley, *Japan's Quest for Autonomy*, 165.
117 Morison, *Turmoil and Tradition*, 397.
118 Rappaport, *Stimson and Japan*, 105.
119 Ibid., 169.
120 Joseph Grew writes in his *Ten Years in Japan*, "Shiratori . . . seems to act independently of his superiors and seems to enjoy giving sensational impressions . . . Shiratori, indeed, is quite an enigma; Shidehara tried to get rid of him and couldn't, as he is apparently supported by the military, with whom he seems to be in entire sympathy. He is also a nephew of Viscount Ishii and is closely connected with Hiranuma, president of the Privy Council and chief of the Kokuhohsha (国本社) reactionary society, which of course renders him impregnable at the foreign office. Joseph Grew, *Ten Years in Japan* (New York: Simon & Schuster, 1944), 36–37.
121 Rappaport, *Stimson and Japan*, 142.
122 Ibid., 170.
123 Ibid., 171.
124 Ibid., 103.
125 Ibid., 103.
126 Herbert Hoover, *The Memoirs of Herbert Hoover: The Cabinet and the Presidency, 1920–33* (New York: Macmillan, 1951), 366–367.
127 Rappaport, *Stimson and Japan*, 170–171. Rappaport writes, "In diplomacy, he seemed to have forgotten, if he ever knew, that one cannot let emotion or morality

*Notes*

be the only guide of conduct. One must neither hate or love, only calculate and weigh." Ibid., 202

128 Ibid., 196.

129 Grew, *Ten Years in Japan*, 79.

130 Morison, *Turmoil and Tradition*, 400.

### 13.5. Japan's Withdrawal from the League of Nations

131 Ogata, *Defiance in Manchuria*, 145.

132 Rappaport, *Stimson and Japan*, 163.

133 Ibid., 163.

134 Ogata, *Defiance in Manchuria*, 158.

135 Ibid., 158–159.

136 Ibid., 159.

137 Nish, *Japan's Struggle*, 159. Following Saitō's announcement of recognition of Manchukuo at the Diet, Uchida made a speech stating that recognition was the only effective way to solve the Manchurian problem. The so-called "scorched earth" talk, in which Uchida said that Japan would not yield an inch even if it were to reduce its territory to "scorched earth," came after the speech when Uchida answered a provocative interpellation from Mori Tsutomu. Ogata, *Defiance in Manchuria*, 159. Kobayashi, *Seitō naikaku no hōkai*, 263.

138 Ogata, *Defiance in Manchuria*, 162–163. Rappaport, *Stimson and Japan*, 174.

139 Ogata, *Defiance in Manchuria*, 171. Rappaport, *Stimson and Japan*, 175. Nish, *Japan's Struggle*, 161.

140 Rappaport, *Stimson and Japan*, 174–175.

141 Ogata, *Defiance in Manchuria*, 171.

142 Ibid., 171.

143 Ibid., 172.

144 Ogata writes, "The recommendations of Lytton Commission might easily have been acceptable to Japan before the Manchurian affair, but in the fall of 1932 they fell far short of what she had decided was her due." Ibid., 172.

145 Stimson had already been criticized by senior American diplomats on the grounds that he had done too much, making the dispute between China and Japan into one between the United States and Japan. Rappaport, *Stimson and Japan*, 187.

146 Ibid., 185. The bitterest critic was Francis Lindley, British ambassador in Tokyo. He confided his belief to Grew that the Manchurian affair was a local affair of no concern to an international organization, which could have been settled by direct negotiations, but the League laid down "dogmatic theories without regard to facts." Ibid., 201.

147 Ibid., 189.

148 When Matsuoka was ordered to head Japan's delegation to the League of Nations, he was no longer an official but a member of the Seiyūkai. He was recommended by Mori and Shiratori as well as Uchida. He was also acceptable to the army. If judged by his place in the Japanese bureaucracy, he was ranked behind the Japan's two existing delegates to the League Council, Nagaoka Harukazu, ambassador to France, and Satō Naotake, ambassador to Belgium. Matsuoka's nomination for the chief delegate

*399*

Chapter 13

was opposed by several Japanese diplomats, including Satō Naotake and Yoshida Shigeru, ambassador to Italy. But Inukai overrode the opposition. Matsuoka had gone to the United States in 1893 when he was thirteen years old under the sponsorship of Methodist missionaries. He returned to Japan in 1902 after graduation from the University of Oregon. In 1904 he joined the Ministry of Foreign Affairs, and in 1922 joined the South Manchuria Railway as a director and was promoted to the post of vice-president in 1927. Nish, *Japan's Struggle*, 185.

149 Rappaport, *Stimson and Japan*, 190.

150 Nish, *Japan's Struggle*, 194–195.

151 Rappaport, *Stimson and Japan*, 189–190.

152 Wellington Koo was newly sent to Geneva as a reinforcement for the existing Guomindang representative in Geneva, Yen Hui-ching, minister to Washington. Nish, *Japan's Struggle*, 183.

153 Ibid., 167–168.

154 Rappaport, *Stimson and Japan*, 190–191.

155 In July 1932, the National Socialist Party (Nazi Party) became the largest (but not majority) single party in the German general election. On January 30, 1933, Hitler was named chancellor.

156 Nish, *Japan's Struggle*, 191.

157 Ibid., 191.

158 Simon pointed out that the Lytton Report stated that the Manchurian incident was not one "in which one country has declared war on another without previously exhausting the opportunities for conciliation provided in the Covenant." He also stated that the report described the rights and interests of Japan in Manchuria as very special and proposed that any solution which failed to recognize them would not be satisfactory. Nish, *Japan's Struggle*, 176.

159 Rappaport, *Stimson and Japan*, 192–193. The American consul in Geneva wrote to Stimson, "The contest is really no longer between China and Japan but between Great Britain and the League of Nations." Ibid., 193.

160 The Committee of Nineteen had been organized in March 1932, when the League Assembly discussed the Shanghai Incident. It consisted of twelve Council members (fourteen members minus China and Japan), representatives from Switzerland, Czechoslovakia, Columbia, Portugal, Hungary, Sweden, and the chairman of the Assembly.

161 Inoue, *Kyōchō gaikō*, 13, 49. Matsuoka remarked that Simon had said "in half an hour in a few well-chosen phrases" what he himself had been trying to say "in his bad English for the last ten days." The Chinese remarked that Simon's speech had announced Geneva's bankruptcy. Rappaport, *Stimson and Japan*, 192–193.

162 The Rehe (Jehol) campaign had long been planned by the Kwantung Army. But central headquarters judged that Japan should refrain from taking any major military actions in Manchuria while the League was in the process of drafting recommendations in Geneva. In early January 1933, "as a limited local operation," the Kwantung Army occupied Changde. Beijing lay only 80 miles away on the other side of the Great Wall. On January 13, the Saitō government reluctantly approved the invasion of Rehe (Jehol) province on condition that no moves should be made beyond the

Great Wall. The Kwantung Army commenced full-scale operations on February 23. Encountering little effective resistance, the Japanese forces of twenty thousand put the whole province under their control in about a week. The area of Jehol was approximately the size of Virginia, Maryland, and West Virginia combined. Inoue, *Kyōchō gaikō*, 39–41. Rappaport, *Stimson and Japan*, 194. Herbert Bix, *Hirohito and the Making of Modern Japan* (New York: HarperCollins Publishers, 2000), 260.

163 Rappaport, *Stimson and Japan*, 195.

164 Paragraph 1 of Article 16 provided: "Should any Member of the League resort to war in disregard of its covenants under Article 12, 13 or 15, it should ipso facto be deemed to have committed an act of war against all other Members of the League, which hereby undertake immediately to subject it to the severance of all trade or financial relations, the prohibition of all intercourse between their nationals and the nationals of the covenant-breaking State, and the prevention of all financial, commercial or personal intercourse between the nationals of the covenant-breaking States and the nationals of any other State, whether a Member of the League or not."

165 Article 15 provided, in paragraph 4: "If the dispute is not thus settled, the Council either unanimously or by a majority vote shall make and publish a report containing a statement of the facts of dispute and the recommendations which are deemed just and proper in regard thereto."

166 Rappaport, *Stimson and Japan*, 199. Inoue, *Kyōchō gaikō*, 49.

167 Ogata, *Defiance in Manchuria*, 163–164, 175.

168 Inoue, *Kyōchō gaikō*, 38.

169 Ibid., 49.

170 Ibid., 36. Paragraph 3 of Article 15 was a provision for settlement of disputes by negotiations between the parties with the help of the Council. It provided: "The Council shall endeavor to effect a settlement of the dispute, and if such efforts are successful, a statement shall be made public giving such facts and explanations regarding the dispute and the terms of settlement thereof as the Council may deem appropriate."

171 Sir Eric Drummond of Britain was the first secretary-general of the League from 1920 to 1933. Sugimura Yōtarō succeeded Nitobe Inazō as undersecretary in 1927. He served in the post and was director of the political section until 1933. Drummond had a very high opinion of Sugimura. Among officials from all nationalities, his skill was especially acknowledged, and Japan acquired through his endeavors and those of Nitobe the reputation of being one of the main supporters of the League's work. Nish, *Japan's Struggle*, 10–11, 203–204.

172 Ibid., 203–208.

# Chapter 14
# Japan's Militarism, War with China, and the US Position

## 14.1. The Rise of the Army in Japanese Politics

### 14.1.1. The Army's Privileges and Public Support for the Army

The prewar Japanese army and navy had privileges which most of other major powers' military did not have. The most important one was the so-called independence of the prerogative of supreme command. The chiefs of the general staff and ministers of the army and navy could directly report to the emperor regarding the prerogative of supreme command without prior consultation with the prime minister.[1] Because of this system, except for budgetary controls, the Japanese military was free of the civil government in its military activities. The Meiji leaders emulated Prussia, which had such a system.[2] While Germany discontinued it after WWI, Japan maintained it until the end of WWII. Strictly, the right of supreme command was the authority to move the armed forces at the time of war, but the Japanese army and navy interpreted it more broadly, as in the case of the London Naval Treaty negotiations (11.4.2). In fact, by invoking this privilege, or threatening to invoke it, the army and navy often acted in defiance of the government intention.[3]

The Japanese military's time-honored practice of *dokudan senkō*, the

*403*

Chapter 14

discretionary right entrusted to the field commanders to act flexibly without waiting for instructions from central headquarters, was also a privilege derived from the rule that they could report to the emperor directly.[4] The Jinan Incident (11.3.3) was a typical *dokudan senkō* case, and the Kwantung Army effectively invoked this privilege in pushing forward its program in the Manchurian affair (12.4.2, 13.1.2).

Because of the privilege given to the army minister and the navy minister as above, there was a rule that they had to be military men.[5] This system decisively made the military's position strong vis-à-vis the government, because it gave the army and the navy veto power over the cabinet. The army leaders often forestalled the formation of a cabinet that they did not like by refusing to send the war minister to the prospective cabinet,[6] or overthrew the cabinet by withdrawing the war minister from the cabinet,[7] or forced the cabinet to accept their demands by threatening to withdraw the war minister from the cabinet.[8]

While the Meiji *genrō* were alive, they did not allow arbitrary acts by the army or navy. In the 1920s, most of them were dead, but under the world trend of peace and disarmament after WWI, the civilian government somehow managed to control the military. As observed in 12.2, however, the civilian government, which had pursued severe deflationary policies under the dire economic circumstances of the late 1920 and early 1930s, lost considerable support from the public, especially from farmers. The anti-government and pro-army sentiment became strong. Additionally, in the Manchurian Incident the army received enthusiastic support from the public (13.1).

These developments in the late 1920s and early 1930s, combined with the Japanese military's historical privileges as observed above, caused the political power balance between the civilian government and the military to shift decisively toward the latter in the 1930s.

### 14.1.2. Terrorism and the Army's Leniency toward the Army Offenders

In the early and mid-1930s, Japan experienced a series of coup attempts and terrorism aiming at wiping out the civilian government. None of these achieved their goal, but most of them helped strengthen the army's position in Japanese politics. In 1931 a group of young army officers attempted a coup in March (12.4.1) and again in October (13.1.3). Then came two assassinations in early 1932 by members of the Ketsumeidan (血盟団 Blood Brotherhood), a civilian terrorist group formed by Inoue Nisshō (井上日召).[9] They murdered

404

Inoue Junnosuke (井上準之助), finance minister from July 1929 until December 1931, on February 9, 1932, and Dan Takuma (団琢磨), the managing director of the Mitsui zaibatsu, on March 5. Though Inoue Nisshō's targets had included Inukai, Wakatsuki, Shidehara, Saionji Kinmochi, Lord Keeper of the Privy Seal Makino Nobuaki, and Mitsui's Ikeda Shigeaki, Nisshō and several other members of the Ketsumeidan were arrested before any more murders were committed.[10] But a group of navy officers who had collaborated with Inoue Nisshō escaped indictment. They, together with military academy students and members of the Aikyōjuku (愛郷塾), a school set up by Tachibana Kōzaburō (橘孝三郎),[11] assaulted Prime Minister Inukai Tsuyoshi (犬養毅) at his residence on May 15 and shot him dead.[12] They expected that their act would prompt further actions by superior officers, but no move was made, and the conspirators were all arrested.[13]

Inukai, as the head of the Seiyūkai (政友会), had voiced a strong stance on the China question, but he had had no intention of following the army's China policy. As observed in 13.1.4, he had sought to have a negotiated settlement of the Manchurian crisis with China without consulting with the army, and refused to grant de jure recognition to Manchukuo (13.1.5). He had also attempted to eliminate the very root of lack of discipline in the military. Inukai's radio speech on May 1 criticizing extremism, both right and left, and emphasizing the importance of finding a solution through parliamentary government had also irritated the prospective assassins.[14]

While the navy authority openly denounced the insurgents, the army leadership treated them extremely leniently. Minister of the Army Araki Sadao issued a statement on the May 15 Incident saying that "they had acted upon the genuine belief that this was for the interest of the imperial country. Therefore, the present case should not be dealt with simply in a narrow-minded and businesslike way."[15] During the proceedings of the court-martial of the May 15 Incident, the accused were given a chance to publicize their cause. This was an unusual practice. They presented the problem of impoverished rural areas, and blamed party politicians, the zaibatsu, and the court circle for disregarding the problem.[16] The newspapers reported their statements in full detail, and there was a surprising level of popular support for the accused.[17]

Sentences for the military men were extraordinarily light, while those for civilians looked normal. In the case of the October Incident, Lt. Colonel Hashimoto Kingorō (橋本欣五郎), the leader of the coup attempt, faced twenty days' confinement; two other officers were given ten days' confinement, and the rest were acquitted after admonition. They were not court-martialed.[18] Inoue Nisshō and the two assassins in the Ketsumeidan Incidents underwent life imprisonment, as did Tachibana Kōzaburō in the May 15 Incident.[19] However, Lieutenant Mikami Taku (三上卓), who pulled the trigger on Inukai on May 15, was sentenced to only a fifteen-year imprisonment despite the navy prosecution's call for the death penalty, and the eleven military academy students were sentenced to only three months' imprisonment. Shortly after the court judgement, Araki pressed for promulgation of an amnesty decree to grant pardon to the convicts.[20] Mikami was released after only five years' imprisonment.

It was regrettable and unfortunate that the army authorities took a very tolerant attitude toward the insurgents as above, and that the public, being influenced by the mass media, supported the army's stance and was critical of the navy, which sternly accused the offenders. The navy prosecutor who had called for the death penalty was widely attacked, and the head of the legal affairs bureau of the navy who had approved the prosecutor's demand was forced to resign.[21] Undoubtedly the army's unusually lenient stance and the public's uncritical acceptance of it gave young military men the wrong message, constituting one of the important causes of the February 26 Incident (14.1.4).[22]

### 14.1.3. The Kōdō Faction vs. the Tōsei Faction and the February 26 Incident

After the May 15 Incident, Saionji Kinmochi (西園寺公望) appointed Admiral Saitō Makoto as prime minister.[23] Though Saionji had first thought of choosing the Seiyūkai's new president, Suzuki Kisaburō (鈴木喜三郎), continuing the customary practice of making party leaders premiers, the army had made it clear that it would oppose a party cabinet,[24] and the parties themselves seemed to be lacking the strength and determination to restore political stability in these difficult times.[25] Having consulted with senior statesmen, Saionji decided on a nonpartisan "national unity" cabinet under a neutral third person,[26] discontinuing the established practice of a party cabinet that had lasted over three decades.[27] In the Saitō cabinet, Araki remained as the army minister despite the involvement of military academy students in the May 15 Incident. It was judged that he alone could keep the young officers under discipline.[28] Since December 1931, when Araki had become the army minister of the Inukai cabinet, he had systematically replaced officers at key posts in central headquarters with men with whom he had close relations, building up his own faction. His closest colleague was Lt. General Masaki Jinzaburō, the vice-chief of the general staff. Araki and Masaki emphasized the principle of national polity and the need for preparation for an immediate war with the Soviet Union.[29] Such policies were opposed by a group of officers who believed that the army should adhere to a long-range program to prepare for an eventual total war and were critical of Araki's extolling the virtues of spiritualism and spouting right-wing rhetoric, using such terms as "imperial way" and "national polity" excessively, as well as his lenient attitude toward the radicals in the army and his partiality to old friends in personnel policy.[30] Araki's group was called the Kōdō faction (皇道派 the imperial way faction); the rival group was called the Tōsei faction (統制派 the control faction), and its leader was Colonel Nagata Tetsuzan (永田鉄山), chief of the military affairs bureau of the Army Ministry.

Though Araki was respected by many young officers in the army, especially those assigned to regiments throughout the country, when it came to policy debate in the cabinet, he was no match for the likes of Saitō and Takahashi.[31] Araki was often unsuccessful in having the cabinet approve plans prepared by the army,[32] and his popularity among the middle-ranking officers started to wane. In January 1934, Araki stepped down on health grounds to be replaced by General Hayashi Senjūrō, whose former post as inspector general of education of the army passed to Masaki.[33] Meanwhile, the Saitō cabinet was obliged to resign in July 1934 because of a scandal involving Teikoku Jinzō Kenshi (帝国人造絹糸),[34] and Admiral Okada Keisuke (岡田啓介), who had been navy minister until January 1933, was chosen as prime minister. This time the decision was made by a council of *jūshin* (重臣 chief retainers), a group composed of inner court officials and former prime ministers and headed by Saionji. This became the pattern for selecting prime ministers in the subsequent prewar period.[35]

The Okada cabinet was essentially a continuation of the Saitō cabinet. Army Minister Hayashi and Foreign Minister Hirota Kōki (広田弘毅) stayed.[36] Takahashi, who had retired, was called back after only half a year as his successor became ill.[37] Three Seiyūkai members and two Minseitō members were in the cabinet.

After Araki's resignation in January 1934, his most favored protégés were quickly replaced under Hayashi's leadership by staff that Nagata selected.[38] Masaki, who was now the leader of the Kōdō faction, resisted every transfer plan. Hayashi and Nagata decided to shift Masaki out.[39] Masaki resisted fiercely, but at a meeting on July 15, 1935, of Hayashi, Masaki, and Prince Kan'in (閑院宮), the chief of the general staff, Masaki was overridden by the other two and transferred to the army council.[40] Kōdō faction officers around the country were infuriated.[41] On August 12, Lt. Colonel Aizawa Saburō (相沢三郎), one of the senior officers of the Kōdō faction, stormed into Nagata's office and stabbed him to death.[42]

Hayashi resigned, taking responsibility for the unprecedented case of an officer killing a superior. At the Kōdō generals' insistence, the Aizawa trial was conducted in an open court-martial like the one after the May 15 Incident. Aizawa and the Kōdō faction defense counsels used the court as a nationwide rostrum to criticize Nagata and the Tōsei faction, and to publicize the Kōdō faction tenets emphasizing the principle of national polity.[43] The trial greatly stimulated radical young officers of the Kōdō faction, who were contemplating an uprising to wipe out the Tōsei faction, to set in motion a national restoration.[44]

Many of those young officers belonged to the First Division stationed in Tokyo. In December 1935, it was decided that the First Division would soon be sent to Manchuria. They decided to carry out their scheme before the departure.[45]

Early on the morning of February 26, 1936, a fully armed force of 1,400 men under the command of the several rebellious Kōdō faction officers of the First Division attacked in various parts of Tokyo. Finance Minister Takahashi Korekiyo (高橋是清), Lord Keeper of the Privy Seal Saitō Makoto, and Inspector General of Education of the Army Watanabe Jōtarō (渡辺錠太郎) were killed.[46] Grand Chamberlain Suzuki Kantarō (鈴木貫太郎) was seriously wounded. Prime Minister Okada Keisuke escaped as the rebels killed his brother-in-law, whom they mistook for Okada. The insurgents occupied the prime minister's residence, the Diet building, the army minister's residence, the army ministry, and police headquarters, and they set up camp in the administrative district of central Tokyo, demanding establishment of a Kōdō-led military government.[47] Araki and Masaki, now both army councilors, urged the new army minister to issue a statement condoning what the rebels had done and advising them to return to their barracks.[48] The insurgents took this to indicate that events were going their way and refused to withdraw.[49]

When the emperor learned of the uprising, he was extremely angry, and ordered it to be suppressed as quickly as possible. The navy landed a contingent of marines at Yokohama in case the army did not move, and about forty warships were assembled off the coast of Odaiba (お台場) with cannons ready for the bombardment of Tokyo.[50] While the army ministry leaders were still hesitant, the army general staff decided to bring troops based in nearby prefectures into Tokyo and had them encircle the insurgents.[51] As of nine o'clock in the morning of the 29th, attacks by all the surrounding forces of 24,000 were to be opened. The insurgents finally surrendered. The army's central command hoped that the officers who had led the insurrection would kill themselves, but only one committed seppuku. The others refused to do so, anticipating an opportunity to argue their case in court.[52] However, this time the trial was speedy. On March 4, a closed-door court-martial started with no defense counsel. On July 5, seventeen officers were sentenced to death, and a week later they were executed by a firing squad. Two civilians, Kita and Nishida Mitsugu,[53] were also sentenced to death in August 1937.[54] Aizawa also met the same fate after a secret court-martial.[56]

The leaders of the Kōdō faction were either transferred to the inactive reserves or barred from future assignment in central headquarters. Araki and Masaki were placed on reserve and were prevented from reentering politics by the revival of the old rule requiring the war and navy ministers to be officers on the active list, which had been abandoned in 1913.[56]

### 14.1.4. Political Developments after the February 26 Incident

All the coup attempts in the early and mid-1930s failed to achieve their goal.[57] The radical young military officers thought of themselves as latter-day *shishi* (志士 men of spirit) of the Bakumatsu period (2.3.2), and sought to bring about a "Shōwa Restoration," but they were not successful. While their scheme did not materialize,[58] those coup attempts, especially the February 26 Incident, had considerable effects on subsequent political developments in Japan. The political leaders whom the emperor and Saionji had relied upon the most were either killed or removed from the active list. There was no longer anyone with the political power to resist army demands.[59] The army now became more outspoken about political matters. It sought to use the incidents as justification for reduction of the role of the party politicians, advocating for

Chapter 14

greater "harmony and unity" in the government and society instead of a broader representative leadership.[60]

In March 1936, when Hirota Kōki was chosen as the successor to Okada and set about forming a cabinet, the army presented with him a series of demands.[61] It wanted to reduce party representation in the cabinet to one man each from the Seiyūkai and the Minseitō (though it finally accepted two each), and rejected four of the minister candidates whom Hirota had selected.[62] It requested military budget increases and strengthening of economic controls. Finance Minister Baba Eiichi (馬場英一) accommodated these demands,[63] though the business community voiced opposition to them. In January 1937, there occurred a serious exchange of accusations at the Diet between a Diet man and Minister of the Army Terauchi Hisaichi (寺内寿一).[64] The Hirota cabinet resigned, taking responsibility for this duel.

The *jūshin* council nominated Ugaki Kazushige (宇垣一成), who now represented the most conservative element in the army and could be counted on to cooperate with the business community and political parties. But the army vetoed Ugaki's cabinet formation by not letting any incumbent general accept the post of army minister. The army recommended Hayashi Senjūrō, the army minister in the Hirota cabinet, as a substitute for Ugaki. The Hayashi cabinet was launched on February 2, 1937. He took a stronger anti-party stand than had been taken by any premier up to this time.[65] He demanded that members of his cabinet discard any political party affiliations.[66] Such a demand evoked strong protest from the parties. Hayashi dissolved the assembly on March 31, and finding the election returns disappointing, resigned on June 3. He had been in office only for four months.

In the April 1937 election, the last competitive election in prewar Japan, the leftist Shakai Taishūtō (社会大衆党 the Social Mass Party), doubled its previous share, capturing 36 Diet seats. The two rightist parties the Hayashi government supported, the Shōwakai (昭和会) and the Kokumin Dōmei (国民同盟), decreased their seats; the former from 20 to 18, and the latter from 15 to 11.[67] The Minseitō and the Seiyūkai remained major parties, gaining 179 seats and 174 seats respectively out of 466 seats in the Diet.[68]

As the election results indicated, a feeling of an unease about extreme nationalism and militarism had clearly risen in Japanese society. But the political parties were not disposed to offer strong resistance against the army any longer. A considerable portion of party men, the Seiyūkai members in particular, had drawn closer to the nationalist-militarist line. Now that the military-led national unity government had firmly been established, there was little the political parties could do. The prospect of a return to party government being now almost nil, no able government officials or businessmen showed interest in joining the political parties.[69] The decline of the political parties continued, being accelerated with the onset of the China Incident in 1937, until 1940, when all the parties voluntarily dissolved to "preserve internal unity" and formed "one great party," the Taisei Yokusankai (大政翼賛会 the Imperial Rule Assistance Association).[70]

## 14.2. Japan's China Policy in the Mid-1930s and the Xian Incident

### 14.2.1. Japan's North China Separation Policy

In the Rehe (Jehol) campaign, which started in mid-February 1933 (13.5.4), the Kwantung Army was forced to engage in a bitter fight with the Chinese army reinforced with troops sent from the south of the Great Wall. In the belief that security along the north side of the Wall could not be maintained unless the south side was cleared of Chinese troops, in May the Kwantung Army sent forces into Hebei province (河北省), pushed the Chinese forces back to the Bei River,[71] and concluded the Tangku Truce (塘沽停戦協定) on May 31, 1933, which created a demilitarized zone, some 30 to 40 miles wide, between the Great Wall and a line running across Hebei just north of Beijing. This zone, known as the Jidong (冀東) demilitarized zone, was the first part of China proper to be brought into the Kwantung Army's orbit of control.[72] No Chinese troops were to be permitted in this zone, and order was to be kept only by a Chinese police force. The Japanese troops were also to withdraw, leaving garrisons permitted by the Boxer Protocol.[73] The Tangku Truce was tantamount to the Nationalists' tacit recognition of the Japanese presence in Manchuria. Thus it marked the end of the Manchurian crisis that had started in September 1931, but it was also the "charter of Japan's later aggressions in North China."[74] In effect, the truce gave the Japanese a foothold in the area, which enabled them throughout the next years to exercise military, political, and economic pressure against both the local administrations in North China and the Nanjing government.[75]

After the establishment of the Jidong demilitarized zone, there was a temporary halt in Japan's military push in China. In fact, Japan's relations with China showed gradual improvement.[76] A direct railroad service between Beijing and Mukden, which had long been cut at the Great Wall, was opened in 1934. In the spring of the same year, the two countries agreed to elevate their diplomatic missions in each capital from ministers to ambassadors. Hirota, who had been nominated foreign minister in September 1933 as successor to Uchida, publicly declared that he was anxious to bring about a normalization of Sino-Japanese relations.[77] The policy that Hirota really intended to pursue in China was, however, not as conciliatory as what was announced. He stated in a cable sent to Minister Ariyoshi Akira (有吉明) in China on April 13, 1934, that "the maintenance of peace and order in East Asia" would "require Japan to act independently and on its own responsibility."[78] On April 17, 1934, Amō Eiji (天羽英二), head of the foreign ministry's information division, publicly issued a declaration in line with Hirota's message to Ariyoshi. The declaration, which warned the powers against interfering in affairs in China, drew strong opposition from the United States and Britain as well as China, as it contradicted the Open Door policy in China.[79]

In 1935, there were fresh separatist movements by the Japanese army in North China and Inner Mongolia. In May, the Japanese forces stationed in Tianjin (the so-called Tianjin Garrison Army),[80] taking advantage of disorder in the demilitarized zone, put pressure on the Chinese authorities and demanded the withdrawal of the Kuomintang Army, as well as all anti-Japanese organizations, from the whole of Hebei province, along with the dismissal of the governor of Hebei province.[81] In late June in Chahar in Inner Mongolia, the Kwantung Army made almost identical demands to what the Tianjin Army had made in Hebei.[82] In both cases, Nanjing government leaders decided to accept the Japanese demands, and the local Chinese authorities and the Japanese field army concluded the Umezu–Ho Ying-chin (梅津・何応欽) agreement in North China and the Dohihara–Qin Dechun (土肥原・秦徳純) agreement in Inner Mongolia.[83]

## 14.2.2. Leith Ross's Monetary Reforms and Japan's Reactions

In the fall of 1935, Britain sent Frederick Leith-Ross, chief economic advisor to the British government, to China to help bring order to China's silver-backed currency system, which was in critical condition. The outflow of silver abroad had been continuing due to chronic current account deficits. In addition, the US silver purchase program of 1934 brought about massive silver shipments to the United States. The Nanjing government imposed a new tax on silver exports, to little avail. It only increased the smuggling of silver. The government banknotes became inconvertible into silver, and the yuan's exchange rate against foreign currency plummeted.

The measures Leith-Ross adopted were: (1) Only banknotes issued by the three state banks would be legal tender; (2) all silver holdings were to be collected in exchange for legal tender notes; and (3) the legal tender not convertible into silver was to be stabilized at its existing exchange value with foreign currencies through unrestricted selling and buying by the government banks.[84] The silver standard was thus abandoned and a managed currency system was introduced, with Britain providing credit to support the new currency.[85] Leith-Ross visited Japan from September 10 to 17 to discuss possible collaboration with Japan in the monetary reform project. It was Neville Chamberlain, the chancellor of the exchequer, who sent Leith-Ross to Japan. Being concerned about Nazi Germany's moves in Europe, Chamberlain hoped to use the opportunity to smooth over London's differences with Tokyo. But Japan did not accept the overtures. The army was opposed, and the foreign ministry decided to stick to its policy of negotiating directly with China.[86] They expected that Britain would discard the program as it had done in the past when Japan had not supported British plans.[87] This time, however, Britain carried it out without Japanese support.

The Japanese hoped that the monetary reform would fail. In fact, the Tianjin Army worked to undermine the program, discouraging Chinese local leaders in north China from transferring silver to the Nationalist government. Soon after the Nanjing government enacted the monetary reform, however, the Tianjin Army bitterly acknowledged that it was being successfully implemented.

Successful monetary reform would mean that all of China, including North China, would come under the control of the Nationalist government.[88] The Japanese army's aim to turn the provinces of North China into a second Manchukuo would be frustrated.[89] It was necessary for the Japanese to expedite the separation of North China from Nanjing. In late November 1935, the Tianjin Army hurriedly set up a puppet government in the demilitarized zone in Hebei, the East Hebei Anti-Communist Autonomous Council (冀東防共自治委員会), installing a pro-Japanese general, Yin Ju-keng (殷汝耕), as its

*413*

head. The Nationalist government immediately branded Yin a traitor and issued orders for his arrest.[90]

The Nanjing government proposed, as a compromise with the Japanese, establishment of a new autonomous political council headed by Ho Ying-chin, giving the council the power to make appropriate modifications to the new monetary system and to settle other pending issues locally. It was a big concession on the part of the Nanjing government. Japan objected the appointment of Ho, however, claiming that the head of the council should be someone actually ruling in North China, and demanded Song Zheyuan (宋哲元) be the chairman.[91] Nanjing gave in, and the Hebei–Chahar Political Council (冀察政務委員会) headed by Song was formed in early December; it was to administer Hebei and Chahar, as well as the cities of Tianjin and Beijing.[92] Technically, the East Hebei Anti-Communist Autonomous Council came under the jurisdiction of the Hebei–Chahar Political Council, but the Tianjin Army expected that the former, with Japanese assistance, could function competitively and independently from the latter. As Sung's organization started to work, however, it proved to be much stronger than Yin's council, and under stronger influence of the Nanjing government than expected. Japan's North China separation policy proved less satisfactory than was originally hoped.

### 14.2.3. The Xian Incident

In the spring of 1936 Zhang Xueliang (張学良) was engaging in the campaign against the Communists in the Xian (西安) area on Chiang Kai-shek's orders, but he began to wonder if the time had not come for making peace with the Chinese Communist Party (CCP) to jointly fight the Japanese. In May 1936, Zhang travelled to the CCP base area in the north Shaanxi mountains to meet Zhou Enlai (周恩来).[93] Zhang was impressed by Zhou's sincerity regarding concerted action against Japan.[94] Chiang, having learned of Zhang's dealings with the CCP, felt that he had to take overall personal charge in the Xian campaign. He flew to Xian in early December and required Zhang to cooperate with Central Army in the campaign against the Communists.[95] Zhang resisted, insisting that Chiang should end the war with the Communists and start a fight with the Japanese. At dawn on December 12, after weeklong talks that revealed the irreconcilability of their views, units of Zhang's army captured Chiang and held him in custody.

The next two weeks saw the most tense and delicate negotiations between

*414*

Chiang and Zhang, in which Zhou Enlai later participated.[96] Zhou had been informed of Joseph Stalin's position: a united national front against Japan should be formed under Chiang's leadership. Negotiations continued until Christmas Day 1936, when Chiang, who had steadfastly refused to issue any written statements, offered a verbal promise that he would "review the situation."[97] Zhang released Chiang and escorted him to Nanjing to remove any suggestion that he had been a "mutineer," and to hold Chiang to his word. In Nanjing, a crowd of 400,000 enthusiastically welcomed Chiang. Throughout the country, there was unrestrained rejoicing at Chiang's safe return. The kidnapping and his own steadfastness clearly revived Chiang's popularity as a national leader.[98] Until then, Chinese opinion had increasingly become critical of Chiang's appeasing stance toward Japan,[99] but his return from his detention suddenly made him a living symbol of national unity amid an outburst of patriotic enthusiasm.[100] Zhang was court-martialed for insubordination and sentenced to ten years in prison, but Chiang requested clemency and put him under house arrest.

Though the Nationalist plenum in February 1937 did not make a full commitment to the united front, Chiang now decided to discard the policy of exterminating the CCP as a prerequisite to fighting against Japan, and resolved to stand up to the Japanese invasion in earnest, not adopting the appeasing policy.[101] Chiang had read clearly Stalin's sign in Xian that, in the event of escalation into a full-scale war with Japan, Chiang could count on Soviet support, while he knew that countries like Britain, France and the United States would offer no help.[102] It was in the interests of the Soviet Union to keep Japan, which had just concluded the Anti-Comintern Pact with Germany in November 1936 (16.1.3), tied down in China. In fact, the Soviet Union was to become the largest supplier of weapons to China in the first four years of the eight-year Sino–Japanese War from 1937 to 1945.[103]

# 14.3. The Sino–Japanese War and US–Japanese Relations

### 14.3.1. Japan's Attempts on New Sino–Japanese Relations before the War

In Japan, a group in the army general staff had followed the Xian Incident and its subsequent developments closely, and accurately assessed its implications. The group saw the rise of the new force of Chinese nationalism, along with

Chinese people's strong support for Chiang Kai-shek. It concluded that the anti-Japan front between the Kuomintang and the Communist Party would change into a genuine campaign to construct a new China,[104] and that whether the creation of a new China would be accompanied by a policy of hostility toward Japan or not would largely depend on the Japanese China policy. The central figure in the general staff who made these arguments was Ishiwara Kanji, who had been transferred to the general staff headquarters in August 1935.[105] He believed that Sino–Japanese cooperation could materialize if Japan discarded its past policy of imperialist aggression.[106] He also considered it necessary for, in dealing with the Soviet Union, Japan to improve relations with the United States and Britain, because Japan needed a supply of war materials from them, and that improving relations with them required Japan to improve relations with China.[107] On January 16, 1937, the general staff operations division forwarded to the army ministry a memo titled "Taishi jikkōsaku kaisei iken" (対支実行策改正意見 Proposal of practical measures toward China) recommending a cessation of North China separation activities and renewing attempts to further Sino–Japanese economic cooperation.[108]

Satō Naotake's (佐藤尚武) assumption of the post of foreign minister in March 1937 was no less significant.[109] He opposed his predecessors' China policy. Whereas Hirota and Arita had tried to reduce Western influence in China, Satō argued that Japan should observe the principle of the Open Door in China and give up the policy of detaching the northern provinces.[110] The Ministry of Foreign Affairs drafted a document titled "Taishi jikkōsaku" (対支実行策 Practical measures toward China), which was adopted as official policy at a meeting of the four cabinet ministers on April 16, 1937. It stated that the Japanese policy in North China should henceforth be primarily economic, no longer aiming at a political separation of the area from the rest of China.[111] In fact, in the spring of 1937 there were high hopes in Tokyo for a new era in Sino–Japanese relations.

These new policies, however, naturally met with strong opposition from those who had so far promoted the policy of the separation of North China. They argued that such new policies would play into China's hands, and Japan would not only lose its special position in North China, but possibly even Manchuria. For them, there was only one plausible policy: to militarily strengthen Japan's hold on North China.[112]

Given this stance on the part of the imperialists, it should have been

*416*

necessary for the Hayashi government to vigorously promote its new approach to China. But unfortunately, the Hayashi government and Satō's tenure in office lasted only until June 3, 1937 (14.1.4), and the aristocrat Konoe Fumimaro (近衛文麿) was appointed prime minister.

Being young—age 46—and a member of one of the five elite families that had traditionally provided regents to the emperors for hundreds of years, Konoe seemed to be the only individual leader capable of bringing some unity to national politics. In fact, he was well connected with elements in the army, the bureaucracy, and the Diet.[113] Expectations were high that he would do something that would solve the China problem. It turned out, however, that he did not have any new policy ideas, and to the disappointment of promoters of the new China policy, he had not discarded an old-fashioned imperialist view on international relations: Japan, being a "have-not" country, should oppose the international system, which was based on a status quo that froze the inequitable distribution of natural resources.[114] He was not a type to be very decisive about things, but, as discussed below, his inclination in this direction, combined with Hirota's appointment as foreign minister, proved to nullify the effect of Ishihara and Satō's efforts to implement new China policies.[115]

## 14.3.2. The Outbreak of the War and Developments at the Early Stage

On July 7, 1937, a minor skirmish occurred between Chinese and Japanese troops at the Marco Polo Bridge near Beijing.[116] The local commanders succeeded in arranging a truce.[117] Chiang Kai-shek, however, was now determined not to take an appeasing policy anymore.[118] On July 17, at a meeting in Lushan which all major political leaders, including Communist leaders, attended, he made an unprecedentedly strong call to the people of China to unite for a long and difficult struggle for national survival. He declared that "the loss of even one more inch of Chinese territory is unacceptable—to tolerate it would be an unpardonable crime against our race."[119] In both tone and content, the address was a clear departure from Chiang's previous speeches, which had contained some words of caution and conciliation.

Three days after Chiang's address in Lushan, Ishiwara proposed to Army Minister Sugiyama Hajime (杉山元) that since there was a great danger that the war was about to become a "general war" and Japan would become "bogged down in China exactly as Napoleon had in Spain," all Japanese troops in North China should be pulled back into Manchuria immediately. Having

Chapter 14

failed to convince Sugiyama, Ishiwara took his arguments to Prime Minister Konoe, and proposed that Konoe undertake a direct talk with Chiang. But the plan was opposed by army leadership and Hirota as well.[120]

Many officers in the army, including Army Minister Sugiyama, were of the opinion that Japan should take an aggressive stance to compel the Chinese to back down. They failed to recognize the Nationalist army's new determination to resist the Japanese invasion, and argued that it could be completely subdued by a small military force deployed for a short period of time.[121]

The argument between Ishiwara's group and the hard-liners was won by the latter. In the next few months Ishihara's position became increasingly beleaguered. Chief of the Operations Section Mutō Akira (武藤章) took a leading role in consolidating the opposition to Ishiwara and pressing for his transfer from the center.[122] By late September 1937, Ishiwara's views were so out of step with the prevailing opinion in both the army headquarters and the field armies that his enemies were able to secure his removal from the general staff. On September 27, he was assigned to the Kwantung Army as vice chief of staff under Tōjō. This transfer was tantamount to exile.[123]

On September 13, 1937, China appealed to the League of Nations, which advised on October 6 that a conference of the Nine-Power Treaty nations would be held in Brussels. Japan refused to attend the conference, but instead prepared its own peace terms and asked Germany to transmit them to China, which Ambassador Oskar Trautmann in Nanjing passed on to Chiang on November 5, 1937. Chiang at first responded negatively, expecting the Brussels conference would come up with some disciplinary measures. But when the conference ended on November 24 without calling for any sanctions against Japan, Chiang decided to accept the Japanese proposal of November 5 as a basis for negotiations.[124] The Japanese proposal was rather moderate, as it was in line with the policy approved by the cabinet on October 1, which still retained Ishiwara and Satō's counsels.[125]

When Chiang's intention to enter negotiations was relayed to Japan on December 7, however, the Japanese army had already gotten Shanghai under its control after two months of fierce fighting, and was advancing on Nanjing.[126]

Nanjing fell on December 13, 1937 giving rise to a feeling of invincibility in Japan. While Vice-Chief of General Staff Tada Hayao (多田駿) and his non-expansionist subordinates in the general staff thought that Japan should

*418*

enter negotiations with China on the November 5 terms, the hard-liners were determined to demand harsher terms for negotiations. They argued that with one more push, the Nationalist government would fall, and that urging peace at this point would revive the Nationalists' morale. Konoe concurred with their view.[127] He ignored Tada's repeated warnings against the expansionist policies.

On December 22, Hirota gave German ambassador Herbert von Dirksen the Japanese government reply to Chiang's response. It looked like peace terms demanded by a victorious nation against a defeated nation.[128] Dirksen, disconcerted by the harshness of the Japanese terms, cabled Berlin saying in some disgust that the Japanese leaders seemed to be looking forward to the Chinese rejection of the Japanese terms.[129]

On January 15, 1938, at a liaison conference between the government and the Imperial General Headquarters (*Daihonei* 大本営),[130] Tada warned again of the disastrous implications of a protracted war, but all other attendants of the conference excepting Navy Vice-Chief of Staff Koga were in favor of taking a resolute stand against China. In fact, Konoe did not understand why Tada was so adamant in insisting on an early settlement of the war, and the next day he announced the *aitenisezu* (相手にせず no longer recognizing) policy.[131] He declared, "The Imperial Government will hereafter have no dealings with the Nationalist government. . . . We will then work with the new Chinese government to improve relations between our two countries and cooperate in the construction of a regenerated China." Refusing contact with the only internationally recognized government of China was a monstrous step.[132] It was a position indicating that only a policy of intimidation could quickly solve the China problem. Konoe took this step largely in response to mounting pressures from the hard-liners as a result of the December military successes in China.

Meanwhile, in December 1937, the Japanese army formed a puppet regime in North China named the Provisional Government of the Republic of China, and in March 1938 created another in Central China called the Reformed Government of the Republic of China.[133] But neither of the regimes was of any help to Japan in "the construction of a regenerated China" that was advanced in the *aitenisezu* declaration. There was no defection to either regime of even marginally important figures from the Kuomintang regime. No local warlords committed their troops to either puppet regime.[134]

Konoe came to regret the *aitenisezu* declaration within a few months, as he realized that the Ishiwara–Tada predictions about a protracted war and an endless drain on national resources were going to come true. Konoe began to seek ways of putting the war strategy in the hands of leaders more conciliatory toward the Chiang regime.[135] He reshuffled the cabinet in late May 1938, and replaced Foreign Minister Hirota, who had been identified with a tough stance toward the Nationalists and the West, with General Ugaki Kazushige, who was known to have strong disagreements with the army's China policy.[136]

Ugaki made his joining the cabinet conditional on Konoe's acceptance of four conditions, one of which was the unification of Japan's China policy.[137] Ugaki served as foreign minister for only four months, until September 29, but while in office, he pursued peace talks with the Nationalists in earnest. He wanted the Nationalists to authorize Kung Hsiang-hsi (孔祥熙), president of the Executive Yuan, to engage in informal peace negotiations with him.[138] Chiang Kai-shek appeared to have encouraged such talks. Kung sent his secretary to Hong Kong to meet with the Japanese consul general there.[139] The negotiations through the two intermediaries began on June 16.

Ugaki had been given a report on Japan's China policy which Ishii Itarō (石射猪太郎), chief of the Asia bureau of the Ministry of Foreign Affairs, had written for his new boss. Ishii argued that the strength of the Kuomintang government was firmly taking root in China, and Chiang Kai-shek was the man responsible for the "national revival" of China, and that Japan should take a "broad-minded attitude" and negotiate an honorable and generous peace with China.[140] Ugaki basically concurred with Ishii's opinion excepting the question of Chiang's retirement, a face-saving action the Konoe cabinet requested as a condition to conclude a peace agreement.

Some headway was made in the Ugaki–Kung negotiations, but they ultimately foundered. They disagreed on the question of Chiang's resignation and special areas in North China.[141] But the more decisive cause was the Japanese army's obstruction of the talks. The army divested the Ministry of Foreign Affairs of control over Japan's China policy by establishing a China Board (later named the Kōain 興亜院) which would centralize decision-making and policy implementation concerning China. When Konoe did not oppose the scheme, yielding to the army, Ugaki regarded Konoe's action as a breach of his promise to unify Japan's China policy.[142] Ugaki submitted his resignation on September 29.

420

### 14.3.3. The US Moves against Japan after the Outbreak of the War

In the United States, Roosevelt's second administration started in March 1937. The foreign policy in his first term had been quite isolationist or anti-interventionist, as exemplified by the Neutrality Act of 1935 (16.1.2). It made no distinction between aggressor and victim, simply characterizing both as "belligerents" in forbidding arms shipments. This stance signified a marked contrast to the previous administration's Stimson diplomacy that had made moral distinctions between disputing nations.[143]

In his second term, however, Roosevelt discontinued the anti-interventionist stance. For example, he declined to invoke the Neutrality Act in the "China Incident" because being neutral to both China and Japan would be unfavorable to China, which he wanted to assist (though it was actually a war).[144] Then came the quarantine speech of October 5, 1937, which clearly showed Roosevelt's departure from isolationism. He declared that the United States was ready to act together with other countries to quarantine the epidemic of world lawlessness. He did not specify which countries were lawless, but everybody knew that he meant Japan, as well as Germany and Italy. The speech, which was made immediately before the League Assembly's call for a conference in Brussels (14.3.2), as well as the US attendance at the conference, greatly encouraged the other nations participating in the conference.[145]

In the United States, the quarantine speech was applauded by interventionists who felt that some sanctions against Japan were necessary. Though it was followed by no specific activist policies, it helped to increase participation in private anti-Japanese boycotts in the United States.[146]

Japan, on the other hand, continued to signal to Washington that it understood the importance of US interests in China, and that it wanted no confrontation with the United States.[147] While Tokyo was cautious not to provoke the United States, a serious incident occurred in China on December 12, 1937, the day preceding the Japanese conquest of Nanjing. Several Japanese military planes attacked a US navy gunboat, the *Panay*, and three tankers of the Standard Vacuum Oil Company on the Yangtze close to Nanjing. American diplomats and residents were on board the *Panay*, which was escorting the tankers with many Chinese evacuees from Nanjing to Shanghai. Two Americans' lives were lost and thirty were wounded. Hundreds of Chinese died.[148] The attack could have led to a serious crisis between the two countries. Outraged, Roosevelt immediately considered reprisals against

Japan, including a ban on foreign-exchange transactions and a naval blockade. The United States wanted to have Britain's cooperation in implementing these two plans, but Britain was not supportive of either of them.[149] Meanwhile, the Japanese government sought a quick settlement of the crisis. No sooner had the news of the attack reached Tokyo than Hirota saw Grew and expressed his profound regret. The incident was settled in less than two weeks, as Americans accepted the Japanese explanation that the pilots of the Japanese planes, despite seeing the American flag flying on the ship, had suspected it was carrying Chinese military personnel and weapons, and that without waiting for orders they had fired at the ship and realized only later the graveness of the act.[150] The terms of the settlement included Japan's official apology and indemnity payments.[151] Such quick action, rather uncharacteristic of Japan, showed how seriously Japan wanted to avoid conflict with the United States.[152] Grew, who played an important role in the settlement, was deeply affected by the letters and gifts that Japanese from all walks of life sent to the embassy in an attempt to make amends. The American public viewed the *Panay* incident with surprising calm. Interventionists raised no loud outcry. One business journal congratulated Roosevelt for not being militaristic after the attack.[153]

Although Japan's prompt redress for the *Panay* losses avoided immediate crisis, US government leaders were becoming increasingly wary of the Japanese aggression in China and Tokyo's war-preparatory measures typified by the national mobilization law enacted in April 1938 (15.3.5). They were distressed in particular by the fact that Japan was availing itself of American materials for its military operations in China. When the Japanese army conducted air raids on Guangzhou in June 1938, causing heavy civilian casualties, Roosevelt and Secretary of State Cordell Hull decided to halt the sale of American bombers and related equipment to Japan. The state department contacted the manufacturers of those items directly and asked them to stop exporting to Japan. By late summer 1938, this "moral embargo" had effectively stopped sales of military aircraft and aeronautical equipment to Japan.[154]

This first step of pressure on Japan, however, fell far short of deterring Japanese military operations and violations of the Open Door policy in China. The Japanese army continued the blockade of neutral navigation of the Yangtze River, which it had imposed during the Hankou campaign even after that city's capture.[155] In northern China, an independent currency system the Japanese army had adopted was causing reductions in all but Japanese imports

*422*

into the area.[156]

The State Department discussed various measures of economic sanctions, including repudiation of the 1911 trade treaty so that the United States could impose restrictions on trade with Japan whenever it wished, but Hull decided as a first step to write a comprehensive letter of protest to Japan. The letter, dated October 1, 1938, was delivered to the Japanese government by Grew on October 6.

In response, Arita stated on November 18, 1938: "It is the firm conviction of the Japanese Government that now, at a time of continuing development of new conditions in East Asia, an attempt to apply to present and future conditions without any changes, concepts and principles which were applicable to conditions prevailing before the present incident does not in any way contribute to the solution of immediate issues."[157] Arita flatly rejected the Washington system, discarding the ambiguous stance which Japan had so far taken concerning the Nine-Power Treaty.[158]

This provocative stance of the Japanese government made the State Department determined to impose stronger sanctions on Japan.[159] The American Committee for Non-Participation in Japanese Aggression, a group of pacifists and friends of China led by former missionaries in China, was more active than ever. Legislators were showered with letters demanding discontinuation of shipments to Japan of materials that were being used by the Japanese army for its military operations in China.[160] On July 18, 1939, a resolution was proposed in the Senate that the United States give Japan the six-month notice required to abrogate the trade treaty. Hull did not await the debate on the proposal in Congress. On July 26, he told Japan that the treaty was to end the following January (16.2.2).[161]

NOTES

14.1. The Rise of the Army in Japanese Politics

1    Article 11 of the Meiji Constitution provided that the emperor had the right of supreme command, and Article 7 of the Ordinance Concerning the Cabinet provided that the ministers of the army and navy should report to the prime minister what had been reported by the chiefs of the general staff of the army and navy directly to the emperor. The expression "by the chiefs of the general staff of the army and navy" was later deleted so that the Article 7 could be read as saying that the army minister and navy minister, as well as the chiefs of the general staff of the army and navy, could make reports directly to the emperor regarding the right of supreme command

Chapter 14

without prior consultation with the prime minister. Itō Takashi and Momose Takashi, *Jiten Shōwa senzenki no Nihon: Seido to jittai* (Tokyo: Yoshikawa Kōbunkan, 1990), 255–257. Ōe Shinobu, *Tōsuiken* (Tokyo: Nippon Hyoron Sha, 1983), 36–38. Hata Ikuhiko, *Tōsuiken to teikoku rikukaigun no jidai* (Tokyo: Heibonsha, 2006), 83. Hata Ikuhiko, *Sekai shokoku no seido, soshiki, jinji* (Tokyo: University of Tokyo Press, 1988), 430, 508. Nakano Tomio, *Tōsuiken no dokuritsu* (Tokyo: Harashobō, 1973), 454–454. Edwin Reischauer, "What Went Wrong," in *Dilemmas of Growth in Prewar Japan*, ed. James Morley (Princeton: Princeton University Press, 1971), 506.

2    Moltke, the chief of the general staff of Prussia, was given the position to report directly to the kaiser in exercising the right to command all the forces on the ground. Prime Minister Bismarck had also direct access to the kaiser regarding the right of supreme command, but he did not interfere with Moltke, letting him perform his duty fully. Bismarck did not attend the supreme war council during the Franco–Prussian War of 1870. The German general staff's strong position was maintained until the end of WWI. After WWI, the president of the Weimar Republic exercised the right of supreme command, being assisted by the defense minister, who was a member of the cabinet, until Hitler took all power into his hands. Hata, *Tōsuiken*, 81. Hata, *Sekai shokoku no seido*, 279–280.

3    For example, Katō Kanji, chief of the navy general staff, waged a public campaign against the 1930 London Naval Treaty and secured from Hamaguchi a commitment not to renew the treaty in 1936.

4    Kawada Minoru, *Manshū jihen to seitō seiji* (Tokyo: Kodansha, 2010), 172. James Crowley, *Japan's Quest for Autonomy* (Princeton: Princeton University Press, 1966), 115. Reischauer, "What Went Wrong," in *Dilemmas of Growth in Prewar Japan*, ed. Morley, 507.

5    A rule was made in 1886 that the war minister or navy minister must be a military officer. In 1900 it was decided that the war minister should be an active-service full general or lieutenant general, and the navy minister an active-service admiral or vice-admiral. In 1913 the active-service requirement was revoked. Though it was revived in 1936, it was not in force in 1931 when Wakatsuki conceded to the army. Even retired officers could become the minister of the army or navy, so long as they were a three- or four-star general or admiral. In practical terms, however, the army had a strong influence in selecting a candidate for the ministry regardless of any active service restriction. Itō and Momose, *Shōwa senzenki no Nihon*, 258–259.

6    For example, the army vetoed the formation of the Ugaki cabinet in 1937 (14.1.4).

7    In 1940 the army overthrew the Yonai cabinet by having Army Minister Hata Shunroku resign from the cabinet (16.1.3).

8    For example, in 1931 the army had the Wakatsuki government accept its Manchurian policy by threatening to withdraw Army Minister Minami (13.1.3).

9    Inoue Nisshō (井上日召) was a Buddhist priest of the Nichiren sect who claimed to have attained enlightenment by shouting out "Nisshō," while practicing zen meditation in 1924 in Ōarai, Ibaraki Prefecture. His career included broad travel experience in northeast Asia, intimate contact with Kwantung Army men, and service as a Japanese spy. He gathered local youths at a temple in Ōarai and indoctrinated them with his own ideas, which were a blend of a nationalism and Nichirenism, colored by

resentment against the ruling clique, political parties, the zaibatsu, and elite social classes, all of whom were responsible for agrarian misery. He came up with the idea that each member of his group would assassinate one tainted leader. He named the group the Ketsumeidan (血盟団 Blood Brotherhood). Nakamura Takafusa, *Shōwashi I, 1926–45* (Tokyo: Tōyōkeizai Shinpōsha, 1993), 148–149. Robert Scalapino, *Democracy and the Party Movement in Prewar Japan* (Berkeley: University of California Press, 1953), 367–368.

10   Ōuchi Tsutomu, *Nihon no rekishi 24: Fashizumu eno michi* (Tokyo: Chuokoronsha, 1974), 336–338.

11   Tachibana Kōzaruō was a leader of the right-wing agrarian-first radical movement. He set up the Aikyōjuku (Institute for Local Patriotism), a school in Mito for the education of rural youth. His teaching was based on an agrarian-centered radical nationalism. He severely attacked party politics and capitalism. Nakamura Takafusa, *A History of Shōwa Japan, 1926–1989*, trans. Edwin Whenmouth (Tokyo: University of Tokyo Press, 1998), 91. Scalapino, *Democracy and the Party Movement*, 357.

12   When the intruders entered Inukai's residence, he was dining with his family. He took them to the drawing room and tried to talk them out of their plot, but they replied, "It's no use talking to you!" and shot him. Fatally wounded, Inukai still insisted that he would talk with the man who shot him. On that day another group attacked Makino Nobuaki's residence, but he escaped assassination. They also attacked electricity substations in central Tokyo, but failed to inflict serious damage. Nakamura, *A History of Shōwa Japan*, trans. Whenmouth, 91.

13   Ibid., 91.

14   Ogata Sadako, *Defiance in Manchuria: The Making of Japanese Foreign Policy, 1931–1932* (Berkeley: University of California Press, 1966), 152. According to *Kido diary*, Suzuki Teiichi, chief of the China section of the military bureau of the Army Ministry, said that the direct cause that stimulated the assassins to resort to the May 15 Incident was Inukai's speech on May 1. Ibid., 154–155.

15   Ibid., 153–154.

16   Sandra Wilson writes, "It is difficult to judge how sincere were any of the various people who spoke out on behalf of the countryside in the early 1930s." Wilson points out that one of the navy officers who collaborated with the May 15 Incident wrote in his diary in 1931 that "the suffering farmers provided a useful justification for a coup to overthrow the bourgeoisie, especially now that conditions in the countryside were so conveniently bad." Sandra Wilson, *The Manchurian Crisis and Japanese Society, 1931–33* (London: Routledge, 2002), 130. As Peter Duus points out, those right-wing activists did not intend to organize a mass movement for the salvation of the people in the rural areas. They expressed concern about the economic distress in the rural districts and blamed the party government for it, but they appeared less concerned about the people's welfare itself as about the effects of the farmers' poor health on the nation's strength. Those activists chose to resort to a military coup d'état or terrorism rather than the tedious process of building mass support. Peter Duus, *The Rise of Modern Japan* (Boston: Houghton Mifflin, 1976), 209.

17   Nakamura, *A History of Shōwa Japan*, trans. Whenmouth, 113.

18   Ogata, *Defiance in Manchuria*, 99.

Chapter 14

19  Nakamura, *A History of Shōwa Japan*, trans. Whenmouth, 113.
20  Ogata, *Defiance in Manchuria*, 154.
21  Nakamura, *A History of Shōwa Japan*, trans. Whenmouth, 113.
22  Ōuchi, *Nihon no rekishi*, 342.
23  Saitō, former governor of Korea and a well-known moderate, was a tolerable choice to all concerned. His cabinet contained four Seiyūkai men, including Takahashi, who stayed on as the finance minister, and three Minseitō (民政党) men, but one from each party came from the House of Peers. Ogata, *Defiance in Manchuria*, 156. Scalapino, *Democracy and the Party Movement*, 371.
24  Suzuki Teiichi told Kido that, should the cabinet again be handed over to a political party, second and third incidents would occur. Ogata, *Defiance in Manchuria*, 154–155.
25  Misawa Shigeo and Ninomiya Saburō, "Teikoku gikai to seitō," in *Kaisen ni itaru jūnen, 1931–41*, eds. Hosoya Chihiro, Saitō Makoto, Imai Seiichi and Rōyama Michio (Tokyo: University of Tokyo Press, 1971), 10.
26  Duus, *The Rise of Modern Japan*, 211–212.
27  Kawada Minoru, *Shōwa rikugun no kiseki* (Tokyo: Chuokoron Shinsha, 2011), 61. The first party cabinet in Japan was the Ōkuma Shigenobu cabinet inaugurated in 1898. Ōkuma was the head of the Kenseitō, a newly formed party in that year combining the Progressive Party headed by Ōkuma and the Liberal Party headed by Itagaki Taisuke. All of Ōkuma's cabinet members except the ministers of the army and navy were members of the Kenseitō. Ōkuma was a member of the House of Peers. The Hara cabinet of the Seiyūkai, established in 1918, was the first cabinet under a prime minister who was an incumbent member of the House of Representatives.
28  Nakamura, *A History of Shōwa Japan*, trans. Whenmouth, 92. Ogata, *Defiance in Manchuria*, 156.
29  Crowley, *Japan's Quest for Autonomy*, 204. Nakamura, *A History of Shōwa Japan*, trans. Whenmouth,120.
30  Duus, *The Rise of Modern Japan*, 212.
31  Nakamura, *A History of Shōwa Japan*, trans. Whenmouth, 96.
32  For example, the "Outline of Basic Imperial Policies" which the army proposed was not adopted by the cabinet, and their plans for assisting agricultural communities were replaced by a self-help program pushed through by Finance Minister Takahashi and Agriculture and Forestry Minister Gotō Fumio. Ibid., 96.
33  Ibid., 96. Masaki's wish to become the war minister succeeding Araki was not fulfilled because of Chief of General Staff Prince Kan'in's opposition. Ōuchi, *Nihon no rekishi*, 434.
34  Nakamura, *A History of Shōwa Japan*, trans. Whenmouth, 97. Two ministers in the Saitō cabinet and Takahashi's son were arrested on charges that they were embroiled in a financial scandal relating to the purchase of Teijin shares. A three-year inquiry led to all the accused being acquitted, and the judge declaring that no crime had been committed and upbraiding the prosecution for fabricating the charges. This could be interpreted as a case of "prosecutor's fascism." Ibid., 97.
35  Ibid., 97. Duus, *The Rise of Modern Japan*, 211. Itō and Momose, *Shōwa senzenki no Nihon*, 14, 19, 23.

*Notes*

36 Nakamura, *A History of Shōwa Japan*, trans. Whenmouth, 97. Hirota had been am- bassador to the Soviet Union until he took over for Uchida as foreign minister in September 1933.

37 Ibid., 97.

38 Crowley, *Japan's Quest for Autonomy*, 256. Hayashi had now become a supporter of Nagata, though he had not been anti-Araki before assuming the portfolio. W. G. Beasley, *The Rise of Modern Japan* (London: Phoenix, 1990), 180.

39 Nakamura, *A History of Shōwa Japan*, trans. Whenmouth, 123. Masaki was a pivotal actor in the attack on Professor Minobe in the controversy over the interpretation of the emperor's constitutional status, and this also earned Hayashi's displeasure. Ibid., 100.

40 Kawada, *Shōwa rikugun no kiseki*, 49. The army council was composed of the mar- shals, the fleet admirals, the ministers of the army and navy, the chiefs of the general staff of the army and navy, and some full-time councilors. Originally it was created in 1903 for coordination between the army and the navy, but in later years councils for that purpose were rarely held, and the army and the navy held councils separately for other unspecific purposes. It functioned mainly as an advisory organ to the war min- ister or the navy minister. Itō and Momose, *Shōwa senzenki-no Nihon*, 264–265.

41 Nakamura, *A History of Shōwa Japan*, trans. Whenmouth, 123.

42 Aizawa had been looked up to by the young Kōdō faction officers, especially by the members of a group called the Kokutai Genri Group (国体原理グループ National Polity Principle Group). They were strongly influenced by Kita Ikki. Nagata had been wary of the Kokutai Genri Group members because of their revolutionary be- liefs. Crowley, *Japan's Quest for Autonomy*, 257, 264. Kawada, *Shōwa rikugun no kiseki*, 100–102, 115. Nakamura, *A History of Shōwa Japan*, trans. Whenmouth, 123.

43 Crowley, *Japan's Quest for Autonomy*, 270–271.

44 Ibid., 269. Nakamura, *A History of Shōwa Japan*, trans. Whenmouth, 124. Masaki and other Kōdō faction leaders were informed of the likelihood of a rebellion, but they did not dissuade the plotters or inform the military police of the incipient re- bellion. Crowley, *Japan's Quest for Autonomy*, 272.

45 Ōuchi, *Nihon no rekishi*, 441.

46 Watanabe Jōtarō was killed after incurring the Kōdō faction officers' enmity because he became the inspector general of education of the army after Masaki was ousted from the post by Hayashi and Nagata. Ibid., 437.

47 The written demands the rebels had prepared did not propose any concrete plan after the overthrow of the government. They only called, in abstract terms, for the creation of a state upholding the national polity. They demanded a government headed by Masaki, but it was after Kita and Nishida suggested that they do so by telephone on February 27. Ibid., 430–431, 448.

48 The new army minister was General Kawashima Yoshiyuki, who did not belong to either the Kōdō faction or the Tōsei faction.

49 Ōuchi, *Nihon no rekishi*, 444–445. Nakamura, *A History of Shōwa Japan*, trans. Whenmouth,125.

50 Ōuchi, *Nihon no rekishi*, 446.

51 Nakamura, *A History of Shōwa Japan*, trans. Whenmouth, 126. Ōuchi, *Nihon no*

Chapter 14

*rekishi*, 443–444. It was Ishiwara Kanji, now the head of the strategy section of the general staff, who proposed bringing troops from the regiments based in nearby prefectures into Tokyo. Ōuchi, *Nihon no rekishi*, 446.

52  Nakamura, *A History of Shōwa Japan*, trans. Whenmouth, 126. Crowley, *Japan's Quest for Autonomy*, 273.

53  Nishida Mitsugi had been a cavalry lieutenant, but he left the army to engage in political activities in response to Kita's revolutionary calling. Ogata, *Defiance in Manchuria*, 29.

54  Ōuchi, *Nihon no rekishi*, 452–453.

55  Crowley, *Japan's Quest for Autonomy*, 274.

56  Masaki was court-martialed, but found not guilty for lack of sufficient evidence. Nakamura, *Shōwa-shi*, 214.

57  Ben-Ami Shillony observes, "It has not been proven that any prime minister in Japan changed his policy because of intimidation by terrorists." Ben-Ami Shillony, "Myth and Realty in Japan of the 1930s," in *Modern Japan: Aspect of History, Literature and Society*, ed. W. G. Beasley (London; George Allen & Unwin, 1975), 84.

58  Duus, *The Rise of Modern Japan*, 210–211.

59  Nakamura, *A History of Shōwa Japan*, trans. Whenmouth, 128.

60  Reischauer, "What Went Wrong?" in *Dilemmas*, ed. Morley, 507–508.

61  Scalapino, *Democracy and the Party Movement*, 386.

62  The four ministers whom the army opposed included Yoshida Shigeru as foreign minister. Ōuchi, *Nihon no rekishi*, 454–455. Arita Hachirō was accepted as foreign minister by the army.

63  Scalapino, *Democracy and the Party Movement*, 384–385. Nakamura, *A History of Shōwa Japan*, trans. Whenmouth, 129.

64  The Diet member was Hamada Kunimatsu of the Seiyūkai. He openly accused the army of foisting a dictatorship upon Japan. Terauchi charged that Hamada insulted the army. Hamada retorted, "Let's check the record. If there's any language in my comments that is insulting to the army, I will commit seppuku. If there's none, you commit seppuku." Scalapino, *Democracy and the Party Movement*, 385. Nakamura, *A History of Shōwa Japan*, trans. Whenmouth, 135.

65  Scalapino, *Democracy and the Party Movement*, 386.

66  Hayashi asked one Minseitō man and one Seiyūkai man to join the cabinet on the condition that they each leave their party. Having been rejected by both, Hayashi admitted to the cabinet only one party man from the Shōwakai, a rightist party. Misawa and Ninomiya, "Teikoku gikai to seitō," in *Kaisen ni itaru jūnen*, eds. Hosoya, Saitō, Imai and Rōyama, 12. The army minister of the Hayashi cabinet was Nakamura Kōtarō, the foreign minister was Satō Naotake, and the finance minister was Yūki Toyotarō. Yūki, a former Bank of Japan official, set about revising Baba's disastrous fiscal policy. Nakamura, *A History of Shōwa Japan*, trans. Whenmouth, 136.

67  Scalapino, *Democracy and the Party Movement*, 386.

68  In the previous election held in February 1936, the Seiyūkai decreased its seats from 303 to 175, while the Minseitō, which used as one of its slogans, "What shall it be, parliamentary government or fascism?" increased its share from 146 seats to 205. The Seiyūkai's decline was largely attributable to its taking sides in 1935 with those who

*Notes*

denounced Professor Minobe Tatsukichi's (美濃部達吉) emperor-as-organ theory as a denial of the principle of national polity. This theory was a well-established part of Japanese constitutional debate. But it was suddenly attacked in the Diet in February 1935; the Seiyūkai joined the attacking group and sought to make the matter an issue to pull down the Okada administration, which first chose to ignore the controversy. In the army, Masaki was a pivotal actor in the opposition to the theory. Minobe was forced to resign from the House of Peers, his professorship, and all other honors. In February 1936 he was shot by a rightist and was seriously injured. Nakamura, *A History of Shōwa Japan*, trans. Whenmouth, 98–100. Scalapino, *Democracy and the Party Movement*, 372–373.

69 Duus, *The Rise of Modern Japan*, 213.

70 Ibid., 213. W. G. Beasley, *The Modern History of Japan* (London: Weidenfeld and Nicolson, 1963), 257. Scalapino, *Democracy and the Party Movement*, 388–389. Nakamura, *A History of Shōwa Japan*, trans. Whenmouth, 165.

14.2. Japan's China Policy in the Mid-1930s and the Xian Incident

71 Jonathan Spence, *The Search for Modern China* (New York: W. W. Norton, 1990), 394. The Bei River flows through central Hebei and enters the Gulf of Bo Hai at Tangku.

72 Nakamura, *A History of Shōwa Japan*, trans. Whenmouth, 94.

73 Dorothy Borg, *The United States and the Far Eastern Crisis of 1933–1938* (Cambridge: Harvard University Press, 1964), 37.

74 Ibid., 37.

75 Ibid., 37–38.

76 Nakamura, *A History of Shōwa Japan*, trans. Whenmouth, 103–104.

77 Shimada Toshihiko, "Designs on North China, 1933–1937," trans. James Crowley, in *The China Quagmire: Japan's Expansion on the Asia Continent, 1933–1941*, ed. James Morley (New York: Columbia University Press, 1983), 76.

78 Ibid., 82.

79 Ian Nish, *Japanese Foreign Policy in the Interwar Period* (Westport, CT: Praeger Publishers, 2002), 104. James Crowley, *Japan's Quest for Autonomy* (Princeton: Princeton University Press, 1966), 197.

80 The Boxer Protocol of 1901 had allowed eleven nations to station 12,200 troops in total in the legation quarter in Beijing and the area between the capital and the sea. Japan was authorized to station 2,600 troops. The powers had unilaterally increased their troops since then to protect greater numbers of resident nationals. By 1936 Japan had increased the number to 5,600. Shimada, "Designs on North China," trans. Crowley, in *The China Quagmire*, ed. Morley, 174–177.

81 Much of the disruption was fomented by the Japanese, but the biggest incident was the assassinations of two pro-Japanese newspaper publishers by Chinese activists. The Tianjin army charged that the acts were violations of the Tangku agreement. Han-sheng Lin, "A New Look at Chinese Nationalist 'Appeasers,'" in *China and Japan: Search for Balance since World War I*, eds. Alvin Coo and Hilary Conroy (Santa Barbara: ABC-Clio, 1978), 231. Shimada, "Designs on North China," trans. Crowley, in *The China Quagmire*, ed. Morley, 102–106.

*429*

Chapter 14

82 Shimada, "Designs on North China," trans. Crowley, in *The China Quagmire*, ed. Morley, 114–122.

83 The Umezu–Ho Ying-chin agreement was signed by Major General Umezu, the commander of the China Garrison Army, and Ho Ying-chin, the military secretary of the Nanjing government and the chairman of the Beijing Military Council. Qin Decun who concluded the Dohihara–Qin agreement, was a subordinate of Song Zheyuan, who was the governor of Chahar province and the commander of the 29th Army. Dohihara was at the time the head of Mukden Special Service Agency. The Nanjing government appeasement policy shown in both agreements caused sentiments to turn against Wang Ching-wei, the head of the executive yuan, and Wang was seriously wounded in an assassination attempt on November 1, 1935. Lin, "A New Look at Chinese Nationalist 'Appeasers,'" in *China and Japan*, eds. Coox and Conroy, 232.

84 Shimada, "Designs on North China," trans. Crowley, in *The China Quagmire*, ed. Morley, 137.

85 Nakamura, *A History of Shōwa Japan*, trans. Whenmouth, 103–104.

86 Leith-Ross asked the Japanese leaders if Japan would share the necessary funds for the currency reform with Britain. He also said that China should recognize Manchukuo, that Manchukuo should pay China a proper share of China's foreign and domestic debt, and that the payment to China should be added to the reserve funds of the Central Bank of China to be used for monetary reform. Leith-Ross met Hirota, Shigemitsu (the vice foreign minister), and Takahashi. Takahashi expressed his acceptance of Leith-Ross' proposal, but Shigemitsu stuck to the principle that Japan should primarily be responsible for the maintenance of order in China, and other powers should be satisfied with the Open Door in China. Usui Katsumi, *Shinpan Nitchū sensō* (Tokyo: Chuokoronsha, 2000), 26. Nakamura, *A History of Shōwa Japan*, 103–104. Shimada, "Designs on North China," trans. Crowley, in *The China Quagmire*, ed. Morley, 137, 140. Michael Barnhart, *Japan Prepares for Total War* (Ithaca: Cornell University Press, 1987), 41.

87 Shimada, "Designs on North China," trans. Crowley, in *The China Quagmire*, ed. Morley, 140.

88 Ibid., 144.

89 Usui Katsumi, *Nitchū sensō* (Tokyo: Chuokoronsha, 1967), 18.

90 Shimada, "Designs on North China," trans. Crowley, in *The China Quagmire*, ed. Morley, 154.

91 Sung was one of the warlords based in northern China and the Chahar area. In the Rehe campaign in March 1933, Sung fought a good fight against the Japanese army as the commander of 29th Army and won nationwide fame. He had good relations with several Japanese generals stationed in China.

92 Usui, *Nitchū sensō*, 32.

93 Zhou Enlai's position in the CCP changed often, When Zhang met him in May 1936, he was vice-chairman of the CCP under Mao Zedong.

94 Spence, *The Search for Modern China*, 420–421.

95 Steve Tsang, "Chiang Kai-shek's 'secret deal' at Xian and the start of the Sino–Japanese War" (Palgrave Communications, published January 20, 2015), 3, 10.

*430*

96 Ibid., 9. Spence, *The Search for Modern China*, 424.
97 Spence, *The Search for Modern China*, 424.
98 Ibid., 424.
99 Akira Iriye, *The Origins of the Second World War in Asia and the Pacific* (London: Longman, 1987), 36–38.
100 Borg, *The United States and the Far Eastern Crisis*, 231.
101 Tsang, "Chiang Kai-shek's secret deal," 2–3.
102 Ibid., 8.
103 Ibid., 1.

### 14.3. The Sino–Japanese War and US–Japanese Relations

104 John Boyle, *China and Japan at War, 1937–1945: The Politics of Collaboration* (Stanford: Stanford University Press, 1972), 48–49.
105 Ishiwara had been transferred back to the general staff headquarters in August 1935 as head of the operations section of the operations division. In June 1936, he was named head of the newly created war guidance section. In March 1937, he was promoted to head of the operations division.
106 Usui, *Shinpan Nitchū sensō*, 53–54. Kawada, *Shōwa rikugun no kiseki*, 138–145. Shimada, "Designs on North China, 1933–1937," trans. Crowley, in *The China Quagmire*, ed. Morley, 226. Boyle, *China and Japan at War*, 48.
107 Kawada, *Shōwa rikugun no kiseki*, 142, 145–146.
108 Ibid., 138–139. Shimada, "Designs on North China, 1933–1937," trans. Crowley, in *The China Quagmire*, ed. Morley. 226. Barnhart, *Japan Prepares for Total War*, 80.
109 Satō had been ambassador to France before he assumed the post of foreign minister on March 3.
110 Satō strongly believed that Japan's salvation lay in an open international economic system in which the nation would promote industrialization and export, and that an open economic system depended on close cooperation and consultation among nations; thus, it was essential for Japan to promote a policy of international cooperation. Iriye, *The Origin of the Second World War*, 37. Barnhart, *Japan Prepares for Total War*, 80.
111 Iriye, *The Origin of the Second World War*, 37. Usui, *Shinpan Nitchū sensō*, 52–56. The members of the four ministers' meeting were the ministers of foreign affairs, finance, army, and navy.
112 For example, Tōjō, chief of staff of the Kwantung Army, submitted a report to Tokyo headquarters that it was now necessary to strike a blow at the Chinese. Usui, *Shinpan Nitchū sensō*, 59. Kawada, *Shōwa rikugun no kiseki*, 142, 148. Boyle, *China and Japan at War*, 49.
113 Duus, *The Rise of Modern Japan*, 220.
114 In 1918, Konoe wrote a magazine article titled "Eibei hon'i no heiwashugi o haisu" (英米本位の平和主義を排す A Rejection of Anglo-American Pacifism). It was an argument of old-fashioned imperialism justifying "have-not" countries' military solutions. He argued that the League covenant, the nine-power treaty, and the pact of Paris had all defined an international system on the basis of the status quo, which tended to freeze national boundaries and did nothing to alter the inequitable

Chapter 14

distribution of natural resources. Richly endowed nations such as the United States and the British empire had every reason to support the status quo, but for a country like Japan it meant perpetual poverty and injustice. Japan, as a "have not" country, needed to secure for itself "the right of survival." In the absence of an overall international system of justice, Japan's continental policy was fully justified. Iriye, *The Origins of the Second World War*, 38–39. Nakamura, *A History of Shōwa Japan*, 137.

115 Iriye, *The Origin of the Second World War*, 38–39. Iriye argues, "Konoe and Hirota, perhaps more than any other civilians, were to confirm Japan's tragic isolation in world affairs." Ibid., 39. Saionji was wary of Konoe's anti-American and anti-British inclinations, but the army leadership was disposed to see either Hiranuma or Konoe succeed Hayashi. Since Saionji wanted to avoid rightist Hiranuma, he had no other alternative. Gordon Berger, *Parties out of Power in Japan, 1931–1941* (Princeton: Princeton University Press, 1977), 120–121.

116 A Japanese army company was engaged in its nightly maneuvers when it suddenly came under fire. It was never confirmed who had fired the first shots. On the part of the Japanese garrison army, there was no conspiracy as in the case of the Mukden Incident. The knowledge that the eventual triumph of the Chinese Communist Party could not have occurred had it not been for the outbreak of the Sino–Japanese War has now given some adherence to the theory that Communist party members were responsible for firing the first shots. David Lu, Introduction to "The Marco Polo Bridge Incident 1937," in *The China Quagmire: Japan's Expansion on the Asian Continent, 1933–1945*, ed. James Morley (New York: Columbia University Press, 1983), 235.

117 On July 11, a truce was worked out locally, and the chief of staff of the Tianjin Army reported that the situation there did not require additional troops. The Japanese government, which had already decided to send reinforcements, stopped the dispatch. But the decision was soon changed with a report that four Nationalist army divisions were heading for Beijing. Within the two-week period between July 11 and July 27, when the final decision to dispatch reinforcements was made, a decision to mobilize was reached and then cancelled three times. Hata Ikuhiko, "Nitchū sensō no gunjiteki tenkai (1937–1941)," in *Taiheiyō sensō eno michi*, vol. 4, ed. Nihon Kokusai Seiji Gakkai Taiheiyō Sensō Gen-in Kenkyūbu (Tokyo: Asahi Shimbunsha, 1963), 8–11.

118 Tsang, "Chiang Kai-shek's secret deal," 2.

119 John Boyle, "Peace Advocacy during the Sino–Japanese Incident," in *China and Japan: Search for Balance Since World War I*, eds. Alvin Coox and Hilary Conroy (Santa Barbara: ABC-Clio, 1978), 252.

120 Hata, "Nitchū sensō no gunjiteki tenkai," in *Taiheiyō sensō eno michi*, vol. 4, ed. Nihon Kokusai Seiji Gakkai, 14. Boyle, in "Peace Advocacy," *China and Japan*, eds. Coox and Conroy, 253.

121 Hata Ikuhiko, "The Marco Polo Bridge Incident 1937," in *The China Quagmire: Japan's Expansion on the Asian Continent, 1933–1945*, ed. James Morley (New York: Columbia University Press, 1983), 251.

122 Hata, "Nitchū sensō no gunjiteki tenkai," in *Taiheiyō sensō eno michi*, vol. 4, ed. Nihon Kokusai Seiji Gakkai, 9, 24. Boyle, *China and Japan at War*, 52.

*Notes*

123 Hata, "Nitchū sensō no gunjiteki tenkai," in *Taiheiyō sensō eno michi*, vol. 4, ed. Nihon Kokusai Seiji Gakkai, 30. Boyle, *China and Japan at War*, 53.

124 Hata, "Nitchū sensō no gunjiteki tenkai," in *Taiheiyō sensō eno michi*, vol. 4, ed. Nihon Kokusai Seiji Gakkai, 35. Usui, *Shinpan Nitchū sensō*, 93. Chiang assembled his leading generals in the half-evacuated capital of Nanjing on December 2 to ask their opinions concerning the Japanese peace proposals. One of the generals replied "If these and these alone are the terms, why should there be war?" Boyle, *China and Japan at War*, 70.

125 Hata, "Nitchū sensō no gunjiteki tenkai," in *Taiheiyō sensō eno michi*, vol. 4, ed. Nihon Kokusai Seiji Gakkai, 35.

126 In the fighting in Shanghai, the Chinese army resisted fiercely; the Japanese army suffered 9,115 casualties and 31,257 injuries. Usui, *Nitchū sensō*, 51.

127 Hata, "Nitchū sensō no gunjiteki tenkai," in *Taiheiyō sensō eno michi*, vol. 4, ed. Nihon Kokusai Seiji Gakkai, 35–36. Boyle, *China and Japan at War*, 71–74.

128 Hata, "Nitchū sensō no gunjiteki tenkai," in *Taiheiyō sensō eno michi*, vol. 4, ed. Nihon Kokusai Seiji Gakkai, 37. Hata, "The Marco Polo Bridge Incident 1937," *China Quagmire*, 285–286.

129 Usui Katsumi, "Nitchū sensō no seijiteki tenkai," in *Taiheiyō sensō eno michi*, vol. 4, *Nitchū sensō*, II (Tokyo: Asahi Shimbunsha, 1963), 128.

130 The Imperial General Headquarters (*Daihonei* 大本営) was a supreme war council to facilitate cooperation between the general staff of the army and the navy.

131 Hata, "Nitchū sensō no gunjiteki tenkai," in *Taiheiyō sensō eno michi*, vol. 4, ed. Nihon Kokusai Seiji Gakkai, 40. Boyle, *China and Japan at War*, 79.

132 Iriye, *The Origin of the Second World War*, 52.

133 Nakamura, *A History of Shōwa Japan*, 146–147. Wang Kemin was installed as the president of the Provisional Government of the Republic of China. Wang Kemin had been Qing dynasty's official and had later served Zhang Xueliang as his government's financial advisor. The Reformed Government of the Republic of China was headed by Liang Hongzhi who had served on the staff of the Duan Qirui government. Spence, *The Search for Modern China*, 452–453. Boyle, *China and Japan at War*, 89.

134 Boyle, *China and Japan at War*, 141–142.

135 Ibid., 81, 139.

136 Iriye, *The Origin of the Second World War*, 59.

137 The four conditions were the consolidation of the cabinet, a speedy decision on a peace policy toward China, a unification of diplomatic policy on China, and not emphasizing the *aitenisezu* declaration. Boyle, *China and Japan at War*, 148. Usui, "Nitchū sensō no seijiteki tenkai," in *Taiheiyō sensō eno michi*, vol. 4, ed. Nihon Kokusai Seiji Gakkai, 147.

138 Boyle, *China and Japan at War*, 156.

139 Iriye, *The Origin of the Second World War*, 59–60.

140 Ishii argued that it was useless to insist on the retirement of Chiang from the political scene in China. Even assuming that the Chinese assented to this demand, Ishii argued, Japan's best interests would not be served. Whoever succeeded Chiang would be "unavoidably weak" and unable to control China. As a result, all China would fall

Chapter 14

into a state of economic and political bankruptcy. In the confusion and disorder, only the Communists would have both the ideology and the organization to take advantage of the situation. Boyle, *China and Japan at War*, 152–155. Usui, "Nitchū sensō no seijiteki tenkai," in *Taiheiyō sensō eno michi*, vol. 4, ed. Nihon Kokusai Seiji Gakkai, 148–149.

141 Ugaki stubbornly demanded Chiang's resignation, but Kung firmly refused to accept it. Concerning Japanese demand for special areas in North China. Kung explained to Ugaki that China was willing to give its tacit agreement to the existence of Manchukuo and to let Japan establish a special zone and garrison its troops in Inner Mongolia, but the area inside the Great Wall was quite a different matter. If Japan tried to "liberate" North China and station its troops there indefinitely, the Chines people would become "obsessed with the notion that Japan eventually plans to annex all of China." Boyle, *China and Japan at War*, 159–160.

142 Usui Katsumi, *Nitchū gaikōshi kenkyū* (Tokyo: Yoshikawa Kōbunkan, 1998), 303. Usui, "Nitchū sensō no seijiteki tenkai," in *Taiheiyō sensō eno michi*, vol. 4, ed. Nihon Kokusai Seiji Gakkai, 147. Iriye, *The Origin of the Second World War*, 61. Boyle, *China and Japan at War*, 160–161

143 Paul Johnson, *A History of the American People* (New York: Harper Perennial, 1999), 774.

144 Thomas Bailey, *A Diplomatic History of the American People* (Englewood Cliffs, NJ: Prentice-Hall, 1980), 704.

145 Akira Iriye, *The Cambridge History of American Foreign Relations, vol. II: The Globalizing of America, 1913–1945* (Cambridge: Cambridge University Press, 1993), 158. Iriye, *The Origin of the Second World War*, 46.

146 Bailey, *A Diplomatic History of the American People*, 704–705. Anti-Japanese boycotts in the United States began after the outbreak of the Sino–Japanese war. The *Far Eastern Survey* estimates that during the first year of the war, US boycotts reduced imports from Japan by around $15 million, or 7.4 percent of the total imports from Japan. "The Anti-Japanese Boycott in the United States," *Far Eastern Survey*, vol. III, no. 5 (New York: American Council Institute of Pacific Relations, March 1, 1939), 52–54.

147 Walter LaFeber, *The Clash: U.S.–Japanese Relations throughout History* (New York: W. W. Norton, 1997), 186–187.

148 Iriye, *The Cambridge History of American Foreign Relations*, vol. II, 158. Bailey, *A Diplomatic History of the American People*, 704–705.

149 Secretary of the Treasury Morgenthau asked John Simon, his British counterpart, to join in a ban on foreign exchange transactions with Japan. Simon's response was that an exchange ban was impossible without special legislation from Parliament. Roosevelt sent the chief of the US Navy's intelligence division to London to discuss with his counterpart a blockade of Japan by US and British ships. Britain did not concur with the idea. Bailey, *A Diplomatic History of the American People*, 705. Barnhart, *Japan Prepares for Total War*, 126–127.

150 Iriye, *The Origin of the Second World War*, 48.

151 Japan paid all of the US demand for $2,214,007.36 in reparations.

152 Iriye, *The Origin of the Second World War*, 49.

*434*

# Notes

153 Borg, *The United States and the Far Eastern Crisis*, 488. Bailey, *A Diplomatic History of the American People*, 705–706. LaFeber, *The Clash*, 188.

154 A circular letter was sent to the firms on July 1. Barnhart, *Japan Prepares for Total War*, 130. LaFeber, *The Clash*, 188.

155 Barnhart, *Japan Prepares for Total War*, 130.

156 Ibid., 130.

157 Iriye, *The Origin of the Second World War*, 67–68. Usui, "Nitchū sensō no seijiteki tenkai," in *Taiheiyō sensō eno michi*, vol. 4, ed. Nihon Kokusai Seiji Gakkai, 170–171.

158 Usui, "Nitchū sensō no seijiteki tenkai," in *Taiheiyō sensō eno michi*, vol. 4, ed. Nihon Kokusai Seiji Gakkai, 171. Usui, "The Politics of War, 1937–1941," in *The China Quagmire*, ed. Morley, 351. Iriye writes, "One could date Japan's formal rejection of the Washington system from this point." Iriye, *The Origin of the Second World War*, 68.

159 Barnhart, *Japan Prepares for Total War*, 132.

160 Ibid., 133.

161 Ibid., 135.

435

Chapter 15
# US and Japanese Economies, Their Economic Policies, and Their Trade Relations in the 1930s

## 15.1. The US Economy in the 1930s

### 15.1.1. The Causes of the Great Depression

As observed in 12.1.1, the US economy, after having experienced the Great Depression from 1929 to 1933, which reduced the GNP in current prices almost by half and that in constant prices by about 30 percent, finally bottomed out in March 1933, but the subsequent recovery process was a protracted one. In 1939, ten years after the start of the downturn and the year when the war in Europe began, retail prices were still about 20 percent lower than the pre-depression level. The real GNP was slightly above the 1929 level, but the nominal GNP was 12 percent lower than it had been in 1929. The unemployment rate was as high as 17.2 percent (table 15.1.1-a). It was the most severe and prolonged depression experienced since 1848, when records began.

In the aftermath of the Great Depression, various explanations were presented for its causes, including the one that it was the unfortunate coincidence of all the different economic cycles troughing at the same time,[1] and another that it was attributable to the fall in investments due to a complex of causes.[2] But after the work by Friedman and Schwartz was published in the 1960s,

*437*

Chapter 15

Table 15.1.1-a. US Retail Prices, GNP, and Unemployment, 1929–1940

|  | 1929 | 1931 | 1933 | 1935 | 1937 | 1938 | 1939 | 1940 |
|---|---|---|---|---|---|---|---|---|
| Retail price indices | 100 | 88.9 | 75.6 | 80.1 | 83.8 | 82.3 | 81.1 | 81.9 |
| Nominal GNP indices | 100 | 73.5 | 53.9 | 70.0 | 87.7 | 82.2 | 87.8 | 96.7 |
| Real GNP indices | 100 | 83.2 | 69.5 | 83.2 | 99.8 | 94.7 | 102.8 | 111.6 |
| Unemployment (%) | 3.2 | 16.3 | 25.2 | 20.3 | 14.3 | 19.1 | 17.2 | 14.6 |

Source: US Department of Commerce, Bureau of the Census, *Historical Statistics of the United States* (Washington, DC: US Government Printing Office, 1975), 210 (retail prices), 224 (nominal GNP, real GNP).

their view was accepted by many economists that the economic collapse of 1929–1933 was largely due to the Federal Reserve's monetary policy failures.[3]

As observed in 12.1.3, the US economy was hit by a series of banking panics in 1930–1933, but the Federal Reserve did nothing to prevent or alleviate them. Policymakers at the Fed considered that monetary conditions were sufficiently loose.[4] They were rather wary that further monetary expansion would ignite another round of stock-market speculation, leading to another crash and even more catastrophic slump.[5] They did not read the signals correctly. Discount rates had successively been reduced from 6 percent in October 1929 to 1.5 percent in April 1931.[6] Yields on Treasury bonds hovered around a little over 3 percent in 1930–1933 (table 15.1.1-b). But, with prices falling at an average annual rate of about 8 percent, real interest rates (interest rate plus the deflation rate) were as high as the teens. Banks had large quantities of excess reserves, which the Fed took as a sign that money was readily available in the banking system. But the banks kept the excess reserves to maintain enough of a cash cushion to protect themselves against runs.[7] The most serious mistake that the Federal Reserve made was its failure to recognize the significance of the bank panics.[8] Bank failures inevitably resulted in a massive decrease in the money supply. Not only were deposits at the failed banks frozen for years, but the banks that did not fail reduced lending in order to increase their liquidity in case of panic withdrawals.[9] The depositors' propensity to hold cash rather than deposits at banks also decreased the money supply, because while deposited funds in banks would be expected to create deposits through lending, withdrawn cash held by individuals did not have any such multiplier effect.[10] Between 1929 and 1933, the money supply declined by about 25 percent and velocity by about 30 percent, reducing GNP almost by half (table 15.1.1-a, table 15.1.1-b).

**Table 15.1.1-b. US Monetary Indicators, 1929–1940**

|  |  | 1929 | 1931 | 1933 | 1935 | 1937 | 1938 | 1939 | 1940 |
|---|---|---|---|---|---|---|---|---|---|
| Discount rates (%) | High | 6.0 | 3.5 | 3.5 | 1.5 | 1.5 | 1.0 | 1.0 | 1.0 |
|  | Low | 4.5 | 1.5 | 2.0 | 1.5 | 1.0 | 1.0 | 1.0 | 1.0 |
| Government bond yields (%) |  | 3.60 | 3.34 | 3.31 | 2.79 | 2.74 | 2.61 | 2.41 | 2.26 |
| M1 money supply ($ bln.) |  | 26.6 | 24.1 | 19.9 | 25.9 | 30.9 | 30.5 | 34.2 | 39.7 |

*Source:* US Department of Commerce, Bureau of the Census, *Historical Statistics of the United States* (Washington, DC: US Government Printing Office, 1975), 210 (retail prices), 224 (nominal GNP, real GNP), 126 (unemployment), 992 (M1 money supply), 1001 (discount rates), 1003 (government bond yields)

The following factors influenced the Federal Reserve. First of all, unlike the Federal Reserve Act of today, the Federal Reserve Act of 1913, on which the Fed's action in the 1930s was based, did not request the Fed to be a lender of last resort, or responsible for stability of the overall macroeconomy.[11] In the bank crisis of 1930, a total of 1,350 banks were suspended from operation, of which 1,162 were state-chartered banks in rural communities in the Midwest. Most of them were small banks and not members of the Federal Reserve system.[12] The Federal Reserve did not consider nonmember banks to be their responsibility, especially those which were on the edge of bankruptcy through poor management.[13]

Second was the Federal Reserve's adherence to the "real bills doctrine." In 1931, 1932, and 1933, there were 2,293, 1,493, and 4,000 bank failures. Many of these banks were members of the Federal Reserve system. Still, the Federal Reserve refused to lend to them when they failed to pledge short-term securities as collateral. By tying the quantity of currency issued by the Federal Reserve to the quantity of business loans extended by commercial banks, the Federal Reserve intended to avoid the recurrence of stock-market speculation, while supplying credit needed by businesses to maintain production and economic operations. But with the economy having been in a recession for well over a year, banks did not have sufficient stock of short-term securities. This doctrine left no room for the Fed to conduct counter-cyclical expansionary financing.[14]

Thirdly, the Schumpeterian or liquidationist view that the depression was a process of cleansing organizational inefficiencies and resource misallocations was widely supported at the time.[15] In fact, many board members believed that further loosening of monetary conditions would not be advisable. There were certain board members who felt otherwise, but the great majority

Chapter 15

considered further monetary ease harmful. They were wary that it would prevent the "liquidation process" from working effectively.[16]

While Friedman and Schwartz and their followers attribute the problem to the Federal Reserve's policy failures, other economists emphasize the role of the gold standard as an important factor in the Great Depression. According to Barry Eichengreen, the priority that the monetary authorities attached to the gold standard prevented them from intervening forcefully in defense of domestic banks.[17] They could inject liquidity into the banking system to head off the collapse of the domestic financial system, but the provision of liquidity on a significant scale would signal that the monetary authorities attached as much weight to domestic financial stability as to the gold system. Realizing that convertibility might be compromised, investors would rush to get their money out of the country. In the end, the Federal Reserve chose to avoid the risk of endangering the gold standard, sitting idly by as the banking system crumbled.[18]

Peter Temin also declares that the Great Depression was a product of the post-WWI gold-standard regime.[19] After the war, the gold-standard system was revived in essentially its prewar form, but the war had made the postwar conditions very different from those in the prewar days, making restoration of the gold standard arduous for many countries. Countries whose price levels were higher and reserves were lower had to deflate their economies more than countries whose price levels were lower and reserves were greater. The latter countries were expected to expand their economies, but they did so inadequately or not at all. The burden of adjustment fell entirely on debtor countries. This asymmetry magnified the global deflationary forces.[20]

WWI greatly strengthened the financial position of the United States and weakened that of the European countries. In the mid-1920s, the external accounts of the European countries were tenuously balanced by the long-term capital outflow from the United States.[21] When US lending to Europe was curtailed as a result of the stringent US monetary policy launched in 1928 (12.1.2), European governments were forced to pursue severe deflationary policies to defend their gold parities as well as to maintain their repayment of war debt to the United States. To make matters worse, the United States, in an attempt to avoid the recurrence of stock-market speculation and inflation, sterilized gold inflows from Europe, intensifying the gold shortage and pushing the deficit countries into tougher deflationary policies.[22] This practice by

440

the United States broke the rules of the game.[23] Despite gold inflows from Europe, prices did not rise in the United States, imports did not increase, and the gold did not flow back to Europe.[24]

In September 1931, Britain went off gold, followed by other countries (12.1.3).[25] The United States and Germany raised the discount rate to defend gold parity. They also implemented a very restrictive fiscal policy.[26] Chancellor Brüning maintained highly contractionary budgets in his deflationary effort. Hoover asked Congress for a tax increase, and the Revenue Act of 1932 increased taxes by one-third, the highest peacetime tax increase in US history. It did contract the economy.[27]

## 15.1.2. Slow Recovery and the Second Recession

The Emergency Banking Act of 1933 gave the president the power to take the United States off the gold standard, and Roosevelt did so in March 1933.[28] He and his colleagues expected that the rise in the dollar price of gold would push prices of other commodities upward and the devalued dollar would increase exports.[29] Throughout the remainder of 1933, they kept buying gold. The price of gold, which had been $20.67 per ounce since 1879, rose until it was fixed at $35 on February 1, 1934. At this point, the United States returned to a gold standard for international settlements, though the holding of gold remained forbidden to private individuals. The Treasury Department continued buying gold afterward. The inflow of gold was converted into reserves in the banking system, increasing the monetary base and in turn increasing the money supply.[30] The Fed did not sterilize the gold inflows this time as it had done in the late 1920s and the early 1930s.[31] Though the rise in gold prices did not raise the prices of other commodities or increase exports due to retaliatory devaluation by the major trading countries,[32] the increase in the money supply did contribute, albeit slowly, to the economic recovery that lasted until 1937.[33] The GNP in real terms reached the pre-Depression level in 1937.

Then came the Fed's untimely action. With the bank reserves having swelled to two times as much as required reserves, in August 1936 the Fed raised the reserve requirement by 50 percent to turn a portion of the excess reserves into required reserves.[34] The Fed was worried that it would be unable to control the growth of the money supply when inflation became a danger.[35] But, banks, with the bitter experience of illiquidity during the monetary contraction in 1930–1933, wanted to maintain enough of a cash cushion, and

Chapter 15

quickly increased their reserves. The Fed, not understanding the banks' liquidity insurance demands, raised the reserve requirement again to the legal limit in two steps in March and May 1937.[36] Gold inflows from Europe were sterilized. Excess reserves decreased, but the banks again increased their reserves, this time by reducing lending. The money supply fell 6.5 percent from March 1937 to May 1938. The economy sank into the second recession of 1937–1938, a short but sharp recession. The real GNP in 1938 was about 5 percent lower than it had been in 1937 (table 15.1.1-a).

In the spring of 1938, the Fed reversed its reserve requirement policy and gold sterilizing policy. The money supply returned to its growth path and the recovery finally got back on track.[37]

In terms of fiscal policy, the US government was not helpful in accelerating economic recovery in 1934–1937. In fact, its contribution to the economic recovery was rather negative. The federal government had no idea of conducting deficit spending to narrow the huge GNP gap (the gap between actual GNP and that which would have been attained under a full-employment economy).

Roosevelt adhered to a balanced budget more adamantly than Hoover. During his presidential campaign in 1932, Roosevelt continually attacked the fiscal deficits of the Hoover administration.[38] In his inaugural address, Roosevelt declared reduction of budget deficits as a major policy objective. He did run deficits, but they were far short of what the economy needed.[39] When the federal deficit increased from $2.79 billion in 1935 to $4.42 billion in 1936 (table 15.1.2-a), he attempted to reverse the trend.[40] The spending cuts and the newly imposed social security tax combined to reduce budget deficits to $2.79 billion in 1937 and to a low of $1.18 billion in 1938. This budget tightening helped to worsen the second recession in 1937–1938. The budget deficit rose to $3.86 billion in 1939, but it was still less than the deficit in 1936.

John Maynard Keynes published an open letter to Roosevelt in the *New York Times* in December 1933, pointing out that the administration had erred in giving priority to reform over recovery and suggesting that Roosevelt abandon the balanced budget policy and replace it with policies to compensate for shortfalls in private spending with increases in the fiscal deficit spending.[41] In June 1934, Keynes met Roosevelt personally,[42] but he had little impact on Roosevelt, who clung to the old doctrine of balancing the budget.[43] Roosevelt's

*US and Japanese Economies, Their Economic Policies, and Their Trade Relations in the 1930s*

**Table 15.1.2-a. Federal Government Finances, 1931–1939 ($ billion)**

|  | 1931 | 1932 | 1933 | 1934 | 1935 | 1936 | 1937 | 1938 | 1939 |
|---|---|---|---|---|---|---|---|---|---|
| Receipts | 3.12 | 1.92 | 2.00 | 3.02 | 3.71 | 4.00 | 4.96 | 5.59 | 4.98 |
| Expenditures | 3.58 | 4.66 | 4.60 | 6.65 | 6.50 | 8.42 | 7.73 | 6.77 | 8.84 |
| Balances | −0.46 | −2.74 | −2.60 | −2.63 | −2.79 | −4.42 | −2.78 | −1.18 | −3.86 |

*Source:* US Department of Commerce, Bureau of the Census, *Historical Statistics of the United States* (Washington, DC: US Government Printing Office, 1975), 1104.

**Table 15.1.2-b. Changes in US Gold Stock, 1932–1940 ($ billion)**

|  | 1932 | 1933 | 1934 | 1935 | 1936 | 1937 | 1938 | 1939 | 1940 |
|---|---|---|---|---|---|---|---|---|---|
| Gold stocks | 4.23 | 4.04 | 8.26 | 10.23 | 11.42 | 12.79 | 14.59 | 17.80 | 22.04 |
| Net gold imports | −0.45 | −0.17 | 1.13 | 1.74 | 1.12 | 1.59 | 1.97 | 3.57 | 4.74 |

*Note:* Gold was valued at $20.67 per fine ounce through January 1934 and at $35 thereafter.
*Source:* US Department of Commerce, Bureau of the Census, *Historical Statistics of the United States* (Washington, DC: US Government Printing Office, 1975), 995.

stubborn adherence to the balanced budget contrasted sharply with the Japanese government expansionary fiscal policy under Finance Minister Takahashi that led to Japan's strong economic recovery from 1933 (15.3.1).

In the meantime, the US government's gold buying after 1933 rapidly increased US gold holdings (table 15.1.2-b). Additionally, the increase in capital inflows from Europe due to financial and political reasons caused US gold stocks to increase. Financially, after the dollar was devalued in 1933, speculation was directed against currencies which were seen as overvalued, and dollar assets were bought in earnest.[44] Politically, the likelihood of war in Europe as a result of the growing threat of Nazi Germany increased the capital flight into the United States.[45]

US gold stocks of $17.80 billion at the end of 1939 represented about 70 percent of the world's $26 billion gold stocks.[46] US gold holdings of $22.04 billion in 1940 were 159 times as much as Japan's gold stock worth ¥593 million in that year (table 15.1.2-b and table 15.3.3).

# 15. 2. The New Deal

## 15.2.1. The NIRA; Measures for Agricultural and Financial Industries
Upon taking office in March 1933, the Roosevelt administration launched a

*443*

Chapter 15

variety of economic policies collectively called the New Deal. With no sign of recovery in sight after three and a half years' decline, it appeared that the American economy was no longer self-correcting, although it had always rebounded within one or two years following the past depressions.[47] They believed that this time the contraction was mainly due to structural problems in many different economic sectors rather than a deficiency in aggregate demand.[48] Thus, the main part of the New Deal was a series of industrial policies rather than macroeconomic policies.

The National Industrial Recovery Act (NIRA) of 1933 was the most controversial economic recovery program in the New Deal. The act primarily aimed to reduce domestic industrial competition in the belief that competition among business firms had sent prices lower, driving many firms out of business and many workers out of work. The act set up the National Recovery Administration (NRA) to foster the establishment of "fair codes" of competition. Under the guidance of the NRA, representatives of industrialists, workers, and consumers in each industry met and drew up rules for minimum prices, quality standards, and trade practices for businesses, as well as working conditions for workers such as minimum wages and limits on working hours.[49] They also agreed to give workers the right to collective bargaining.

Those codes had a significant upward impact on wholesale prices and wages. From 1933 to 1935, wholesale prices rose by 21 percent and wages by 26 percent.[50] But with aggregate demand remaining weak and retail prices rising only 6 percent during the period (table 15.1.1-a), corporate profits faltered, and employers remained hesitant to increase workforces and investments.[51]

The NIRA was an order to cartelize, suspending antitrust laws.[52] In 1935, the Supreme Court declared the NIRA unconstitutional. Simulations conducted later by economists suggest that the NIRA's programs significantly slowed the recovery of the US economy.[53]

In the New Deal, measures for agricultural problems were very important, as American farmers were in an extremely dire state in the early 1930s. After having suffered from a decade of low farm prices through the 1920s, they were hit still harder by the Great Depression.[54] The Agricultural Adjustment Act (AAA) of 1933 aimed at price increases in farm products by reducing supplies. This was to be achieved by acreage allotments to reduce the plantings of specific crops and by government payments for taking land out of production,

*444*

as well as for the destruction of crops and animals.[55] The program was financed by taxes on the processing of agricultural products, which were borne by consumers who paid higher prices.[56] In 1935, the US Supreme Court declared the AAA unconstitutional. Soon thereafter, however, a second AAA was established with stronger crop control and income support provisions than the first AAA under the Soil Conservation and Domestic Allotment Act.[57] This time, the US Supreme Court had no objections.[58]

The Commodity Credit Corporation (CCC) established in 1933 also functioned as an institution for supporting farm prices. It lent funds to farmers for crops in storage, and when repayment time came, if crop prices exceeded the target level, the farmer would sell the crops on the market and repay the government loan. If crop prices were below the target, the farmer gave the crops to the government as payment for the loan. The program has continued to the present day.[59]

The Farm Credit Administration (FCA) lent farmers money against the collateral of their real property on more liberal terms than had been achieved by the federal land banks.[60] Within two years of its inauguration in 1933, the FCA had lent out more than had been lent in the prior sixteen years by the federal land banks. The FCA would go on to become one of the largest lending institutions of any kind in the United States.[61]

For the Roosevelt administration, most immediately pressing was the banking crisis. Upon taking office, Roosevelt declared a national "Bank Holiday." From March 6, 1933, all banks were closed for a week and were examined by auditors. Banks declared to be sound were reopened shortly. Insolvent banks were ordered to improve their position, and the Reconstruction Finance Corporation (RFC), which had been created in 1932 under the Hoover administration, was now entrusted with task of getting these banks back on their feet by providing them with enough liquidity. The RFC then also provided loans to many New Deal institutions,[62] as well as to railroads, power companies, and industrial companies.[63]

The RFC was wound down at the end of WWII, but some New Deal financial institutions still exist today. The Federal Deposit Insurance Corporation (FDIC) is one of them. The Banking Act of 1933 (the so-called Glass–Steagall Act) called for the establishment of federal deposit insurance, which had often been tried and had never fully succeeded. Well-run large banks opposed a system in which they subsidized their inefficient

*445*

competitors. Despite their opposition, however, a deposit insurance system was installed by 1935. Within the year, more than 90 percent of the nation's banks joined the insurance.[64] The number of bank failures, which was in the thousands per year in the early 1930s, shrank to sixty-one in 1934, and the annual rate did not again reach the triple-digit level until the 1980s. The Glass–Steagall Act also separated the banking business from stock brokerages and investment banking.[65]

Another financial institution that exists today is the Securities Exchange Commission (SEC), which was established in 1934. The SEC was assigned to monitor the stock markets, insider trading, and reporting requirements for firms issuing stock, as well as to enforce rules governing market trades.[66]

## 15.2.2. Social Security and Measures for Labor Problems

Unemployment was one of the most urgent problems for the Roosevelt administration. During its first hundred days, the Roosevelt administration established the Federal Emergency Relief Administration (FERA), which offered direct relief payment (with no work requirement) and work relief that required a family member to work for the funds.[67] The FERA was taken over by the Work Progress Administration (WPA) in 1935. In November 1938, the public work projects sponsored by the WPA employed 3.24 million workers.[68]

The Social Security Act of 1935 established long-term programs for old-age insurance and unemployment insurance.[69] The retirement portion was constructed as a compulsory insurance program with contributions from both the employee and the employer. The unemployment insurance was paid by federal taxes on payrolls.[70] Many of the social insurance systems that are largely still in place today, including social security numbers, were initiated in 1935–1936.[71]

Another lasting legacy of the New Deal was the National Labor Relations Act (Wagner Act) of 1935. When the NIRA was declared unconstitutional, Section 7a of the act providing the workers' right to collective bargaining was reenacted as the Wagner Act in 1935. It provided that employees had the right to organize, elect their own bargaining agents, and bargain collectively. The Wagner Act produced a wave of unionization in the mass-production industries and the establishment of the Congress of Industrial Organizations (CIO) in 1938.[72]

### 15.2.3. The Legacy of the New Deal

The New Deal was a grand scheme aiming at both economic recovery and reforms of American economic systems. Many of the New Deal programs were, however, too extensive and ambitious to be economically effective. Some of them worked at cross-purposes, and some even proved counterproductive.[73] In terms of economic recovery, those programs failed to achieve their purpose. But in terms of structural reforms, many of the programs seem to have worked reasonably well.[74] Several of them were widely approved by contemporaneous Americans, and were woven into the fabric of American society.[75] By the end of WWII, many New Deal programs had ended, but several of them remain in place today in such areas as social security, the labor market, the financial industry, and the agricultural industry.[76] The Social Security Act, for example, provided the Americans with a social right to minimum standards of living, on top of civil rights and property rights traditionally guaranteed by the US Constitution.[77] By this act, which introduced the idea of collective responsibility for human welfare in place of the American tradition of dynamic and rugged individualism, the United States became a welfare nation like other major European countries.[78]

Another New Deal legacy was the expanded role of the federal government. Through implementation of the various New Deal programs, the federal government became a much more important player in the national economy than before. Federal spending increased from 1.3 percent of GNP in 1929 to 5.6 percent in 1939. Having seen the chaos brought by free-market capitalism, the federal government opted for more planning and control of the economy in a way that was unprecedented. In this extensive government intervention, socialist elements can clearly be seen. In the depths of the Depression, the United States turned from its traditional liberalism, or unmixed capitalism, to a form of mixed capitalism, and this type of capitalism was the one that was introduced into Japan by the United States during the occupation days after WWII.[80]

## 15.3. The Japanese Economy and Economic/Industrial Policies in the 1930s

### 15.3.1. Takahashi's Economic Policies and Japan's Economic Recovery

Upon taking office as the finance minister of the Inukai Tsuyoshi

Chapter 15

Table 15.3.1-a. Japan's Monetary and Fiscal Policies, 1929–1940

| | Exchange rates ($=¥100) | | | BOJ discount rates (%) | Central government expenditures (¥ mil.) | | | Bond issues (¥ mil.) |
|---|---|---|---|---|---|---|---|---|
| | High | Low | Avg. | | General a/c | Total | Military | |
| 1929 | 49 | 43-3/4 | 46.07 | 5.48 | 1,736 | 3,737 | 497 | 194 |
| 1930 | 49-3/8 | 49 | 49.37 | 5.11 (10) | 1,558 | 4,001 | 444 | 80 |
| 1931 | 49-3/8 | 34-1/2 | 48.87 | 5.84 (10) 6.57 (11) | 1,477 | 3,509 | 462 | 213 |
| 1932 | 37-1/4 | 19-3/4 | 28.12 | 5.84 (3) 5.11 (6) 4.38 (8) | 1,950 | 4,279 | 705 | 834 |
| 1933 | 31-1/4 | 20-1/4 | 25.23 | 3.65 (7) | 2,255 | 5,080 | 886 | 920 |
| 1934 | 30-3/8 | 28-1/2 | 29.51 | 3.65 | 2,163 | 5,710 | 953 | 866 |
| 1935 | 29-1/8 | 27-3/4 | 28.57 | 3.65 | 2,206 | 5,817 | 1,043 | 784 |
| 1936 | 29-1/2 | 27-1/2 | 28.95 | 3.29 (4) | 2,282 | 8,432 | 1,089 | 719 |
| 1937 | 29-1/4 | 28-1/2 | 28.81 | 3.29 | 2,709 | 9,195 | 3,299 | 2,259 |
| 1938 | 29-1/4 | 27 | 28.50 | 3.29 | 3,288 | 13,124 | 5,984 | 4,549 |
| 1939 | 27-3/8 | 23-5/16 | 25.98 | 3.29 | 4,494 | 12,273 | 6,495 | 5,568 |
| 1940 | | | 23.44 | 3.29 | 5,860 | 15,704 | 7,967 | 6,983 |

*Notes:* 1. Figures in parentheses in the BOJ's discount rates indicate the month when the rates changed.
2. "Total" in central government expenditures is an aggregate of the general account (一般会計) and the special account (特別会計). Duplications between the general account and the special account are deducted.

*Source:* Nippon Ginkō Tōkeikyoku, ed., *Meiji ikō honpō shuyō keizai tōkei* (Tokyo: Namiki Shobō, 1999), 257 (BOJ discount rates), 320 (exchange rates). Ōkurashō Shōwa Zaiseishi Hensanshitsu, ed., *Shōwa zaiseishi*, vol. 6 (Tokyo: Tōyōkeizai Shinpōsha, 1966), 3 (government bonds). Emi Kōichi and Shionoya Yūichi, Ōkawa Kazushi, ed., *Zaisei shishutsu* (*Chōki keizai tōkei*, vol. 7) (Tokyo: Tōyōkeizai Shinpōsha, 1966), 163 (central government expenditures), 186–189 (military expenditures).

administration in December 1931 (13.1.4), Takahashi Korekiyo embarked on a set of expansionary economic policies.[81] It was a complete reversal of his predecessor Inoue Junnosuke's deflationary policies (9.3.3, 9.3.4). On December 13, the day when the Inukai cabinet started, Takahashi declared abandonment of the gold standard. This made it possible for him to pursue a series of expansionary policies. The yen rate was allowed to fall to a natural level. It dropped from a high of $49⅜ per ¥100 in 1931 to a low of $19¾ at the end of 1932 (table 15.3.1-a).[82] The Bank of Japan lowered the discount rates four times between December 1931 and July 1933, from 6.57 percent to 3.65 percent, the lowest level in the BOJ's history to that point.

In terms of fiscal policy, Takahashi conducted deficit spending on a large

448

*US and Japanese Economies, Their Economic Policies, and Their Trade Relations in the 1930s*

Table 15.3.1-b. Japan's Economic Indicators, 1929–1940 (¥ billion)

| | GNP | | Consumption | Investment | Exports | Imports | WPI |
|------|---------|-------|-------------|------------|---------|---------|------|
| | Nominal | Real | | | | | |
| 1929 | 16.29 | 16.29 | 11.78 | 1.09 | 2.83 | 2.81 | 1.00 |
| 1930 | 14.67 | 16.46 | 10.85 | 0.95 | 2.05 | 2.07 | 0.82 |
| 1931 | 13.31 | 16.53 | 9.75 | 0.70 | 1.63 | 1.69 | 0.70 |
| 1932 | 13.66 | 17.26 | 9.80 | 0.57 | 2.05 | 2.00 | 0.77 |
| 1933 | 15.35 | 19.01 | 10.85 | 0.86 | 2.63 | 2.60 | 0.89 |
| 1934 | 16.97 | 20.66 | 12.10 | 1.22 | 3.01 | 3.00 | 0.90 |
| 1935 | 18.30 | 21.98 | 12.67 | 1.50 | 3.65 | 3.34 | 0.93 |
| 1936 | 19.32 | 22.25 | 13.33 | 1.84 | 3.72 | 3.59 | 0.96 |
| 1937 | 22.82 | 23.66 | 15.12 | 1.85 | 4.41 | 5.06 | 1.17 |
| 1938 | 26.39 | 24.57 | 16.01 | 2.44 | 4.08 | 4.80 | 1.23 |
| 1939 | 31.23 | 26.04 | 17.91 | 4.85 | 4.78 | 4.98 | 1.36 |
| 1940 | 36.85 | 27.10 | 20.29 | 6.77 | 5.54 | 6.04 | 1.53 |

*Source:* Ōkawa Kazushi, Takamatsu Nobukiyo and Yamamoto Yūzō, "Kokumin shotoku," in *Chōki Keizai Tōkei*, eds. Ōkawa Kazushi, Shinohara Miyohei, Umemura Mataji (Tokyo: Tōyōkeizai Shinpōsha, 1974), 178 (GNP, consumption). Nakamura Takafusa, *Senzenki Nihon keizai seichō no bunseki* (Tokyo: Iwanami Shoten, 1971), 333 (private investments, exports and imports). Nippon Ginkō Tōkeikyoku, ed., *Meiji ikō honpō shuyō keizai tōkei* (Tokyo: Namiki Shobō, 1999), 80 (retail prices).

scale. Revenue from bond issues accounted for 41 percent of the general account budget on average in 1932–1934 (table 15.3.1-a). The ratio was 10 percent on average in 1929–1931. He had the Bank of Japan buy government bonds directly from the government (not through the market) to avoid siphoning private funds off the market.[83] Historically, government borrowing for deficit spending had been done for specific purposes, such as public works, reconstruction, or war. But Takahashi used fiscal deficits for general government expenditures. Takahashi repeatedly said that it was a temporary expediency, and that when the economy recovered, he would have the private commercial banks buy the bonds from the BOJ. In fact, as the economy recovered, the BOJ sold the bonds to the private sector without difficulty,[84] and Takahashi gradually reduced the bond issues.

The economy rebounded with the increase in fiscal spending as well as the expansion of exports due to the depreciation of the yen. Between 1931 and 1933, government spending increased by ¥1.5 billion and exports by ¥1 billion, helping raise the GNP by ¥2 billion (table 15.3.1-b). Induced by increases in exports and government expenditures, consumption and private

Chapter 15

investments started to increase vigorously from 1933. The GNP grew in real terms by 10.1 percent in 1933, 8.7 percent in 1934, and 6.4 percent in 1935. Japan got out of the Great Depression well ahead of any other major country.

Hugh Patrick describes the policies pursued by Takahashi as "one of the most successful combinations of fiscal, monetary, and foreign exchange rate policies, in an adverse international environment, the world has ever seen."[85]

The expansionary economic policies pursued by Takahashi had a Keynesian nature. Takahashi justified increased government expenditures in terms of the expenditure multiplier. This does not mean that his ideas predated Keynes. Keynes had already advocated a policy of public works expenditure because of its multiplier effect in 1929.[86] It is quite likely that Takahashi, being an avid reader of foreign publications, had read the Keynesian description of it by 1929.[87]

The main expenditure increases in Takahashi's budgets were for farm village relief as well as for the military. The annual average military expenditures in 1932–1934 were ¥848 million, which was ¥380 million more than they had been in 1929–1931 (table 15.3.1-a). In 1932–1934, meanwhile, Takahashi allotted about ¥180 million yearly on average for relief for farm villages in the central government budget, and he also had the local governments spend about ¥200 million additional yearly for that purpose.[88] While the increase in military expenditures in 1932–1934 over the previous three years equaled the aggregate expenditures for rural relief in 1932–1934, in terms of effects on the Japanese economy and society, the latter was far more important.[89] It signified a crucial shift from the past Japanese government stance, which had almost totally ignored economic difficulties in the rural communities.[90]

The problem was, however, that Takahashi's fiscal policy came when the army was becoming increasingly assertive in the Japanese politics (12.2.3, 14.1.1). Takahashi at first acceded to the army's demands for greater military expenditures. His thinking was that if, in the political context of the time, one had to spend money on the military anyway, it was "better than nothing" in terms of its economic effect.[91]

Meanwhile, he knew that financing government expenditures by issuing debt was limited by the ability of the public to absorb it. He saw that this limit had been reached in 1934. In that year, for the first time, the Bank of Japan could not sell all its treasury bills. With the economic expansion, companies' demand for capital had expanded to such a level that the bonds had to

*450*

compete with private borrowing for available capital.[92]

Takahashi drew up the 1935 budget, in which military expenditures were less than those in the 1934 budget. But facing strong resistance from the army and navy, he added ¥100 million more to the draft budget to avoid a head-on confrontation with the military. Instead, however, he had to discontinue expenditures for rural relief.

Takahashi was now firmly determined to cut the 1936 military budget. The *Tokyo Asahi Shimbun*'s reportage during the final weeks of the budget-formation process gave the reader a feeling of Takahashi's almost suicidal resolve to control military spending.[93] The army insisted that the government should increase the issuance of deficit bonds. Takahashi was firmly committed to reducing it, and he rejected any increase in military spending. In the end, an agreement was reached whereby the army and the navy accepted 30 million yen that other ministries proposed to transfer from their coffers to the army and navy ministries.[94]

The general election held on February 20, 1936 gave Takahashi a powerful vote of confidence. In spite of the strong opposition to cuts in military spending by the Seiyūkai (政友会) as well as by the military and right wing, the Minseitō (民政党), which supported Takahashi's efforts to reduce budget deficits, won the most seats, 205 seats against the Seiyūkai's 175 seats (14.1.4).[95]

Military spending as a percentage of GNP stayed steady at around 5.7 percent in all four Takahashi budgets from 1933 until 1936 (table 15.3.1-a, table 15.3.1-b). Only after Takahashi's death (14.1.4) did military spending as percentage of GNP grow dramatically.[96]

## 15.3.2. The Japanese Government's Industrial Policies in the 1930s

While Takahashi's macroeconomic policies effectively brought about Japan's economic recovery, there were also important moves in the 1930s by the Japanese government in terms of industrial policy.[97]

The idea of industrial rationalization was at that time widely supported in many countries, among which Germany was the most earnest performer of industrial rationalization measures, including improvements in manufacturing processes, introduction of uniform standards for many products, and efficiency studies to trim the amount of time wasted.[98] Another important characteristic of German industrial rationalization was the drive to strengthen and expand key industries by creating powerful monopolies and cartels.[99] Seventy

*451*

Chapter 15

iron and steel makers were merged in Vereinigte Stahlwerke AG, leaving Friedrich Krupp GmbH as its only major domestic competitor. In the chemical industry too, six large firms were merged to form IG Farben. These came to account for more than 80 percent of Germany's total industrial output.[100]

In Japan, the ministry of commerce and industry (MCI) was the center for the industrial rationalization movement. In June 1930, the MCI created the Temporary Industrial Rationalization Bureau (TIRB 臨時産業合理局) to promote industrial rationalization.[101] The central MCI bureaucrats who promoted the move were Yoshino Shinji (吉野信次), the chief of the industrial affairs bureau, and Kishi Nobusuke (岸信介), Yoshino's subordinate. Yoshino sent Kishi to Germany twice, in 1926 and 1930, and Kishi reported back on the industrial rationalization movement there. In April 1931, the TIRB's recommendations were embodied in the Important Industries Control Law (重要産業統制法). The law gave the government power to encourage compulsory cartelization with the goal of rationalizing industry and increasing government control over industry through those cartels and trade associations.[102] As of the end of 1932, as many as eighty-three cartels had been formed in twenty-two industries.

The Important Industries Control Law also led to several important mergers and acquisitions in the early 1930s. For example, three paper companies merged to form Ōji Paper (王子製紙) in 1933, and Yawata (八幡) and five steel mills united to become Nippon Iron and Steel (日本製鉄) in 1934.[103]

Then came a series of industry-specific control laws. The Petroleum Industry Law, passed in 1934, gave the government authority to license the business of importing and refining petroleum, and it required importers to stockpile at least a six-month supply of petroleum in Japan, though the Japanese government could not expel foreign oil companies which did not comply with the stockpile requirement from the Japanese market. Oil was Japan's Achilles' heel.[104] In 1936, the Automobile Manufacturing Industry Law was passed, which required that all automakers in Japan receive government licenses to produce more than 3,000 cars per year so as to gain special government support and avoid various restrictions.[105] Only Toyota and Nissan were licensed, and by 1939 the law had put Ford and GM out of business in Japan.[106] Other laws passed during the late 1930s were the Artificial Petroleum Law (1937), the Steel Industry Law (1937), the Machine Tool Industry Law (1938), the Aircraft Manufacturing Law (1938), the Shipbuilding Industry

452

Law (1939), the Light Metals Manufacturing Industry Law (1939), and the Important Machines Manufacturing Law (1941). These laws did much to promote the particular industries concerned by providing special government protective measures.[107] At the same time, these laws, as well as the Important Industrial Control Law, were used by the Japanese government to increase its industrial controls.

### 15.3.3. The Japanese Government's Stronger Economic Controls after the China Incident and the Enactment of the National General Mobilization Law

After the February 26 Incident in 1936, Finance Minister Baba of the Hirota cabinet did not resist the army's demand for an increased military spending.[108] The military spending of the FY1937 budget proposal amounted to ¥1.4 billion, about 30 percent more than Takahashi's last budget.[109] In anticipation of increases in domestic demand, prices soared and imports mushroomed. In January 1937, the Hirota cabinet resigned on account of the dispute between Army Minister Terauchi and a member of the Diet (14.1.4). But with his cabinet economic policy having reached an impasse, it was highly probable that Hirota used the dispute as an excuse to surrender control of the government.[110] From February 1937, Finance Minister Yūki of the Hayashi administration set about revising Baba's disastrous fiscal policy, cutting the budget and amending the taxation system. But before Yūki's reforms had any effect, the Hayashi cabinet resigned on June 4, 1937 (14.1.4).

Then came the China Incident on July 7 (14.3.2). The Japanese Diet approved a supplementary military budget amounting to ¥2.5 billion,[111] and the military expenditures for 1937 came to be three times as much as those for 1936 (table 15.3.1-a). Fears of inflation and widening of the trade deficit grew. The most serious problem was foreign exchange. The Japanese military and the military industries were heavily depended on imports, and military imports were mostly from the non-yen area countries, for which settlements were made in international currencies or in gold. The surge in military spending in 1937 greatly widened the deficit with those countries (table 15.3.3),[112] making a massive outflow of gold inevitable.

The government intensified its efforts to increase gold output in mines in Japan proper, Korea, and Taiwan. It even purchased privately owned gold at higher prices than market rates. But those efforts did not help solve the gold

**Table 15.3.3. Japan's External Accounts Position, 1932–1941 (¥ million)**

| | | 1932 | 1935 | 1936 | 1937 | 1938 | 1939 | 1940 | 1941 |
|---|---|---|---|---|---|---|---|---|---|
| Exports | ¥ block | 175 | 488 | 631 | 795 | 1,234 | 1,838 | 1,867 | 1,659 |
| | Other areas | 1,291 | 2,340 | 2,166 | 2,252 | 1,661 | 2,091 | 1,789 | 992 |
| Imports | ¥ block | 175 | 291 | 410 | 469 | 637 | 728 | 756 | 855 |
| | Other areas | 1,349 | 2,403 | 2,515 | 3,485 | 2,198 | 2,398 | 2,697 | 2,043 |
| Trade balance | ¥ block | 0 | 197 | 221 | 326 | 597 | 1,110 | 1,111 | 804 |
| | Other areas | −58 | −63 | −349 | −1,233 | −537 | −307 | −908 | −1,051 |
| Current a/c balance | | 102 | 178 | 233 | −18 | −797 | −977 | −789 | −1,342 |
| Gold outflow | | 112 | −0 | −0 | 866 | 660 | 663 | 320 | 152 |
| Gold newly mined | | 47 | 105 | 139 | 178 | 206 | 313 | 287 | 288 |
| Gold purchased | | | | | 4 | 86 | 190 | 72 | 38 |
| Gold holdings | | 554 | 531 | 577 | 890 | 582 | 586 | 593 | 549 |

*Source:* Nakamura Takafusa, *Economic Growth in Prewar Japan*, trans. Robert Feldman (New Haven: Yale University Press, 1971), 259–260 (exports, imports, trade balance, current account balance, and gold outflow). Nakamura Takafusa, *Senzenki Nihon keizai seichō no bunseki* (Tokyo: Iwanami Shoten, 1971), 225 (gold outflow). Mitani Katsumi, *Kokusai shūshi to Nihon no seichō* (Tokyo: Heibonsha, 1957), 207 (gold holdings), 255 (gold newly mined), 256 (gold purchased). Takahashi Kamekichi, *Taishō Shōwa zaisei hendōshi* (Tokyo, Tōyōkeizai Shinpōsha, 1955), 1784 (gold purchased).

shortage problem.[113] There was no other choice but to directly control foreign trade.[114]

In September 1937, the government enacted three laws, intending to control all aspects of the economy. One was the Temporary Import-Export Grading Measures Law (輸出入品等臨時措置法), authorizing the government to restrict or prohibit the import or export of any commodity[115] and to control the manufacture, distribution, transfer, and consumption of all imported raw materials.

The second was the Temporary Funds Adjustment Law (臨時資金調整法), which enabled the government to examine the long-term financial needs of enterprises and regulate their procurement of capital. It classified industries into categories according to their national importance, and channeled limited resources into the military-supply sector and, on a case-by-case basis, into other less important sectors that required investment for expansion.

The third was the Law Concerning Implementation of the Military Industries Mobilization Law (軍需工業動員法の適用に関する法律), which stipulated the means by which the army and navy could manage, utilize, and even expropriate factories under the Armament Industry Mobilization Law of 1918. It put all important supply industries under military control.[116]

Direct interventions by the government as above were inevitable emergency measures, but it should be noted that there was a prevailing view in Japan at the time which was supportive of a government-controlled economy and critical of laissez-faire economic policies. It was shared by new bureaucrats, junior military officers, and some members of the private sector. The Great Depression, as well as the recent economic development of the Soviet Union, fostered those people's support of such a socialist view.[117] Above all, they were encouraged by the experiment in Manchukuo, where a planned economy was well underway. What the Japanese government started doing in 1937 was not identical to policies pursued in Manchuria, but it was in the same direction.[118]

In October 1937, the cabinet planning board (CPB, 企画院) was established as the economic control tower to command and coordinate the activities of the various ministries for the expansion of total production.[119] The National General Mobilization Law (国家総動員法) enacted in April 1938 was the CPB's most important work.[120] National mobilization meant that in times of war, the government would control and manage human as well as material resources. In fact, it was more than an economic law. It provided the government with the power to carry out a complete reorganization of society.[121] The law covered virtually all aspects of social activities, including industry, finance, labor, education, and publishing.[122] Despite the control of vast areas, its fifty articles contained very few concrete rules or stipulations. All details of implementation were left to Imperial ordinances, which the bureaucracy could issue on its own initiative without reference to the Diet.[123] During the debate of the bill in the Diet, business leaders expressed opposition to many of the business regulations, but they were eventually quieted with the government assurance that the law would be used only during a state of war, which did not include the China Incident.

In the beginning after the passage of the National General Mobilization Law, the government was prudent in its implementation. For example, in November 1938, when one of the ministers in the Konoe cabinet made a suggestion to restrict corporate dividend payments in a cabinet meeting, another minister was strongly opposed, and a compromise was worked out.[124] But after 1939, the government ceased to show restraint. The provisions of the National

Chapter 15

General Mobilization Law were applied in rapid succession, pushing Japan toward totalitarianism.[125]

## 15.4. Trade Relations between the United States and Japan in the 1930s

### 15.4.1. The US Position in Japan's Trade and Japan's Position in US Trade

In Japan's export trade, the United States had been the largest market for Japanese goods ever since the middle of the 1870s (table 5.2.1-c), when Japan's exports to the United States exceeded those to Britain. The United States remained the best buyer of Japan's exports until 1938, when Japan's exports to Manchuria exceeded those to the United States. Of Japan's total exports, the US share accounted for about one-third in the early part of the 1930s, but it declined to one-fifth to one-sixth in the latter part of the 1930s (table 15.4.1-a).

The United States, meanwhile, was the largest supplier to Japan in the 1930s, as it had been since the onset of WWI. During the 1930s, US exports to Japan accounted for one-third, on average, of Japan's total imports. Japan's imports from China and Manchuria combined was half as much as those from the United States.

In US foreign trade (table 15.4.1-b), Japan stood third next to Britain and Canada as a market for US exports for most of the 1930s.[126] Of total US exports, Japan's share was 7 to 9 percent during the decade. Meanwhile, Japan remained the second-largest supplier to the United States (after Canada) during most of the 1930s. Japan supplied about 10 percent of US imports in the early 1930s and about 7 percent in the rest of the decade.

China ranked ninth to tenth as a trading partner of the United States in the 1930s. Despite Americans' historical claim of the importance of trade with China, either as a market of American exports or as a supplier to the US market, China's share of American foreign trade had never exceeded 4 percent at any time in the pre-WWII years.[127]

In terms of balance of trade, Japan maintained a favorable balance of trade with the United States in the 1910s, 1920s, and the first two years in the 1930s, but in 1932 the bilateral balance of trade became unfavorable for Japan and remained so for the rest of the prewar years. This reversal was mainly

456

*US and Japanese Economies, Their Economic Policies, and Their Trade Relations in the 1930s*

Table 15.4.1-a. Japan's Trade with US, China, and Manchuria (¥ million)

| | Japan's exports | | | | Japan's imports | | | |
|---|---|---|---|---|---|---|---|---|
| | Total | US | China | Manchuria | Total | US | China | Manchuria |
| 1930 | 1,470 | 506 | 366 | 87 | 1,546 | 442 | 162 | 121 |
| 1931 | 1,147 | 425 | 144 | 77 | 1,236 | 342 | 104 | 132 |
| 1932 | 1,410 | 445 | 130 | 147 | 1,431 | 509 | 77 | 128 |
| 1933 | 1,861 | 492 | 108 | 303 | 1,917 | 620 | 113 | 168 |
| 1934 | 2,172 | 399 | 117 | 403 | 2,283 | 769 | 120 | 192 |
| 1935 | 2,499 | 536 | 149 | 426 | 2,472 | 809 | 134 | 216 |
| 1936 | 2,693 | 594 | 160 | 498 | 2,764 | 847 | 155 | 239 |
| 1937 | 3,175 | 639 | 179 | 612 | 3,783 | 1,270 | 144 | 294 |
| 1938 | 2,690 | 425 | 313 | 853 | 2,663 | 915 | 165 | 400 |
| 1939 | 3,576 | 642 | 456 | 1,292 | 2,918 | 1,002 | 216 | 467 |
| 1940 | 3,656 | 567 | 681 | 1,186 | 3,453 | 1,241 | 339 | 417 |

*Note:* "Total" means total Japanese exports or imports in each year.
*Source:* Nippon Ginkō Tōkeikyoku, ed., *Meiji ikō honpō shuyō keizai tōkei* (Tokyo: Namiki Shobō, 1999), 292–296. Yamazawa Ippei and Yamamoto Yūzō, "Bōeki to kokusai shūshi," in *Chōki keizai tōkei*, eds. Ōkawa Kazushi, Shinohara Miyohei, and Umemura Mataji (Tokyo: Tōyōkeizai Shinpōsha, 1977), 208, 212 (figures for Manchuria).

Table 15.4.1-b. US Trade with Canada, UK, Japan, and China ($ million)

| | US exports | | | | | US imports | | | |
|---|---|---|---|---|---|---|---|---|---|
| | Total | Canada | UK | Japan | China | Total | Canada | UK | Japan | China |
| 1930 | 3,843 | 659 | 678 | 165 | 90 | 3,061 | 402 | 210 | 279 | 101 |
| 1931 | 2,424 | 396 | 456 | 156 | 98 | 2,091 | 266 | 135 | 206 | 67 |
| 1932 | 1,611 | 241 | 288 | 135 | 56 | 1,323 | 174 | 75 | 134 | 26 |
| 1933 | 1,675 | 211 | 312 | 143 | 52 | 1,450 | 185 | 111 | 128 | 38 |
| 1934 | 2,133 | 302 | 383 | 210 | 69 | 1,655 | 232 | 115 | 119 | 44 |
| 1935 | 2,283 | 323 | 433 | 203 | 38 | 2,047 | 286 | 155 | 153 | 64 |
| 1936 | 2,456 | 384 | 440 | 204 | 47 | 2,423 | 376 | 200 | 172 | 74 |
| 1937 | 3,349 | 509 | 536 | 289 | 50 | 3,084 | 398 | 203 | 204 | 104 |
| 1938 | 3,094 | 468 | 521 | 240 | 35 | 1,960 | 260 | 118 | 127 | 47 |
| 1939 | 3,177 | 489 | 505 | 232 | 56 | 2,318 | 340 | 149 | 161 | 62 |
| 1940 | 4,021 | 713 | 1,011 | 227 | 78 | 2,625 | 424 | 155 | 158 | 93 |

*Note:* "Total" means total US exports and imports of each year.
*Source:* US Department of Commerce, Bureau of the Census, *Historical Statistics of the United States* (Washington, DC: US Government Printing Office, 1975), 903 (exports), 905–906 (imports).

Chapter 15

attributable to the fall in prices of raw silk, Japan's major export item to the United States, and the increase in US exports to Japan of raw cotton, the major US export item to Japan.[128]

## 15.4.2. Main Commodities in Japanese Exports to the United States

Japan's exports to the United States, the historical preponderance of raw silk continued in the 1930s as well,[129] though its share of total Japanese exports to the United States, which had been over 80 percent in the 1920s, declined substantially, mainly because of the decline in raw-silk prices. Raw silk from Japan accounted for three-quarters of American raw-silk imports by the 1920s, about 80 percent by the 1930s, and over 90 percent on average in the 1930s.[130]

During the 1910s and 1920s Japan greatly expanded exports of cotton fabrics in the world market,[131] and in 1932 Japan took over Britain as the world's leading exporter of cotton cloth, capturing from Britain a large part of the world cotton-goods market, first in China, and then India and Southeast Asia. Japanese low-priced cotton cloth sold well in those relatively low-income economies.[132] In the US market, Britain had historically been the leading supplier of cotton goods, except in 1931–33 when imports from Switzerland exceeded those from Britain. From 1934, however, Japan became the main supplier to the United States. The Japanese share of US cotton-cloth imports was 2.7 percent in 1933, but it increased to 57.3 percent in 1935 and 72.3 percent in 1937.[133] Compared to US domestic production of cotton cloth, imports from Japan accounted for only 0.6 percent in 1935 and 1.2 percent in 1937. But the rapid increase in Japan's share of US cotton-cloth imports created great alarm in the American cotton textile industry.[134]

For one thing, most of the imports from Japan were medium-quality goods that competed directly with domestic goods. Imports from Europe consisted mostly of better-quality goods not directly competitive with domestically produced goods.[135] In addition, the US textile manufacturers were complying with the provision of the National Industrial Recovery Act (NIRA) to improve wages and working conditions (15.2.1). With the cost of production being thus raised, they thought that it was the government's responsibility to protect them from foreign competition.[136] The State Department negotiated with the Japanese government in the latter part of 1935 and the early part of 1936, but they could not reach an agreement.[137] In May 1936, the US government raised the duties on cotton cloth by an average of 42 percent

458

Table 15.4.2. Main Commodities in Japan's Exports to US ($ thousand)

| | 1931 | 1933 | 1935 | 1937 | 1939 |
|---|---|---|---|---|---|
| Raw silk | 167,369(81.2) | 89,734(70.1) | 93,967(61.4) | 99,573(48.8) | 108,925(67.7) |
| Silk fabrics | 2,208 (1.1) | 1,402 (1.1) | 1,936 (1.3) | 3,402 (1.7) | |
| Cotton fabrics | 28 (0.0) | 327 (0.3) | 2,330 (1.5) | 4,274 (2.1) | 2,779 (1.7) |
| Tea | 2,577 (1.3) | 3,725 (2.9) | 1,280 (0.8) | 3,725 (1.8) | 3,304 (2.1) |
| Ceramics, etc. | 3,242 (1.6) | 3,351 (2.6) | 4,507 (2.9) | 3,351 (1.6) | 2,072 (1.3) |
| Hats, etc. | 2,998 (1.5) | 1,491 (1.2) | 1,001 (0.7) | 1,491 (0.7) | 1,199 (0.7) |
| Marine products | 3,816 (1.9) | 4,498 (3.5) | 4,803 (3.1) | 4,822 (2.4) | 5,079 (3.2) |
| Electric bulbs | 1,423 (0.7) | 772 (0.6) | 685 (0.4) | 610 (0.3) | n/a |

*Notes:* (1) Figures in parentheses show percentages of each item of total Japan's exports in each year.
(2) Marine products are canned tuna fish and crab meat.
*Source: An Economic Analysis of United States–Japanese Trade* (San Francisco: Japanese Chamber of Commerce, 1970), 34 (figures for 1937, 1938, and 1939). Matsumizu Yukuo, "Nichibei keizai kankei no saikentō," *Hiroshima Daigaku Keizai Ronsō* (Hiroshima: Hiroshima University, 1980, vol. 3, no. 4), 262. *Far Eastern Survey* (New York: American Council Institute of Pacific Relations, Nov. 23, 1938), 270. *Far Eastern Survey* (New York: American Council Institute of Pacific Relations, Jan. 3, 1940), 6.

by invoking the so-called flexible tariff clause of Section 336 of the Smoot–Hawley Act, which provided that the president could impose special duties on imported goods whose production cost was deemed to be lower than that of domestic goods of the same kind.[138] The higher tariffs, however, did not stop the influx of Japanese imports. In 1937 a new agreement was concluded between US cotton-textile industry representatives and their counterparts in Japan. This time, however, Japanese cotton-textile exports fell short of the quota provided by the agreement, mainly due to the inability of Japanese manufacturers to acquire enough raw cotton, which had been placed under the Japanese government import restrictions (15.3.5).

In addition to high import duties, some Japanese goods were subject to dumping duties. For example, in 1934, Japanese incandescent electric lamps were levied a 30 percent dumping duty under the Anti-Dumping Act of 1921 on top of the 20 percent ad valorem duty imposed on imports of this products.[139] Japanese incandescent electric lamps continued to be exported over these steep import barriers.

As regards raw silk, since there was virtually no sericulture industry in the United States and American silk manufacturers depended entirely on imported raw silk, raw silk carried no US import duty, and it was immune to any forms of protectionist duties. But it was subject to anti-Japanese boycott movements, which started to be active after the Mukden Incident and became widespread after the onset of the Sino–Japanese war. The movements were promoted by several private groups, including a group of university presidents and faculty members.[140] The Chinese-American community in particular was active. American public opinion about the boycotting of Japanese imports was divided, however. A poll conducted in October 1938 indicated that 37 percent of the American people were in favor of boycotting Japanese goods. But not all of them translated their sentiments into action.[141] Another public survey showed that about 22 percent of families refused to buy Japanese goods (except silk), and another 40 percent supported the boycott in principle but applied it only occasionally in practice, while 10 percent objected to the boycott, mainly on the grounds that it hurt American exports.[142] After the USS *Panay* incident (14.3.3), *Business Week* reported, "In the last two months, fifty-five hosiery manufactures in the United States have turned to the production of lisle hose," but these did not represent the bulk of the industry, which continued to depend on silk from Japan.[143] Some retail stores supported boycotts. After the *Panay* incident, four of the nation's largest chain stores—F. W. Woolworth, S. S. Kresge, S. H. Kress and Co., and McCrory Stores Corp.— announced that they were discontinuing the purchase of Japanese goods. But before long they resumed imports from Japan, albeit on a modest level.[144] The *Far Eastern Survey* estimated that during the first twelve months of the Sino–Japanese war, as compared with the previous twelve-month period, US boycotts cost Japan around $15 million, or 7.4 percent of its total prewar exports to the United States, which accounted for about 28 percent of the total decline in Japan's exports to the United States during the period.[145]

### 15.4.3. Main Commodities in US Exports to Japan

While there were some declines in US exports to Japan in the early 1930s, they were much smaller compared to the declines in US exports to other countries (table 15.4.1-b). The declines in US exports to Japan were largely due to the fall in the market price of raw cotton. In fact, in terms of quantity, US exports of raw cotton to Japan more than doubled from 1930 to 1932. Japan's growing exports of cotton goods to world markets in the early 1930s required larger and larger purchases of long-staple American raw cotton. From 1931 to 1936, Japan was the largest foreign consumer of American raw

*US and Japanese Economies, Their Economic Policies, and Their Trade Relations in the 1930s*

Table 15.4.3. Main Commodities in Japan's Imports from US ($ thousand)

|  | 1931 | 1933 | 1935 | 1937 | 1939 |
|---|---|---|---|---|---|
| Raw cotton | 75,113 (48.1) | 96,253 (67.3) | 106,266 (52.3) | 61,724 (21.4) | 42,448 (18.3) |
| Petroleum products | 23,983 (15.4) | 14,803 (10.4) | 27,204 (13.4) | 42,402 (14.7) | 44,057 (19.0) |
| Iron and steel scrap | 403 (0.3) | 4,204 (2.9) | 18,622 (9.2) | 39,386 (13.6) | 32,593 (14.0) |
| Automobiles and parts | 7,729 (5.0) | 3,351 (2.3) | 8,929 (4.4) | 13,581 (4.7) | 6,420 (2.8) |
| Aircraft and parts | n/a | n/a | n/a | 2,484 (0.9) | n/a |
| Metalworking machinery | 7,921 | 5,508 (3.9) | 11,114 (5.5) | 11,904 (4.1) | n/a |
| Copper and copper products | 310 (0.2) | 2,267 (1.6) | 10,241 (5.0) | 17,997 (6.2) | 27,567 (11.9) |

*Notes:* (1) Figures in parentheses show percentages of total Japan's imports for each item in each year.
(2) Figures for aircraft and parts are not available for 1931, 1933, 1935 or 1939, but the figure for 1934 is $4,804,000 and that for 1938 is $11,069,000.
(3) Japan's import figures for metal working machinery in 1939 are not available. Imports in 1938 were $23,614,000, and those in January through September in 1939 were $19,524,000, which was 13 percent larger than corresponding figure in 1938.
*Source: An Economic Analysis of United States–Japanese Trade* (San Francisco: Japanese Chamber of Commerce, 1970), 34 (Figures for 1937, 1938, and 1939). Matsumizu Yukuo, "Nichibei keizai kankei no saikentō," *Hiroshima Daigaku Keizai Ronsō* (Hiroshima: Hiroshima University, 1980, vol. 3, no. 4), 262. *Far Eastern Survey* (New York: American Council Institute of Pacific Relations, Nov. 23, 1938), 270. *Far Eastern Survey* (New York: American Council Institute of Pacific Relations, Jan. 3, 1940), 6.

cotton, taking as much as a quarter to 30 percent of American raw-cotton exports,[146] which in turn represented 50 to 60 percent of Japan's total raw-cotton imports during the period. From 1937, however, raw-cotton imports were curtailed by the Japanese government's import restrictions under the Temporary Import-Export Grading Measures Law, which classified raw cotton as raw materials of peacetime industry whose imports were subject to severe curtailment (15.3.5). Acute foreign-exchange difficulties compelled Japan to confine its imports to war materials such as oil, metals, and machinery. Of Japan's total imports from the United States, raw cotton accounted for 67 percent in 1933, but the proportion declined to 21 percent in 1937 and 18 percent in 1939. In contrast, the share of petroleum and its products increased from 10 percent in 1933 to 19 percent in 1939, and that of iron and steel

Chapter 15

scrap from 3 percent to 14 percent during the same period (table 15.4.3).

With respect to petroleum, by the late 1930s Japan produced only about 7 percent of its requirement.[147] Standard Vacuum and Royal Dutch Shell supplied 60 percent of Japan's oil imports, and the rest was supplied by about thirty Japanese companies which imported their oil from a number of American producers.[148] In terms of the countries of production, about 80 percent of crude oil supplied to the Japanese market were produced in the United States, about 10 percent in the Dutch East Indies, and the remainder in the British possessions.[149] In 1937, of US crude oil production, exports accounted for 5 percent, of which one-fifth was exported to Japan. Japan's imports represented 1 percent of the total produced in the United States.[150]

Japan depended on imported iron and steel scrap for half of its total consumption in the late 1930s, and imports from the United States accounted for 70 to 80 percent of Japan's total iron and steel imports. Japan was by far the largest purchaser of US iron and steel scrap, taking an increasing percentage of US exports of the material—48 percent in 1938 and 59 percent in 1939.[151] Because the US iron scrap market was so large, exports to Japan had little impact on supply and demand in the United States.[152]

With respect to copper, Japan was self-sufficient until 1932, but by 1937 Japan had to depend on imports for over half of its total consumption. In that year, Japan's imports of copper from the United States accounted for 65 percent of its total imports. US exports of copper to Japan represented 24 percent of its total exports and 8 percent of its total production.[153]

Japan's $10 million worth of metalworking machinery imports from the United States in 1937 all but equaled the value of Japan's domestic output of metalworking machinery in that year, and represented one-quarter of US exports of the machinery to the world.[154] From 1937 to 1938 Japanese imports of metalworking machinery from the United States nearly doubled, and imports from January through September 1939 were about 10 percent larger than those in the corresponding period in 1938.[155]

As noted above, Japan was increasingly dependent on imports from the United States for procurement of war materials in the 1930s, and this dependence increased with the onset of the war in Europe in November 1939. Of Japan's imports from the United States, the proportion of wartime materials increased from one-fifth in 1933 to more than half in 1939 (table 15.4.3). A growing number of Americans were now supportive of some restrictions on

462

*Notes*

the export of those materials to Japan. Military aircraft and aeronautical equipment were placed on a "moral embargo" in the summer of 1938 (14.3.4). After the abrogation of the 1911 treaty in January 1940, a series of "mandatory embargoes" were to follow, as observed in the next chapter.

NOTES

15.1. The US Economy in the 1930s

1   This unfortunate coincidence view explains the 1929 Depression as a depression in a Kondratieff long cycle covering as long as forty to fifty years, which arrived simultaneously with a depression in a Juglar intermediate nine-year cycle and a short-range Kitchin cycle in inventories. This is the Schumpeter view. Charles Kindleberger, *The World in Depression, 1929–1939* (Berkeley, Los Angeles: University of California Press, 1973), 3. Geoffrey Wood and Forrest Capie, eds., *The Great Depression Critical Concepts in Economics*, vol. I (London: Routledge, 2011), introduction, 6.

2   Keynes attributed the Depression to a fall in investments due to a complex of causes, including high interest rates, diminishing returns on investments, tight Federal Reserve policies, gold scarcity outside the United States, and falling American foreign investments. Peter Temin, *Lessons from the Great Depression* (Cambridge: MIT Press, 1989), 7.

3   Milton Friedman and Ann Schwartz, *A Monetary History of the United States, 1867–1960* (Princeton: Princeton University Press, 1963), chapter 7. Peter Temin writes, "The account of 'The Great Contraction' in chapter 7 of Friedman and Schwartz's classic *Monetary History of the United States* stands without peer among narratives of the early 1930s. It is scholarly, detailed, insightful, and fascinating. As might be expected, it has had an enormous influence on our views of the Depression. It has become something like the standard history of the Depression for students of economics." Peter Temin, *Did Monetary Forces Cause the Great Depression?* (New York: W. W. Norton, 1976), 14. Bernanke describes the argument of Friedman and Schwartz as "the most persuasive explanation of the worst economic disaster in American history." Benjamin Bernanke, "Remarks," Milton Friedman and Anna Schwartz, *The Great Contraction, 1929–1933* (Princeton: Princeton University Press, 2008), 228.

4   Wood and Capie, eds., *The Great Depression Critical Concepts in Economics*, vol. I, 6. Friedman and Schwartz quote Irving Fisher's comment as follows. "I thoroughly believe that if he [Benjamin Strong] had lived and his policies had been continued, we might have had the stock market crash in a milder form, but after the crash there would not have been the great industrial depression." Benjamin Strong was the governor of the Federal Reserve Bank of New York from 1914 until his death in 1928. Friedman and Schwartz, *Monetary History*, 413.

5   Barry Eichengreen, *Golden Fetters: The Gold Standard and the Great Depression, 1919–1939* (New York: Oxford University Press, 1995), 251.

6   The discount rate was reduced from 6 percent to 5 percent in October 1929, to 4.5 percent in November 1929, to 4 percent in February 1930, to 3.5 percent in March

Chapter 15

1930, to 3 percent in April 1930, to 2.5 percent in June 1930, to 2 percent in December 1930, and to 1.5 percent in April 1931. It was raised to 3.5 percent in October 1931 after the British withdrawal from the gold standard, but it was reduced to 2.5 percent in June 1932. It was raised again to 3.5 percent in March 1933, but it was reduced to 1.5 percent in 1934 and remained at that level until 1937, when it was reduced to 1 percent. Friedman and Schwartz, *Monetary History*, 304, 513.

7   Kenneth Weiher, *America's Search for Economic Stability: Monetary and Fiscal Policy Since 1913* (New York: Twayne Publishers, 1992), 64–65.

8   Friedman and Schwartz, *Monetary History*, 352. Wood and Capie, *The Great Depression*, vol. I, 6–10. Thomas Hall and David Ferguson, *The Great Depression: An International Disaster of Perverse Economic Policies* (Ann Arbor, MI: University of Michigan Press, 1998), 84–85.

9   Between 1929 and 1933 the monetary base rose 17 percent, reflecting increases in bank reserves in the Federal Reserve in anticipation of runs by depositors. Hall and Ferguson, *International Disaster*, 10, 85.

10  Weiher, *America's Search for Economic Stability*, 63. Hall and Ferguson, *International Disaster*, 85.

11  As a result of several reforms after the Great Depression, the Federal Reserve of today is tasked with such macroeconomic goals as achieving full employment, stable price levels, and the growth of national production. But in the 1930s the Federal Reserve was not assigned such roles, though it was expected to give the nation a more uniform currency, supervise the US banking system, and nip financial crises in the bud through the injection of liquidity into illiquid but solvent banks. The Fed's limited power and responsibility in the 1930s reflected the US government's historical disinclination to have a powerful central bank. There had been eight decades of no central bank after 1836, when the second Bank of the United States, which had received a twenty-year charter in 1816, ceased functioning because the renewal of its charter was vetoed by President Jackson. The first Bank of the United States also lasted for only twenty years from 1791 to 1811, when Congress refused to renew its charter. Richard Sylla, "Reversing Financial Reversals: Government and the Financial System since 1789," in *Government and the American Economy*, ed. Price Fishback (Chicago: University of Chicago Press, 2007), 121, 125, 129, 137–138.

12  While all nationally chartered banks were members of their regional Federal Reserve, most state-chartered banks were not, except those which met certain standards to become members. Hall and Ferguson, *International Disaster*, 83.

13  Friedman and Schwartz, *Monetary History*, 358–359. A basic principle of the Federal Reserve's behavior was that loans were to be made to banks that were sound and profitable, but temporarily short of liquid funds due to being faced with unexpectedly large withdrawals of cash. Hall and Ferguson, *International Disaster*, 77.

14  Hall and Ferguson, *International Disaster*, 82–85.

15  Philippe Aghion and Peter Howitt, *Endogenous Growth Theory* (Cambridge: MIT Press, 1998), 239. Hoover called a number of conferences of manufacturing and financial leaders and asked them to resist the temptation to cut wages or decrease employment. This attempt of his was criticized by supporters of the liquidationist view as preventing the market from causing necessary liquidations of marginal enterprises.

*464*

## Notes

James Willis and Martin Primack, *An Economic History of the United States* (Englewood Cliffs, NJ: Prentice-Hall, 1980), 369. Bernanke, in his speech on July 10, 2013, stated that the liquidationist view and the real bills doctrine, both of which were prevalent in the late 1920s and early 1930s, were clearly counterproductive. Ben Bernanke, "The First 100 Years of the Federal Reserve: The Policy Record, Lessons Learned, and Prospects for the Future," speech at a conference sponsored by the National Bureau of Economic Research, Cambridge, Massachusetts. http://www.federalreserve.gov/newsevents/speech/bernanke20130710a.html.

16  Eichengreen, *Golden Fetters*, 253. Takemori Shumpei, *Keizai ronsen wa yomigaeru* (Tokyo: Tōyōkeizai Shinpōsha, 2002), 6–7.

17  Eichengreen, *Golden Fetters*, 262.

18  Ibid., 18, 262.

19  Temin, *Lessons from the Great Depression*, 38.

20  Ibid., 33–34.

21  Eichengreen, *Golden Fetters*, 12

22  Ibid., 247–248. Temin, *Lessons from the Great Depression*, 30. Wood and Capie, *The Great Depression*, vol. I, 10.

23  Hall and Ferguson, *International Disaster*, 89. Noguchi Asahi and Wakatabe Masazumi, "Kokusai kinhonisei no ashikase," in *Shōwa kyōkō no kenkyū*, ed. Iwata Kikuo (Tokyo: Tōyōkeizai Shinpōsha, 2004), 40–43.

24  Hall and Ferguson, *International Disaster*, 88–89.

25  Ibid., 89. Britain left the gold standard on September 21, 1931. By the end of September, nine countries, including Sweden, Denmark, Norway, and Canada, had suspended convertibility. In October, they were joined by Finland, Portugal, Bolivia, and El Salvador; in December, by Japan. Eight additional nations defected from the gold standard in the first half of 1932. At its height in 1931, forty-seven countries had been on gold. By the end of 1932 the only significant holdovers were Belgium, France, Italy, the Netherlands, Poland, Switzerland, Germany, and the United States. Eichengreen, *Golden Fetters*, 298–299.

26  Temin, *Lessons from the Great Depression*, 29.

27  Ibid., 29–31. There is a view that Hoover wanted the tax increase not so much to deflate the economy as to balance the budget to discourage gold outflows. The tax increases enlarged the budget deficit rather reducing it, as table 15.1.2-b shows. Willis and Primack, *An Economic History of the United States*, 370.

28  Weiher, *America's Search for Economic Stability*, 79.

29  Keynes commented that the gold-buying program had been "foolish" because there was no "mathematical relation between the price of gold and the prices of other things." Gary Best, *Pride, Prejudice, and Politics: Roosevelt versus Recovery, 1933–1938* (New York: Praeger Publishers, 1991), 51.

30  Weiher, *America's Search for Economic Stability*, 81.

31  Ibid., 81.

32  Willis and Primack, *An Economic History of the United States*, 377.

33  Weiher, *America's Search for Economic Stability*, 82.

34  In 1936, excess reserves were in the $2.5–3.0 billion range, which was larger than the Fed's portfolio of securities at $2.4 billion. Ibid., 83.

Chapter 15

35  The discount rate hike would have little effect on banks which had ample reserves and little need to borrow from the Fed, and the Fed did not own enough securities for open market operation either. Ibid., 82.

36  Ibid., 84.

37  Ibid., 83–85.

38  Willis and Primack, *An Economic History of the United States*, 375.

39  Weiher, *America's Search for Economic Stability*, 90.

40  Willis and Primack, *An Economic History of the United States*, 375.

41  Best, *Pride, Prejudice, and Politics*, 51.

42  Keynes journeyed to the United States to accept an honorary degree from Columbia University and to confer with Roosevelt in the White House through the good offices of Felix Frankfurter. Best, *Pride, Prejudice, and Politics*, 65.

43  Price Fishback et al., *Government and the American Economy* (Chicago: University of Chicago, 2007), 390. Keynes once claimed, "Madmen in authority, who hear voices in the air, are distilling their frenzy from some academic scribblers of a few years back." Ibid., 390.

44  US Department of Commerce, *The United States in the World Economy* (Washington, DC: US Government Printing Office, 1943), 120.

45  Ibid., 9, 122.

46  The figure does not include gold in circulation, or certain unreported or irregularly reported holdings. Ibid., 134.

15.2. The New Deal

47  Fishback et al., *Government & the American Economy*, 385.

48  Weiher, *America's Search for Economic Stability*, 73. Robert Puth, *American Economic History* (Chicago: Dryden Press, 1982), 383.

49  Fishback et al., *Government and the American Economy*, 404.

50  Weiher, *America's Search for Economic Stability*, 88.

51  Keynes pointed out in an essay that "the important but intangible state of mind which we call business confidence, is signally lacking." A major cause of this, he concluded, was "the menace of possible labor trouble," but more important was "the perplexity and discomfort which the business world feels from being driven so far from its accustomed moorings into unknown and uncharted waters" by the New Deal. Best, *Pride, Prejudice, and Politics*, 65.

52  Jeremy Atack and Peter Passel, *A New Economic View of American History* (New York: W. W. Norton & Company, 1979), 672–673. Willis and Primack, *An Economic History of the United States*, 378–379.

53  Fishback et al., *Government and the American Economy*, 405. Weiher, *America's Search for Economic Stability*, 88.

54  American farmers' total cash incomes decreased from $14.5 billion in 1919 to $4.7 billion in 1932, while their total outstanding debt increased from $7.1 billion to $9.1 billion during the same period. US Department of Commerce, Bureau of the Census, *Historical Statistics of the United States* (Washington, DC: US Government Printing Office, 1975), 483, 491.

55  In 1933, 6 million pigs were slaughtered and buried in an effort to cut pork supplies.

*466*

## Notes

Willis and Primack, *An Economic History of the United States*, 380.

56 Ibid., 380.

57 The most spectacular of all Roosevelt's conservation measures was the Tennessee Valley Development Act (May 18, 1933). The idea was to dam the river and its tributaries, thus providing flood regulation, navigable reaches and an important source of power. The plan covered an area of about 40,000 square miles (100,000 square kilometers) in seven states. Before long, the TVA assumed second place among American electric supply systems. Peter Jones, *An Economic History of the United States* (London: Routledge & Kegan Paul, 1964), 251.

58 Fishback et al., *Government and the American Economy*, 402. Jonathan Hughes and Louis Cain, *American Economic History* (Boston: Addison Wesley, 2003), 486. Kusui Toshirō, *Amerika shihonshugi to Nyūdīru* (Tokyo: Nihon Keizai Hyōronsha, 2005), 108–109.

59 Fishback et al., *Government and the American Economy*, 402.

60 Hughes and Cain, *American Economic History*, 486.

61 Hughes and Cain, *American Economic History*, 486. Fishback et al., *Government and the American Economy*, 402.

62 The institutions to which the RFC provided loans included the FCA, the Public Works Administration (PWA), the Home Owners' Loan Corporation (HOLC), the Federal Housing Administration (FHA), the Rural Electrification Administration (REA), and the Works Progress Administration (WPA). Fishback et al., *Government and the American Economy*, 394.

63 Ibid., 394. Willis and Primack, *An Economic History of the United States*, 381.

64 Weiher, *America's Search for Economic Stability*, 77.

65 Ibid., 78. The provisions separating commercial and investment banking were repealed in 1999. The regulations on interest rates, except for the ban on demand-deposit interest, were phased out during the period 1981–1986. The prohibition on interest-bearing demand-deposit accounts was repealed in 2011.

66 Fishback et al., *Government and the American Economy*, 411.

67 Ibid., 396.

68 Gilbert Fite and Jim Reese, *An Economic History of the United States* (Boston: Houghton Mifflin, 1973), 599.

69 Ross Robertson and Gary Walton, *History of the American Economy* (New York: Harcourt Brace Jovanovich, 1979), 500–501.

70 Willis and Primack, *An Economic History of the United States*, 383. Fishback et al., *Government and the American Economy*, 385. Neither Medicare nor Medicaid were envisaged at this stage. They were created when Lyndon B. Johnson signed amendments to the Social Security Act in 1965.

71 Hughes and Cain, *American Economic History*, 495.

72 Ibid., 489. Willis and Primack, *An Economic History of the United States*, 384–385.

73 Puth, *American Economic History*, 383. Weiher, *America's Search for Economic Stability*, 73. Fishback et al., *Government and the American Economy*, 385.

74 Fishback et al., *Government and the American Economy*, 417.

75 Hughes and Cain, *American Economic History*, 498.

76 Fishback et al., *Government and the American Economy*, 409, 420.

Chapter 15

77  Kusui, *Amerika shihonshugi to Nyūdīru*, 144.
78  Hughes and Cain, *American Economic History*, 490.
79  Willis and Primack, *An Economic History of the United States*, 383.
80  Kusui, *Amerika shihonshugi to Nyūdīru*, 4.
81  Takahashi, then seventy-seven, was called back from retirement by Inukai to become the finance minister for the fifth time.

### 15.3. The Japanese Economy and Economic/Industrial Policies in the 1930s

82  Mark Metzler, *Lever of Empire* (Berkeley: University of California Press, 2006), 250.
83  Nakamura Takafusa and Odaka Kōnosuke, eds., *The Economic History of Japan, 1600–1990*, vol. 3, *Economic History of Japan 1914–1955: A Dual Structure* (New York: Oxford University Press, 1999), 40.
84  Dick Nanto and Shinji Takagi write, "This constituted the beginning of open market operations." Dick Nanto and Shinji Takagi, "Korekiyo Takahashi and Japan's Recovery from the Great Depression," in *The Interwar Economy of Japan: Colonialism, Depression, and Recovery, 1910–1940*, ed. Michael Smitka (New York: Garland Publishing, 1998), 372.
85  Hugh Patrick, "The Economic Muddle of the 1920s," in *Dilemmas of Growth in Prewar Japan*, ed. James Morley (Princeton: Princeton University Press, 1971), 256.
86  Nanto and Takagi, "Korekiyo Takahashi," in *The Interwar Economy*, ed. Smitka, 372.
87  Takahashi kept abreast of theoretical developments in economics abroad, and used them in his public statements. In a 1933 speech, for instance, he quoted Irving Fisher and used the results of a University of Chicago research group arguing for countercyclical fiscal policy. Nanto and Takagi, "Korekiyo Takahashi," in *The Interwar Economy*, ed. Smitka, 372. Richard Smethurst, *From Foot Soldier to Finance Minister: Takahashi Korekiyo, Japan's Keynes* (Cambridge: Harvard University Press, 2007), 275.
88  Nakamura Takafusa, *Economic Growth in Prewar Japan*, trans. Robert Feldman (New Haven: Yale University Press, 1971), 236–237. The relief expenditures for farm villages were a package of public investments largely comprising land reclamation, irrigation, drainage, dikes, roads, and river repairs. David Flath, *The Japanese Economy* (New York: Oxford University Press, 2000), 59.
89  Nakamura, *Economic Growth in Prewar Japan*, trans. Robert Feldman, 237.
90  A special summer session of parliament was called in 1932 to deal with supplemental spending for rural relief. Smethurst, *Takahashi Korekiyo*, 275.
91  Ibid., 273–274. When asked by Ishibashi Tanzan whether an increase in military allocations was the best kind of spending policy to stimulate economic recovery, Takahashi answered, "Of course, military spending is not directly productive . . . Warships do not produce other goods, but the money used to build warships is used productively. . . . If in the political context of the time one has to spend money on the military anyway, it is better than nothing." Smethurst, *Takahashi Korekiyo*, 273–274.
92  Ibid., 286.
93  Ibid., 288. After he joined the Okada cabinet in November 1934, Takahashi told an acquaintance, "If I were young, I would worry about the young officers, but at my age I have no future. I have to do my service now, I entered the government again think-

*Notes*

ing that this is my last chance to serve. I am prepared to die now." Ibid., 295.

94 Ibid., 293.

95 Ibid., 295. The Shōwakai and the Kokumin Dōmei, which the military and the right wing supported, obtained only twenty seats and fifteen seats respectively out of the 466 Diet seats.

96 Smethurst, *Takahashi Korekiyo*, 274.

97 Nakamura Takafusa, *A History of Shōwa Japan, 1926–1989*, trans. Edwin Whenmouth (Tokyo: University of Tokyo Press, 1993), 108.

98 Chalmers Johnson, *MITI and the Japanese Miracle: The Growth of Industrial Policy, 1925–1975* (Stanford: Stanford University Press, 1982), 105.

99 Nakamura, *A History of Shōwa Japan*, trans. Whenmouth, 74.

100 Ibid., 74.

101 Johnson, *MITI*, 104. Nakamura, *A History of Shōwa Japan*, trans. Whenmouth, 74.

102 The law stipulated that once a cartel included more than half of the companies in any key industry, it should be registered with the government. When such a group had signed up two-thirds of the companies in the industry, nonmembers were also to be subject to its directions. Nakamura, *A History of Shōwa Japan*, trans. Whenmouth, 75.

103 Johnson, *MITI*, 110–111. The law also brought about the zaibatsu's expansion of its operations through mergers and acquisition, though it was not the original intention of the law. Ibid., 110.

104 For example, Standard Vacuum Oil Company kept defying the stockpile provisions, but the company had the least difficulty obtaining foreign-exchange or import licenses in Japan, according to the survey by the US consulate in Yokohama in 1939. Mark Mason, *American Multinationals and Japan: The Political Economy of Japanese Capital Controls, 1899–1980* (Cambridge: Harvard University Press, 1992), 96. Mira Wilkins, *The Maturing of Multinational Enterprise: American Business Abroad from 1914 to 1970* (Cambridge: Harvard University Press, 1974), 230–232. Johnson, *MITI*, 120–121.

105 Mason, *American Multinationals*, 86.

106 Johnson, *MITI*, 132.

107 Nakamura, *A History of Shōwa Japan*, trans. Whenmouth, 108. Johnson, *MITI*, 133.

108 Nakamura, *Economic Growth in Prewar Japan*, trans. Feldman, 266. Nakamura, *A History of Shōwa Japan*, trans. Whenmouth, 131.

109 Nakamura, *A History of Shōwa Japan*, trans. Whenmouth, 132. Nakamura, *Economic Growth in Prewar Japan*, trans. Feldman, 266.

110 Nakamura, *A History of Shōwa Japan*, trans. Whenmouth, 209.

111 Ibid., 148.

112 Japan's current account balance had long run a surplus because non-trade accounts, especially shipping, were in surplus. But in 1937 the large trade deficit exceeded the non-trade surplus, turning the current account balance to a deficit.

113 Mitani Katsumi, *Kokusai shūshi to Nihon no seichō* (Tokyo: Heibonsha, 1957), 207, 255, and 256. Takahashi Kamekichi, *Taishō Shōwa zaisei hendōshi* (Tokyo, Tōyōkeizai Shinpōsha, 1955), 1784.

114 Nakamura, *Economic Growth in Prewar Japan*, trans. Feldman, 286.

*469*

Chapter 15

115 The Temporary Import-Export Grading Measures Law (輸出入品等臨時措置法) passed by the Diet in September 1937 classified all imports into four classes to ensure preferential treatment for materials needed by the munitions industry. Class A contained the leading raw materials of peacetime industry, whose imports were subject to severe curtailment from normal levels. Raw cotton was listed in this class. Class B listed articles of a nonessential or luxury nature, or which could be manufactured in Japan. Imports of articles in this category were generally prohibited. Class C contained articles used for exports which were prohibited. Class D specified articles whose imports were given preferential position. See Miriam S. Farley, "The Impact of War on Japan's Foreign Trade," *Far Eastern Survey*, vol. VIII, no. 11 (New York: American Council Institute of Pacific Relations, May 24, 1939), 124.

116 Nakamura, *A History of Shōwa Japan*, trans. Whenmouth, 148. Nakamura, "The Age of Turbulence," in *The Economic History of Japan*, eds. Nakamura and Odaka, 56, 58. Nakamura, *Economic Growth in Prewar Japan*, trans. Feldman, 288.

117 Nakamura, "The Age of Turbulence," in *The Economic History of Japan*, eds. Nakamura and Odaka, 59.

118 Ibid., 58–59. The Kwantung Army prepared a proposal titled "Principles of Manchurian Economic Construction," and had it approved by the government in Japan. For example, industries were classified in the proposal into three categories: those that should be encouraged through central planning, those that could be left relatively free of control, and those that should be actively discouraged. In the first group, only one company was to be permitted in each field, and its development was to be closely regulated by the state. Nakamura, *A History of Shōwa Japan*, trans. Whenmouth, 102.

119 Nakamura, "The Age of Turbulence," in *The Economic History of Japan*, eds. Nakamura and Odaka, 58.

120 Johnson, *MITI*, 109. Another important product of the CPB was the Electric Power Control law of 1938. It gave the state control over all thermal power stations and all electricity transmission facilities bringing them under the unified management of the new Japan Electric Power Generation and Transmission Company. Nakamura, *A History of Shōwa Japan*, trans. Whenmouth, 152.

121 Johnson, *MITI*, 133.

122 Ibid., 139. Nakamura, *A History of Shōwa Japan*, trans. Whenmouth, 151. Nakamura, "The Age of Turbulence," in *The Economic History of Japan*, eds. Nakamura and Odaka, 59.

123 Johnson, *MITI*, 139.

124 Janis Mimura, *Planning for Empire Reform: Bureaucrats and the Japanese Wartime State* (Ithaca: Cornell University Press, 2011), 141. It was Admiral Suetsugu, home minister, who demanded in the cabinet meeting that dividends should be controlled. He asserted that if this were not done, he would have great difficulty maintaining public peace. At this Ikeda Shigeaki, a Mitsui executive who held the ministerial portfolios of both finance and commerce, said to him, "Do you really think a factory worker knows how much stockholders receive as dividends? . . . Why do you say such a damned foolish thing? Is there any connection between a stockholder's dividends and the public peace?" Ikeda also said at a press conference, "If you limit stock

*Notes*

profits, you will destroy the entrepreneurial spirit and there will be no hope for the very important expansion of production our country now needs." Suetsugu pressed Konoe to get rid of Ikeda or else face his own resignation. Finally, Navy Minister Yonai intervened, and it was agreed to limit regular dividends to 10 percent a year. Ikeda had set a pattern for making the controls on the business community lighter than otherwise. Arthur Tiedemann, "Big Business and Politics in Prewar Japan," in *Dilemmas of Growth in Prewar Japan*, ed. James Morley (Princeton: Princeton University Press, 1971), 310–311.

125 Nakamura, *A History of Shōwa Japan*, trans. Whenmouth, 152. Johnson, *MITI*, 139.

126 German imports from the United States were $278 million in 1930 and $166 million in 1931. French imports from the United States in 1930 were $224 million.

15.4. Trade Relations between the United States and Japan in the 1930s

127 US Department of Commerce, *Historical Statistics*, 903–904.

128 In 1929, the United States imported from Japan 70 million pounds of raw silk, which amounted to $356 million. The price per pound was $5.08. In 1932, US imports of the commodity were 69 million pounds, amounting to $106 million. The price per pound was $1.54. US Tariff Commission, "Recent Developments in the Foreign Trade of Japan Particularly in Relation to the Trade of the United States," in *The United States in World Trade during the Inter-War Period* (Washington, DC: US Government Printing Office, 1936. Reprinted in Tokyo by Gozando Books, 1992), 8.

129 At the early stage of Japan's trade with the United States, tea was Japan's leading export item, but it was replaced by raw silk in the mid-1880s, and after that raw silk continued to be the leading export (see table 5.2.2-a, table 9.2.4-b).

130 In 1930–1934, Japan supplied 90.4 percent of American raw silk imports, China 6.1 percent, Italy 3.1 percent, and France 0.4 percent. Giovanni Federico, *An Economic History of the Silk Industry, 1830–1930* (Cambridge: Cambridge University Press, 1994), 214. Japan's share of US raw silk imports was 92.7 percent in 1936, 93.4 percent in 1937, 94.9 percent in 1938, and 88.4 percent in 1939. Japanese Chamber of Commerce, San Francisco, *An Economic Analysis of United States–Japanese Trade* (San Francisco: Japanese Chamber of Commerce, 1970), 53.

131 Between 1910–13 and 1936–38 Japan's share of world cotton cloth exports rose from 2 percent to 39 percent. In 1935 Japanese cotton textiles' major purchasers were China and Hong Kong (12 percent), British India and Ceylon (21 percent), the Dutch East Indies and Malaya (21 percent), Africa (10 percent), South America (7 percent), and Australia (3 percent). Christopher Howe, *The Origins of Japanese Trade Supremacy* (London: Hurst & Company, 1996), 216–217.

132 Ibid., 205.

133 Kenneth L. Bauge, "Voluntary Export Restriction as a Foreign Commercial Policy with Special Reference to Japanese Cotton Textiles," in *Foreign Economic Policy of the United States*, ed. Stuart Bruchery (New York: Garland Publishing, 1987), 64–65.

134 Ibid., 63–65.

135 Ibid., 89.

136 Ibid., 40–66, 86–91.

137 Ibid., 60.

Chapter 15

138 Ibid., 52. Besides cotton cloth, the US government raised duties, for example, on Japanese wool knit gloves (by 100 percent) and frozen swordfish (50 percent) invoking Section 336 of the Tariff Act of 1930. *Far Eastern Survey*, vol. V, no. 8 (New York: American Council Institute of Pacific Relations, April 8, 1936), 70.

139 Ikeda Michiko, *Tainichi keizai fūsa* (Tokyo: Nihon Keizai Shimbunsha, 1992), 102–103.

140 Ikeda Michiko, *Japan in Trade Isolation* (Tokyo: I-House Press, 2008), 102–103.

141 Nathan M. Becker, "The Anti-Japanese Boycott in the United States," *Far Eastern Survey*, vol. VIII, no. 5 (New York: American Council Institute of Pacific Relations, March 1, 1939), 52.

142 This survey was conducted in Toledo, Ohio. Nathan M. Becker, "The Anti-Japanese Boycott in the United States," *Far Eastern Survey*, vol. VIII, no. 5 (New York: American Council Institute of Pacific Relations, March 1, 1939), 52.

143 Mira Wilkins, "The Role of U.S. Business" in *Pearl Harbor as History*, eds. Dorothy Borg and Shumpei Okamoto (New York: Columbia University Press, 1973), 346.

144 Ibid., 346.

145 The *Far Eastern Survey* divided Japanese imports into three categories: Class A, goods which were easily recognizable as made in Japan and readily replaceable by substitutes or supplies from other sources; Class B, raw silk; and Class C, goods which were not recognized as Japanese, or for which there was no available substitute, or raw or semi-manufactured materials sold at the wholesale level where the boycott was not effective. The survey estimated that the boycott decreased imports of Class A, Class B, and Class C by approximately 55 percent, 15 percent, and 5 percent respectively, costing Japan, as a result, around $15 million during the first twelve-month period. Becker, "The Anti-Japanese Boycott in the United States," *Far Eastern Survey*, vol. VIII, no. 5, 52–54.

146 William Lockwood, "American–Japanese Trade: Its Structure and Significance," *The Annals of the American Academy of Political and Social Science*, 215 (Philadelphia: Sage Publications, 1941), 87.

147 Daniel Yergin, *The Prize: The Epic Quest for Oil, Money, and Power* (New York: Simon & Schuster, 1992), 307.

148 Among the Japanese oil companies that imported oil from the United States, Mitsubishi Sekiyu, a fifty-fifty oil-refining joint venture between Mitsubishi Shōji and Associated Oil, headquartered in San Francisco, was the biggest supplier with about a 10 percent market share in Japan (10.3.3).

149 Yergin, *The Prize*, 307–308. Robinson Newcomb, "Japanese–American Trade in Its Latest Phase," *Far Eastern Survey*, vol. IX, no. 23 (New York: American Council Institute of Pacific Relations, Nov. 20, 1940), 268.

150 Eliot Janeway, "Japanese Purchases in the American Economy," *Far Eastern Survey*, vol. VII, no. 11 (New York: American Council Institute of Pacific Relations, June 1, 1938), 126. Robinson Newcomb, "Japanese–American Trade in Its Latest Phase," *Far Eastern Survey* vol. IX, no. 23 (New York: American Council Institute of Pacific Relations, Nov. 20, 1940), 268.

151 Japanese Chamber of Commerce, San Francisco, *An Economic Analysis of United States–Japanese Trade* (San Francisco: Japanese Chamber of Commerce, 1970), 39.

*Notes*

152 Newcomb, "Japanese–American Trade in Its Latest Phase," *Far Eastern Survey*, vol. IX, no. 23, 269.

153 Janeway, "Japanese Purchases in the American Economy," *Far Eastern Survey*, vol. VII, no. 11, 125. Ohara Keiji, ed., *Nichibei bunka kōshōshi* (Tokyo: Yōyōsha, 1954), 50.

154 Janeway, "Japanese Purchases in the American Economy," *Far Eastern Survey*, vol. VII, no. 11, 127.

155 Miriam Farley, "Japanese–American Commercial Agreement Expires," *Far Eastern Survey*, vol. IX, no. 1 (New York: American Council Institute of Pacific Relations, Jan. 3, 1940), 6.

## Chapter 16
# Japan, the United States, and China on the Eve of the Pacific War

## 16.1. The War in Europe

### 16.1.1. Hitler and the European War

Adolf Hitler became the German chancellor in 1933. His first goal was to unite all areas inhabited by ethnically German people who had been dispersed by the Versailles Treaty. In March 1938, he annexed Austria without much protest from the other powers. When he attempted in the autumn of that year to annex the Sudetenland in Czechoslovakia with its large minority of ethnic Germans, however, he met strong resistance from the Czechs. The British and French governments sought a negotiated settlement. In late September 1938, an agreement accepting German annexation of the Sudetenland was signed at Munich by the leaders of Great Britain (Chamberlain), France (Daladier), Italy (Mussolini), and Hitler. When Hitler renounced his treaty commitments and annexed the rest of Czechoslovakia in March 1939, Britain and France announced that they would no longer acquiesce to any more German violations of the Versailles Treaty.

On September 1, 1939, Germany launched the invasion of Slavic Poland,[1] implementing the quest for *Lebensraum*—territory and resources in Slavic

Central and Eastern Europe that Nazi ideology held were needed for Germany's natural and destined development. On September 3, Great Britain and France declared war on Germany and the Second World War began. After a seven-month "phony war" period, during which there was little fighting on the Western Front,[2] the Germans launched a massive spring offensive. They overran Denmark and Norway in April 1940.[3] In May they occupied Belgium and Holland. France surrendered on June 22.

Hitler then assaulted Britain in July 1940 with a major bombing campaign in preparation for a projected invasion of the British Isles. He was met with strong British resistance, which had US support (16.1.2). As early as September 1940, Hitler essentially acknowledged defeat in the air war by discontinuing preparations for his invasion of the British Isles (Operation Sea Lion).

In the East, having subjugated Germany's half of Poland, Hitler decided to strike his principal target for *Lebensraum*: the Soviet Union. On June 22, 1941, the German forces moved into Russia. Initially they made rapid progress, but the Russians resisted stubbornly despite heavy casualties and the loss of vast stretches of territory. Like the forces of Napoleon before him, Hitler's army bogged down before the gates of Moscow in early December 1941 as the fearsome Russian winter came on. A subsequent Soviet offensive eventually drove the German forces out of the country. The Russians lost over 20 million lives in total.

### 16.1.2. The United States and the European War

In the United States, isolationist sentiment was dominant in the 1930s. The overwhelming majority of Americans wanted to avoid any involvement in external entanglement, preferring to retreat into neutrality. They believed that the first priority of the Roosevelt administration was to turn its energies inward and do something about the Great Depression, avoiding any foreign complications.[4]

The enactment of a series of neutrality acts demonstrated American isolationism in the 1930s. The Neutrality Act of 1935 empowered the president to declare an embargo on shipments of arms and war materials to warring nations, making no distinction between aggressor and victim. The Neutrality Act of 1936 added a prohibition on extending loans or credits to belligerents. The Neutrality Act of 1937 extended the embargo on arms and war materials

*476*

shipments to civil wars, but was later amended with the cash and carry provision that authorized the president to list certain war materials, other than arms, which had to be paid for upon delivery and taken away in the ships of the buyer, belligerent or non-belligerent. This provision made the United States less isolated and less neutral in that it was more favorable to naval powers, notably Great Britain.[5]

After the Munich conference in September 1938, the United States moved toward more active support of democracies opposing the dictators. Soon after Hitler's invasion of Poland in September 1939, Congress passed the Neutrality Act of 1939 which permitted the embattled Allies to buy, for cash, arms from the United States, but it prohibited American ships from navigating in danger zones.[6]

After the German spring offensive in April 1940, American public opinion clearly turned against Germany and in favor of Britain. Americans were now coming to the realization that, should totalitarian Germany defeat Britain, democracy in Europe and elsewhere would be in danger. Moreover, if Japan were formally tied to Germany, the threat would become even more formidable.[7] The Roosevelt administration set about taking decisive steps to rescue Britain. The "destroyer deal" of September 1940 during the London Blitz was an unprecedented exercise of presidential executive power by Roosevelt. In an effort to help the British in their battle against German submarines, fifty US destroyers were transferred to Britain in return for the US lease of British bases in Newfoundland, Bermuda, and Trinidad.

By the end of 1940, Britain had used up its foreign exchange reserves and had no more money to negotiate new cash-and-carry contracts for arms. The Roosevelt administration placed a bill before Congress authorizing the president to lend "defense articles" to those governments "whose defense the president deems vital to the United States."[8] The Lend-Lease Act was passed in March 1941 in the Senate with a two-thirds majority and with a more one-sided vote of 317 to 71 in the House.[9] The Lend-Lease Act was among the most momentous laws ever passed by Congress. British morale was greatly boosted. Britain was the immediate beneficiary of the new law. In May 1941, China, too, became a recipient of lend-lease goods, and in November it was applied to Russia. When Lend-Lease was terminated on August 21, 1945, over $50.6 billion of aid had been sent to Britain, China, and Russia.[10] The enormous amount of $50.6 billion was equivalent to about one-quarter of the

US GNP in 1945.[11]

### 16.1.3. Japan's Alliance with Germany

Germany and Japan pursued their expansionary policies independently, without any form of coordination, until November 1936, when they signed the Anti-Comintern Pact. The ostensible purpose of this pact was to contain the spread of communism, but it had a secret protocol which required both parties to consult with a view to safeguarding their common interests if either Germany or Japan was attacked by the Soviet Union. The Anti-Comintern Pact was negotiated between Ōshima Hiroshi (大島浩), the military attaché of the Japanese Embassy in Berlin and Joachim von Ribbentrop, at the time Hitler's principal adviser on foreign affairs. It had required eighteen months to negotiate it because the senior members of the Japanese leadership saw no reason to alienate the Soviet Union needlessly and were aware of the distaste of the United States and Britain for the Nazi regime.[12]

In early 1938, Germany sought to transform the anti-Comintern pact into a military alliance targeted against Britain and France as well as the Soviet Union. Negotiations started unofficially between Ribbentrop, who was now the German foreign minister, and Ōshima. In an attempt to conciliate Japan, Germany recognized Manchukuo and withdrew its military advisors from China.[13] In Japan, a group called the Axis faction, mainly mid-level officials of the foreign ministry and the army, was eager to identify Japan with Germany against Britain, France, and the United States, and argued fervently for the alliance with Germany. The leader of the Axis faction in the foreign ministry was Shiratori Toshio.[14]

In the first Konoe Fumimaro cabinet, which started on June 4, 1937, Foreign Minister Arita Hachirō (有田八郎) and Navy Minister Yonai Mitsumasa (米内光政) strongly opposed a treaty which was likely to antagonize Britain and the United States. They were against any form of pact that was targeted against any country other than the Soviet Union. But Army Minister Itagaki Seishirō insisted on including Britain and France as secondary targets.[15]

The Konoe cabinet was dissolved on January 4, 1939, owing to a division of opinions over the question of the alliance with Germany. Hiranuma Kiichirō (平沼騏一郎) took over as premier. Arita, Yonai, and Itagaki remained in the cabinet. Hiranuma was close to the militarists and let negotiations with

Germany go on. But the abrupt conclusion of the German–Soviet Nonaggression Pact on August 23, 1939 (see note 1) shocked Hiranuma so much he resigned in confusion. In the general mood of distrust of Germany in Japan, the political influence of the Axis faction greatly declined.

General Abe Nobuyuki (阿部信行), who replaced Hiranuma as prime minister in late August 1939, appointed pro-American admiral Nomura Kichisaburō (野村吉三郎) as foreign minister. Nomura was negative about an alliance with Germany that would most certainly harden America's policy against Japan. He had negotiations with US Ambassador to Japan Joseph Grew seeking a new trade treaty, but any alteration to US policy was not possible without major changes in Japan's China policy. Nomura's efforts proved fruitless. In January 1940, the Abe cabinet resigned, taking responsibility for lack of progress on the diplomatic front. Abe was replaced by Yonai and Nomura by Arita. Yonai had been regarded as a "most undesirable person" as prime minister by the Axis faction.[16]

The astounding success of the 1940 German spring offensive, however, revived the Axis faction. They now criticized the Yonai government for its lack of enthusiasm for an alliance with Germany.[17] In July 1940, the army had the army minister, General Hata Shunroku (畑俊六), resign from the cabinet, a standard tactic to overthrow the government (14.1.1). Yonai resigned July 16. The army made it clear that they would not accept any government which was against an alliance with Germany. On July 22, 1940, the second Konoe cabinet was launched. Konoe appointed Matsuoka Yōsuke (松岡洋右) as foreign minister as Arita's replacement. Matsuoka was an advocate of a military alliance with Germany targeted against the United States as well as Britain.[18]

In early September, Hitler sent Minister Plenipotentiary Heinrich Stahmer to Tokyo and the alliance discussions resumed. Stahmer and German ambassador Eugen Ott in Tokyo demanded a pact which would automatically obligate treaty signatories to enter into a war against a treaty counterparty.[19] This automatic obligation was strongly opposed by the Japanese navy. Matsuoka proposed a compromise; while the automatic obligation provision would be included in the treaty, mention would be made in a supplementary protocol and an exchange of notes that each contracting party would retain its freedom to choose independently the time and method of fulfilling the obligation. Stahmer and Ott accepted this compromise,[20] and the Tripartite Pact was signed in Berlin on September, 27, 1940. Article III of the Pact demanded

that Japan, Germany and Italy "undertake to assist one another "with all political, economic and military means when one of the three Contracting Parties
is attacked by a power at present not involved in the European War or in the
Sino–Japanese Conflict." Germany sought to prevent the United States from
intervening in the European war by demonstrating the determination of
Germany, Italy, and Japan to stand together.[21] Likewise, Matsuoka believed
that the pact would prevent the United States from intervening against Japan's
policies in Asia (16.3.3).

## 16.2. Japanese China Policy and the US Reaction in the Late 1930s

### 16.2.1. Japanese China Policy in the Late 1930s

After the outbreak of the Sino–Japanese war in 1937, the expansionists in the
Japanese army pushed forward with aggressive China policies, disregarding
Ishiwara's warning of the danger of being stuck in the morass of a long war.
The fall of Nanjing in December emboldened the government as well as mili-
tary leaders, leading to the *aitenisezu* declaration on January 16, 1938 (14.3.2).

In the spring of 1938, the Japanese army launched the massive Xuzhou
(徐州) campaign. Xuzhou fell on May 19 after fierce fighting. Then the Japanese
army assaulted Hankou (漢口) and Guangzhou (広州), conquering
Guangzhou on October 21 and Hankou on October 26. Within sixteen
months after the outbreak of the war, all major cities in China had fallen to
Japanese forces, yet there was hardly a feeling of victory on the Japanese side.[22]
These campaigns proved very costly. Especially casualties in the Xuzhou campaign were heavy.[23] The Nationalists refused to surrender and moved their
government to Chongqing (重慶), where they were ensconced beyond the
Yangtze River gorges and safe from the Japanese army's land attack.[24] The war
was likely to drag on for a long time.

It was in these circumstances that a document titled "Policies for Adjusting
to New Japan–China Relations" (*Nisshi shin kankei chōsei hōshin* 日支新関係
調整方針) was drafted, which stated conditions under which Japan could end
the war by negotiations with the Kuomintang government after certain military achievements following July 1937.

The "Policies" offered to renounce claims for territory and indemnities,
but demanded: (a) Creating separate regional regimes in China (the policy of

*bunji gassaku* 分治合作) and assigning Japanese advisors to such regional regimes; (b) Japan's maintaining a necessary number of troops for an unlimited length of time in Inner Mongolia and North China; (c) Japan's "special privileges" in economic matters in North China and Central China; and (d) Japan's right of strategic requisition and supervision of railroads, aviation, communication, and important harbors and waterways where Japanese troops were stationed.[25]

The original draft of the "Policies" prepared by the army general staff War Guidance Section in the spring of 1938 was moderate and fair, but while it was passed on up through the various departments of the army and navy bureaucracy for discussion, amendment, and the seals of endorsement for six months until it was finally brought before an imperial conference on November 30, it had become a document demanding old-fashioned imperialist rights and special interests in China.[26]

Being an internal document, the "Policies" was not published externally as it was. But Japan's China policies officially announced and actually implemented in1938 and after were all based on the "Policies." Foreign Minister Arita's provocative declaration of November 18 (14.3.3) was a corollary to the new China policy stated in the "Policies."[27]

On November 3, 1938, Konoe issued a declaration that Japan would aim at establishing a "New Order in East Asia" (*Tōa shin chitsujo* 東亜新秩序) by forming a mutually assisting link among Japan, China, and Manchukuo to ensure permanent stability in East Asia. Being a diplomatic statement, the "New Order" declaration did not mention the hard conditions of the "Policies." As discussed in 16.2.3, Wang Ching-wei believed that he could engage in peace negotiations with Japan based on the proposals in this declaration, but he later learned that Japan's China policy was strictly bound by the conditions of the "Policies." Wang strongly resisted accepting them, but to no avail.[28]

After the occupation of Hankou and Guangzhou, the Japanese army was not able to mount any further large-scale land offensives. In 1939, excepting the Nomonhan Incident as described below, the Japanese military actions in China and its vicinity were limited to air raids on Chongqing and the occupation of the Hainan Island (海南島) and the Spratly Islands. Bombing on Chongqing started in January 1939. While many civilians were killed and many buildings were destroyed, military facilities in Chongqing being small in scale and scattered, the bombardments' military effect was limited. Air attacks

*481*

Chapter 16

were discontinued in October.[29] In February 1939, the Japanese navy occupied Hainan Island, off the southern China continent, and in the next month the Spratly Islands, 700 miles south of Hainan. The taking of these islands showed the navy's interest in extending its sway over the South Seas even at the risk of creating tensions with Britain, France, and the United States.[30]

At Nomonhan, on the border between Manchukuo and Outer Mongolia, the Kwantung Army fought with the Soviet Army in the spring through the fall of 1939. The fighting started when several hundred troops from Outer Mongolia crossed the border into Manchukuo in May. The Kwantung Army repulsed them and crossed the border for punitive expeditions, where it encountered the vastly superior Soviet artillery and tanks. The Kwantung Army suffered a total defeat. Approximately 56,000 Japanese forces were committed and the overall casualty rate reached 32 percent.[31] The Soviets, who were then facing a serious situation in the west after the German occupation of Czechoslovakia in March 1939, evidently intended to warn the Japanese against any military operations in the east.[32]

As of December 1939, the total number of Japanese troops deployed in China reached some 850,000. The number of war dead up to the beginning of the Pacific War exceeded 185,000, with the injured numbering 325,000. Even having so many soldiers and having sacrificed so many victims in China, Japan could still not win the war. The Japanese army was now shifting its focus of interests from the battlefields of China to Southeast Asia, leaving the settlement of the Sino–Japanese war primarily to diplomatic measures.[33]

### 16.2.2. The US Reaction to Japan's China Policy in the Late 1930s

In the United States, while activists in the State Department argued that the Japanese invasion had to be stopped by any means necessary, otherwise it would dominate all of East Asia,[34] moderates maintained that Asia's usefulness to the United States was limited and the defense of the region would not be worth a war. Secretary of State Cordell Hull, a proponent of world peace based on the rule of law and respect of treaties, embraced a stance which was close to that of the activists, but he "subordinated his feelings of righteous indignation at Japan's aggression in China to the less emotional criteria of national interest."[35] He took the view that the United States should not risk a confrontation with any country for anything less than a vital national interest. The Japanese invasion of China was undesirable, but it did not threaten a vital

*482*

American interest.[36] President Roosevelt accepted Hull's argument, but temperamentally he shared the activists' view. His annoyance at a policy that let Japan get away with blatant aggression in China prompted him to deliver the quarantine speech in October 1937 (14.3.3). This presidential leadership encouraged the activists greatly, but Hull was determined to prevent Washington "hotheads" from provoking a confrontation with Japan. The quarantine speech was followed by no specific activist policies. Hull considered that the longer Japan fought a futile war in China, the more precarious the position of the Japanese military would become at home.[37]

As the year 1938 progressed, however, Hull started to have sympathy with the view harbored by activists that the crisis in China was not an isolated phenomenon, but was part of a developing world crisis.[38] As the likelihood of war in Europe increased in 1939, Hull clearly shifted his stance closer to that of the activists. In July, Hull told the Japanese ambassador, " . . . we draw the line between honest, law-abiding, peaceful countries and peoples, without reference to their form of government, on the one hand, and those who are flouting law and order and officially threatening military conquest . . . " He divided countries into two camps—peace-loving countries and aggressors—and implied that the United States would come to the aid of China in its fight with Japan, as it would help British and French resist Germany.[39]

By the summer of 1939, growing number of Americans came to support economic sanctions against Japan. In June 1939, Gallup polls showed that 72 percent of the American people favored an embargo on war materials shipment to Japan.[40] In Congress, Senator Key Pittman, chairman of the Senate Foreign Relations Committee, proposed that the next neutrality act empower the president to embargo the sale of war materials to any nation that violated the Nine-Power Treaty—in other words, Japan. Republican senator Arthur Vandenberg, on the other hand, introduced a resolution calling for the abrogation of the 1911 US–Japan commercial treaty (14.3.3).[41]

Hull was put in a delicate diplomatic and political situation. Passage of the Pittman resolution would mean confrontation with Japan. Its defeat, on the other hand, would convince Japan that isolationist sentiment was still strong in the United States. Hull did not want either to happen. The Vandenberg resolution would give the administration a more leeway, but the Democrats would probably attack it on partisan grounds. If it failed, Hull's Asian policy alternatives would be restricted. Whether those two resolutions passed or failed, debate on them in Congress would cause unnecessary strain on US–Japanese relations. Roosevelt and Hull decided to avoid these dangers by pre-empting the legislation. On July 26, the Roosevelt administration served Japan the required six months' notice for termination of the 1911 commercial treaty before Congress passed the resolution[42]

### 16.2.3. The Wang Chingwei Government—An Abortive Peace Effort

In China, from the mid-1930s, a group of politicians and scholars called the Low-Key Club began to meet regularly in Nanjing to discuss means of counteracting the deteriorating relationship with Japan.[43] The group's prominent members included Chiang's aide-de-camp Chou Fo-hai (周仏海),[44] the Foreign Ministry's Asian bureau chief Kao Tzung-wu (高宗武),[45] the Foreign Ministry's Asian section chief Tung Tao-ning (董道寧),[46] economic historian Tao Hsi-sheng (陶希聖),[47] and the Hong Kong office manager of an organization of the Kuomintang Government, Mei Szu-p'ing (梅思平).[48] After the outbreak of the Sino–Japanese Incident in 1937, they questioned the official all-out resistance-to-the-death slogans, and contended that diplomatic channels to Japan should be explored fully to attain peace.

In Japan, a group of people mainly in the army general staff responded positively to these Chinese moves. They were Colonel Kagesa Sadaaki (影佐禎昭), the chief of the Stratagem Section, which was newly created for the express purpose of finding a solution to the China Incident;[49] chief of the China Unit of the Stratagem Section Imai Takao (今井武夫), and Inukai Takeru (犬養健), councilor in the Ministry of Communication, who was determined to complete his father's unfinished tasks to help China become a democratic modern state.[50]

In the first half of 1938, there were two visits to Japan from the Chinese side. One was by Tung Tao-ning in mid-January 1938.[51] In Japan, Tung met Vice-Chief of General Staff Tada Hayao (多田駿) as well as Kagesa and Imai, and gained the impression that the *aitenisezu* statement could be modified.[52] Chiang Kai-shek was pleased with the results of Tung's trip,[53] and indicated that a ceasefire with Japan would be possible if Japan acknowledged territorial and administrative integrity of China south of the Great Wall.[54]

The second trip was made in July by Kao Tzung-wu. Kao was convinced in Japan that there was a chance that Japan might negotiate with Wang Ching-wei, at the post of deputy director-general at the time.[55]

*484*

When Wang first learned that the Japanese were considering peace negotiations with him, not with Chiang, he summarily rejected the idea.[56] However, his rejection changed to cautious interest as the year wore on. A major factor in this change was his dismay at the agonizing cost of the war of resistance against Japan, as exemplified by the destruction of the Yellow River dikes in June 1938 at the cost of a million Chinese lives.[57] Chagrin over the Western powers' lack of willingness to help China also caused Wang to change his mind.[58]

Then came Konoe's announcement on November 3 that Japan would look forward to cooperating with China in establishing a new order in East Asia. Wang considered it conciliatory enough to have further exploration and discussion. Wang ordered Kao and Mei Szu-p'ing to initiate peace talks with Japan.[59] Kao and Mei met with Kagesa, Inukai, and Imai in Shanghai on November 12–13 and 19–20.

The Chinese representatives presented the following scheme: As soon as an agreement was reached between the two sides, Wang would leave Chongqing and Japan would make public the basic terms of the peace agreement. Then Wang would organize a new government embracing Yunnan (雲南), Sichuan (四川), Guangdong (広東) and Guangxi (広西). Yunnan and Sichuan had not been occupied by Japan, but Wang had already made pacts with Lung Yun (竜雲) of Yunnan and various warlords in Sichuan. Guangdong and Guangxi could serve as the basis of a new government with the partial withdrawal of Japanese troops. To the Japanese this seemed an epoch-making and encouraging scheme.[60]

On November 20, 1938, they agreed on the "Minutes of a Sino–Japanese Understanding," which listed the following points of agreement: (a) China's recognition of Manchukuo; (b) Japan's stationing of troops in Inner Mongolia and in the Tianjin–Beijing area; (c) Japanese citizens' rights to reside in the interior of China and to engage freely in commerce, and in this connection Japanese consideration of the abrogation of its extraterritorial rights and relinquishment of its concessions; (d) Japan's priority rights in developing and utilizing the resources of North China; and (e) the withdrawal of Japanese troops not specifically covered by agreements within two years after the restoration of peace.[61]

Wang accepted all the items and on December 18 flew to Kunming (昆明), the capital of Yunnan, accompanied by his wife and his secretary Tsen

Chung-ming (曾仲鳴).[62] At Kunming, the headquarters of Lung Yun, Wang had a long and decisive discussion with Lung, but Wang was evidently unable to extract a firm promise of support from Lung.[63] On December 19, the Wang party, now joined by Chou Fo-hai and T'ao Hsi-sheng, flew to Hanoi. Meanwhile, Lung wavered for some weeks after the December 18 talks, and in the end cast his lot with Chiang.[64]

On December 22, Konoe issued an agreed statement that generally followed the lines of the November 20 "Understanding." Significantly, however, having yielded to the pressure from the army hard-liners, Konoe omitted mention of the troop withdrawal plan which had been agreed on November 20.[65] Wang's reaction came on December 29. He generally supported Konoe's statement, but insisted that the garrisoning of troops in Inner Mongolia must be limited to a period concurrent with the proposed anti-Communist pact, and as for China proper, Japanese troops must be withdrawn from Chinese soil promptly.[66]

By early 1939, Wang had become fairly discouraged about the prospects for his movement. He was expelled from the Kuomintang on January 1; the response from the generals of southwestern provinces to his appeals for support was disappointing; Japan appeared reluctant to commit itself to his cause. Were it not for the murder of Tsen Chung-ming, Wang's confidential secretary and longtime friend, on March 21, Wang might have abandoned the peace movement.[67]

The Japanese government offered to provide Wang with necessary security in Shanghai. He accepted the offer, and he and his party moved to Shanghai in early May on a vessel chartered by the Japanese government.[68]

Wang decided to visit Japan to talk directly with Japanese leaders. He and a small entourage including Chou Fo-hai and Kao Tzung-wu arrived in Japan on June 2, 1939.[69] Meanwhile, on June 6, the Five Ministers Conference decided that the Wang regime would be one of the regimes under the *bunji gassaku* scheme of the "Policies," and that Wang was not to be told of this policy for the time being.[70] The Japanese leaders avoided referring to the *bunji gassaku* policy in their meetings with Wang, but Itagaki hinted at one of the meetings with Wang that Japan would allow the Provisional and Reformed Governments to remain (14.3.2). Wang retorted strongly that a new government should be central, united, and sovereign. In the end, however, Wang gave in and accepted the existence of an "administrative council" for North China.[71]

*486*

In late June through early July, Wang met Wang K'o-min (王克敏) of the Provisional Government in Beijing and Liang Hung-chih (梁鴻志) of the Reformed Government in Shanghai, but these meetings were more discomfiting than his Japanese trip. Both were totally unproductive.[72] In July and August, Wang made an attempt to form a government in Guangzhou, where in May 1931 he had once established a short-lived separate government with the support of an anti-Chiang warlord, Chang Fa-k'uei (13.2.1). The Japanese South China Expeditionary Army offered to support the scheme. Wang made a radio speech on August 9 appealing for the support of the warlord generals as well as the citizenry at large. However, the support from the supposedly wavering generals did not materialize. The scheme to form a government in Guangzhou was quietly dropped.[73] On August 28, Wang convened a gathering of supposed Kuomintang supporters in Shanghai. The meeting, heralded for several weeks by Wang's press agents as the Sixth Kuomintang Congress, proved to be one more dismal failure. Few important members of the Kuomintang joined him, and his reputation declined markedly.[74]

Meanwhile, it became necessary to let the Wang group know about the conditions of the "Policies." Talks with the Wang group began on November 1, 1939, in Shanghai.[75] The Wang group was astonished at the differences from the November 20, 1938 "Understanding." The Japanese said that the "Understanding" was not a formal agreement binding on the government, and that if the Wang group had succeeded in the planned uprising in Sichuan and Yunnan, agreements in the "Understanding" could have been implemented. But since the plan had failed and the Wang government was to be formed in the Japanese occupied territory, Japan had to demand of the Wang regime similar restrictions to those imposed on other regional regimes.[76] The Chinese side argued in vain that they had to be given "persuasive power" sufficient to cause the Chinese people to change their support from the Chongqing government to the new government, if the formation of the latter was to end the war with the former.[77] An agreement was signed on December 30, which represented an almost complete capitulation by Wang to Japanese demands.[78]

Kao and T'ao, totally disenchanted by these developments, fled Shanghai on January 4 for Hong Kong, where they handed over secret documents used at the negotiations to a Hong Kong newspaper. The revelation of the documents sent a shock wave through the Wang camp.[79] It represented a great propaganda victory for Chongqing.[80] They not only undermined Japan's prestige, but showed the people of China that Wang's new central government was a puppet of the Japanese.[81]

Meanwhile, the Wang government was established on March 30, 1940, in Nanjing; the Reformed Government was absorbed into the Wang government, but the Provisional Government became the North China Political Council, with a high degree of autonomy for North China.[82]

The formal recognition of the Wang government by the Japanese government, however, was held up until November 30, 1940, as there were protracted negotiations on a treaty between the Wang government and the Japanese government,[83] and two abortive Tokyo–Chongqing peace talks. One of the two peace talks started in late September 1939 and continued intermittently until the end of August 1940, when the Japanese became convinced that the Chinese approach was a stratagem to frustrate the Wang scheme.[84] The other one was initiated by Matsuoka, who became the foreign minister of the Konoe cabinet in July 1940, but with the Tripartite Pact having linked the Sino–Japanese War to the European War and greatly strengthened the Chinese position vis-à-vis Japan, there was little likelihood of Chiang agreeing to the conditions Matsuoka offered.[85] Matsuoka had to abandon his attempt.

The establishment of the new government on November 30, 1940, however, had little practical meaning.[86] There were no defections of important leaders or shifts of influential warlord support to the Wang government. Chiang Kai-shek, now a powerful symbol of the new Chinese nationalism, successfully brought dissidents into the fold. The Chongqing government had firmly taken root in a new China, and it had become unified and committed to resistance as never before.

In contrast to Japanese nationalism, which had a somewhat artificial quality in the sense that it was instilled in the citizenry by the government, Chinese nationalism, which had grown out of a bitter century of experience, had great vitality and depth. The Japanese, without a history of humiliation at the hands of foreigners, could not appreciate the feelings of the contemporaneous Chinese. For example, the *bunji gassaku* program was very insensitive to Chinese nationalism. It was an anachronistic policy. No Chinese leader could expect the support of the Chinese people by associating himself with the dismemberment of his nation. Wang's acceptance of it foredoomed the failure of his regime.[87]

The Japanese who were associated with Wang's scheme, men like Kagesa and Inukai, were bent on building the Wang regime around Ishiwara's concept of cooperation with China.[88] They sought to reduce Japanese demands on Wang and free him of the puppet stigma. But in the end, they yielded to the hard-liners.

However, given the Chinese people's strong support for Chiang, the bitter rivalry between Wang and Chiang, and the Communists' strong position in Chinese domestic politics,[89] even if a more independent and viable government under Wang had been formed, there seemed to be little assurance that it would have provided a peaceful solution to the troubled Sino–Japanese relations.

## 16.3. Japan's Southward Advance and the Tripartite Pact, and the US Reaction in 1940

### 16.3.1. Japanese Negotiations in the Dutch East Indies

On January 26 1940, the 1911 US–Japanese commercial treaty expired, but the US administration had no immediate program in mind for trade restrictions against Japan. Exports to Japan, including oil, continued. In a letter to Ambassador Grew, Roosevelt wrote that the US government had so far been patient and cautious and would continue to be so. He also said in the letter, " . . . it will be a good thing to have this Government's hands free, . . . and the uncertainties which may prevail may cause the Japanese to think more deeply and more liberally."[90]

Then came the German spring offensive in April. Hitler's sweeping victories over France and the Netherlands gave Japan a golden opportunity for its southern expansion.[91] As early as April 15, 1940, less than one week after Hitler's invasion of Norway, Foreign Minister Arita issued a statement contending that Japan was intimately related with "the South Sea regions, especially the Netherlands East Indies," and Japan could "not but be deeply concerned over any development . . . that may affect the status quo of the Netherlands East Asia."[92] This statement, being vague, could be interpreted in many ways, and it raised the question whether Japan intended to take some action in the East Indies. On April 17, Hull announced that "Intervention in the domestic affairs of the Netherlands Indies or any alteration of their status quo by other than peaceful processes would be prejudicial to the cause of stability, peace, and security not only in the region of the Netherlands Indies but in the entire Pacific area."[93] Hull later wrote, "If we had not adopted a firm attitude from the very outset, Japan might well have made a forceful move toward the East Indies in the summer of 1940."[94]

The Japanese army and navy considered Arita's approach too weak. In mid-May, the navy dispatched the Fourth Fleet to the Palaus, anticipating a development that would affect the status quo of the East Indies. It hoped to take advantage of such a situation to launch its planned southward advance. In June, the army general staff prepared a paper titled "Outline of the Main Principles for Coping With the Changing World Situation" (世界情勢の推移に伴う時局処理要綱), which advocated that Japan "should take advantage of America's indecision and Britain's difficulties in Europe to attack Malaya and Hong Kong and expel British forces from the Far East and the southern areas," and put "the resources of the Dutch East Indies under Japan's control." The "Outline" was approved by the Liaison Conference on July 27, 1940.[95]

Meanwhile, no developments occurred which the Japanese navy and army had expected in the South Seas. The Netherlands had been overrun by Hitler's armies, but their government had not surrendered. They were still carrying on the struggle as allies of Great Britain and a direct attack upon the Netherlands East Indies might well involve Japan in hostilities with Britain, and possibly with the United States. The Netherlands had also considerable forces in the East Indies which could conduct fights for long enough to allow for the destruction of the equipment for the production of oil as well as oil stocks.[96]

The Japanese army and navy now decided that "for the present, efforts will be made to acquire needed resources" of the Dutch East Indies "by diplomatic means," refraining from taking any military action to avoid the risk of direct conflict with the Western powers.[97]

Negotiations between the Dutch East Indies government and a Japanese mission headed by Commerce and Industry Minister Kobayashi Ichizō (小林一三) started on September 13, 1940 in Batavia. Kobayashi proposed to buy annually 3,000,000 tons of oil (which was five times as much as Japan's recent annual imports from the Dutch East Indies) for five years.[98] The Dutch East Indies government rejected the proposal on the ground that such a drastic increase would necessitate reduction of exports to other customers, and took the stand that Japan should discuss its oil import proposals with oil companies. In the negotiations between Mukai Tadaharu (向井忠晴), chairman of Mitsui & Co., and the representatives of Royal Dutch Shell and Standard

*Japan, the United States, and China on the Eve of the Pacific War*

Vacuum Oil from early October, Mukai was offered a spot sale of 726,500 tons of oil. The amount was a little more than Japan's annual imports from the Dutch East Indies. He reluctantly accepted it in the end.[99] The US government had encouraged the Dutch East Indies government and the oil companies to limit the quantity of oil to be sold and the length of contract with Japan to the best of their ability.[100] Kobayashi was summoned back to Tokyo on November 30, and was replaced by former foreign minister Yoshizawa Kenkichi (芳沢謙吉), who started the talks with the Dutch authorities from January 2, 1941. He presented a wide-ranging list of proposals as an agenda for negotiations. But the Netherlands authorities stubbornly evaded discussion of the proposals. They were following advice from the US and British governments not to accede to any ideas that would lead to creation of a Japan-centered East Asian bloc, or what was later called the Greater East Asia Co-Prosperity Sphere.[101] On June 14, 1941, Tokyo instructed Yoshizawa to end the talks with the Netherlands East Indies government.

### 16.3.2. Japan's Invasion of the North Indochina and the US Reaction

In French Indochina, unlike in the East Indies, the risk of incurring the powers' military intervention was considered much smaller.[102] On June 17, 1940, when the French government of Marshal Pétain was negotiating an armistice with Germany at Vichy, Japan demanded that the French close the French Indochina supply route to China and admit the stationing of the Japanese inspectors at the border. The Vichy government had no choice but to yield to Japanese pressure in such a time of crisis.[103] Among the major supply routes to China, the French Indochina routes (Haiphong to Kunming, Haiphong to Paise, and Haiphong to Nanning) were the most important (table 16.3.2).[104]

In August, the Japanese additionally demanded of the French the right of transit for Japanese forces through northern Indochina, the construction of airfields in Tonkin, and an economic arrangement which would bind Indochina securely to the Japanese sphere.[105] The negotiations were unexpectedly protracted, as the French did what they could to delay and restrict their concessions to the Japanese. Finally, on August 29, 1940, Foreign Minister Matsuoka and the Vichy ambassador in Tokyo Charles Arsène-Henry signed a political accord, under which the Tokyo government recognized the "permanent French interest in Indochina," while the Vichy government in its turn recognized the "preponderance of Japanese interest in that area." This

Chapter 16

Table 16.3.2. Supply Routes to Nationalist China as of June 1940

| Supplier | Route | Course | Monthly traffic (tons) | % |
|---|---|---|---|---|
| USSR | Northwest | Xinjiang–Gansu | 500 | 2 |
| France | Indochina | Haiphong–Kunming, Paise, Nanning | 15,000 | 48 |
| UK | Burma | Rangoon–Kunming | 10,000 | 31 |
| UK | Coast | Hong Kong and others | 6,000 | 19 |

*Source:* Hata Ikuhiko, "The Army's Move into Northern Indochina," trans. Robert Scalapino, in *The Fateful Choice: Japan's Advance into Southeast Asia, 1939–1941* (Japan's Road to the Pacific War series), ed. James Morley (New York: Columbia University Press, 1983), 157.

agreement was to go into effect only after the conclusion of a military arrangement to be negotiated later at Hanoi. Negotiations started on August 30 between Major General Nishihara, the head of the inspection team stationed at the border, and governor general of French Indochina Jean Decoux. Japan again encountered repeated resistance from the French, but on September 22, after some military actions and an ultimatum, it finally secured French acceptance of the stationing of 5,000 to 6,000 Japanese troops for guarding air bases and supplies to Japanese troops in China, and the passage of 25,000 Japanese troops through Tonkin province.[106]

In the face of these Japanese moves, the United States did not remain passive. On July 2, 1940, the Congress enacted the National Defense Act, which gave the president authority to put important materials and products on the defense list, subjecting them to license for export. Roosevelt embargoed top grade scrap iron on July 26, and aviation gasoline on July 31. And at the news of the conclusion of the Tripartite Pact (16.3.3), an embargo on all types of scrap iron was proclaimed on September 26, 1940.[107]

The United States was determined to block Japan's southern expansion taking advantage of German military achievements in Europe.[108] Japan's taking over of British colonies would reduce British power to resist against Germany, and the survival of Britain itself would be threatened. The collapse of the British Empire would decidedly threaten the US security. It had to be prevented by all means. The belief that American and British security were interdependent became the guiding principle of American policy and strategy from this time on.[109]

492

### 16.3.3. The Tripartite Pact—Controversy in Japan and US Reaction

Japan's advance into North Indochina brought about US economic sanctions as observed above, but the Japanese action that caused US–Japanese relations to deteriorate more than anything else in 1940 was the conclusion of the Tripartite Pact on September 27. As discussed in 16.1.3, with the successful German spring offensive, there suddenly arose a possibility that Japan might gain control over the European powers' colonies in Asia. Matsuoka believed that the Tripartite Pact would warn the United States away from intervention in Asia by the threat of war with all three Axis powers and enable Japan to complete its southward drive.[110]

The Japanese army officers, the Axis faction officers in particular, were ardent advocates of the pact. But the navy was negative. Navy Minister Yoshida Zengo (吉田善吾) was firmly convinced that Japan should not take any actions that would incite the United States, but Yoshida fell ill and was replaced by Oikawa Koshirō (及川古志郎).[111] Oikawa was also opposed to the pact. He did not believe Matsuoka's brink-of-war logic that allying with Germany was the only way to avoid war with the United States. But when Matsuoka stated that a firm understanding had been reached with Germany that Japan would be free to make its own decision whether or not to enter the war, and when he saw the general public turning in favor of the Tripartite Pact, he considered that he lost grounds to continue his opposition. He was also under strong pressure from middle-ranking officers in the navy that supported the alliance as backing for the drive to the south.[112]

Many government leaders and critics were naturally wary of harmful effect of the pact on US–Japanese relations.[113] In fact, Matsuoka and Konoe had difficulty in securing support from those who had misgivings about allying with Hitler. At a cabinet meeting in September, Matsuoka made a long plea for his colleagues to trust him. The speech was greeted at first by silence, but then there was weak support from two of the cabinet members. One of them said, " . . . it may be that the United States will change its recent insulting attitude toward us. This isn't very likely to happen, but it is our chance."[114]

On September 19, when the Imperial Conference met in the presence of the emperor to review the draft treaty, Hara Yoshimichi (原嘉道), the chairman of the Privy Council, pointed out that thus far the United States had been holding back, lest pressure on Japan drive it into alliance with Germany, but the proposed pact, far from serving as a warning to the United States, might stiffen its attitude and lead to war.[115] Matsuoka challenged this view by arguing that Japanese–American relations had now deteriorated to the point where no improvement could be expected through courtesy or a desire for friendship, and that all Japan could do to prevent war with the United States was to strengthen its position by allying firmly as many countries as possible.[116] At the conference, navy chief of staff Prince Fushimi Hiroyasu (伏見宮博恭), who was not a firm opponent of the pact, raised the question of Japan's automatic obligation to enter war. Matsuoka explained about the freedom of action, referring to the secret note appended to the treaty. The prince also asked about the effect of the Pact on the oil supply. Army Minister Tōjō replied that Japan would try to secure oil from the Dutch East Indies through diplomatic means, but it would resort to the use of force if necessary. At the end of the conference, both chiefs of staff—Prince Kan'in Kotohito (閑院宮載仁) and Prince Fushimi—and Hara gave their consent to the draft pact.[117] Thus the pact was signed on September 27, 1940 in Berlin.

Grew, who was not usually pessimistic, was deeply disturbed. He stated, "Japan has associated herself with a team or system of predatory Powers, with similar aims and employing similar methods." He also argued, "It will be the better part of wisdom to regard her no longer as an individual nation, with whom our friendship has been traditional, but as part and parcel of that system which, if allowed to develop unchecked, will assuredly destroy everything that America stands for."[118]

A public opinion poll indicated a remarkable change in the feeling of Americans as a result of the Tripartite Pact. Before the Tripartite Pact, 12 percent of the Americans queried answered that the United States should risk a war to block Japanese control of China. After the pact, the percentage increased to 39 percent (table 16.3.3). To the question, "Do you approve of Roosevelt's embargo on scrap iron?," 88 percent were in the affirmative on September 30.[119]

Within the Roosevelt administration, Secretary of War Stimson, who had long been convinced that force was the only weapon which Tokyo understood and that the deterrent measures thus far taken against Japan had been altogether inadequate, insisted that an embargo on oil shipments was now imperative. Other cabinet officers, such as Secretary of the Treasury Henry Morgenthau and Secretary of the Interior Harold Ickes also vehemently urged stronger measures against Japan, including the oil embargo. Stanley

Table 16.3.3. American Public Opinion before and after the 1940 Tripartite Pact

|  | Jul. 20 | Sept. 30 |
| --- | --- | --- |
| The US should let Japan control China | 47 | 32 |
| The US should risk a war not to let Japan control China | 12 | 39 |
| Others | 16 | 16 |
| No opinion | 25 | 23 |

Source: Herbert Feis, *The Road to Pearl Harbor: The Coming of the War Between the United States and Japan* (Princeton: Princeton University Press, 1950), 122.

Hornbeck, Secretary Hull's adviser, also suggested that the United States should act before it was too late. Hull, though sympathizing with those activist arguments within the government and especially Grew's view, decided after all to continue shipments of oil to Japan (except aviation gasoline).[120]

During the next few months, important changes were in process in America's Asia policy. The United States began preparing for the use of armed force in the Southwest Pacific.[121] Informal Anglo–American naval conversations began in the autumn of 1940, which were expanded later to military conferences between American, British, and Dutch officers, who drew up joint plans for possible Far Eastern defense.[122] The United States also increased financial assistance to China in line with its policy to keep Japan embroiled on the mainland of China. Up to September 25, 1940, US loans to China had been $44 million in total. On September 25, in response to the news of the Japanese–German alliance talks as well as the Japanese move into North Indochina, the United States made a loan of $25 million, and another $50 million on November 30. This loan was also an expression of the US government's disapproval of the Wang government, which the Japanese government formally recognized on November 30 (16.2.4).[123] These loans were modest in scale, but they gave not a little encouragement to the Chongqing government.[124]

Matsuoka had expected that the Tripartite Alliance would discourage the United States from intervening into Asia conflicts. But, as noted above, the reactions of the United States were in an entirely different direction from what he had expected. The United States was now more firmly determined to show that the Japanese could not expect the United States to be impressed with such an alliance.[125] American public opinion reacted sharply against the Japanese decision (table 16.3.3). This was important in the long run. And crucially, in terms of American diplomacy, American requirements for peace hardened

*495*

markedly, though this did not become fully apparent until the peace talks began in the spring of 1941 (16.4.1). Japan was asked to adhere more than ever to the principles such as the Four Points of Hull as a base of foreign policy.[126]

## 16.4. US–Japanese Relations in 1941

### 16.4.1. Nomura–Hull Talks from March to July 1941

When Ambassador Nomura called on President Roosevelt to present his credentials on February 14, 1941, Roosevelt suggested to Nomura that he should "sit down with Cordell Hull to review the important phases of relations between the two countries" and to "see if our relations could not be improved."[127] Hull and Nomura had their first meeting on March 8, which was to be followed by more than forty meetings until Pearl Harbor.[128]

Mending relations between Japan and the United States seemed an almost impossible task. Nomura was well aware of this. Japan's alliance with the Axis, its war on China, and its southward expansion policy were apparently incompatible with the American policy of support of Britain, aid to China, and the preservation of the status quo in Southeast Asia.[129]

As far as the strategic aims of Japan and the United States were concerned, however, as Schroeder points out, there was no irreconcilable conflict between the two countries. America's attention was focused chiefly on Europe, while Japan was preoccupied exclusively with Asia. In Europe, America's primary interest was a British victory in the war. Japan was concerned about the European war insofar as its outcome affected Japan's East Asian policy. Japan's purpose in entering the alliance with Germany and Italy was to deter the United States from intervening against Japan's southward expansion. In East Asia, Japan was intent on securing materials necessary for its national security as well as for its economic development. On the other hand, America's concern about preserving the status quo in East Asia was basically to maintain Britain's Far Eastern lifeline. As for China, America's strategic interest was distinctly subordinate, though there was a great deal of American sympathy for the Chinese based on sentiment and American ideals.[130] Japan had strategic interests in China as it sought to make China a member of the inner Co-Prosperity Sphere of Japan–Manchukuo–China to cope with the threat of the Soviet Union as well as to serve as a supply source of food and raw material. If Japan had retreated on the issues of the Tripartite Pact and of its southward expansion, and if the United States had compromised on China, some agreement could have been worked out between the two countries.[131]

The trouble was that the philosophy of Hull's diplomacy and that of Japan were different. Whereas Hull's diplomacy was based on lofty idealism, Japan's was based on realism. Whereas Hull demanded a comprehensive agreement based on clear principles, Japan wanted any kind of agreement that would prevent a Japanese–American war.[132] Hull regarded everything less than a sweeping agreement with Japan as a futile appeasement.[133]

Hull insisted on a sincere and wholehearted subscription by Japan to his four principles, which read:

1. Respect for the territorial integrity and sovereignty of each and all nations.
2. Support of the principle of non-interference in the internal affairs of other countries.
3. Support of the principle of equality, including equality of commercial opportunity.
4. Non-disturbance of the status quo in the Pacific, except as the status quo may be altered by peaceful means.

Hull's four principles were much like Elihu Root's four principles, which had been incorporated in Article 1 of the Nine-Power Treaty concluded in February 1922 at the Washington Conference (7.4.3). But since then, Japan had acquired Manchuria and placed many areas in mainland China and East Asia under Japanese control. Japan had no idea at all of giving them up. Besides, in 1941, even among the allies of the United States no nation fully subscribed to Hull's free-trade formula. Economic nationalism and autarky, trade barriers and restrictions were the order of the day. Japan had no intention of abandoning its self-sufficiency policy until a liberal commercial world order was established. It was only after WWII that Hull's goals were realized by the establishment of such an order under the GATT system. Utley declares that expecting Japan to return to the situation of the 1920s through diplomatic talks was "reaching for the moon."[134]

A policy to seek a modus vivendi, a limited and temporary agreement settling some issues and leaving others in abeyance to avert war without involving sacrifice of principle, would have been the only realistic approach that the

United States and Japan could have adopted then. But Hull tenaciously pursued a policy of seeking a comprehensive agreement based on his four principles.[135] At the last stage Hull sought a modus vivendi, but to no avail (16.4.6).

Hull's insistence on his four principles worried Nomura, as he knew that his government was not prepared to accept them. He feared that emphasizing them to the Japanese government would wreck the peace talks.[136] Nomura decided to send the four principles to Tokyo in such a way as they did not look very important. He sent them together with a certain controversial draft proposal of understanding between the United States and Japan, which had recently been prepared in the course of informal talks by American and Japanese individuals. The draft had first been written by two American Catholic priests from the Japanese viewpoint as they understood it; later, an America politician, a Japanese businessman, and a Japanese officer in the Japanese embassy in Washington joined the discussion.[137] The final draft was presented to the US government on April 9, 1941.[138] Hull agreed to use it as an informal basis for further discussion on the condition that Japan would accept the four principles.[139] But Nomura forwarded the April 9 draft to Tokyo as if it had been approved by the US government independently from the four principles. Nomura made no mention of relationship between the April 9 draft and the four principles.[140]

The Japanese government saw what Hull regarded as a conditionally acceptable and unofficial proposal as an unconditionally acceptable and official proposal. More seriously, the importance the United States placed on the four principles in the negotiations with Japan was not duly conveyed to the Japanese.[141] This caused the Japanese to believe that the United States had abruptly escalated its demands in the later negotiations, though the United States basically continued to take same stance.[142]

Meanwhile, Konoe and some army officers found what they believed to be a formal proposal from the United States acceptable. But Matsuoka, who had just returned from his European trip in late April, was not pleased with the proposal. He redrafted it and had it approved by the cabinet, and then sent it to Hull through Nomura on May 12. The Matsuoka version, which totally ignored the spirit of the four principles and emphasized the importance of the Tripartite Pact,[143] disheartened Hull. Though he almost lost hope for further negotiations, on June 21 he submitted a counterproposal emphasizing the four principles, along with an "oral statement" that clearly criticized

Matsuoka. Matsuoka reacted furiously and insisted that the talks be broken off. Konoe and the other ministers decided that the time had come to rid themselves of Matsuoka. The cabinet resigned in a bloc on July 16 and was reconstituted the next day without Matsuoka; Retired Admiral Toyoda Teijirō took his place.[144]

## 16.4.2. Japan's Move into South Indochina

When Germany launched its invasion of the Soviet Union on June 22, 1941 (16.1.1), the Japanese army and navy pressed hard for the occupation of southern French Indochina, as they judged that the danger from the north had virtually diminished. At this time, Matsuoka argued for an attack on the Soviets, abrogating the Russo–Japanese nonaggression treaty which he himself had negotiated and concluded on April 13.[145] He contended that the southern expansion would entail an American intervention, whereas the operations in the north would not; and besides, the attack on the Soviets would contribute to the cause of the alliance with Germany. But he was opposed by a large majority in the Japanese government as well as the army, which, stalled in China, did not want to use up forces and supplies in the vast plains of Siberia.[146]

A liaison conference on June 25 between the representatives of the military high command and the government decided on a policy calling for the occupation of South Indochina, and this policy, "Outlines of National Policies in View of the Changing Situation" (情勢の推移に伴う帝国国策要綱), was approved by the Imperial Conference on July 2. In the excitement of the German–Russo war, the wording suggested by the middle-ranking military officers was adopted unaltered without careful deliberation.[147] It was now official policy to advance into South Indochina, even at the risk of war with the United States and Britain.[148] Schroeder states that Konoe was not agreeable to the draft policy, but he accepted it largely as a "sop" to the militarist extremists who wanted to go much farther.[149] He did not fight in earnest with the extremists before or during the liaison conference of June 25. His failure to do so allowed the army to have its way.[150]

On July 12, Tokyo instructed Ambassador to France Katō Sotomatsu to open negotiations with the Vichy government. On July 14, Katō handed to Admiral Darlan, the vice premier and foreign minister, a note demanding French consent to Japan's dispatch of 'the necessary number' of troops, fleet units, and air units to southern Indochina; establishment of naval base at Cam

Chapter 16

Ranh Bay and Saigon.[151] On July 21, having no choice but to submit, Darlan accepted the demands. On July 24, Japanese troops began to move into southern Indochina, which thus came under Japanese control.[152]

In Washington, Nomura met with Acting Secretary of State Benjamin Sumner Welles on July 23,[153] and said to him that the Japanese move into South Indochina had been necessitated by reasons of the economic situation in Japan and military security. In reply, Welles stated that "the United States must assume that Japan was taking the last step before proceeding upon a policy of totalitarian expansion in the South Seas through the seizure of additional territories in that region." That being so, he said, Secretary Hull "was unable to see that any basis was now offered for continuing the talks," which had begun in March.[154]

On July 24, Roosevelt, receiving Nomura, said that if Japan would withdraw its forces from Indochina, he would seek to obtain an agreement of Britain, China, and the Netherlands to regard Indochina as a "neutralized" country.[155] Hull wrote in his memoir, "Japan's explanation for occupying Indo-China having been that she wanted to defend its supply of raw materials there, the President's proposal took the props from under this specious reasoning."[156]

### 16.4.3. The Oil Embargo and Japan's Preparations for War

Roosevelt felt that the time for words had passed, and he decided to accept Welles' suggestion to freeze Japanese assets in the United States and bring all trade with Japan under US government control.[157] Roosevelt assured navy officials that, since the embargo was not total but selective, it would not prompt the Japanese to strike at either the United States or the Netherlands East Indies. Japan could obtain some petroleum products and would hesitate to cut off this last source of oil by rash action.[158]

The freeze was formally announced on July 26, and to implement the plan, Welles prepared a program: Export licenses would be issued by the State Department for exports which were not prohibited by trade regulations, and exchange licenses would be issued by the Treasury Department to release the dollars from the frozen accounts to finance the licensed exports after approval by the State–Treasury–Justice Foreign Funds Control Committee (FFCC).[159]

Issuing export licenses was automatic. In the case of oil export to Japan, export licenses would be issued for non-aviation petroleum products up to the amount Japan had imported during 1935–1936.[160] But issuing exchange

500

*Japan, the United States, and China on the Eve of the Pacific War*

licenses was not automatic. Each request was to be considered independently by the FFCC, and the FFCC chairman Assistant Secretary of State Dean Acheson had one significant reservation. Acheson was determined not to allow Japan to make payments from blocked Japanese accounts if Japan had unfrozen funds elsewhere that were convertible into American dollars.[161]

The Treasury Department had been monitoring the transfer of Japanese funds from the United States to various Latin American countries since January 1941. It estimated that by August Japan had hoarded at least six million US dollars in Latin America, and about half that amount was circulating in the United States. Acheson was determined to have Japan exhaust these funds before releasing any funds blocked in the United States.[162]

When the freeze was imposed, Japan had filed applications for 2 million dollars' worth of exports. By the US guidelines, then, the amount Japan could purchase from the United States per month was $600,000 worth of goods.[163] On August 1, the State Department issued an export license for $300,000 worth of oil for Japan,[164] for which Japan expected that the FFCC would grant release of a corresponding amount of dollars from their frozen account. But Acheson was determined that it should be paid in currency or from their bank accounts in Latin America.[165] "The FFCC engaged in an administrative 'run-around' to camouflage its refusal of releasing the blocked funds."[166]

It was not until September 4 that Hull became aware of Acheson's "de facto" oil embargo. By then, it was too late. Hull had been resting away from Washington until August 4, and after his return to his office he was too busy to check what Acheson was doing.[167] He considered that starting to issue licenses after a month's refusal would have sent the wrong message to Tokyo and reinforced the position of the Japanese hard-liners, who would have claimed that the United States had given in. All Hull did was order that no new restrictive measures be taken and that the present attitude not be relaxed.[168]

What Roosevelt had planned was a selective and partial embargo, not a total embargo. But in the end, no exchange license was issued after August 1 when the licensing system was introduced as a result of the policy that Acheson had adopted.[169] Acheson might have believed his actions were in keeping with the spirit of the freeze, and thought he was doing the country a favor. Like Morgenthau and Ickes, with whom he associated, Acheson believed that Japan would never go to war with the United States, so the application of economic sanctions was safe.[170] Utley argues, "In effect, the Acheson

*501*

Chapter 16

**Table 16.4.3. Japanese Petroleum Imports**

| | Crude oil | | Refined products | | Total | | US portion (% of total) |
|---|---|---|---|---|---|---|---|
| | Million barrels | Million tons | Million barrels | Million tons | Million barrels | Million tons | |
| 1931 | 6.4 | 0.92 | 13.3 | 1.69 | 19.7 | 2.61 | |
| 1935 | 12.8 | 1.83 | 20.6 | 2.62 | 33.5 | 4.45 | |
| 1937 | 20.2 | 2.89 | 16.6 | 2.11 | 36.9 | 5.00 | 79 |
| 1939 | 18.8 | 2.69 | 11.8 | 1.50 | 30.6 | 4.19 | 85 |
| 1940 | 22.0 | 3.15 | 15.1 | 1.92 | 37.1 | 5.07 | 62 |

*Note:* Estimated tonnage of crude oil and refined product are calculated based on: (1) One barrel of oil is 159 liters. (2) Specific gravity of crude oil is 0.9 and refined product 0.8.
*Source: Far Eastern Survey,* vol. IX, no. 23 (New York: American Council Institute of Pacific Relations, Nov. 20, 1940), 268. Herbert Feis, *The Road to Pearl Harbor: The Coming of the War Between the United States and Japan* (Princeton: Princeton University Press, 1950), 268.

embargo placed a time limit on peace in the Pacific."[171]

Japan's domestic oil production supplied only about 7 percent of its total oil requirement by the late 1930s (15.4.3). Of the total petroleum imports into Japan, the United States supplied roughly 85 percent in 1939 and 62 percent in 1940 (table 16.4.3). In 1940, the Dutch East Indies supplied about one quarter.[172]

The Japanese army and navy leaders had not expected that their actions in South Indochina would bring about a total oil embargo.[173] They now realized that if nothing were done, they would soon run short of oil.[174] They decided that they must seize control of oil production in the Dutch East Indies, even if that meant war with the United States.[175]

Although war with the United States had been envisaged for some time, and each general staff office of the army and the navy had a war plan, no integrated plan had been prepared as of early August.[176] The navy, which was comparatively more prepared for a war with the United States than the army, presented its "Plan for Carrying Out the Empire's Policies" (帝国国策遂行方針) at the August 16 army–navy conference of division and bureau chiefs. It proposed that Japan should pursue preparations for war, to be completed by late October, and at the same time conduct diplomacy. If a diplomatic agreement could not be reached by the middle of October, Japan should exercise force.[177]

Konoe agreed that the army and the navy would make all dispositions for war, while he got the military to consent to his plan to have a summit conference with the United States. Konoe had harbored the idea of a personal meeting with Roosevelt and had recently secured the consent of his cabinet.[178] The machinery of war was to be placed in gear, and it was to be stopped only when Japan came to terms with the United States by the middle of October.[179] This dual initiative approach was approved by the leadership of both the army and navy, and written into a document entitled "Essentials for Carrying Out the Empire's Policies" (帝国国策遂行要領), which was adopted at the Imperial Conference on September 6.[180] It stated:

> In view of the critical situation at present, in particular the offensives that such nations as the United States, Britain and Holland are taking against Japan, the situation in the Soviet Union, and the resiliency of the Empire's national strength, we shall carry out the policies toward the south contained in the "Outline of National Policies in View of the Changing Situation" as follows:
> 1. To achieve self-preservation and self-defense, the Empire shall complete preparations for war by the approximate deadline of late October, based on the resolve not to flinch from war with the United States (Britain and Holland).
> 2. Concurrently, the Empire shall strive to obtain its demands by exhausting all possible diplomatic means vis-à-vis the United States and Britain. The minimum objectives the Empire shall achieve in negotiations with the United States (Britain) and the limits on what the Empire can agree to therein are set forth in the Supplement.
> 3. In the event that by early October there is still no prospect of obtaining our demands through diplomatic negotiation, we shall immediately resolve to go to war with the United States (Britain, Holland).[181]

Japan's minimum demands and maximum concessions spelled out in the appendix were that the United States and Britain should desist from extending military and economic aid to the Chiang Kai-shek regime; that they should refrain from establishing military facilities within Thailand, the Dutch East Indies, China, or the Far Eastern provinces of the Soviet Union and from augmenting their forces in the Far East beyond their existing strength; and that

*503*

Chapter 16

they should provide Japan with resources needed for its existence by restoring trade relations. In return for such concessions on the part of the United States and Britain, Japan would not undertake further military expansion in Asia and withdraw its troops from Indochina "upon the establishment of a just peace in East Asia."[182]

On September 5, when Konoe informed the emperor of the contents of the "Essentials," the emperor asked Konoe: "The order in which the particulars of the plan are set down is a bit strange. Why aren't diplomatic negotiations put first?" Konoe replied lamely that the draft "did attach primary importance to diplomatic negotiations, just as if diplomatic negotiations were put first in the plan." The emperor, being unsatisfied with Konoe's answer, summoned Chief of General Staff Sugiyama Hajime (杉山元) in the evening of the same day and asked his opinion. His response was more unconvincing than Konoe's.[183] Though both Konoe and Sugiyama learned the emperor's strong wish for peace and his misgivings about the bellicose imagery of the "Essentials," they went before the Imperial Conference on the following day with the draft "Essentials" unchanged.[184]

At the conference on September 6, the emperor again expressed his strong wish for peace and read out a tanka poem composed by Emperor Meiji: "Across the four seas / All are brothers. / In such a world / Why do the waves rage, the winds roar?" And he declared, "I have always heeded the words of this poem and strived to bear in mind the spirit and love of peace of the late, great emperor."[185]

The army was the most keenly impressed by the emperor's strong inclination for peace. Upon returning to his office from the conference, Tōjō exclaimed: "His Majesty's wish is for peace, I tell you." And Mutō blurted out excitedly to a member of the Military Affairs Bureau, "His Majesty told us to reach a diplomatic settlement on this, no matter what it takes. We've got to go with diplomacy."[186] Tsunoda argues that that was the one and only golden opportunity that would have allowed Japan to change its orientation from going to war to negotiating peace. If, at the September 6 conference, Konoe had withdrawn the "Essentials," there might have been a good chance that he might have succeeded in reworking it along the lines the emperor called for. But he did not do it. Instead, he increased his efforts to materialize a summit meeting with Roosevelt.[187]

504

## 16.4.4. Konoe's Proposal for a Summit Meeting

Hull had decided to break off negotiations with Japan in July 1941 when Japan invaded South Indochina, but he reconsidered and met Nomura again on August 6, as Nomura wanted to hand him a Japanese reply to Roosevelt's July 24 proposal of neutrality for Indochina (16.4.2).[188]

Hull took a glance at the Japanese proposal and blandly commented that it did not respond to Roosevelt's neutralization proposal. It was at this juncture that Nomura announced that Konoe wanted to have a meeting with Roosevelt, perhaps at Honolulu.[189] Hull's reaction was negative. He stated that such a meeting would be useless without policy changes on the Japanese side.[190] But when Nomura met Roosevelt, who had just returned from the Atlantic Conference with Churchill, Roosevelt reacted favorably to the idea of a meeting with Konoe. He even suggested Juneau, Alaska, as a site rather than Honolulu.[191]

Ambassador Grew urged that the proposal be given profound consideration. He argued, "The good which may flow from a meeting is incalculable."[192] Encouraged by these positive responses, Konoe wrote an urgent and conciliatory letter to Roosevelt. The president, impressed by Konoe's message, commented that he was "keenly interested" in the meeting, and said, "I am looking forward to having approximately three days' talk."[193]

However, Roosevelt met Hull's determined opposition. Hull had many reasons for opposing the summit meeting: distrust of Konoe,[194] fear of causing uneasiness in China, unwillingness to see his own theoretical diplomacy and firm principles laid aside for the personal diplomacy of Roosevelt, and fear of a Far Eastern Munich resulting in a weakening of the American moral position in the world.[195] In addition, his desire to protect his bureaucratic turf also made him negative about the meeting. Hull considered Japanese–American relations his peculiar domain and did not like Roosevelt usurping him. The unsatisfactory (to Hull) Atlantic Conference in mid-August, where Roosevelt proceeded to deviate from the careful policy Hull had prescribed, also made him cautious about the idea of a Pacific conference.[196]

Among the various reasons above, the most important one was his firm conviction that any talks with Japan should not be conducted unless they were based on fundamental principles, and that any agreement should not be had with Japan unless it was a comprehensive agreement, not a partial or temporal agreement. For example, he was convinced that an agreement which

Chapter 16

would leave Chinese questions in abeyance should be avoided. Furthermore, he insisted that no summit meeting be held until preliminary agreement was reached on all the basic issues through regular channels. This policy would effectively wreck the plan, since the whole idea behind the summit meeting was that agreements which could not be reached through normal diplomatic channels could be reached through a leaders' conference.[197] Grew kept sending cables to the State Department in support of the summit meeting, arguing that if the US government wanted the preliminary agreement on both principle and in concrete detail, "the conversations will almost certainly drag on indefinitely," and that if the outlook for an agreement was deemed hopeless, the present government would fall and be replaced by a military dictatorship.[198] Grew's view was supported by British ambassador Robert Craigie, who reported to London, "It seems apparent that the United States does not comprehend the fact that by the nature of the Japanese and also on account of the domestic conditions in Japan no delays can be countenanced . . . (Grew) and I are firmly of the opinion that on balance this is a chance which it would be inexcusable folly to let slip."[199]

However, these views were not accepted by the officials of the Division of Far Eastern Affairs for the State Department, Hornbeck in particular. Hornbeck argued that Konoe did not control the military, and the proposal for a summit meeting by Konoe was a confession of his weakness in the domestic politics. He insisted that the course that the United States should pursue would be that of making "every effort toward ensuring a complete discrediting of the armed efforts" of the militaristic leadership.[200] Hull was more influenced by Hornbeck's opinions than by Grew's frequent reports from Tokyo.[201]

On September 3, Roosevelt summoned Nomura and read to him a reply to Konoe's message which pointed out that it would be difficult to agree to a summit conference without preliminary talks. He also said that the US government could not enter into any agreement which would not be in harmony with the principles in which the US government and the American people believed.[202] Roosevelt had given in to Hull's policy.[203]

Konoe cast about for any concession that would help the summit to materialize. When he met with Grew on the evening of September 6, Konoe indicated that if a summit could be arranged quickly, he could commit the leaders of the army and navy to a settlement based on Hull's four principles.[204] In the

*506*

light of the army and navy's sign of subjugation to the emperor's strong wish for peace expressed at the September 6 conference (16.4.3), Konoe might have believed that he would be able to make the military accept a settlement based on the four principles.[205]

As Tsunoda argues, for Konoe to drastically change decisions that had just been adopted at the Imperial Conference was not an easy job. Therefore, he thought of gutting the conference decision at a meeting with Roosevelt that would be held away from Japan. But it was certainly unusual for a prime minister to attempt to change a state policy sanctioned at the conference over which he presided with the help of an overseas summit meeting.[206] Grew trusted Konoe and supported his initiative, but Hull and Hornbeck did not.[207]

By October, Konoe was becoming desperate. On September 25, when Sugiyama and Nagano Osami (永野修身), the chiefs of staff of the army and navy, had jointly presented to the Liaison Conference a proposal that, in accordance with the September 6 decision, whether it would be politics or war "shall be decided by October 15 at the latest," Konoe commented, "I understand this proposal." But in actuality, the proposal came as quite a shock to Konoe.[208] He confined himself to his private villa at Kamakura from September 27 to October 1. All he did before going to Kamakura was to send a cable to Nomura, saying, "At this point, time is of the essence in every respect, . . . we would be much obliged if you were promptly to obtain a definite answer one way or the other; it would be most convenient for us if in due course the date of the meeting were to be set between October 10 and October 15."[209]

While Army Minister Tōjō was rigidly faithful to the September 6 decision, Navy Minister Oikawa was sympathetic to Konoe. When Oikawa was invited to Kamakura on October 1, Oikawa told Konoe, "We must be prepared to swallow whole the US proposal. If the prime minister is prepared to move forward on this basis, the navy will of course lend its full support, and I am convinced that the army will also follow suit." Konoe said, "That's a relief; that's where my thinking also lies."[210]

Toyoda, who had been expected to accompany Konoe to the summit, said years later, "We were ready to settle everything on the spot, even the withdrawal of troops from China, and then seek the emperor's sanction."[211] The army's war guidance office observed that if the summit talks took place, a negotiated settlement would be reached based on a temporary compromised adjustment. Naval Affairs Bureau Chief Oka Takazumi (岡敬純) also opined that "once Konoe meets with Roosevelt, things might get settled on the spot, so something may come out of it if he goes."[212]

On October 2, Hull met Nomura and conveyed to him the US position on the summit question. In a long oral statement, Hull presented a lengthy list of reasons why he could not agree on a meeting between Konoe and Roosevelt. He particularly emphasized that Japan's action in China and the southwestern Pacific hardly squared with his four principles, and insisted that a fundamental agreement on basic principles prior to a meeting was necessary. The October 2 statement virtually ended the bilateral negotiations over the summit meeting.[213]

Grew later wondered why Konoe had not been given more encouragement, and why the matter of the "transcendent importance of preserving peace had to depend on an unproductive effort to find a mutually satisfactory formula."[214]

### 16.4.5. Tōjō and Tōgō's Efforts to Avert War

Nomura sent Hull's statement of October 2 to Tokyo, saying, "It is my sense that Japanese–United States negotiations have finally reached a deadlock . . . I think there will be no change in US policy toward Japan . . . unless Japan does an about-face in its policies."[215]

The chiefs of the army ministry and general staff division and bureau met on October 5 and urged that an Imperial Conference be promptly convened to decide to go to war.[216] The navy was more cautious than the army. Naval Affairs Bureau Chief Oka stated that there were prospects for obtaining our demands through diplomacy, if Japan reconsidered the matter of stationing troops.[217] Navy Minister Oikawa indicated that he wanted to avoid a war with the United States, but he stated that the navy could not declare that it opposed this war, because deciding on whether or not to go to war being a political issue, it was proper for the prime minister to decide on it.[218]

Tōjō insisted that Japan should set about preparing for a war with the United States. However, as he had a series of meetings with Oikawa, he came to doubt that the navy stood a chance of winning a war with the United States. If the navy, which was to have the leading role in the war with the United States, had no confidence about the war, that meant that they had obtained the emperor's consent at an Imperial Conference on September 6 to a

*508*

proposal that was "premature and insufficiently examined," and that those responsible for advising the emperor in the government and the high command "bore a grave responsibility for having done so."[219] He insisted that once they were all clear about their responsibility, what had to be changed would have to be changed, and that bringing new personnel into the government as well as both services was the prerequisite for starting all over again. And he suggested that Prince Higashikuni Naruhiko (東久邇宮稔彦), in the role of prime minister, would be the only person capable of managing the present situation.[220]

Tōjō argued that if the decision by the new government was that there could be no way out in relations with the United States other than to accept the American demands indicated on October 2 and conduct a full-scale withdrawal of troops from China, the prestige of the army and navy would plummet and morale would collapse, and there would almost certainly be an emotional explosion among the Japanese people. To control such situations, there would be no other way than putting Japan under the command of an imperial prince invested with the authority of the emperor.[221]

Konoe supported Tōjō's argument and his suggestion of a new government led by Prince Higashikuni. But Lord Keeper of the Privy Seal Kido Kōichi (木戸幸一) opposed the idea on the ground that making a member of the imperial family prime minister and having him decide issues of war and peace would risk undermining the authority of the emperor.[222] Konoe, meanwhile, presented his resignation on October 16 without ensuring the basic course to be taken by the succeeding cabinet.[223]

Kido then decided to recommend Tōjō as the new premier. Kido judged that Tōjō had recently changed his mind concerning a war with the United States, and considered that Tōjō would not advocate going to war, so far as the navy remained opposed to it. If war could be avoided, Tōjō would be the best man to keep the military under control, and if war could not be avoided, he would be preferable to Prince Higashikuni.[224]

The council of senior statesmen, the successor body to the genrō of the past, approved Tōjō's premiership on October 17.[225] The next day, when Tōjō received a command from the emperor to form a cabinet, Kido conveyed to him the emperor's message that Japan's situation should be examined without being bound by the September 6 Imperial Conference decision.[226] In order to control the army's opposition and the public's outbursts that were anticipated in the event that Japan should accept American conditions for peace, Tōjō

Chapter 16

appointed himself army minister and home affairs minister. He appointed Tōgō Shigenori (東郷茂徳) foreign minister. Tōgō had served in Berlin and Moscow as ambassador before he was "purged" by Matsuoka, who had pursued pro-Axis diplomacy. Tōgō joined the cabinet after having made sure that the new cabinet was to work to come to terms with the United States.[227]

After the formation of the Tōjō cabinet, the Liaison Conference met nearly every day, to resurvey the Imperial Conference decision of September 6. The Conference discussed three alternatives; 1. "perseverance and patience" without war; 2. an immediate decision for war; and 3. A combination of negotiation with preparations for war. The first alternative was unacceptable to the military. It was supported only by Tōgō and Finance Minister Kaya. They argued that if Japan could not win a war, there was little point in going into it. The army general staff insisted on launching hostilities immediately (the second alternative), but many, including the navy as well as Tōjō, preferred the third alternative. The third alternative was tantamount to the September 6 decision with the postponed deadline of negotiations.[228]

Thus, Tōjō asked Tōgō to prepare proposals to the United States to make final diplomatic efforts. Tōgō came up with two proposals, Plan A and Plan B. Plan A aimed at a comprehensive settlement of the major issues with the United States. It did not differ much from Japan's previous position. Plan B was a modus vivendi, or temporary agreement, to avoid conflict between the two countries for the time being.

Plan A, which was approved by the Liaison Conference on October 30, was as follows: 1. Japan would agree to withdraw its forces from most areas of China within two years of the establishment of a truce, concentrating them in certain parts of North China, Mongolia, Xinjiang (新疆), and Hainan Island. They would stay in those areas for up to twenty-five years. 2. After settlement of the China Incident, all Japanese troops would be withdrawn from Indochina. 3. Japan would accept the principle of non-discrimination in trade in the Pacific and in China if the same principle were applied throughout the world. 4. As for the Axis alliance, Japan would act "in accordance with its own decisions."[229]

Plan B proposed the following: 1. The two countries were to undertake not to advance by force into Southeast Asia or the South Pacific (Indochina was excepted, since Japan had already occupied that area). 2. The two countries were to cooperate to ensure acquisition of the raw materials each might

510

*Japan, the United States, and China on the Eve of the Pacific War*

require from the Netherlands East Indies. 3. The United States was to restore US–Japanese trade relations to the state that had existed prior to the asset freeze; and 4. The United States was to cut aid to China.[230]

The Plan B that Tōgō had originally drafted was much less demanding. As to oil, Japan requested the United States to supply annually 1,000,000 tons of aviation fuel and to cooperate with Japan in its procurement of oil from the Dutch East Indies. There was no proviso that the United States should end aid to Chiang.[231] However, Tōgō was forced to revise his original Plan B by the strong demand of the chief and vice-chief of the army general staff. They were opposed to the idea itself of presenting a modus vivendi to the United States and hoped that these revisions would increase the chances of the plan being rejected.[232] The Liaison Conference which discussed Plan B lasted from 9:00 a.m. on November 1 until 1:30 a.m. on November 2. The conference decided that if diplomacy failed to produce a settlement by December 1, Japan would make the final decision for war regardless of the status of the negotiations at that time.[233] On November 5, the Imperial Conference sanctioned those decisions by the Liaison Conference.

### 16.4.6. Hull Note

Tōgō instructed Nomura to present Plan A to Hull on November 7. Hull found it totally unacceptable. He made no counterproposal.[234] Instead, he lectured Nomura on the importance of Japan's adopting a policy of conciliation and friendship with China.[235] Tōgō had been sure that Plan A would stand no chance of Hull's acceptance, as it conflicted with Hull's four principles. On November 19 he instructed Nomura and newly arrived special envoy Kurusu Saburō (来栖三郎) to present Plan B to Hull, giving up on Plan A.

Plan B was also unacceptable to Hull, but he decided to prepare a response.[236] He felt that if he rejected the Japanese proposal, the Japanese army might use the rejection as a pretext for making war.[237] In fact, Hull was then under pressure from the American military and Roosevelt to buy time to continue building up US naval power in the western Pacific.[238]

Accordingly, the State Department prepared a modus vivendi as a counterproposal to Plan B, and also drafted the outline of a general agreement to accompany the modus vivendi. The modus vivendi was to last for three months, during which period conversations were to continue on the general agreement for an eventual comprehensive settlement.[239]

*511*

Chapter 16

The outline of a general agreement consisted of following ten basic proposals; 1. A multilateral nonaggression pact among the governments principally concerned in the Pacific; 2. An agreement among the principally interested governments to respect the territorial integrity of Indochina and equality of economic opportunity therein; 3. No support of any government in China other than the Nationalist government (Chiang Kai-shek); 4. Relinquishment of extraterritorial rights in China; 5. A trade agreement between the United States and Japan on liberal lines; 6. Removal of freezing measures; 7. Stabilization of the dollar–yen rate; 8. An agreement not to interpret any agreement which either country had concluded with any third power or powers in such a way as to conflict with the fundamental purpose of the proposed basic accord (reference to the Tripartite Pact); 9. The United States and Japan would use their influence to cause other governments to accept and apply the principles set forth in the proposed agreement (reference to the Four Principles); 10. Japan would withdraw its armed forces from China and Indochina.[240] The US version of the modus vivendi was as follows: 1. Japan would withdraw its forces from South Indochina. 2. Japan would reduce the total of its forces in North Indochina to 25,000—the number present on July 26, 1941. 3. There would be no limit on Japanese exports to the United States, the proceeds from which would go into a clearing account to be used for Japanese imports from the United States. 4. The United States would export raw cotton in the value of $600,000 per month, petroleum solely for civilian use in an amount to be determined after consultation with the British and Dutch, and food and medical supplies subject to limitations on commodities in short supply in the United States.[241] As the Japanese modus vivendi excluded the question of the withdrawal of Japanese troops from China, so did the US modus vivendi.

Hull intimated to Nomura and Kurusu that a US counterproposal to Plan B had been drafted and the United States would officially present it to Japan shortly. Both ambassadors were delighted at this US move.[242]

Hull showed the US modus vivendi to Britain, the Netherlands, and China to obtain their consent. But their reactions were not encouraging. It was only the Netherlands that expressed an agreement. China strongly opposed it, saying that the United States was appeasing Japan at the expense of China.[243] Britain did not oppose the US policy, but Churchill expressed his sympathy for China's objection.[244]

*512*

On the afternoon of November 26, Hull called in Nomura and Kurusu to his office. The two ambassadors had expected to receive a proposal for a modus vivendi, but instead they were given the ten-point proposal for the general agreement (later called the Hull Note). Nomura and Kurusu were astounded.[245] To their question of why the United States had dropped the modus vivendi, Hull simply replied that he had done his best in the way of exploration, lamely placing the blame on the agitated state of public opinion.[246] On the ten-point proposal, he did not make any strong rebuttals against the Japanese protests, nor did he give any further explanation. He simply suggested that Japan should study the documents carefully before discussing them further.[247] Hull was totally unapproachable.[248]

What caused Hull to change the policy overnight is not clear. At the meeting with Nomura and Kurusu on November 26, he mentioned the agitated state of public opinion. It is true that the Chinese recognized the Roosevelt government's sensitivity to public opinion and had considerable success in a vigorous anti-Japanese campaign through lobbying and working on mass media.[249] But apparently public opinion was not a decisive factor in the abrupt change of policy.

There is a widely held view that Churchill played an important role in the US decision to drop the modus vivendi.[250] According to *The Memoirs of Cordell Hull*, Roosevelt received a cable from Churchill on the night of November 25 in which Churchill warned Roosevelt that it would be dangerous to weaken the Chinese will to keep fighting, because "a Chinese collapse would hugely augment our common dangers." And Hull writes, "I came to the conclusion that we should cancel out the modus vivendi. Instead, we should present to the Japanese solely the ten-point proposal."[251] But as demonstrated by his subsequent testimony that "we had no serious thought that Japan would accept our proposal [the ten-point proposal],"[252] he was well aware that forcing fundamental principles on Japan would wreck the talks. In fact, up to November 25 Hull had attempted to achieve a modus vivendi with Japan. On that day he had persuaded Stimson and obtained his consent to presenting a modus vivendi to Japan, albeit on condition that it would be rescinded upon any new Japanese military moves.[253] After having delivered the basic ten-point proposal (the Hull Note) to the Japanese, he voiced a strong complaint to British ambassador Halifax that Churchill had used Chiang Kai-shek's plea to influence Roosevelt's decision.[254] Churchill was anxious to avoid by any means

Chapter 16

a situation in which Britain alone would have to fight against Japan.[255] Hull was resentful at Churchill's maneuvering to have Roosevelt drop the modus vivendi, expecting that dropping the modus vivendi would certainly lead to a US–Japanese war.

Roosevelt's statement at the meeting with Nomura and Kurusu on November 27 provides a clue about another important factor of the last-minute decision not to enter modus vivendi negotiations. On that day, Roosevelt said to the two ambassadors that he was wary of the recurrence of a development like the one in July when Japan invaded south Indochina while the Hull–Nomura negotiations were going on.[256] During the night of November 25, Roosevelt might have been provided with information from Churchill or through Magic intercepts (a secret operation that had broken the Japanese diplomatic code) about new moves by the Japanese navy.[257]

The Hull Note was presented in the form of a proposal; it began with the description, "Tentative and without commitment outline of proposed basis for agreement." Regardless of its wording, however, the Hull Note could be taken as notification of the termination of diplomatic negotiations, and in terms of conventional diplomatic usage, this was virtually an ultimatum without a deadline for response.[258] On November 27, Hull told Stimson, "I have washed my hands of it and it is now in the hands of you and Knox—the Army and the Navy."[259]

In Tokyo, Tōjō declared at the Liaison Conference on November 27 that the US memorandum of November 26 was an ultimatum, and that Japan could not accept it.[260] Tōjō and Tōgō had been prepared to retreat to some extent from Plan B, and had up to that point opposed the arguments for war, but having received the Hull Note, they had no alternative but to accept the Japanese army activists' argument.[261] The Liaison Conference for the first time lined up behind war.[262]

At the Imperial Conference held on December 1, Tōjō stated that "the empire has come to the point where going to war against the United States, Britain, and Holland is inevitable."

The next day, December 2, the two chiefs of staff jointly reported to the throne and were given imperial sanction to commence operations. At 5:30 p.m. on that day, Admiral Yamamoto Isoroku (山本五十六), the commander-in-chief of the combined fleet, telegraphed the task force, which had sailed for Pearl Harbor from Etorofu Island on November 26 subject to his order to

514

*Notes*

turn back, telling them to go ahead with the attack as planned.

NOTES

16.1. The War in Europe

1   Germany had signed a nonaggression pact with the Soviet Union on August 23, 1939, which had a secret agreement by which both agreed to partition Poland. The Soviet Union invaded Poland on September 17 and annexed eastern Poland.

2   The Soviet Union was active during the "phony war" period. It invaded Finland in November 1939. The fighting continued until March 1940. The exhausted Finns made peace on Soviet terms, which included the Finns' concession of 11 percent of their territory to the Soviet Union.

3   Chamberlain resigned in May 1940, taking responsibility for failing to defend the Scandinavian countries. He was replaced by Winston Churchill.

4   Historically, isolationism in American foreign policy stems from George Washington's Farewell Address of 1796 (1.3.5). After WWI, many Americans harbored the view that they had been dragged into the war by bankers and munition manufacturers who reaped fabulous profits. In the mid-1930s, aviation hero Charles Lindbergh argued that the European war was a "civil war" that had no moral implication for America. T. R. Fehrenbach, *F.D.R.'s Undeclared War, 1939 to 1941* (New York: David McKay, 1967), 189.

5   Akira Iriye, *The Cambridge History of American Foreign Relations*, vol. III, *The Globalizing of America, 1913–1945* (Cambridge: Cambridge University Press, 1933), 165.

6   Thomas Bailey, *A Diplomatic History of the American People* (Englewood Cliffs, NJ: Prentice-Hall, 1968), 715. Because of this prohibition clause, US arms sold to Britain were transported to Halifax, Canada, for onward shipment to Britain.

7   Iriye, *The Cambridge History of American Foreign Relations*, 177. Bailey, *A Diplomatic History*, 718–719.

8   Iriye, *The Cambridge History of American Foreign Relations*, 182. Bailey, *A Diplomatic History*, 722. Roosevelt used the analogy of lending a garden hose to a neighbor whose burning house endangers one's own, and then expecting it back when the fire is out. Bailey, *A Diplomatic History*, 721.

9   Iriye, *The Cambridge History of American Foreign Relations*, 182.

10  Ibid., 182. Paul Johnson, *A History of the American People* (New York: HarperCollins Publishers, 1999), 776–777.

11  In view of the fact that the buildup of war debts after WWI bedeviled the world economy in the 1920s and 1930s, the Lend-Lease bill gave the president broad discretion to determine the conditions of the repayment. On February 23, 1942, the United States and Britain agreed on the Mutual Aid Agreement, whose article VII provided that the signatories should confer together to determine the means of the Lend-Lease settlement. The Americans used the leverage given them by this provision to negotiate with the British for elimination of the imperial tariff preferences. Richard Gardner, *Sterling-Dollar Diplomacy in Current Perspective: The Origin and*

Chapter 16

*the Prospects of Our International Order* (New York: Columbia University Press, 1980), 55–57. Bailey, *A Diplomatic History*, 777.

12 Ōhata Tokushirō, "Nichidoku bōkyō kyōtei, dō kyōka mondai (1935–1939)," *Taiheiyō sensō eno michi*, vol. 5, *Nanpō shinshutsu*, ed. Nihon Kokusai Seiji Gakkai Taiheiyō Sensō Gen-in Kenkyūbu (Tokyo: Asahi Shimbunsha, 1963), 18–31. Ōhata Tokushirō, "The Anti-Comintern Pact, 1935–1939," in *Deterrent Diplomacy: Japan, Germany, and the USSR, 1935–1940* (Japan's Road to the Pacific War series), ed. James Morley (New York: Columbia University Press, 1976), 24–37.

13 Akira Iriye, *The Origin of the Second World War in Asia and the Pacific* (London: Longman Group UK, 1987), 51–52. Ōhata, "Nichidoku bōkyō kyōtei," in *Taiheiyō sensō eno michi*, vol. 5, *Nanpō shinshutsu*, ed. Nihon Kokusai Seiji Gakkai, 60. Paul Schroeder, *The Axis Alliance and Japanese American Relations, 1941* (Ithaca, New York: Cornell University Press, 1958), 110–111.

14 Shiratori was a former Information Bureau director (from 1930 to 1933) and ambassador to Sweden (from 1933 to 1936). He maintained a view that Japan should join forces with other "have-not" nations and rectify the existing injustices in international affairs. He was appointed ambassador to Italy in September 1938 and cooperated closely with Ōshima, ambassador in Berlin since October 1938. Iriye, *The Origin of the Second World War*, 52. In August 1932, when Secretary of State Stimson delivered a speech condemning the Japanese military actions in Shanghai, Japanese newspapers made offensive remarks against the speech. Ambassador Grew attributed the Japanese newspapers' offensive remarks to the then Information Bureau director Shiratori's provocative interpretation of Stimson's speech, and reported that Shiratori had intentionally aroused anti-American feeling among the Japanese (13.4.1).

15 Ōhata "Nichidoku bōkyō kyōtei," in *Taiheiyō sensō eno michi*, vol. 5, ed. Nihon Kokusai Seiji Gakkai, 92–94. Ōhata, "The Anti-Comintern Pact 1935–1939," in *Deterrent Diplomacy* (Japan's Road to the Pacific War series), ed. James Morley, 76, 78.

16 Iriye, *The Origin of the Second World War*, 89.

17 Ibid., 103. The Yonai cabinet began to assume a positive posture toward a "southern advance," but it was inclined to avoid the use of force, and firmly opposed a military alliance with Germany directed against the Anglo–American nations. Hosoya Chihiro, "Sangoku dōmei to Nisso chūritsu jōyaku" in *Taiheiyō sensō eno michi*, vol. 5, *Nanpō shinshutsu*, ed. Nihon Kokusai Seiji Gakkai Taiheiyō Sensō Gen-in Kenkyūbu (Tokyo: Asahi Shimbunsha, 1963), 174, 177. Hosoya Chihiro, "The Tripartite Pact, 1939–1940," in *Deterrent Diplomacy: Japan, Germany, and the USSR, 1935–1940* (Japan's Road to the Pacific War series), trans. and ed. James Morley (New York: Columbia University Press, 1976), 207, 211.

18 Iriye, *The Origin of the Second World War*, 106–107.

19 Hosoya, "The Tripartite Pact," *Deterrent Diplomacy*, trans. and ed. Morley, 236.

20 It was later known that Stahmer and Ott accepted this compromise on their own responsibility without the knowledge and against the instructions of Berlin. Stahmer promised Ott when he left Japan for Germany early in October that he would obtain Ribbentrop's approval, but he did not carry out his promise. Hosoya, "Sangoku dōmei to Nisso chūritsu jōyaku," in *Taiheiyō sensō eno michi*, vol. 5, ed. Nihon

*Notes*

Kokusai Seiji Gakkai, 254. Meskill, *Hitler & Japan*, 18–20. Takeda Tomoki, "The Path to the Tripartite Alliance of Japan, Germany, and Italy," in *Fifteen Lectures on Showa Japan*, ed. Tsutsui Kiyotada (Tokyo: Japan Publishing Foundation for Culture, 2016), 207–208. Hosoya argues, "Thus, in spite of the high-sounding outward solidarity of the alliance, its foundation was extremely fragile." Hosoya, "Sangoku dōmei to Nisso chūritsu jōyaku," in *Taiheiyō sensō eno michi*, vol. 5, ed. Nihon Kokusai Seiji Gakkai, 219. Hosoya, "The Tripartite Pact," in *Deterrent Diplomacy*, ed. Morley, 254–255. Morley writes that he had an occasion to call on Ott in 1966, who was living in retirement in Munich. Ott said to Morley, " . . . every effort had to be made to keep America out of the way: That is why I felt entitled to go my own way if the negotiations became difficult." James Morley, Introduction to *Deterrent Diplomacy Japan, Germany, and the USSR, 1935–1940* (Japan's Road to the Pacific War series), trans. and ed. James Morley (New York: Columbia University Press, 1976), 187–189.

21   Iriye, *The Origin of the Second World War*, 115.

16.2. Japanese China Policies and the US Reaction in the Late 1930s

22   Iriye, *The Origin of the Second World War*, 67.

23   At the battle of Xuzhou, the vital transportation center, in the spring of 1938, the Chinese made a major defense effort at Taierzhuang, a town about 35 miles northeast of Xuzhou. The Chinese claimed that the battle at Taierzhuang was the first major Chinese victory of the war. It humiliated the Japanese military's reputation as an invincible force. Though the Japanese finally captured Xuzhou, Japanese infantry took huge casualties. The Japanese army deployed about 200,000 troops and suffered about 12,000 deaths. The Chinese deployed 600,000 troops and suffered about 60,000 deaths. John Boyle, *China and Japan at War, 1937–1945* (Stanford: Stanford University Press, 1972), 138.

24   Peter Duus, *The Rise of Modern Japan* (Boston: Houghton Mifflin, 1976), 217.

25   Ibid., 216. Usui Katsumi, *Nitchū gaikōshi kenkyū* (Tokyo: Yoshikawa Kōbunkan, 1998), 310.

26   Boyle, *China and Japan at War*, 215.

27   Usui Katsumi, "Nitchū sensō no seijiteki tenkai," in *Taiheiyō sensō eno michi*, vol. 4, *Nitchū sensō II*, ed. Nihon Kokusai Seiji Gakkai Taiheiyō Sensō Gen-in Kenkyūbu (Tokyo: Asahi Shimbunsha, 1963), 171.

28   This declaration was also a revision of the *aitenisezu* statement (14.3.2) in that it proposed the Nationalist government to participate in establishing the new order in East Asia. Boyle, *China and Japan at War*, 192.

29   Sometimes over a hundred airplanes participated in one air attack. About fifty airraids were carried out between January and October in 1939. Usui Katsumi, *Shinpan Nitchū sensō* (Tokyo; Chuokoronsha, 2000), 130–132.

30   Iriye, *The Origin of the Second World War*, 76.

31   Japanese casualties rose to 8,440 killed and 8,766 wounded, for a total exceeding 17,000. The 23rd division, in particular, suffered an annihilating blow: more than 11,000 casualties, or 73 percent of its entire strength. The overall casualty rates of 32 percent compared with 28 percent at Mukden during the Russo–Japanese War and 6

*517*

percent casualty rates at the Xuzhou campaign in the spring of 1938. Hata Ikuhiko, "The Japanese–Soviet Confrontation, 1935–1939," in *Deterrent Diplomacy Japan, Germany, and the USSR, 1935–1940* (Japan's Road to the Pacific War series), ed. James Morley (New York: Columbia University Press, 1976), 175.

32  Iriye, *The Origin of the Second World War*, 77–78.

33  Tobe Ryōichi, "The Deepening Quagmire of the Sino–Japanese War and the Declaration of a New Order in East Asia," in *Fifteen Lectures on Showa Japan*, ed. Tsutsui Kiyotada (Tokyo: Japan Publishing Foundation for Culture, 2016), 173.

34  The most outspoken among the hard-liners was Stanley Hornbeck, advisor on political affairs, an office from which he continued to dominate Asian affairs. Utley, *Going to War with Japan*, 9.

35  Ibid., 9.

36  Ibid., 10.

37  Ibid., 33–35.

38  James Thomson, Jr., Peter Stanley, and John Curtis Perry, *Sentimental Imperialists* (New York: Harper & Row, 1981), 191. Akira Iriye, *Across the Pacific: An Inner History of American–East Asia Relations* (Chicago: Imprint Publications, 1967), 201–202.

39  Iriye, *Across the Pacific*, 203, 205. Komatsu argues that this oversimplified and subjective view of Hull toward the Far Eastern issue contributed to his failure to reach an agreement with Japan based on rational thinking. Keiichiro Komatsu, *Origins of the Pacific War and the Importance of 'Magic'* (London: Routledge, 1999), 320.

40  Utley, *Going to War with Japan*, 55.

41  Ibid., 62.

42  Ibid., 63. Iriye, *The Origin of the Second World War*, 78–79.

43  Han-sheng Lin, "Chou Fo-hai," in *Diplomats in Crisis*, eds. Richard Dean Burns and Edward Bennett (Santa Barbara, CA: American Bibliographical Center–Clio Press, 1974), 175–177.

44  Chou Fo-hai served as the deputy director of propaganda of the Kuomintang, and was a trusted aide-de-camp of the generalissimo. Of all those who defected with Wang Ching-wei, Chou was closest to Chiang. Boyle, *China and Japan at War*, 168–169. Ryū Ketsu, *Nitchū sensōka no gaikō* (Tokyo: Yoshikawa Kōbunkan, 1995), 319. Chiang Kai-shek was not a member of the club, but his position on peaceful relations with Japan had been compatible with the club's until the Xian Incident. After that incident, Chiang was no longer in a position to talk openly of peace, and Chou, as a member of Chiang's inner cabinet, took over the peace diplomacy. Lin, "Chou Fo-hai," in *Diplomats in Crisis*, ed. Burns and Bennett, 175.

45  Shortly after the fall of Nanjing, Chou Fo-hai sent Kao to Hong Kong for gathering intelligence on Japan. Ryū, *Nitchū sensōka no gaikō*, 319. Boyle, *China and Japan at War*, 173.

46  Kao sought Tung's assistance in late 1937 when Kao was forced to suspend his activities in order to recuperate from tuberculosis. Boyle, *China and Japan at War*, 170.

47  T'ao Hsi-sheng was a former professor at Beijing University and assumed several important posts in the government. He organized the Institute of Art and Literature (芸文社), which was actually a small bureau of the government that fought the

*Notes*

Communist Party. Ibid, 168.

48 Mei Szu-p'ing was one of the few participants in the Wang movement who had never been to Japan to study. (Chou and Tung studied at Kyoto Imperial University and Kao at Kyūshū Imperial University). In early 1938 he was sent by T'ao Hsi-sheng to Hong Kong to manage the Hong Kong office of the Institute of Art and Literature. Ibid., 168, 194–195.

49 Kagesa was made Chief of the China Section of the General Staff in August 1937 at the behest of Ishiwara, whose view of China greatly influenced Kagesa. In December 1937, when the Stratagem Section was created Kagesa was made its Chief. Kagesa had deep respect for Chinese nationalism and was determined to find a peaceful solution to the Sino–Japanese War. Boyle, *China and Japan at War*, 175.

50 Ibid., 183.

51 In mid-January 1938, Tung contacted his old friend Nishi Yoshiaki (西義顕), manager of the South Manchuria Railway's Nanjing office. Tung conveyed to Nishi his frustration at failing to find a diplomatic solution to the Sino–Japanese conflict. Nishi suggested that Tung visit Japan, where he would be able to see certain members of the Army General Staff who would lend a sympathetic ear to the cause of the Low-Key Club. Nishi then went to Tokyo himself and obtained Kagesa's agreement about Tung's trip to Japan. Ibid., 175.

52 Usui, *Nitchū gaikōshi kenkyū*, 361.

53 When Tung left Tokyo on March 5, Kagesa gave him letters addressed to Chief of Staff Ho Ying-ch'in and Chang Ch'un, then vice president of the Executive Yuan. Both were Kagesa's classmates at the Japanese military academy. Tung did not deliver Kagesa's letters to Ho or Chang, but gave it to Chou Fo-hai instead. Chou in turn submitted it to Chiang Kai-shek. Chiang said that "as a soldier" he was deeply moved by Kagesa's sincerity and courage, and that Tung's report reflected the most sincere attitude he had encountered in many years of negotiating with the Japanese. Boyle, *China and Japan at War*, 179. Lin, "Chou Fo-hai," in *Diplomats in Crisis*, eds. Burns and Bennett, 178.

54 Boyle, *China and Japan at War*, 179. Usui, *Nitchū gaikōshi kenkyū*, 362.

55 Kao was encouraged to make a trip to Japan by Matsumoto Shigeharu (松本重治), the head of the Dōmei news service operations in central and south China. Financial interests in China which were anxious for peace with Japan also supported Kao's trip. Boyle, *China and Japan at War*, 181–186.

56 Kao did not report to Chiang directly because the trip was made without Chiang's consent. He knew that in the midst of the Xuzhou–Hankou–Guangzhou campaign, Chiang would not allow him to visit Japan. Kao passed on his report to Chou, who discussed it with Wang. Wang was shocked to learn that the Japanese authority was wishing him to turn against Chiang. He flatly rejected the idea and turned the report over to Chiang. Chiang's reaction was "more one of annoyance than rage." He simply said, "Absurd!" Ibid., 187.

57 Chiang's policy of wasting the land in retreat was exacting an enormous toll. For example, the dikes on the Yellow River near Zhengzhou were dynamited in June 1938, releasing the silt-filled waters to ravage three provinces before finding a new channel. Eleven cities and some 4,000 villages were flooded, millions of acres of farmland

*519*

Chapter 16

were submerged, about three million people were left homeless, and 400,000–500,000 Chinese died as result of the floods. The scorched-earth policy followed by fleeing soldiers, while not halting the advance of the Japanese troops, was also causing unnecessary sacrifices merely destroying the lives, property, and livelihoods of the Chinese people. Ibid., 186–187.

58  Ibid., 191.

59  Ibid., 193.

60  Usui, *Nitchū gaikōshi kenkyū*, 363–364.

61  Ibid., 364. Usui Katsumi, "The Politics of War, 1937–1941," in *The China Quagmire: Japan's Expansion on the Asian Continent, 1933–1941* (Japan's Road to the Pacific War series), ed. James Morley (New York: Columbia University Press, 1983), 383.

62  After Wang had decided to undertake peace negotiations with Japan, he made several attempts to change Chiang's mind, but Chiang remained unconvinced of the wisdom of a conciliatory policy. Chiang was concerned that if resistance was abandoned, the Communists would use anti-Japanese slogans to build public support for their opposition to the government, with a new eruption of civil war being the inevitable result. The only way to forestall that war was to continue to resist the Japanese. On the other hand, continued resistance meant maintaining a united front and providing a sanctuary for the Communists, thereby enhancing their chances of success at war's end. Between the two evils, Chiang decided to take the latter. Boyle, *China and Japan at War*, 208–209. On December 18, when Wang left Chongqing, he advised Chiang that he was going to Chengdu to address a gathering, but it is rather natural that Chiang knew about Wang's real purpose in making the trip, and he could have prevented Wang's departure if he had wanted to. Ibid., 212.

63  Lung was the archetype of the independent Chinese warlord. He had his own army, issued his own currency, and controlled the lucrative opium industry. He was given the title of governor of Yunnan, but he paid little heed to the central government. Ibid., 211.

64  Ibid., 211.

65  Usui, *Nitchū gaikōshi kenkyū*, 365–366. Konoe had yielded to pressure from the hard-liners like Lieutenant-general Nakajima Tetsuzō, who had just succeeded General Tada as vice-chief of staff, and Nakajima's subordinate Major-general Tominaga Kyōji. Boyle, *China and Japan at War*, 214.

66  Boyle, *China and Japan at War*, 224.

67  Tseng Chung-ming was murdered in the private house in Hanoi in which Wang and his immediate party resided. A reconstruction of the events strongly suggested that Wang was the intended victim. Boyle, *China and Japan at War*, 228. Wang now declared that he would work for peace for the sake of comforting Tseng's soul as well as for the nation. Ibid., 229.

68  Kagesa and Inukai accompanied Wang and his party from Hanoi to Shanghai. The trip by sea afforded them each an opportunity to become acquainted with the other's view. Wang talked about the difficulty of gaining a sympathetic audience in China for a peace settlement. Appeals for a war of resistance were manifestly patriotic, he said, but it was hard to convince anyone that the advocacy of peace could also spring from a love of China. Such a course would be severely criticized at first, but if

*520*

*Notes*

Sino–Japanese cooperation should proceed well, the public would see that the war of resistance was pointless. He emphasized the importance of a fair and just policy on the part of Japan, without which the Sino–Japanese collaboration could not have a persuasive power. Ibid., 233.

69    Prior to his decision to visit Japan, Wang had summoned his followers to ask them about the wisdom of making such a trip. Kao was against the trip. He was wary of Wang being pressured to accept a regime which was a virtually Japanese puppet. Kao was convinced that the proposed Wang regime should be free of Japanese control, being located in unoccupied areas with its own military base in the form of a native army. In fact, he had made repeated requests for Japanese diversionary attacks to free Lung Yun, Chiang Fa-k'uei, and others to join Wang's movement, but the Japanese army remained unresponsive. On the other hand, Chou's idea was to establish a government in the occupied area. He had once hoped the Japanese Army would help Wang set up an independent regime in unoccupied China, but now, since that was apparently no longer an option, he felt there was nothing to do but set up a government in occupied Nanjing and carry on the peace movement from there. He believed that Wang's government could prove its usefulness if it could secure the return, in one form or another, of the businesses, factories, and homes the Japanese Army had taken over to Chinese owners. Wang decided to go to Japan, rejecting the counsel of Kao. Kao decided to accompany Wang after much deliberation. In Tokyo, however, Kao was literally pushed into the background by the Japanese authorities, who resented the cautionary advice he was giving Wang. The troublemaker was not housed with the main body of the Wang entourage in the Tokyo suburb of Ōji, but instead was given quarters in Asakusa. Ibid., 231, 234, 245, 248–249.

70    The June 6 government decision stated: (a) Basic policy would be the *bunji gassaku* program. (b) The regional regimes would include, besides the Wang government, the existing regional governments in North China and Central China. A reformed Chongqing government could also be included. (c) Any regime must subscribe to the "Policies for Adjusting to New Japan–China Relations." Boyle, *China and Japan at War*, 242–243. Usui, *Nitchū gaikōshi kenkyū*, 370.

71    Boyle, *China and Japan at War*, 242–246.

72    Wang held these meetings, since the Japanese had suggested that he do so. In Beijing, Wang K'o-min refused to support Wang, and declared that he would not participate in any regime Wang would establish. In Nanjing, Liang said that he would join Chiang when the situation permitted Chiang's return to Nanjing. He believed that Wang was in collusion with Chiang. Boyle, *China and Japan at War*, 249–250.

73    Ibid., 250–252.

74    Ibid., 252.

75    The participants included Kagesa and Inukai from the Japanese side and Chou Fo-hai, Mei Szu-p'ing and T'ao Hsi-sheng from Chinese side.

76    Usui, *Nitchū gaikōshi kenkyū*, 379.

77    Boyle, *China and Japan at War*, 275–276.

78    Inukai later admitted that Wang yielded too much and compromised away the chance of his own future success. Ibid., 261, 270–271. Usui, *Nitchū gaikōshi kenkyū*, 382.

Chapter 16

79   Kao and T'ao were quickly castigated in the Wang press and the authenticity of their disclosures was denied. The documents which were disclosed were not those that finally emerged from the conferences, but those which Kagesa presented to the Wang group on November 1. Nevertheless, many of the things they revealed were intended to remain forever buried in secret protocols. Boyle, *China and Japan at War*, 279.

80   Chiang sent a letter to Kao applauding him as the genius of Zhejiang. A few months later Kao received a passport from Chongqing and sailed for the United States where he lived ever since. Ibid., 280.

81   Usui, *Nitchū gaikōshi kenkyū*, 384.

82   Ibid., 384. The North China Political Council was allotted a large share of China's customs fees, salt revenues, and excise taxes, and it was also allowed to issue bonds. The Council even had the right to raise its own army. Boyle, *China and Japan at War*, 271.

83   The Chinese had expected that a new treaty would be drafted on the basis of the December 30 agreement, but the Japanese added newly some new conditions on the grounds of "military necessity." Boyle, *China and Japan at War*, 297.

84   A Chinese who claimed to be a younger brother of T. V. Soong and Soong Meiling (Madame Chiang Kai-shek) approached a Japanese officer on an intelligence mission in Hong Kong. Soon Colonel Imai Takeo, now a staff officer of the China Expeditionary Army, was involved. The Imperial Army in Tokyo gave the green light to the talks and sent another officer from Tokyo to join the Japanese team. When Imai was later engaged in intelligence work in Zhejiang, he met the man he had known as T. L. Soong, now a prisoner of war. Imai learned that the man was a key member of a guerrilla organization. Iriye says, "This clutching at straws shows how pessimistic the Japanese army was becoming about its ability to settle the war through military efforts alone. Iriye, *The Origin of the Second World War*, 92.

85   Matsuoka presented to the Chongqing government peace terms that were substantially more generous than those the Wang regime had been forced to accept. For example, Matsuoka agreed to the withdrawal of all Japanese troops sent to China after the Marco Polo Bridge Incident within six months after a cease-fire was effected. Boyle, *China and Japan at War*, 302. Usui, "The Politics of War, 1937–1941," in *The China Quagmire*, ed. Morley, 422.

86   Usui, *Nitchū gaikōshi kenkyū*, 388.

87   Boyle, *China and Japan at War*, 337, 339.

88   Ishiwara proposed a loose association with China based on equality and mutual assistance that would ensure Japan the security and economic strength that was needed to defend against the Soviet Union. Ishiwara held that by disavowing aggrandizement and the fruits of past aggression, Japan would have no difficulty in inducing China to support such association with Japan. Its purposes were thus not only compatible with but beneficial to the growth of Chinese nationalism. Ibid., 338.

89   The coalition between the Nationalists and the Communists was working well while they continued to fight against Japan. But it was highly probable that a civil war would start between the Nationalists and the Communists once the war with Japan ended. In that case, Japan might be involved in the civil war. Ibid., 338.

*Notes*

### 16.3. Japan's Southward Advance and the Tripartite Pact, and the US Reaction in 1940

90  Jonathan Utley, *Going to War with Japan, 1937–1941* (Knoxville: University of Tennessee Press, 1985), 79.

91  William Langer and S. Everett Gleason, *The Undeclared War, 1940–1941* (New York: Harper & Brothers, 1953), 3.

92  Nagaoka Shinjirō, "Nanpō shisaku no gaikōteki tenkai (1937–1941)," in *Taiheiyō sensō eno michi*, vol. 6, *Nanpō shinshutsu*, ed. Nihon Kokusai Seiji Gakkai Taiheiyō Sensō Gen-in Kenkyūbu (Tokyo: Asahi Shimbunsha, 1963), 75. Nagaoka Shinjirō, "Economic Demands on the Dutch East Indies," trans. Robert Scalapino, in *The Fateful Choice: Japan's Advance into Southeast Asia, 1939–1941* (Japan's Road to the Pacific War series), ed. James Morley (New York: Columbia University Press, 1980), 128. Hull, *The Memoirs*, 888.

93  Hull, *The Memoirs*, 889.

94  Ibid., 893.

95  Tsunoda Jun, "Nihon no taibei kaisen," in *Taiheiyō sensō eno michi*, vol. 7, *Nichibei kaisen*, ed. Nihon Kokusai Seiji Gakkai Taiheiyō Sensō Gen-in Kenkyūbu (Tokyo: Asahi Shimbunsha, 1963), 22–23. Tsunoda Jun, "The Navy's Role in the Southern Strategy," trans. Robert Scalapino, in *The Fateful Choice: Japan's Advance into Southeast Asia, 1939–1941* (Japan's Road to the Pacific War series), ed. James Morley (New York: Columbia University Press, 1980), 247–248. Yoshida Yutaka, *Ajia Taiheiyō sensō* (Tokyo: Iwanami Shoten, 2007), 3.

96  F. C. Jones, *Japan's New Order in East Asia: Its Rise and Fall, 1937–45* (London: Oxford University Press, 1954), 238–239.

97  Tsunoda, "Nihon no taibei kaisen," in *Taiheiyō sensō eno michi*, vol. 7, ed. Nihon Kokusai Seiji Gakkai, 44. Tsunoda, "The Navy's Role in the Southern Strategy," trans. Scalapino, in *The Fateful Choice*, ed. Morley, 253. Hull, *The Memoirs*, 895.

98  Langer and Gleason, *The Undeclared War*, 7–8. In the late 1930s, Japanese oil imports averaged about 5 million tons annually. They were mostly from the United States (table 16.4,3).

99  The Japanese wanted to buy 400,000 tons of aviation gasoline annually, but the Dutch promised the Japanese a spot sale of 33,000 tons. The Japanese demand for 1,100,000 tons of aviation crude was scaled down to 120,000 tons, and 1,500,000 tons of other crude oil was reduced to 573,500 tons. Langer and Gleason, *The Undeclared War*, 8.

100  Ibid., 7. Nagaoka "Nanpō shisaku," in *Taiheiyō sensō eno michi*, vol. 6, ed. Nihon Kokusai Seiji Gakkai, 89. Nagaoka, "Economic Demands on the Dutch East Indies," trans. Scalapino, *The Fateful Choice*, ed. Morley, 143.

101  Langer and Gleason, *The Undeclared War*, 8. The Greater East Asia Co-Prosperity Sphere was based on the idea that the world was to be divided into four zones; The Greater East Asian zone, the European zone (including Africa), the American zone, and the Soviet zone (including India and Iran). Japan was to be the political leader of the Great East Asian zone with the responsibility for the maintenance of order and achieving prosperity of all the nations within the area. This would entail securing a

Chapter 16

superior position in the procurement of raw materials necessary for national defense. Iriye, *Japan and Wider World*, 80.

102 Jones, *Japan's New Order*, 238. The French ambassador in Washington reported to the Vichy government that "the United States would not use military or naval force in support of any position which might be taken to resist the Japanese attempted aggression on Indochina." Langer and Gleason, *The Undeclared War*, 10.

103 Hull, *The Memoirs*, 896. Iriye, *The Origin of the Second World War*, 101.

104 Japan demanded of Britain closure of the Burma route, and it was closed on July 17, 1940. But in late September Churchill decided to reopen it on October 17, judging that there was no point in continuing to submit to Japanese pressure anymore as American resolve was becoming clearer. Hata Ikuhiko, "Futsuin shinchū to gun no nanshin seisaku" in *Taiheiyō sensō eno michi*, vol. 6, *Nanpō shinshutsu*, ed. Nihon Kokusai Seiji Gakkai Taiheiyō Sensō Gen-in Kenkyūbu, (Tokyo: Asahi Shimbunsha, 1963), 187. Hata Ikuhiko, "Army's Move into Northern Indochina," trans. Robert Scalapino, in *The Fateful Choice: Japan's Advance into Southeast Asia, 1939–1941* (Japan's Road to the Pacific War series), ed. James Morley (New York: Columbia University Press, 1983), 156.

105 Schroeder, *The Axis Alliance*, 17. Langer and Gleason, *The Undeclared War*, 9.

106 Hata, "Futsuin shinchū," in *Taiheiyō sensō eno michi*, vol. 6, ed. Nihon Kokusai Seiji Gakkai, 225. The date of the passage, the route, and the method of transportation were to be decided in consultation between Japan and French Indochina. Ibid., 225–226.

107 Schroeder, *The Axis Alliance*, 18.

108 Ibid., 14. Iriye, *The Origin of the Second World War*, 97.

109 Iriye, *Across the Pacific*, 207. Iriye, *The Origin of the Second World War*, 97.

110 Schroeder, *The Axis Alliance*, 20–22.

111 Yoshida was hospitalized with nervous exhaustion from anxiety over Matsuoka's policies. Nakamura Takafusa, *Shōwashi I, 1926–1945* (Tokyo: Tōyōkeizai Shinpōsha, 1993), 255.

112 Hosoya Chihiro, *Ryō-taisenkan no Nihon gaikō, 1914–1945* (Tokyo: Iwanami Shoten, 1988), 172–174.

113 Ishibashi Tanzan wrote an editorial in the *Tōyōkeizai Shinpō* saying that the pact would make the US Japanese war inevitable. Nakamura, *Shōwashi*, 258.

114 Hosoya Chihiro, "Sangoku dōmei to Nisso chūritsu jōyaku," in *Taiheiyō sensō eno michi*, vol. 5, *Sangoku dōmei, Nisso chūritsu jōyaku*, ed. Nihon Kokusai Seiji Gakkai Taiheiyō Sensō Gen-in Kenkyūbu (Tokyo: Asahi Shimbunsha 1963), 210. Hosoya Chihiro, "Tripartite Pact, 1939–1940," in *Deterrent Diplomacy: Japan, Germany, and the USSR, 1935–1940* (Japan's Road to the Pacific War series), trans. and ed. James Morley (New York: Columbia University Press, 1976), 242–243.

115 Hosoya, "Sangoku dōmei," in *Taiheiyō sensō eno michi*, vol. 5, Nihon Kokusai Seiji Gakkai, 212. Hosoya, "Tripartite Pact," in *Deterrent Diplomacy*, trans. and ed. Morley, 246. Langer and Gleason, *The Undeclared War*, 26.

116 Hosoya, "Sangoku dōmei," in *Taiheiyō sensō eno michi*, vol. 5, ed. Nihon Kokusai Seiji Gakkai, 212. Hosoya, "Tripartite Pact," in *Deterrent Diplomacy*, trans. and ed. Morley, 246–247.

*524*

117 Hosoya, "Sangoku dōmei," in *Taiheiyō sensō eno michi*, vol. 5, ed. Nihon Kokusai Seiji Gakkai, 214. Hosoya, "Tripartite Pact," in *Deterrent Diplomacy*, trans. and ed. Morley, 249.

118 Joseph Grew, *Turbulent Era: A Diplomatic Record of Forty Years, 1904–1945* (New York: Books for Libraries Press, 1952), 1231.

119 Herbert Feis, *The Road to Pearl Harbor: The Coming of the War Between the United States and Japan* (Princeton: Princeton University Press, 1950), 122.

120 Langer and Gleason, *The Undeclared War*, 34–35, 37. Schroeder, *The Axis Alliance*, 22.

121 Feis, *Road to Pearl Harbor*, 123.

122 Schroeder, *The Axis Alliance*, 26.

123 Utley, *Going to War with Japan*, 133.

124 Schroeder, *The Axis Alliance*. 27.

125 Iriye, *The Origin of the Second World War*, 85, 114. Hosoya, *Ryō-taisenkan no Nihon gaikō*, 293. It is said that when he was told of the outbreak of the war, Matsuoka shed bitter tears, saying, "The conclusion of the Tripartite Pact was the greatest mistake of my life." Hosoya, "Tripartite Pact," in *Deterrent Diplomacy*, trans. and ed. Morley, 254.

126 Schroeder, *The Axis Alliance*, 24.

### 16.4. US–Japanese Relations in 1941

127 Utley, *Going to War with Japan*, 142.

128 Hull writes, "I held my first extended conversation with Nomura on March 8 in my apartment at the Carlton Hotel. This was the first of some forty to fifty conversations between us until Pearl Harbor . . . Joseph Ballantine, an outstanding Japanese expert of the Department, used to appear at my apartment at seven-forty-five, bring whatever documents were necessary, and talk them over with me. Nomura and his advisers came in shortly before eight-thirty, and the conversations usually went on until ten o'clock, sometimes ten-thirty. Ballantine then returned to the State Department to prepare a memorandum of the conversation." Hull, *The Memoirs*, 988.

129 Schroeder, *The Axis Alliance*, 29. When Foreign Minister Matsuoka asked Nomura to assume the ambassadorship to Washington in August 1940, Nomura refused because he opposed Matsuoka's policy toward the United States. Nomura said to one of his friends, "My conscience does not allow me to serve as ambassador to a country toward which our government maintains a policy totally contrary to my own views . . . A person like Matsuoka who only sees matters superficially can hardly be depended upon; to take anything such a person says is out of question." He also said to Navy Minister Yoshida, " . . . it is impossible to rectify diplomatic relations between Japan and the United States by trying to juggle both Germany and the United States at the same time." Despite having expressed such strongly critical views, Nomura had finally accepted Vice Admiral and Vice Navy Minister Toyoda's ardent plea that he should take the post on behalf of the Japanese navy. He conveyed his consent to Oikawa, the new navy minister, " . . . my ties to the navy make it impossible for me to refuse. Worth it or not, succeed or not, . . . I feel I have to go." Tsunoda Jun, "Nihon no taibei kaisen," in *Taiheiyō sensō eno michi*, vol. 7, ed. Nihon Kokusai Seiji Gakkai

525

Taiheiyō Sensō Gen-in Kenkyūbu (Tokyo: Asahi Shimbunsha, 1987), 129–130. Tsunoda Jun, "Confusion Arising from a Draft Understanding Between Japan and the United States," trans. David Titus, in *The Final Confrontation Japan's Negotiations with the United States, 1941* (Japan's Road to the Pacific War series), ed. James Morley (New York: Columbia University Press, 1994), 15.

130 Schroeder, *The Axis Alliance*, 30.

131 Ibid., 31.

132 Ibid., 30, 207.

133 Utley, *Going to War with Japan*, 144–145.

134 Ibid., 143–144.

135 Schroder argues that Hull's attitude of complete settlement or open conflict, or all or nothing, constituted one of his major shortcomings as a diplomat. Schroeder, *The Axis Alliance*, 207. Utley is also critical of Hull's rigid stance. Utley, *Going to War with Japan*, 144, 178–180.

136 Utley, *Going to War with Japan*, 144.

137 The proposed memorandum of understanding was written by two American Catholic priests who sought peace between America and Japan. They were Father James Drought, secretary general of the Catholic Foreign Mission Society of America and Bishop James Walsh, the society's chairman. The two visited Japan in November 1940, and met Ikawa Kunio, director of Industrial Guilds Central Saving Union, who was also a Catholic, and the three met Japanese government officials including Matsuoka. In February 1941, Drought, Walsh, and Ikawa met again in New York and, with the understanding of Ambassador Nomura and US postmaster Frank Walker, who was also a Catholic, worked out a draft agreement of understanding. Michael Barnhart, *Japan Prepares for Total War: The Search for Economic Security, 1919–1941* (Ithaca: Cornell University Press, 1987), 220, 222–223. Nakamura, *Shōwashi*, 262–263.

138 In April a revised version was prepared by Drought and the Japanese army's military affairs department chief Iwakuro, who was then stationed in Washington to help Nomura, and it was presented to the US government. The document did not renounce the Tripartite Pact, but it would have rendered it a worthless scrap of paper. The United States was to mediate in the settlement of the war in China, and Japan would promise to respect the independence of other Asian nations in exchange for the revitalization of trade with the United States and new loans from Washington. Nakamura, *Shōwashi*, 262–263.

139 At any earlier time, Hull would have rejected it out of hand, but the Hull–Nomura talks being at a standstill, Hull agreed reluctantly that the proposal would be used as starting place for discussion. Utley, *Going to War with Japan*, 142.

140 Barnhart, *Japan Prepares for Total War*, 223. Gaimushō, ed., *Nihon gaikō bunsho Nichibei kōshō, 1941*, vol. I (hereafter cited as *Gaikō bunsho Nichibei kōshō I*) (Tokyo: Gaimushō, 1990), 20–24.

141 Utley, *Going to War with Japan*, 144.

142 Ibid., 144.

143 *Gaikō bunsho Nichibei kōshō I*, 39–41.

144 Schroeder, *The Axis Alliance*, 141.

*Notes*

145 When Matsuoka visited Germany in March 1941, Hitler indicated nothing of his plan of invading the Soviet Russia to Matsuoka, though he had decided on it in the fall of 1940. On the trip back to Tokyo from Berlin, Matsuoka dropped by Moscow and held talks with Stalin and Molotov and concluded the Russo–Japanese nonaggression treaty on April 13. Iriye, *The Origin of the Second World War*, 142. Schroeder, *The Axis Alliance*, 137.

146 Feis, *Road to Pearl Harbor*, 214.

147 Nakamura, *Shōwashi*, 266. In arriving at this bold decision, Tokyo might have been influenced by the breakdown of the long negotiations with the Netherlands East Indies Government from September 1940 through June 1941 (16.3.1). Langer and Gleason, *The Undeclared War*, 631.

148 *Gaikō bunsho Nichibei kōshō I*, 130.

149 Schroeder, *The Axis Alliance*, 138.

150 Feis, *Road to Pearl Harbor*, 213, 217.

151 Nagaoka Shinjirō, "Nanka taisei no juritsu," in *Taiheiyō sensō eno michi*, vol. 6, *Nanpō shinshutsu*, ed. Nihon Kokusai Seiji Gakkai, Taiheiyō Sensō Gen-in Kenkyūbu (Tokyo: Asahi Shimbunsha, 1963), 136–137. Nagaoka Shinjirō, "The Drive into Southern Indochina and Thailand," trans. Robert Scalapino, in *The Fateful Choice: Japan's Advance into Southeast Asia, 1939–1941* (Japan's Road to the Pacific War series), ed. James Morley (New York: Columbia University Press, 1980), 236.

152 Nagaoka, "Nanka taisei no juritsu," in *Taiheiyō sensō eno michi*, vol. 6, *Nanpō shinshutsu*, ed. Nihon Kokusai Seiji Gakkai, 140. Nagaoka, "The Drive into Southern Indochina and Thailand," trans. Scalapino, in *The Fateful Choice*, ed. Morley, 240.

153 Hull was convalescing at White Sulphur Springs in West Virginia.

154 Hull, *The Memoirs*, 1014. Langer and Gleason, *The Undeclared War*, 644.

155 *Gaikō bunsho Nichibei kōshō I*, 169–170.

156 Hull, *The Memoirs*, 1014. Nomura added to his report about Roosevelt's proposal of neutralization of Indochina his feeling that the United States was contemplating imposing some economic sanctions against Japan shortly. *Gaikō bunsho Nichibei kōshō I*, 170.

157 Utley, *Going to War with Japan*, 151, 153. *Gaikō bunsho Nichibei kōshō I*, 181–184.

158 Utley, *Going to War with Japan*, 153–154.

159 Barnhart, *Japan Prepares for Total War*, 230.

160 Utley, *Going to War with Japan*, 153.

161 Barnhart, *Japan Prepares for Total War*, 231.

162 Ibid., 231.

163 Ibid., 231.

164 Utley, *Going to War with Japan*, 154.

165 Barnhart, *Japan Prepares for Total War*, 231.

166 Utley, *Going to War with Japan*, 155.

167 Roosevelt's conference with Churchill in August 9–12 (the Atlantic Conference) created some diplomatic problems for Hull, and he had neither the time nor the inclination to "peer over Acheson's shoulder." Ibid., 155.

168 Ibid., 156. Barnhart writes, "Hull, still a thoroughly tired man and increasingly pessimistic about chances for peace, simply accepted the freeze as implemented for what

*527*

Chapter 16

it was. Barnhart, *Japan Prepares for Total War*, 232.

169 Utley, *Going to War with Japan*, 156. Japan made one last try to transfer funds from Latin America to pay for oil for two tankers in San Francisco, but Japan gave up the purchase because Japan's mobilization for the southward advance compelled the withdrawal of all Japanese shipping from the United States, including tankers. Complications involving the financial obligations of Japanese banks in the United States also hampered Japanese attempts to buy oil using Latin American balances. Barnhart, *Japan Prepares for Total War*, 231–232.

170 Utley argues, "As late as a week before the Pearl Harbor attack, Acheson was still pressing Hull for a tough line against Japan, and Hull had to rein him in by pointedly asking him if he knew what the naval force could do in the Far East. Acheson had no idea, but it was just that sort of ignorance that gave him the arrogance to alter a presidential order." Utley, *Going to War with Japan*, 156.

171 Utley, *Going to War with Japan*, 156. Utley argues, "Acheson was not the first high-ranking government official to try and change policy at the level of implementation. A variety of people within the government had given it a try. In each of those cases, however, Hull or Roosevelt had become aware of what was going on and intervened before any serious damage could be done to national policy. What was different about Acheson's exploit was that he got away with it." Ibid., 156.

172 *Far Eastern Survey*, vol. IX, no. 23 (New York: American Council Institute of Pacific Relations, Nov. 20, 1940), 268. Despite the embargo on aviation gasoline since July 31, 1940, Japan imported from the United States over 6.3 million barrels (nearly 1 million tons) of petroleum products in October–December 1940. Nagaoka Shinjirō, "Arita seimei to Nichi Ran-in keizai kōshō" in *Nanpō shinshutsu, Taiheiyō sensō eno michi*, vol. 6, ed. Nihon Kokusai Seiji Gakkai, 91. Nagaoka Shinjirō, "Economic Demands on the Dutch East Indies," trans. Robert Scalapino, in *The Fateful Choice: Japan's Advance into Southeast Asia, 1939–1941* (Japan's Road to the Pacific War series), ed. James Morley (New York: Columbia University Press, 1980), 145.

173 Nakamura, *Shōwashi*, 268.

174 The Japanese government during the 1930s had imported far more than required for current use. Much had been put into reserve. Toward the end of 1939, the reserve stock had been highest—about 55 million barrels, enough to last a year and a half. But thereafter use—especially for military operations and training—had grown, while it had become much harder to import. The reserve had shrunk—probably to less than 50 million barrels by September 1941. At the time of Pearl Harbor, stock had fallen to about 43 million barrels. Feis, *Road to Pearl Harbor*, 268–269.

175 Nakamura, *Shōwashi*, 268.

176 Iriye, *The Origin of the Second World War*, 150.

177 Tsunoda Jun, "Kaisen eno keisha," in *Taiheiyō sensō eno michi*, vol. 7, ed. Nihon Kokusai Seiji Gakkai Taiheiyō Sensō Gen-in Kenkyūbu (hereafter cited as "Kaisen eno keisha") (Tokyo: Asahi Shimbunsha, 1963), 244. Tsunoda Jun, "Leaning Toward War," trans. David Titus, in *The Final Confrontation* (Japan's Road to the Pacific War series), ed. James Morley (hereafter cited as "Leaning Toward War") (New York: Columbia University Press, 1994), 165.

178 Schroeder, *The Axis Alliance*, 55.

528

*Notes*

179 Feis, *Road to Pearl Harbor*, 264.

180 The Essentials for Carrying Out the Empire's Policies was almost same as the Plan for Carrying Out the Empire's Policies. One of a few changes made in drafting the "Essentials" was from "If a diplomatic agreement could not be reached by the middle of October," in the "Plan," to "If there is no prospect of obtaining our demands through diplomatic negotiations by early October," in the "Essentials." "Kaisen eno keisha," 247–248, 256. "Leaning Toward War," 169, 179.

181 "Kaisen eno keisha," 248. "Leaning Toward War," 170, 364–365.

182 Iriye, *The Origin of the Second World War*, 160.

183 The emperor asked Sugiyama, "If something happens between Japan and the United States, how long does the army really believe it will take to clear things up?" Sugiyama replied, "If limited to the South Seas, I would expect to clear things up in three months." The emperor said, "You were army minister at the time the China Incident broke out, and I remember you saying: 'The incident will be cleared up in about a month.' But it still hasn't been cleared up after four long years, has it?" Sugiyama replied, "China opens onto a vast hinterland and military operations could not be conducted as planned." Then the emperor said, raising his voice in reproach, "If the hinterland of China is vast, isn't the Pacific Ocean even more vast? What convinces you to say three months?" Sugiyama lowered his head, unable to reply. "Kaisen eno keisha," 252. "Leaning Toward War," 174.

184 "Kaisen eno keisha," 254–255. "Leaning Toward War," 177.

185 Nakamura, *Shōwashi*, 268. "Kaisen eno keisha," 253–254. "Leaning Toward War," 175–176.

186 "Kaisen eno keisha," 255. "Leaning Toward War," 177.

187 "Kaisen eno keisha," 253–256. "Leaning Toward War," 175–179.

188 Barnhart, *Japan Prepares for Total War*, 232. The Japanese reply of August 6 was that Japan would withdraw from Indochina at the conclusion of the China Incident and respect Philippine neutrality. In return, the United States would relax its economic pressure on Japan, recognize special status for Japan in Indochina after the withdrawal, and suspend its military buildup in the southwest Pacific. Ibid., 232, Schroeder, *The Axis Alliance*, 55.

189 *Gaikō bunsho Nichibei kōshō I*, 197–200. Barnhart, *Japan Prepares for Total War*, 233.

190 *Gaikō bunsho Nichibei kōshō I*, 203.

191 *Gaikō bunsho Nichibei kōshō I*, 234. Schroeder, *The Axis Alliance*, 56.

192 Schroeder, *The Axis Alliance*, 57.

193 *Gaikō bunsho Nichibei kōshō I*, 259.

194 Hull's distrust of Konoe was largely attributable to the fact that the political philosophy of the two were totally incompatible. Whereas that of Hull was a lofty idealism based on fundamental political principles, that of Konoe was a kind of old imperialism. Konoe's declaration of the New Order in East Asia denied Hull's Four Principles.

195 Schroeder, *The Axis Alliance*, 57.

196 Utley, *Going to War with Japan*, 159.

197 Schroeder, *The Axis Alliance*, 58.

198 "Kaisen eno keisha," 267. "Leaning Toward War," 192.

Chapter 16

199 "Kaisen eno keisha," 268. "Leaning Toward War," 193.

200 "Kaisen eno keisha," 264–265. "Leaning Toward War," 188.

201 When Grew met with Hull following his return to the United State, he wondered whether all of his dispatches had actually been forwarded to Hull for him to read. "Kaisen eno keisha," 268. "Leaning Toward War," 194.

202 At this meeting, Roosevelt consoled Nomura, saying, "Prince Konoe, Your Excellency, and the Secretary of State are all working for peace in the Pacific. But both Japan and the United States have vocal publics, and I have received a stream of telegrams demanding that there be no changes in our policy in order to accommodate Japan. I am therefore very sincerely sympathetic toward Prince Konoe." "Kaisen eno keisha," 264–265. "Leaning Toward War," 189.

203 Schroeder argues that Roosevelt's fault, if any, was that of allowing Hull and others to talk him out of impulses and ideas which, had he pursued them, might have averted the conflict. Schroeder, *The Axis Alliance*, 203. Iokibe argues that Roosevelt chose to give up a meeting with Konoe, because Roosevelt was anxious to avoid to make Hull, an influential figure in the American politics, so displeased as to quit the cabinet. Iokibe Makoto, *Nihon no kindai 6—Sensō, senryō, kōwa, 1941–1955* (Tokyo: Chuokoron Shinsha, 2013), 143–144.

204 Barnhart, *Japan Prepares for Total War*, 233.

205 Grew writes in his *Ten Years in Japan* that Konoe said to Grew that he and his cabinet "conclusively and wholeheartedly" agreed with "the four principles enunciated by the Secretary of State as a basis for the rehabilitation of relations between the United States and Japan." As to Washington's misgiving about Konoe's ability to resist the attacks of opposing elements in Japan, Grew writes that Konoe "voiced the conviction that since he had the full support of the responsible chiefs of the Army and Navy it would be possible for him to put down and control any opposition which might develop among those elements." Grew also writes that Konoe stated that he was "determined to bring to successful conclusion the proposed reconstruction of relations with the United States regardless of cost or personal risk." Joseph Grew, *Ten Years in Japan* (New York: Simon & Schuster, 1944), 425–428.

206 "Kaisen eno keisha," 266, 271. "Leaning Toward War," 191, 197.

207 Hull was also skeptical, if an agreement was reached, about how faithfully the agreement would be implemented by the Japanese government. Hull saw his skepticism vindicated by the interception of Toyoda's cable to Nomura on October 4 in which Toyoda said that while the premier accepted the four principles in principle, there would be differences of opinion when it came to actually applying these four principles. Gaimushō, ed., *Nihon gaikō bunsho Nichibei kōshō, 1941*, vol. II (Tokyo: Gaimushō, 1990), (hereafter cited as *Gaikō bunsho Nichibei kōshō II*), 16. Utley, *Going to War with Japan*, 161.

208 After the conference he asked Tōjō if that proposal was really meant to be a strong demand. Tōjō replied, " . . . it is not so much a demand as merely a faithful statement of what was decided at the Imperial Conference." Konoe appeared nonplussed. "Kaisen eno keisha," 277. "Leaning Toward War," 209–210.

209 "Kaisen eno keisha," 278–279. "Leaning Toward War," 209–210.

210 "Kaisen eno keisha," 277–278. "Leaning Toward War," 209–210.

*Notes*

211 "Kaisen eno keisha," 268. "Leaning Toward War," 193.

212 "Kaisen eno keisha," 268. "Leaning Toward War," 193. F. C. Jones argues that "had Roosevelt and Konoe met, they might have been able to agree on a relaxation of the embargo in exchange for satisfactory assurances on the Tripartite Pact and southward expansion, with the China issue laid aside." See Schroeder, *The Axis Alliance*, 207.

213 Barnhart, *Japan Prepares for Total War*, 234. Schroeder, *The Axis Alliance*, 64. "Kaisen eno keisha," 272. "Leaning Toward War," 197. Iriye, *The Origin of the Second World War*, 163.

214 Utley, *Going to War with Japan*, 160.

215 "Kaisen eno keisha," 279. "Leaning Toward War," 211. *Gaikō bunsho Nichibei kōshō II*, 14–15.

216 "Kaisen eno keisha," 280. "Leaning Toward War," 212.

217 "Kaisen eno keisha," 281. "Leaning Toward War," 213.

218 "Kaisen eno keisha," 287. "Leaning Toward War," 222.

219 "Kaisen eno keisha," 284–285. "Leaning Toward War," 218.

220 "Kaisen eno keisha," 294–297. "Leaning Toward War," 231–235.

221 Tōjō told Oikawa, "We have lost 200,000 souls in the China Incident, and I cannot bear to give it all up just like that. But when I think of all the lives that will be further lost if there is a war between Japan and the United States, we must even think about withdrawing troops. "Kaisen eno keisha," 297. "Leaning Toward War," 235.

222 Nakamura, *A History of Shōwa Japan*, trans. Whenmouth, 178.

223 "Kaisen eno keisha," 297. "Leaning Toward War," 235–236.

224 "Kaisen eno keisha," 298. "Leaning Toward War," 237.

225 Barnhart, *Japan Prepares for Total War*, 254.

226 Tsunoda argues that this "wiping the slate clean" idea (白紙還元案) was what Suzuki Teiichi had suggested and Kido had adopted, but Tōjō took it as a "formalistic process," as Kido failed to tell Tōjō that the emperor wanted to avert a war with the United States "under any circumstances." "Kaisen eno keisha," 303–305. "Leaning Toward War," 243–244.

227 Iriye, *The Origin of the Second World War*, 169. "Kaisen eno keisha," 307.

228 Iriye, *The Origin of the Second World War*, 173.

229 Ibid., 175. Tsunoda Jun, "Nihon no taibei kaisen," in *Taiheiyō sensō eno michi*, vol. 7, *Kaisen no kettei*, ed. Nihon Kokusai Seiji Gakkai Taiheiyō Sensō Gen-in Kenkyūbu (hereafter cited as *Kaisen no kettei*), (Tokyo: Asahi Shimbunsha, 1963), 312. Tsunoda Jun, "The Decision for War," trans. David Titus, in *The Final Confrontation* (in Japan's Road to the Pacific War series), ed. James Morley (hereafter cited as "The Decision for War") (New York: Columbia University Press, 1994), appendix 9.

230 Robert Butow, *Tōjō and the Coming of the War* (Princeton; Princeton University Press, 1961), 322. Barnhart, *Japan Prepares for Total War*, 235, 259.

231 Butow, *Tōjō*, 322. Barnhart, *Japan Prepares for Total War*, 259.

232 Butow, *Tōjō*, 323. Barnhart, *Japan Prepares for Total War*, 259.

233 "Kaisen no kettei," 312–319. "The Decision for War," 257–264.

234 Utley, *Going to War with Japan*, 168.

235 Hull, *The Memoirs*, 1058.

236 Utley, *Going to War with Japan*, 171.

*531*

Chapter 16

237 Hull, *The Memoirs*, 1072.
238 Barnhart, *Japan Prepares for Total War*, 235.
239 Hull, *The Memoirs*, 1073.
240 Ibid., 1083. *Gaikō bunsho Nichibei kōshō II*, 187–188.
241 Hull, *The Memoirs*, 1072–1073.
242 Iguchi Takeo, *Kaisen shinwa: Taibei tsūkoku wa naze okuretanoka* (Tokyo: Chuokoron Shinsha, 2008), 119.
243 On November 22 Hull called in British and Chinese ambassadors and the Dutch minister to his office and went over with them in detail the Japanese modus vivendi and the US counterproposal. Chinese ambassador Hu Shih asked if the Japanese military actions in China could be prohibited by the US modus vivendi during the three-month period. Hull's reply was negative. He said that it would be only possible under the permanent agreement which the United States was seeking to conclude with Japan. On November 24, Hull called them back again to hear their home government responses. Chiang Kai-shek expressed strong opposition to the modus vivendi, saying that any relaxation of US restrictions against Japan would lead to a collapse of Chinese morale and the Chinese army. Hull, *The Memoirs*, 1073, 1076–1077.
244 Iguchi, *Kaisen shinwa*, 125, 128–129. Iokibe, *Nihon no kindai 6*, 145. Edwin Layton, with Roger Pineau and John Castello, *And I Was There* (New York: William Morrow, 1985), 198.
245 Utley, *Going to War with Japan*, 173. Layton, *And I Was There*, 199. Winston Churchill, *The Second World War*, vol. III, *The Grand Alliance* (London: Cassell & Co., 1959), 531.
246 Utley, *Going to War with Japan*, 173.
247 Hull, *The Memoirs*, 1085.
248 *Gaikō bunsho Nichibei kōshō II*, 188.
249 Iguchi, *Kaisen shinwa*, 119, 139–140.
250 Iguchi, *Kaisen shinwa*, 128. Layton argues that new documentations cast serious doubt on Hull's memoirs in which he writes that he initiated the dropping of the modus vivendi. Layton argues that Hull was a reluctant follower of Roosevelt's order, referring to Hornbeck's letter to Hull in which Hornbeck wrote, " . . . in days to come you will look upon the decision which was made and the action you took yesterday with great satisfaction." Layton argues that the description of "the decision which was made" showed that the president made the decision and had Hull follow it. Layton, with Pineau and Castello, *And I Was There*, 200.
251 Hull, *The Memoirs*, 1081.
252 "Kaisen no kettei," 357. "The Decision for War," 313.
253 Iguchi, *Kaisen shinwa*, 122. On the morning of November 25, Hull showed Stimson and Knox a final draft of the US modus vivendi and obtained their consent to presenting it to the Japanese, and on the afternoon of that day a war council at the White House attended by Roosevelt, Hull, Stimson, Knox and the two chiefs of staff approved the decision reached in the morning. "Kaisen no kettei," 350. "The Decision for War," 305. Keiichiro Komatsu, *Origins of the Pacific War and the Importance of 'Magic'* (London: Routledge, 1999), 315–316.

*Notes*

254 Iguchi, *Kaisen shinwa*, 128.

255 Ibid., 128–129. Iokibe, *Nihon no kindai 6*, 145.

256 Iokibe, *Nihon no kindai 6*, 147. *Gaikō bunsho Nichibei kōshō II*, 203.

257 *Nihon no kindai 6*, 146–147. Layton argues that Roosevelt was provided with the intelligence report about the Japanese naval concentration in Hitokappu Bay of Etorofu in the Kurile Islands from the British and the Dutch intelligence agencies. Though there was no decryption that the Japanese fleet had sailed for the mid-Pacific, it is possible that Roosevelt expected an imminent massive Japanese naval operation, and that expectation prompted him to decide to drop the modus vivendi to Japan. Layton, with Pineau and Castello, *And I Was There*, 202, 206–207. Iokibe writes that, although neither the US nor British intelligence service decoded the Japanese cables prior to Pearl Harbor, it is possible that the British obtained intelligence about the Japanese navy's moves to a considerable degree. Iokibe, *Nihon no kindai 6*, 146.

258 "Kaisen no kettei," 358. "The Decision for War," 314.

259 Utley, *Going to War with Japan*, 173.

260 "Kaisen no kettei," 362. "The Decision for War," 319.

261 Tōgō was discouraged in particular at point 10 of the Hull Note, which demanded without any condition a withdrawal of the Japanese troops from China, while there was an expression "amicable negotiations regarding Manchuria" in the US proposal of June 21. Iguchi, *Kaisen shinwa*, 141.

262 "Kaisen no kettei," 362. "The Decision for War," 320.

# Chronology of Events in Japan, China, US, and Other Areas from the 1850s to 1941

(Numbers in parentheses indicate the month)

| | Japan, China, and Asia | US, Europe, and other areas |
|---|---|---|
| 1853 | Perry visits Uraga. (7) | |
| 1854 | Kanagawa Treaty opens Japan. (3) | US supplies more than 70% of world's |
| 1856 | Harris arrives in Shimoda. (8) Arrow War in China. (10) | raw cotton in the 1850s. |
| 1857 | Convention of Shimoda with Harris. (6) | US railroad mileage expands threefold |
| 1858 | Treaty of Amity and Commerce with Harris provides for extraterritoriality and 20% duty for majority imports. (7) | in the 1850s; by late 1850s represents over 40% of world's railroad mileage. |
| 1860 | Ii killed at Sakurada Gate. (3) | UK–France Free Trade Treaty. (1) Japanese treaty ratification mission visits Washington. (2) US southern states form the Confederacy. |
| 1861 | Heusken assassinated. (1) | American Civil War begins. (4) |
| 1862 | Harris returns to US. (5) Satsuma samurais kill UK tourist. (8) | Homestead Act enacted; 270 million acres of land (10% of total US land) eventually given to 1.6 million settlers. |
| 1863 | Chōshū fires on US, French, and Dutch ships in the Shimonoseki Straits. (5) UK bombs Satsuma. (8) | Military deaths in American Civil War: 620,000 to 750,000. |
| 1864 | UK, France, Holland, and US bomb Chōshū, request $3 million indemnity. | |
| 1865 | | Lee surrenders to Grant. (4) Lincoln assassinated. (4) 13th Amendment (ban on slavery) passed. |
| 1866 | Japanese tariffs set at 5% by UK. | Ku Klux Klan organized. |
| 1867 | Price of rice ten times that in 1860. | |
| 1868 | Restoration of emperor to power declared. (1) | 14th Amendment (citizenship) passed. |
| 1869 | Four-tier social rank system abolished. Feudal lords surrender their fiefs. | 15th amendment (suffrage) passed. Transcontinental railway completed. (5) The Suez Canal opens. |
| 1870 | | Franco–Prussian War. (7) |

*534*

## Chronology of Events

| | Japan, China, and Asia | US, Europe, and other areas |
|---|---|---|
| 1871 | Griffis arrives in Fukui. (3) Prefectures replace feudal domains. (8) | Iwakura Mission departs on a tour of US and Europe. |
| 1874 | | Telephone invented in US. |
| 1876 | | Arai Ryōichirō arrives in New York. (3) |
| 1877 | Mitsui & Co. opens office in Shanghai and New York. | |
| 1878 | UK rejects Bingham's tariff treaty. (7) | |
| 1879 | | Incandescent light bulb invented in US. |
| 1880 | Yokohama Specie Bank opens office in New York. | Bismark tariff ends free trade in Europe. |
| 1881 | Matsukata pursues deflation policies. | In raw-silk exports to US, Japan surpasses China in the early 1880s. |
| 1882 | K. Inoue's treaty revision talks fail. Osaka Cotton Spinning built. | |
| 1886 | Inoue's second treaty revision talks fail. | |
| 1887 | Inoue resigns; Ōkuma takes over. | By the 1890s, 90% of Africa partitioned by UK, France, Germany, and other European powers. |
| 1889 | Meiji Constitution promulgated. (2) Ōkuma bombed (10); treaty revision talks stop. | |
| 1894 | Japan enters war with China. Japan signs treaties with powers to end exterritoriality in 1899. | US southern states enact Jim Crow laws in the 1890s, mandating racial segregation in all public facilities. |
| 1895 | China cedes Liaodong and Taiwan, pays 200 million taels indemnity. Russia, France, and Germany advise Japan to return Liaodong to China. | |
| 1897 | | US annexes Hawaii. |
| 1898 | Dalian/Port Arthur leased by Russia, Jiaozhou by Germany, Guangzhou by France, Weihaiwei and northern part of Kowloon by Britain. | US acquires the Philippines, Cuba, Puerto Rico, and Guam. |
| 1899 | Western Electric invests in NEC. | John Hey proclaims Open Door. |
| 1900 | Boxers attack Beijing legation district (6); Japanese troops win international fame for their discipline. | Hey's second Open Door. |
| 1902 | Anglo–Japanese Treaty signed. (1) | |
| 1903 | | Henry Ford forms his company. |
| 1904 | Japan goes to war with Russia. (2) | Japan's £82 million bond issues in UK, US, and Germany in 1904 and 1905 finance 65% of total war costs. |
| 1905 | Itō becomes resident general in Korea. GE invests in Tokyo Electric. | Portsmouth Peace Treaty signed. (5) |

535

## Chronology of Events

| | Japan, China, and Asia | US, Europe, and other areas |
|---|---|---|
| 1906 | Anti-Japanese riots increase in Korea. | Roosevelt asks San Francisco school board to halt segregation of Japanese students. |
| 1907 | Russia recognizes Japan's "political solidarity" with Korea. | Roosevelt blocks alien land bill. |
| 1908 | US business leaders visit Japan. | Japan–US gentleman's agreement on immigration. Far Eastern Division established in US State Dept. Ford introduces Model T. |
| 1909 | Knox proposes neutralization of Manchurian railways. (3) Itō assassinated by Korean nationalist. (10) | Roosevelt again blocks alien land bill. Japanese business leaders visit US. |
| 1910 | Japan and Russia sign agreement on division of spheres in Manchuria. Japan annexes Korea. (8) | US has twice as many cars as Europe. |
| 1911 | Riots against the Qing government policy for Hukuang railway project spreads in south China. Yuan Shikai crushes riot, but suggests the Qing rulers abdicate. | Taft blocks alien land bill. |
| 1912 | Sun Yat-sen yields presidency to Yuan. Nationalists win election. (12) | Standard Oil ordered to break up. |
| 1913 | Song Jiao-ren assassinated. (3) | Wilson recognizes Yuan regime. (5) Alien Land Law enacted. (5) |
| 1914 | Yuan dissolves Parliament. (1) Japan occupies Shandong. (12) | WWI begins. (9) |
| 1915 | Japan issues Twenty-One Demands. (1) UK criticizes Katō's approach, but asks China to accept revised Demands. | US minister in Beijing insists on total rejection of Twenty-One Demands. Bryan issues "non-recognition" note. |
| 1916 | Yuan dies. (6) | |
| 1917 | Nishihara loan to Duan Qirui. Goodrich invests in Yokohama Gomu. | Lansing–Ishii agreement. (11) |
| 1918 | | Siberia expedition by US and Japan. |
| 1919 | May Fourth Movement in China. (5) Inoue raises discount rate to 8.03%. (11) | Versailles Peace Conference (1–6) creates the League of Nations. Japan's Shandong claim accepted. (4) |
| 1920 | | US Senate rejects Versailles Treaty. (3) |

## Chronology of Events

| | Japan, China, and Asia | US, Europe, and other areas |
|---|---|---|
| 1921 | Hara assassinated. (11) | Alien Land Law enacted by ballot. (11) Washington Conference (Dec. 1921 to Feb. 1922) agrees on ending UK–Japan treaty, naval disarmament, and settling China issue. |
| 1922 | | Ozawa's neutralization petition rejected. |
| 1923 | The Great Kantō Earthquake. (9) Sun–USSR joint statement of alliance. | |
| 1924 | | Anti-Japanese Immigration Act enacted. (5) |
| 1925 | Riots and boycotts in Shanghai. (5) | UK returns to gold standard. (5) |
| 1926 | Tariff talks in Beijing end in failure. (4) Northern Expedition starts. (7) Saburi meets Chiang Kai-shek. (11) | Chamberlain's Christmas message. (12) |
| 1927 | Shidehara's statement on China. (1) Earthquake bills cause monetary panic. (3–4) Consulates in Nanjing attacked. (3) Eastern Conference held in Tokyo. (6–7) Yoshizawa visits Nanjing. (8) Chiang visits Japan. (9–11) | Kellogg's statement on China. (1) US produces 90% of world's passenger cars. |
| 1928 | Jinan Incident occurs. (5) Zhang Zuolin assassinated. (6) Nationalists conquers Beijing. (7) Zhang Xueliang pledges allegiance to Chiang. (12) | US approves Nanjing regime by granting tariff autonomy. (7) Kellogg–Briand Pact signed. (8) UK approves Nanjing regime and grants tariff autonomy. (12) |
| 1929 | Japan approves Nanjing regime. (6) Tanaka resigns. (7) Hamaguchi starts deflation policy. (7) Saburi killed. (11) | New York stock market crashes. (10) |
| 1930 | Japan returns to gold at prewar par. (1) Japan grants China tariff autonomy. (3) J. Inoue maintains deflation policy. | Naval disarmament agreed in London. (4) Hoover signs Smoot–Hawley Tariff. (6) |
| 1931 | Mukden Incident occurs. (9) Wakatsuki taken over by Inukai. (12) Takahashi ends gold standard. (12) | Creditanstalt bank collapses. (5) UK goes off gold. (9) |

537

## Chronology of Events

| | Japan, China, and Asia | US, Europe, and other areas |
|---|---|---|
| 1932 | Ketsumeidan kills Inoue and Dan. (2, 3)<br>Three Manchurian province governors declare formation of Manchukuo. (3)<br>Young naval officers kill Inukai. (5)<br>Saitō recognizes Manchukuo. (8) | Stimson criticizes Japan. (1, 2, and 8)<br>US stock market at 1/6 of its peak. (6)<br>US nominal GNP half of its peak.<br>British Imperial Preference launched. (7) |
| 1933 | Jehol operation pursued. (2)<br>Japan leaves the League of Nations. (3)<br>Tangku Truce demilitarizes south side of the Great Wall. (5)<br>Takahashi economic policies raise real GNP by 10.1% in 1933, 8.7% in 1934, and 6.4% in 1935. | Litton Report adopted. (2)<br>US unemployment rises to 26.4%.<br>US launches the New Deal, enacting National Industrial Recovery Act (NIRA), Agricultural Adjustment Act (AAA), and Banking Act. |
| 1934 | Amō's statement of Japan's independent China policy issued. (4)<br>Petroleum industry control law enacted.<br>Enactment of other industry-specific control laws follows in succession until 1941. | Keynes suggests, without avail, that FDR drop budget-balancing policy. (6)<br>Reciprocal Trade Agreement Act<br>World trade falls by 2/3 from 1929. |
| 1935 | Umezu and Ho Yingqin agree on security measures in Hebei. (6)<br>Aizawa kills Nagata. (8)<br>Leith-Ross imposes monetary reforms in China. | Wagner Act (for labor movement) and Social Security Act enacted.<br>The Neutrality Act enacted. (8) |
| 1936 | Takahashi, Saitō, and two others killed; Suzuki seriously injured. (2)<br>Japan signs the Anti-Comintern Pact with Germany. (11)<br>Zhang confines Chiang at Xian (12), and Chiang changes his policy on CCP. | Fed raises reserve requirement. (8) |
| 1937 | Sino-Japanese War starts. (7)<br>Ishiwara opposes war; is exiled. (9)<br>Three economic laws enacted in Japan.<br>Paney incident occurs. (12)<br>Nanjing falls (12); Nationalist government moves to Chungking. | Fed raises reserve requirement. (3, 5)<br>US allows cash-and-carry on certain war materials other than arms.<br>Roosevelt delivers quarantine speech. (10) |

## Chronology of Events

| | Japan, China, and Asia | US, Europe, and other areas |
|---|---|---|
| 1938 | Konoe issues *aitenisezu* statement. (1)<br>National General Mobilization Law enacted. (4)<br>Japanese army occupies Xuzhou (5), Hankou, and Guanzhou. (10)<br>"Policies for Adjusting to New Japan–China Relations" approved. (11)<br>"New Order in East Asia" issued. (11)<br>Wang Ching-wei decides to have talks with Japan, leaves Chungking. (12) | Hitler annexes Austria. (3)<br>In Munich, UK, France, and Italy accept German annexation of Sudetenland. (9)<br>US "moral embargo" on sales of bombers to Japan.<br>US real GNP drops 5% (second recession). |
| 1939 | Nomonhan incident. (5–9)<br>Wang visits Japan. (6)<br>Japan tells Wang that his regime would be one of regional regimes. (11) | US gives Japan the six months' notice of ending the 1911 trade treaty. (7)<br>Hitler invades Poland (9), starting WWII.<br>US allows cash-and-carry on arms. (11) |
| 1940 | Japanese army has Hata resign to oust Yonai. (7)<br>Talks with Dutch East Indies start (9); end without result.<br>Japan seizes North Indochina. (9)<br>The Tripartite Pact signed. (9) | Germany launches spring offensive. (4)<br>US enacts National Defense Act. (7)<br>Top-grade scrap iron and aviation gasoline embargoed against Japan. (7)<br>All types of scrap iron embargoed. (9)<br>US transfers 50 destroyers to UK. (9) |
| 1941 | Japan moves into South Indochina. (7)<br>"Essentials for Carrying Out the Empire's Policies" adopted. (9)<br>Konoe proposes summit (8), but is rejected by Hull (10). | Nomura–Hull talks begin. (3)<br>US Congress passes Lend-Lease Act. (3)<br>Germany invades USSR. (6)<br>Japanese assets in US frozen. (8)<br>De facto oil embargo against Japan. (8)<br>Hull Note requesting Japan to move out of China presented (11). Modus vivendi holding China issue in abeyance not presented.<br>Japan bombs Pearl Harbor. (12) |

*539*

# Index

## A

Abe Masahiro 29
Abe Nobuyuki 479
abrogation of the 1911 US–Japan
commercial treaty 423, 483
Acheson, Dean 501
Agricultural Adjustment Act (AAA)
444–445
Aikyōjuku 405
*aitenisezu* (no longer recognizing) policy
419
Aizawa Saburō 408–409
Aizawa Seishisai 4
Alcock, Sir Rutherford 36–37, 39–40
Alien Land Law of 1913 200
Alien Land Law of 1920 202
American citizens 196
American public opinion 313, 483, 495,
513
American Revolution 13–14
Amō Eiji 412
Anglo–French treaty of 1860 124
Anglo–Japanese Alliance 133, 172,
175–177
Anglo–Japanese Treaty 133, 175
Anti-Comintern Pact 478
anti-lynching bill 208
Aoki Shūzō 84
Arai Ryōichirō 106–108
Araki Sadao 374, 405, 407
Aramco 272
Arita Hachirō 423, 428, 478, 489
army as a savior 230
Army's leniency 404
Army's Manchurian policy 357–359
Army's privileges 403
automobile 226
aviation gasoline 492

## B

Axis faction 478

*bakufu* 1
balanced budget policy 442
Balfour, Arthur J. 174
bank failures 439
Bank of Japan 98, 243, 448–449, 450
Bank of Taiwan 247, 317
banking panics in 1930–1933 341, 438
battleship *Mutsu* 175
Bayer 267
Bell Telephone Company 269
Bill of Rights 14
Bingham, John 76, 89
Bingham Treaty of 1878 76–77
Bismarck tariff 124
"Black Codes" 16
Borah, William 173, 383
Boxer expedition and indemnities 151
Boxer Uprising 132–133
boycott movements 314, 379, 382, 388,
460
Britain's conciliatory policy 314
Britain's recognition of the Nationalist
government 315
British and American reactions to the
Twenty-One Demands 163
British J. & P. Coats group 266
British resistance against Germany 476
British withdrawal from the gold
standard 341, 441
Bryan, William Jennings 164
Bryan Note 166
Buddhism 3, 19
*bunji gassaku* 481, 486, 488
*Bunmeiron no gairyaku* 57

*540*

## C

cabinet planning board 455
California Arabian Standard Oil
   Company 272
Californians 191
cash and carry 477
Chamberlain Christmas message 314
Chengde 388
Chiang Kai-shek 306–308, 316, 318–
   320, 323, 375–376, 414, 416, 418,
   420, 484, 489
Chiang's address in Lushan 417
Chiang's instructions to Zhang 376
Chiang's popularity 415
China's appeal to the League of Nations
   377
China's tariff autonomy 323
Chinese Communist Party (CCP) 307
Chinese Exclusion Act of 1882 192
*chiso kaisei* 97
Chongqing 480
Chōshū 1, 40, 42–43
Chou Fo-hai 484
Christianity 1–2, 61
Churchill, Winston 512–514
city upon a hill vii, xii, 11, 17
Civil War 14–15
Clark, William Smith 66
coal 225
Cobden–Chevalier Treaty 7, 125
Commodity Credit Corporation (CCC)
   445
commodity prices 339–340
comparative advantage 114, 237
complementary US–Japanese trade 114
Confederacy, the 15
Confucianism 3, 6
Constitutional Convention in
   Philadelphia 14
Convention of 1866 on tariffs 41

## D

Convention of Shimoda of 1857 30
Cotton cloth in China 113
cotton fabrics in US 458–459
cotton gin 14
cotton industry in Japan, UK and US
   108–114, 225, 227–228
coup attempt in October 373
Credit-Anstalt 341
Curzon, Lord 172
customs duty share of government
   revenues 75

Daewongun 127
*Daihonei* 419
Dan Takuma 405
Declaration of Independence 13
"de facto oil embargo" 501
deficit spending 448
deflation 98
deflationary atmosphere 243, 247–248
deflationary policies 248, 344, 440–441
Denison, Henry Willard 64
"destroyer deal" 477
"Diligence and Thrift" 245
Dirksen, Herbert von 419
disagreements among Japanese leaders
   over the Manchuria policy 138
discount rate 243, 438, 448
Disraeli, Benjamin 7
Division of Far Eastern Affairs 157
division of spheres in Manchuria 159
division within the Army 370
Dohihara Kenji 392
*dokudan senkō* 320, 371, 403–404
dollar diplomacy 157
downfall of the Qing dynasty 160
Drummond, Eric 389
Duan Qirui 307
dumping duties 459

*541*

Dutch, the 2
Dutch East Indies 490, 502

**E**
"earthquake bills" 247
East India Company 7
Eastern Conference 317
Edison Telephone Company 268
Edo 3
Eichengreen, Barry 440
electricity 226
Elgin, Lord 33
emperor's strong wish for peace 504
emperors 4
empress dowager 132
Enlightenment thought 12–13
"Essentials for Carrying Out the Empire's
   Policies" 503–504
exceptionalism 18
exchange licenses 500
exchange of Japanese shipping for
   American steel 240–242
export licenses 500
extraterritoriality 9, 74, 77–84, 86

**F**
Farm Credit Administration (FCA)
   445
farm village relief 450
February 26 Incident 406
Federal Deposit Insurance Corporation
   (FDIC) 445–446
Federal Reserve Act of 1913 439
Federal Reserve system 439
Federal Reserve's monetary policy 438
Fed's untimely action 441
fiat currency system 35
Fifteenth Amendment 16
financial crises in 1930–1933 341
First Amendment 14

five-article charter oath 43
Five-Power Treaty 175
fleet faction 325
Ford 269
Ford, Henry 226
Ford Japan 280
foreign direct investments in Japan
   275–282
Foreign investments in Japan 272–282
foreign investments in the United States
   265–268
foreign judges 80
Foreign portfolio investments in Japan
   272–275
Four-Power Consortium 168
Four-Power Treaty 175
Fourteenth Amendment 16
Franco–Prussian war 124
freeze of Japanese assets 500
Friedman and Schwartz 437–439
Fujioka Ichisuke 297
*fukoku kyōhei* 6
Fukuda Hirosuke 319–320
Fukuzawa Yukichi 54, 56–57
fundamental principles 505
Futabakai 356
Fuzhou 376

**G**
Gallagher, John 8
Gallup polls 483
GDP, GNP 93–94, 223-224, 244. 338–
   339, 345, 437, 438, 442, 449, 450
Geary, John 277
general agreement (ten-point proposals)
   511–512
General Electric 269, 276
General Motors 269
General Motors Japan 280
Gentlemen's Agreement of 1908 197–

*542*

Index

198, 205–207
German industrial rationalization
 451–452
German spring offensive 477, 479, 489
German–Russo war 499
German–Soviet Nonaggression Pact
 479
gold reserve (stock) 346, 443, 454
gold shortage 440 (in Europe), 453 (in
 Japan)
gold standard 128, 440, 448
Goodrich, B. F. 277
Grant, Ulysses 17
Great Awakening 12–13
Great Depression 337–344, 437–441
Great Kantō Earthquake 245
Great Wall 411, 484
Grew, Joseph 494, 505–506, 508
Grey, Edward 161–163, 166
Griffis, William E. 64–66
Guangzhou 480
Gulf Oil 272
Gulick, Sydney 212

**H**
*haihan chiken* 97
Hainan Island 481
Hamaguchi Osachi 245, 327
Hamilton, Alexander 14
Hanihara Letter 204–206
Hanihara Masanao 174, 204, 207, 214
Hankou 480
*hansatsu* 37
*hanseki hōkan* 97
Hanyehping Company 162
Hanyehping iron and steel 288
Hara Takashi 169, 244
Hara Yoshimichi 493
Harriman, E. H. 152, 158
Harris, Townsend 30–37, 39

Hart, Robert 11
Hashimoto Kingorō 405
Hata Shunroku 479
"have-not country" 417
Hawaii 142
Hay, John 144
Hayashi Daigaku no Kami 29
Hayashi Senjūrō 370, 407, 410
Hebei–Chahar Political Council 414
hegemonic Britain 7–11
hegemonic stability 343
Hepburn, James 62
*Hesperia* incident 79
Heusken, Henry 30, 42, 52
Higashikuni Naruhiko 509
Hiranuma Kiichirō 478
Hirota Kōki 410, 412, 418, 420
Hitler, Adolf 475–476
Homestead Act of 1862 96
Hong Kong 9
Honjō Shigeru 358
Hoover, Herbert 378, 382, 441
Hornbeck, Stanley 506
Hotta Masayoshi 30
House of Representatives 14
Hughes, Charles Evans 173, 205, 207,
 209, 212, 222
Hukuang railway loan 160
Hull, Cordell 215, 482, 496–498, 501,
 505–506, 508, 511–514
Hull Note 513
Hull's four principles 497

**I**
*ichibu* 35
Ii Naosuke 34
Imai Takao 484–485, 522
immigration disputes 137, 192–193,
 195–207, 210–215
Immigration from Europe to US 267

*543*

Imperial Conference on September 6
503, 508–509, 531
Imperial Preference System 343
imperialism 123–125
imperialism in the late 19th century 7–
8, 43, 123–125
imperialist view of Konoe 417
Important Industries Control Law 452
income disparity 229–230
India 7–8, 159
industrial development of US and Japan
224–228
industrial policies of US 444
industrial products 225
industry-specific control laws 452
inflation 37–38, 42, 97
informal empire 8, 10
Inoue Junnosuke 243, 344, 350, 405
Inoue Kaoru 80
Inoue Nisshō 404
International Business Machine 281
Inukai Takeru 484–485, 489
Inukai Tsuyoshi 374, 405
investments in China by country 286
investments in US railways 265–266
iron and steel 225
Ishibashi Tanzan 210–211, 524
Ishida Baigan 5
Ishii Itarō 420
Ishii Kikujirō 167
Ishiwara Kanji 357–359, 416–418, 428
isolationism 17
Issekikai 356
Itagaki Seishirō 357–358, 371, 478, 486
Itō Hirobumi 35, 58, 69, 127, 133, 138–
139, 141
Iwadare Kunihiko 275, 283
Iwakura Embassy of 1871 58–62
Iwakura Tomomi 58–59

# J

Jackson, Andrew 13–15
Japan–Manchukuo Protocol 385
Japanese cotton industry and trade
110–114
Japanese cotton-spinning mill 112
Japanese Exclusion Law of 1924 203–
215
Japanese foreign trade 99–102, 231, 235–
237, 457
Japanese government's industrial policies
in the 1930s 451–453
Japanese government's stronger economic
controls 453–456
Japanese population in California 193
Japan's financial position 251–252
Japan's foreign direct investments 283–
291
Japan's investments in China by industry
286
Japan's per-capita GNP 3
Japan's population 2
Japan's raw-silk industry and exports
104–106, 236–239
Japan's recognition of the Nationalist
government 323
Japan's return to the gold standard
242–245, 248
Japan's suspension of the gold standard
342
Japan's tea industry and exports 103–
104, 238–239
Jardine Matheson & Co. 99
Jiaozhou 161
Jidong demilitarized zone 411
Jilin 370
Jim Crow laws 17
Jinan Incident 318–320, 404
Jinzhou 372
Jinzhou bombing 372, 377

Index

John Manjirō 28
Johnson, Albert 203
Johnson, Andrew 16
Johnson, Hiram 199, 209
judicial autonomy 73
*jūshin* 407

**K**

Kagesa Sadaaki 484–485, 488
Kanagawa Treaty 29
Kanaya Hanzō 359, 369, 373
Kanegafuchi Spinning 113
Kaneko Kentarō 196, 210
Kan'in Kotohito 374
*Kanrin-maru* 54
Kao Tzung-wu 484–487
Katō Kanji 325–326
Katō Takaaki 162, 245
Katō Tomosaburō 173–175, 245
Katsu Kaishū 54, 56
Katsura Tarō 134, 140, 152
Kellogg, Frank 311–312
Kellogg announcement on January 27,
   1927 315
Kellogg's chilly reception of Uchida 313
Kellogg's unilateral approaches
   311–313
Kennan, George 146
Kenseikai 243, 246–247
Ketsumeidan 404
Keynes, John Maynard 442, 450
Kido Kōichi 509
Kido Takayoshi 58
Kindleberger, Charles 343
Kishi Nobusuke 452
Kita Ikki 356, 409
Knox, Philander 157
Knox's Manchurian railway
   neutralization proposal 159
Kōain 420

Kobayashi Ichizō 490
*kōbu-gattai* 42
Kodama Gentarō 138, 150
Kōdō faction 407
Koiso Kuniaki 359, 371
Kokugaku 4
Kokuryūkai 163
*kokutai* 4, 6
Kōmoto Daisaku 321
Komura Jutarō 134, 152
Konoe Fumimaro 417, 479, 499, 502,
   505–509
Koo, V. K. Wellington 164, 170, 387
Korea 125, 136, 139
Korean Army commander 370
Korean protectorate 140
Korean resistance 139
Korea's annexation 141
Ku Klux Klan 16
Kume Kunitake 59
Kunming 485
Kuomintang 306–308, 322
Kurusu Saburō 511
Kwantung Army 357–359, 369–372,
   373, 375, 386, 388, 404, 418

**L**

Lamont, Thomas 248
land tax 75
Lansing, Robert 165
Lansing–Ishii agreement 167
League of Nations 170, 377–378, 381,
   388–390, 418
*Lebensraum* 475
Leith-Ross, Frederick 412
Lend-Lease Act 477
lender of last resort 343
Li Hongzhang 127–128
Liaodong Peninsula 128
liquidationist view 350, 439

*545*

Index

literacy rate 3
Lodge, Henry Cabot 174, 204, 206, 209
London Blitz 477
London Naval Agreement 325
London Naval Conference 324
London Protocol of 1862 39
Louisiana 18
Lung Yun 485
Lytton Commission 378
Lytton Report 385–388

**M**
MacMurray, John Van Antwerp 205, 311–312
Madison, James 14
main commodities in Japanese exports to the United States 238–239, 458–460
main commodities in US exports to Japan 239–240, 460–463
Makino Nobuaki 170
Manchukuo 375
manifest destiny 18
manufacturing of US 224
Marco Polo Bridge Incident 417, 432
Masaki Jinzaburō 374, 407–408
Mason, George 14
Matsudaira Yoshinaga 64
Matsukata Masayoshi 98
Matsuoka Yōsuke 387, 389, 479–480, 493, 495, 498–499
May Fourth Movement 171
Mei Szu-p'ing 484
Meiji Constitution 83
Meiji, Emperor 43
Meiji government revenues 76
Meiji government's political, social, and economic reforms 97–99
*Memoirs of Cordell Hull, The* 513
metalworking machinery 462
Mexican silver dollar 35

Mikami Taku 406
military conquest of Beijing 312
Military Industries Mobilization Law 454–455
Military spending in Japan 448–449, 451
militias 14
Min, Queen 127, 130
Minami Jirō 359, 369, 373
ministry of commerce and industry (MCI) 452
Minseitō 248–249, 355
Minutes of a Sino–Japanese Understanding 485
"missionary-mind diplomacy" 165
Mito school 4
Mitsubishi Denki 278
Mitsubishi Sekiyu 282
Mitsui & Co. 284
Miura Gorō 130
mixed capitalism 447
Miyake Mitsuharu 359
mobocracy 57
Model T 226, 269
modus vivendi 497, 511–514
Mokuyōkai 356
money supply 345, 438, 441–442
"moral embargo" 422
Mori Arinori 69
Mori Tsutomu 374
Morioka Shōhei 316
Motoori Norinaga 4
Mukai Tadaharu 490
Munich 475, 505
Muragaki Norimasa 55
Muraoka Chōtarō 321
Murray, David 65
Mutō Akira 418, 504
Mutsu Munemitsu 82, 86

546

## N

Nagano Osami 507
Nagata Tetsuzan 356, 358, 407–408
Naigaimen 287
Nakahama Manjirō 54
Namamugi Incident 52
Nanjing 418
Nanjing Incident of March 1927 308,
   316
National Defense Act 492
National General Mobilization Law
   455–456
National Industrial Recovery Act
   (NIRA) 444
national unification 308
Nationalist government 312
Nationalist government's problems 375
Nationalist revolutionary diplomacy
   314
naval disarmament 174
negotiations in the Dutch East Indies
   489–491
Netherlands East Indies 489
Neutrality Act of 1935 476
Neutrality Act of 1937 476
Neutrality Act of 1939 477
New Deal 443–447
"New Order in East Asia" 481
Nihon Kinsen Tōrokuki 280
Nihon Seikōsho 277
Nihon Watson Tōkei Kaikeiki 280
Nihon Yūsen 284
Nine-Power Treaty on China 177, 423
Ninomiya Harushige 371
Nippon Electric (NEC) 275
Nippon Iron and Steel 452
Nishida Mitsugu 409
Nishihara loans 251, 308
Nitobe Inazō 210
Nogi Maresuke 135

Nomonhan 482
Nomura Kichisaburō 398, 479, 498,
   500, 506, 508, 525
Nomura–Hull talks 496–498, 500, 505
*Normanton* 81
North China separation policy 411–
   412
North Indochina 491
Northern Expedition 307
notice to abrogate the trade treaty 423

## O

offensive in Rehe province 388
Oguri Tadamasa 67
Oikawa Koshirō 493, 507–508
oil embargo 500–502
Okada Keisuke 407
Okamura Yasuji 356
Ōkawa Shūmei 356
Oki Shōkai 275
Ōkubo Toshimichi 58, 69
Ōkuma Shigenobu 63, 81–84, 98
open court-martial 405, 408
Open Door 144–145
Opium Wars 8–11
Osaka Cotton Spinning 112
Ōshima Hiroshi 478
Ott, Eugen 479
outflow of gold 35–37
"Outline of the Main Principles for
   Coping With the Changing World
   Situation" 490
"Outlines of National Policies in View of
   the Changing Situation" 499
Ōyama Iwao 135

## P

Palmerston, Lord 10
*Panay* 421
Paris Peace Conference 169

Parkes, Sir Harry 9, 41, 79
partitioning of Africa 123
party cabinet 406
Patrick, Hugh 450
pension payments to former samurai 97
Perry, Matthew C. 28
petroleum (oil) 225, 270–271, 490–
491, 494, 528
Philippines 143
"picture brides" 198
Pittman, Key 483
Plan A 510
Plan B 510
Poland 475
"Policies for Adjusting to New Japan–
China Relations" 480
policy of nonresistance 376
political background of the enactment of
the 1924 law 207–209
population 2–3, 94, 223–224
Portsmouth 136
"Practical measures toward China" 416
Presbyterian Scots-Irish 12
pro-army sentiment 350
pro-Japanese governors 375
"Proposal of practical measures toward
China" 416
protectionist US trade policy 233–235
Provisional Government 419
Puritanism 11

**Q**
Qing dynasty 161, 305
Qiqihar 372
quarantine speech 421, 483

**R**
racial equality 170–171
Radical Republicans 16
railroad construction 265–266

railroad mileage 96
railway between Shinbashi (Tokyo) and
Yokohama 98
Rangaku 5
Ratification Embassy of 1860 54–57
ratification of the Treaty of Versailles
171
raw cotton 240, 460
raw-cotton production 95
raw silk 227, 239, 348, 350, 458
raw-silk exports 236, 237, 238–239,
349, 459
"real bills doctrine" 439
Reciprocal Trade Agreement Act 235,
344
reciprocal visits by representatives of the
chambers of commerce 237, 259
recognition of Manchukuo 385
Reconstruction Finance Corporation
(RFC) 445
Reed, David 204
Reformed Government 419
*Regulations Under Which American
Trade Is to Be Conducted with Japan*
32
Reinsch, Paul 164
resident-general 139, 141
Revenue Act of 1932 441
Ribbentrop, Joachim von 478
rice in Japan 38, 347–349
right of supreme command 326, 403
rivalry between the Senate and the State
Department 209
Robinson, Ronald 8
*rōjū* 29
Roosevelt, Franklin 442
Roosevelt, Theodore 135, 196
Root, Elihu 174, 177
Root–Takahira agreement 138
Royal Dutch Shell 268

*548*

rural depression 347
rural distress 350–352
Russia (Soviet Union) 83, 130, 132, 133–136, 140, 372, 476, 477, 482, 499
Russia's recognition of Japan's annexation of Korea 140
Russo–Japanese Agreement of 1910 159
Russo–Japanese War 134–136

S
Saburi Sadao 323
Saburi's meeting with Chiang 316
Saigō Takamori 57, 126
Saitō Makoto 385, 406, 408
Sakamoto Ryōma 50
*sakoku* 1, 5
Sakuma Shōzan 5
Sakurada Gate 34
Sakurakai 356
Salisbury, Lord 83, 85
San Francisco School Incident 195–197
Sanjō Sanetomi 58
Satō Naotake 416
Satsuma 42–43, 52
Schiff, Jacob 136
scrap iron 461–462, 492
Second Amendment 14
second recession of 1937–1938 441–443
Second World War 476
Securities Exchange Commission (SEC) 446
Seinan War 97
*Seiyō jijō* 57
Seiyūkai 243, 246, 317–318, 326–327, 355
Senate 14
separation of church and state 14

September 6 Imperial Conference decision 509–510
Shandong 161–162, 170–171
Shandong expedition 319
Shanghai Cotton Manufacturing Company 287
Shanghai Incident 379–382
Shanghai Incident on May 30 311, 314
*shi-nō-kō-shō* 97
Shiba Gorō 132
Shibaura Seisakusho 276
Shibusawa Eiichi 112, 259
Shidehara Kijūrō 173, 213, 369, 373–374
Shidehara message 315
Shidehara's China policy 354
shift in the government position 373
Shima, George 194
Shimonoseki 40
Shimonoseki indemnity 53
Shimonoseki treaties 40 (with four powers), 128 (with China)
Shingaku 5
Shinto 3
shipbuilding 227–228
Shirakawa Yoshinori 380, 398
Shiratori Toshio 384, 478
*shishi* 41, 409
Shōkasonjuku 5
Shortridge, Samuel 204
Shōwa Depression 344–346
shrinkage in foreign trade 340–341
Shushigaku 3, 6
Siberia Expedition 168–169
Simon, John 384, 388
Singer Sewing Machine 268, 283
Sino–Japanese War 127–130, 415–423
Slater, Samuel 108
slavery 14–17
slaves 15

*549*

slow recovery 441
Smoot–Hawley Tariff Act 342
Social Security Act of 1935 446
Song Jiaoren 306, 327
Song Zheyuan 414
*sonnō jōi* 4, 30
Soong Mei-ling 308
South Indochina 499
South Manchuria Railway 136
South Manchuria Railway Company 289–291
Stahmer, Heinrich 479
Standard Oil 269
Standard Oil of California (Socal) 272
Standard Oil's breakup 270
Stimson, Henry 377–378
Stimson's challenge to Japan 382–384
Straight, Willard 158
Sudetenland 475
Suetsugu Nobumasa 325
Sugimura Yōtarō 389
Sugiyama Hajime 417, 504, 507
suicidal resolve to control military spending 451
Sumitomo Electric Wire and Cable Works 278
summit conference (meeting) 502, 504–508
Sun Yat-sen 305–307
supply route to China 491
Suzuki Kantarō 408
Suzuki Shōsan 21
Suzuki Shōten 247
Swift, Franklin 84

**T**
Tada Hayao 418–419
Taft, William 157
Taft administration's anti-Japanese policy 157

Taft–Katsura memorandum 140
Taisei Yokusankai 411
Taiwan 128
Takahashi Korekiyo 136, 243–245, 408
Takahashi's economic policies 447–451
*Takao Ozawa v. the United States* 204
Tanaka Giichi 246, 308, 311–318, 321–322
Tangku Truce 411
Tao Hsi-sheng 484
Tariff autonomy of China 312, 315, 323
tariff autonomy of Japan 73–76, 87
tariff conference in Beijing 311
Tatekawa Yoshitsugu 358, 370
tea 101–104, 238–239
Tea Party incident 13
Temin, Peter 440
Temporary Funds Adjustment Law 454
Temporary Import-Export Grading Measures Law 454
Tennessee Valley Development Act 467
*terakoya* 3
Terashima Munenori 77
Terauchi Masatake 141
terrorism 404
terrorist attack in Shanghai 397–398
Thayer, Henry 275
Thirteenth Amendment 16
Tocqueville, Alexis 62
Tōgō Heihachirō 135
Tōgō Shigenori 510
Tōjō Hideki 418, 507, 508–510, 514
Tōjō and Tōgō's Efforts to Avert War 510–512
Tokugawa government 1
Tokugawa ideologies 3–6
Tokugawa Iesato 173
Tokugawa Mitsukuni 20
Tokugawa Nariaki 34
*Tokumei zenken taishi Beiō kairan jikki*

59
Tokutomi Sohō 125, 137, 351
Tokyo Electric 276
Tokyo Shibaura Denki (now Toshiba) 277
Tonghak ("Eastern Learning") sect 127
Tōsei faction 407
Tōyō Carrier Corporation 279
Toyoda Teijirō 499, 507, 525
Trautmann, Oskar 418
Treaties of Tianjin of 1858 9
treaty faction 325
Treaty of Amity and Commerce 31–33
Treaty of Commerce and Navigation (of 1894 with Britain) 86
Treaty of Kanghwa of 1876 126
Treaty of Nanjing of 1842 9
Treaty of Paris in 1783 13
treaty port system 10
Treaty Revision 73–87
Tripartite Pact 479, 493–496
Triple Intervention 130–131
truck crops grown in California 195
Tsen Chung-ming 486
Tsuda Umeko 69
Tung Tao-ning 484
Turkish Petroleum Company (TPC) 272
Twenty-One Demands 161–166

## U

Uchida Yasuya 313, 385
Ugaki Kazushige 410, 420
ultimatum without a deadline 514
Umezu–Ho Ying-chin agreement 412
unemployment 340–341, 437–438
Union, the 15
United Fruit Company 270
US annual raw-silk imports 105
US cotton industries and trade 108–
110
US direct investments in Latin America 270
US economic contraction 337–339
US exports and imports 232
US financial position 249–251
US foreign direct investments 268–272
US foreign trade 95, 231–235, 457
US gold stock 443
US–Japan trade relations 99–101, 237–240, 451–463
US oil investments in the Middle East 271–272
US opposition to the Anglo–Japanese alliance 172, 175
US "popularity-courting policy" 313
US tea imports 103

## V

Vandenberg, Arthur 483
"veiled threat" 206
Verbeck, Guido 62
Versailles Peace Conference 310
veto power over the cabinet 404
Victor Talking Machine of Japan 280

## W

Wagner Act in 1935 446
Walsh, Hall & Co. 99
Wang Ching-wei 375–376, 484–489
Wang, C. T. 170
war materials 461, 477
War of 1812 13
Washington Conference 172–174
Washington, George 17
Watson, Thomas 283
Welles, Benjamin Sumner 500
Western Electric 269
whaling 27–28
wheat production 95

*551*

Whitney, Eli  14, 108
Wilson, Huntington  157
Wilson, Woodrow  164, 169–171, 309–310
Winthrop, John  xii, 11
"wiping the slate clean idea"  531
withdrawal of troops from China  507
Woods, Cyrus  212–213
Work Progress Administration (WPA)  446
World War I  161
Worldwide Depression  339–341
Wu Peifu  308

**X**
Xian Incident  414–415
Xuzhou campaign  480, 517

**Y**
Yamagata Aritomo  126

Yamamoto Isoroku  514
"Yankee inventiveness"  96
"Yellow Peril"  137, 193
yen rate  242, 244, 345, 448–449
Yokohama Gomu  277
Yokohama Specie Bank  284
Yōmeigaku  4
Yoshida Shōin  5, 20, 47
Yoshida Zengo  493
Yoshino Shinji  452
Yoshizawa Kenkichi  313, 321, 491
Yoshizawa's visit of Nanjing  318
Yuan Shikai  127, 164, 305–306
Yuan's appeal to Christian churches  309

**Z**
Zhang Xueliang  309, 353, 371–372, 376, 414
Zhang Zuolin's assassination  320–322
Zhou Enlai  414

# About the Author

Tsunao Nakamura, a former professor at Takushoku University, was born in 1936 in Osaka, Japan, and graduated from Kyoto University (Faculty of Law) in 1959. He then worked for the Sumitomo Corporation, a Japanese trading company, for 38 years, engaging in business transactions in Osaka, New York, and Tokyo (1959–1975), in overseas office administration in Tokyo and in Beirut and Istanbul offices (1975–1987). In his last ten years with Sumitomo (1987–1997), he headed the research department of the company. Between 1997 and 2007 he taught trade policy at Takushoku University. He co-authored *Subarashii Amerika bijinesu* (Tokyo: Yūhikaku Publishing, 1988), *Going Global* (Tokyo: The Japan Times, 1996), and *Nichibei keizai handbook* (Tokyo: The Japan Times, 1996). He is a member of Japan Academy for International Trade and Business and The Japan Association of International Relations.